BANKING OPERATIONS

STUDY AND REVISION MANUAL

M. J. Henderson M.A., A.C.I.B., Cert. Ed.

Mike Henderson worked in banking for a number of years and qualified as an Associate of the Chartered Institute of Bankers. He is currently in charge of banking courses at the Polytechnic, Wolverhampton.

He has previously had work published for the Stage Two subject 'Nature of Management'.

DP PUBLICATIONS LTD
Grand Union Industrial Estate – Unit 6
Abbey Road
London NW10 7UL
1988

Acknowledgements

The author would like to express thanks to the Chartered Institute of Bankers for permission to reproduce sample examination questions, and to National Westminster Bank, Royal Bank of Scotland, Standard Chartered Bank and Trustee Savings Bank England and Wales for permission to include sample documents.

Special thanks are also due to Paul White for his assistance during the writing of the text, and to my wife Pat for her support.

ISBN 0-905435-98-2

Typeset by
Alphaset
65A The Avenue
Southampton SO1 2TA

Printed in Great Britain by
The Bath Press
Lower Bristol Road
Bath

Contents

Preface

AIMS OF THE MANUAL

1.   This manual is designed to cover the syllabus of Banking Operations 1 and Banking Operations 2 of the Chartered Institute of Bankers Certificate examinations. (It contains all the material necessary for study and revision purposes.)

NEED

2.   The need was seen for a *new* textbook to cover the different requirements of the *new* syllabus. Apart from covering the syllabus comprehensively, material has been included to give practice in a *new feature* of the examinations – *multiple choice questions* and *comprehensive exercises*. A *revision* section is *also* included, thus providing the lecturer and student with the *complete course text*.

LAYOUT AND SCOPE OF THE MANUAL

3.   The manual is divided into five sections as outlined below.

Section 1
Main contents:-
> Syllabus of BANKING OPERATIONS 1;
> Syllabus of BANKING OPERATIONS 2;
> Sample examination paper for BANKING OPERATIONS 1;
> Sample examination paper for BANKING OPERATIONS 2;
> Commentary on the sample papers.

Section 2
Main contents:-
This is the STUDY Section of the manual and consists of:-
> a.   study hints;
> b.   self-contained chapters sub-divided into short, easily absorbed paragraphs illustrated, where appropriate with diagrams and tables;
> c.   end of chapter summaries;
> d.   self review questions cross-referenced to the relevant paragraphs;
> e.   sample questions with answers in Section 4.

Section 3
Main contents:-
This is the REVISION Section of the manual and consists of:-
> a.   examination technique hints;
> b.   revision check lists of essential knowledge;
> c.   sample question papers with commentary;
> d.   mock examination papers with answers.

Section 4
Main contents:-
> Answers to all end of chapter questions and exercises.

Section 5
Main contents:-
> A selection of questions without answers.

HOW TO USE THE MANUAL EFFECTIVELY

4.   Students are recommended to make themselves familiar with the information in Section 1 about the requirements of the syllabus, and to refer to this regularly to ensure that their studies are directed carefully at what the syllabus demands.

For students learning by private study the text should be read in sequence since later chapters often build on ideas contained in earlier chapters. The text does not begin with Banking Operations 1 and then go on to Banking Operations 2 because many of the basic ideas of banking are relevant to both areas. In general the syllabus for Banking Operations 1 is covered in Chapters 11 to 23, and the material for Banking Operations 2 appears in Chapters 1 to 10 and 24 to 27.

For students using the text as part of a course of study the sequence of chapters is likely to be modified to meet the requirements of individual lecturers. In order to assist the reader each chapter is self-contained; where previous knowledge is assumed reference is made to the appropriate chapter.

When working through a chapter ALWAYS tackle the self review questions and the exercises. This is an essential part of the learning process.

When you have completed the STUDY SECTION you can go on to Section 3 of the manual. This provides a thorough revision of the material.

SPECIAL NOTES FOR LECTURERS

5.   When the manual is used as a course text for Banking Operations 1, Banking Operations 2 or both subjects the lecturer will want a range of questions to set as homework assignments. These are included in Section 5 of the manual and a separate answer guide is available free to lecturers who adopt the manual as a course text.

Section 1

In order to get a broad view of the knowledge required for each of the Banking Operations papers, students should read carefully through this section of the manual before going on to Section 2, the Study Section. The syllabuses and past papers included here should be used throughout the course of study for reference. When using the Study Section students should REFER BACK to this section to make sure that they see how each chapter of the study material fits into the overall syllabus and to get an idea of the variety of questions which can be asked. The commentary on the past papers should give a clearer understanding of what the examiners are looking for.

Syllabus of BANKING OPERATIONS 1

Syllabus of BANKING OPERATIONS 2

Sample examination paper for BANKING OPERATIONS 1

Sample examination paper for BANKING OPERATIONS 2

BANKING OPERATIONS 1: Syllabus 1988
(reproduced by kind permission of the Chartered Institute of Bankers)

Banking Operations 1 – International and Lending

Objective

To instil more detailed knowledge of the background against which banking practices in "international" and lending fields are carried out, and to promote a broad understanding of these practices.

Aims

To give an insight into the aspects of international business enabling staff not directly involved in this area to assess the relative risks/benefits of the various services available and controls to safeguard the bank's position.

To examine the general principles of bank lending and the range of borrowing services available, with the objective of safety, liquidity and profitability.

To be aware of causes and warning signs for potential bad debts and methods of termination and recovery.

To interpret balance sheets as a management tool.

To be aware of alternative sources of finance.

Content

1. **Travel Facilities**
    Systems, benefits and drawbacks of alternatives:
    Travellers Cheques
    Foreign Currency
    Credit Cards, Euro Cheques and Cards
    Cheque, Drafts
    Travel Insurance
    Passports and Visas

2. **Remittance/Receipt of Funds**
    Benefits and drawbacks:
    Telegraphic Transfer, International Money Order, International Payment Order.
    SWIFT

3. **Inter-Bank Accounts (Nostro/Vostro)**
    To be aware of the way accounts operate between UK and Overseas Banks.

4. **Rates of Exchange**
    To be aware of the effects of various factors on rates of exchange.
    To understand the procedures for the system.
    To understand the benefits and drawbacks of Exchange Risk Protection (Spot and Forward Exchange Transactions).
    To be aware of the benefits and drawbacks of maintaining currency accounts — loans and deposits.

5. **International Trade: Exporters/Importers**
    Exporters: to be aware of various methods of settlement.
    Exporters: to be aware of documentation procedures and requirements (financial/commercial).
    To appreciate the role of Export Credits Guarantee Department for Buyer and Country Risk guarantee.
    To be aware of Exchange Control restrictions.
    To be aware of other potential services.
    Importers: to be aware of types and procedures for inwards collections.
    Importers: to be aware of methods of dishonour of inwards collections.
    Importers: to be aware of methods for protection of goods.
    Importers: to understand the considerations and procedure for taking produce as security.

6. **Acceptance Credits**
    To understand the purpose and method of operation of this service.

7. **Other Services**
    To be aware of the benefits and drawbacks of bank guarantees/bonds, forfaiting, LIFFE.

8. **Canons of Lending**
    To understand the basic canons of lending.

9. **Personal Borrowers**
    To define the purpose for borrowing by a customer.
    To understand the advantages and disadvantages of various types of borrowing.
    To understand the procedures for credit scoring and inherent benefits.
    To be aware of special considerations for student accounts.

10. **Other Borrowers**
    To define the purpose for borrowing.
    To be aware of special considerations for various types of borrowing Customers.

11. **General Principles of Security**
    To define the rights and duties of a creditor.
    To understand the banker's position if plans for repayment go wrong.
    To define the difference between first and third party security.
    To be aware of features of ideal security.
    To understand the suitability and methods of valuation of various types of security and the parties involved.
    To understand the terminology and highlight the benefits and drawbacks of certain types of charges.
    To be aware of other technical considerations for taking security.
    To be aware of methods for discharge/release of security.

12. **Review and Control of Accounts**
    To understand the reasons and procedures for reviewing and controlling borrowing accounts.

13. **Bad and Doubtful Debts**
    To identify causes and warning signs for potential and bad debts.
    To be aware of various methods of recovery of lending.
    To be aware of problems/drawbacks of realisation of security.

14. **Interpretation of Balance Sheets**
    To understand the requirements for comparison of trends in balance sheet analysis.
    To identify strengths/weaknesses in areas of the balance sheet with particular regard to: safety, liquidity, profitability, other factors.
    To define the purpose and content of profit budgets for both customer and bank.
    To identify the basis of assumptions in preparation of profit budgets.
    To be aware of the need for implementing monitoring systems for checking customer produced information.
    To define the purpose and content of cash flow forecasts for both customer and bank.
    To define the basis of assumptions and effect of changes in significant factors for monitoring cash flow forecasts.
    To understand the purpose and content of source and application of funds statements.

15. **Alternative Source of Finance**
    To be aware of specialist alternative sources of finance.

BANKING OPERATIONS 2: Syllabus 1988
(reproduced by kind permission of the Chartered Institute of Bankers)

Banking Operations 2 — Customer Services and Marketing

Objective

To develop fuller understanding of the banker/ customer relationship; to provide greater knowledge of the influences which affect the current financial market and to promote a broad understanding of the banks' marketing practices.

Aims

To understand the make-up of bank profits and to be able to identify any regulatory or organisational constraints.

To understand the nature of the changing financial services market and why banks need to develop non-interest related products.

To understand the basic principles of the marketing of financial services.

To know what services and types of account are available to customers; to identify the needs of a customer and match them against a suitable service.

To know the variety of the ways in which bankers and customers can communicate with each other and to be aware of the various techniques which assist each method of communication.

Examiner's Comment

The subject builds upon the foundation knowledge acquired in the study of The Business of Banking. It therefore explores similar areas in more detail and examines current experiences in the financial services market.

1. **Understand the present organisation of the banking system and appreciate the pressures which have led to its recent diversification.**
   Identify the present financial institutional relationships in the UK between the banks, insurance companies, finance houses, discount houses, and accepting houses.
   Outline the development, and explain the role, of the UK central banking system.
   The special function of the Bank of England

in implementing a monetary policy, including the major controls exercised.
Competition and Credit Control and its aftermath.
The development of the euro-markets and the arrival or foreign bank competition.
The declaration of true profits and the clearing bank mergers.

2. **Understand monetary policy and government intervention**
   Current monetary policy and the reasons for the present position.
   The importance of bank liquidity, and how it may be affected by Bank of England constraints.
   Outline the different types of interest rates and the effect on bank lending when rates change substantially.
   Explain the operation of the money markets and the Bank of England's intervention.
   Describe and define the financial instruments used in the market.
   Interpret the market reports that appear in the national press.
   Understand the importance of the money markets to the banks with special reference to bank liquidity and profitability.
   The implications of interest rate movements for bank profitability.

3. **Understand the structure of the balance sheet and profit and loss account of a bank.**
   Explain and describe in broad detail the main liabilities of a bank's balance sheet.
   Describe the main sources of funds.
   Explain, with reference to the order of liquidity, the various assets.
   Relate the items of the balance sheet to the reports of the directors and chairman.
   Understand the principal contributors to bank profits, and the overhead structure of the banks with reference to return on capital employed.
   Understand the needs of the banks to diversify into non-interest related products.
   Understand the overhead pressures associated with branch network costs.

4. **Basic Marketing Knowledge**
   Understand the concept of "marketing mix" as it applies to financial services, and who in a bank has control of these elements:-

Place, Price, Personnel, Promotion, Product
Understand the factors which can be used to analyse customer type and need:

Segmentation of the market into corporate and personal
Socio-economic categories
Acorn analysis
Life Style
Life Cycle
Attitudes to money and financial institutions

5. **Understand the banker/customer relationship**
State and explain the various banker-customer relationships.
Be aware of the need for secrecy about the customers' affairs.
Explain occasions when secrecy may be breached.
Describe the procedure for opening the account of a corporate and non-corporate customer and be aware of the reasons why references are important and circumstances in which they need not be relied on.
Describe the procedure for closing the account of a customer and the precautions that should be taken.

6. **Demonstrate a broad knowledge of the services available to customers and the competition faced.**
Corporate Services
Including computer based cash management services, performance bonds, discounting, money transmission, BACS.
Personal Services
Covering savings and investment opportunities, credit cards, cash dispensers, home banking, insurance, pensions and executor/trustee services, unit trusts.
Competition, with reference to its impact on various areas of bank services
Building societies, licensed deposit takers, foreign banks, finance companies, National Savings, Gilts, local authority stock, ordinary and preference shares, debentures, unit trusts and investment trusts.
Understand the basic tax implications of the various forms of investment.

7. **Provide a knowledge of the basic skills of interviewing relevant to the candidate's own work and a better understanding of the needs of senior colleagues.**
Consider the various types of interview, both formal and informal, to include:—
Selling, negotiating, problem accounts and customer complaints, staff interviews, telephone and enquiries.
Emphasise the importance of preparation to cover the following:-
Gathering information on interviewee
Assessing interviewee's objectives
Appropriate product knowledge
Setting objectives and success criteria
Assessing balance of authority of parties to interview
Physical setting for interview
Will there be a "winner"?
Understand main phases of an interview.

Opening/setting out background
Gathering information—questioning techniques.
      —establish full picture of customer needs.
Giving information   —have full knowledge of facts clear, concise, relevant.
Conflict
Compromises and settlement
Close—summarise agreement
      —determine follow-up action
      —monitor

7.1 Cover further interviewing issues.
Control of the interview—arrange for no interruption
      —allow time/be aware of passing time
      —remain prepared to change tack
      —listen
Non-verbal communication.
Persuasion styles, dealing with objections, closing techniques.
Benefit statements re products and use of concessions.

BANKING OPERATIONS 1; Examination Paper
May 1987
(reproduced by kind permission of the Chartered Institute of Bankers)

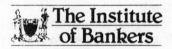
The Institute of Bankers

STAGE 1

BANKING CERTIFICATE EXAMINATION–
FINAL SECTION

BANKING OPERATIONS I–
INTERNATIONAL AND LENDING

14 May, 1987

N.B. 1. Read the instructions on the cover of the answer book.

2. **Answer FIVE questions: TWO from Section A, THREE from Section B.**

3. CANDIDATES MUST SATISFY THE EXAMINER IN BOTH SECTIONS OF THE PAPER.

4. The number in brackets after each question indicates the marks allotted. Where questions are subdivided, the figure shown after each subdivision indicates the number of marks allotted to that part of the question.
   In awarding marks the examiner will look for answers which show (*a*) an appreciation of the significance of the question and (*b*) a reasoned practical approach to the problem.

5. Tabulated answers (i.e. statements in listed note form) are acceptable.

6. Silent electronic calculators may be used in this examination. Whether or not candidates use them, it is in their interest to show the basic figures from which their calculations are made.

7. Time allowed: three hours.

8. 15 minutes' reading time is allowed at the beginning of the examination when candidates may write on this paper but NOT in the answer book.

SECTION A

Answer TWO questions from this Section

1.—Please answer ALL of the following questions. Only the question number and the letter beside the correct answer should be written in your answer book. (Thus if the answer to number (i) is (B), then write '(i)(B)' in the answer book.)

(i) The following US$ bank buying rates for fixed forward contracts have been quoted by the bank:
SPOT 1.5730
One month 1.5770
Two months 1.5790
Three months 1.5800
Are the forward rates quoted above:
(A) at a premium to sterling? or
(B) at a discount to sterling?

(ii) S.W.I.F.T. is a computer based system which allows banks to transmit messages quickly. S.W.I.F.T. stands for:
(A) Society for World-Wide Interbank Financial Telecommunications;
(B) Society for World-Wide International Financial Telecommunications;
(C) Society for World-Wide Interbank Financial Transfers.

(iii) For travellers, which service provides the greatest safety in case of loss or theft?:
(A) Currency;
(B) Travellers cheques
(C) Letter of credit.

(iv) A Government body established in 1919 to assist exporters by providing insurance for country/buyer risks is called:
(A) I.C.F.C.
(B) E.C.G.D.
(C) B.O.T.B.

(v) A bank guarantee provided on behalf of an exporter of capital goods is a:
  (A) Letter of introduction;
  (B) Documentary credit
  (C) Performance bond.

(vi) A bank customer asks the bank to buy a documentary bill. Is this:
  (A) A negotiation;
  (B) A collection;
  (C) A documentary credit.

(vii) A credit card can be used:
  (A) at any organisation offering goods and/or services;
  (B) at any place displaying the credit card logo;
  (C) at any shop

(viii) A factoring company operates by:
  (A) loaning to its clients funds against their invoiced debts;
  (B) buying from its clients their invoiced debts;
  (C) buying from its clients their bad debts.

(ix) LIFFE opened in the City's old Royal Exchange in September 1982 and trades in short term currency time contracts. What does LIFFE stand for?:
  (A) London International Financial Futures Exchange;
  (B) London and International Forward Futures Exchange;
  (C) London and International Financial Futures Market.

(x) Which of these is eurocurrency?:
  (A) Swiss Francs held in Germany by a German resident;
  (B) Dollars held in New York by an American Resident;
  (C) Sterling held in France by a Swiss Resident.
  (20)

2.—Your customers, Johns Jeans Ltd, have recently exported for the first time to a new buyer in Spain, introduced through a mutual acquaintance. Although they invoiced the purchaser some five weeks ago they have still not received payment and they have come to you for advice.

State briefly:
  (a) the major benefits and drawbacks of various alternative methods of financing exports;   (16)
  (b) what advice you can offer to the Directors, Mr and Mrs James, for any future contracts they may have with the buyer. (4)

3.—(a) Define briefly all the following terms:
  (A) SPOT transactions;
  (B) FORWARD transactions;
  (C) Foreign currency options;
  (D) Tender to contract;
  (E) Financial futures.
  (10)

(b) In Foreign Exchange Markets what do we mean by the following glossary of terms?:
  (A) Closing Rate;
  (B) Discount;
  (C) Premium;
  (D) Spread;
  (E) SWAP.
  (10)

SECTION B

Answer THREE questions from this Section

4.—(a) Mr Timothy Wilkins has been known to you as a good personal customer for several years. You are aware that his present employers in the retail trade think highly of him in his middle management post with them.

Mr Wilkins has been saving for several years and now wishes to set up a new business for himself in the High Street, Timothy Wilkins (Lighting) Limited. He has asked the bank to lend him £15,000 towards the £40,000 required for the lease, fixtures and fittings and initial stock. You feel happy to lend to him against his personal guarantee as sole director, supported by the deeds of his home.

State briefly the **technical considerations** necessary before lending. (10)

(*b*) Your customer, Maggie Charles, wants to borrow £500 towards the purchase of some hi-fi equipment against the security of her building society pass book, (balance £651.40). She would prefer not to withdraw those funds for the purchase.

Assuming you are happy to grant the loan:

(i) What action would you take to protect the bank's position? (4)

(ii) What are the benefits and drawbacks of this type of security? (6)

5.—(*a*) The account of one of your customers, Mr Matthews, has an overdraft limit of £4,000 and a loan of £7,500. Recently, his account has appeared regularly on your morning computer print-out of irregular accounts and you have warned him that the limits must be strictly observed, failing which you will have to return cheques unpaid.

On this morning's print-out, the balances as at the end of close of business last night are shown as:

Current account: £4,675 debit

Loan account: £7,500 debit

The five items debited in yesterday's general clearing are:

i. a crossed cheque in favour of A Smith for £49, dated 10 April, 1987 with Mr Matthews' cheque card number 825439 on the reverse;

ii. a crossed cheque in favour of Dale Austin for £183 dated 4 April, 1987;

iii. a direct debit for £32 in favour of Sure Life Assurance;

iv. a crossed cheque in favour of J Garwood for £79, dated 6 June, 1987;

v. a crossed cheque in favour of J Round for £47, dated 4 April, 1986.

Your bank is a member of the London Bankers' Clearing House.

State briefly:

(i) what actions you will take with regard to the five items debited in yesterday's general clearing,

(ii) what action will you take on hearing that there is a gentleman tendering a Bank Giro Credit for his account at your City Branch of £250. The credit is made up of cash and a crossed cheque for £100 drawn by your customer, Mr Matthews, dated 11 April 1987. The gentleman is asking whether the cheque is paid.(15)

(*b*) Edward Simpkins guarantees the account of his son, George who runs a sandwich bar. George banks at your branch and at present has a debit balance of £1,004.17.

You have just received notice of the death of Mr Simpkins' senior. What action must the Bank take to protect its position? (5)

6.—(*a*) You have discovered that a credit card has been issued to your student customer, John Brown, age 17½, in the mistaken belief that he was at least 18. There is an outstanding balance of £560 now on the credit card account.

What action can you take? Give your reasons.(5)

(*b*) Your customer, Mary Smith, has been on a spending spree using her cheque book, accompanied by a cheque guarantee card, for amounts up to £50. Her account stands at £1,205 debit without prior agreement or arrangement. What is the bank's position? (5)

(*c*) For what purposes are personal loans normally granted to individuals? Briefly, describe the characteristics of personal loans and state the advantages and disadvantages to the customer and the bank. (5)

(*d*) What are the basic canons of lending? (5)

7.—Please answer ALL of the following questions. Only the question number and the letter beside the correct answer-should be written in your answer book. (Thus if the answer to number (i) is (C), then write '(i)(C)' in the answer book).

(i) A Finance House is likely to provide finance to individuals for:

(A) purchase of industrial shares;

(B) hire purchase of a consumer durable;

(C) house purchase.

(ii) A bank advance for a business to purchase trading stock will:
  (A) reduce the outstanding liabilities of the business;
  (B) increase the fixed assets of the business;
  (C) increase the current assets of the business.

(iii) Interest charged on an overdraft and paid for the year will be shown in:
  (A) the trading account;
  (B) the profit and loss account;
  (C) the profit and loss appropriation account.

(iv) The period of credit given to debtors is calculated by:
  (A) $\dfrac{\text{debtors} \times 365 \text{ No. days}}{\text{Turnover}}$ = days
  (B) $\dfrac{\text{creditors} \times 365 \text{ No. days}}{\text{Turnover}}$ = days
  (C) $\dfrac{\text{debtors} \times 365 \text{ No. days}}{\text{Purchases}}$ = days

(v) In a balance sheet for a manufacturing company, plant and machinery are shown as:
  (A) fixed assets;
  (B) current assets;
  (C) working capital.

(vi) A paramount consideration before lending money is that:
  (A) the customer has more than adequate security;
  (B) the customer has the ability to repay;
  (C) the customer has a good safe job.

(vii) A bridging loan from the bank's point of view is often:
  (A) simple, profitable and self-liquidating;
  (B) profitable and self-liquidating but needs registering;
  (C) simple, profitable, but is usually repayable in the long term.

(viii) One of the first questions asked by a banker when confronted with a request for a loan is:
  (A) how much security is available?
  (B) do you own your own house or business?
  (C) what is the source of repayment?

(ix) What is usually the cheapest form of bank lending?
  (A) personal loan;
  (B) credit card;
  (C) overdraft.

(x) What do we mean by a firm's gearing?:
  (A) relationship between loan and equity capital;
  (B) relationship between current/fixed assets;
  (C) level of plant and machinery.

(20)

BANKING OPERATIONS 2: Examination Paper
May 1987

(reproduced by kind permission of the Chartered Institute of Bankers)

 **The Institute of Bankers**

STAGE 1

BANKING CERTIFICATE EXAMINATION—
FINAL SECTION

BANKING OPERATIONS II

18 May, 1987

N.B. 1. Read the instructions on the cover of the answer book.

2. This examination paper has **FOUR** Sections. Candidates should attempt all four sections.
Section A: Answer **ALL** questions (**One** mark per question)
Section B: Answer **ALL** questions (**FIVE** marks per question)
Section C: Answer **TWO** questions only (**Fifteen** marks per question)
Section D: Answer **ONE** question only. Your answer should be in essay form. (**Twenty-five** marks).

3. Tabulated answers (i.e. statements in listed note form) are acceptable, except in Section D.

4. Time allowed: three hours.

5. 15 minutes' reading time is allowed at the beginning of the examination when candidates may write on this paper but NOT in the answer book.

SECTION A

*Answer **ALL** questions. Each question carries **ONE** mark. In your answer book, write the question number **and** the option (a, b, c or d) that you think is correct.*

1.—Replies to status enquiries are not signed on behalf of the bank providing them. This is because:

(a) The individual member of staff who signed the reply could be held responsible;

(b) The bank seeks to avoid a claim of fraudulent misrepresentation in the information given;

(c) The bank acts as a credit reference agency;

(d) The bank accepts no responsibility to its customer for the accuracy of the reply.

2.—Treasury Bills are usually issued for a tenor of:

(a) 31 days;

(b) Six months;

(c) 91 days;

(d) A year.

3.—Which of the following form part of a bank's liquid assets in calculating its liquidity ratio:

(a) Money at call;

(b) Advances;

(c) Investments;

(d) Premises?

4.—Which of the following is a feature of preference shares:

(a) A variable dividend;

(b) Security by way of specific assets;

(c) Priority in the event of liquidation;

(d) Lower rates of tax on yield?

5.—The advantage of buying gilt-edged securities on the Post Office register is:

(a) A higher rate of interest is paid;

(b) Purchases can be completed more quickly;

(c) Purchases are free of commission;

(d) Interest is paid gross.

6.—The Bank of England has not set a formal Minimum Lending Rate since:

(a) 1969;

(b) 1971;

(c) 1981;

(d) 1979.

7.—Investments which pay interest net of composite rate tax are of maximum benefit and convenience to:

(a) Children;

(b) Pensioners;

(c) Higher rate tax payers;

(d) Standard rate taxpayers.

8.—Which of the following has to seek permission from the Bank of England before accepting funds from the public:

(a) Insurance companies;

(b) Stockbrokers;

(c) Clearing banks;

(d) Local authorities?

9.—Which of the following might be referred to as 'below the line' advertising:

(a) Television commercials;

(b) Leaflets;

(c) Newspaper advertisements;

(d) Direct mail letter?

10.—How many of the partners should sign a normal partnership mandate:

(a) only the senior partner;

(b) The partners who operate the account;

(c) At least half the partners;

(d) All the partners?

11.—What does the expression 'ultra vires' mean with reference to the board of directors of a company:

(a) that each director has the same power;

(b) that an action is within their power;

(c) that the directors must act together;

(d) that an action is beyond their authority?

12.—If the market price of fixed interest securities has fallen then:

(a) market rates of interest have risen;

(b) money supply has increased;

(c) banks have increased their lending;

(d) market rates of interest have fallen.

13.—Does the expression 'administrator' (with reference to accounts with banks) usually mean a person employed:

(a) in the civil service;

(b) by the court to deal with a deceased's estate;

(c) in local government administration;

(d) in any administrative capacity?

14.—Which of the following is normally accepted to be a duty of a banker:

(a) to give interest on accounts;

(b) to give a receipt for all cheques paid in;

(c) to know the signature of customers;

(d) to ensure that a cheque payable to cash is endorsed?

15.—What is the maximum number of partners allowed in a partnership of solicitors:

(a) 20;

(b) 50;

(c) No maximum;

(d) 5?

16.—Discount houses usually borrow money:

(a) short term;

(b) by the use of debentures;

(c) by the issue of shares;

(d) long-term.

17.—As a paid bailee of items lodged in safe custody, a bank must:

(a) take maximum possible care;

(b) take reasonable care;

(c) insure the items lodged;

(d) be aware of the contents of packages lodged.

18.—The principal advantage of a budget account is that:

(a) reduced interest rates are usually available;

(b) bills can be paid by standing order;

(c) planning is aided by regular statements of account;

(d) large bills can be spread over twelve months.

19.—Acting as an 'issuing house' involves:

(a) issuing government securities;

(b) trading on the stock exchange;

(c) assisting companies in selling their shares;

(d) providing notes and coin.

20.—If the Bank of England wishes to make more funds available to the money market it:

(*a*) calls for special deposits;
(*b*) lends money to the clearing banks;
(*c*) buys eligible bills;
(*d*) increases the rate of interest charged to the discount houses.

SECTION B

Answer ALL questions.
Each question carries FIVE marks

Read the following extract from the *Financial Times* and answer all the questions.

MONEY MARKETS

Little overall change despite firm pound

UK clearing bank base lending rate 11 per cent since October 15

INTEREST RATES were hardly changed in the London money market yesterday. Sterling finished the day on a firm note but there was a general lack of confidence, highlighted by the flat interest rate structure from one month out to one year. Dealers stressed a number of factors currently governing market sentiment which could easily change, such as the performance of sterling, oil prices and to some extent the implications of Mr Nigel Lawson's autumn statement.

Three-month interbank money was unchanged at $11\frac{1}{16}-10\frac{15}{16}$ per cent while overnight money touched a high of $11\frac{1}{2}$ per cent from an opening level of $11\frac{1}{4}-11$ per cent before touching a low of 8 per cent and finishing very late at 11 per cent bid.

The Bank of England forecast a shortage of around £250m with factors affecting the market including maturing assistance and a take up of Treasury bills together draining £217m and a rise in the note circulation a further £100m. In addition banks brought forward balances £55m below target. These were offset by Exchequer transactions which added £110m. The forecast was revised to a shortage of around £300m and the Bank gave assistance in the morning of £126m through outright purchases of £126m of eligible bank bills in band 2 at $10\frac{13}{16}$ per cent.

Further help was given in the afternoon of £89m through outright purchases of £17m of eligible bank bills in band 1 at $10\frac{7}{8}$ per cent and £72m in band 2 at $10\frac{13}{16}$ per cent. Late help came to £85m, making a total of £300m.

21.—Explain the meaning of the phrase 'flat interest rate structure from one month out to one year'.

LONDON MONEY RATES

Nov. 5	Over-night	7 days notice	Month	Three Months	Six Months	One Year
Interbank	$11\frac{1}{2}-8$	$11-10\frac{3}{4}$	$11-10\frac{7}{8}$	$11\frac{1}{16}-10\frac{15}{16}$	$11\frac{1}{16}-10\frac{15}{16}$	$11\frac{1}{16}-10\frac{15}{16}$
Sterling Cds	—	—	$11-10\frac{7}{8}$	$11-10\frac{7}{8}$	$11-10\frac{7}{8}$	$11-10\frac{3}{4}$
Local Authority Deposits	$11-10\frac{1}{2}$	$10\frac{7}{8}-10\frac{1}{2}$	$10\frac{15}{16}-10\frac{7}{8}$	$11\frac{1}{16}-10\frac{15}{16}$	$11-10\frac{15}{16}$	$10\frac{15}{16}$
Local Authority Bonds	—	—	$11\frac{1}{4}$	$11\frac{1}{4}$	$11\frac{1}{4}$	$11\frac{1}{8}$
Discount Market Deposits	$10\frac{1}{2}-7\frac{1}{2}$	$10\frac{3}{4}$	$10\frac{3}{4}$	$10\frac{3}{4}$	—	—
Company Deposits	$11-10\frac{7}{8}$	$10\frac{7}{8}$	$11\frac{1}{16}-10\frac{15}{16}$	$11\frac{1}{16}-10\frac{15}{16}$	11	11
Finance House Deposits	—	—	$10\frac{7}{8}$	11	11	11
Treasury Bills (Buy)	—	—	$10\frac{13}{16}$	$10\frac{5}{8}$	—	—
Bank Bills (Buy)	—	—	$10\frac{13}{16}$	$10\frac{11}{16}$	$10\frac{1}{2}-10\frac{15}{32}$	—
Fine Trade Bills (Buy)	—	—	$11\frac{7}{16}$	$11\frac{5}{16}$	$11\frac{3}{32}$	—
Dollar CDs	—	—	5.90-5.85	5.85-5.80	5.85-5.80	6.00-5.95
SDR Linked Deposits	—	—	$6\frac{1}{8}-5\frac{7}{8}$	$6\frac{1}{4}-6$	$6\frac{5}{16}-6\frac{1}{16}$	$6\frac{3}{8}-6\frac{1}{8}$
ECU Linked Deposits	—	—	$7\frac{7}{16}-7\frac{5}{16}$	$7\frac{1}{2}-7\frac{3}{8}$	$7\frac{1}{2}-7\frac{3}{8}$	$7\frac{7}{16}-7\frac{5}{16}$

22.—What reason is given for this 'flat interest rate structure'?

23.—How did the Bank of England deal with the shortage of liquidity in the market?

24.—Explain the main features of 'eligible bank bills' and 'certificates of deposit'. Identify the differences between these two instruments.

25.—Describe the main function of the inter-bank market.

SECTION C

*Answer TWO questions only.
Each question carries FIFTEEN marks.*

26.—Your branch has recently carried out a direct-mail promotion of credit cards and one of your customers has replied that he has no need to borrow money. From an investigation of branch records, you find that the customer keeps an average balance of £550 credit on current account, but does overdraw occasionally. His account is very active and bank charges are some £25 per quarter. You are also aware that your customer travels frequently. The account has been opened for over 10 years but there is no indication that this customer has made use of any additional bank services.
Draft a letter for your manager to sign outlining some of the relevant advantages of a credit card and persuading the customer to change his mind.

27.—Your manager tells you that he wishes to carry out a review of the branch's promotional activity.
Prepare brief notes for a meeting, identifying a maximum of five products/services which would be promoted 'in-branch'. You should indicate which times of the year you would consider more appropriate for each promotion and note your reasons for the choice.

28.—Mrs. Brown has called at the enquiry counter and told you that she has inherited £5,000 worth of equities. She is concerned that the money is presently invested in only two companies and has been advised that unit trusts would spread the risk. Mrs. Brown is most interested in a general fund giving a balance of income and capital growth. From your knowledge of her financial affairs you believe that this is sensible, but Mrs. Brown is worried about the cost of selling her recently inherited shares and confused about the significance of the 'bid' and 'offer' prices for unit trusts shown in the morning newspaper.
Mrs. Brown asks for guidance, as she has no idea how to acquire a suitable unit trust. In short paragraphs, outline your response to Mrs. Brown, setting out the explanations she requires.

SECTION D

*Answer ONE question only in essay form.
TWENTY-FIVE marks*

29.—Outline the 'life-cycle' segmentation of personal customers. Give examples of bank services which would benefit each segment you identify.

30.—State the principal methods which a clearing bank may use to attract personal customers. Discuss how far an individual branch of a bank can exercise any control over these methods.

31.—Before entering a meeting to negotiate upon any matter, you should have devoted some time to preparation.
Discuss the main areas you would consider during this preparatory work.

BANKING OPERATIONS 1: Commentary on May 1987 paper

The paper is divided into two sections, Section A concentrating on international banking and Section B concentrating on lending services. Candidates must pass in both sections of the paper, but greater weight is given to lending which carries 60% of the marks. Note that calculators are permitted and questions may be set which require some calculation. In this paper most candidates would not have needed to use a calculator.

Q1. Multiple choice

This question consists of a 10-part multiple choice test intended to cover a wide range of aspects of the syllabus. The use of such questions means that no subject area included in the syllabus can be safely ignored.

Q2. Financing exports

This question deals with the different approaches to paying for exports from open account to payment in advance. Suitable advice might include checking on the buyer with a status enquiry, choosing a method of payment which gives adequate protection and taking out credit insurance.

Q3. Definitions

Like a multiple choice question this questions picks out different parts of the syllabus to test. Unlike multiple choice questions inspired guesswork is unlikely to be of much help.

Q4. Security for lending

Part a) is a potential source of confusion because the examiner uses the phrase 'technical considerations' to refer to security and the legal background to it. The basic requirements of the security are reasonably straightforward, but extra marks might be earned by referring to the legal requirements for opening the company account and the possibility that the borrowing might be outside the manager's discretionary powers.

Part b) deals with a personal loan (which would normally have been offered unsecured), but goes on to ask about the benefits and drawbacks of a building society passbook as security.

Q5. Returning cheques and the death of a guarantor

Part a) of the question is a problem about how to deal with a variety of items drawn by a customer beyond his overdraft limit, and a full answer requires detailed knowledge of the Clearing House rules as well as the basic principles.

In part b) the examiner asks for a brief explanation of what happens when a guarantee has been taken and the guarantor dies.

Q6. Miscellaneous lending questions

The four parts of this question deal with minors, misuse of a cheque guarantee card, personal loans and the principles of lending.

Q7. Multiple choice

This question consists of a ten-part multiple choice test covering a number of areas relating to accounting and accounting ratio analysis as well as asking about the role of finance houses, a topic which could equally have been included in Banking Operations 2.

BANKING OPERATIONS 2: Commentary on May 1987 paper

The instructions for the Banking Operations 2 paper are rather complex and candidates should take great care in following them. The examiner emphasises that tabulated answers are acceptable, but this is not relevant to Section A or to Section D.

Section A. Multiple choice (for 20x1 marks)

This section contains twenty multiple choice questions on a range of topics including some, such as the advantages of budget accounts, which could equally have been included in the Banking Operations 1 paper. As with Banking Operations 1 the use of such questions means that candidates need to be familiar with all areas of the syllabus. Because all questions in Section A are compulsory there is even less opportunity for missing out any part of the material than there is with Banking Operations 1.

Section B. Comprehension (for 5x5 marks)

This section requires the student to read a passage, in this case from the Financial Times, then answer questions connected with the text. It is not purely a comprehension exercise because the student is expected to comment on ideas which are used in the passage but not explained by it. There is no choice in this section.

Section C. Short case studies (for 2x15 marks)

The three questions in this section describe situations which may arise in branch banking. The candidate can choose two out of the three and is expected to explain how the problem described should be tackled.

The first example is about the benefits of using a credit card. The second example deals with in-branch

promotion of services (allowing the student to choose which services to include). The third example is about buying unit trusts.

Section D. Essay (for 25 marks)

Candidates are given a choice of one essay out of three. The titles are intended to be fairly open-ended. Topics covered in this paper are market segmentation, attracting personal customers and preparation for interviews. In each case the title is fairly precise and students need to take care to keep to the subject. Careful planning should ensure that there is no difficulty in having enough material to include.

Section 2
The Study Manual

27 Chapters covering all aspects of the
Chartered Institute of Bankers syllabuses
for BANKING OPERATIONS 1
and BANKING OPERATIONS 2.

EXAMINATION AND STUDY TECHNIQUE

The examinations of the Banking Certificate will be the final examinations which some students will take and are therefore not intended to be easy to pass. Determined effort over a continuous period of study is needed in order to be sure of success.

For more ambitious students the Banking Certificate represents only a first stage towards qualifying as an associate of the Chartered Institute of Bankers. For such students it is even more important that the material studied is thoroughly absorbed rather than being hastily revised at the last moment in order to scrape through the examination. The knowledge required for the two Banking Operations papers forms the basis of much of what is studied in the Stage Two Diploma. A carefully planned programme of study is therefore essential as a means of building up the required level of knowledge.

HINTS ON HOW TO STUDY

1. Allocating your time

Begin by being realistic. Decide how much time you will be able to spend on study each week and plan to devote specific hours of specific days each week to studying. Make sure your allocated hours do not clash with favourite television programmes or other regular leisure activities. The hours you choose should also not be so late at night that you will be unable to concentrate properly.

An effective method is to divide you study time into periods of 45 minutes to an hour followed by a break. To try to concentrate for longer periods usually leads to a reduction in the quality of the work you are doing. If you are taking several different subjects try to vary the work systematically, both because this will reduce the likelihood of boredom and because you will be less likely to devote too much time to one of the subjects at the expense of others.

2. Using the Syllabus

For each topic that you are tackling look up what the syllabus requires. This helps you to think about the kind of questions you should be finding answers to in your reading of the text.

The syllabus can also be a guide to the amount of time to spend on each topic area. This is particularly useful when you are revising because it becomes very easy to look at the revision material, assume that you understand it all and move on to the next topic without spending time testing your knowledge.

3. How to learn

Because your time is valuable you should make sure that when you are studying you are making the most of the time. Simply reading through a text is not the same as learning, particularly if there are distractions. In order to learn you need to adopt a more active approach to study.

This means that you should study with a pen and paper. For each chapter that you tackle begin by skimming through briefly and then re-read more actively:—

MAKE NOTES ON THE CHAPTER AS YOU READ;

INVENT QUESTIONS WHICH YOU EXPECT THE CHAPTER TO ANSWER FOR YOU;

TACKLE THE SELF REVIEW QUESTIONS;

REVIEW THE CHAPTER BY MAKING YOUR OWN SUMMARY OF KEY POINTS.

These techniques will help you to understand the information. You should also tackle the questions and exercises set because these are part of the learning process too. They will help you to identify areas which you have failed to understand as well as getting you used to analysing what questions are getting at, a vital skill for examinations.

4. Revision and the Examination

Section 3 of the Manual provides a basis for your revision programme, and includes guidance on how to revise and how to tackle the examinations. Again your own realistic timetable of study is essential.

1. The Banking System

INTRODUCTION

1. This chapter looks at how banks are defined. The major provisions of the Banking Act 1979 and the Banking Act 1987 are outlined to show how legislation has changed the structure of the banking system. Different approaches to the categorisation of banks are considered before going on to look at the major categories of importance today in the United Kingdom.

The categories to be considered are:-
a) The Central Bank;
b) Clearing Banks;
c) Foreign Banks;
d) British Overseas Banks;
e) Merchant Banks;
f) Discount Houses;
g) Fringe Banks;
h) The National Savings Bank.

THE TRADITIONAL DEFINITION

2. Before 1979 there was no legal or official definition of a bank and where laws applied to banks or referred to banks it was not always certain which institutions were covered by the term 'bank'.

In general it was considered that a bank:-
a) accepted deposits from customers and looked after their money;
b) offered cheque books to customers to enable them to make payments to other people;
c) provided at least some other financial services.

Any organisation which could show that it met those three basic requirements would probably have felt entitled to claim to be treated as a bank.

RECOGNITION AS A BANK

3. For the well known banks with branches in high streets throughout the country there is no problem of identity; they have never needed to prove that they are banks. For smaller institutions which are only involved in providing a few financial services,

possibly of a fairly specialised nature, to be seen as a bank may offer special benefits. These include:-
a) the possible use of the name 'bank' in promotional material, encouraging depositors to have greater confidence that they will get their money back;
b) wider recognition by customers that the institution is a competitor with other banks;
c) specific legal privileges or protections which are only available to banks, particularly to do with the legal risks involved in dealing with cheques.

THE DEFINITION IN THE 1979 BANKING ACT

4. In 1979 when new legislation was brought in to regulate the banking system it was important to identify clearly the institutions to be covered by the new rules.

The type of definition adopted was a very simple one. Since the 1979 Act an institution has been defined as a bank and is allowed to use the name 'bank' as part of its official company name only if it is recognised as a bank by the Bank of England (which was given this responsibility because of its role as the central bank of the United Kingdom, described later in this chapter).

This method of defining banks has two important implications.
1. The Bank of England has great power over banks because it can remove them from the list of banks by withdrawing its recognition (an extreme penalty, unlikely to be imposed very often).
2. Any institution wishing to become known as a bank has a clear and simple method of achieving this aim; it applies to the Bank of England for recognition.

Clearly the Bank of England does not accept all applications. The general principles it uses to decide whether a bank should be recognised or not are similar to the ideas of the traditional view of what constituted a bank. The Bank of England will look at a range of factors, in particular whether the applicant:-
a) accepts deposits;
b) offers loans;

c) deals with import and export finance and foreign exchange;

d) provides investment services and advice on business finance.

If an institution does all of this, is managed by capable people and has a minimum level of capital, set at £5 million in the 1979 Act, the Bank of England will normally grant recognition. It is also possible to be recognised as a bank without meeting all of these criteria, but exceptions are rare. Among the exceptions are the discount houses, described later in this chapter.

INSTITUTIONS NOT RECOGNISED AS BANKS UNDER THE 1979 ACT

5. Some institutions asking for recognition as banks under the 1979 Act were not considered suitable by the Bank of England because of their limited range of services. The 1979 Act therefore included a second, lower level of recognition. Institutions could be granted the status of Licensed Deposit Takers or Licensed Deposit Taking Institutions (often abbreviated to LDTs or LDTIs). This title also depended on the approval of the Bank of England and was intended to apply to specialist organisations rather than to 'banks' which were in any way second-rate. Nevertheless the status of LDT was often seen as being inferior to that of recognised banks.

An institution did not, of course, have a permanent place on one of the Bank of England's two lists. As an example the Commercial Bank of Wales was originally only allowed to be a licensed deposit taker. Later the Bank of England gave approval for Commercial Bank of Wales to become a recognised bank, though it was later taken over by the Bank of Scotland (in 1986).

During 1985 five licensed deposit takers had their licences revoked by the Bank of England, though all of these were businesses with liabilities of less than £10 million. No major institutions have yet suffered this fate.

To be deprived of recognition as either a bank or a licensed deposit taker is clearly a serious problem because recognition allows an institution to advertise for and accept deposits from the general public. Unrecognised institutions are not allowed to ask the public to deposit money with them unless they are already subject to other legal controls. (Local authorities and building societies, for example, are not governed by the Banking Acts because they are controlled by other legislation).

BACKGROUND TO AND PROVISIONS OF THE 1979 BANKING ACT

6. The basic purpose of the 1979 Banking Act was to make sure the whole banking system was safe and well controlled so that the general public would have confidence that their money deposited with banks was secure.

The need for such legislation had become apparent in 1973 and 1974 when many smaller banks got into difficulties because they had lent too much to businesses specialising in buying property. As property prices fell and depositors wanted to get their money back a major operation affecting even the big high street banks was needed to prevent the whole banking system from collapsing. This so-called 'lifeboat' operation coordinated by the Bank of England involved large banks lending money to smaller banks to pay out to their worried customers and it succeeded in saving most of the banks involved, though some have taken many years to recover from the crisis.

The Banking Act was passed in 1979 with the aim of preventing a recurrence of the problem by imposing tighter supervision. In addition a directive of the European Economic Community on the standardisation of banking regulation within the Common Market had made some form of new legislation necessary.

The major provisions of the Act were that:-

a) the Bank of England would only recognise as banks institutions which met certain criteria (considered above);

b) the Bank of England would recognise as licensed deposit takers institutions which only met some of the required criteria;

c) the Bank of England would require regular information from banks and LDTs to monitor the risks they were taking and would be entitled to carry out supervisory visits (though in practice only a small proportion of banks or LDTs have received such visits);

d) a deposit protection scheme would be set up to give depositors greater certainty of getting their money back if the bank with which they had placed money got into difficulties.

THE DEPOSIT PROTECTION SCHEME

7. The following table summarises the features of the Deposit Protection Scheme (sometimes referred to as a deposit insurance scheme) set up as a result of the 1979 Banking Act.

1. All banks and LDTs contributed a proportion of their total deposits (which the high street banks saw as unfair because they claimed to be at least risk of failure but had to pay in the largest amounts).

2. The fund collected, which initially amounted to over £5 million, was controlled by a Deposit Protection Board under the Bank of England.

3. Protection related to any deposit up to maximum of £10,000 with any one institution.

4. The deposit protection fund would pay out compensation of 75% of any protected deposit.
   e.g. a deposit of £8,000 –
   compensation of £6,000
   a deposit of £18,000 –
   compensation of £7,500
   (the maximum)

5. As the fund was depleted by paying out compensation the contributors would be asked for more funds.
   This happened during the 1980s as payments were made following the failures of a number of very small licensed deposit takers (for example, Merbro Finance with 271 depositors owed a total of less than £700,000).

THE BANKING ACT 1987

8. Just as the banking crisis in the 1970s was a stimulus for the passing of the 1979 Banking Act, so the collapse of Johnson Matthey Bankers in 1983-84 encouraged government to pass the 1987 Banking Act.

The main aim of the new legislation was to improve still further the control which the Bank of England is able to exercise over the banking system. The main changes brought about by the act were:-

a) the ending of the two-tier system of banks and licensed deposit-takers so that all of them come under the same rules;

b) greater powers for the Bank of England to require information from banks about their activities;

c) the setting up of a supervisory board including outside experts to assist the Bank of England in its work;

d) greater influence for the Bank of England in restricting takeovers of banks.

The provisions of the 1979 Act have not been swept away by the new legislation. The deposit protection scheme remains in place (though it has been amended to cover deposits of £15000, with maximum refunds therefore now amounting to £11,250), and the Bank of England still has its power to decide whether institutions can be considered as banks.

CATEGORISATION OF BANKS

9. As we have seen, in the broadest sense institutions which provide banking services can be categorised according to official guidelines as under the 1979 Banking Act. However the range of organisations which have obtained approval from the Bank of England to be considered as banks is wide; at the time of the 1979 Act there were around 300 recognised banks and the number is now greater. To understand the banking system it is therefore useful to classify banks rather than thinking of them as all being the same. Such classification involves identifying particular shared characteristics that only some banks have. A number of different broad categories have been commonly identified but these are not necessarily completely separate and distinct.

One commonly made distinction is between retail banking and wholesale banking. Retail banking means banking provided through branches, offering services to the general public who can come in and open accounts. Wholesale banking means dealing with money on a large scale, usually in millions of pounds and often for periods as short as a day or a week. Wholesale banking takes place between banks or other financial institutions rather than with the general public. Some banks specialise in retail banking or in wholesale banking but the large United Kingdom banks operate in both areas.

The clearest division between different kinds of banks, and one to which the Bank of England gives official recognition is the distinction between 'eligible' banks and other banks. Like recognition as a bank this depends entirely on the approval of the Bank of England. Eligible banks, which include the main high street banks and other particularly important or influential banks, have a special privilege of being able to raise money from the money markets at rates slightly more favourable than those which other banks have to pay. The word 'eligible' is used to describe them because the documents they use to raise money are eligible (or acceptable) for purchase by the Bank of England. It is the backing of the Bank of England which enables the eligible banks to raise money cheaply.

Other subdivisions of the banking system do not usually relate to such technical differences, but are more general.

The major categories are considered in turn.

THE CENTRAL BANK

10.   Banking systems in all countries of the world have a central bank which plays a part in controlling the other banks. In the United Kingdom this central bank is the Bank of England.

The basic functions of the central bank are:-

a)   to act as a bank for other banks and financial institutions, providing deposit and loan facilities. (Because the central bank lends, directly or indirectly, to other banks when they are short of money it is commonly referred to as the 'lender of last resort');

b)   to act as a bank for the government providing deposit and loan facilities and often offering advice on government financing and economic affairs;

c)   to help to implement government monetary policy, in particular by influencing interest rates;

d)   to represent the country in international meetings of central banks to discuss such areas as banking supervision.

These functions would normally be carried out to some extent by all central banks. In addition the Bank of England, in common with many other central banks has responsibility for:-

a)   issuing notes and coins (although some Scottish banks also issue their own notes);

b)   operating the Exchange Equalization Account, looking after the country's reserves of gold and foreign currency to help to make sure that the value of the pound remains fairly stable in relation to the currencies of other countries;

c)   advising the government about raising money through issues of government stock or the sale of nationalised industries (though other banks in the private sector have also been involved in the programme of denationalisation);

d)   operating a deposit protection scheme (the scheme set up under the 1979 Banking Act and amended by the 1987 Act);

e)   supervising the whole banking system by deciding which institutions can be banks, and by collecting statistical information from them at regular intervals in order to anticipate any likely problems.

The Bank of England, although owned by the government, does operate on a commercial basis. In 1985 it made a profit of £106 million, but since it does not have private shareholders any dividend paid out goes to the government. For 1985 this amounted to almost £40 million, a record level. Although the Bank of England does have some private customers these are few in number and the Bank does not compete for deposits with the other banks, or try to gain new customers, and its profits therefore arise largely from its dealings with other financial institutions.

TRADITIONAL ENGLISH CLEARING BANKS

11.   The term clearing bank (often abbreviated to 'clearer') refers to any bank which is directly involved in a system for exchanging payments, a clearing system.

Payments made between non-clearing banks or other financial institutions need to pass through a clearing bank, and this special influence within the banking system adds to the high status of the clearers.

The traditional clearing banks include the most well-known names in United Kingdom banking. In 1983 the National Consumer Council in its report 'Banking Services and the Consumer' described as Traditional London clearing banks:

Barclays Bank plc;
Lloyds Bank plc;
Midland Bank plc;
National Westminster Bank plc;
Coutts and Co;
Williams and Glyns Bank plc.

The first four of these, the 'big four', have been the most widely represented banks in the high streets of this country since small local banks joined together in bigger and bigger groups, the last main changes taking place by the beginning of the 1970s. The 'big four' are the largest United Kingdom banks in terms of capital and total assets. Of the other two listed Coutts & Co is a wholly owned subsidiary of National Westminster Bank, but has its own direct representation in the clearing house in London, and Williams and Glyns has merged with the Royal Bank of Scotland to form one bank operating throughout Great Britain.

The domination of high street banking by the 'big four' arose because of the mergers by which they were formed. The reorganisation of National Westminster Bank provides an example of how the changes took place. In the other major banks similar developments occurred but National Westminster Bank probably ended up with the greatest duplication of branches because both National Provincial Bank and Westminster Bank had very extensive branch networks at the time of the merger in 1970.

The Formation of National Westminster Bank

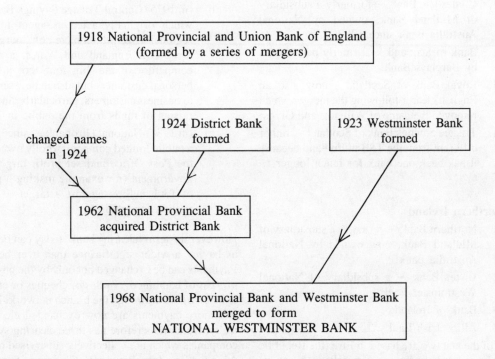

The new bank began operations in 1970 with 3,600 branches

Rationalisation by combining branches has been continuing since 1970 and by the end of 1984 the number had fallen to 3217, still the largest of the 'big four' since the others had been carrying out similar programmes to cut costs. Note that closures have taken place at the same time as the opening of new branches. In 1984, for example, National Westminster opened 33 branches but closed 51.

OTHER TRADITIONAL CLEARING BANKS

12.   Apart from the clearing banks which operate the clearing house for exchanging cheques and credits in London there are cheque and credit clearing operations in Scotland and Northern Ireland.

This means that in addition to the traditional English clearers the following banks can also be considered as clearing banks.

In Scotland

1.   Clydesdale Bank − formerly a subsidiary of Midland Bank, owned by National Australia Bank since 1987;

2.   Bank of Scotland − formerly part-owned by Barclays Bank;

3.   Royal Bank of Scotland - now also an English clearer following the merger which removed the name of Williams and Glyns;

4.   Trustee Savings Bank of Scotland − rather different from the TSB in England because it has been one bank for much longer.

In Northern Ireland

1.   Northern Bank − formerly a subsidiary of Midland Bank, now owned by National Australia Bank;

2.   Ulster Bank − a subsidiary of National Westminster Bank;

3.   Bank of Ireland;

4.   Allied Irish Banks.

Both of the last two are based in Eire (the Republic of Ireland) but have branch networks in Northern Ireland.

NEWER MEMBERS OF THE CLEARING SYSTEM

13.   The domination of the banking system by very large banks which jointly operated a clearing system for the exchange of payments was seen by banks outside the system as very unfair and a restriction on true competition. Banks which were not part of the clearing system had to pay fees to a clearing bank to get their cheques cleared. This encouraged some of the non-clearing banks to apply for membership of the clearing house. There were three main aims in applying:-

a)   to save on the cost of regular fees to a clearer;

b)   to reduce the delay in processing payments;

c)   to have some say in the future development of the system.

This last reason has become particularly important as new methods of payment and of exchanging payments have been developed.

Successful applicants to join the London cheque and credit clearing system were:-

a)   (in 1975) Cooperative Bank plc;

b)   (in 1975) Central Trustee Savings Bank − which originally acted as agent for the regional TSBs which have now merged to form TSB England and Wales, a major competitor of the 'big four' not just for personal customers but also in new services to business customers, particularly since the raising of funds from the public in 1986;

c)   (in 1981) National Girobank − since 1985 a public limited company wholly owned by the Post Office and set profit targets by government (for example making a profit of £3.1 million against a target of £3.0 million for 1985/86).

However the term 'clearing bank' today can be seen as having a wider significance than ever before. Payments can be exchanged not only by the physical process of handing over piles of cheques or credits to be distributed through the branch network. More and more payments are now exchanged electronically. London therefore has three clearing system companies which are collectively supervised by the Association for Payment Clearing Services (APACS). These clearing systems are:-

a) The Cheque and Credit Clearing Co. Ltd. (which is the traditional clearing house dealing with the exchange of paper);

b) BACS Ltd (formerly Bankers Automated Clearing Services Ltd, a company set up to exchange automated payments, in particular regular standing order instructions which can be fed into a computer memory to be acted upon at predetermined dates);

c) CHAPS and Town Clearing Co. Ltd. (which includes the Clearing House Automated Payments System, a network of linked computers which can be used to send and check messages about urgent payments, usually of high value, from one bank to another, a system described in Chapter 24).

All of these systems handle the transfer of payments between banks and are therefore clearing systems. Banks involved in any of the systems can be seen as clearing banks. Citibank, for example, was the first American owned bank to become a clearing bank in this broad sense. Although Citbank had not been successful in its earlier applications to join the traditional clearing house the development of new technology made the American bank's claim to be represented much harder to resist. The volume of cheque payments handled by Citibank was not high enough to justify its acceptance as an equal by the traditional clearers, but the volume of electronic payments was sufficient to earn Citibank a place. In spite of this Citibank would more usually be categorised as a foreign bank rather than as a clearing bank.

By July 1987 there were 17 members of APACS including two building societies, Abbey National and Halifax, as well as banks which are not always seen as clearing banks like Standard Chartered and Yorkshire Bank.

FOREIGN BANKS

14. Generally the term foreign bank refers to banks which operate in the United Kingdom but which are controlled from a head office in a foreign country.

This is certainly the case, for example, with Citibank, part of the Citicorp group based in the United States, even though, as we have seen, this does not exclude Citibank from being in one sense a United Kingdom clearer.

Within the broad category of foreign banks it is possible to distinguish between different forms of representation.

1. Some foreign banks have branch networks in the United Kingdom to meet the needs of local communities here. These include the two Irish banks already identified as Northern Ireland clearers. In addition there are branch networks of some of the banks from India and Pakistan.
Example: Bank of Baroda.

2. More commonly representation of a foreign bank is in the form of a single branch or office intended to provide a service for business customers coming to the United Kingdom. Very often such offices do not provide a full range of banking services.
Example: Bulgarian Foreign Trade Bank.

3. Other foreign banks come to London for reasons specifically associated with London's role as an international banking centre, the major market outside the United States for borrowing and lending dollars and the major market in the world for buying and selling foreign currency. (This role is discussed more fully in Chapter 18).
Example: Security Pacific National Bank (which has had a branch in London since 1969 but now has a range of financial interests in London including securities dealing and factoring).

4. Where a foreign bank does not have the resources to allocate to setting up a full branch or office it may be possible to join with other banks in a consortium.
Example: Credito Romagnolo (as a member of the ItaB Group).

Foreign banks have become of enormous importance in the British banking system because of their presence here in such large numbers, more than in any other international banking centre, and because of their involvement on a large scale in international lending carried out through London. They have also gained a strong position as dealers in the financial markets in London; for example over half the primary dealers in the important market for United Kingdom government stocks are foreign owned.

BRITISH OVERSEAS BANKS

15.   At one time a major category in the analysis of the British banking system was the group known as British Overseas Banks. These banks had head offices in Britain but their branch networks and offices were located abroad. They had their origins in Britain's history as a leading trading nation and world power. Now they have largely disappeared.

Some were taken over by traditional clearers. Example: Bank of London and South America (which became part of Lloyds Bank).

Of the remainder most are now more accurately considered as foreign banks because control is no longer based in London.

The main examples of note are:-

a)   Hong Kong and Shanghai Banking Corporation – now strictly a foreign bank because it is controlled from Hong Kong;

b)   Grindlays Bank – now strictly a foreign bank because it was taken over in 1984 by Australia and New Zealand Banking Group;

c)   Standard Chartered Bank – an exception, perhaps the only true example today of a British Overseas bank, though proposals for a takeover by Lloyds Bank nearly ended its independence in 1986.

MERCHANT BANKS

16.   The term 'merchant bank' is one of the most difficult to define in categorising banks.

Merchant banks can be distinguished from other banks because they provide different services but there are no clear guidelines about which services need to be provided in order to establish that an organisation is a merchant bank.

In general merchant banks can be seen as financial advisers for companies. They help to decide what financial services a client company needs and then arrange to provide those services. If, for example, a company needs a major loan the merchant bank will not necessarily provide all or any of the funds itself but will arrange for other people or other institutions to supply the money. Having the right contacts and putting over a convincing case to wealthy investors may be as crucial as judging whether the borrowing company will be able to repay.

Since merchant banks will not often be lending their own funds the main source of their income is not interest but fees for making the arrangements or giving advice. The American term 'investment bank' gives a more clear indication of some of the work involved; a merchant banker links up companies needing money with investors who have funds to place with companies, whether as loans or as the purchase price of new shares. The English term 'merchant bank' does not have exactly the same meaning because the banking systems of the two countries are different, in particular because until 1986 banks in the United Kingdom did not have the same rights as United States investment banks to own and trade in stocks and shares. The use of the name 'merchant bank' in the United Kingdom reflects the more historical view of the British banking system because the merchant bankers were traditionally wealthy merchants whose financial standing as traders enabled them to give financial advice and backing to other businesses.

Merchant banks are very often seen as specialists in particular aspects of company finance, for example in takeover bids or in management buy-outs, and success in previous deals is an important means of establishing a reputation. Merchant banks which deal in the issue of new shares or in the acceptance of bills of exchange will usually provide many other services too and if banks call themselves issuing houses or accepting houses these terms are of historical significance rather than reflecting what functions the members now perform.

For well established merchant banks status has traditionally been reflected in membership of the Issuing Houses Association (IHA) or the even more exclusive Accepting Houses Committee (AHC). ISSUING HOUSES are banks (or 'houses' since they were often originally family owned businesses) which deal in the issuing of new shares on behalf of client companies. ACCEPTING HOUSES are banks which 'accept' or put their names to bills of exchange as a special way of providing finance to companies, particularly those involved in foreign trade where bills of exchange (described in Chapter 4) are still widely used.

At the end of 1985 the members of the Accepting Houses Committee were:-

Baring Brothers & Co Ltd;
Brown Shipley & Co Ltd;
Charterhouse Japhet plc;
Robert Fleming & Co Ltd;
Guinness Mahon & Co Ltd;
Hambros Bank Ltd;
Hill Samuel & Co Ltd;
Kleinwort Benson Ltd;
Lazard Brothers & Co Ltd;
Samuel Montagu & Co Ltd;
Morgan Grenfell & Co Ltd;
Rea Brothers plc;
N M Rothschild & Sons Ltd;
J Henry Schroder Wagg & Co Ltd;
Singer & Friedlander Ltd;
S G Warburg & Co Ltd.

These sixteen banks also belonged to the much larger Issuing Houses Association, which has about fifty five members. Students are not advised to try to memorise these names but they should recognise at least some of them. During 1988 a new, broader organisation was set up to represent merchant banks, the British Merchant Banking and Security Houses Association (BMBA), reflecting the wider range of banks, including many foreign banks, now involved in merchant banking.

Major areas in which the merchant banks are involved apart from issuing shares and handling bills of exchange include foreign exchange dealing, investment management and various forms of lending. These topics are considered in later chapters.

DISCOUNT HOUSES

17.   The discount houses are a unique feature of the British banking system. For many years their role has been as a kind of buffer between the Bank of England and the commercial banks. Other banking systems do not have a separate tier of institutions between the central bank and commercial banks which want to borrow from it.

When the banking system becomes short of money, for example because the government sells shares in a nationalised company and the money from buyers' bank accounts goes to the government, the banks do not approach the Bank of England directly to obtain loans. In many countries central banks do lend directly to other banks (as illustrated in the diagram below), usually requiring fairly formal and well-documented loan applications. In the United Kingdom the Bank of England has been willing to lend to the discount houses with very little formality. As there have been only about a dozen discount houses the people involved have had close personal contact with the Bank of England officials, so formal procedures have not been as important as they would be for a system permitting any of the hundreds of commercial banks to borrow. The discount houses in return for the privilege of being allowed direct access to the Bank of England have undertaken to provide short-term finance to the government when required.

The British Banking System

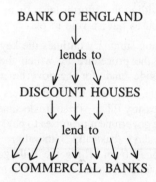

BANK OF ENGLAND

lends to

DISCOUNT HOUSES

lend to

COMMERCIAL BANKS

Other Banking Systems

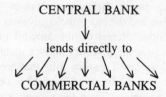

CENTRAL BANK

lends directly to

COMMERCIAL BANKS

The special status of the discount houses means that although they are recognised as banks they do not need to use the name bank. Traditionally they were independent companies, and the Bank of England seemed opposed to the idea of any of them being taken over but the number of discount houses had declined as a result of a series of mergers to 13 in 1980 and the number has continued to fall. Outside takeovers seemed an acceptable way of preventing too much control ending up in too few hands. Agreements were therefore reached to enable larger organisations to own discount houses and by 1985 3 out of only 9 left were in the hands of larger financial institutions.

HOW THE DISCOUNT HOUSES PROVIDE FUNDS TO THE GOVERNMENT

18.   The government's main sources of income are taxation and borrowing. Most government borrowing is in the form of issues of government stocks, which are in effect loans over a number of years. It is also important for the government to have access to shorter-term borrowing to enable normal expenditure to be maintained while waiting for major loans or tax payments to be received.

It is in providing this shorter term finance that the discount houses have a role to play.

The following summary outlines the key points to note about the procedure by which the discount houses provide funds for the government.

1.   The Bank of England offers for sale Treasury Bills — these are documents which the government promises to pay, usually in 91 days (basically 3 months) — and the money from selling the Bills goes to the government to meet its short term financial needs, rather like an overdraft taken by a personal customer of a bank.

2.   The discount houses put in a bid for the Treasury Bills — this is an offer to buy at below face value (or at a 'discount') and the discount or difference between the face value and the bid is the equivalent of three months interest on the amount involved. Because the discount houses undertake to bid for any Treasury Bills that are offered for sale the Bank of England is certain of being able to raise the money it needs.

3.   The Bank of England sells some or all of the Bills to the discount houses, which then re-sell some to banks or other financial institutions which want to hold them as a short-term investment.

4.   The discount houses have money available at all times because major banks normally keep money with the discount houses as a short-term, highly liquid investment. Until 1986 it was a requirement that 'eligible' banks (referred to earlier in this chapter) kept some of their funds with the discount houses, an amount based on a percentage of their eligible liabilities, a technical term which roughly speaking means the amount of money deposited by customers.

5.   The discount houses also have liquid funds of their own in the form of other 'paper' which they can sell. 'Paper' in this context means documents issued by companies, by local authorities or by financial institutions which promise to pay the bearer at a future date just as Treasury Bills are promises by the government to pay at a future date. All of these items pay interest in one form or another and are readily saleable because institutions with spare cash would rather earn some interest than none. (The different forms of 'paper' are described more fully in Chapter 4.)

6.   The sale of Treasury Bills takes place each week and some of the money raised is used, in effect, to pay back the holders of the Bills issued 91 days earlier. If the government needs extra money a larger value of Bills will be sold but if the government has enough other money available then a smaller issue of Bills will be sold than at the corresponding 'auction' 91 days earlier.

The special status of the discount houses has been threatened to some extent by the changes in the Stock Market following the de-regulation in October 1986 (the so-called 'Big Bang') because the government's methods of raising money have been affected. The procedure is intended to bring in more competition than before and although the Stock Market does not deal in such short-term government borrowing as the 91 day Treasury Bills short-term government stock, known also as short-dated gilts (similar in effect to Treasury Bills but dated at anything from one to five years) may be an alternative source of funds.

FRINGE BANKS

19.   At the opposite end of the banking spectrum from the highly respected discount houses with their

close links with the Bank of England are the small and often new entrants to the banking industry.

The term 'fringe bank' or 'secondary bank' like 'merchant bank' lacks precision but is usually applied to suppliers of financial services which do not provide the full range of services expected of a bank. They are generally small in terms of capital and the total amounts they lend.

Historically the fringe banks developed to meet a gap in the market, offering a service to people who would not normally have used a bank account because of the formal image of banks. They were highly innovative in their marketing techniques, using methods only now being adopted by larger banks. They came more dramatically to the attention of the general public and the authorities concerned with supervising the banking system during the 1970s when the financial problems experienced by many of them threatened the whole banking system.

The causes of the secondary banking crisis, or fringe banking crisis, were varied but probably the most significant was the extent of overlending to property speculators. At the beginning of the 1970s a rise in property prices encouraged investors to buy with borrowed funds. In 1973 property prices fell sharply and by the end of that year banks which had lent money found that they could not get the money back to pay out to their depositors. The first casualties were London and Counties Securities and Cedar Holdings. Their problems led to fears of a 'domino' effect spreading to other secondary banks and then to larger banks. There were rumours that major clearing banks could be hit by similar problems but in the end it was the clearing banks which saved the situation by contributing money to a fund, commonly referred to as the 'lifeboat', which was lent out by the Bank of England to banks in need. This totalled some £1,200 million of lending by August 1974. The seriousness of the crisis was one of the major factors leading to the passing of the 1979 Banking Act.

The worst hit banks closed down but many others survived as a result of the 'lifeboat' operation and are still in business today.

Today the term 'fringe banks' is less widely used than in the 1970s but many of the smaller institutions recognised under the 1979 Banking Act as licensed deposit takers could be seen as secondary banks.

Because of their limited resources and their lack of national reputation they often market their services very strongly in order to compete with larger rivals.

NATIONAL SAVINGS BANK

20. The National Savings Bank, which was founded in 1861 and today employs around 3000 staff, is something of an oddity in the banking system. The name bank is perhaps inappropriate because it does not offer the range of services other banks provide. Unlike the state-owned National Girobank the National Savings Bank does not compete on equal terms with other commercial banks.

Instead the National Savings Bank is one of the three operating divisions of the Department of National Savings. (The other two divisions are the Savings Certificates division and the Bonds and Stocks division.) The National Savings Bank provides two types of account, the Ordinary Account and the Investment Account (or Invac), both of which are similar to bank deposit accounts in taking in a depositor's money and paying interest on it. Cheque books are not provided so withdrawals from the accounts normally have to be in cash. The main feature which makes National Savings Bank accounts attractive is that the interest is paid Gross (which means without deduction of tax, though taxpayers would still need to declare the income and pay tax on it). The government has reserved this privilege for its own institution having denied it to all other deposit takers including the banks. This makes the National Savings Bank particularly suitable for people who do not have to pay any tax, such as children or others on very low incomes. (In contrast many other National Savings products are tax free which means they are of special benefit to high rate taxpayers.)

The Department of National Savings as a whole is set annual targets by government for the amount of money to be raised from the public. The money is then lent to the government to be spent together with the money raised through taxation and other borrowing. Out of an overall target of £3,000 million of new money the National Savings Bank contributed over £800 million in the financial year 1983/84. In 1984/85 this had fallen to £400 million even though the target for all National Savings remained at £3,000 million. This gives some indication of a decline in the role of the National Savings Bank relative to other forms of National Savings.

NEWCOMERS TO THE BANKING SYSTEM

21.   One of the most prominent characteristics of the banking system in recent years is the rate at which change is taking place. Traditional categories such as 'clearing banks' are now rather different from what they used to be. New foreign banks are continuing to 'set up shop' in the United Kingdom and non-bank institutions are moving into the banking system.

Although the Bank of England will still continue to confer banking status under the 1987 Banking Act and treat banks as separate and different from other organisations, from the point of view of customers banking is no longer restricted to banks. The building societies, as explained in the next chapter, are taking on many of the roles traditionally reserved for banks. Non-financial institutions like major retailers are also offering some banking services and therefore beginning to influence the banking system in a way which may lead to a need for new controls and closer supervision. In the United Kingdom the launch of the Marks and Spencer charge card was a significant step in this direction, but in the longer term the Discover card offered by the United States retailing giant Sears Roebuck may have an even bigger impact if, as proposed, it becomes accepted by a wide range of independent shops. Similarly money transmission services offered by the banks at present may be by-passed by new electronic payments systems if the banks are not quick enough in setting up their own version of EFTPOS, Electronic Funds Transfer at Point of Sale (described in Chapter 24).

Competition is turning the banking industry into a much broader financial services industry. For a banker knowledge of the banking system is no longer enough; a good understanding of competitor financial institutions is vital too.

SUMMARY

22. a)   Banks can be categorised according to the services they offer and generally in order to be considered as a bank an institution should:-

      1.   take deposits;

      2.   offer loans;

      3.   provide some other financial services.

b)   The advantages of being seen as a bank include certain specific legal benefits as well as the more general status which may help in promotion of the institution's services.

c)   Under the 1979 Banking Act the Bank of England acquired the power to determine which institutions could call themselves banks.

d)   The 1979 Act also allowed the the Bank of England to recognise other institutions as licensed deposit takers, though this distinction has been removed by the 1987 Banking Act.

e)   To protect depositors in the event of a failure of a bank a deposit protection scheme was set up under the supervision of the Bank of England.

f)   Recognised banks can also be granted the status of 'eligible' banks by the Bank of England.

g)   The Bank of England as the central bank of the United Kingdom has a number of specific functions common to most central banks. It also carries out certain duties which are not necessarily shared by other central banks.

h)   The traditional clearing banks include the largest United Kingdom based banks, the 'big four'. They became dominant as a result of mergers of what had originally been small local banks. Scotland and Northern Ireland have their own traditional clearing banks too, but they are rather smaller.

i)   There are also newer entrants to the clearing system which participate in the London clearing systems, including the systems set up to deal with electronic methods of payment. Building societies are now among the participants in payment clearing.

j)   Foreign banks are very important in the United Kingdom banking system with more foreign banks operating in London than in any other city in the world. Foreign banks operate in the United Kingdom for a number of reasons but the importance of London as an international financial centre is one of the main explanations.

k) British Overseas Banks are now of diminishing importance as a category within the British banking system.

l) Merchant banks include some of the old established banking businesses. They are concerned with providing a wide range of financial services to companies. These include share issues and acceptance of bills of exchange (as suggested by the names of the main groups of merchant banks) but they perform many other functions too.

m) Discount houses are unique to the British banking system, acting as intermediaries between the Bank of England and the commercial banks in providing loans when they are needed. When it is the government that needs money the discount houses buy the weekly issue of Treasury Bills. When the commercial banks need money the discount houses can obtain funds from the Bank of England as 'lender of the last resort'.

n) Fringe banks or secondary banks are mostly small banks with much less capital than the 'big four'. The problems that arose in 1973-74 for the fringe banks, which led to the Bank of England's 'lifeboat operation', encouraged the government to pass the 1979 Banking Act. Some of the fringe banks which survived the crisis took many years to become profitable again.

o) The National Savings Bank is an oddity in the banking system because it is part of the Department of National Savings, it does not offer ordinary banking services and it has special tax advantages compared to other banks.

p) The nature of the banking system is changing as a result of broader changes in the financial services industry. There is far more competition with a far wider range of institutions actively involved in banking.

STUDENT SELF-TESTING

Self Review Questions

1. What were the main provisions of the 1979 Banking Act? (4 − 7)

2. What changes have there been to these provisions as a result of the 1987 Banking Act? (8)

3. State three of the functions of the Bank of England. (10)

4. Name eight traditional clearing banks. (11, 12)

5. Co-operative Bank, National Girobank and Trustee Savings Bank have all joined the London Clearing House since 1970. Which one joined most recently? (13)

6. What is the basic difference between a Foreign Bank and a British Overseas Bank? (14, 16)

7. What do the letters IHA and AHC stand for? (16)

8. Why is a discount house so called? (17, 18)

9. What was the fringe banking crisis in 1973-74? (19)

10. What makes the National Savings Bank rather an unusual bank? (20)

Exercises (answers begin page 321)

A1. Read this passage and answer the questions which follow.

The 1979 Banking Act can be seen as a consequence of the fringe banking crisis in 1973-74; this was one of the events which prompted the Bank of England to tighten its control over the banking system.

The 1987 Banking Act may also be judged to be the result of a major crisis in the banking industry, the Johnson Matthey affair, when a banking company which also operated one of the country's leading gold bullion dealers found itself in extreme financial difficulties, apparently as a result of overlending to one group of borrowers.

The 1987 Act emphasises prudential supervision. One of the essential criteria for being authorised to accept deposits from the public under the Act is that the business must be conducted in a prudent manner, maintaining adequate accounting and other records. It is the Bank of England which has the role of judging whether an institution meets the criteria laid down in the Act.

One of the main changes brought in by the Act was to remove the two-tier system of deposit-takers established in the 1979 Act, though there is still a restriction on smaller institutions calling themselves banks. Another important power which the Bank of England now has is the power to block changes in the control of banks if it judges that the people trying to take control are not suitable.

1. What was the fringe banking crisis?

2. What is prudential supervision?

3. What two categories of deposit-takers existed under the 1979 legislation?

4. Why is it helpful for the banking system as a whole if the Bank of England can influence who owns banks?

5. What do you consider to be the most important of the changes brought in by the 1987 Act and why?

A2. What are the functions of a central bank ? What other roles does the Bank of England perform?

A3. 'There is no longer any such thing as a British Overseas Bank.' Discuss.

A4. What is a clearing bank? How and why has the concept of a clearing bank changed?

2. Financial Intermediaries

INTRODUCTION

1. Banks are not the only institutions which provide banking services or compete with other banks. This chapter looks at the other organisations which play a major role in the financial services industry.

They range from very small local groups, the credit unions, to major multinationals bigger than most banks. The main categories to be considered fit somewhere between these two extremes. They are:-

    a) building societies;

    b) insurance companies and pension funds;

    c) unit trusts and investment trusts;

    d) finance houses.

The chapter also considers the relationship between lending and securities and the changing role of the Stock Exchange in helping to ensure that industry obtains the funds that it needs.

THE NEED FOR FINANCIAL INTERMEDIARIES

2. Some people have money available which they do not wish to spend immediately. Other people want to spend but do not have the money available. In some circumstances those with money can lend directly to those wanting to spend, but there are a number of difficulties in the way. In particular the people concerned may not know one another or, if they do, may not trust one another.

To get round these difficulties both groups of people can make use of a financial intermediary. A bank is a good example. Savers feel safe putting their money in a bank. Borrowers know that banks have money to lend. The bank judges whether the borrower is suitable, so that the saver or depositor does not need to consider who is using the money deposited. In this way the bank acts as a go-between or intermediary between saver and borrower. (In this context savers and borrowers may be businesses as well as individuals, many of them being both at different times or even the same time.)

Within the United Kingdom as a whole the largest users of borrowed funds are businesses and one of the main roles of major financial institutions is to channel funds to those businesses which need to borrow.

The financial institutions, large financial intermediaries, in particular insurance companies, pension funds, unit trusts and investment trusts, provide funds to companies either by lending or by buying shares. People who save with such institutions cannot usually get repayment on demand as bank depositors can; the methods of repayment vary according to the type of investment, but investors should be aware in placing funds with a financial intermediary of the requirements they must meet in order to get their money back.

Some types of saving clearly involve the risk of a fall in value, rather than guaranteeing payment of a known sum of money. This is normally the case where stocks and shares quoted on the Stock Exchange are the basis of the investment, but even with pensions and life insurance policies which may specify guaranteed payouts the underlying assets are likely to include stocks and shares. It is through pension funds and insurance companies that most people have an interest in the companies which are quoted on the stock market. Although direct personal investment in Stock Exchange companies has been increasing over the last few years it is still a small minority of the population which owns shares directly (estimated to be around 1 in 8 of the population by the end of 1985 though perhaps as high as 1 in 5 by the end of 1987).

CREDIT UNIONS

3. Among the smallest financial intermediaries are the credit unions. These are usually locally based organisations where savers and borrowers do have some shared interest, perhaps through a club or other social organisation, perhaps through working for the same employer.

The rules of Credit Unions are controlled by the Credit Unions Act 1979 which permits any group of at least 21 people with some common interest to set up a credit union, a scheme by which the participants save money which can then be lent out to members. The main limitation is that very large loans are not permitted.

Advantages include:-

    a)   a low risk of bad debts because people borrowing are using their friends' money;

    b)   a low cost of borrowing because the aim of a credit union is *not* to maximise profit;

    c)   a good return on saving because although basic interest paid on savings is by law fairly low any surpluses made by the credit union are paid out as bonuses;

    d)   a sense of helping the local community by putting savings into a fund to be used to meet the needs of local borrowers;

    e)   democratic control over how the organisation is run.

Although credit unions are small there are national organisations which can give advice and guidance to new credit unions. These are:-

    a)   The Credit Union League of Great Britain *and*

    b)   The National Federation of Credit Unions.

FRIENDLY SOCIETIES

4. Most Friendly Societies are also fairly small institutions but they are a little better known than the credit unions, partly because like most of the major financial organisations they use national advertising to promote themselves (and are not restricted to members with a common interest).

Friendly Societies raise funds from the general public mainly through savings plans linked to life insurance.

Advantages of Friendly Society savings plans are that:-

    a)   all benefits paid out to the saver are free from tax, which means no liability for income tax or for capital gains tax;

    b)   savings can be made by regular payments each month or each year;

    c)   a small amount of life insurance cover is included.

The main limitation is that the maximum annual investment is £100 per person. No-one can have more than one tax exempt Friendly Society plan. This restriction has helped to make sure that the Friendly Societies have stayed small.

BUILDING SOCIETIES

5. Building Societies, unlike banks, are supervised by the Building Societies Commission rather than by the Bank of England. Both Building Societies and Friendly Societies had their origins in local schemes aimed at encouraging relatively poor people to save. In the case of the Building Societies the purpose of the saving was to help the savers to buy their own homes. In essence the organisations were nonprofitmaking, aimed at helping the members. Even today Building Societies are owned by their members, people who have money in share accounts, and the published annual accounts of a building society do not show a figure for profit but refer instead to surplus. This may change for some Societies if they choose to convert to limited companies as they are now legally empowered to do by the Building

---

Characteristics of Building Societies before 1980

1. Deposits were almost entirely obtained from account holders.

2. The majority of account holders had passbook share accounts (entitling them to voting rights as members of the Society).

3. Lending was only for the purchase of domestic property and had to be fully secured by mortgages over the houses bought by borrowers.

4. Deposits could only be withdrawn at the counters of branches or agencies.

5. Building Societies were all organised as mutual institutions owned by the members.

6. All interest paid was subject to Composite Rate Tax, a disadvantage compared to banks.

7. The range of services offered included arranging insurance for house buyers but little else apart from lending and taking deposits.

Characteristics of Building Societies after 1986

(following the passing of the Building Societies Act)

1. Deposits are frequently raised from the money markets (for example by issuing Certificates of Deposit, first used in 1983) as well as from account holders.

2. More depositors have accounts other than traditional share accounts: examples include high-interest accounts, accounts with cheque books and accounts with cash dispenser cards.

3. Loans are offered for purposes other than house purchase (though mortgage business still remains the main source of income).

4. Apart from making withdrawals at branch counters deposits can be withdrawn by writing out cheques, by payment of standing orders and through cash dispensers (including some bank cash dispensers for Building Societies which belong to the LINK network, a group of financial institutions with a sharing agreement).

5. It is now possible for larger Building Societies to convert to limited company status provided a high enough proportion of members vote for such a change.

6. Interest payment is now on equal terms with banks:-
   a)   because banks now have to deduct tax from interest paid to their United Kingdom depositors;
   b) because Building Societies no longer have to deduct tax from interest paid to depositors who are not residents of the United Kingdom.

7. The range of services is now widening as the Building Societies' legal powers are extended to permit them, for example, to acquire estate agents, to build houses for rent and to sell a range of different investments.

Societies Act 1986, but such conversions are expected to be rare in the foreseeable future.

In many respects the Building Societies seem old fashioned, but the reality is very different. Making profit, even if it is not called profit, is a major concern, and the Building Societies have become the biggest competitors of the banks in obtaining deposits from the general public. The rate of change within the Building Society industry has been enormous as can be seen by a comparison of the main features of the industry in the past and in the present. Change had been taking place over a number of years but the Building Societies Act 1986 has been a particularly significant step.

Clearly the Building Societies are now providing much stronger competition for the banks than ever before. The fact that two Building Societies joined the Association for Payment Clearing Services in 1987 (see Chapter 1) shows just how similar the two types of institution are becoming. By entering many of the banks' existing markets Building Societies present a serious threat to any bank which does not adapt quickly to new market conditions.

The six leading building societies at the end of 1985 were:-

		Assets £ millions	Branches
1.	Halifax	24365	718
2.	Abbey National	19552	674
3.	Nationwide/Anglia	15664	927
4.	Alliance & Leicester	7175	451
5.	Leeds Permanent	6905	479
6.	Woolwich Equitable	6791	402

(Source: CBSI)

INSURANCE COMPANIES

6.   At first sight Insurance Companies may not seem to be financial intermediaries in the same way as banks or building societies. However a large proportion of the money which Insurance Companies take in as premiums can be seen as a form of saving because the people taking out the insurance do expect to get their money back.

There are of course many forms of insurance which do not represent savings, but the types of insurance which are forms of saving involve much larger sums of money.

Note on Terminology

Insurance – payment of a premium or premiums to obtain a financial recompense if or when a particular event occurs, whether the event is certain or not.

Assurance – insurance relating to an event which is certain to happen (and used mostly to refer to life insurance since death is a certainty for everybody).

The more general term insurance is used throughout this chapter.

Types of insurance which do not involve saving

1. Motor policies – only paid out if a road accident occurs.
2. Personal accident insurance – only paid out if injury occurs.
3. Marine policies – a large market which can involve very large claims if ships sink or collide.
4. Term life policies – only paid out if the person insured dies within the specified term.

There are of course many other examples; what they have in common is that there is no certainty of obtaining a payout. The premiums do not represent money set aside to be used on some later occasion.

Types of insurance which do involve saving
(where the insurance company acts as a financial intermediary)

1. Whole life policies – an agreed sum is paid out when the insured person dies. In the case of a 'with profits' policy the sum is a minimum with additional bonuses related to the profit made by the insurance company.
2. Endowment policies – an agreed sum is paid out at a particular date or at death if this occurs first. This is similar to a whole life policy except that the insured can benefit from the savings in person rather than leaving the money as part of the estate, the assets left at death. Endowment policies are commonly used in connection with the purchase of houses. The buyer borrows money

from a bank or building society and pays interest over the period of the loan together with the premiums on the endowment policy, but no repayments are made until the end of the period at which time the endowment policy matures and the money received pays off the borrowing, usually leaving some money over for the borrower.

3. Personal pension plans – originally devised for self-employed people who would not otherwise have any pension apart from the minimum state pension. These plans are based on the concept of an endowment policy maturing at the retirement date to give the insured a lump sum. This lump sum can then be used to buy an annuity, which is a way of converting a lump sum into income. The insurance company agrees to pay a set sum per annum for life. This is cheaper for older people because the cost is based on how long the purchaser of the annuity is expected to live. (See also Chapter 25.)

Anyone of retirement age or above can buy an annuity if they have a lump sum to invest (although below the age of seventy the cost is very high). Some people do this by remortgaging their houses, but personal pension plans offer tax advantages which are restricted at the moment to those who earn income without acquiring pension rights. The government has proposed measures to extend the idea of personal pensions to everybody as a way of making the whole pensions system more flexible, and this could provide a big growth area for the Insurance Companies.

4. School fees plans – regular premiums are paid into a plan so that when a child reaches the age to be sent to a fee-paying school funds can be drawn out to cover the cost. If the person taking out the plan dies a lump sum payment is made, so the element of life insurance is included.

These are all forms of insurance which enable the Insurance Companies to act as financial intermediaries by providing them with funds which they can lend out or invest. The list is far from complete but gives an indication of some of the possibilities.

PENSION FUNDS

7.   For most people putting money into a pension scheme does not feel like saving because they have no choice about it. But compulsory saving is just as much saving as the forms of voluntary saving which take place when money is paid into an account with a bank or a building society, or when regular premiums are paid for an endowment policy.

The pension funds therefore handle savings (paid in by both employers and employees) and these funds are available to lend or invest until the money has to be paid out as pensions. Interest earned and dividends received help to make sure the recipients of the pensions are able to take out more than they put in. Judging when the money will be needed is usually fairly straightforward for pension funds because in most cases approximate retirement ages are known well in advance. Banks, in contrast, find it very difficult to predict on a long term basis when their depositors will want their money back, so pension funds are in a stronger position than banks to offer loans over very long terms.

Among the largest pension funds in the United Kingdom are those of the nationalized industries like the Post Office and the National Coal Board. Major companies including the big banks also have very large pension funds.

Decisions about investments are usually made by fund managers answerable to independent trustees. For the larger pension funds the managers are full-time staff of the fund, but for many smaller companies financial institutions act as paid fund managers looking after the employees' pensions. Merchant banks, including subsidiaries of the clearers, and insurance companies are among the leading fund managers dealing with company pension funds. The independent trustees are very often major banks or insurance companies too.

UNIT TRUSTS

8.   In terms of organisation Unit Trusts are rather similar to pension funds since they also involve managers making decisions about investments with independent trustees ensuring that savers' interests are protected. Leading financial institutions including banks and insurance companies often act as managers of some funds and trustees of others. There are also specialist unit trust management groups, most of which offer a range of different unit trusts, just as there are independently managed pension funds.

In other respects however Unit Trusts are very different from pension funds. Unit Trusts provide a form of investment which offers the advantages of investing on the stock market but with reduced risk. *Investors buy units in a fund which is then invested by the Unit Trust fund managers in a range of stocks and shares.* The decisions made by the fund managers are controlled by a trust deed (which means that Unit Trusts are trusts in the strict legal sense). Each Unit Trust deed must be approved by the Department of Trade and Industry so the whole system is regulated by government.

Features of investment in Unit Trusts

1.   The investor does not require knowledge of the stocks or shares of specific companies.

2.   Expert investment managers make the decisions about what companies to invest in.

3.   Even when small sums are invested *risk is spread* rather than being concentrated in one company.

4.   The investor buys 'units' from the Unit Trust managers and can sell them back to the managers to raise money.

5.   The buying price (or 'offer' price at which the managers sell to the investor) is always higher than the price for selling back units (the 'bid' price). This means that a loss is made immediately a purchase takes place, so unit trusts should not be seen as a form of short-term investment.

6.   The value of the units is related to the value of the underlying investments bought by the fund managers.

7.   For many unit trusts regular savings plans are available so that units can be accumulated over a period of time (and because the sum invested is a fixed amount more units are bought when prices are low than when prices are high).

Unit trusts are particularly suitable for investors who:-

a)   are concerned to reduce risk, because the money can be spread among a range of stocks and shares which are unlikely to all do badly at the same time;

b) do not take a close interest in the workings of the stock market and want to leave decisions to an expert, paying for his/her skills;

c) want to invest in a particular sector of the world economy in which they do not have personal expertise for example an experienced investor with a range of shares in major British companies might want to invest in small businesses or in the Far East and might therefore choose a unit trust with that particular specialisation.

Six of the leading unit trust management groups at the end of 1985 were:-

		Funds under management (June 1986) £m
1.	Save and Prosper Securities Ltd	2841
2.	M and G Investment Management Ltd	2306
3.	Allied Dunbar Unit Trusts PLC	1914
4.	Henderson Unit Trust Management	1500
5.	Barclays Unicorn Ltd	1383
6.	TSB Unit Trusts Ltd	1030

(Source: Unit Trust Association)

INVESTMENT TRUSTS

9. In contrast to Unit Trusts which are legally trusts, and have trustees to look after the interests of the savers, Investment Trusts, in spite of the name, are not trusts at all. They are in fact limited companies quoted on the stock market.

Like Unit Trusts they invest in a range of companies as a way of making a return on their shareholders' investment. Decisions about the stocks and shares to buy or sell are made by investment managers, who are either employed directly by the investment trust company or outside advisers, often merchant banks.

Features of investment in Investment Trusts

1. The investor is buying shares in the Investment Trust company and will normally have to go through the Stock Exchange to do this.

2. Expert investment managers make the decisions about what companies the Investment Trust should invest in.

3. Risk is spread in the sense that the underlying investments can be wide ranging.

4. The investor can sell the shares in the Investment Trust through the stock market or any recognised securities dealer.

5. The costs of dealing on the stock market mean that buying and then selling immediately could be very expensive (and a high proportion of the value for deals involving only a few hundred pounds) so Investment Trusts are not a good form of short term investment.

6. The value of the shares in an investment trust is determined by supply and demand on the stock market rather than by the value of the underlying shares. Very often the shares held by the investment managers are worth more than the price of the investment trust shares would suggest; the assets of the investment trust can be 'bought' by shareholders at a discount.
Example: £100 of shares in an investment trust might represent £110 worth of shares in the companies invested in by the investment trust. The investor cannot gain this extra £10 but may benefit from higher dividend payments because the dividend on shares worth £110 will normally be more than the dividend on £100 of shares.

7. Regular savings plans are rarely available so an investor in an Investment Trust must have a lump sum available.

Although Investment Trusts may be general or concentrated on specific sectors just like Unit Trusts the great growth of the number of different Unit Trusts during the 1980s means that Unit Trusts now offer a far wider choice than Investment Trusts.

One of the most important differences between Unit Trusts and Investment Trusts is that Investment Trusts cannot normally advertise. This means that they are generally seen as more suitable for experienced investors, a view which may give Unit Trusts an unjustified advantage in the market for savers' funds.

The six leading investment trusts at the end of 1985 were:-

	Assets £ millions
1. Globe Investment Trust	846
2. Foreign and Colonial Trust	833
3. Edinburgh Investment Trust	610
4. T R Industrial General Trust	590
5. Scottish Mortgage Trust	564
6. Witan Investment Trust	543

(Source: The Banker)

FINANCE HOUSES

10.   A finance house is a financial intermediary which specializes in providing funds to buy major assets. At a personal level this means lending to buy household goods such as washing machines, stereo systems or cars. More important than this for most finance houses is the business market where cars and office equipment are at the bottom end of the price range. At the top end are ships, aircraft, major computer systems and complete factories.

Deposits for finance houses come partly from individual depositors with accounts, but more often from money market investments (which are large sums, at least £10,000, deposited short term, sometimes repayable on demand, sometimes for fixed periods of a number of months).

Funds obtained are transferred to the users of the money in the form of loans or through leasing or hire purchase as described in later chapters. Finance houses do not often buy shares in the businesses they are assisting, in contrast to unit trusts, investment trusts and insurance companies which often do.

In general finance houses charge higher interest rates than banks but have no security apart from any claim over the assets financed. They will often take on lending which is not agreed by a branch manager of a bank, the higher interest reflecting the higher risk of the business. The lending services of finance houses can be seen as complementary to, rather than competing with, the loans offered by branch banking. The major banks, recognising that finance house services could help them to provide a more complete range of options for customers, therefore acquired existing finance houses.

The following table shows the six leading finance houses. The banks which own them are shown in brackets.

The six leading finance houses at the end of 1985 were:-

	Capital £ 000s	Profit in 1985 (before tax, interest) £ 000s
1. Lombard North Central (National Westminster)	2990	390
2. Mercantile Credit (Barclays)	3548	321
3. Lloyds Bowmaker (Lloyds)	2184	217
4. Forward Trust (Midland)	2142	178
5. United Dominion Trust (Trustee Savings Bank)	1118	103
6. North West Securities (Bank of Scotland)	638	60

Most of the top finance houses are bank owned, with Irish banks and American banks among the major owners along with the United Kingdom clearers. There are some exceptions to this general pattern, with high rankings for Ford Motor Credit and a few independent specialists such as Welbeck Finance and Wagon Finance.

From the point of view of the major clearing banks the importance of the finance house subsidiaries is that they have specialist lending skills and experience which it would have taken the banks a long time to develop for themselves. The big banks have been able to dominate the finance house market simply by buying established finance houses, in some cases more than one. National Westminster, for example, bought North Central Finance and Lombard Finance, which had been separate companies, forming them into Lombard North Central, and also acquired the separate Tricity Finance.

LENDING AND SECURITIES

11.   As explained some financial intermediaries pass funds on to users of the money in the form of loans while others provide capital by buying shares in companies. The distinction is not always very clear because some methods of funding combine elements of the two.

However the two approaches can be represented diagrammatically:-

1. Traditional Lending

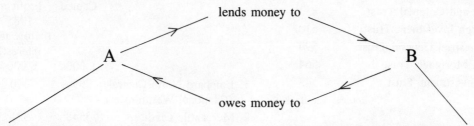

There is usually only one lender.

A relies on B to get the money back.

B must make repayment to A.

B must pay regular interest even if no profit is made.

2. Securities Issues

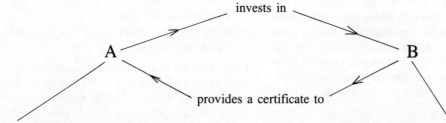

There may be a large number of investing institutions or individuals.

A can get money back by selling part or all of the investment to third parties.

B *may* not need to repay at all if the investment is permanent capital.

If repayment is made it is not necessarily to A, the original investor.

B *may* make dividend payments related to profit rather than paying interest.

The first approach is clearly the simplest, but from the point of view of the business (B) using the money it may not be the most suitable, particularly as interest rates may be high when profits are low.

The second approach is more flexible. It does not exclude the possibility of paying interest and making repayment to the original lender, but allows for more variety. The 'Securities' approach also copes better with larger amounts of money than one bank could lend on its own.

The certificates issued are referred to as securities. SECURITIES in this context can be defined as marketable financial claims. The certificates represent money lent or invested (a liability from the borrower's point of view or an asset from the certificate holder's point of view) and the certificates can be sold (often on an organised market like the Stock Exchange). Traditionally certificates have literally been pieces of paper which the owner of the security could see, but the growth in computer technology may make this idea obsolete. Future share 'certificates' may be no more than data entries in computer records. The term covers a wide range of possibilities, and further details of some more specialised securities are given in later chapters. The following list describes some of the most important forms.

1. Share certificates

   These represent a 'share' or part ownership of a limited company and are often referred to as 'equities'. In the case of a public limited company (usually abbreviated to PLC or plc) the shares can be freely bought and sold. Many large public companies have their shares quoted on the Stock Exchange. This makes it easier for buyers and sellers to find one another, usually through a securities dealer, and agree a price. On the Stock Exchange companies are divided into four categories.

   a) Alpha stocks − the most widely traded stocks;

   b) Beta stocks − rather less widely traded stocks;

   c) Gamma stocks − stocks of less important quoted companies;

   d) Delta stocks − the least traded stocks for which market makers only provide prices on request.

   The terms 'stocks' and 'shares' are identical in meaning when applied to the ownership of companies. Some companies prefer to refer to their owners as stockholders and issue them with stock certificates but most now use the term shareholders.

   Funds invested as share capital are not repayable and do not receive interest. The dividends paid to shareholders depend on the company's profit, but with successful companies the shares do become more valuable as the company expands, giving the shareholders a return in the form of capital growth in addition to any dividend. The capital gain can only be converted into cash by selling some of the shares.

2. Loan stock certificates

   These represent loans, as the name implies. Holders of loan stock receive interest, often at a fixed rate, unaffected by changes in other interest rates. Unlike traditional lending it is not necessarily the original lenders who get the money back because the certificates change hands, being bought and sold on the Stock Exchange like shares. (Government stocks or 'gilts' are similar in effect but with the government as borrower they are considered to be free from any risk of default when due for repayment. The volume of buying and selling of gilts is much greater than for company securities.)

3. Convertible certificates

   These represent loans which can later be changed into shares at predetermined prices. This gives the lender (or investor) the opportunity to get interest in the early stages but later obtain a capital gain if the shares have risen in value.

SECURITIES FOR MAJOR COMPANIES

12.   Major companies raising money today may consider many possible types of security. The following are among the key questions which the company's decision makers or financial advisers need to consider.

1. Who to approach to raise funds − a single lender, a group of lenders, the general public and institutions of one particular country or the stock markets of several countries?

2. Whether to raise permanent capital or to set a date or series of dates for repayment?

3. Whether to offer a return to investors linked to profit, or to pay interest?

4. If interest is paid whether to pay at a fixed rate or a variable rate linked to the general interest rates in a particular country?

5. What to set as the minimum size for each investment − which could mean excluding most private individuals and only allowing for institutional investors if the level is high?

The answers to these questions will determine what type of security meets the company's needs. It may be one of the well-known categories, shares or a loan stock, or it may be a more complex form of security. New variations are being developed by imaginative merchant banks, but these new securities are not always as easy to sell as familiar types. This extra difficulty is only justified if there are significant benefits in the tailor-made security.

For smaller companies the straightforward methods of issuing shares or loan stock to be quoted on a stock market may be the only possibility. Investors may be very suspicious of unusual forms of security issued by companies which do not already have a sound reputation.

BANKS AND THE SECURITIES INDUSTRY

13.   For a number of reasons banks have a particular interest in the securities industry and how it develops.

1.   Traditional bank lending to companies is being threatened by the increased use of securities as a form of financing. Companies obtaining funds from the general public and share-buying financial institutions can cut out the 'middleman', the bank acting as an intermediary. Banks still have a role to play because they can help to arrange securities issues for their customers and earn income from fees, but income in the form of interest on loans is likely to decline. This process of increasing use of securities as a source of funds is often referred to as 'securitisation', and it has been one of the most important influences on banks in the 1980s.

2.   Banks have an important function as advisers to clients with funds to invest. In some cases these funds can be directed to a bank's own deposit accounts or to unit trusts managed by the bank. The new regulations brought in by the Financial Services Act 1986 make it harder for banks to do this since there is a potential conflict of interest where a bank claims to be giving impartial advice but also has its own products to sell. Banks therefore need to be aware of the way in which they may be affected by rules designed to control the whole securities and investments industry. (See also Chapter 7 on the Financial Services Act.)

3.   Buying and selling securities is a major industry in itself and one which is growing in importance, not least because of the Conservative government's measures to transfer state owned organisations into private hands and to encourage wider share ownership. Of particular significance for banks was the deregulation of the Stock Exchange, the so-called 'Big Bang' on 27 October 1986, when it became possible for banks to acquire 100% holdings in dealers in securities.

By the time of the 'Big Bang' Barclays Bank, for example, had already arranged to buy the stockbrokers De Zoete and Bevan and the stockjobbers Wedd Durlacher Mordaunt and Co. to form a new securities dealing company, Barclays de Zoete Wedd. Many other banks adopted a similar policy in order to ensure that they could be directly involved in securities dealing.

Note on Terminology

The Big Bang

On 27th October 1986 the rules of the Stock Exchange were altered radically, the name Big Bang meaning extreme and rapid change. Three measures in particular were of great importance.

1.   Fixed minimum commission charges were abolished making all commissions negotiable between client and dealer.

2.   The separation between stockbrokers (agents of the client wishing to buy or sell shares) and stockjobbers (market makers owning and making a 'market' in shares by quoting prices for them to brokers) was ended. Now members of the Stock Exchange are dealers who can buy or sell for clients or for themselves.

3.   The rule that member companies could not be wholly owned by outsiders was removed, enabling banks to become fully involved for the first time.

DEREGULATION OF THE SECURITIES INDUSTRY

14.   The term 'de-regulation' implies a removing of rules and regulations, but in the context of the securities industry this is not strictly accurate. Some of the old rules were removed by the Big Bang but they are being replaced by a complex system of self-regulation supervised by the Securities and Investments Board (SIB) which is authorised to oversee the selling of investments and the giving of investment advice. It carries out this role through:-

a)   Recognised Professional Bodies which control their own individual members (for example Chartered Accountants);

b)   Self-Regulating Organisations (SROs) which control individual and company members through their internal rules and disciplinary procedures.

The number of proposed SROs has varied from time to time. The following list shows the position at the end of 1986.

Proposed self-regulating organisations (SROs) at December 1986

1. Association of Futures Brokers and Dealers **(AFBD)**
2. Financial Intermediaries, Managers and Brokers Regulatory Organisation **(FIMBRA)**
3. Investment Management Regulatory Organisation **(IMRO)**
4. Life Assurance and Unit Trust Regulatory Organisation **(LAUTRO)**
5. The Securities Association (covering international securities dealers and the Stock Exchange)

MARKETS FOR SECURITIES

15. The range of terms which appear in the list of self-regulating organisations shows clearly that the business of buying and selling investments is not restricted to the Stock Exchange. Although the Stock Exchange is seen as the leading market for stocks and shares and its list of quoted companies includes most of the big names of British Industry there are other markets for different types of investment. Even for stocks and shares the Stock Exchange has no monopoly.

The Stock Exchange deals only with a limited list of company and government securities, around 7,000. There are many companies which do not qualify for a full Stock Exchange listing but their shares may still be traded in one of a number of ways.

1. On the Unlisted Securities Market (an offshoot of the Stock Exchange set up in 1980). In spite of its name this is a list, and one open to public companies which do not quite meet the requirements of the full stock market listing. The companies on the USM, over 500 by the end of 1986, are often smaller or newer than their counterparts with full listings.
2. On the 'Third Market' set up by the Stock Exchange in 1987 for public companies which are so small or new that they cannot meet the requirements laid down for admission to the USM list. When trading began on the Third Market dealing was possible in the shares of less than ten companies although nearly 70 had expressed interest in the idea.
3. Through the 'Over-the-Counter Market', a system of buying and selling shares in unlisted public companies, companies which are not included in any of the Stock Exchange lists referred to above. The dealers operate only by telephone links and the OTC market is an informal one which has never had a set place of business like the Stock Exchange floor.
4. By private agreement. This is the usual system for shares in private companies though it is theoretically possible to sell public company shares in this way.

The Unlisted Securities Market, the Third Market and the Over-the-Counter Market are relatively recent developments indicating the way in which the possibilities for buying and selling investments have broadened in the 1980s. Possibly even more significant is the growth of an international market entirely outside the stock market system dealing in bonds, company securities like loan stocks issued for very large amounts. (See also Chapter 23.)

THE STOCK MARKET AS A FINANCIAL INTERMEDIARY

16. Most of the major financial intermediaries considered in the first part of this chapter, the Building Societies, the Insurance Companies, the Unit Trusts and the Finance Houses act fairly directly as intermediaries. They take funds from the investing public as deposits or premiums and then pay out the money to users of funds, industry or individual consumers.

The Stock Exchange, although sometimes seen as a financial intermediary, is rather different. Investors on the Stock Exchange buy shares from people who already own those shares and the Stock Exchange is sometimes referred to as a secondary market because the securities traded are second-hand rather than new.

Where a company wants to raise new money in the form of share capital it must find its own buyers; it cannot leave this to the mechanism of the stock market, although stock market dealers are likely to have a part to play in advising the company.

The main methods available for raising new share capital which can later be traded on the Stock Exchange are listed below.

1. Rights Issues
    These operate by offering existing shareholders the right to buy more shares, usually at a favourable price. The National Westminster Bank rights issue in 1986 was the largest which had taken place up till that time, raising over £700 million.

2. Placings
    These are less formal because securities dealers acting on behalf of the company contact possible investors, in particular the big institutions, to 'place' shares with them.

3. Sales by tender
    This method consists of an invitation to the general public to buy, leaving the would-be buyers to name a price which they are willing to pay.

By handling these types of new issue, whether for an existing quoted company or for a company new to the stock market, the Stock Exchange does indirectly act as a financial intermediary, but this is not its main role.

The chief benefits to companies from having their shares quoted on the stock market are:-

a) improved credit rating (since the Stock Exchange is perceived as only accepting creditworthy companies for a quotation) which means it is easier to raise loans;

b) greater marketability of shares (so that investors know they are not tied to the company indefinitely but can sell out) which means it is easier to raise new share capital.

Without an efficient stock market investors would be much more reluctant to buy shares in companies because of the difficulty of getting money back when it is needed.

OTHER FINANCIAL INTERMEDIARIES

17.   Apart from the securities industry and institutions which specialise in taking deposits in order to lend them there are a number of other types of organisation which have some role as financial intermediaries. These include:-

a) major retailers − some of which take deposits in the form of regular payments into charge card schemes or Christmas savings clubs, and allow credit to customers for their purchases;

b) multinational groups of companies − some of which operate in-house 'banks' which take deposits from wealthy subsidiary companies in order to finance other companies within the group, reducing the need to borrow from external financial intermediaries such as banks.

These types of financial intermediary are becoming increasingly sophisticated. They have access to the same computer technology as the banks and other specialist financial intermediaries. This means that they have less need of banking services than ever before and can often become competitors of established banks without too much difficulty or expense.

A COMPARISON OF MAJOR FINANCIAL INTERMEDIARIES

18.   Financial intermediaries have faced increasing pressure during the 1980s because of:-

a) the desire by investors and users of funds to avoid financial intermediaries (choosing securitisation instead) *and*

b) the growth of competition from organisations which are not primarily financial intermediaries.

In spite of this pressure the major institutions have continued to grow as the following table indicates. Note that the figures are not strictly comparable because financial intermediaries operate in different ways so the assets of one type of institution are not necessarily like those of other institutions.

	Assets £m 1980	Assets £m 1985
Banks	(*) 331705	587692
Pension Funds	55745	157376
Insurance Companies	65260	(**) 134135
Building Societies	53793	120763
Unit Trusts	4629	18654
Investment Trusts	8352	17126

(*) 1981 figure   (**) 1984 figure

(Source: Annual abstract of statistics 1987)

SUMMARY

19. a) Banks face competition from a wide range of financial intermediaries apart from other banks.

b) A financial intermediary is any organisation which takes in funds from one group of people and passes them on to other groups of people.

c) Credit Unions are among the smallest financial intermediaries.

d) Friendly Societies also have limits on the business they can do but their special feature is that they are able to offer tax-exempt saving.

e) Building Societies are major competitors of the banks. Great changes have taken place in their business during the 1980s and the rate of change has increased with the passing of the Building Societies Act 1986.

f) Insurance Companies provide insurance-linked forms of saving on a large scale, making them very important financial intermediaries. The main savings products which they offer are whole-life policies, endowment policies and personal pension plans.

g) Pension funds take in regular contributions from employees and employers and since this money is not needed immediately to pay out pensions it is invested by the fund managers, who are often merchant banks or insurance companies.

h) Investors can spread risk rather than investing all their money in one company by buying unit trusts or investment trusts.

i) Unit Trusts are trusts, supervised by trustees. A unit trust holder buys units from the managers and can sell them back to the managers. Unit trusts invest in a range of companies and the value of the units depends on the value of those underlying investments.

j) Investment Trusts are *not* trusts, but public limited companies. Managers invest in a range of companies but the value of the shares in the investment trust is not directly related to the value of the underlying investments. Investors can only get money back by selling shares in the investment trust at the going price on the stock market.

k) Finance houses specialise in financing the purchase of major assets, both by domestic consumers and by industry. Most of the major finance houses are owned by banks. They help the banks to offer a full range of lending services.

l) Financial intermediaries can provide funds in the form of traditional loans or by buying securities. The issuing of securities has become more important than ever before during the 1980s.

m) Major traditional types of security include shares, loan stocks and convertibles. Other securities to meet the specific needs of companies are also possible.

n) Banks are becoming more involved in the securities industry because it is a growing area (through the process of securitisation), because the banks can offer expert advice and because the deregulation of the Stock Exchange has allowed banks to acquire securities dealing companies.

o) Supervision of the securities industry now comes under the Securities and Investments Board.

p) Securities can be traded in a variety of ways and do not need to have a traditional stock market listing in order to be marketable. Some of the high value securities, international bonds, are traded entirely outside the stock market system.

q) The Stock Exchange itself is a secondary market for shares which have already been issued. Although its existence helps to make new shares more acceptable to investors, the raising of new capital is not carried out through the mechanism of the stock market. A number of methods are available to companies wanting more share capital.

r) Retail chains and multinationals may act as financial intermediaries to a limited extent even though this is not their main role.

s) The large financial institutions have continued to grow in spite of the trend towards securitisation and the development of new competitors.

STUDENT SELF-TESTING

Self Review Questions

1. How would you define a financial intermediary? (2)

2. What is a Credit Union? (3)

3. What are the advantages of saving with a Friendly Society? (4)

4. What major changes have taken place during the 1980s in the way in which Building Societies operate? (5)

5. Name three types of insurance product which are forms of saving? (6)

6. What types of investor might choose to buy unit trusts, and why? (8)

7. State three of the differences between a unit trust and an investment trust. (8,9)

8. Name three common types of security. (11)

9. What was the 'Big Bang'? (13)

10. What are the main benefits for a company of having its shares quoted on the Stock Exchange? (16)

Exercises (answers begin page 322)

A1. How do investment trusts differ from unit trusts, and why do these differences matter?

A2. In what sense are credit unions competitors of the clearing banks?

A3. Is the Stock Market a financial intermediary? Discuss.

A4. Companies can raise money by borrowing from financial intermediaries or by cutting out the middlemen and issuing securities directly to investors. What advantages and disadvantages are there in taking the latter course?

3. The Control of The Banking System: Monetary Policy

INTRODUCTION

1. The banking system, as explained in Chapter 1, is supervised by the Bank of England under the powers given to it through the Banking Acts of 1979 and 1987. Ultimate control of the system therefore stems from the government. Government policies determine how the banking system is to operate, and the government has used a wide range of methods to influence the behaviour of banks. This chapter examines the government's reasons for controlling the banking system, describes the methods which have been used and considers how controls may develop in the future.

The main methods of control to be considered are:-

    a) cash ratios;

    b) special deposits;

    c) directives;

    d) control over interest rates.

These methods are commonly described as the tools of monetary policy, policy designed to control the amount of money in the country.

THE AIMS OF GOVERNMENT

2. The government attempts to control the banking system for a variety of reasons. The relative importance of these reasons depends on the particular views and beliefs of the government in office, but the following aims would be seen as significant by governments of most political persuasions.

    1. To encourage economic growth and higher employment.
    Banks, by their lending to growing businesses, play a major part in promoting growth which, in turn, is expected to create new jobs. Without control growth might be restricted, for example because of high interest rates, or might be in the wrong sectors of the economy from the government's point of view.

    2. To reduce inflation.
    Banks create money by their lending and if this process is not limited, either by government or by the banks themselves, the total amount of money rises faster than the the volume of goods and services produced. Prices then rise. Although governments have great difficulty in measuring the amount of money in the economy (the money supply) it is generally accepted that ending inflation depends on preventing the money supply from rising faster than the output of goods and services.

    3. To maintain confidence in banks.
    If depositors do not believe that the banks are able to meet requests for repayment they may try to withdraw their money, as happened in the 1973-74 fringe banking crisis. It is important to appreciate that since the total amount of cash in the country is far less than the deposits of the major banks the system depends entirely on confidence.

These broad aims are met by a range of government policies some of which have little direct impact on banks or the banking system. Government policy on taxation (fiscal policy) or on specific schemes for helping particular industries or businesses in special areas may have some effect on banks and the lending they are able to do, but the main way in which banks are affected by government is through monetary policy, based on measuring and controlling the money supply.

The main difference between the measures of the money supply is that they include different financial assets, so the overall total of one aggregate may rise faster than the total for another. (The definitions given are an indication of the assets included under different headings during 1987 but are not the full technical definitions). Governments have used different aggregates as targets at different times, often choosing those which seemed easiest to control, and have also altered the definitions of aggregates from time to time.

Note on Terminology

Monetary Policy

Monetary policy is the term used to describe the measures taken by government to control the amount of money in the economy. This includes the issue of notes and coin but control over bank lending is far more important.

Money Supply

Money supply can be defined as the amount of money in the economy. There are a number of different measures used to calculate the money supply which means that there is no one agreed right answer to the question of how much money is in circulation. These measures of the money supply (also known as monetary aggregates) include:-

M0 − notes and coins in circulation including money in bank tills and operational deposits with the Bank of England;

M1 − notes and coins in circulation and privately owned United Kingdom current accounts (officially known as sight deposits);

M2 − notes and coins and privately owned building society and bank deposits including National Savings Bank ordinary accounts;

M3 − M1 plus privately owned long-term bank deposits and Certificates of Deposit (see Chapter 4);

M3c − M3 plus privately owned foreign currency bank deposits;

M4 − M3 adjusted to allow for building society accounts and building society deposits with banks;

M5 − M4 plus privately owned National Savings accounts and money-market 'paper' (explained in Chapter 4).

THE DEVELOPMENT OF CONTROLS FROM THE 1960S

3.   During the 1960s control of the banks and their ability to create money by lending was mainly carried out by the setting of 'ceilings' or maximum amounts which each bank was permitted to lend. Other financial institutions were controlled by quite different methods. It is only more recently that the need for some uniformity of approach has been recognised, and given legal backing in the Financial Services Act 1986.

Prior to 1980 the most significant change in government policy on the control of the banking system came in 1971. This was when the Bank of England's consultative document 'COMPETITION AND CREDIT CONTROL' came into force.

The aims of the new policy laid down in the 'Competition and Credit Control' document were to:-

a)   make banks more competitive with one another;

b)   increase the role of market forces;

c)   reduce the influence of government decisions;

d)   reduce the need for specific controls over bank lending;

e)   give greater importance to interest rates.

Following the implementation of the new policy the Bank of England used two main techniques for controlling bank lending. These were the reserve asset ratio and the special deposit scheme.

1.   **The Reserve Asset Ratio**
   Under 'Competition and Credit Control' all banks with eligible liabilities (a technical term which refers to most deposits from customers) of £5 million or above were required to keep an amount equivalent to 12½% of their eligible liabilities in the form of specified Reserve Assets. Reserve Assets were assets which could be fairly easily 'realised' or turned into cash if depositors wanted their money back. This rule meant that as banks gained new deposits they had to increase their holdings of Reserve Assets rather than lending out all the deposits accepted.

2.   **The Special Deposit Scheme**
   'Competition and Credit Control' also confirmed the Bank of England's power to instruct banks to make Special Deposits. These were deposits placed with the Bank of England on which interest was paid at the same rate as on Treasury Bills. The purpose was to take away money which banks could have held in the form of Reserve Assets. This in turn meant that money which could have been lent out would have to be held as Reserve Assets, so the higher the level of Special Deposits required the more lending would be restricted.

These two measures were intended to ensure that confidence in the banking system was maintained since a high level of assets that could be turned into cash should have safeguarded depositors. In view of the 1973-74 fringe banking crisis the policy may be regarded as unsuccessful in its failure to cope with the smaller lending institutions.

One major strengthening measure introduced in 1973 was the Supplementary Special Deposits Scheme. This scheme, often referred to as the 'corset' because of its tight control, required banks to place deposits with the Bank of England if deposits from customers grew above a predetermined level. These Supplementary Special Deposits, unlike the ordinary Special Deposits, were held by the Bank of England without payment of interest. The drawbacks of the scheme, referred to later in the chapter, led to its abandonment in 1980.

CONTROL OF INTEREST RATES IN THE 1970S

4.   The 'Competition and Credit Control' proposals had been intended among other things to give greater prominence to interest rates and to market forces. In order to achieve these aims the Bank of England in October 1972 ended its practice of announcing Bank Rate, the rate at which it would lend to the discount houses. This had always been seen as a major influence on the banking system affecting the decisions of all other lenders about the interest rates they would charge.

Bank Rate was replaced by Minimum Lending Rate (MLR), which was different because:-

a)   it was linked to market rates;

b)   a predetermined formula was used, which meant that the Bank of England no longer influenced other lenders as it had before;

c)   changes in MLR were automatic so the Bank of England could not delay or speed up changes in interest rates.

However the influence of the Bank of England on interest rates remained strong because:-

a)   the formula (the average rate offered by the discount houses in bidding for Treasury Bills plus ½% rounded up to the nearest ¼%) had been set by the Bank of England;

b)   the Bank of England could persuade discount houses to modify their bids for Treasury Bills;

c)   the Bank of England could *and did* suspend the predetermined MLR when it chose to do so;

d)   the whole scheme could be abandoned at the Bank of England's discretion (which is what happened in May 1978 when the Bank of England took over responsibility for determining the Minimum Lending Rate again).

THE DEVELOPMENT OF CONTROLS SINCE 1980

5.   A government review of monetary control methods in 1979 formed the basis of a number of proposals for change. The most significant reforms took place in August 1981 when the Bank of England document 'MONETARY CONTROL − PROVISIONS' came into effect.

Following the 1979 Banking Act the Bank of England was concerned about licensed deposit takers as well as banks and one of the main changes was to make the rules on monetary control apply to a wider group of institutions than before. This *New Monetary Sector* became the basis of government statistics on banking, and included:-

a)   all recognised banks;

b)   all licensed deposit takers;

c)   the National Girobank;

d)   the Trustee Savings Banks;

e)   the banking department of the Bank of England;

f)   any banks in the Channel Islands or the Isle of Man which chose to join the cash ratio scheme (described below).

Note that National Girobank and the Trustee Savings Banks had been exempted from the registration requirements of the 1979 Banking Act.

The main methods available to control the monetary sector and restrict the creation of money by lending after 1981 were the following.

1.   A Cash Ratio scheme.

2.   A Special Deposit scheme.

3.   Rules applied to eligible banks.

4.   Directives.

5.   Controls over interest rates.

CASH RATIOS

6. The basic principle underlying a cash ratio requirement imposed on banks is that banks which have to keep a proportion of their assets in cash are restricted in the amount they can lend. This was certainly the case before 1980 when the Reserve Asset Ratio applied, but when the Reserve Asset Ratio was finally abolished in August 1981 the idea of a cash ratio was retained for a rather different purpose.

From 1981 all institutions in the new monetary sector with eligible liabilities of over £10 million were required to place a sum equal to 0.5% of their eligible liabilities with the Bank of England. The official definition of eligible liabilities was amended at this time but in essence it still covers deposits from customers (excluding deposits banks make with one another so that customer deposits do not get counted twice over). The aim of this new cash ratio based on a small proportion of eligible liabilities was to provide the Bank of England with funds for its operations. In October 1986 the 0.5% ratio was reduced to 0.45% giving banks even less restriction on the use of their assets.

As with any method of monetary control there are advantages and disadvantages which the government needs to assess in deciding on its policy. For cash ratios these can be summed up as:-

Advantages

1. Easy to implement.
2. Gives Bank of England interest free balances.
3. May be used to restrict lending.

Disadvantages

1. Only affects specified institutions.
2. Level of eligible liabilities may be manipulated by banks.
3. No direct penalties for overlending.

THE SPECIAL DEPOSIT SCHEME

7. The purpose of a Special Deposit scheme is to give the Bank of England the power to take money out of circulation so that it cannot be used by the commercial banks to increase the amount of money in the economy.

The Bank of England is authorised to do this by instructing all institutions in the new monetary sector with eligible liabilities of over £10 million to make Special Deposits. As outlined above these deposits are held at the Bank of England until released (as monetary conditions improve) and the depositing banks receive interest at about the same rate as paid on Treasury Bills.

Although the Bank of England has not chosen to call for Special Deposits since the new monetary sector was established, the scheme is still in force. This is in contrast to the Supplementary Special Deposits scheme which was officially abandoned in 1980.

A comparison of Special Deposits and Supplementary Special Deposits:-

Special Deposits

1. Scheme still available to Bank of England (though not used).
2. An integral part of Competition and Credit Control from 1971.
3. Related to amount of eligible liabilities.
4. Interest paid at the Treasury Bill rate.

Supplementary Special Deposits

1. Scheme officially abandoned in March 1980.
2. An addition to the 1971 system to tighten it up when problems occurred.
3. Related to increase in eligible liabilities.
4. No interest paid.

In general terms Special Deposit schemes, whether in the form of the scheme currently available to the Bank of England or the much more severe 'corset' can be seen as having the following advantages and disadvantages.

Advantages

1. Very rapid in taking money out of circulation.
2. Can help to provide extra cash for the Bank of England.
3. Can boost Bank of England profits if no interest is paid.

Disadvantages

1. Disrupts sensible planning by banks.

2.   Does not allow market forces to adjust the level of lending.

3.   Gives non-banks a competitive advantage.

Since little use has been made of the scheme during the 1980s it is clear that government currently sees the disadvantages of reduction in free competition as outweighing the short-term advantages to the Bank of England.

RULES APPLIED TO ELIGIBLE BANKS

8.   As explained in Chapter 1 certain major banks are granted the status of Eligible Banks by the Bank of England. This gives them the advantage of being able to raise money on bills of exchange a little more cheaply than other banks.

Any bank can apply to become an eligible bank if it is already involved in accepting (or putting its name to) bills of exchange, and has established a good reputation in the field. If the Bank of England agrees to the application the eligible bank will then agree in turn to place funds with the discount houses or with approved money brokers (dealers who arrange loans between banks). When the rules for eligible banks were introduced the amount to be kept was set at 6% of eligible liabilities on average (over a period of either six or twelve months chosen by the bank) with no less than 4% at any one time without Bank of England approval. The eligible liabilities figure was to be based on the statistics provided to the Bank of England beforehand.

In 1983 the requirements were relaxed to 5% of eligible liabilities with a minimum of 2½%. More recently, in September 1986, the requirement to keep a minimum proportion of eligible liabilities with the discount houses was removed, though banks still use the discount houses as a place where they can keep funds which they may need to turn into cash again at short notice.

The purpose of the original requirement on eligible banks was to make sure the discount houses always had enough funds. This is essential for the smooth working of the banking system because of the key role of the discount houses as intermediaries between the commercial banks and the central bank.

The Bank of England needs to make sure the mechanism of lending and borrowing works efficiently because this enables changes in interest rates to affect the whole banking system. However the rules relating to eligible banks were not generally seen as a means of monetary control in themselves.

DIRECTIVES

9.   Well before the reforms in monetary control in the 1980s, and even before 'Competition and Credit Control' in 1971, the Bank of England had tried to regulate the amount of money in the economy by issuing directives to banks.

Banks cannot normally ignore directives from the Bank of England because of the central bank's enormous influence on all aspects of the banking system, but the amount of control which directives can give is generally considered to be fairly limited because directives are by their very nature broad and imprecise. They are more likely to outline areas of priority rather than to provide absolute rules.

Traditionally they have been categorised as either:-

a)   quantitative − setting ceilings for lending (a system abolished in 1971) *or*

b)   qualitative − emphasising particular sectors of the economy to support or to avoid. (After 1971 this type of directive was first applied to restrict support for property speculation, which may have helped to prevent the major banks from being drawn into the fringe banking crisis, but from 1986 the Bank of England has also abandoned the use of qualitative directives.)

In general directives can be considered to have the following advantages and disadvantages.

Advantages

1.   Easy to implement.

2.   Fairly strong because of the Bank of England's influence.

3.   Can specify lending ceilings or deal with particular sectors of the economy.

Disadvantages

1.   Setting ceilings on banks allows competitors to step in.

2.   Banks involved in unacceptable lending are those most likely to ignore restrictive directives.

3.   Positive directives depend for their success on the customers e.g. exporters coming forward to borrow.

Since directives are now no longer officially included among the range of tools which the Bank of England uses to implement the government's monetary policy it seems that the current view is that the disadvantages outlined here are seen as outweighing the advantages.

CONTROL OVER INTEREST RATES

10. Money can be seen as a commodity like anything else which can be bought and sold. Its price is determined by supply and demand, and interest rates can be considered to be that price. If more people want to borrow than to lend this will tend to push up the price of money, the interest rate, until more lenders are attracted and borrowers are discouraged. In theory an equilibrium level of interest rates would then be achieved.

In practice the market for money is not a freely competitive market because of many outside pressures, in particular the government's concern to maintain interest rates at a fairly stable level in order to achieve policy goals.

The government's reasons for trying to regulate interest rates are varied and to some extent contradictory. In general the government aims to:-

a) maintain stable interest rates to help businesses develop (since planning is clearly much harder if interest rates keep changing);

b) keep interest rates low enough to prevent businesses from cutting back on investment;

c) keep interest rates high enough to discourage a huge expansion of consumer credit which could accelerate inflation;

d) keep interest rates low enough to prevent the cost of borrowing from adding to inflation;

e) keep interest rates high enough to discourage foreign investors from drawing out their money, selling pounds and affecting exchange rates;

f) keep interest rates low so that the cost of government borrowing is not increased.

It is important to note that expectations of inflation tend to keep interest rates high because lenders will want to make sure that the money they are paid back is not worth a lot less than the amount lent.

Given that government does aim to influence interest rates, in particular because of the effects on inflation and on the money supply, it is important to understand how this influence works.

In theory the government has a wide choice of possibilities in setting a policy on interest rates.

1. The strongest form of control is direct control by setting interest rates for all types of lending and borrowing. This is not a practical possibility in an economy which is open to pressures from outside agencies, including foreign lenders and borrowers.

2. The central bank, as lender of last resort, can impose minimum interest rates on other banks by compelling them to borrow. The methods by which commercial banks can be made short of funds so that they need to turn to the central bank include calls for special deposits. Sales of government assets or government stock to take money out of accounts held with commercial banks can also force the banks to borrow.

3. The central bank can recommend a particular level of interest rates. This is often done by publishing official rates, which banks are then expected to follow, though they are not compelled to do so.

4. Allowing free market forces to determine interest rates is the opposite end of the spectrum from strict control. This approach is generally in line with the philosophy of Conservative governments but is not always a practical possibility because of the implications for exchange rates or other aspects of the economy.

The policy adopted by most United Kingdom governments is likely to be within the broad categories 2 and 3 listed above, but these do give some scope for making choices in implementing policy.

THE STRUCTURE OF INTEREST RATES

11. When a government sets or recommends a particular rate of interest it does not expect all other interest rates within the country to be the same. Different circumstances and types of borrowing and lending demand different rates.

In general terms it is expected that short-term rates will normally be lower than long-term rates. This is because lenders prepared to commit their money over a long period expect to be rewarded better than if they only tied up the money for a short time.

This 'normal' pattern of interest rates over time can be represented graphically as below.

A 'Normal' Rising Yield Curve

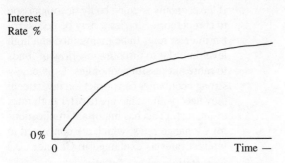

This kind of graph is described as showing a rising yield curve, because the yield or return increases as the period of lending is increased.

In contrast to this a falling yield curve occurs when short-term interest rates have become higher than long-term rates. This might occur if long-term rates were expected to fall.

A Falling Yield Curve

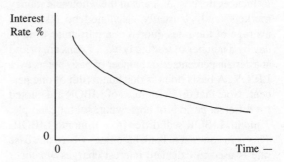

Government has to be aware of the importance of the period of lending when considering how interest rates are changing. Equally the type of lending has an influence. The inter-relationships between different interest rates and the types of lending or borrowing to which they are applied are complex. The following diagram suggests how some rates influence others so that decisions made by the

The Structure of Interest Rates

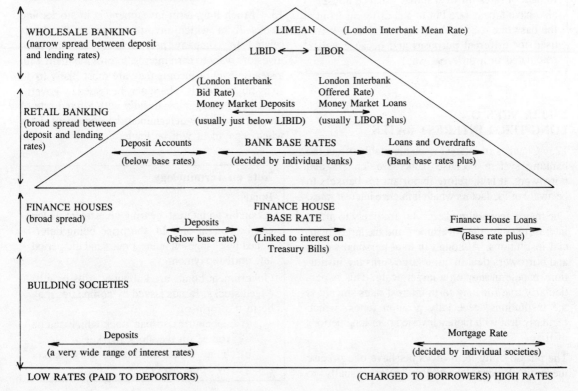

government and implemented by the Bank of England are likely to be far-reaching in their effect.

Among the most important of the rates shown here is LIBOR, London InterBank Offered Rate, which influences the cost of loans in the wholesale money markets (and is usually calculated by taking an average of the rates quoted at a particular time of day by a number of leading banks). Loans are priced at a certain percentage or number of basis points over LIBOR. A basis point is one hundredth of one percent. Note that different rates of LIBOR are quoted for different periods of borrowing, so, for example, 3-month LIBOR will differ from 6-month LIBOR. This is in contrast to bank base rates where one base rate is used to calculate interest charges whatever the period of borrowing.

Note on Terminology

Base Rate

A base rate is simple a rate on which other rates are based. In the context of the British banking system the term is most commonly applied to the base rate set by clearing banks as the determinant of rates for overdrafts. Finance houses also have a base rate but this is different from the base rate used by banks (both because it is used for different purposes and because it is calculated in a different way).

INFLUENCES ON LONG-TERM INTEREST RATES

12.   Changes in interest rates inevitably affect the banking system because banks are lenders and borrowers. It is therefore important for bankers to be aware of the factors which influence interest rates.

The major decision-makers who are likely to affect interest rates are the government and the large financial institutions. Although in total personal savers and borrowers deal in quite large sums the institutions handle money on a larger scale. This is particularly true for long-term interest rates since it is the institutions, especially pension funds, which regularly deal with money invested over long periods of time.

The phrase 'long-term' does not have one precise meaning. Where 'short-term' refers usually to

periods of up to one year, 'long-term' may be interpreted as over five years, over ten years or even longer.

The following broad areas can be seen as the most important factors affecting rates in the long-term (however this is defined).

1.   General Economic Performance
     If the economy is doing badly in comparison to competitor countries it may be necessary for interest rates to be maintained at a high level in order to discourage a flow of funds to more successful economies. Conversely strong economies can attract the investment they need without having to offer high rates of interest. (This has important implications for exchange rates, which are connected to interest rates as explained in Chapter 20.)

2.   Expectations about Inflation
     If inflation is expected to be high borrowers will be prepared to pay more and lenders will expect to receive more than where prices are stable.

NOMINAL RATES AND YIELDS

13.   Much long-term investment is in stocks and shares from which investors receive dividends related to company performance. If long-term investors want to earn interest to provide them with a steady level of income they are most likely to do so by buying bonds. These may be issued by government or by companies, usually with a fixed rate of interest and a pre-determined date or set of dates when repayment will be made.

Note on Terminology

Bonds

A bond is an interest- bearing investment which can be bought or sold, the price being determined by changes in interest rates and the period left until repayment.

Government bonds are known as gilts or gilt-edged stocks. Bonds issued by companies may be in the form of:-
   a)   debentures or loan stock which can be traded on the stock market *or*
   b)   bonds traded outside the stock market by bond dealers.

Modern developments in the markets for bonds have included variable rate bonds and bonds on which no interest is paid (where the return to the investor arises from the difference between the purchase price and the amount repaid). However fixed interest bonds with set repayment dates remain the most common form.

It is important to recognise that the stated or nominal rate of interest is not an accurate reflection of the return to the investor.

Example Treasury Stock 8% 2009

This is a government stock repayable in 2009. Interest is paid at a fixed rate (also known as 'coupon') of 8%. A holder of £100 nominal value of stock will therefore receive £8 a year in interest. If current interest rates are much higher, for example at 12%, the holder would not be able to sell his £100 certificate for as much as £100. The price would be expected to fall to £66.67. The interest paid would remain at £8 so at that price the rate of interest would be

$(8 \div 66.67 \times 100)\% = 12\%$

This figure, relating the amount of interest to the price paid, is known as the yield. It is fairly unlikely that any holder of £100 nominal value of stock will have paid exactly £100 to obtain it, and the yield is therefore nearly always different from the 'coupon' or nominal rate of interest. (Note that a more precise calculation of yield would also include an adjustment for the length of time until the repayment date).

If prices of bonds are very high this will reflect very low yields. Price and yield move in opposite directions so if interest rates fall a holder of fixed rate bonds will be able to make capital gains by selling the bonds at a higher price then he or she paid for them.

REAL INTEREST RATES

14. The preceding section of the chapter suggested that yield is a better indicator of the return on an investment than the nominal interest rate. However even yield can be misleading. A yield of 10% may sould like a good return, but if prices are rising at 11% a year the investor will see the value of the investment falling.

Interest rates or yields adjusted for inflation are described as real rates.

Example Yield 5%   Inflation at 4% per annum
Real Rate of Interest 1%

If inflation is higher than the yield the real rate will be negative, as was the case with some bank deposit accounts during much of the 1970s. From 1974 to 1977 the annual inflation rate was consistently above clearing bank base rates and therefore well above what the banks paid to depositors.

INFLUENCES ON
SHORT-TERM INTEREST RATES

15. The connections between different interest rates mean that short-term and long-term rates are subject to similar pressures.

If, for example, long-term rates become very high borrowers will tend to borrow short term if possible. This will cause short-term rates to rise and long-term rates to fall. So although there normally will be differences between interest rates over different periods of time general trends in interest rates are identifiable.

For long-term rates the main influences are the long-term factors, the economy and political expectations about the control of inflation, which are also important for short-term rates.

Key factors having an effect on interest rates in the short term are:-

a) long term rates;

b) exchange rates, which in turn are affected by a wide range of broader issues from the level of imports and exports to speculative dealing;

c) government borrowing, in particular through the Bank of England's decisions about what bids to accept for the weekly Treasury Bill issue;

d) opinion in the money markets where lending and borrowing takes place on a large scale.

These factors are, of course, not separate and independent but closely interrelated and constantly in interaction with one another.

INTEREST RATES AND THEIR EFFECT ON BANKS

16.   The government's aims in controlling the economy include ensuring the stability of the banking system, but in other respects government decisions are not intended to take special account of the needs of banks.

Nevertheless changing levels of interest rates clearly do affect banks. Research into the overall effects is inconclusive, but in general changing rates can be expected to have the following advantages and disadvantages.

Rising interest rates

Advantages for banks

1.   More income will be earned from loans at variable rates (e.g. overdrafts linked to base rate).
2.   There is a likelihood of a wider spread between rates paid to depositors and rates charged to borrowers.
3.   More deposits will be attracted (from abroad or from people holding cash).

Disadvantages for banks

1.   Greater cost will be incurred in interest paid out to depositors.
2.   There will be a reduction in the amount of borrowing, cutting income.
3.   There is a risk of 'trading up', with current account customers being tempted to transfer money to accounts on which interest is paid.

Falling interest rates

Advantages for banks

1.   Less interest will be paid out to depositors.
2.   Demand for loans will increase, adding to income from fees as well as interest.

Disadvantages for banks

1.   Less income will be earned from existing loans (except those at fixed rates).
2.   There is a likelihood of a reduced spread between deposit and loan rates.
3.   There will be outflows of money abroad.

To some extent the disadvantages can be overcome, for example by having a reasonable mixture of fixed rate and floating rate loans and deposits. The risk of money flowing abroad can also be countered by offering accounts in other currencies; interest on U.S. dollar accounts is linked to interest rates in the United States rather than to United Kingdom rates.

In general terms stability of interest rates probably meets the needs of banks best because there are savings in cost if promotional literature and documentation do not need to be changed very often. Stability also means that the level of lending can be matched more easily to the level of deposits. Athough no bank maintains an exact balance between attracting new money and selling new loans any sudden or extreme change in rates may create a severe imbalance.

It is important to recognise too that banks are not purely passive participants in the processes which decide the level of interest rates. Banks themselves make decisions about the base rate on which they calculate overdraft interest and about the rate they pay to depositors. When general interest rates rise no bank can resist the rise by refusing to pay extra to depositors because deposits would start to fall and more and more people would want to borrow at the exceptionally low rates charged. What banks can do is to delay any change they make. The speed at which banks react to changes in general interest rates may in turn influence other institutions, so cautious reactions by banks can help to increase stability.

CONTROLS IN THE FUTURE

17.   The emphasis of the Conservative government on the influence of the market is likely to continue in the future because of the increased internationalisation of financial services. Banks all over the world compete for deposits, offer loans to multinational companies and deal with one another. Major banks have subsidiaries in all the leading financial centres of the world. This means that future controls and supervision will need an international dimension. The Bank of England, along with other central banks, regularly discusses issues of concern to the international banking community, but jointly agreed policies are only just beginning to emerge.

Until there is more agreement any central bank trying to impose strong restrictions on its own banking system, in order to influence the national economy, will find that banks abroad will circumvent the regulations. Today major United Kingdom based companies can borrow sterling in New York or Paris just as easily as in London. Restrictive measures applied to United Kingdom lending banks can therefore only work if either:-

a) the whole economy is regulated so that British companies or their foreign subsidiaries cannot borrow without permission (an extremely unlikely development)

b) the banking regulators in other countries co-operate with the United Kingdom authorities (a more likely option, but one which has a long way to go).

SUMMARY

18. a) Government has a range of aims in trying to control the banking system. These include the encouragement of economic growth, the control of inflation and the maintenance of confidence in banks.

b) Before 1980 monetary control was based on rules laid down in the Bank of England document 'Competition and Credit Control'. The measures available included a reserve asset ratio and the Special Deposit scheme.

c) In October 1972 Bank Rate was replaced by Minimum Lending Rate.

d) At the beginning of the 1980s new monetary control systems were brought in, including the creation of the New Monetary Sector to include institutions other than banks.

e) Major methods of control available from 1981 were:-
1.   a cash ratio requirement (0.5% of eligible liabilities to be placed with the Bank of England, 0.45% from 1986);
2.   the Special Deposits scheme (which already existed);
3.   rules applied to 'eligible' banks about placing funds with the discount houses (removed 1986);
4.   qualitative directives (abandoned 1986);
5.   controls over interest rates through buying and selling 'paper'.

f) Government tries to influence interest rates in order to maintain stability, prevent inflation and protect exchange rates.

g) Interest rates vary according to the period of borrowing to which they relate. In general interest rates are higher for longer term borrowing, but there are exceptions.

h) Different interest rates are also applied to different types of borrowing with banks basing some rates on their own base rate and some rates on money market interest rates. Other lending such as house purchase loans may pay interest which is not directly connected with either of these main influences.

i) Long-term interest rates tend to be affected by the underlying strengths and weaknesses of the economy.

j) Quoted interest rates are now always what they seem. This is because:-
1.   very often a nominal rate, for example on a bond, is quite different from the yield, the return on the amount of money invested *and*
2.   rates of interest cannot be judged in isolation from the value of money; if inflation is at a higher rate than the interest rate the real return can be negative.

k) Short-term interest rates are affected by broad economic factors just as long-term rates are, but there may be other more immediate influences such as the level of government borrowing through the Treasury Bill issue.

l) When interest rates change banks are affected in a variety of ways, for example finding reduced demand for loans if interest rates rise. Stable interest rates probably suit banks best because any change in rates costs banks money.

m) The growing internationalisation of banking means that in future tight control of one economy through monetary policy is unlikely to succeed without international co-operation.

STUDENT SELF-TESTING

Self Review Questions

1.   What is monetary policy? (2)

2.   What were the main aims of the 'Competition and Credit Control' policy? (3)

3.   What was the purpose of changing from Bank Rate to Minimum Lending Rate? (4)

4.   What were the terms of the cash ratio system introduced in 1981? (6)

5.   What were the differences between Special Deposits and Supplementary Special Deposits? (7)

6.   What are 'eligible' banks? (8)

7.   What are the advantages and disadvantages of using directives as a means of controlling bank lending? (9)

8.   Why are long-term interest rates normally higher than short-term rates? (11)

9.   What is a base rate? (11)

10.   What is the difference between the nominal rate of interest on a bond and the yield? (13)

Exercises (answers begin page 323)

A1.   Read this passage and answer the questions which follow.

Following reforms in August 1981 the Bank of England required all institutions in the new monetary sector with eligible liabilities of £10 million or more to keep ½% of the value of their eligible liabilities in non-interest bearing balances at the Bank.

At the same time the mechanism for carrying out monetary policy remained little changed. The Bank of England continued to influence interest rates in the market by buying bills from the discount houses when they needed funds. Although MLR was no longer publicly announced except on rare occasions this did not mean that market forces were free from government influence.

Even the Special Deposits scheme was maintained as a mechanism available for use, although it had not been used since 1979.

1.   What does the phrase 'new monetary sector' mean?

2.   What are eligible liabilities?

3.   How does the Bank of England influence interest rates by buying bills from the discount houses?

4.   What was MLR and why had the regular announcement of it been important?

5.   What was the purpose of the Special Deposits scheme?

A2.   To what extent do banks decide their own interest rates?

A3.   What arguments are there against the view that banks like interest rates to rise so that they can charge more for their loans?

A4.   Special deposit schemes and cash or liquid asset ratio controls are designed to restrict bank lending. How do they do this and what alternatives are available to the authorities?

4. The Money Markets

INTRODUCTION

1.　The markets in which money is bought and sold are perhaps more important than ever today. The government has chosen to emphasise the role of market forces in influencing monetary conditions so the operations of the money markets affect the financial affairs of everybody who deposits or borrows money.

The government, through the Bank of England, actively affects the price of money in the markets because it is a user of borrowed money and a supplier of money when the system is short.

This chapter looks at what different money markets there are, and at what is bought and sold. In particular there are four main types of 'paper' traded in the money markets.

1.　Certificates of Deposit.
2.　Local Authority Bills.
3.　Commercial Bills.
4.　Treasury Bills.

Following an explanation of these terms and a very important concept associated with them, negotiability, the chapter looks at the kind of information provided in press reports on the money markets, defining some of the commonly used expressions.

THE MONEY MARKETS

2.　A money market consists of financial institutions buying and selling large sums of money, or documents representing claims on money (in other words borrowing or lending). There is no market place in the sense of a physical location where buyers and sellers can meet. Instead deals are normally by telephone, although in the future it may well become normal practice for trading to take place through networks of linked computers.

Money markets are usually referred to in the plural to indicate that there are markets in different types of 'paper' and markets in which different organisations participate. Major banks are participants in most of the money markets. It is sometimes considered that the official money market is the system operated by the discount houses (described in Chapter 1). Other money markets are therefore sometimes referred to as 'parallel money markets' because they operate alongside the discount house market.

If the government takes steps to encourage a rise in interest rates it is likely to be felt first either as a formal announcement of interest rate policy or through a change in the price of paper which the government sells or buys. Other buyers and sellers in the money markets will be affected in turn. Because the scale of lending and borrowing in the money markets is so great opinions and attitudes of dealers in money can also be a significant influence on interest rates.

The major categories of money market apart from the discount house system are:-

    a)　the Certificate of Deposit Market;
    b)　the Local Authority Bill Market;
    c)　the Commercial Bill Market;
    d)　the Treasury Bill Market;
    e)　the Interbank Market;
    f)　the Intercompany Market;
    g)　the Commercial Paper Market.

The first four of these are defined primarily in terms of the type of paper being bought and sold. The remaining three are fairly simply explained.

The interbank market refers to the lending which takes place between banks. Deals are often on a very large scale, and the participants are often put in touch with one another by money brokers who take a commission for their part in the process of transferring money from banks with a temporary surplus to those with a shortage.

The intercompany market (which became important in the 1970s but has almost entirely disappeared) involved lending between companies during a period when bank credit was highly restricted (particularly whily the 'corset' or Supplementary Special Deposit Scheme was in force).

The commercial paper market is the newest of the markets, having begun in May 1986 following a relaxation of certain restrictions. It deals with bonds issued by companies for periods of a year or more, in contrast to the well-established commercial bill market which is based on Bills of Exchange rarely dated more than six months ahead. The longer time scale means that the commercial paper market could be considered rather different from the true money markets which deal mainly in short-term claims.

A broader definition of FINANCIAL MARKETS would also include markets in stocks and shares and in foreign exchange. Money markets specialise in claims on money, but the distinction between money market paper and other claims such as company loan stocks is not always very clear.

CERTIFICATES OF DEPOSIT

3.   The market in Certificates of Deposit began in the United Kingdom in 1966 when depositors with American banks were issued with certificates if they made deposits of U.S. $10,000 or more for a fixed term. The most significant feature of these certificates was that they were negotiable.

Note on Terminology

Negotiability

Negotiable documents (commonly referred to as negotiable instruments) can be transferred from one holder to another with the special feature that the the new holder can obtain a better legal title than the previous holder.

Such documents are said to have the quality of negotiability, and this makes them more acceptable to buyers than documents which may prove to have no value if they have been stolen.

Example

If you take a ten pound note from someone in payment for goods and it turns out that the money was stolen the original owner cannot claim it back from you. You have a good title because the ten pound note is negotiable.

In contrast if you accept a watch worth ten pounds as payment for goods the original owner of the watch can claim it back from you even though you did not know it was stolen, because watches, in common with almost all other goods and documents, are not negotiable. You cannot obtain a good title to them if they have been stolen because you cannot have a better title than the previous holder.

This quality of negotiability meant that holders of Certificates of Deposit could be fairly sure of getting their money back if they needed it even though the deposit was for a fixed term. The bank issuing the certificate would not repay early but other investors or financial institutions would be willing to acquire the certificate knowing that they could obtain a good

title to it and be able to claim the money when the certificate matured (or, of course, sell it to another holder).

The idea of negotiable Certificates of Deposit (commonly known as CDs) originated in New York in the early 1960s. After introducing dollar certificates into the United Kingdom in 1966 American banks also issued sterling certificates from 1968 and the idea was taken up by the clearing banks in 1971. Eventually many banks became issuers. In 1983 Building Societies also issued Certificates of Deposit for the first time.

The issue of a Certificate of Deposit takes place when a depositor places funds with an issuing institution. The market in Certificates of Deposit is a market in second-hand certificates since if the original investor simply holds on to the the certificate until the maturity date no buying or selling takes place. Within the market major buyers are financial institutions and large companies with cash surpluses. Certificates of Deposit are a short-term investment, and because they are highly liquid (which means they can be converted into cash again very quickly) they are ideal for investors needing to get their money back at short notice.

Characteristics of Certificates of Deposit

1.   Issued by major financial institutions.
2.   Negotiable and readily saleable.
3.   Set maturity date, usually between 3 months and 5 years.
4.   Issued for fixed round sums, in dollars from $10,000 and in sterling from £50,000
5.   Interest paid, usually at a fixed rate added to the sum paid at maturity. Floating rate certificates are possible.
6.   Tax not deducted at source as it is for most bank deposits.

LOCAL AUTHORITY BILLS

4.   The market in local authority paper is similar to the Certificate of Deposit market. Local authorities raise money like central government by issuing promises to pay at a future date. Buyers are willing to acquire these bills because the risk of a failure to pay is very small and the interest paid is normally a little more than on Treasury Bills.

The market is more complicated than with Treasury Bills because the local authorities do not issue bills weekly. Each authority can issue bills when it chooses to do so, according to specific needs, although government restrictions on spending by local authorities have reduced the market to some extent during the 1980s.

Characteristics of Local Authority Bills

1. Issued by local authorities.
2. Readily saleable through a well-established market.
3. Set maturity date.
4. Issued in sterling.
5. Interest paid, usually at a fixed rate.

BILLS OF EXCHANGE

5.   The term Bill of Exchange in the context of the paper bought and sold in the money markets refers to documents issued by companies, normally in connection with their trade. These commercial bills, like Certificates of Deposit, Local Authority Bills and Treasury Bills, are promises to pay in the future.

> ### Note on Terminology
>
> Under the Bills of Exchange Act 1882 the technical definition of a Bill of Exchange is given as:-
>
> "An unconditional order in writing addressed by one person to another, signed by the person giving it, requiring the person to whom it is addressed to pay on demand, or at a fixed or determinable future time a sum certain in money to, or to the order of, a specified person or to bearer."
>
> Bills of Exchange are of special significance to bankers, not only because of their importance in the money markets but also because of their use in international trade.
>
> In effect the drawer of a Bill of Exchange, the person giving it, is the person who expects to receive money. Only when the person to whom it is addressed, the drawee, has signed it to agree to pay in the future does the piece of paper become of any value. This agreement to pay is known as acceptance of the bill and the drawee in making it becomes the acceptor of the bill. It is the acceptor, not the issuer of the bill, who is making a promise to pay although the issuer will be liable to pay if the drawee accepts the bill but then defaults at the due date.

(For an example of a Bill of Exchange see Chapter 14.)

Characteristics of Bills of Exchange

1. Issued (or 'drawn') by companies.
2. Negotiable and readily sold (or 'discounted') to banks (as explained in Chapter 14).
3. Traded in the Commercial Bills market if accepted by known drawees, often banks.
4. Set maturity date, usually below six months.
5. Issued in sterling or in foreign currency for any amount (although the bills traded in the money markets are usually for large round sums).
6. Traded at a discount (the amount of the discount being the equivalent of interest) as no interest is added on at maturity.

Note that many Bills of Exchange are not traded in the money markets and are not considered suitable as money market 'paper', for example because the amounts are too small or the parties to the bill are not well known names.

TREASURY BILLS

6.   The fourth important form of paper traded in the money markets is the government-issued Treasury Bill. Treasury Bills are normally sold through the Bank of England each week.

Characteristics of Treasury Bills

1. Issued by central government.
2. Negotiable and readily saleable.
3. Set maturity date, usually 91 days after issue.
4. Traded at a discount as no interest is added to the face value.
5. Issued in sterling in round amounts.

THE FORMS OF PAPER USED IN THE MONEY MARKETS

7.   The four categories of 'paper' described above give financial institutions a choice of short-term investments which they can acquire in preference to leaving surplus cash idle.

Holding paper is a deliberate policy for banks and other financial intermediaries which may have to pay out to depositors at short notice, because the paper can be sold quickly if cash is needed. This is in contrast to more profitable fixed term deposits or loans to customers which cannot normally be reclaimed very quickly.

The balance between the different categories of paper can vary considerably as the different groups of borrowers who issue the paper have varying needs for money. The following approximate figures give some indication of the variations that do take place in the total amounts handled by the money markets.

The Money Markets:
 estimated value of paper in circulation

	End of year	
	1979	1983
	£ million	£ million
Certificates of Deposit	23500	73000
Local Authority Bills	5000	6000
Commercial Bills	3500	9000
Treasury Bills	2500	3000

For Commercial Bills in particular the figure can never be more accurate than an estimate because companies are continuously issuing bills of exchange and paying off earlier bills, some of them passing through the money markets and some being handled by trading partners of the issuing companies.

Similarly for Certificates of Deposit the issuers, banks or financial institutions, are also holders of Certificates of Deposit and may, in some circumstances, buy back their own certificates before the maturity date, so reducing the amount in circulation.

PRESS REPORTS ON
THE MONEY MARKETS

8.   Because interest rates in the money markets have an influence to some degree on all other interest rates the financial columns of leading newspapers include reports on the money markets. The language used by financial journalists should be familiar to bankers.

The following list of commonly used terms should prove helpful.

1.   Paper
    The various types of document bought and sold in the money markets are referred to as paper.

2.   Interbank
    This is the short name for the rate at which banks borrow from one another. For example, 3 month interbank means the rate for loans lasting for a period of 3 months while overnight interbank is the rate for lending repayable the next day.

3.   Assistance
    Assistance is the provision of funds for the markets from the government; the Bank of England buys paper, which puts cash into the banking system.

4.   Bands
    When the Bank of England buys bills it usually chooses particular ranges of maturity date. These ranges are known as bands, with band 1 covering paper near to maturity. The bands cover the period from overnight to 12 months.

5.   Bank Bills
    Bills of exchange drawn by commercial companies become bank bills when they are signed by banks as acceptors, and this makes them more readily saleable in the money markets. Such bills are often issued as a form of bank financing known as an 'acceptance credit', described in Chapter 14.

6.   Eligible Bills
    These are bills of exchange signed by banks which the Bank of England recognises as eligible banks. They are considered particularly safe, that is certain to be paid at the due date, so they sell at higher prices than other bank bills. This is the same as saying that eligible banks can borrow more cheaply.

7.   The Authorities
    This term refers to the Bank of England and the Treasury acting on behalf of the government.

A PRESS REPORT INTERPRETED

9.   The following example illustrates the kind of language and ideas which may be encountered in press reports about the operations of the money markets.

Example

"The London money markets continued to anticipate a cut in clearing bank base rates yesterday. Three-month interbank was lower by one sixteenth suggesting base rates

might fall by a half to one percent. In early trading the discount houses were reluctant to sell bills at the dealing rates offered and the authorities found it hard to obtain paper.

Shortages of funds in the market led to late assistance, with buying of bank bills in the lower bands. By the close overnight inter-bank had regained its opening level."

Key points to note about this report are listed below.

1. If buyers and sellers in the money markets expect general rates of interest, for example the clearers' base rates, to fall, they will lower their rates in advance. This means that rate changes do not occur all at once, and rates may be out of alignment with one another for some time.

2. One sixteenth means one sixteenth of one percent. Rates are still often described in these fractions rather than in their decimal equivalents.

3. The journalist's stated view that base rates may fall by between half a percent and one percent means one or the other since base rates are normally set to the nearest half percent.

4. The writer comments that there is a connection between the fall in interbank rate and base rates, but predicting the size of the fall assumes a detailed knowledge of the markets because it depends on knowing the current level of market rates and base rates. The information which the report gives about the interbank rate falling cannot in itself point to a corresponding fall in base rates.

5. Dealing rates offered are what the Bank of England will pay the discount houses for bills, usually eligible bills of exchange.

6. As this article indicates conditions in the markets change during the day so the Bank of England may find banks or discount houses unwilling to sell early on but keener to do so later on when cash is more urgently needed.

7. The Bank of England's decisions about which bands of bills to buy depend upon its own plans and predictions about the market.

8. Like most other markets trading normally takes place within limited times. Opening prices are not necessarily similar to closing prices on the previous day because important news affecting the markets may have been received in the meantime. This is increasingly true as markets become more international and events abroad have a great influence on prices.

SUMMARY

10. a) Government measures to alter interest rates usually have their effect initially through the money markets.

b) Money markets are usually defined either in terms of the documents (or 'paper') bought and sold, or in terms of the organisations involved in the market.

c) The interbank market means the market for loans between banks and the intercompany market (a temporary phenomenon created by restrictions on bank lending) meant the market for loans between companies.

d) The Certificate of Deposit market involves banks and other financial institutions but deals in Certificates of Deposit. In the United Kingdom these were first issued in 1966.

e) Certificates of Deposit are negotiable instruments issued by financial institutions, mainly banks. They can be bought or sold until the final maturity date when the issuer pays back to the holder of the certificate the sum originally deposited plus interest.

f) Local authority bills, issued by local authorities to raise money, can also be traded in the money markets.

g) For banks the form of 'paper' which has most significance is the Bill of Exchange. Commercial bills traded on the money markets are important in their own right, but bankers also have to deal extensively with Bills of Exchange in their foreign trade operations.

h) The drawer of a Bill of Exchange instructs the drawee to make payment. The payee who is to receive the money will often be the same company as the drawer. The procedure is similar to writing out a cheque payable to 'Self' in order to draw money out of a bank account, except that very often the payment date is in the future. Term bills, which do allow a period of credit in this way, are often dated up to six months ahead.

i)   Treasury Bills issued each week by the Bank of England to mature 91 days later, are a major source of short-term finance for the government. They are normally bought by the discount houses, but regularly sold on to other institutions.

j)   Bankers need to understand press reports on the money markets. These deal with the rates of interest and the Bank of England's activity in the markets.

STUDENT SELF-TESTING

Self Review Questions

1.   What is a money market? (2)

2.   What is the difference between the commercial bill market and the commercial paper market? (2)

3.   What is the significance of the word 'negotiable' in the phrase 'negotiable instrument'? (3)

4.   What is a negotiable Certificate of Deposit? (3)

5.   What are the characteristics of local authority bills? (4)

6.   What is the definition of a Bill of Exchange? (5)

7.   What does an acceptor of a Bill of Exchange do? (5)

8.   What is the usual maximum maturity period for a Bill of Exchange? (5)

9.   Which are bought and sold in larger quantities on the money markets, Commercial Bills or Treasury Bills? (7)

10. What do financial journalists mean by 'assistance' in the money markets? (8)

Exercises (answers begin page 324)

A1.   What is a money market, and what kinds of money market are there today in the United Kingdom?

A2.   Why are Certificates of Deposit important in the money markets?

A3.   What differences are there between Certificates of Deposit, Local Authority Bills and Commercial Bills used in the money markets?

A4.   What are Treasury Bills, and how important are they in the money markets?

5. The Balance Sheet of a Bank

INTRODUCTION

1. This chapter looks at the information contained in the annual accounts produced by banks. In reading the chapter students will find it useful to refer to the latest set of accounts from their own bank or from a bank with which they are familiar.

The beginning of the chapter considers the nature of balance sheets and an example is used to illustrate the major categories of assets and liabilities which banks include in their balance sheets. These different items are explained in turn. Various kinds of analysis of bank balance sheets are considered and the chapter also describes the accounting data and statements included in a set of published accounts.

BALANCE SHEETS

2. A balance sheet is a statement of the assets and liabilities of a business at a particular point in time. Assets are the claims a business has, either on other people or in the form of objects owned. Liabilities are amounts owed to other people. Banks, for example, owe large sums to their depositors so deposits feature as a major liability in a bank's balance sheet.

For all businesses except those in severe difficulties assets are of greater value than liabilities. The difference is the capital of the business. Capital could be seen as a liability in the sense that it is owed to the owners of the business (the shareholders if the business is a limited company). Usually it is considered different from other liabilities because the owners do not expect to get their capital back from the company.

For example a major bank might have a balance sheet with the following structure.

	£ millions
Total Assets	60000
(mainly money owed to the bank by borrowers)	
Total Liabilities	57500
(mainly money owed by the bank to depositors)	
Capital	2500
	60000

Note that the assets and liabilities are constantly changing. As a customer draws out money the assets are reduced because the amount of cash held has fallen. At the same time the liabilities fall by an equal amount because the bank no longer owes that amount of money.

Capital changes as the bank makes profit. When interest charges are made for loans that interest adds to the asset of money owed to the bank but there is no corresponding increase in liabilities. The interest is profit which belongs to the owners of the bank.

The following table lists some of the differences between a bank balance sheet and a balance sheet of a manufacturing company.

Bank	Manufacturing Company
Assets	
1. The list of assets usually has fixed assets last.	1. The list of assets usually has fixed assets first.
2. The major asset is money lent.	2. The major asset is often fixed assets.
3. No stock is held.	3. Stock is often a large item.
4. A wide range of short-term assets is held.	4. Cash in hand and at the bank are the only highly liquid assets.
Liabilities	
5. Money owed is very large, often over 75% of total assets.	5. Money owed is usually less than 25% of total assets.
Capital	
6. Capital is likely to be less than a tenth of total assets.	6. Capital is likely to be over a quarter of total assets.

Since a change in any one part of the balance sheet must involve a change in another part the balance sheet will always balance. The important point to note is that it represents a static view of the business, the position on just one day. This may be untypical of the normal situation.

TYPES OF BALANCE SHEET

3.   The balance sheets of banks are often rather different from the balance sheets of manufacturing or trading companies, as shown in the table on the previous page. Banks should be aware of these differences, not only as a means to understanding their own industry better but also because they have to appreciate the significance of the balance sheets of businesses to which they lend money.

The differences arise because of the business banks are in. This provides useful evidence for bankers that set rules about how balance sheets should appear are meaningless. What is important is that the balance sheet should be appropriate to the business.

EXAMPLE OF A BANK BALANCE SHEET

4.   The following balance sheet is based on the balance sheets produced by the major United Kingdom clearing banks.

Consolidated Balance Sheet of 'Typical Clearer' at 31 December 1985

Assets	£ millions
Cash and short-term funds	10000
Cheques in course of collection	500
Investments	1000
Advances to Customers	47500
Trade Investments	500
Premises and Equipment	500
	60000

financed by:
Liabilities

Deposits and customers accounts	56000
Other liabilities	1500
	57500

Capital

Loan Capital	500
Share Capital and Reserves	2000
	60000

The figures shown indicate the approximate size of the leading clearers. The largest, Barclays and National Westminster, have bigger balance sheets. Note that the heading, 'Consolidated Balance Sheet', means that all of the subsidiary companies owned by the bank are included in the figures. In other words the balance sheet represents the bank as a group of companies rather than as an individual company.

Some banks do not use the same terms as those in the example, and even where they do they may not interpret them in quite the same way as their competitors. This means that the balance sheets of different banks cannot be considered as directly comparable with one another. However in most cases bank balance sheets are broadly similar in appearance.

In the actual published accounts of a bank many of the items will be accompanied by reference numbers to footnotes. These usually give additional detail about what is included.

The following sections of the chapter look at all of the items in the balance sheet in turn, commenting on their meaning and importance.

CASH AND SHORT-TERM FUNDS

5.   The first of the assets shown in most bank balance sheets is the money available to pay out to depositors who want to be repaid. This is not held entirely as cash but takes a number of forms.

For normal day-to-day transactions the banks have money in their tills, their branch safes and the bullion centres which distribute funds to the branches. All of this 'till money' in the form of actual cash cannot earn interest. It is lying idle, waiting to be drawn out, and in the meantime costing money rather than earning money because it requires expensive security measures to protect it. The banks therefore aim to keep their holdings of cash to the minimum level which they regard as safe. This is the level at which they will always be able to meet demand for withdrawals without having to tell any customers that they cannot have their money back. To keep too little could lead to a loss of confidence.

Equally unprofitable but less of a security risk are the working balances which banks maintain at the Bank of England. These are needed to settle up with other banks when payments are exchanged through the clearing system.

> **Example**
>
> Bank A transfers to Bank B cheques totalling £50 million drawn on B and Bank B transfers to Bank A cheques totalling £45 million. This leaves Bank B owing Bank A £5 million to settle up for the cheques which have been paid into Bank A drawn by customers of Bank B. The transfer of £5 million can be made from Bank B's account with the Bank of England to Bank A's account.

Note that the working balances (or operational balances) are in addition to the cash deposits (or non-operational balances) required by the Bank of England as part of the cash ratio scheme described in Chapter 3. The cash ratio balances are also part of a bank's short term funds.

Although the senior management of a bank can estimate the level of cash and Bank of England balances needed to be fairly sure of meeting normal demands for money, it is also important to allow for exceptional circumstances. Other short-term funds help to provide for unexpected needs.

The essential quality shared by the various short-term assets held by banks is their high level of liquidity. This means that they can be turned into cash very quickly. Bank of England balances can be considered the most liquid of the non-cash assets because they can be used just like cash to settle debts owed to other banks, or used to buy cash from other banks.

Almost as liquid are loans to other financial institutions (in particular the discount houses described in Chapter 1) through the money markets, a form of lending described as money 'at call'. 'Call money', as it is known, can be asked for without notice and will be repaid the same day. Other short-term money market loans range from overnight lending to loans over a period of a few months. The longer the period the higher the interest earned in most cases, so by losing a little liquidity extra profit can be made.

Similarly highly liquid are the banks' holdings of the kinds of 'paper' described in Chapter 4. Banks hold a range of Treasury Bills, Local Authority Bills, Commercial Bills and Certificates of Deposit. These earn interest but can be converted into cash quickly by selling them to other financial institutions or companies with cash to invest.

Note that the Certificates of Deposit held by banks are issued by other banks. Where a bank has issued Certificates of Deposit the liability to repay is included in the total of deposits and customers' accounts in the balance sheet.

Within a bank's published accounts there is likely to be a footnote to the item for cash and short-term funds giving a breakdown into broad categories. This might show, for example:-

	£ million
Notes, coin, Bank of England balances	1100
Money at call and short notice	4400
British Treasury Bills	200
Other Bills	3400
Certificates of Deposit	900
	10000

In some balance sheets cash and short-term funds will cover only the first two or the first four items with Bills or Certificates of Deposit as separate categories.

CHEQUES IN COURSE OF COLLECTION

6.   When a bank customer pays in a cheque drawn on another bank that cheque adds to the customer's bank balance, an increased liability from the point of view of the bank. The bank is able to treat the cheque as a claim on the other bank and therefore a corresponding asset. For the bank as a whole the total value of cheques drawn on other banks and not yet paid for can be substantial, even though the collection period is short.

The basic procedure for handling cheques paid in is outlined overleaf.

This means that on any day on which a bank, in our example Midland Bank, chooses to draw up its balance sheet, among the assets will be cheques paid in at its whole network of branches. These will include cheques paid in on the balance sheet date to be despatched to the clearing house and any cheques at the clearing house for which settlement has not been received through the Bank of England. Cheques written by customers of branches of Midland Bank do not represent an asset since they are only transferring funds from one account to another.

Although in the balance sheet this asset is usually listed among the first as a highly liquid asset this

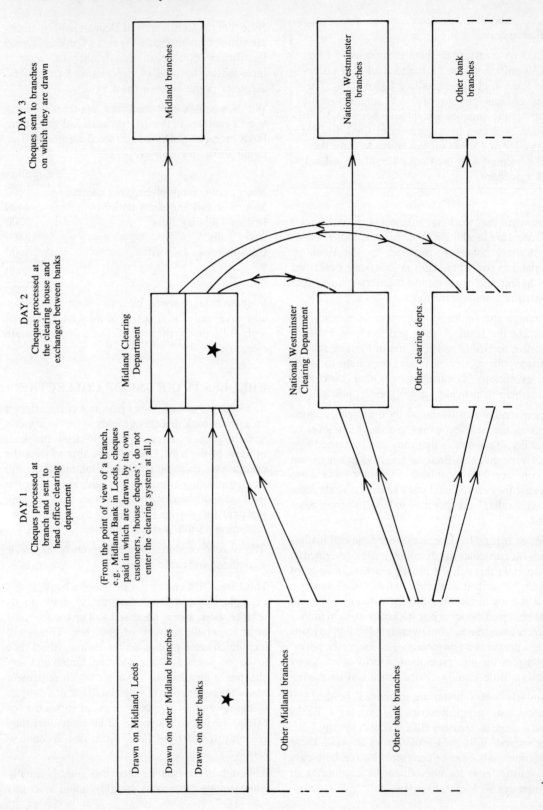

DAY 1
Cheques processed at branch and sent to head office clearing department

(From the point of view of a branch, e.g. Midland Bank in Leeds, cheques paid in which are drawn by its own customers, 'house cheques', do not enter the clearing system at all.)

Drawn on Midland, Leeds

Drawn on other Midland branches

Drawn on other banks ★

Other Midland branches

Other bank branches

DAY 2
Cheques processed at the clearing house and exchanged between banks

Midland Clearing Department ★

National Westminster Clearing Department

Other clearing depts.

DAY 3
Cheques sent to branches on which they are drawn

Midland branches

National Westminster branches

Other bank branches

★ = claims which Midland Bank has on other banks

52

may be a little misleading. The specific cheques included in the balance sheet will be turned into cash within a matter of days by being paid for by the banks they are drawn on. Further cheques paid in will create a new asset. The size of the figure is determined by what customers of the bank do, and cannot easily be reduced by any action the bank takes. This means that cheques in course of collection cannot be used to improve the bank's overall cash position as other liquid assets can.

INVESTMENTS

7. The third category of fairly liquid assets held by the banks is investments. This item covers stocks and shares, very often including a high proportion of government stocks. These can be considered highly liquid because most can be sold readily on a recognised stock market. They are also a means of earning income for the bank in the form of interest payments or dividends. If the bank's investment managers make good buying and selling decisions the investments held may also rise in value giving the bank capital gains. Some banks which emphasise the profits from buying and selling refer to investments used in that way as dealing assets, distinguishing them from assets held for income. Most banks use only the more general term 'investments' in their balance sheets.

The kind of breakdown of investments in the footnotes to a bank balance sheet does not usually give any precise information except to show that the figures in the balance sheet, known as the 'book value', may differ from the market value.

For example the notes might indicate:-

	Book Value £m	Market Value £m
Listed Investments		
Government Stocks	460	442
Other U.K. Stocks	220	258
Foreign Stocks	270	281
Unlisted Investments	50	53
	1000	1034

The fact that the valuation of the government stocks is below the book value in this example does not present any particular problem for the bank because market values fluctuate as interest rates go up and down (as explained in Chapter 3). Some banks might prefer to show the lower figure in the balance sheet but this depends on the bank's stated accounting policies.

Usually market values will be greater than the book values, as is the case for the other investments shown here.

ADVANCES TO CUSTOMERS

8. This balance sheet heading covers all the different kinds of lending by the bank. Some banks recognise this broad meaning by referring to advances and other accounts. Some of the bank's subsidiaries may be involved in other types of business rather than lending money and the money they are owed by debtors is usually lumped into this enormous asset, by far the largest in the balance sheet. For a typical clearing bank the amount is likely to be over three quarters of the bank's total assets.In our example with total assets of £60,000m and advances of £47,500m the ratio is 79%, a high figure but not unbelievable in a competitive environment, since in spite of an increasing emphasis on income from the fees for services lending money remains the major source of profit for banks.

The footnotes to the section on advances are among the most keenly studied by banking analysts since it is usually here that banks give some clues to their lending problems. The notes normally show provisions for bad debts, divided into:-

a) specific provisions − related to particular loans for which repayment is not expected *and*

b) general provisions − related to sectors of the world economy from which bad debts are likely to be experienced.

The only advances and debts owed to the bank which are not included in this advances figure are the short-term items referred to under the heading of cash and short-term funds.

TRADE INVESTMENTS

9. Having identified one section of investments in the balance sheet it seems a little surprising to find another only slightly further down the list of assets. The position is significant because it indicates that these investments, again stocks and shares, are not

seen by the bank as liquid assets to be sold if extra cash is needed. These investments, the trade investments, are part of the bank's overall business.

Longer term investments can be of four main types.

1. Investment in unrelated companies.
    Some shareholdings are purely an investment, essentially no different from the shorter-term investments considered above. Many banks would not see such investments in unrelated companies as trade investments, although others do, particularly where the bank owns shares because it has provided share capital (or 'venture capital') as a form of finance.

2. Trade investments.
    Banks may invest in companies involved in the financial services industry or related industries by acquiring fairly small shareholdings which do not give any control or direct influence on the policies of the companies concerned.

3. Investment in associated companies.
    Associated companies are businesses in which the bank owns a shareholding which does not give outright control but which does allow some measure of influence. Quite commonly such organisations are jointly owned by a number of banks. Leading examples include:-
    a) the Agricultural Mortgage Corporation plc (which specialises in farming finance);
    b) the International Commodities Clearing House Ltd (which deals with the processing of transactions arranged on the commodity markets between dealers in basic commodities such as foodstuffs).

4. *Investment in subsidiaries.*
    Subsidiaries are companies in which the bank owns over 50% of the shares. For example most major banks own a finance house as a subsidiary. *The consolidated balance sheet includes the actual assets and liabilities of the subsidiary companies rather than showing the parent company's shareholding as an asset.*

The balance sheet category 'trade investments' may include any of the first three types of long-term investment, though some banks do show shareholdings in associated companies as a separate balance sheet item.

PREMISES AND EQUIPMENT

10.   The last in the list of assets is the least liquid. The fixed assets cannot be easily or quickly disposed of, and getting rid of fixed assets will usually restrict a business in carrying out its normal trading operations.

The fixed assets of banks include large amounts of property, from huge head office buildings like the famous National Westminster tower to the smallest of sub-branches as well as properties which the banks own and let out to other businesses. The banks' computer systems are also a significant item in the total figure here, but banks have a wide range of other equipment from calculators to fleets of cars. Many of the banks have spent large sums in recent years on video equipment, both for in-branch publicity and for staff training. All of this is included in the premises and equipment section of the balance sheet.

Most other business organisations do not show these vital resources in last place on the list of assets, but this is normal practice for banks because of their aim of emphasising the liquidity of their assets by putting liquid assets first.

DEPOSITS AND CUSTOMERS' ACCOUNTS

11.   This section of the liabilities, the amounts owed by the bank to its customers, is the largest of all the balance sheet items. For the major clearers the figure in recent years has generally been around 90% of the balance sheet total, and in our example with deposits of £56,000 and a balance sheet total of £60,000 the figure is over 90%.

Some banks give a breakdown of the deposits into sterling and foreign currency. Such an analysis is of interest because banks within the British banking system hold a very high level of foreign currency deposits. This is partly accounted for by the fact that a large number of foreign banks operate in London, but even the United Kingdom clearers have substantial currency deposits.

In our example a breakdown might show:-

	£ million
Sterling Deposits	39000
Currency Deposits	17000
	56000

This kind of ratio of nearly a third of the deposits in foreign currencies would be reasonably typical of the major clearers.

In addition banks record for their own purposes when deposits are due to be repaid. Although many deposits are repayable on demand large deposits often have fixed maturity dates. A bank can therefore draw up a table of maturities, for example grouping all deposits repayable within one year as a category. This helps the bank to make sure that funds are available when they are needed. Published accounts may include a maturity table of this kind but often the information is not made public.

OTHER LIABILITIES

12.   This section of the balance sheet is rather a mixture, including items which in the balance sheets of most companies would usually be specified separately.

Part of the figure is for creditors, which will mainly relate to the suppliers of subsidiaries which carry out activities other than banking. Banks themselves do not normally do much buying on credit since they carry no stocks of goods to process or sell, although some of their buying of supplies and equipment may be on credit terms.

Another major item will be the tax liability of the bank. The total amount of the tax related to the year's profit will be shown more clearly in the consolidated profit and loss statement. Within the balance sheet the relevant figure is any tax owed but not yet paid.

Liabilities shown here will also include dividends to be paid out to shareholders. The usual practice is to announce and pay out an interim dividend half way through the financial year, and then to announce a final dividend when the annual report, including the end-of-year balance sheet, is produced. What goes into the balance sheet in this section is therefore the final dividend, the part of the total dividend for the year which has been announced but not yet paid.

The broad heading of liabilities may include one or two other minor liabilities too, but these three areas, creditors, tax and dividend will make up the main part of the amount in most cases.

LOAN CAPITAL

13.   The term capital in a precise sense means the funds permanently invested in a business by the owners of the business, but most large companies like to have some fairly permanent investment from other people.

Loan capital is this kind of long-term investment. The banks, like any other commercial company can issue securities in a variety of forms. In the balance sheet those which are not shares are categorised as loan capital. The owners of such securities are paid interest instead of a dividend, and therefore obtain a return on their investment even if the business makes no profit.

Most loan capital has a set date for repayment and a set rate of interest. A note to the accounts will often contain a list of the different issues of securities, showing the maturity date and interest for each.

Some loan capital may be undated and may have a variable rate of interest. Securities of this type, often referred to as perpetual floating rate notes, are more common among banks than most other companies. The variable rate paid to providers of loan capital is helpful to banks because bank income often depends on the level of interest rates in the world's money markets, and by matching expenditure to income the risk of lending at a loss is reduced.

A further measure which banks adopt to reduce the likelihood of financial problems is to raise loan capital in a variety of different currencies. This helps to cope with the fact that for some banks major assets are acquired in foreign countries or in foreign currencies. A breakdown of a bank's loan capital will therefore show the currencies of the various loans as well as payment dates and interest. (So far only Scandinavian Bank Group plc has gone the stage further of issuing shares which are denominated in multiple currencies.)

SHARE CAPITAL AND RESERVES

14.   This section of the balance sheet indicates what the business owes to its owners, the shareholders. It does not mean that they can get back the amount shown, because as shareholders they are not normally able to get their investment back from the company unless it ceases trading (an unlikely event, and one which would quickly alter the values of other

items in the balance sheet). Shareholders do expect to be able to make money from any rise in the value of the shares because they are entitled to sell to other investors. They also obtain a return on their investment in the form of a dividend if the business is profitable.

The share capital figure included in the balance sheet is the face value of the shares issued, and this has no direct relationship with the market value of the shares. As with any other quoted company the market value is determined purely by supply and demand on the stock market, influenced by the latest news believed likely to affect the success of the company.

The reserves represent increases in value of the business. The primary reason for an increase in value is profit. Where a business trades profitably and the profit is not all paid out to shareholders in dividends the extra value of assets kept in the business to make it grow is shown among the reserves as accumulated profit. Reserves are not cash which the company can use but can be considered as simply the bookkeeping double entry to assets on the other side of the balance sheet.

There may also be reserves for a variety of more specialised reasons, for example as a result of issuing shares at more than their face value (a share premium reserve) or through updating the values of property owned by the company (a revaluation reserve).

The share capital and reserves can be seen as a kind of 'buffer' between the assets and liabilities. If the assets fall in value the company will still be able to pay off all the liabilities unless the fall in value is greater than the total amount of share capital and reserves.

THE LAYOUT OF THE BALANCE SHEET

15. In comparison to the balance sheets of most commercial companies bank balance sheets are a little unusual in layout. The purpose of the layout is to emphasise the liquid assets by putting them first. When other commercial balance sheets start with the assets, which is not always the case, the normal order is to start with the fixed assets and work down in order of increasing liquidity. The reverse arrangement, as illustrated below, is used by most banks.

Consolidated Balance Sheet of 'Typical Clearer'

Assets

Cash and short-term funds	Very liquid
Cheques in course of collection	Low profit
Investments	Fairly liquid
Advances to Customers	Most profitable
Trade Investments	Supporting profit
Premises and Equipment	Very illiquid

financed by:-

Liabilities

Deposits and customers accounts
Other liabilities

Capital

Loan Capital
Share Capital and Reserves

The key items, advances and deposits, do not need special emphasis because they stand out as exceptionally large figures.

The second half of the balance sheet shows the sources of funds, where money has come from to finance the bank's assets. For banks share capital and loan capital is far less significant than the funds provided by customers in the form of deposits; for most businesses shareholders are the main source of funds.

THE CONFLICT BETWEEN LIQUIDITY AND PROFITABILITY

16. Traditionally the advances to customers have been the basic source of profit for any bank. Even though there is now an increasing emphasis on income from services other than lending interest on advances remains the main source of profit.

In view of this the shareholders in banks are keen to see a high level of lending because profit is likely to be higher if a high proportion of the money deposited with the bank is lent out again to earn as much interest as possible. In contrast to this depositors with a bank prefer to see a high level of deposits kept in the form of cash and other liquid assets. These produce less profit but help to ensure that if a depositor wants to get money back there is little risk of the bank being short of cash.

There is therefore a conflict of interests in the running of any bank. Protecting the needs of depositors tends to reduce or hold back the bank's capacity to make profit. Resolving this conflict is an important issue for senior management.

For a large and successful bank the conflict may not be a serious one. A known and trusted name is enough for most depositors since they do not normally analyse the balance sheet of the bank they use. With a good name a bank can afford to lend out a high proportion of deposits and make good profits because the risk of a 'run on the bank' when depositors all demand their money back is very small. For smaller banks the failure to maintain adequate liquidity can easily lead to collapse, something which happens to a number of banks each year in the United States.

ANALYSIS OF THE BALANCE SHEET

17. Because of the importance of the choice between holding liquid assets or lending money to customers, balance sheet analysis of banks is often based on ratios or relationships involving these items.

In our example of a typical balance sheet liquid assets including cheques in course of collection amounted to £10500m. Total assets were £60000m so liquid assets as a percentage of total assets were $(10500 \div 60000 \times 100) = 17.5\%$. This ratio is fairly typical for clearing banks though some do risk a slightly lower level. Smaller banks will often feel they need a higher proportion of liquid assets of 20 to 30%.

Advances in our example amounted to £47500m while deposits were £56000m. This gives an advances to deposits ratio of $(47500 \div 56000 \times 100) = 85\%$. This figure is certainly higher than most banks would have expected at the beginning of the 1980s but now the emphasis on profit has encouraged large and secure banks to lend out far more than before, in some cases showing a ratio in excess of 90%.

It seems likely that in the next few years the pattern of bank balance sheets will change again, this time towards a higher level of other assets, as banks become more involved in services other than lending.

THE IMPORTANCE OF CAPITAL

18. Because capital can be seen as a 'buffer' which makes sure that people owed money by the bank are protected from loss even if the bank makes losses, analysis of bank balance sheets regularly includes the assessment of ratios related to the capital.

Often seen as being of particular importance is the ratio of total capital (loan capital plus shareholders' capital) to the total of other liabilities. This ratio is important because the higher the level of other liabilities the greater the risk that they will not be met if the bank does badly. A low ratio of capital to liabilities indicates less stability for the bank. In our example there is £2500m of capital to £57500m of other liabilities. This gives a ratio of $(2500 \div 57500 \times 100) = 4.3\%$, rather lower than most of the major banks over the last few years. They have mostly maintained a level of around 7%

Another important concept in analysing bank capital is the idea of 'free equity'. This is the amount of shareholders' funds which is left after paying for all the fixed assets. This is seen as important because it is what could be used up if there were any unexpected losses. In our example with shareholders' capital of £2000m and fixed assets of £500m the free equity is £1500m. Free equity can then be shown as a ratio of advances. In our case with advances of £47500m the free equity to advances ratio is $(1500 \div 47500 \times 100) = 3.2\%$, not very different from the figures for most clearing banks during the 1980s.

Absolute freedom from risk for depositors is not possible, but if free equity amounted to 100% of advances even a complete failure by all borrowers to repay would not force the bank to sell up its fixed assets. In practice a level of 2 to 4% of free equity to advances gives adequate protection, and is not seen by depositors, borrowers or shareholders as a risky approach.

If, however, advances and deposits rise very quickly, either because:-

a)   the bank increases its volume of business *or*

b)   inflation leads to greater amounts of money deposited and lent,

then the capital base of the bank may fall in relation to the assets and liabilities in the balance sheet.

A gradual rise in advances and deposits is not usually a problem because the bank's capital grows through retaining profits. A rapid rise may mean that new capital is required.

The methods which banks use to raise new capital include those referred to in Chapter 2. The National Westminster Bank rights issue announced in May 1986, for example, was designed to ensure that National Westminster's ratios of capital to liabilities and capital to advances did not fall too much below those of the other major banks. Issues of perpetual floating rate notes (referred to above) are also part of a bank's range of measures for improving capital ratios.

Because of its responsibility under the 1979 and 1987 Banking Acts the Bank of England is concerned about whether banks have enough capital. The rules which it applies to defining capital for banks do allow a proportion of the capital to be in less traditional securities like perpetual floating rate notes rather than having to be entirely in the form of shares. As new forms of capital are devised and new forms of risk are taken on by banks (as alternatives to conventional lending), the Bank of England's calculations of capital adequacy are becoming more complex and sophisticated. Different kinds of risk are given different weightings to reach an overall calculation of how much capital a bank needs in order to be acceptably safe.

THE BALANCE SHEET OF
THE PARENT COMPANY

19. All of the aspects of bank balance sheets discussed so far have been related to the consolidated balance sheet of the bank as a group of companies. Within the annual report there are figures for the group as well as for the parent company which owns the various subsidiaries. The difference in name between the parent company and the leading subsidiaries may be very small but legally they are separate companies with one owning the others. The main operating subsidiary of the Royal Bank of Scotland group plc, for example, is the Royal Bank of Scotland plc.

For a parent company the main assets will be the investments in subsidiary companies. In many cases all of the other assets are owned through subsidiaries and the parent will have no assets except for the shares it owns. The liabilities will be correspondingly small, again because deposits will be placed with the subsidiaries rather than with the parent company.

Even capital may be smaller for the parent company than for the group because the capital figure for the group could include loan capital raised by subsidiaries rather than by the parent.

PROFIT AND LOSS STATEMENTS

20. Just as the published accounts include two balance sheets, one for the group and one for the parent company, so there may be two profit and loss statements or profit and loss accounts, one for the group and one for the parent. Where only one profit and loss statement is included this will be for the group.

Accounting rules about what information should be disclosed in published profit and loss statements allow companies to remain fairly secretive about many of their costs. Although, for example, companies must show how much they have paid the auditors for checking the accounts they do not have to include figures for the total wages bill. If you want to get some idea about that you will need to read the report of the directors which will usually state the average number of employees of the company and how much, on average, they were paid.

It is also impossible to check from the profit and loss statement how much the bank received in interest on loans, the main source of the bank's income, although interest paid out is shown in the notes as an expense of the business. Banks have traditionally been cautious about revealing information about profit. Although they are no longer allowed to hide profit in secret reserves and are required to show 'true' profits, the range of information which they provide is deliberately kept to a minimum. This helps to prevent competitors from knowing too much about their methods of operation and, perhaps more important, makes it possible to minimise the bad publicity which might arise from serious problems. This limited disclosure of information does not mean that banks hide all their problems. If major bad debts need to be written off this will be shown in the profit statement. In 1987 and 1988, for example, the leading United Kingdom banks wrote off large sums because of debts from poorer countries, mainly in South America. Many experts believe that further write-offs will be necessary over the next few years.

THE REPORT AND ACCOUNTS

21. The annual report and accounts of a bank is more than just a balance sheet and profit and loss account. A number of other items are commonly included.

1. Funds Flow Statement.
   This shows the movement of funds coming into the business and going out of the business during the accounting year.

2. Current Cost Accounts.
   These are a set of final accounts (a balance sheet and profit and loss account) calculated on the basis of current prices as a way of adjusting the figures to allow for inflation.

3. Chairman's Statement.
   This is likely to cover broad policy issues, major changes in the past year and major plans for the future.

4. Report of the directors.
   This normally deals with the general range of activities of the group together with details of a variety of aspects of the bank's operations, in particular profit and dividends, shareholdings of the directors and the way in which the company communicates with its employees.

5. Accounting Policies.
   A summary is provided of the way in which accounting rules have been applied to calculate the figures shown in the accounts. This often provides evidence that one bank's set of accounts cannot be directly compared with another's because items described in the same way are not necessarily calculated in the same way.

In addition banks, like other public companies, frequently include further information they want their shareholders to be aware of. For example a detailed review of operations will show what new services the bank is promoting. Statistical data about past performance will often be presented in the form of graphs to emphasise past performance and highlight any trends of continuing improvement.

The following table summarises the information you might expect to find in your bank's report and accounts. Items marked 'yes' form part of a standard annual report; the others will not necessarily be present.

Accounting Information

Consolidated Balance Sheet	Yes
Consolidated Profit and Loss	Yes
Parent Company Balance Sheet	Yes
Parent Company Profit and Loss	Often
Funds Flow Statement	Yes
Current Cost Balance Sheet	Usually
Current Cost Profit and Loss	Usually
Notes to Accounts	Yes
Statistics of Past Performance	Usually
Analysis of Costs (e.g. wages)	Not Usually

Other Information

Chairman's Statement	Yes
Directors' Report	Yes
Review of Operations	Often
Analysis of Shareholders	Usually
Geographical Analysis of business	Usually
List of Subsidiaries	Yes
List of Associated Companies	Yes

Apart from the full set of accounts produced once a year public companies, including banks, publish an interim report in rather less detail showing the balance sheet at the end of the half-year with a profit and loss statement for half a year's trading.

SUMMARY

22. a) A balance sheet is a statement of the assets and liabilities of a business at a particular point in time. The assets and liabilities themselves are constantly changing.

   b) Bank balance sheets are different from the balance sheets of most other businesses for a number of reasons. Money deposited and money lent are major balance sheet items for banks, and the layout of bank balance sheets is usually different from that of other businesses such as manufacturing companies.

   c) The summary of a bank's assets and liabilities is contained in the consolidated balance sheet, which treats the bank as a group including all subsidiary companies.

   d) Cash and short-term funds are the most liquid assets held by banks and enable the bank to pay back money to depositors when it is needed. Among these liquid short-term funds are certificates of deposit and bills which can be sold on the money markets.

   e) Cheques in course of collection are paid for by the banks they are drawn on a day or two after they appear in a bank's balance sheet, but because other cheques will have been paid in, the amount may fluctuate but will not disappear.

f) Investments by the bank are liquid but are also an important means of earning income for the bank through payments of interest or dividends.

g) The main source of income for most banks is the interest paid on advances to customers, by far the largest of the assets in the balance sheet.

h) Some of the banks' investments are long term, not treated as liquid assets. These are mainly shareholdings in businesses which are connected with banking.

i) Premises and equipment are the least liquid of a bank's assets, and banks normally show them last in their list of assets.

j) The main liability and largest item in a bank's balance sheet is the deposits from customers, which may be as much as 90% of the balance sheet total.

k) Other liabilities include creditors, tax due and dividend due.

l) Loan capital represents long-term investment on which interest is paid. Banks can raise some of their long-term capital in the form of floating rate notes.

m) Share capital and reserves can be seen as what the bank owes to its owners. Reserves are created in a number of ways, of which making profit and keeping it in the business is the most important.

n) Bank balance sheets are presented to emphasise the liquidity of the range of assets, with the less liquid but more profitable assets lower down the list. Shareholders are more concerned with profit than liquidity, while depositors are more likely to be concerned about liquidity. Banks with a good reputation can overcome the apparent conflict of interest because they are seen as safe by depositors and can lend out a high proportion of deposits.

o) Analysis of bank balance sheets by ratios often makes use of the following ratios.
   1. Liquid Assets/Total Assets %.
   2. Advances/Deposits %.
   3. Total Capital/Total Liabilities %.
   4. Free Equity/Advances %.

p) Because capital is so important to banks in showing that depositors are not at risk,

banks need to raise extra capital if their capital ratios fall significantly below the standards set by competitors.

q) Published annual reports include a range of other accounting and general information apart from the balance sheet of the group. Main items include the parent company's balance sheet, the profit and loss account, the chairman's statement and the report of the directors.

STUDENT SELF-TESTING

Self Review Questions

1. What is the major asset in a bank's balance sheet? (3)

2. What is the largest liability in a bank's balance sheet? (3)

3. What factors encourage banks to keep their holdings of cash low even though high cash levels are better for maintaining confidence? (5)

4. How are investments in associated companies defined? (9)

5. In what category of the consolidated balance sheet would you expect to find the dividend due to be paid to shareholders? (12)

6. What are perpetual floating rate notes? (13)

7. What is meant by the conflict betweeen liquidity and profitablility? (16)

8. Why do capital ratios matter for banks? (18)

9. Which does a bank show in the notes to its profit and loss account, interest received on loans or interest paid on deposits? (20)

10. Name four types of information other than accounting information which you would expect to find in a bank's annual report and accounts. (21)

Exercises (answers begin page 325)

A1. Read this balance sheet and answer the questions which follow.

Consolidated Balance Sheet of Omega Bank at 31 December 1986

£ millions

Assets

Cash and short-term funds	2900
Cheques in course of collection	500
Investments	310

Advances to Customers	*3090*
Trade Investments	*400*
Premises and Equipment	*500*
	7700

financed by:-

Liabilities

Deposits and customers accounts	*5500*
Other liabilities	*7000*

Capital

Loan Capital	*100*
Share Capital and Reserves	*600*
	7700

1. Calculate the ratio of liquid assets to total assets.

2. Calculate the ratio of advances to deposits.

3. How much free equity does Omega Bank have?

4. Describe two ways in which the figures for Omega Bank differ from what you would expect to see for a major clearing bank.

5. What kind of bank do you think Omega Bank is, and why?

A2. What features of bank balance sheets make them different from the balance sheets of other companies?

A3. It is often argued that there is a conflict between liquidity and profitability in banking. To what extent is this true?

A4. Describe the main methods used for assessing the capital adequacy of banks.

6. The Range of Banking Business

INTRODUCTION

1.   This chapter looks at the range of basic services offered by banks and at how and why that range has been expanded. Major emphasis is given to deposit-taking and lending. Specific details of bank services are dealt with in later chapters. Here the aim is to examine the pressures which have led to change and the direction of the changes taking place.

The chapter assesses the advantages and disadvantages to major banks of operating a national payments system and a large branch network, and outlines possible strategies for banks, giving particular attention to the reasons for adopting a strategy of diversification.

NEEDS OF DEPOSITORS

2.   The original purpose for which customers used banks was to have a safe place to keep their money. Cash could be lost or stolen but if members of the public handed over their money to a trusted person with well-protected premises they could be fairly sure of getting it back when it was needed.

Security was therefore a primary requirement of any bank customer. Today that seems to be very much taken for granted with few customers of the major clearers thinking twice about the safety of their money in the bank. Risk of loss is still present, but in practice it is smaller financial institutions rather than large banks which fail to repay their customers.

Another important consideration for customers depositing funds is the ease with which the money can be used again. Traditionally customers got back their deposits in cash by going into the branch or office at which the deposit was made. Today there is a much wider range of possibilities open to depositors, and the different methods of withdrawing deposits are an important factor for customers in choosing which type of deposit to place with a bank.

Linked to ease of access is the question of speed of access. From the customer's point of view a liquid investment, a deposit which can be drawn out very quickly, is preferable to one for which a period of notice is required. The disadvantage of having to give notice is therefore usually matched by the compensating advantage of interest at a higher rate.

As explained in Chapter 3 the general level of interest rates is determined by broad economic factors, but for depositors the specific amount of interest paid, if any, is related to the factors just described.

1.   Security
   Smaller, potentially less secure institutions, will often have to pay extra interest to attract deposits.

2.   Ease of access
   Interest is more likely to be paid on deposits which can only be drawn out at branches and is less likely to be paid where the customer has a choice of methods of using the money deposited.

3.   Speed of access
   Where the customer can withdraw funds immediately the interest is normally lower than for deposits which can only be withdrawn after a period of notice.

There are exceptions to these general principles, in particular for large sums of money where interest may be combined with quick and easy access. Because the cost of handling one large deposit is so much less for the bank than dealing with many small amounts, preferential terms can be offered to depositors with large sums.

CURRENT ACCOUNTS AS DEPOSITS

3.   The most popular type of account through which customers deposit funds with banks is the current account. A current account is an account into which the customer can deposit funds at any time and draw out those funds without notice. Deposits in this form offer security, ease of access and speed of access.

Ease of access was provided traditionally by the use of a cheque book so that the customer could write out cheques as a means of payment without having to go to a branch of the bank. As a result of improved technology, and because of greater competition between banks ease of access has increased in a number of ways. To make cheques more acceptable to shops banks now provide cheque guarantee cards. Customers can also use their funds to pay regular bills by automated transfers carried out through the banks' computer systems. Cash can be obtained through cash dispensers at branches, or in some cases through machines at shops or factories. These machines, often referred to as automated teller machines (ATMs) from the American term for a cashier, a bank teller, are also becoming more sophisticated in the range of services which they offer.

The provision of a wide choice of methods of making instant use of the funds deposited in current accounts means that speed of access is excellent. From a customer's point of view money can be obtained or spent without notice and therefore without the money being 'tied up' or unavailable for use. In addition if a cheque is used as a method of payment the records of the bank may not be updated until several days later when the cheque has passed through the clearing system, an advantage which many customers consciously use. Newer electronic methods of payment, which could eventually replace cheques as a way of spending current account deposits, might not have this advantage.

While technological change may be helping banks as much as their customers, competitive pressure is benefitting customers rather at the expense of the banks. Traditionally current accounts with cheque books provided the banks with deposits on which they did not pay interest. These 'free' deposits are, of course, quite costly to banks because of the work involved in processing the various types of payments which customers can use (which is why bank charges have not been completely abandoned). Some banks have estimated that the costs of running a typical current account are equivalent to a rate of interest of 8 to 10% per annum, which means that when general interest rates are below that level current accounts are an expensive form of deposit-taking.

A significant change in the mid 1980s was the development of cheque-book accounts on which interest is paid. Very often such accounts require a minimum initial deposit, sometimes as much as £2500, but competition between banks and other financial institutions has led to a reduction in the restrictive terms applied to some of these interest-bearing accounts. The interest paid is often above the rate on ordinary deposit accounts, making the overall cost to the bank inclusive of the processing of payments very high. Such high interest cheque accounts (sometimes abbreviated to HICAs) are now provided by all the major banks.

DEPOSIT ACCOUNTS

4.   Ordinary deposit accounts offered by banks are usually described as seven-day notice accounts. In theory customers should give seven days' notice before withdrawing the funds deposited, but in practice the money is instantly available with the customer losing interest for the seven days.

The pressures which have affected the way in which banks attract current account deposits have also influenced deposit accounts. During the 1970s bank deposit accounts offered lower interest rates than building society accounts and as a result personal deposits with building societies grew while personal deposits with banks fell. To compete banks began to offer a wider range of deposit accounts including special accounts for children, accounts which paid different levels of interest as the balance in the account rose and deposit accounts with improved access to cash by means of automated teller machines.

These innovations have made the funds held in deposit accounts more expensive for the banks, although improved technology has helped to control the increase in costs.

MONEY MARKET DEPOSITS

5.   The overall total of funds deposited in banks includes the deposits in current accounts and in deposit accounts, but also takes in the larger sums deposited by wealthy individuals or business customers to earn high rates of interest from the money markets. These deposits, usually of at least £10,000, are placed with the bank on agreed terms, which could be for a fixed period so that the customer gets the money back on a predetermined date (e.g. 1 month fixed or 3 months fixed) or with a set period of notice so that the money remains on deposit until notice is given (e.g. 7 days notice). The interest rate offered will be determined by money market rates at the time the deposit is placed with the bank or renewed. With a 'notice' deposit the rate of interest can keep changing.

With deposits of this type the bank is providing good interest in exchange for reduced liquidity. The customer will not be able to obtain repayment earlier than the agreed date. Access to the deposit at the end of the period usually involves the sum being credited to a current account from which the customer can then make payments as normal.

The disadvantage of lack of access to the funds is one which competition has begun to reduce; customers can now opt instead for high interest cheque accounts (HICAs), which pay interest at or near to money market rates provided the balance on the account is high enough. As customers become more financially sophisticated they are more willing to 'shop around' to find deals which suit their needs as fully as possible. One result of this is that it is increasingly difficult for banks to acquire their deposits cheaply.

NEEDS OF BORROWERS

6.   When bankers first discovered that they had the power to lend out other people's money and charge interest for it the loan business was very clearly a lender's market. For many years banks have looked at lending in this traditional way, and the basic principles of lending safely, described in later chapters, have remained unchanged. Borrowers have found it hard to raise the money they need, in spite of the importance of ease of access to funds.

During the 1980s more institutions have been offering loans to borrowers in the United Kingdom, and some of these institutions have been more flexible and perhaps less prudent in agreeing to lend. This has suited borrowers in the short term because funds have been available, though there are longer term dangers as the cost to borrowers can become so high that even interest payments cannot be met; the amount owed then grows bigger even though no further borrowing is taken.

It would therefore be unrealistic to assume that all that borrowers require from lenders is ease of access to funds. Flexibility in repayment programmes is also an important factor. Whether the borrower expects to repay from weekly or monthly income, from a lump sum payment or from irregular inflows of cash he or she will be best able to repay if the required repayments match the income received.

Borrowers are also concerned that interest and any other costs to be paid, such as arrangement fees for setting up the loan, should be as low as possible (though there do seem to be some exceptions to this, where borrowers pay far more than they need to because of ignorance or because they prefer the convenience of a more expensive kind of borrowing). The factors already referred to do, of course, influence the interest and other costs.

1.   Ease of access
Where funds are made quickly and easily available the interest charge is likely to be higher than where the lender examines the background to the borrowing very carefully to identify and eliminate risks.

2.   Flexibility of repayments
Where the customer agrees to a rigid programme of repayment which the lender can monitor easily to see if any problem has occurred, the cost is likely to be lower than if the borrower chooses when and how to repay.

Rather more important than either of these considerations in determining the interest rate is the lender's view of the borrower. A sound, well-established business which has borrowed before and repaid according to an agreed programme is more likely to be able to borrow cheaply than a borrower with a past bad record and no regular income. As with the interest on deposits the size of the sum involved may also make a difference. Small scale borrowing in general is more costly per pound borrowed than large scale borrowing, because from a lender's point of view the costs of arranging and administering a small loan are just as great as for a large loan.

OVERDRAFTS

7.   Before 1970 the main form of bank lending to personal customers and to industry in the United Kingdom was the overdraft. It still remains an important form of lending because British borrowers are used to it. This is not the case throughout the world since in some countries overdrafts are not legally permitted. An overdraft enables a customer with a current account to carry on spending money from the account when the balance has fallen below zero. An overdraft limit is set by the bank as the maximum negative balance which the customer is allowed; if cheques are written out which would increase the overdraft above the limit the bank can refuse to pay them.

The main advantage of the overdraft is that interest is paid only on the money that is used. With a loan interest is paid on the whole amount borrowed even if it is not all spent. The overdraft therefore remains a valuable form of borrowing for many bank customers, though alternatives have become available to meet differing needs.

Access to an overdraft depends on contacting the branch to obtain the bank's agreement to the arrangement, and this usually takes the form of approval for a specified limit for a limited time, often a few months and normally no more than a year. (Unauthorised overdrafts do occur, but banks usually charge customers far more for them.) As an alternative which improves on ease of access many banks now offer revolving credit accounts which, once set up, provide the customer with an automatic right to an overdraft with a known limit without reference to the bank. Credit cards can also be considered a more accessible form of borrowing because they can be used without asking the bank's permission every few months. (See Chapter 12 on personal lending.)

The cost of an overdraft, which is charged for at an interest rate related to the bank's base rate, has also encouraged some of the more creditworthy borrowers to look for alternative sources of finance. Instead of using overdrafts some companies now obtain short-term funds by means of acceptance credits, a form of borrowing described in Chapter 14. The cost of the borrowing is linked to the rates of interest in the market for bills of exchange, referred to in Chapter 4, rather than being linked to base rate. This is often cheaper than overdraft borrowing.

STRUCTURED LOANS

8.   Structured loans are loans which have set repayments, decided when the loan is taken out. This means that the interest, the cost of borrowing, is determined at the beginning. If general interest rates change the borrower with a structured loan is not affected.

These loans, also referred to as 'term loans' because the repayments cover an agreed term, became increasingly important in the 1970s. By 1981 term lending to industry had become greater than lending on overdraft. Personal lending also moved towards the use of structured loans; term loans to personal customers are generally described as Personal Loans. Banks and other lenders produce tables showing the monthly repayments on personal loans of different sizes over different periods, so it is easy for a customer to find out whether he or she can afford a personal loan.

The basic drawbacks to structured loans are:-

  a)   inflexibility, though early repayment of the amount still owing is normally a possibility;

  b)   the risk of being 'locked in' to a high rate of interest when other interest rates have fallen.

Banks have not been forced to make major changes to overcome these problems because borrowers can choose other types of borrowing if they see the drawbacks as too serious. For many borrowers the rigid structure of set repayments is a valuable benefit, making it easier to plan future financial commitments. Repayments are usually monthly, and for most personal customers and many businesses this fits in well with the timing of the income they receive.

LOAN ACCOUNTS

9.   Apart from structured loans with fixed interest banks also offer loan accounts for which the interest is related to base rate. This type of variable rate borrowing (varying with changes in base rate) is suitable where repayment is not expected to come from a regular flow of income but from a lump sum or from a series of irregular payments. When such a loan account is opened the money lent is credited to a current account and interest is immediately payable on the full amount of the borrowing.

In comparison to using an overdraft the loan account offers less flexibility since the amount of the borrowing, represented by the balance on the loan account, can only be reduced. Once repayments have been made, any further borrowing increasing the loan to its original level would need to be agreed separately with the bank.

Loan accounts do have some of the advantages of structured loans since they can be used by both bank and customer to monitor progress in reducing the level of borrowing. At the same time they are more flexible since different amounts can be paid off as money becomes available.

ALTERNATIVES TO TRADITIONAL LENDING

10.   Overdrafts are often very suitable for borrowers who need money in the short term, and structured loans may be equally appropriate in the medium term, from two years to as much as fifteen years. Until the 1970s banks did not often lend for periods longer than that. Today, as banks have expanded their range of business to meet customers' needs more fully, longer-term lending has become

more common. Borrowers needing funds for fifteen years, twenty years or more are less willing to take structured loans because of the interest rate risk, the danger of being tied to high rates of interest when general interest rates have become much lower.

One of the ways to reduce this problem for borrowers is to allow them to switch from fixed interest borrowing to variable rate borrowing at intervals, for example every five years, a facility which banks now offer. This enables the borrower to judge how interest rates are moving and choose accordingly.

Another major alternative for borrowers is to raise money through the issue of securities as described in Chapter 2. Interest can then be fixed, related to a variable rate or replaced by dividend payments, but whichever is chosen the borrower maintains the extra flexibility of being able to buy back the securities through the stock market on which they are traded. This possibility is not open to small-scale borrowers but many other ideas developed by the banks and their competitors can be used by small businesses or by individuals. Further details of many of the options available are included in the later chapters on lending.

THE NEED FOR A NEW ROLE FOR BRANCHES

11.   As the range of deposit-taking and lending services changes banks are having to look carefully at the role of their branches. The major banks with large branch networks have used the branches in the past as places where deposits could be received and loans provided.

Today deposits can be obtained at only a slightly higher cost in interest through the money markets. Raising deposits in that way instead of through the branches could lead to very great savings, in particular in staff costs. By closing down branches there would also be some savings in running costs like heating and lighting. Money could also be gained by selling off unwanted property.

In support of this trend towards reduced dependence on branches customers paying into their accounts can now often do so through machines. Postal credits have also been available to customers for a long time to enable them to pay in cheques without calling at a branch. At the same time more and more 'savers' are looking at alternatives to banks for their savings;

for example more people are buying shares than ever before. This too reduces the role of branches as collection points for deposits. Personal deposits would therefore not necessarily be lost any more quickly even if branches closed.

Loans are also increasingly being provided by means other than the branch network. Many personal borrowers use credit cards or revolving credit accounts, which, once established, can be used over and over again to borrow money without further need to contact a branch of the bank. Personal loans are regularly offered by post or by telephone. Even for larger scale business borrowing the customer does not always need to visit a branch since banks are beginning to make greater use of calling officers, staff who visit the customers at their own premises in order to discuss their financial needs.

Given these changes banks are forced to consider either branch closures or new roles for branches. Most of the largest banks are pursuing both paths. Citibank, one of the most strongly established American banks in the United Kingdom, has stated that it would consider a branch network of 250 branches adequate to cover the whole country. For the banks with over ten times as many branches as that such a target is not likely in the forseeable future, but Citibank's view does emphasise the importance of finding a new role for branches.

THE BRANCHES AND PAYMENTS SERVICES

12.   The idea of branches as places at which customers can pay in money is still very important. Although branch staff still spend a high proportion of their time handling payments, this labour-intensive work is being reduced by increased automation at all stages in the process.

1.   **Receiving deposits**
     Cashiers sitting at counters waiting for customers are not particularly productive but it is never possible to match the supply of cashiers exactly to the needs of customers coming into the branch. By getting more people to pay in through automated teller machines receipts can be issued for deposits automatically and cashiers checking the deposits can do so at times convenient for the bank rather than as customers happen to arrive.

2. **Updating accounts**

Modern real-time computer systems can update customers' accounts at the moment that a cashier accepts a deposit and keys the details into the computer. This approach reduces the need for back-office staff concerned with processing payments. Of the major banks Trustee Savings Bank has been the first to use a real-time system but many other smaller financial institutions are also very advanced in their computer equipment.

3. **Sending cheques for clearing**

Most banks are now trying to reduce the volume of paper moved through clearing departments. One method of achieving this is 'truncation'. This consists of keeping the cheques at the branch where they have been paid in and sending details to the account-holding branch in the form of a computer message. So far it has only been used to a limited extent mainly because of the difficulty of verifying signatures, though the technology is available, at a cost, to enable signatures to be recorded in digital form so that they could be checked at any branch.

4. **Processing cheques from the clearing house**

Cheques paid in at other banks (and at other branches if they have not been truncated) come through the clearing system to the account-holding branch in order to be debited to the appropriate account. Machines at the clearing house which read the Magnetic Ink Character Recognition (MICR) details on cheques mean that most cheques can now be debited automatically to customers' accounts with only non-standard or damaged cheques needing to be processed manually. This relatively old technology is now very familiar to banks; further advances using Optical Character Recognition (OCR) are likely in the future.

In addition to these technical improvements in handling paper payments great advances have been made in promoting methods of payment which use computer messages as an alternative to paper. Automated standing orders, direct debits, transfers between accounts and cash withdrawals from machines reduce the amount of paper and with it the need for a large clerical staff spread through a large number of branches. A central computer department can deal with automated payments more efficiently than branches can because one of the great strengths of computers is that they cope well with large volumes of routine transactions. The development of a national system of electronic payments at shops will also reduce considerably the need for bank branches to act as collecting points for payments.

So it is not only in dealing with loans and deposits that branches have a reduced role. This is equally true of the branches as providers of payment services. If services were only available in these three areas through branches there would be a serious risk that the branches would have no job left to perform even though there are some important advantages to institutions which operate a national payments system. The following table shows some of these with corresponding disadvantages.

Banks as providers of a national payments system

Advantages

1. Banks can control how the system operates.
2. Banks can charge other users.
3. Banks may be able to restrict newcomers wishing to provide payments systems.

Disadvantages

1. Others use the system but do not incur all the costs.
2. Full charges to cover all costs may not be possible. (The real cost of processing a cheque is estimated at over 60p).
3. Lower cost systems can be set up in competition with the banks.

Given that new and competing payments systems are being developed with the help of new technology it is harder for banks to justify running branches simply because they are needed in order to deal with customers' payments. Instead banks are taking a more positive approach, changing the way branches are used in order to emphasise the services which they can offer.

CHANGES IN THE BRANCH NETWORK

13.   Bank branches are changing. The provision of a wide range of new services (described in later chapters) has meant that branches will not retain their

traditional characteristics of formality, impersonality and very evident security.

Some branches have already adopted a more informal, friendly layout, with much of the cash handling behind the scenes (a style originally introduced by some secondary banks as long ago as the 1960s). Bandit-screens of bullet-proof glass are being replaced by desks with computer terminals. Security is still important but is becoming more discreet.

The purpose of such changes is to attract more customers who may be interested in buying the bank's services. As customers have less and less need to come into bank branches to pay in or draw out money they may go elsewhere too for their loans, insurance or other financial requirements. By making bank branches more attractive and friendly banks hope to prevent this loss of business.

At the same time branches have started to become more specialised. Instead of offering a full range of personal and business services at every branch banks now often distinguish between branches for personal customers and branches for business customers. One main advantage of doing this is that the bank does not need to have highly trained staff with specialist knowledge of business finance in every branch. Many types of work can be concentrated in specialist centres to which customers can be referred if they need particular services.

One development in operating the branch network is for specialist centres to offer a full range of banking services with all the smaller branches in the same area only providing a limited service. The small branches become 'satellites' of the main branch. Banks which adopt the satellite banking system are able to save on the cost of branch managers' salaries since a manager of a satellite does not need to be paid as well as a manager of a full branch. For staff joining the bank there is the drawback that there are less opportunities for promotion to well-paid posts if the number of full branches is reduced.

ADVANTAGES AND DISADVANTAGES OF LARGE BRANCH NETWORKS

14.   The leading British banks already have large branch networks for reasons rooted in their early history. Changes are now taking place in how the branches are used but the strategies which banks adopt cannot ignore the existence of the branches.

Some assessment of what the branches can offer and what problems they create is an important first step in deciding what should be done next. The following table summarises some of the main advantages and disadvantages of operating large branch networks.

Large Branch Networks

Advantages
1.   Easy access to a wide number of customers.
2.   Potential outlets for selling varied services.
3.   Ability to adapt to local needs.

Disadvantages
1.   Resources tied up in the form of buildings and equipment.
2.   High running cost, particularly in terms of staff.
3.   Difficulty of maintaining standards across the organisation.

Since the major clearing banks cannot immediately escape from all the disadvantages of having large branch networks they are concerned to make the most of the possible advantages. The environment has changed in terms of:-

a)   wider choice for depositors (not only different types of bank accounts but also alternatives like direct investment in shares);

b)   wider choice for borrowers;

c)   technological improvements.

This has led to increased emphasis on the marketing of banking services. As part of the marketing philosophy attention has been paid to the range of services offered, and branches are now being used to sell new products designed carefully to meet the needs of customers. (For more detailed discussion of the effects of this marketing philosophy see Chapter 10, Marketing Financial Services.)

DIVERSIFICATION BEYOND THE BRANCH NETWORK

15.   The desire to diversify, to offer more variety of services, which is encouraging banks to find new roles for their branches also has a wider significance. As Chapter 5 described, the major banks are groups of companies which may operate in a number of different fields. If the senior management of a bank decides that the bank will be most successful if it

diversifies its range of products this will not be a policy restricted to the branches.

New services may also be offered by acquiring businesses in other industries. One of the most striking examples of this has been the acquisition of a chain of estate agencies by Lloyds Bank. This move was soon followed by competitor financial institutions including other banks such as Hambros and the Trustee Savings Bank as well as building societies and insurance companies.

Such steps alter the structure of a bank's balance sheet because a smaller proportion of the assets are held in the form of advances to customers. So far where financial institutions have bought into other businesses the size of the acquisitions has been small in proportion to the total assets of the buyer. If the process continues the balance sheets of the major banks may start to look rather different from the way they look now.

The main pressures for change identified in this chapter, competition, technology and customer sophistication, will not go away. In addition the changing legal environment examined in the next chapter will force banks to re-examine some of their practices.

BANK STRATEGIES

16.   The history of banking shows banks as being flexible and adaptive in their response to the environment in which they operate. The specific changes taking place in deposit, lending and payment services are only examples of much more general changes rapidly taking place in the field of financial services and in the broader area of providing and using information (which encompasses financial services). These changes call for major responses from banks if they are to be successful in the future.

In order to plan new approaches, for example in dealing with the changing role of branches, banks, like any other business need a strategic view, a view which considers what the overall aims of the bank should be. This will take in the broad question of what kind of business the bank should become. A number of possibilities may be considered.

1.   **Specialisation**
Some banks will choose to concentrate on the services in which they are strongest. In

this way they can build up a reputation for expertise which will attract customers who may normally deal with other banks. This kind of strategy, sometimes referred to as a 'niche' strategy, is probably most suited to banks which already have a high level of expertise in a limited number of fields.

2.   **Localisation**
Some banks will prefer to direct their attention to particular areas of the world or regions within one country. This strategy assumes that local reputation will be strong enough to discourage too many customers from turning to larger outside financial institutions.

3.   **Diversification**
The larger banks in the United Kingdom, in common with major foreign banks, seem to be adopting a strategy of widening the range of services to meet all of a customer's financial needs. This 'financial supermarket' philosophy is most suited to banks which already offer a wide range of products, and is particularly appropriate for banks which have a network of branches through which to sell services.

The basic strategy of offering more and more services linked to the basic services of deposit-taking and lending means that branches can be seen as having a new role. It also explains why major banks, and their competitors including building societies and insurance companies, are acquiring interests in other financial services businesses.

SUMMARY

17. a)   Banks were originally places where depositors could leave their money safely. Ease and speed of access were important considerations for depositors. Earning interest could be a compensation for not having immediate access to the money deposited.

b)   Current accounts use a cheque book as the main method of access to the funds deposited, but new technology now provides other means of using the funds. Interest may also be paid on current accounts even though access is immediate.

c) Deposit accounts have also been changed because of new technology and competition.

d) Money market deposits are usually placed with banks for fairly short periods of time. The interest, based on rates in the money markets, is high, but cheap deposits are now becoming rare as customers become more financially sophisticated.

e) During the 1980s it has become easier for borrowers to obtain money. Borrowers require access to funds when needed, but also look for flexibility of repayment and low interest.

f) Traditional borrowing by means of overdraft remains an important service offered by banks but alternative forms of flexible borrowing such as revolving credit accounts are available instead.

g) Structured loans are less flexible than overdrafts and may leave borrowers 'locked in' to high rates of interest, but they do help with planning because repayments are made in regular fixed amounts.

h) Loan accounts are more flexible than structured loans but do not allow for borrowing to go up and down as overdrafts do.

i) As banks are prepared to lend for longer periods and customers want to borrow long term, alternatives to traditional lending are being developed, including the use of securities rather than loans as a means of finance.

j) Branches used to be places at which deposits were collected and loans given. Changes in deposit services and loan services mean that the role of branches must change.

k) Payment services have also been a major part of the traditional role of the branch network. New technology has meant that providing a payments service is now far more automated than ever before.

l) Branches are changing, both to attract more customers and to specialise in particular aspects of the bank's business.

m) Since major banks cannot ignore their branch networks they need to consider the advantages and disadvantages of having a large number of branches, including the important positive opportunity to sell services to a wide number of customers.

n) Diversification involves not only new roles for branch networks, but also acquisitions of businesses providing services such as estate agency which bank branches do not provide.

o) Important pressures for change include legal requirements as well as competition, new technology and customer sophistication.

p) More general changes in the field of financial services mean that banks need a strategic view of overall aims. Different types of strategy suit different banks. The major United Kingdom banks seem to be adopting a strategy of diversification.

STUDENT SELF-TESTING

Self Review Questions

1. What are the main factors of concern to depositors in placing their money with the bank? (2)

2. What are HICAs and how do they differ from ordinary current accounts? (3)

3. What are the main factors of concern to borrowers in obtaining advances from banks? (6)

4. What is an overdraft limit? (7)

5. What are the drawbacks of structured loans? (8)

6. In what ways are banks making it easier for customers to borrow money without going to a branch of the bank? (11)

7. What technological changes in processing payments have reduced the role of the branch? (12)

8. What are the main disadvantages for banks of providing a national payments system? (12)

9. What are the main advantages to banks of having a large branch network? (14)

10. Why is a strategy of diversification particularly appropriate for the major British clearing banks? (16)

Exercises (answers begin page 325)

A1. Deposit-taking is one of the basic activities undertaken by banks. How and why are deposit-taking services changing?

A2. What kind of factors do customers need to consider when choosing a form of bank lending?

A3. What advantages and disadvantages are there for banks in having a large branch network? Do the advantages outweigh the disadvantages?

A4. What do you understand by the concept of diversification in the financial services industry? Illustrate your answer by reference to changes in the major clearing banks.

7. Bank and Customer: The Legal Relationship

INTRODUCTION

1. This chapter explains briefly the nature of the law of contract as it applies to banks and examines the idea of the contract between the bank and its customer. The importance of some of the terms of the contract is considered and the legal background to the contract is explored by reference to leading cases which have had an influence on the rights and duties of bank and customer.

In particular the principle that banks must maintain secrecy about their customers is emphasised while outlining the circumstances in which a bank can and should give information to third parties, for example in providing bankers' references.

Further sections of the chapter consider the legal risks faced by banks in their dealings with customers and the legislation which affects banks. Finally there is an assessment of how the contract between bank and customer may develop in the future.

THE COMPONENTS OF A CONTRACT

2. A contract is quite simply an agreement between two parties which is enforceable by a court of law. The essential requirements for the formation of a contract are:-

a) an offer by one party;

b) an acceptance of the offer by the other party;

c) 'consideration', which means something given or done by one party to the contract in exchange for the benefit provided by the other party;

d) an intention to enter into a legal relationship.

The exact meaning of these four factors has been developed over many years by the legal decisions of the courts (which have also considered such issues as the illegality of certain contracts or the unenforceability of contracts where parties do not have the legal right to enter into contracts).

One of the important implications of the four requirements listed is that there are just two parties to a simple contract, and English law has recognised this by the doctrine of 'privity of contract' which means that (with very limited exceptions) when a contract is created the only parties which have any rights or duties as a result of the contract are the parties to it; third-parties are excluded.

As far as the contract between the bank and a customer is concerned there has been little case law dealing with problems in interpreting what is needed to create a contract. When a potential customer comes to the bank to open an account he or she can be seen as making an offer to the bank which the bank accepts by opening the account; consideration is then provided by the bank in promising to look after the customer's money and by the customer in allowing the bank the use of the money until it is needed again. It would be surprising if either bank or customer later claimed that there had been no intention to enter into a legal relationship, so the process of opening an account seems to meet the basic requirements which create a legally enforceable agreement.

It is in deciding just what the agreement includes that case law has had to deal with problems and areas of doubt. Most case law concerned with the nature of the banker-customer relationship has looked at situations in which a customer has an account in which funds have been deposited and from which, by writing a cheque as an instruction to the bank, money can be drawn out by the account holder in person or transferred to a third party. This situation can be seen as a framework upon which the legal relationship is built, although it is, of course, possible for a bank to have a contractual relationship with a customer in other ways.

THE DEBTOR AND CREDITOR RELATIONSHIP

3. It is generally accepted that a bank will undertake to receive money from anyone for whom an account has been opened. Customer deposits may take the form of cash or cheques (which need to be collected, that is sent to the bank they are drawn on in order to obtain payment). Such deposits are normally a first stage in a banker-customer relationship. Given that the account holder has placed money with the bank it has been accepted by law that the bank is a debtor of the customer, that is someone owing money to the customer. Corresponding to this the customer is a creditor, someone to whom the money is owed by the bank. This principle was clearly established in the case of Foley v. Hill in 1848, a case which remains valid today in the sense

that no customer of a bank could now claim any different relationship.

Foley v Hill (1848)

Facts

F. deposited money with H. and later sued for the money claiming that H. was an agent and should have kept him informed about how the money was used.

Judgement

The claim was not one the court could deal with.

Comments

In summing up the judge held that the bank is not an agent for the customer but a debtor, able to use the customer's money as if it were its own but obliged to repay an equivalent sum.

In one sense, however, the relationship of bank and customer is not one of debtor and creditor because the law normally requires the debtor to seek out and pay the creditor to whom the money is owed. Clearly it would be nonsense for the bank to do this since the customer very deliberately pays money into the bank in order to leave it there until it is needed; he or she does not want the bank to hand back the money as soon as it is paid in.

IMPORTANT TERMS OF THE CONTRACT

4.   A customer opening an account with a bank may well consider that the contract created is extremely simple involving no more than the debt that the bank owes for the money paid in. However judges in their decisions about cases have emphasised strongly that the basic debtor and creditor contract incorporates a number of implied terms, terms which are not specifically stated by either party or agreed between them but which nevertheless are legally enforceable.

One of the most important cases in which implied terms were described was the case of Joachimson v. Swiss Bank Corporation (1921). The judgement in the case was wide-ranging, but brought out a number of duties and obligations on both sides, as outlined below.

Duties and obligations of the customer
(as identified in the Joachimson case) were:-
  a)   to apply to the bank to get back money deposited;
  b)   to exercise care in drawing up written instructions to the bank so that fraud is made difficult.

Duties and obligations of the bank
(as identified in the Joachimson case) were:-
  a)   to repay the customer's money during banking hours at the branch where the account is kept (which suggests that if a cash dispenser is out of order this will not constitute a breach of contract);
  b)   to repay money against the customer's written instructions, authorising the bank to debit the account;
  c)   to give reasonable notice before ceasing to do business with the customer, that is closing the account (an aspect of the contract analysed in more detail in the case of Prosperity Ltd v. Lloyds Bank Ltd described below).

Prosperity Ltd v. Lloyds Bank Ltd (1923)

Facts

The bank were unhappy with the nature of the business which P. was carrying out and gave one month's notice for the account to be closed.

Judgement

It was held that in view of the complex nature of P.'s financial affairs one month was not long enough to constitute reasonable notice. The bank was liable for breach of contract.

Although the Joachimson case made it clear that there are implied duties and obligations imposed on a bank and its customers the judgement in the case did not give an exhaustive list of the terms of the contract. Later cases have added further important ideas.

The case of Burnett v. Westminster Bank Ltd, for example, suggested that where the bank changes its procedures there must be adequate notice to customers before they are legally affected by the new terms.

Burnett v. Westminster Bank Ltd (1966)

Facts

B. had accounts at two different branches and gave instructions to one branch to stop a cheque he had issued. It had been drawn on the cheque book issued by the other branch and had been sent back there and paid because the automated cheque processing equipment did not recognise that B. had manually altered the branch address.

Judgement

The bank was liable because B. had no reason to suppose that the bank would pay the cheque at the wrong branch and had given valid instructions to stop the cheque.

OPENING ACCOUNTS

5.   When a customer wants to open an account the bank in agreeing to this undertakes to carry out all of the duties associated with operating an account. Some of these are the obligations outlined in the Joachimson case. More fundamentally the bank agrees to accept cash and cheques into the account, and here there is a potential legal problem for banks.

If a bank receives a cheque into an account of someone who is not the true owner of the cheque the bank will unknowingly be depriving the true owner of the money to which he was entitled. This is an act of conversion; the true owner of the cheque may sue the bank for conversion and if the bank loses the case it will have to pay back the money. The bank may have acted quite innocently but this is no defence against the claim of the rightful owner and the bank may lose money, as shown in the example.

The risk to a bank of such a sequence of events is small if the bank knows the customer well, but it could be very difficult to detect anyone deliberately intending to commit a crime. The law has recognised the problem which banks face in these circumstances, and it has been enacted that if a bank acts 'without negligence' (Cheques Act 1957, section 4) this will be a defence against a claim of conversion provided certain other conditions are met. Case law suggests that banks usually have little difficulty in meeting the other requirements of section 4, for example that the cheque should be collected for a customer. Showing that there was no negligence is

Example

Thief steals a cheque payable to P. Williams.

Thief opens an account with Commercial Bank *in the name of P. Williams*.

Thief pays in the stolen cheque.

The stolen cheque is passed through the clearing system and paid.

Thief draws out the money from Commercial Bank.

The real P. Williams finds out what has happened.

P. Williams sues Commercial Bank for conversion.

Bank loses case and pays out to P. Williams.

Bank has a claim against the thief, but he has disappeared.

more of a problem, and the most important piece of evidence seems to be a reference taken when the account was opened. There have been a number of cases on the conditions in which such references can give protection. One of the most important of these is the Marfani case.

Marfani & Co Ltd v. Midland Bank Ltd (1968)

Facts

M. was persuaded by the office manager of the company to sign a cheque payable to E. The manager then opened an account in the name of E. giving as a reference someone to whom he had earlier pretended to be called E. The company sued for conversion.

Judgement

Although the bank had only obtained one reference instead of the usual two this was satsifactory and provided evidence that the bank had not been negligent. The claim for conversion was unsuccessful.

This case demonstrates the value to a bank of taking references. However banks are very conscious of the costs incurred, mainly in the form of staff time, where references are taken on all new customers.

As a result most major banks have adopted a policy of only taking references where there seems to be a particular reason for doubt about the identity of the new customer. In other cases accounts are opened simply on the basis of some form of identification produced by the intending account holder. This does mean that the bank would not have the protection of section 4 of the Cheques Act. Banks following this policy do so on the assumption that the saving in costs will be greater than the losses incurred on the rare occasions when the bank is sued for conversion.

Other legal risks which can occasionally arise for banks when operating accounts for customers are:-

a)   a liability to a Trustee in Bankruptcy if a new customer is an undischarged bankrupt; (See Chapter 8 for further explanation of the effects of bankruptcy on the relationship between bank and customer.)

b)   a liability for payments made from a company account if the business has not completed the formalities for becoming a company. (See Chapter 9 for further explanation of the requirements when opening a company account.)

Apart from the legal considerations in opening new accounts there are a number of important practical matters to attend to. The following example of an account opening checklist indicates the kinds of information which a bank would require before opening an account.

Note that staff using this form are reminded by point 10 that it may be necessary to take up references.

The questions asked are those which are needed in order to complete the account opening procedure such as the details of the type of cheque book required and those which help the bank to decide whether to open the account. For example if the potential customer is unemployed the bank may feel that opening an account is a risk. Information about the applicant's address is relevant in both respects because it is needed in order to send out correspondence, but can also be used to check that the applicant is not known to have any outstanding debts for which he has been taken to court.

Some banks carry out a full credit-scoring procedure (of the type normally used in assessing loan applications) before opening any account and people

judged unsuitable are turned down. Credit-scoring, described in Chapter 12 on personal lending, helps to reduce the risk of troublesome accounts by offering banking facilities only to the most creditworthy.

In addition banks are becoming more conscious of the role of branch staff in marketing bank services, and the procedure on opening an account is also intended to help identify financial services which the customer may require.

CLOSING ACCOUNTS

6.   Closing a customer's account marks the end of the normal banker-customer relationship, but like opening an account is not something which the bank should do lightly without giving thought to the legal implications. As the case of Prosperity v. Lloyds Bank (1923) showed the bank must allow a reasonable time for the customer to deal with the closure of the account.

There may be cheques the customer has written out which have not yet been presented for payment, and there is a risk that if the bank simply returns them with the answer on them 'Account closed' or 'No account' this may be considered libellous. Implying that a customer has written out cheques after the account has been closed may make the customer appear untrustworthy in his business affairs.

There may also be difficulties about closing accounts for customers who are borrowing from the bank, particularly where the borrowing is in the form of a loan requiring regular repayments rather than an overdraft which is technically repayable on demand.

SECRECY

7.   Banking has a tradition of maintaining secrecy about the affairs of customers, and bank staff are required to sign a confirmation that they will not reveal any information about customers to people outside the bank. Great care is taken, for example, to ensure that staff do not give away information by telephone about the amount of money in a customer's account unless they have obtained positive identification in some way. This is because it has been held that if a banker does give away confidential information the customer can sue the bank for breach of contract.

SPECIMEN *(by kind permission of Royal Bank of Scotland plc)*

The Royal Bank of Scotland plc

Opening Current Account — Checklist

Date _____

1   Name in full

2   (a) Address/Registered Office address

      (b) Home address if different from above

3   Designation

4   Employers

5   Telephone number:—   Private

                          Business

6   Statement address:—   2(a)   2(b)

      Other

7   Statement frequency:—   Daily   /Weekly   /Monthly

8   Introduced by

9   Details of any other previous or current Banking connection

10   References to be taken up

11   Obtain specimen signature

12   Operating instructions

13   Service charge details

14   Borrowing requirements

15   Interest details

16   Obtain as necessary Private Account:—   Joint Account Letter, Mandates

                 Business Account:—   Memorandum and Articles of Association
                                          Certificate of Incorporation (sight only)
                                          Mandates, Minutes
                                          Certificate of Registration of Business Name
                                          Law Agents/Accountants
                                          Night Safe Indemnity

17   Country of residence

18   Cheque book details

19   Obtain mandates for:—   Bank Cheque Card   *Yes/No
                             Cashline Card   *Yes/No
                             Access Card   *Yes/No

20   Obtain Standing Order details

21   Salary details (if mandated, destination of salary when received)

22   Other accounts to be opened eg D/A

23   Safe Custody items

24   Dividend instructions

Notes

*Delete as necessary
01127   (4/85)

Front page

SPECIMEN *(by kind permission of Royal Bank of Scotland plc)*

The Royal Bank of Scotland plc	Opening Current Account — Checklist							Action taken (Initials)
Account number								
Complete Title Card								
Prepare opening entry								
Complete input of new account number								
Complete input of account details								
Complete input of Statement and address details								
Complete Cheque Plate Personalising Data (01414) or Requisition for Rapid Data Personalising Plate (01448 — London Branches only)								
Complete Cheque Book Frequency Card (01446)								
Issue pay-in book								
Issue Statement wallet								
Issue Cheque Book and wallet								
Prepare Voucher File divider card and Cheque Book divider card (if applicable)								
Prepare Annotation sheet (if applicable) (01908)								
Complete BTDA Account Relationship Details (if appropriate) (01409)								
Set up the following when necessary	Standing Orders							
	Bank Cheque Card							
	Cashline Card							
	Access Card							
	Stop Payments							
	Safe Custody Records							

Back page

As with other implied terms of the contract between bank and customer a clear understanding of what this means can be best obtained by consideration of relevant case law. The leading case here is Tournier v. National Provincial.

Tournier v. National Provincial and Union Bank of England (1924)

Facts

A manager of N.P. revealed to T.'s employer details of T.'s account including the facts that it was overdrawn and that cheques had been written to bookmakers.

Judgement

The bank was liable for damages to T.

Comments

Although secrecy is not an absolute duty of the bank disclosure of information is permitted only in certain circumstances, which the judge listed as four specific categories.

The importance of the Tournier case arises from the fact that the judge did give a clear list of the reasons for which a bank can give away information about a customer without risk of a claim for breach of contract. These are described below.

1. **Under compulsion of law**

   This refers to information given out by the bank in order to comply with the law. A request for information by the police would not normally be sufficient reason for disclosing information but the requirements of an Act of Parliament would protect a bank from any claim from the customer. Examples include the Income Tax Act 1952 (where a bank has to give information about interest earned), the Bankers' Books Evidence Act 1879 (often in connection with criminal proceedings) and more recently the legislation on drug trafficking.

2. **Through public duty**

   This category of disclosure seems to occur very rarely in practice but might include such matters as the bank having evidence of a customer acting as a spy for a foreign government.

3. **In the interests of the bank**

   The most common situation in which a bank discloses information about a customer in its own interest is where legal proceedings are taken to recover a debt. By going to court the amount owed is made public and this is therefore a disclosure of information to outsiders.

4. **With the customer's consent**

   a) *Express consent*

   The customer may authorise the bank to disclose certain information, for example in instructing the bank to send out copy statements to an accountant.

   b) *Implied consent*

   Implied consent is more difficult to describe but might arise at a meeting of the customer, his accountant and the bank manager at which the accountant was able to learn about the customer's bank transactions by being involved in the discussion.

   There is, however one important aspect of implied consent to disclose information which in itself forms an accepted part of the contract between the bank and the customer. Although most customers might be surprised to learn this a bank has an implied right to answer enquiries about a customer's creditworthiness provided these 'status enquiries' meet certain conditions. The customer is not normally consulted about the replies made but the bank is not at risk of a claim for breach of contract because it is assumed that in opening the account the customer has given an implied consent to answer such enquiries.

STATUS ENQUIRIES

8. Businesses often want to sell on credit, allowing time to pay rather than insisting on cash payment, because giving credit is seen as a way of getting more sales. If a business wishes to know whether a potential purchaser should be offered credit terms an important consideration is whether payment is likely to be made at the end of the credit period or whether there is any risk of default. The most commonly used means of establishing that the purchaser will be a good risk is to take up a banker's reference. These references are commonly known to the banks themselves as status enquiries.

By tradition a bank will not reply to anyone except a bank or a recognised credit-reference agency (for example U.A.P.T., the United Association for the Protection of Trade). This means that the usual procedure is for an enquirer to go to his own bank to deal with the matter. As shown in the diagram below the exchange of information does not involve the subject of the enquiry, in this case Arnold Green Ltd.

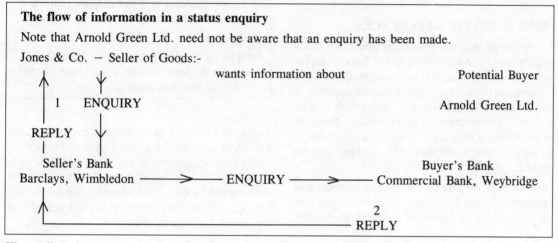

The flow of information in a status enquiry

Note that Arnold Green Ltd. need not be aware that an enquiry has been made.

Jones & Co. − Seller of Goods:-

wants information about   Potential Buyer

1   ENQUIRY   Arnold Green Ltd.

REPLY

Seller's Bank   Buyer's Bank
Barclays, Wimbledon ——→—— ENQUIRY ——→—— Commercial Bank, Weybridge

2
REPLY

The replies given to status enquiries adopt fairly standard phrases which may mean little to an outsider but have fairly clear meanings for the banks themselves. A reply might take the following form.

Commercial Bank plc
West Road
WEYBRIDGE
Surrey

1 The reply is not to the true enquirer but to the bank which has forwarded the enquiry.

1 The Manager
Barclays Bank plc
4 High Street
Wimbledon

14 June 1988

Dear Sir,

PRIVATE AND CONFIDENTIAL

2 A disclaimer clause is included to protect the bank against a claim for negligence.

2 For you private use and without responsibility on the part of the bank or its officials.

3 The name of the customer is not given in full to prevent any disclosure in breach of contract.

3 **A.G. Ltd**

4 The format of the answer uses standard phrases. Here the reply is favourable.

4 Respectably constituted private limited company. Considered good for you figures and purpose.

5 The terms of the enquiry are usually repeated to avoid misunderstanding.

5 Monthly credit of £1,500

6 The reply is unsigned to prevent any personal liability from arising.

6

7 A reference to the Consumer Credit Act is included implying that the customer does not have the right to see the reply given.

7 The bank is not a credit reference agency under s.145 of the Consumer Credit Act 1974.

This particular form of words including the phrase 'considered good for you figures and purpose' indicates that the bank considers the customer creditworthy.

RISKS IN GIVING REFERENCES

9.   Although little information is given in a status enquiry reply there are risks to the bank in replying. If too much is stated, for example the amount of money in the account, this would be a breach of the contractual duty of secrecy. If the reply is misleading and misrepresents the customer's financial position so that the enquirer suffers a loss through perhaps offering credit unwisely, the bank may be liable for negligence.

The case of Hedley Byrne and Co Ltd v. Heller and Partners Ltd described below suggests that the risk can be reduced by means of a disclaimer clause.

Hedley Byrne & Co Ltd v. Heller & Partners Ltd (1964)

Facts

The bank gave a misleading reply to an enquiry and this resulted in loss by H.

Judgement

The disclaimer clause included in the reply was effective and meant that the bank was not liable for the loss.

Although in the Hedley Byrne case all liability was avoided by the bank there are two important reasons why such disclaimers may not remove all of the risk.

1.   Since the case was decided there has been new legislation, the *UNFAIR CONTRACT TERMS ACT, 1977*, and this may make such a disclaimer clause completely unenforceable. No case has yet occurred to settle the matter one way or the other.

2.   If the bank's reply is particularly misleading it may be considered a fraudulent misrepresentation, and a court might follow the decision in the following leading Australian case.

Commercial Banking Company of Sydney Ltd v. R H Brown & Co (1972)

Facts

A highly misleading status enquiry reply was given, but a disclaimer clause was included.

Judgement

In spite of the disclaimer clause the bank was liable for the loss because its reply constituted fraudulent misrepresentation.

These risks have not prevented banks from regularly providing information to third parties through the status enquiry system, relying for their basic protection on the fairness of the replies made and on the view put forward in the Tournier case that having implied consent from customers is a defence against any claim for breach of contract.

AGENCY

10.   In some of the more specialised services which banks perform for their customers the bank acts as an agent, for example in buying and selling stocks and shares.

Banks also regularly act as agents for one another. If a customer with an account at Midland Bank pays in cheques at a branch of Lloyds Bank because it is more convenient to do so, Lloyds Bank in collecting those cheques, obtaining the proceeds from the banks on which the cheques are drawn, is acting as agent for Midland Bank. If the staff of Lloyds Bank did not carry out their job properly Midland Bank may have a claim against Lloyds Bank for any loss incurred. For any other outsider, such as the rightful owner of one of the cheques wishing to make a claim for conversion, it is the principal, Midland Bank, against whom any claim should be made.

The law of agency is complex and many aspects of it can only be understood with reference to the leading cases. From a banker's point of view the main principles to be aware of are that:-

a)   an agent acts on behalf of a principal and should make this known;

b)   the principal should give clear instructions to the agent;

c)   the agent should normally carry out his duties without delegating tasks to others;

d) the agent will incur no personal liability when following instructions;

e) any profits made by an agent belong to the principal except for the agent's known and agreed remuneration.

LEGAL RISKS FOR BANKERS

11. As the earlier sections of this chapter have illustrated, banks, in their dealings with customers, are at risk of legal claims for a number of reasons. Some of these are associated with the contractual nature of the relationship between a bank and its customers. Others form part of the general law of tort. A tort is a civil wrong; no criminal penalty is incurred but anyone suffering as a result of a tortious act can sue the person committing the act.

The main categories of legal claim against banks are described below.

1. **Breach of Contract**
   Customers may sue a bank if it does not meet its obligations as identified in various past cases. The most likely problem is a breach of the duty of secrecy.
   Where a breach of contract occurs the bank will normally try to put matters right as far as possible without recourse to the law. By apologising and trying to take any appropriate corrective action the damages which a court might award for breach of contract would be minimised.

2. **Defamation**
   Anyone whose reputation is damaged by the unjustified spoken or written communication of another can take legal action for defamation. A bank would clearly not intend to libel one of its customers by putting anything in writing to discredit him or her, but a bank may refuse to pay a customer's cheques in the mistaken belief that there is no money available to pay them. In these circumstances the reply written on the cheque, for example 'Refer to Drawer', will be considered libellous. A customer who sues successfully for libel will be awarded damages related to the seriousness of the loss suffered. This means that for a trader who is dependent on credit the damages are likely to be greater than for a private individual, for whom nominal damages may be considered sufficient.

3. **Conversion**
   Conversion occurs when the rightful owner of goods is deprived of those goods. This may arise when a bank collects a stolen cheque or where a bank has undertaken to look after a customer's valuables in safe custody and releases them to the wrong person by mistake. The damages awarded are based on the loss suffered, as in claims for defamation.

4. **Negligence**
   Negligence, as a tort for which a bank can be sued, means a failure to carry out a duty of care which was owed to someone with the result that he or she has incurred loss. This is in contrast to the more general meaning of the word negligence in law which simply means a lack of reasonable care, as, for example, when a bank tries to prove that it acted without negligence in opening an account; if the bank was negligent it loses the protection of section 4 of the Cheques Act and may therefore lose a case for conversion, but it has not committed the tort of negligence.
   A claim against the bank for the tort of negligence might occur where a misleading status enquiry reply has been given. This was the basis of the claim in the Hedley Byrne case, though it failed because of the bank's disclaimer clause. Similarly a bank may be sued for negligence where it has held goods in safe custody but allowed them to be lost or stolen.
   Any award for damages is related to the extent of the loss.

MAJOR LEGISLATION AFFECTING BANKERS

12. Banks, like other business organisations, need to be conscious of the legal constraints affecting them. The line between what is legally safe and acceptable and what is legally a risk is determined partly by case law (as the earlier sections of this chapter have shown) and partly by statute law.

This section outlines some of the main statutory provisions which affect banks, not only in their relationship with customers but also in their general operations. Clearly any laws which apply to society as a whole are of some relevance to banks, both as organisations with a social context and because of their dealings with customers who are members of society. Specialist departments of the banks also need very detailed knowledge of particular aspects of law, for example law on taxation, the law dealing with trusts and the law of succession, covering wills and executorship. More directly banks are affected by legislation designed to regulate businesses. This includes the law on employment and the rights of employees as well as the very important *COMPANIES ACT 1985* (a consolidating act, repealing and replacing earlier Companies Acts). Some of the provisions of the Companies Act are considered in the chapter on companies as customers, but it is important to remember that the rules apply to banks as well as to the companies with which they deal.

Apart from the vast amount of general legislation which concerns banks there are laws which have a very special and direct impact, affecting banks more than most other organisations. The following list summarises some of the most important of them.

1. **Bills of Exchange Act 1882**
    As indicated in Chapter 4 Bills of Exchange are important to bankers both because of their use in the money markets and because of their role in international trade. The Bills of Exchange Act is still in force although it is now over a hundred years old, and the provisions of the act still have a bearing on the day-to-day operations of banks.

2. **Cheques Act 1957**
    Although cheques are technically a type of bill of exchange and come within the terms of the Bills of Exchange Act, changes in banking practice meant that banks were seen to need special protection from the risks attached to handling large quantities of cheques. As explained in the fifth section of this chapter one of the areas of risk was of claims for conversion when collecting cheques, from which a bank can now obtain protection under section 4 provided the legal requirements are met. The Cheques Act also gives protection to banks which pay cheques, for example where the payee has failed to endorse the cheque by signing it on the back. This protection comes from section 1 of the act.

3. **Consumer Credit Act 1974**
    The purpose of the Consumer Credit Act was to protect borrowers from unscrupulous lenders. This was to be achieved in a number of ways including giving borrowers time to change their minds about loan agreements, ensuring that lenders provide full details of the cost of borrowing and making excessive interest rates illegal. From the banks' point of view the legislation meant far more paperwork in handling loans, without necessarily providing any significant benefit to their customers. (See also Chapter 12.)

4. **Data Protection Act 1984**
    The Data Protection Act is not as specifically associated with banking as the other acts in this list (and is so far ranging that it seems unlikely that all organisations affected will be aware of their responsibilities under the Act). Essentially any person or organisation which stores data about other people in non-manual records, for example in computer files, must register with the Data Protection Registrar. If the people about whom the data is recorded, the data subjects, request details of the information on record they will be entitled to be provided with copies on payment of a fee. Although accounts and records of transactions are exempt the passing of the Act does mean that banks could receive demands from their customers for personal data, particularly where requests for loans or other facilities are turned down.

5. **Financial Services Act 1986**
    The main purpose of the Financial Services Act is to provide a framework for regulating the financial services industry, partly with the aim of protecting investors. The act has authorised the setting up of the Securities and Investments Board which will have power vested in it by the government to supervise the Self-Regulating Organisations referred to in Chapter 2. For banks the main impact has been the *polarisation* rule which means that financial institutions cannot be independent advisers and sellers of their own products at the same time.
    Midland Bank was the first of the major

banks to decide that its branches would be tied to selling the bank's own products, and this approach has been followed by most banks with only National Westminster choosing to keep its branches as independent financial advisers. In contrast most building societies have chosen to operate their branches as independent advisers, with Abbey National a notable exception, entering into an agreement to be tied to selling insurance products offered by the Friends Provident insurance company.

6. **Insolvency Act 1986**
   The importance of insolvency law for banks is that they are often at risk in dealing with customers near to insolvency. Because they may be lending to such people they may lose money if their interests are not well protected. For many years the main legislation dealing with people becoming bankrupt was the Bankruptcy Act 1914, and many of its provisions also applied to companies going into liquidation. In 1985 a new law was passed replacing the earlier laws and bringing in a number of changes. This 1985 Insolvency Act was soon followed by the 1986 Insolvency Act in an attempt to modify and improve what had been enacted in 1985. (Further information on the effects of insolvency on different types of customer is included in Chapters 8 and 9.)

7. **Banking Act 1987**
   The Banking Acts of 1979 and 1987 both affected the status of banks and some of their rights and obligations. (More details of the legislation are provided in Chapter 1.)

These brief examples indicate the importance of the legal background to banking. A thorough understanding of banking practice requires detailed knowledge of the relevant law.

THE DEVELOPMENT OF THE BANKER-CUSTOMER CONTRACT

13. Just as past legal decisions have built up a picture of what the contract between bank and customer entails, so future legal decisions and Acts of Parliament can modify that picture. Acts like the Consumer Credit Act and the Data Protection Act impose new obligations on banks. The Insolvency

Act may restrict some of a bank's rights against customers.

Future case law could similarly modify the terms of the banker-customer contract. For example, it seems likely that if challenged in the courts over the right to deduct bank charges from a customer's account without express authority banks would claim successfully that this, too, is an implied term of the contract.

However, rather than leaving matters to chance or to the considered views of eminent judges banks would prefer to know exactly where they stand in relationship to their customers over all issues concerning the operation of accounts. One way in which the uncertainty can be reduced is by basing the contract on express terms, terms written down and agreed by both parties when the contract is made. For example, customers can be issued with a notice about bank charges and how they are calculated, together with a reminder that any changes will be advertised. The customer cannot then claim that the bank has no right to make charges.

For more complex types of account or for services connected with the use of an account, like a cheque guarantee card, it is becoming common for specific contractually binding documents to be drawn up by the bank for signature by the customer. Terms written into such documents then clearly form part of the banker-customer contract. Eventually the traditional contract with its implied terms may disappear, since all implied terms can be replaced by clear express terms. For example, the idea of reasonable notice is sometimes specifically modified to state an exact period of notice which the bank will give if the account is to be closed. All other implied terms could be incorporated in this kind of way.

Certainly agreements to borrow from the bank are already normally recorded in writing since the right to borrow is not an implied term of the traditional contract between bank and customer. The development of legislation to protect consumers (and the climate of opinion which has encouraged the passing of such laws) has been an important influence on the banks, encouraging or compelling them to provide more detailed information. Midland Bank was first to try a written contract, in 1987, but it was not widely welcomed by consumer groups because it seemed complicated and confusing for ordinary customers. There seems little likelihood in the near future that existing customers will be asked to re-negotiate the terms on which they do business with their banks, though consumerists are watching to make sure that any written contract does not offer worse terms than the present unwritten contract. (See Chapter 25 for further information about consumer protection in banking.)

SUMMARY

14. a) A contract is an agreement between two parties which is enforceable by a court of law.

b) The basic contractual relationship between a bank and a customer is that of debtor and creditor, except that the bank is not obliged to seek out the customer in order to repay money deposited.

c) The implied terms of the contract between bank and customer have been illuminated by a number of legal cases of which the most important is *Joachimson v. Swiss Bank Corporation* (1921).

d) Opening an account for a customer is normally the beginning of the contract between bank and customer, and the bank needs to be aware of the legal implications. In particular there is a danger that if the bank is negligent and opens an account for someone who has stolen a cheque the bank may face a claim for conversion.

e) In spite of the need to take references in order to avoid liability for claims of conversion banks often choose not to do this. They do, however, ask for a range of other information, some of it designed to assist in operating the account, some to help market bank services and some to help protect the bank.

f) Closing an account, ending the banker-customer relationship, also entails legal problems, for example of returning cheques.

g) One of the most important terms of the contract between bank and customer is that the bank will keep the affairs of the customer secret, except in limited circumstances which were specified in the case of *Tournier v. National Provincial and Union Bank of England* (1924) as being:-

1. Under compulsion of law;
2. Through public duty;
3. In the interests of the bank;
4. With the customer's consent, express or implied.

h) A common and accepted form of disclosure of information is the giving of bankers' references (or replies to status enquiries) from one bank to another. The wording of such replies is cautious, and banks take care to minimise the risk of claims for negligence.

i) Banks often act as agents in carrying out business for their customers or for other banks.

j) Major legal risks for banks in their normal dealings with customers are claims for:-
1. Breach of contract;
2. Defamation;
3. Conversion;
4. Negligence.

k) The law affects banks very broadly, not just in their relationship with customers. Apart from legislation like the Companies Act 1985 which applies to all companies including banks, there have been many statutes of special importance to bankers, from the Bills of Exchange Act 1882 up to the present day.

l) There is now a tendency for banks to make the contract with the customer more formal by putting in writing many of the terms relating to particular services, a development partly encouraged by the passing of laws to protect the rights of consumers.

STUDENT SELF-TESTING

Self Review Questions

1. What are the basic requirements for forming a contract? (2)

2. By what principle does the bank have the right to deal with a customer's money as if it were its own? (3)

3. What was the importance of the case of Joachimson v. Swiss Bank Corporation in establishing the relationship between bank and customer? (4)

4. How can a bank lose money if it commits conversion in collecting a cheque for a customer? (5)

5.   In what circumstances does a bank have a right to disclose information about a customer to third parties? (7)

6.   Why do status enquiry replies:-
   a)   have no signature;
   b)   include a reference to the Consumer Credit Act;
   c)   include a disclaimer clause?   (8)

7.   Give an example of a situation in which one bank acts as agent for another. (10)

8.   Give an example of a situation in which a bank may be sued for the tort of negligence? (11)

9.   Why is the Bills of Exchange Act 1882 of special importance to bankers? (12)

10.   What advantages might there be for banks in using written contracts to determine the relationship between bank and customer? (13)

Exercises (answers begin page 326)

A1.   Read this document and answer the questions which follow.

Commercial Bank plc
14 Market Place
LICHFIELD
Staffordshire

The Manager
Lloyds Bank plc
12 High Street
Colchester

Dear Sir,

PRIVATE AND CONFIDENTIAL

For you private use and without responsibility on the part of the bank or its officials.

B.P. & Co Ltd

Respectably constituted private limited company. The figure you mention is higher than we are used to seeing but we do not feel that they would enter into a commitment they could not see their way clear to fulfil.

Monthly credit of £20,000

The bank is not a credit reference agency under s.145 of the Consumer Credit Act 1974.

---

1.   Why is Commercial Bank not in breach of its duty to its customer Brian Peters & Co Ltd in giving this reply?

2.   Status enquiries are said to include a disclaimer clause; which words here are the disclaimer clause?

3.   What possible effect has the Unfair Contract Terms Act 1977 had on the use of disclaimer clauses?

4.   Does the reply indicate that Lloyds Bank, Colchester are considering offering credit to Brian Peters & Co Ltd?

5.   How would you interpret the reply given?

A2.   A customer who opens an account with a bank enters into a contract. What do you consider the terms of that contract to be?

A3.   What legal risks do banks face in:-
   a)   opening accounts;
   b)   closing accounts?

A4.   To what extent are status enquiry replies an exception to the general rule that banks must maintain secrecy about their customers?

8. Types of Customer

INTRODUCTION

1. This chapter looks at the very wide range of customers for whom banks provide services. Company customers (also known as corporate customers) are considered in Chapter 9.

The information in the chapter develops some of the ideas from Chapter 7 about the contract between the bank and the customer by describing some of the ways in which the contract may come to an end, through the death, bankruptcy or mental incapacity of a customer. Attention is also paid to the specific problems or features of accounts for different categories of customer, from the relatively straightforward personal accounts of individual customers to the complexities of accounts for business partnerships, particular kinds of business accounts and accounts for executors and trustees.

PERSONAL ACCOUNTS

2. The term personal account can be interpreted in a number of different ways. For example banks can use the phrase to mean any account belonging to a customer, in contrast to impersonal accounts with account titles such as Cleaning Expenses or Inter-Branch Settlements, which help banks to keep their internal book-keeping in order.

More commonly personal accounts are considered to be those which members of the general public use for their personal financial transactions, as opposed to any bank accounts used for business purposes. It is in this narrower sense that the term is used here.

The vast majority of personal accounts are current accounts in the names of individual account holders, and they are commonly used to deposit regular income and to pay for normal day-to-day living expenses. There are also large numbers of joint accounts in the names of married couples or others who live together and share some of their regular expenses. Personal accounts also include various types of deposit accounts and loan accounts, both unstructured loans and, more commonly, personal loans with their structure of regular monthly payments.

For personal accounts, whether in the name of one person or more than one, banks normally have a standard scale of charges, a tariff which is available for customers. The major banks, following the lead set by a number of smaller banks and then by Midland Bank in 1984, make no charges if a personal account is maintained continuously in credit. This does mean that a day or two 'in the red' can prove very expensive because charges are then incurred for all transactions during a charging period, which is often as much as three months. Customers discovering this the hard way may often be upset or annoyed that the bank can simply deduct its charges without reference to the customer; the contract between bank and customer can seem very one-sided.

SOLE ACCOUNTS

3. A sole account, an account in the name of just one person, is the simplest form of banker-customer relationship, and should present relatively few problems for the bank. Although some individual customers will be seen as more valuable to the bank than others, for example because of their known wealth or because of their connections with other important customers, all should be treated equally. This is not merely a matter of providing a high standard of service to all but, in some respects, a legal requirement. At one time a married woman would have been asked about her husband's employment when opening an account; now it is not legally acceptable to discriminate in this way. If this information is needed both men and women should be asked about their spouses; in practice most banks have abandoned the question.

While an account is being operated the main practical problems are likely to take the form of requests for borrowing (and banks' lending services are discussed in later chapters). Apart from providing loans one of the major changes which may occur during the course of the banker-customer relationship is a change of name. This occurs most commonly when a woman gets married, but divorce may be the reason too. A customer may also simply choose to be known by another name, though a bank will not normally be willing to alter the title of an account without some form of documentary evidence that the customer's name has changed. This is because the purpose of the change of name could be to pay in stolen cheques; if this happened the bank could face a claim for conversion from the rightful owner of the cheques.

The other events which are of special importance

to bankers in operating customers' accounts are ones which, in one way or another, bring the contract to an end. These are considered in the following sections.

DEATH OF A CUSTOMER

4.   When a customer dies the contract between the bank and the customer comes to an end, but the bank still has an account in the name of the deceased person. It is therefore important for banks to know what procedures to follow in dealing with the money that is left.

The law dealing with a deceased person's estate (the term used to describe the assets and liabilities left at death) is designed to take into account the wishes of the deceased. In most cases this may be fairly easy to judge, but disputes can and do arise. In order to prevent problems a court of law appoints personal representatives to deal with the estate, and because their decisions are backed by a court anyone acting on their instructions is protected from claims from any other interested parties.

Note on Terminology

Personal Representatives

This is the general term used to describe the people appointed by a court to administer the estate of a deceased person. Those appointed are often friends or relatives of the deceased, but paid experts such as banks or solicitors can be appointed. There are two categories of personal representative.

1.   Executors

Executors are named in the deceased's will and act in accordance with the instructions given by the testator (the term used for a person making a will).

2.   Administrators

Administrators are appointed if there is no executor. This could be because:-

   a)   the deceased person made no will (known as dying 'intestate'), in which case set legal procedures determine how the estate will be divided *or*

   b)   the named executors do no want to act or cannot act, in which case the administrator carries out the instructions in the will.

From the bank's point of view, when it becomes clear that a customer has died it is necessary to prevent any further use of money in the account until the court has appointed the personal representatives. Evidence of death may come from a relative or even from the obituary column of a newspaper. Cheques written just before death and presented for payment after notice of death has been received should be returned unpaid. The payee may then request payment from the personal representatives. There are some exceptions to this general rule, for example payments backed by a cheque guarantee card, but as a matter of principle it is considered that notice of a customer's death brings to an end the bank's authority to pay the customer's cheques. The bank must therefore see the court order appointing the administrators (known as Letters of Administration) or the order appointing the executors (known as a Letter or Grant of Probate) before releasing any money.

The bank can ignore this general rule if the amounts involved are very small where:-

   a)   the risk to the bank is very small because the family background is well known *or*

   b)   the total estate is known to be under £5,000 (since such estates can be dealt with without seeing proof of appointment under the Administration of Estates Small Payments Order 1984).

If in doubt the bank should make sure that it has the backing of the court before disposing of any funds, because it is only the formally appointed representatives who can give valid instructions about the deceased's estate.

BANKRUPTCY OF A CUSTOMER

5.   The idea that when a customer dies the assets that he or she owned pass into the control of someone else is, in some ways, similar to what happens when a court decides that a person is bankrupt.

If people are unable to pay their debts because what they owe is more than what they own, they are insolvent. If the creditors, the people owed money, do not mind about this, because they expect to be repaid in the longer-term future, insolvency may be temporary and not particularly serious. If the creditors are not so tolerant or optimistic a likely development from the general state of insolvency is to be made bankrupt. This usually occurs where a creditor owed at least £750 takes legal action to recover the money (though the debtor, the insolvent person, can also go to court to ask to be adjudged bankrupt).

The main purpose of insolvency law, now laid down in the INSOLVENCY ACT 1986, is to make sure that all the creditors are treated fairly. They will not be able to get back all their money because the debtor, being insolvent, does not have enough money to repay them in full, but they should all get paid in proportion to what they are owed. The main exception to this is that any secured creditor, someone who has acquired rights over particular assets as security for the money owed, is able to use the security to obtain repayment rather than joining the unsecured creditors in taking a share of what is left.

Example

A debtor owes £10,000 but only owns assets worth £7,000.

Creditor A is owed £4,000 (secured by assets worth £4,000).

Creditors B, C, and D are owed £2,000 each.

If all the creditors were treated equally each would get 70p in the pound.

Instead A uses £4,000 of the assets, leaving only £3,000 to share between the other creditors. They are owed £6,000 but only receive half that amount, so they are paid 50p in the pound.

This principle is particularly important for banks when lending and taking security as it puts them in a very strong position. The implications are considered in more detail in the chapters on taking security.

In this chapter the most important consideration is what happens when a bank has money in the account of someone who is declared bankrupt. The money and any other assets kept by the bank are no longer the bankrupt's to deal with as he or she pleases. Instead the court places all assets under the control of a Trustee in Bankruptcy. The Trustee will usually be an accountant whose appointment is acceptable to the creditors, and by law must be a qualified insolvency practitioner. His role is to collect in all the assets and use them to raise money to share out among the creditors.

This is potentially more difficult for a bank to deal with than the death of a customer because:-

a) the mandate is considered to be terminated when bankruptcy begins, which is when the court issues a Bankruptcy Order (rather than when the bank is notified of it) so the bank is at risk of paying cheques which it should return and may face a claim from the Trustee in Bankruptcy for repayment of the value of the cheques;

b) the customer may deliberately try to take money out of the account after being made bankrupt, for example by continuing to write cheques.

The most recent legislation on insolvency, firstly the Insolvency Act 1985 which repealed the Bankruptcy Act 1914, and subsequently the Insolvency Act 1986 replacing the 1985 Act, has given the bank a little more protection than in the past. If a bank deals with a bankrupt's assets after a Bankruptcy Order has been made the Trustee will not automatically claim the value of the assets from the bank. How useful this protection will be remains to be seen as the new law is tested in the courts.

Banks often have difficulty in dealing with bankrupt customers, either because the bank is owed money and wants to get it back or because of the need to stop an account of a customer who may not want the account stopped. The important rule for banks is that the Trustee in Bankruptcy has the court's backing for his decisions and the bank cannot afford to ignore this.

MENTAL INCAPACITY OF A CUSTOMER

6.   Another situation where a court can appoint a representative to look after a customer's assets is when the person concerned has become mentally ill so that he or she is incapable of making important decisions, and therefore cannot cope with running a bank account.

Where a bank knows that a customer is mentally incapacitated the account should be stopped. The difficulty is in deciding at what point this should be done. A customer who has been compulsorily detained in a psychiatric hospital can clearly be judged to be incapable of running his financial affairs. More often the decision is not so clear cut, and some form of medical certificate may be needed.

A bank faces some risk whichever approach is adopted. If cheques are returned when a customer is not in fact incapacitated there is a risk of an action for breach of contract or for defamation. If cheques are paid when they should not have been the customer may sue to get his money back when he recovers from illness.

The best course of action for the bank is to get a relative of the customer to apply to be appointed as a Receiver by the Court of Protection, a special court of law for dealing with such cases. A receiver appointed by the Court of Protection will be able to produce a court order, a document showing what powers he or she has been given to operate the customer's bank account or take funds from it. If the bank acts in accordance with the court order it will be protected from claims by the customer.

An alternative solution is available where the customer, before becoming ill, drew up a power of attorney under the ENDURING POWERS OF ATTORNEY ACT 1985.

Note on Terminology

Power of Attorney

A power of attorney is a document drawn up by one person (often called the donor or grantor) authorising another (the donee, grantee or attorney) to act on his or her behalf generally or in connection with specific acts. The document must be signed and sealed. Powers of Attorney in general are governed by the POWERS OF ATTORNEY ACT 1971.

An enduring power of attorney is a newer idea designed specifically to solve the problem that normal powers of attorney are cancelled if the donor is mentally incapacitated, which is precisely the time when they would be of most use. A power of attorney expressed as being drawn up under the Enduring Powers of Attorney Act remains valid when the donor becomes mentally ill, subject to objections by close relatives. The attorney can therefore usually continue to act.

Of the three major events which terminate the banker-customer relationship the mental incapacity of the customer is perhaps the most delicate and awkward to handle. The recent Enduring Powers of Attorney Act has helped to reduce the difficulties a little but enduring powers of attorney are not widely used; the general rule of stopping the account and returning the customer's cheques still applies.

JOINT ACCOUNTS

7.   The major problems identified in the last three sections have a similar effect from a bank's point of view whether the account holder has a sole account or a joint account. The main difference is that the bank also has to make allowance for the needs of the other party or parties to the account.

Most joint accounts are in the names of just two people, though there is no limitation on numbers. What a bank does need is an agreed set of rules about how the people concerned will operate the account, for example whether only one signature is needed or whether two or more are required on cheques or other instructions to the bank. Such an agreement, a document signed by the parties to the account, is known as a mandate.

The mandate will outline the terms and conditions which apply to the account. For a joint account one of the most important considerations is that all parties to the account should be fully liable for any debt owed to the bank. If one of the two people using a joint account writes a cheque taking the account overdrawn it is not just that person who is liable to repay. Both are equally committed to meet the debt. In addition the bank's position is strengthened in the mandate by stating that the bank can sue each party individually; even if it sues one of the parties unsuccessfully this will not prevent it from taking legal action against the others. This right to pursue legal actions against all parties individually or together arises from the account holders' agreement to accept JOINT AND SEVERAL LIABILITY.

Traditionally this has been distinguished from JOINT LIABILITY where an action against one party prevents action against the others. Since the passing of the CIVIL LIABILITY (CONTRIBUTION) ACT 1978, which virtually removed this restriction, the distinction has become unimportant, but bank mandates continue to require customers of joint accounts to formally agree to joint and several liability.

If a party to a joint account dies the bank can allow the other account holder or holders to continue to use the money in the account. There is no statute law to permit this but banks rely on the common law principle of 'Survivorship'. This idea that the survivor is entitled to any money which the bank owed to the joint account holders has been confirmed by a number of past cases, but this does not over-rule the legal rights of the deceased's personal representatives to deal with the estate. It is the survivor who is answerable to the personal representatives rather than the bank. Where the joint account is overdrawn, because of the principle of joint and several liability, the bank can choose how to try to get its money back. For example, if the deceased was the only wealthy account holder the personal representatives can be asked to repay. A choice of this kind can be made whatever the reason for stopping the account to seek repayment.

If a party to a joint account is made bankrupt the account should be stopped and any money released only on the joint instructions of the Trustee in Bankruptcy and the solvent party or parties to the account.

Similarly if a party to a joint account becomes mentally incapacitated the account should be stopped and money only released on the joint instructions of the receiver and the solvent parties.

Bank staff should be familiar with these kinds of requirements for dealing with particular problems related to different types of account, though the bank's own internal rule books or books of instruction are available for reference.

ACCOUNTS OF MINORS

8.   Just as there are special requirements and procedures for operating joint accounts so there are particular matters to pay attention to if a customer is aged under eighteen, and therefore legally a minor.

The most important consideration for banks is that if money is lent to a minor the minor can refuse to repay, though the position of banks has been improved by the MINORS' CONTRACTS ACT 1987. Legally a minor may not be responsible for his or her debts and in some circumstances cannot be forced to pay back borrowed money. This makes it essential to mark the bank's records to show that a customer is under eighteen, so that loans, overdrafts and credit cards are not provided. Even cheque guarantee cards are not normally issued to minors because of the risk that they can be used to create unauthorised borrow-ing simply by writing cheques which the bank would be committed to paying even if the customer had no money.

Under the Consumer Credit Act 1974 it is an offence to offer credit to minors, to 'canvass' them to suggest that they should borrow money. To know when a customer reaches the age of eighteen is therefore very useful. From that time the full range of banking services can be offered without legal penalty, enabling the bank to market its products to the full.

Particular care is needed when dealing with students because many of them are adults and will expect to be treated like any other customer, while others are below the age of eighteen. Students are generally seen as particularly valuable customers because of the assumption that they will end up in well-paid jobs, making wide use of banking services. It is, of course, a risk that a student customer will open an account at another bank as soon as he or she starts full-time employment.

BUSINESS ACCOUNTS

9.   The accounts considered so far in this chapter have been personal accounts, but banks have a much wider role than simply providing financial services for personal customers. For major banking groups, which include investment banking and numerous specialist departments and subsidiaries, business customers are a far more important source of profit than personal customers.

At branch level banks are moving towards a separation of 'business' branches and 'personal' branches, but in branches with both types of customer personal customers are usually in the majority. In spite of this it is often the business customers who use most banking services and borrow the largest amounts of money. Business customers are also likely to take up a high proportion of managerial time discussing their financial needs.

On a practical level the operation of accounts for businesses may be little different from the operation of personal accounts; there may be a need to deal with higher volumes of cash and cheques paid in as business takings and there may be more cash drawn out to pay wages, but these are largely a matter of degree rather than different services. In contrast some services are designed more specifically for business customers, from the use of night-safe facilities enabling a business to pay in when the branch is closed to large-scale lending designed to meet the needs of multi-national companies, one of the many business services offered through a specialist department rather than by the local branch manager.

One of the important distinguishing features of business accounts is that they are charged for the bank's services in a different way from personal customers. Most banks today offer personal customers the use of a current account free from charges if the account is maintained in credit; when charges are incurred they relate to the number of transactions, sometimes with different rates applied to different kinds of item (with cheques usually more expensive than computerised payments like standing orders). For business customers charges are more commonly related to the amount of money passing through the account, usually measured by adding up the value of all the items debited to the account, the debit turnover. A percentage of the debit turnover is deducted as charges, though adjustment may also be made to charge more if a lot of cash is handled or if there have been large numbers of cheques drawn. For both business and personal customers charges may be reduced if high credit balances are maintained in the account.

The particular charging system may be pre-programmed into the bank's computer but the level of charges will vary from business to business. For personal customers a standard set of rules applies and the computer records will simply need to show that an account is to be charged at the normal personal tariff.

SOLE TRADERS

10.   When individuals go into business on their own they are known as sole traders. From a bank's point of view there are no particular difficulties about operating an account for a sole trader since this will be much like a personal account except for the charging system and the volume of transactions.

Sole traders may employ other people but their businesses are unlikely to grow to very great size because they are limited by the lack of outside capital. Banks do lend to sole traders to help their businesses to expand but a bank will not usually put more of its own money into an enterprise than the owner has put in. This means that if a businessman or businesswoman wants to trade on a larger scale it may be necessary to organise the whole business

in a different way to bring in more capital, for example by going into partnership with someone else or by setting up a limited company with other people.

PARTNERSHIPS

11. A partnership is defined as an agreement:-
   a)   entered into by two or more people;
   b)   to carry on business;
   c)   with a view to profit.

A group of people forming a partnership are therefore likely to need a bank account since only the smallest of businesses can operate on a basis of using only cash, and one of the likely reasons for forming a partnership is to trade on a larger scale than a sole trader can cope with.

Partnerships are ruled by the PARTNERSHIP ACT 1890 unless the partners agree to adopt different conditions. A partnership can be created quite informally just by two people working together, provided they do so with the intention of making a profit. There is no need for any written agreement because the Partnership Act can be applied in the event of any dispute.

If the partners do not want to be restricted to the principles laid down in the Partnership Act they can choose instead to draw up their own agreement, known as Articles of Partnership or a Partnership Deed. From a bank's point of view such a document is not of particular importance because if a bank account is opened for a partnership the bank will require the partners to sign a mandate. This, like a joint account mandate, will spell out clearly the liability of all parties for any bank borrowing, giving the bank maximum protection from loss if the partnership is unsuccessful. The bank will not want to see any written agreement between the partners because if it does see such a document it may be legally obliged to act in accordance with it. It is much simpler for the bank to operate on the basis of its own standard mandate, and there is no penalty or risk to the bank in acting in ignorance of the terms of the partnership agreement.

THE DISSOLUTION OF A PARTNERSHIP

12. Because a partnership is simply an agreement between people it can be brought to an end by agreement. When a partnership ceases to exist this is often referred to as dissolving, terminating or determining the partnership.

A partnership may be determined, in this sense of the word, because the partners have achieved their objectives or because there was some pre-arranged date at which the agreement came to an end. There are also specific events which may lead to the termination or dissolution of the partnership. The most important of these are linked to ideas already referred to during this chapter.

1. **Death of a Partner**

   If one member of a partnership dies this may bring the partnership to an end or the remaining partners may be able to carry on business, depending on the terms of the partnership agreement. From a bank's point of view if a partner dies the most important consideration is whether the deceased's assets are needed by the bank to repay borrowing. If this is the case the account will be stopped and a request for repayment will be directed to the personal representatives.

2. **Bankruptcy of a Partner**

   If a member of a partnership is made bankrupt the bank will have to be careful to ensure that any borrowing is not allowed to increase and that assets including money in the bank account which might be claimed by a Trustee in Bankruptcy are not released. The usual procedure is therefore to stop the account. If the other partners want to continue in business a new account can be opened for them.

3. **Bankruptcy of the Partnership**

   In some cases the partnership itself may be made bankrupt because of its failure to meet its debts. Where this happens the partnership will cease business and the bank will need instructions from the Trustee in Bankruptcy before releasing any money or other assets of the partnership. Usually the bankruptcy of the partnership will mean that each partner is made bankrupt but since the Insolvent Partnerships Order 1986 this is no longer necessarily the case.

4. **Mental Incapacity of a Partner**

   If one partner becomes mentally ill and unable to carry on in business this does not automatically dissolve the partnership, but the bank will not be able to treat the mentally incapacitated partner as liable for any new borrowing by the partnership. If the account is overdrawn when the bank hears of a partner's mental illness the important question is whether the other partners will be able to repay; if there is any doubt about this the bank can request repayment from the mentally ill partner through the receiver appointed by the Court of Protection.

The general principle which a bank applies in dealing with any of these problems is that the bank may be at risk of losing money and action may be needed to remove or reduce that risk. For a highly reputable, financially sound partnership the bank will make a great effort to ensure that business as normal is permitted as far as possible.

SPECIFIC BUSINESS ACCOUNTS

13. All businesses have their own particular needs or requirements, but for banks these special factors are usually of most prominence only when a business wants to borrow money. However there are some businesses which are unusual in their normal banking operations because of the legal restrictions imposed on them in their handling of other people's money. Most notable are solicitors, highly valued as bank customers because they regularly have large credit balances and because they may well introduce new business to their bank. Most firms of solicitors will use a bank account called an Office Account for their own money but by law must have a separate account or accounts for money which belongs to the firm's clients. Similar rules apply to a number of types of business and the most important examples are included in the following list.

1. **Solicitors**

   The account(s) must be designated 'Clients' Account'.

   Only a solicitor can operate such an account, and on the death of a sole practitioner a Law Society nominee will act unless the executor is also a solicitor.

   Solicitors' clients accounts are governed by the Solicitors' Accounts Rules based on a series of SOLICITORS ACTS.

2. **Insurance Brokers**

   The account(s) must be designated 'Insurance Broking Account'.

   Only brokers who are members of Lloyds

are exempted from the requirement to operate a separate account for clients' money. Insurance Broking accounts are regulated by the INSURANCE BROKERS (REGISTRATION) ACT 1977.

3. **Estate Agents**
The account(s) are normally designated 'Clients' Account'.
Usually accounts will be deposit accounts because the estate agent has to pay the client interest on deposits held unless the sum is below £500 or the interest below £10.
These accounts are regulated by the ESTATE AGENTS ACT 1979.

4. **Licensed Dealers in Securities**
The account(s) are normally designated 'Clients' Account'.
Although there are some businesses which deal in securities without being required to operate special accounts for clients' funds it is always advisable to separate the dealer's own money from clients' money.
Accounts which are regulated are those which come under the Licensed Dealers Conduct of Business Rules 1983.

5. **Investment Advisers**
Under the Financial Services Act 1986 businesses engaged in giving investment advice or arranging investments for clients must satisfy the Securities and Investments Board that arrangements have been made to keep clients' money separate. Again the term 'Clients' Account' may well be used.

The common feature of these types of business is that they hold money in trust for other people. It is not really their own money, and this has important implications.

1. If businesses like these borrow money from the bank the bank cannot use the clients' money to repay the business debts.
2. Similarly if such a business goes bankrupt the Trustee in Bankruptcy cannot claim the clients' money to pay out to other creditors. It must be returned to the clients.

Note that the specific business accounts referred to here are often partnerships, but this is not necessarily the case. Estate agents, insurance brokers and securities dealers may be incorporated as limited companies and might therefore have been considered in Chapter 9 instead of this chapter.

Similar considerations about the nature of trusts apply to the accounts of personal representatives and trustees, which are considered in the next two sections.

PERSONAL REPRESENTATIVES

14. As described in the section of this chapter dealing with the death of a customer, after death the assets of a deceased person are dealt with by personal representatives, either executors named in the will or administrators.

Banks are therefore regularly required to operate accounts for executors or administrators. (Banks themselves can also act as executors; this service is considered in Chapter 24.)

Before opening an account for an executor the bank will need to see the Letter of Probate by which a court has confirmed the validity of the will in which the executor is named. Seeing 'probate' is necessary because the testator may have made more than one will. If the bank pays out money to a named executor only to find out that a later will appoints a different executor the bank may be liable to refund the money wrongly released. Once court approval has been given to an executor this risk is removed. A subsequent will which the court did not know about may override the approved will but the bank will not be liable for any money paid out.

Similarly if there is no will or no-one agreeing to act as executor the bank can open an account for administrators, but will first need to see Letters of Administration. This too is a court document formally appointing the personal representatives, and gives similar protection to the bank even if it later appears that the administrators should not have been appointed.

When dealing with joint executors or administrators, as is commonly the case, banks will take a mandate similar to a joint account mandate. This will specify, for example, whether one signature or more than one is required.

TRUSTEES

15. Banks regularly operate accounts for trustees, people who have the power to deal with assets for the benefit of others. As described above solicitors

dealing with their clients' money are acting as trustees.

The law of trusts is extremely complicated, but the basic idea of a trust is simply that:-

    a)   a trustee (or a group of trustees) has control;

    b)   over an asset or assets held in trust;

    c)   for a beneficiary or beneficiaries.

The rights of the beneficiaries may include obtaining an income from the assets or coming into full possession of the assets at some particular date or following some specified event in the future. In many cases the trust will be created by a specific document, a trust deed, which states how the trust will work. In other cases no such document exists but the law may accept that there was an intention to create a trust and this can be sufficient to impose obligations on the trustees and give rights to the beneficiaries.

One of the most common reasons for opening an account for trustees is because executors under a will have dealt with all the transactions involving disposal of assets and are left with some assets to keep in trust for beneficiaries named in the will, very often children who are to receive the assets when they are older. In these cases the terms of the trust are decided by the wording of the will. One of the difficulties for banks is that there is no clearly defined point at which executors become trustees, though the difference between them is important. Where a number of trustees are acting together the bank mandate should require all of them to sign all instructions to the bank. Executors can delegate signing authority but trustees are not allowed to. Banks therefore need to watch the transactions on executors' accounts to see if they are dealing, for example, just with regular payments to one or two specific people. In such cases the signatories on the account are probably trustees and should be asked to complete a new mandate.

Many charities operate as trusts, but the beneficiaries are normally a particular group or category of people rather than named individuals. Here the bank would expect there to be a trust deed.

Banks may also have accounts in the names of individual people which are, in fact, trust accounts. For example, the treasurer of a club may open an account in his or her own name on behalf of the club and act as a trustee, with the club members as beneficiaries of the trust.

UNINCORPORATED BODIES

16. Any group of people or any organisation which handles money may want to have the use of a bank account. Rather than leaving all banking matters to a treasurer operating an account in trust for the other people a more formal arrangement may be made by opening an account in the name of the organisation. The bank will then be able to get a mandate completed so that there are clear rules about who can operate the account.

The range of organisations which work in this way is enormous (though most major businesses choose to form limited companies for a number of reasons considered in the next chapter).

1. **Clubs and Societies**
    The smallest clubs and societies may simply open an account in the name of the treasurer, but there may be difficulties in dealing with the money if anything happens to the treasurer. A club account with a mandate makes it a simple matter to deal with changes in the club's officials.

2. **Friendly Societies and Building Societies**
    The role of friendly societies and building societies as financial intermediaries means that their banking operations are often very complex (to the extent that some building societies may choose to become limited companies under the provisions of the Building Societies Act 1986). In essence however the signatories on a building society's account with a bank are representatives of the society named in a mandate.

3. **Churches**
    Although different religious denominations have their own particular approaches to their banking arrangements, most churches do have bank accounts. Exactly who can sign on behalf of the church is defined in a bank mandate.

4. **Trade Unions**
    Trade unions may choose to have their bank accounts operated by full-time paid officials or by elected representatives. Whatever the rules of the union the officials concerned will need to complete a bank mandate.

5. **Local authorities**
    Local authorities operate very active bank accounts since they collect in large sums of

money from local rates and make payments for many local services. Their accounts are operated by full-time paid officials named in the bank mandate.

The general principle for banks that all kinds of organisations can operate accounts provided a bank mandate is completed means that banks offer their services very widely. They are often a little more restricted in providing loans to customers because many clubs and societies do not have the same clear legal status as local authorities or building societies. If a club wants to borrow money it may only be possible for the bank to lend to the committee of the club. A lender cannot rely on the members of the club to repay any borrowing unless they specifically agree to do so, for example by completing guarantees.

SUMMARY

17. a) Most personal accounts, accounts used for personal financial transactions rather than business purposes, are current accounts.

   b) When a customer dies the assets he or she owned, known as the deceased's estate, are taken over by personal representatives, either executors or administrators. The assets are then disposed of as specified in the will or, in the absence of a will, in accordance with set legal rules.

   c) If a customer is made bankrupt his or her assets are taken over by a trustee in bankruptcy to divide out the proceeds fairly between the creditors.

   d) If a customer becomes mentally incapacitated and therefore unable to make valid decisions about financial matters a court known as the Court of Protection may appoint a receiver, usually a relative, to take over the customer's assets.

   e) Where more than one person operates an account a bank mandate needs to be completed to specify who is to sign on the account and to confirm the principle of joint and several liability if the customers owe money to the bank.

   f) If a customer is a minor, aged under eighteen, this needs to be shown clearly in bank records because of the legal problems of lending money to minors.

   g) If an account is used for business purposes the system of charges will normally be different from that applied to personal customers.

   h) When a bank operates an account for a partnership the bank will not usually want to see the partnership deed or agreement, but will prefer to apply the bank's own standard mandate. Particular problems may arise when a partnership comes to an end as a result of death, bankruptcy or mental incapacity.

   i) Some businesses have special banking needs, particularly businesses of professional advisers like solicitors who regularly handle other people's money.

   j) There are special considerations for banks in dealing with the accounts of executors, administrators and trustees because of the differing legal rules which apply to these types of account.

   k) A very wide range of unincorporated bodies operate bank accounts. In each case a mandate controls who can sign on the account.

STUDENT SELF-TESTING

Self Review Questions

1.   When are administrators appointed instead of executors? (4)

2.   What is the role of a trustee in bankruptcy? (5)

3.   In what circumstances would the Court of Protection appoint a receiver? (6)

4.   What is a Power of Attorney? (6)

5.   What is a mandate? (7)

6.   What Act of Parliament has made the idea of joint liability less important than it used to be? (7)

7.   Why are banks cautious about lending to minors? (8)

8.   Why would a bank prefer not to see any written agreement between people setting up a partnership? (11)

9.   Why do solicitors have to keep clients' money in a separate account from their office account? (13)

10. Why is the mandate for a trustees' account likely to be different from the mandate for an executors' account? (15)

Exercises (answers begin page 327)

A1. What is a mandate? Why is it needed and what kind of information does it include?

A2. When a customer dies the estate is dealt with by personal representatives. What does this mean and how does it affect the bank?

A3. Some bank accounts are trust accounts. What are the implications of this? Give three examples of circumstances in which trust accounts are needed.

A4. What problems does a bank face if it believes that one of its customers is mentally ill?

9. Corporate Customers

INTRODUCTION

1. This chapter concentrates on one particular category of customer, the company. Companies are sometimes referred to as corporate bodies and from a bank's point-of-view they can be classified as corporate customers.

The chapter looks at the general features of companies, the documents needed when setting up a company or opening a company bank account, the role of the directors and the possible problems in operating company bank accounts. There is also an explanation of the measures taken when a company is in financial difficulties. This leads on to a description of the various officials who may take over company assets when a company is in trouble or is closing down.

CORPORATE STATUS

2. A company is referred to as a corporate body because it is incorporated as a legal person or legal entity, separate from the individual people who are the owners or members of the company. This is an important distinction because it means that a company can make contracts and own assets in its own right; these legal powers are not affected by changes in the membership of the company.

Companies are not the only corporate bodies. Some public offices are referred to as 'corporations sole', for example the Official Receiver; if the office holder dies this does not terminate all official contracts but allows them to be carried on by a successor without a break. Nationalised industries are also usually corporate bodies, incorporated by Act of Parliament.

However by far the majority of corporate bodies are companies, and are registered as companies under the Companies Acts. The current legislation, the Companies Act 1985, replaced all earlier legislation but existing companies remain registered under previous legislation, which may continue to affect their internal regulations though not their dealings with other people.

The idea that incorporation makes a company a separate legal person was first recognised to be of importance in the case of Salomon v. Salomon and Co. Ltd.

> **Salomon v. Salomon & Co Ltd (1897)**
>
> *Facts*
>
> S. sold his business to a company owned by himself and his family. He then lent money to the company using the assets as security. The company went into liquidation.
>
> *Judgement*
>
> S. was entitled to sell the company assets for his own benefit rather than for the creditors of the company because he was legally a separate person from the company and had a good legal claim against it which had priority over other claims.

This principle, established in the Salomon case, may mean that shareholders are more willing to invest in companies knowing that they cannot be held personally responsible for a company's actions merely because they are members of the company. In addition most companies also adopt the principle of limited liability, meaning that the financial risk to an investor in a company is limited to a specified sum.

TYPES OF COMPANY

3. It is possible to form companies with unlimited liability but these are now extremely rare. Most companies are incorporated with limited liability to make sure that the members of the company do not have to use their personal assets to meet the debts of the separate legal entity, the company, beyond the known limit of their liability.

Limited companies can be established in two ways.

1. **Companies limited by guarantee**
   The members of a company limited by guarantee do not hold shares in the company but simply agree to guarantee the debts of the company up to an agreed sum of money. The details of the amount guaranteed are written into the the documents governing the running of the company.
   Trade associations or educational bodies may choose to operate as companies limited by guarantee, but profitmaking businesses rarely do so.

2. **Companies limited by shares**
By far the majority of companies for which banks operate accounts are companies limited by shares. The members of the company are shareholders and their liability for the debts of the company is limited to the amount still unpaid on any shares they own. In most cases shares are fully paid for at issue or shortly afterwards so the risk to shareholders is only that they will not get their money back or not get any return on their money if the company does badly.

Limited companies can also be categorised as either public companies or private companies. In general public companies are larger because the purpose of 'going public' is to raise money from a wider circle of investors, but there are some very large private companies which choose not to become public companies. The main difference is that public companies are entitled to offer their securities to the public; private companies are more restricted. The following table outlines some of the differences.

Private Company	Public Company
1. Not allowed to raise capital by offering securities to the public.	1. Can offer securities to the public subject to certain requirements.
2. Name ends with limited (Ltd) or Welsh equivalent (cyf).	2. Name ends with public limited company (plc) or Welsh equivalent (ccc).
3. No minimum share capital.	3. Minimum share capital of £50,000.
4. Only one director and a secretary needed.	4. Two directors and a qualified secretary needed.

Any limited company which does not meet the requirements of a public limited company is considered to be a private company.

NEW COMPANIES

4. When a company is formed the Registrar of Companies at Companies House issues a certificate of incorporation which is the evidence that the company has legally come into being.

The Registrar will only issue the certificate when he has been supplied with all the necessary papers relating to the proposed company. These include a statement about the numbers and value of shares being issued, details of the proposed directors and an official declaration that the requirements of the Companies Act 1985 have been met. From a bank's point of view the two most important documents which a company submits to the registrar are:-

a) the Memorandum of Association *and*

b) the Articles of Association.

The bank itself will want to see these together with a certificate of incorporation when opening an account for a company.

THE MEMORANDUM AND ARTICLES

5. The Memorandum and Articles of Association, usually bound together in one booklet, provide the rules by which a company must operate. The bank will need to see these rules and will keep a copy of them in its file. (Note that this is different from the rules of a partnership, which a bank would prefer not to see.) If the bank fails to see a company's Memorandum and Articles of Association it will not have proper evidence of who the directors are or what powers they have to borrow money.

1. **The Memorandum of Association**
The memorandum deals with the external affairs of a company. It contains:-
a) the correct name of the company;
b) a statement of whether the company is public or private;
c) a statement of the country in which the registered office is located (England or Wales);
d) the amount of the authorised share capital;
e) the 'objects clause'.
The objects clause is of special significance because it outlines in very broad terms what the company is empowered to do. This is important to banks because if money is lent for a purpose not covered by the objects clause the company may not be obliged to repay the debt. Any actions carried out by a company which are not allowed for in the objects clause are described as 'ultra vires' the company. This means beyond the powers of the company. Problems in lending in such circumstances are described in Chapter 13.
Note that there are proposals to change the current law and remove the concept of 'ultra vires' actions so that all companies would

be empowered to carry out any activity without having to rewrite their rules. Under section 9 of the European Communities Act 1972 it is already possible for people dealing with a company to enforce contracts with the company provided they did not know the contract was not covered by the objects clause (though banks see the Memorandum and therefore cannot make this claim). Recently incorporated companies often try to avoid problems by making sure that the objects clause is as full as possible, running to perhaps a couple of pages of text outlining different things the company can do.

2. **The Articles of Association**
The articles of association deal with the internal rules of the company. In particular they describe how the directors of the company are authorised to act on behalf of the company, outlining the circumstances in which decisions can be made by the directors and the circumstances in which only the members of the company can take action.

In small companies this difference may be of little significance; if there are two directors who own all the shares between them they can make decisions as members of the company by holding a general meeting even if they do not have the power to take a particular decision as directors.

The difference may matter more to a bank which will sometimes need to have instructions for its actions from the company rather than from the directors. An incorrectly worded document may not be legally valid. Because of the need to make sure that the rules by which companies are regulated cover all sorts of possible problems governments have included in their legislation (the Companies Act 1985 and the Companies Acts which preceded it) standard wordings for the articles of association which companies can adopt in part or completely.

THE DIRECTORS

6. The directors of a company are the representatives of the company who are given delegated authority to make collective decisions on behalf of the company. From a bank's point of view it will usually be the directors who complete a mandate when an account is opened. The directors then act as signatories on the account, possibly in conjunction with the company secretary (who may also be a director).

In some companies the directors are known by different titles but recent legislation, in particular the Company Directors Disqualification Act 1986, has emphasised that it is decision-making power rather than the name which is important.

Directors are not employees of the company though they may be employed to act as executives as well as being directors. Most major companies have a board of directors consisting of some full-time working directors and some non-executive directors, often from other industries. The major banks themselves have this kind of board structure. Smaller companies may have as few as two officers, one director and a secretary. More commonly there are two directors if only as a precaution against accident or illness which might cause delay in making urgent decisions.

PROBLEMS WITH COMPANY DIRECTORS

7. Anyone acting as a director in making decisions for a company while claiming not to be a director is considered in law to be a 'shadow director'. Such 'shadow directors' face the same legal penalties as appointed directors if acting improperly, for example in committing the offence of wrongful trading (continuing to run a business knowing that it cannot meet its debts). Some banks have become concerned that the definition of 'shadow directors' might include bank staff advising a company about its financial problems. In practice it seems unlikely that courts will consider bankers liable as 'shadow directors'.

Banks should also be aware that company directors are at risk of being involved in 'insider trading', dealing with the shares of the company on the basis of inside knowledge which gives them an unfair advantage over other investors. 'Insider trading' is illegal and may lead to criminal proceedings or to civil claims for compensation from other shareholders.

Chapter 8 showed the problems for a bank if a customer becomes mentally ill or dies. These events do not happen to companies but they can affect the directors. Where a director is affected the bank will need to see whether the Articles of Association make any provision for such events in order to decide what action to take about the company's account. As a general principle the separate legal identity of the company means that it should be able to continue to use its bank account in spite of anything which happens to a particular director. For example if a director who becomes mentally ill is barred from office by the rules of the company the bank will only have a problem if the company does not have other directors who can act instead, in which case a new director will need to be appointed.

If a director is made bankrupt it is usual for this to lead to disqualification from all company director-ships. Exceptions to this rule are very rare. Care should, of course, be taken to make sure that new company accounts are not opened for directors who are undischarged bankrupts.

OPENING A COMPANY ACCOUNT

8.   The procedure for opening a company account is similar to the procedure for any other account, but the separate legal identity of companies does make some difference. The steps to be taken are to:-

   a)   obtain a copy of the Memorandum and Ar-ticles of Association;

   b)   check what the objects clause covers;

   c)   see the certificate of incorporation;

   d)   see a certificate to commence trading (if the company is a new public company rather than a private company 'going public');

   e)   ask for details of the directors and their bankers;

   f)   take references on directors not already known;

   g)   obtain a resolution from the company appointing the bank as its banker;

   h)   arrange for the mandate to be completed;

   i)   take specimen signatures from all of the named signatories;

   j)   open the account and issue a paying-in book;

   k)   issue a cheque-book when funds have been paid in.

If the account is for a company which already has an account with another bank it will also be standard practice to ask for a reference from the account-holding bank or to at least see previous bank statements. Very often if a company wants to transfer its account it will also want to arrange borrowing; the matters to consider on taking over borrowing from other banks are considered in the chapters on lending.

OPERATING THE ACCOUNT

9.   In the normal course of business there should be no particular difficulties in operating accounts for company customers.

Payments out of the account must comply with the mandate and if they do the bank is unlikely to face any legal problems. One exception to this general principle is that banks should exercise caution where payments are made to the signatories of the cheques; directors might divert funds from the company account to their own personal accounts. A bank could be liable to the company for conversion if it was negligent in not noticing this. Ideally cheques payable to any of the directors, for example as remuneration for their services, should be signed by other authorised signatories rather than the payee.

Payments into a company account will usually be cheques payable to the company. If, however, cheques payable to a company are signed on the back to enable them to be paid into a different account the bank receiving such cheques should ask why the transfer is being made. There is risk here too of a claim for conversion if the bank does not obtain an adequate explanation.

CLOSING A COMPANY ACCOUNT

10.   A company account, like any other account, can be closed for a variety of reasons. The follow-ing list covers some of the main possibilities.

   1.   The bank does not want to operate the account.
        As explained in Chapter 7, if an account is in credit and the bank wants to close it reasonable notice must be given. If an account is overdrawn the debt is repayable on demand and once a formal demand for repayment has been made the account can be closed, though the bank may not get its money back very quickly or at all.

   2.   The company ceases trading.
        If a company is set up for a specific purpose and that purpose is achieved the members may decide to simply cease trading. The company itself does not need to be closed

down but remains as what is sometimes described as a 'shell' company, because there is no longer any real business behind the company name. In such circumstances the bank account will no longer be needed.

3. The company closes down.

   If the members of a company decide that they do not want the business to continue the more correct formal procedure is to put the company into liquidation.

   If the company is solvent, having enough assets to pay off all the people to whom it owes money, the liquidation process is known as a members' voluntary winding up. This means that it is the members who have chosen to close down the company and who control how it is done, by appointing a liquidator of their choice.

   If the company is insolvent, unable to pay all its debts in full, the creditors to whom money is owed will control the liquidation. It is in such circumstances that an insolvency practitioner may take over the assets of the company (as described below).

4. An insolvency practitioner takes over the company assets.

   This reason for closing a company bank account is not necessarily separate and different from closing down a company, though the appointment of an insolvency practitioner to deal with the company assets may be used as a way of getting the business going again rather than closing it down. Under the Insolvency Act 1986 only properly qualified experts, usually accountants with experience of insolvency work, are authorised to act as insolvency practitioners. This general term covers people in a number of different roles (including Trustees in Bankruptcy who deal with individual insolvency rather than corporate insolvency). When an insolvency practitioner is appointed to take over the assets of a company the bank will not normally continue to operate an account for the company but will act on the instructions of the insolvency practitioner. This may mean transferring the balance on the account to an account at another bank or altering the name of the account.

The following section of the chapter looks at the different titles which insolvency practitioners may take on in dealing with insolvent companies.

INSOLVENCY PRACTITIONERS

11. One of the main purposes of the new legislation on insolvency brought in during 1985 and 1986 was to try to reduce the number of companies forced to close down because of what might have been temporary difficulties. In order to achieve this objective a new procedure was introduced in addition to the formal winding up procedures which were already available (and only slightly modified by the new law). The new measure allows the appointment of an Administrator whose aim would be to try to salvage a company in trouble.

Banks in dealing with insolvent companies may therefore come across insolvency practitioners in three different roles.

1. **Administrators**

   An Administrator is appointed by a court order known as an Administration Order following a petition, a request to the court, from the company or from the company's creditors. The role of an Administrator is to help the company to solve its problems. Once an Administrator is appointed no legal action can be taken against the company to get debts repaid or to realise security. This last point is of particular importance to banks because they may have lent money expecting to be able to sell particular assets if the company failed to repay; if an Administration order is made the bank will not be able to sell the assets taken as security until the Administrator has finished his work.

2. **Administrative Receivers**

   One of the forms of security which banks or other lenders can take is a floating charge, which means that the assets used as security are not individually identified. In order to realise this kind of security the lender appoints an Administrative Receiver to deal with the assets (for example to sell off stock owned by the company) using the money raised to pay off the loan. Anyone appointed as an Administrative Receiver must be a qualified insolvency practitioner.

It is also important to note that once an Administrator has been appointed this prevents the bank from appointing an Administrative Receiver.

3. **Liquidators**

   If a company or its creditors do not want to appoint an Administrator, or if an Administrator has failed to rescue the company from its difficulties, a Liquidator can be appointed. Like an Administrator or Administrative Receiver a Liquidator must be a qualified insolvency practitioner. His role is to close down the business in a way which ensures that the creditors get as much of their money back as possible.

Note that banks may be asked to operate bank accounts for insolvency practitioners in any of these three roles, though liquidators usually have to keep an account with the Bank of England rather than with a commercial bank.

SUMMARY

12. a) A company is a separate legal person from the individuals who are the owners or members of the company.

   b) Companies are governed by the Companies Act 1985 which replaced a series of earlier Companies Acts.

   c) The majority of companies are companies limited by shares.

   d) Limited companies can be either public or private. A company must meet certain requirements including having a minimum share capital of £50,000 in order to qualify as a public limited company. Companies which do not meet all the conditions to qualify as public companies are automatically considered as private companies.

   e) A company comes into being when it is issued with a certificate of incorporation by the Registrar of Companies.

   f) The main documents which a company needs to produce to the Registrar of Companies, and then to a bank in order to open a bank account are:-
   1. the Memorandum of Association (the external rules) *and*

   2. the Articles of Association (the internal rules).
   These are usually bound together in one booklet.

   g) Directors are the officials who are given delegated authority to make decisions on behalf of a company.

   h) When opening a company bank account the bank should take up references on the directors as well as asking for a copy of the Memorandum and Articles.

   i) Banks have to be watchful in dealing with company accounts to make sure that the funds belonging to the company are not diverted into other accounts, for example the personal accounts of the directors.

   j) A company account may be closed for a number of reasons. If a company is solvent the members may choose to close it down by a members' voluntary winding up.

   k) If a company is insolvent a qualified insolvency practitioner may be appointed by the court as an Administrator to try to get the business going again.

   l) Banks, or other lenders, with security for their lending in the form of a floating charge, may appoint an Administrative Receiver to deal with the assets covered by the floating charge. This means that the assets can then be disposed of to help to get the lender's money back.

   m) Liquidators are appointed to deal with companies which are being wound up. Their role is to dispose of the assets to get as much money as possible for the creditors.

STUDENT SELF-TESTING

Self Review Questions

1. What was the significance of the case of Salomon v. Salomon and Co Ltd? (2)

2. What is a company limited by guarantee? (3)

3. What are the main differences between public and private companies? (3)

4. What is the objects clause of a company, and where would you find it? (5)

5. What are the Articles of Association of a company? (5)

6.   What is a 'shadow director'? (7)

7.   When would a bank see a certificate to commence trading? (8)

8.   What is a members' voluntary winding up? (10)

9.   What is the difference between an Administrator and an Administrative Receiver? (11)

10.   What is the main function of a liquidator? (11)

Exercises (answers begin page 328)

A1.   Read this passage and answer the questions which follow.

Banks do not require to see the terms of a partnership agreement when opening a partnership account because the terms of the bank mandate are adequate. Not seeing the partnership agreement means that the bank is not legally bound to take note of its terms.

In the case of accounts opened for limited companies the bank does need to see the Memorandum and Articles of Association because this document is one of the pieces of evidence that the company exists and can operate a bank account as a legal 'person', separate and different from its members or its directors. One of the disadvantages of seeing the Memorandum and Articles is that it is unlikely that the bank can benefit afterwards from section 9 of the European Communities Act 1972, and may suffer if company borrowing is 'ultra vires'.

1.   State three of the key points covered by a bank mandate for a partnership account.

2.   What is the main piece of legislation covering the operation of limited companies?

3.   What is the basic difference between the Memorandum of Association and the Articles of Association?

4.   What does the phrase 'ultra vires' mean?

5.   What is the significance of section 9 of the European Communities Act?

A2.   In what ways is an Administrator different from an Administrative Receiver? In what circumstances would each be appointed?

A3.   What is limited liability and what advantages does it offer:-

a)   for members of a company;

b)   for the company itself?

A4.   If a company director dies this does not necessarily have the same effect on the company as far as a bank is concerned as the death of a partner would have on a partnership. Why is there this difference and what implications does it have for banking procedures in opening and operating accounts?

10. Marketing Financial Services

INTRODUCTION

1. This chapter is concerned with the idea of marketing and how it can be applied by financial institutions. Special features of marketing services, and in particular financial services, are considered and the chapter goes on to examine some of the important concepts in marketing, including the marketing plan, marketing research, the marketing mix and market segmentation. The increased importance of the marketing philosophy in banking makes this a specially important chapter.

MARKETING

2. When marketing was first introduced into the major clearing banks it was seen by many members of staff as being the same as selling, and therefore something to which many bank employees were initially rather hostile. It is important to recognise that although marketing does include selling the idea of marketing is very much broader. Essentially marketing consists of three main elements:-

   a) identifying the needs of customers;
   b) providing goods or services to meet those needs at the right price, at the right time and in the right place;
   c) making a profit from meeting customers' needs.

This definition of marketing makes no specific reference to selling or to advertising, but the implication that both advertising and selling skills are important is contained in the three elements. How they fit in is considered later in the chapter.

MARKETING SERVICES

3. Since the definition of marketing given above is a general definition it applies to both goods and services. In banking it is rare for goods to be marketed (although some banks have included physical objects like money boxes in their range of products from time to time). The emphasis in banking is therefore on marketing services, and it is useful to consider some of the specific features of services which create particular marketing problems.

The following list highlights a number of important issues to consider.

1. Intangibility
   Services are intangible (which means they cannot be touched) so potential buyers cannot usually look at or try out what they are going to buy.

2. Individuality
   Services are often specific to the individual buyer rather than identical. A buyer of a tin of beans gets an item which is the same as, and could be exchanged for, a tin bought by anyone else. A customer at a hairdressers does not get the same haircut as the next customer.

3. Lack of Standardisation
   Although few goods today are individually hand-made it still remains common for services to involve at least some personal element. Bank services are often seen as personal by customers because they judge the bank by the way staff treat them. This cannot be standardised in spite of training aimed at achieving a uniformly high level of customer care.

In addition to these general features of services, which are not necessarily separate and distinct from one another, many services are characterised by a client relationship where the customer uses a particular service because he or she likes the sales staff. Buyers of goods are less often influenced in this way; they are more likely to decide what to buy before deciding where to go rather than deciding first which supplier is the best.

FINANCIAL SERVICES

4. Banks as providers of financial services need to be conscious not only of the general features of marketing services but also of unusual problems or characteristics of financial services.

Financial services like other services are normally intangible, specific to each individual buyer and non-standard. In addition financial services are special because of the importance of money as a source of the power to make decisions. People who are seen as experts on money matters are considered to have a high level of responsibility towards the people with whom they deal. With the passing of the Financial

Services Act 1986 this special kind of responsibility has been recognised in law. The Securities and Investments Board, which has powers under the Financial Services Act, has attempted to establish the principle that financial institutions should choose either:-

    a)   to sell only their own brand services (so that buyers would know that they were dealing with sales staff rather than advisers) *or*

    b)   to sell only other people's services (acting as impartial advisers and disclosing any commissions earned).

This principle (known as 'polarisation') has affected the major banks more than most other providers of financial services because before the Act was passed it was normal practice for banks to give general investment advice, but also to sell their own brand products such as unit trusts.

THE ROLE OF THE MARKETING PLAN

5.   Any planned attempt at marketing must take into account the kind of legal constraints referred to in the preceding section. Rather more important is the overall strategy of the organisation, a concept considered in Chapter 6.

The marketing plan of any company, like the basic strategy, arises from a view of what business or businesses the organisation should be in, and how it should compete in those fields. The first stage of the marketing plan for any bank is to know what the present position is. This means preparing a situation analysis which identifies clearly:-

    a)   the range of businesses the bank is currently engaged in;

    b)   the strengths and weaknesses of the bank;

    c)   opportunities available to the bank;

    d)   threats which the bank will have to face;

    e)   the different kinds of customer which the bank wants;

    f)   the reasons why customers choose the bank in preference to others;

    g)   what financial needs customers have which the bank does not meet;

    h)   what competition the bank faces in all its different services.

This information about all the different factors affecting current business can then be put together by planners in summary form, in conjunction with the views of senior managers about strategy for the future, to form the basis of a plan. To convert a mass of data and broad strategic goals into policies which can be of value in deciding on action means that some narrowing down is needed. For example the aim of providing loans to personal customers is very broad; to identify particular types of customer and particular types of loan may make it easier to choose appropriate advertising and methods of selling.

The essential role of a marketing plan is therefore to turn the general into the particular, to create action plans out of broad objectives. Resources, both time and money, then need to be allocated to the steps that are to be taken and staff need to be given responsibility for each of the activities agreed on.

FEATURES OF THE MARKETING PLAN

6.   A marketing plan is a document or series of documents intended to help an organisation to be more successful in meeting the needs of customers profitably. It is not a rigid set of rules but a range of proposals arising out of an analysis of the organisation's situation. Changes in the situation, which may be the result of such factors as trends in fashion, new technology or increasing competition, must lead to changes in plan. To ignore the real world would make the plan pointless. The documents to be used by different departments or sections therefore need to be re-written as circumstances alter. For large businesses this re-writing may be a continuous process; more commonly a revised set of proposals is produced each year. Usually the aim is to adapt what was previously put forward rather than to start from scratch because to ignore previous plans would mean treating much past effort as a waste of time.

The marketing plan, whether as a new plan or a revised version of a previous plan, will usually contain sections dealing with:-

    a)   the current situation including the strengths and weaknesses of the business and all its competitors (e.g. market share in specific markets);

    b)   broad strategy (e.g. diversification into new markets) together with reasons for choosing the strategy;

    c)   the specific groups or types of customers whose needs the organisation is trying to meet (e.g. the student market);

d) the range of products to be offered, prices of those products (e.g. charges for current accounts) and the methods of promotion to be used;

e) the distribution methods to be used for different products and to different markets;

f) the kind of marketing staff needed in the organisation;

g) the training needs of those staff;

h) the costing of the marketing process, including budgets (e.g. for advertising);

i) any constraints on marketing (e.g. legal restrictions).

Many of these areas are considered in more detail in later sections of this chapter. This summary indicates the wide scope of the marketing plan. Successful marketing affects all aspects of a bank and marketing can be seen as a philosophy, a way of looking at things, rather than as a specialist function separate and different from the other things banks do.

MARKETING RESEARCH

7. Gathering information is an essential first stage, since the marketing plan begins by looking at the bank's current position in terms of markets, competition and strengths and weaknesses. This information can come from a broad range of sources, some purely internal like the bank's own records of numbers of customers and accounts. Other data about the market as a whole and about the quality of competition may come from the competitors or from independent surveys.

Understanding the bank's own customers may require specific research because banks in the United Kingdom are only just beginning to build up detailed records on computer of the characteristics of their client base and the services which customers use.

Research may also be important when a new product is being launched. By getting views from potential customers beforehand the risk of a costly mistake is reduced.

The diversity of sources of data used for different marketing problems has led marketing experts to distinguish between market research and marketing research. Market research is research into the qualities and features of a specific market. Marketing research is the systematic collection and analysis of all information about the marketing process. The following table lists some of the main differences between the two ideas.

Marketing Research	Market Research
1. Covers all areas in which the organisation operates.	1. Looks at a specific area or part of the market.
2. Provides continuous updating of data.	2. Usually takes the form of a survey at a particular point in time.
3. Uses market research as one of a range of tools and techniques.	

When marketing research is systematically recorded and analysed in order to form a complete database of marketing intelligence this is often referred to as a marketing information system. Banks are moving towards the introduction of such systems to enable them to make decisions based on a full understanding of their target markets.

THE MARKETING MIX

8. Although background knowledge is being continuously updated, when a marketing plan is drawn up predictions about the market have to be made on the basis of what is known at the time. From these predictions and the strategic goals laid down by senior management decisions can be made about key aspects of the business.

From a marketing point of view four crucial areas about which decisions need to be made are:-

a) Product;

b) Price;

c) Place;

d) Promotion.

These four areas need to be considered together in order to achieve the basic goal of marketing, meeting customers' needs profitably. If the product is wrong, inadequately promoted or not available in the right place or at the right time it will fail to meet customers' needs. If the price is wrong the bank may not make any profit even if the customers are happy.

Because of the interaction between these four elements (sometimes referred to as the four Ps of marketing) they are known collectively as the marketing mix. The following sections look at each in turn, but in practice they cannot be considered in isolation because each affects the others, an improved product for example being able to command a higher price.

More recently writers on marketing have begun to look more critically at the limitations of the idea of the marketing mix. There have been suggestions that other elements should be included. For example personnel is commonly considered as a separate influence on marketing decision-making. This is a most important factor for service industries like banking where a customer's view of the bank is determined by how he or she is treated by the bank's staff. It has also been proposed that the list of components of the marketing mix should include Public Relations, since bad publicity can counteract the effects of the most careful planning on product, price, place or promotion.

PRODUCT

9.   In the context of banking the term product does not mean a physical object but a service provided by the bank. One of the difficulties about defining bank products is that many banking services do not exist on their own. For example the use of a cheque guarantee card is a service the bank can offer, but it cannot sell this service to someone who does not

already have an account and a cheque book. For banks, therefore, it is very important to consider the product range rather than individual items in the product range.

In broad terms banks have product ranges in the five areas of:-

a)   cash handling;
b)   money transmission;
c)   investment;
d)   lending;
e)   financial advice.

Although some services fall clearly into one or other of these categories there is considerable overlap; a well established service like the current account overdraft could fit into several of these product ranges.

What is important from a marketing point of view is how the customers see the product. At the very least the customer should appreciate the basic benefits. Marketing may be more successful if additional features can be built in. Even more effective is to construct a package of associated features which extend the customer's dependence on the product, establishing a lasting relationship between the customer and the bank. This idea of different levels of perception about products can be represented diagramatically as a series of circles, as shown below.

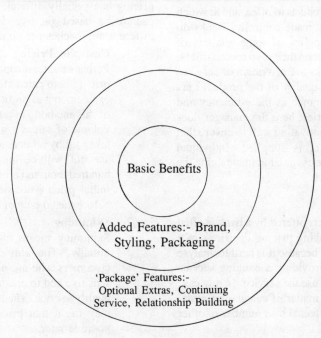

Basic Benefits

Added Features:- Brand,
Styling, Packaging

'Package' Features:-
Optional Extras, Continuing
Service, Relationship Building

As an example a bank might devise a savings account for young people. The basic benefits are those of any savings account. Funds are kept safely and interest is paid. These benefits are seen by any potential customer and are represented by the inner circle in the diagram. To sell this product the bank may offer additional features such as free gifts incorporating the bank's name or the brand name of the account. These features are outside the basic benefits and are shown as the second circle. The outer circle represents anything which extends beyond what is initially perceived by the buyer, for example a follow up letter of welcome to an account holders' club with further special offers. These package features are partly aimed at increasing the customer's use of the service and partly at reassuring the customer that the decision to open the account was a good one.

Part of the role of marketing is to devise new products as customers needs change or existing needs are recognised for the first time. Equally important, though usually less emphasised, is the removal of products from the product range as they become unprofitable. Products are often seen as having a life cycle of development, maturity and eventual decline, but some like current accounts do continue over very long periods, and are more likely to be improved or amended than dropped from a bank's product range.

Decisions about what products to offer, and at which branches, are normally made centrally. Banks do not usually adopt the policy of some retailers of allowing managers to put on their own special offers. However, because banks are providers of services rather than goods, the quality of the product may vary from branch to branch as the efficiency and friendliness of staff varies; here the manager does have a role to play in motivating staff to ensure that a high quality product is supplied. Individual members of staff too are essential in maintaining the standard of the product.

PRICE

10.   Pricing the products offered by a bank is often more difficult than making pricing decisions in a manufacturing business because it is hard to analyse the costs incurred in providing a banking service until customers start to use the service. In any case pricing is not simply a matter of calculating costs. Pricing decisions are affected by a number of other factors.

1.   Relationships
   A customer who comes from a wealthy family may be offered services at a lower cost because of the importance of maintaining the family connection. At a more general level two services offered together may be priced more competitively than if they were provided separately; this helps to increase sales and strengthen the customer's relationship with the bank.

2.   Special Offers
   Where a bank wants to encourage the use of a particular service it may lower the price, as some banks have done for house buyers, offering mortgages at lower rates than usual for the first year.

3.   Customer Attitudes
   A bank may specifically want to alter its customers' attitudes. For example lower charges for automated payments than for cheques are intended partly to encourage greater use of new technology.

These kind of factors make the pricing of any bank service a complex matter. For established products banks can modify prices or systems of pricing to achieve desired profit margins or to meet targets for market share (although one of these goals is likely to be at the expense of the other). For new products pricing is especially difficult because the decision cannot be based on experience. A number of different approaches are commonly used.

1.   **Cost-plus Pricing**
   Perhaps the least sophisticated approach to pricing is to calculate costs and add on an extra amount as profit. One major weakness of this method is that cost depends on the volume of sales; if a new account is only taken up by a hundred people the cost per account will be much greater than if a hundred thousand accounts are opened. The initial pricing decision needs to be made before the take-up of the service is known.

2.   **Skimming**
   Skimming means charging a high price initially. The aim of this is to attract customers who are not particularly price-sensitive and to create an image of a high-quality service. The high revenue early on may mean that price reductions will be possible later.

3. **Penetration Pricing**

    Penetration pricing means setting a low price so that customers will be attracted in large enough numbers to build up market share quickly. If a mass market is needed in order to justify offering a particular service penetration pricing is more likely than skimming. Profit may be improved later if prices can be raised or if other services can be sold to the new customers.

4. **Value pricing**

    When new products are launched market research is carried out, often by survey or a pilot scheme. One of the aims of this research is to find out how valuable customers think a new service will be. Value pricing means pricing determined by what customers judge is the right price acccording to such research. If this price is too low the bank may abandon the new product or try to reduce the cost of supplying it.

Decisions about price, like decisions about products, are generally made initially at head office level. However for many services managers do have some discretion, within general guidelines, to vary the price charged. Normal fees for some services may be waived in certain circumstances. Head offices generally try to discourage such waivers because of the reduced profit and because of the risk that customers who complain most about charges pay least. As managers become more profit conscious than ever before they are likely to share this reluctance to let customers off paying reasonable charges, but it is important to recognise that in some cases making a loss on a service may be justified if it helps to sell other more profitable services.

PLACE

11. To introduce new products priced at a level which customers are willing to pay is not enough to ensure that customers buy. It is also essential to make sure that the products are readily available.

Although the term place is often used to refer to the systems by which services are made available to users this ignores the importance of time. Services need to be provided at the right time as well as in the right place. Distribution may therefore be a more suitable general term to use, and distribution is an aspect of the marketing mix to which banks have given considerable attention.

For some services place is the more critical factor. Making insurance and mortgage products available at estate agents' offices, for example, is clearly an improvement for a customer seeking the convenience of dealing with a complete house-buying transaction at one place. For other services time may be just as important as place. To be able to obtain cash only from bank branches during opening hours was a very limited service. Now automated teller machines operating for eighteen or twenty four hours a day give customers much better access to their money. In addition agreements between some of the major banks have created networks which mean that cardholders can draw cash at many sites other than branches of their own bank. (See Chapter 25.)

A bank's policy on distribution systems, providing ways for customers to use the bank's services, needs to come from senior management because of the importance of a co-ordinated approach. Branch managers are clearly not in a position to judge, for example, when and where new branches should be opened. They may have some influence where changes are to be made within a branch, for example in automating some services, but their role is limited. Their powers and decisions are related to one particular delivery system, the branch. Where decisions are taken to distribute bank services through systems other than the branches such decisions must be made at high level.

PROMOTION

12. Promotion is concerned with getting customers and potential customers to be more aware of the bank and its products, and to make more use of the products. Traditionally banks have considered their services good enough to 'sell themselves' without promotion. During the 1970s and 1980s promotion of banks and their services has become much more prominent because of:-

a) the greater competition between banks;

b) the increase in new services to bring to customers' attention;

c) the loss of personal deposits, mainly to building societies;

d) the increased sophistication of customers;

e) the acceptance by banks of marketing as a philosophy.

The most obvious form of promotion is advertising, but just as marketing research is much broader than market research, so promotion is much broader than advertising. Promotion is often divided into two categories:-

a) **Above the line** promotion (which means advertising in the press and through radio, television and cinema) *and*

b) **Below the line** promotion (covering all forms of promotion other than media advertising).

Advertising ranges from the very general, like the Midland Bank's claim to be the 'Listening Bank' or the Trustee Savings Bank slogan 'The bank that likes to say yes', to advertising specific to a particular product like the regular television advertising campaigns for Barclaycard.

Although the ultimate aim of any advertising is to increase profitable business the objectives of any advertising campaign need to be more narrowly defined because winning customers depends on the whole marketing mix, not just on advertising. Typically success might be measured by the number of newspaper coupons being returned to ask for more information or by before-and-after surveys showing an increased number of people aware of the existence of a particular service. If advertisements achieve these limited aims a failure to increase sales will indicate a weakness in some other area of the marketing mix.

For banks most advertising will be centrally controlled, partly because of the aim of co-ordinating plans and partly because the cost of some forms of advertising, in particular television, is so high that smaller local units might not be able to justify the expense. Advertising regionally or at branch level is rare though the use of the local press to publicise specific events is not unknown. If, for example, a branch has a new automated teller machine an advertisement in the local paper might bring this to people's attention, though where possible banks prefer to obtain free publicity by making an event of this kind into a news item.

FORMS OF PROMOTION

13.   Although advertising is the form of promotion on which banks spend the largest amounts of money, other, below-the-line, promotions are of considerable importance. It is much more difficult to generalise about these than about advertising, but the following list indicates some of the possibilities which banks have tried.

1. Free Gifts
    This type of promotion is most common in petrol retailing but banks have made use of the idea, mainly in trying to attract younger customers, for example with Midland Bank's highly successful Griffin Young Savers Account where new account holders received sports bags, clipboards and dictionaries.

2. Mail Shots
    Because banks have the names and addresses of the people who buy their services (an advantage many other suppliers of goods and services do not have) they are able to communicate with them regularly to keep them informed about new products or to encourage them to make greater use of existing products. Promotional materials sent out with customers' regular statements of account (often known as 'statement stuffers') do not even involve extra postage costs, so they provide a very cheap form of communication.

3. Point-of-Sale Displays
    All banks make some use of displays of information within branches. This may take the form of posters on the walls or racks of leaflets to which customers can help themselves. More recently banks have used video screens to show brief promotional videos which customers can watch while they are waiting to be served. TSB Scotland has led the way in introducing interactive video in some branches so that customers can make enquiries about loans without the risk of being turned down by a member of staff.

4. Incentive schemes
    Many banks have tried out the idea of offering prizes to staff or to branches who are most successful in selling the bank's services. Because some customers may be a little suspicious of special offers and promotions aimed at them these indirect schemes aimed at staff may be more acceptable.

Policy decisions about these forms of promotion will usually be made at head office rather than at branch level though branches may run specific campaigns to promote particular services which are seen to be under-used locally. In these circumstances selective mailing is a common approach though personal selling techniques are also likely to be important. Personal selling may therefore be seen as a form of promotion too, though some marketing experts would categorise it as a means of distribution.

PERSONAL SELLING

14.   It is in the use of personal selling that policy decisions at branch level are of most significance. All staff have a role in marketing because the quality of service, the product, is influenced by how well staff do their jobs; getting things right behind the scenes matters to customers. Apart from this general responsibility shared by all staff, many staff have the additional marketing role of contact with customers. This may take the form of letters, answers to telephone enquiries or face-to-face communication at a cash desk, at an enquiry counter or in a formal interview.

Direct personal contact is particularly important in the financial services industry because customers believe that banks will provide honest and accurate advice about matters of great concern (and the importance of interviewing in banking is considered in more detail in Chapter 27).

In looking at the role of customer contact in the marketing process what is important is that marketing is about meeting customers' needs profitably. In order to do this staff who have contact with customers must be aware of the bank's product range and must be alert in identifying situations where a customer is likely to need particular services. Taking an interest in a customer's personal circumstances can be a way to spot selling opportunities.

Within branches staff training can play a major part in improving selling techniques, product knowledge and awareness of selling opportunities. Branch managers can also do a lot to increase the level of effective selling by the ways in which they encourage and motivate staff.

PUBLIC RELATIONS

15.   Public relations can be distinguished from advertising because it is not fully controlled and paid for by the bank. This does not mean that it requires no expenditure by the bank; to issue a press release, for example, takes up staff time in deciding the wording and managerial time to approve the purpose and content of the communication. If, however, journalists then choose to make use of the information there is no extra cost for the space in the newspaper as there would be if advertising space had been purchased.

The purpose of public relations is to create a favourable image for the organisation. Because reporting is considered by the public as more objective than advertising any praiseworthy behaviour by a bank or its staff can create a good impression if it is reported; to advertise similar behaviour would be less effective because it would be less widely believed.

Apart from making the most of newsworthy items a bank can develop a public relations programme, for example by sponsoring sporting or cultural events. Here the publicity which is obtained depends on how successful and well promoted the events are. The choice of types of event to sponsor depends on the particular image the bank is trying to create for itself. For example several of the major banks feel that they wish to attract the kind of customers who listen to classical music or opera and have sponsored performances. In contrast the Trustee Savings Bank has sponsored young rock musicians.

MARKET SEGMENTATION

16. The belief that banks need to have a clear idea of the kinds of people at whom they are directing their marketing efforts is the basis of what is known as market segmentation. This means dividing up the total market into clearly defined groups of customers, segments of the market, so that decisions about the marketing mix are appropriate to the chosen target.

The most basic form of segmentation is the division of the overall market for banking services into personal customers and business customers, a division now beginning to be reflected in branch networks with some branches specialising in banking services for the business sector.

However segmentation can be much more detailed, and may prove to be a worthwhile exercise provided that any segment identified as a target at which to direct marketing efforts is:-

a) a large group (for whom it may be profitable to develop specific products);

b) a coherent group (whose common factors are such that their banking needs are likely to be similar);

c) a targetable group (with whom it will be possible to communicate without too much difficulty or too much expense);

d) a measurable group (so that objectives can be set in terms of market share).

Segmentation of the commercial market is likely to be on the basis of such factors as company size, type of industry and possibly decision-making procedure.

Traditionally the main form of segmentation of the personal market in the United Kingdom has been by means of government statistics on social class. The standard socio-economic groupings which are used can be considered broadly accurate but they are based on the employment of heads of households, not always an appropriate way to measure needs for marketing purposes. The categories are:-

1. A . . . higher managerial, professional and administrative;

2. B . . . intermediate managerial, professional and administrative;

3. C1 . . . supervisory, clerical and junior administrative;

4. C2 . . . skilled manual;

5. D . . . semi-skilled and unskilled manual;

6. E . . . others (students, pensioners, unemployed etc.).

To use such categories for marketing does assume a belief that most people within a particular socio-economic group will have roughly similar needs, for example for banking services. This is clearly not the case for group E, but may be more true of the other groups.

APPROACHES TO MARKET SEGMENTATION

17.   Because socio-economic categories A to E are considered rather broad a number of more specific ways of segmenting the personal customer market have been devised.

1. **Life Cycle Segmentation**
This approach to segmentation assumes that most people's lives form similar patterns. From a stage as young singles, people move on to become 'nest-builders', settling down to buy a home and have children. Later income rises to a level above what is needed for ordinary living expenses and the couple can save towards their retirement. General changes in society, such as increasing levels of divorce, mean that this pattern is far from universal but may occur commonly enough to form the basis of a useful kind of segmentation. Banking products can be specifically directed at people in different stages of this life cycle.

2. **Psychographic Segmentation**
The idea of psychographics is to analyse people in terms of the kind of life-style they adopt. This makes it more detailed than life-cycle segmentation, which treats everyone alike. Categories identified include the quiet family man, the traditionalist and the achiever. In terms of marketing banking services there may be advantages in directing new high technology products at the kind of people seen as most adaptable and ready to accept change. The difficulty is in identifying such customers and directing marketing communications to them.

3. **ACORN Segmentation**
In the United Kingdom one of the most sophisticated methods of dividing up the market is by post-code areas, each of which is assessed according to the main type of housing within the area. Since each postcode covers only a small number of households this gives a fairly precise analysis. Using this form of segmentation assumes that people living in similar houses are likely to have similar needs for goods and services; this will not invariably be the case but it may be a valid assumption often enough to be useful. Because the technique is specific to small areas it can be used at branch level if required, as well as on a national basis.

The name ACORN is simply an acronym: A Classification Of Residential Neighbourhoods. The system uses nearly forty different categories but these are grouped into bands A to K from agricultural areas to better retirement areas.

Different methods of segmentation may be appropriate for different kinds of marketing. Marketing of financial services requires a form of segmentation which groups people according to their attitudes and beliefs about their financial needs. The methods outlined above may give some guidance but not all financial products can be targetted on specific market segments.

THE MARKETING PHILOSOPHY

18.   In the past banks offered a range of products or services which they had the resources or skills to provide. If customers wanted to use the banks' services they could choose to do so and would pay what the bank decided was a fair price. As conditions became more competitive banks tried harder to sell their products, to find customers who wanted to buy what was on offer. The basic philosophy was product-centred. Marketing was seen as a technique which could help to sell the products.

The marketing philosophy is rather different from this because it assumes as a starting point that customers have needs. The first step for any business adopting marketing as a philosophy rather than just a technique is to find out what customers need. Any products should then be planned to meet those needs, assuming that customers are willing to pay a price which allows some profit to be made.

Marketing is very different from selling because of this difference in where the process starts. People involved in selling need to know about the products that they sell so that they can identify prospective customers and communicate effectively with them. Marketing decision-makers have to consider the whole process of planning including research and the elements of the marketing mix, product, price, place and promotion.

The major banks in the United Kingdom are still moving towards a full acceptance of the marketing philosophy. This is partly because of their long tradition of providing a familiar range of products. Newer, smaller banks are often more marketing-orientated because they do not have the same history. The building societies are also unlikely to be highly product-orientated as they begin to compete more fully in the financial services industry because their

traditional fairly narrow product-range has forced them to ask what customers need.

SUMMARY

19. a)   Marketing involves identifying customer needs and providing goods or services to meet those needs profitably.

b)   Marketing services may be different from marketing goods because services are intangible, different for each individual buyer and often dependent on the person providing the service.

c)   Successful bank marketing needs to be related to the bank's overall strategy. Marketing should be based on a plan which uses an analysis of the present situation to identify objectives which can in turn lead to action plans. This marketing plan needs to be flexible enough to meet the needs of different levels of the organisation as circumstances change.

d)   Research needs to be carried out to make sure marketing plans are relevant to customer needs. This may take the narrow form of market research or the broader marketing research. More thorough research forming a complete database is referred to as a Marketing Information System.

e)   Most marketing decisions are related to four key areas, the four elements of the marketing mix, product, price, place and promotion.

f)   In banking the term product refers to the services offered to customers. Product ranges need to be changed continuously as new products are developed and old products dropped.

g)   Pricing decisions are not simply a matter of calculating costs and adding on some profit. A number of factors influence pricing decisions, in particular customer attitudes. Different pricing methods are used according to the circumstances.

h)   To enable customers to use banking services they have to be provided in the right place and at the right time. New distribution systems are helping to ensure that products are more widely available than ever before.

i)   Promotion of financial services has increased enormously. The most important form of promotion is advertising; for the major banks this includes extensive television and press advertising. Banks have also tried a number of other forms of promotion.

j)   Personal selling is of special importance in financial services because customers expect good advice and may see branch staff as financial experts.

k)   Banks may promote a good image of themselves by public relations. The use of media reports of sponsorship or other newsworthy events is often more convincing than paid advertising.

l)   In order to direct marketing efforts more precisely at customers banks make assumptions about groups of people and their needs. The use of such groups as a tool of marketing is known as market segmentation. Although socio-economic groupings have been used as the basis for segmenting the personal market other more detailed kinds of segmentation are now available.

m)   The marketing philosophy is based on the belief that the customers' needs rather than the bank's products come first. This is why marketing is much broader in scope than selling.

STUDENT SELF-TESTING

Self Review Questions

1.   What is marketing? (2)

2.   State three factors which usually distinguish the marketing of services from the marketing of goods. (3)

3.   What is 'polarisation'? (4)

4.   State four of the areas covered by a situation analysis in a marketing plan. (5)

5.   What are the main differences between market research and marketing research? (7)

6.   What are the four crucial elements of the marketing mix? (8)

7.   What is penetration pricing? (10)

8.   What is the main difference between advertising and public relations? (15)

9.   What is life cycle segmentation? (17)

10.   How does the marketing philosophy differ from selling based on a range of products? (18)

Exercises (answers begin page 330)

A1.   To what extent is the traditional summary of the marketing mix as the four Ps an adequate explanation of what banks need to consider in order to market their services?

A2.   What is a situation analysis, and what part does it play in a bank marketing plan?

A3.   What is market segmentation? What approaches to segmentation do you consider to be most appropriate for marketing banking services?

A4.   What is market research and how is it used in banking? In what ways is marketing research a wider concept?

11. Principles of Lending

INTRODUCTION

1. The next seven chapters concern one of the most important parts of a bank's product range, lending services. This chapter deals with some of the background issues, the importance of lending, the risks of lending and ways in which banks can approach lending. The main part of the chapter deals with the key factors which bankers need to consider when making decisions about whether to lend.

Note that this chapter is the first chapter relating specifically to the syllabus of the Banking Operations 1 syllabus rather than Banking Operations 11. If you have not already studied Chapter 6 on the range of banking business that would be a useful chapter to read as background to this part of the text.

THE IMPORTANCE OF LENDING

2. In general banks obtain most of their income from charging interest on the money they lend. A bank does, of course, have to pay interest to many of the depositors who have provided the money, but even when this is deducted from interest earned the profit left over is, for most banks, more than the profit from all of the rest of the bank's business.

In a sense the importance of lending has declined as income from other sources has become relatively more important, but the actual amounts of money earned by the major United Kingdom banks from lending have continued to rise. The rise in interest income has generally exceeded the rate of inflation, and therefore represents a real increase in profit. The following example gives some indication of how the relationship between interest and other forms of income has been changing for major clearing banks over recent years.

In the case of Barclays taking in and lending out money still accounted for two thirds of income by the end of 1986. With some foreign bank groups, particularly in Switzerland, the income from lending has fallen to well below the income from fees for other services. British banks are moving in the same direction by increasing fee income faster than they are increasing interest income, but as the Barclays figures show there is no prospect of lending becoming an unimportant part of banking in the foreseeable future.

Example

Barclays PLC
(Source: annual report and accounts)
Comparative figures on sources of income

	1982 £ million	1986 £ million
Interest received	6285	7287
Interest paid out	4633	4812
NET INTEREST INCOME	1652	2475
NON-INTEREST INCOME	657	1259
TOTAL INCOME	2309	3734
Interest as % of total	71.5	66.3

It should also be emphasised that deposit-taking is a counterpart to lending. One cannot exist without the other, and since a bank's depositors are often also the customers who buy other financial services like insurance it would be a mistake to see lending as a separate and distinct activity unconnected with the rest of the bank's business. A loan is a service like any other financial service and needs to be marketed in an appropriate way.

THE RISKS OF LENDING

3. Any explanation of the nature of profit includes some consideration of the question of risk. Profit may also be associated with the reward for using particular skills, entrepreneurial skills of bringing together the resources which can create wealth, but in general it is accepted that businesses can expect to earn high profits if they take high risks or lower profits if they take lower risks.

Banks, as lenders of money, are risk-takers. The traditional view of bankers as cautious and afraid to take risks arises because the activity of lending is so risky that only a sensible approach to risk can ensure survival. To be incautious in risk-taking would soon put a bank out of business.

Sensible lending therefore involves making a reasoned attempt to measure risk and decide whether the return to be made justifies the risk being taken. Because of the long history of banking useful guidelines have been developed for looking at lending propositions, but the final decision, to lend or not to lend, must be a matter of judgement.

Clearly a banker who never loses any money when lending is being over-cautious and missing opportunities for profit. To lose money frequently is even worse because it uses up all the profit made on loans which are repaid.

REDUCING RISK

4.   Since banks are in business to make profit they are keen to lend money (even if some customers find this hard to believe). Their aim is to reduce the risk that they will not get their money back so that profits can be as high as possible.

The following list outlines some of the major methods of reducing risk.

1.   **Insurance**
Some specific risks which could prevent a borrower from repaying can be covered by insurance. For example if a bank lends money to buy a house and the house burns down the customer is unlikely to have the money to repay. If the bank has arranged, or required the customer to arrange, insurance, then the loss may be avoided. Here the cost of insurance may reduce the bank's profit or add to the borrower's costs.

2.   **Staff training**
By making sure that staff who lend money know what to look for in assessing proposals from borrowers risk can be reduced. The training costs reduce total profit.

3.   **Setting lending limits**
This takes the idea of training further by allowing for experience. Young, inexperienced staff only deal with lending on a small scale. With more experience lenders can operate up to higher limits. This system can be applied at all levels of the bank. Branch managers are set discretionary limits (sometimes referred to as DPs or discretionary powers) according to their status, and can only lend above their limit with approval from a higher level, like a regional office. The very largest loans may require approval from the Board of Directors. Within branches staff below managerial level may be authorised by the manager to agree to loans, but usually not up to the manager's own discretionary limit.

Here the cost of reducing risk arises from the time and effort taken in setting up and operating the system of limits.

4.   **Monitoring lending**
When money has been lent the bank can reduce the risk of not getting repaid by checking up on how the money has been used and what the customer is doing about repayment.
Again any procedures for checking on borrowers add to the bank's costs, and therefore affect profit.

5.   **Spreading risk**
This is perhaps the most important concept. If a bank lends all its money to one customer who fails to repay the bank goes out of business. If a bank lends all its money to one industry which goes into recession the bank may go out of business. If a bank lends all its money to one country and that country's economy is destroyed the bank may go out of business. Banks, being aware of these potential problems, try to lend as widely as possible. In order to achieve this objective they need to measure their 'exposure' to different industries or different countries. If the level of 'exposure' to one country becomes too high further lending will be restricted to reduce the risk.
The cost of reducing risk in this way arises from:-
a)   any profitable business turned down;
b)   the administrative cost of measuring 'exposure' and of setting appropriate limits based on views about risks.

Most banks would agree that the kind of measures suggested here are appropriate ways of reducing risk provided that the reductions in profit do not exceed the savings. As far as training about lending is concerned, for example, there has certainly been a change in attitude as banks have begun to use more automated systems for making decisions about lending; such systems mean more judgements are made at higher levels in the organisation.

Another important factor in reducing risk is that very often bank staff have a close knowledge of their customers' financial affairs, for example through operating a bank account, through making visits to the business premises or even through local gossip.

This is an advantage which many other lenders do not have because they do not have such extensive networks of local branches.

APPROACHES TO LENDING

5.   In theory decisions about lending can be tackled in a variety of different ways. These can be categorised in terms of what the lender sees as the predominant issue.

1.   **The borrower**
Many customers expect banks to look at lending simply in terms of who is borrowing. They may even ask 'How much will you lend me ?' or 'How much am I good for?' In some circumstances banks do, in effect, answer this question, for example when setting a spending limit for a credit card. In more complicated situations knowledge of the borrower may not be an adequate basis for a decision.

2.   **The use of the money**
If a bank has fairly close control of how money is to be used this may be a determining factor in agreeing to lend. For example a bank might agree to lend money for the purchase of a house where it would not advance a similar sum for any other purpose.

3.   **Security**
Customers often expect banks to lend just because adequate security is being offered, and there are some special cases where this is more or less true (considered in Chapter 17). In practice few lenders consider security as the predominant issue when lending because getting money back by selling security is uncertain, complicated and time-consuming. (For more detailed consideration of security and the forms it takes see Chapter 16.)

4.   **The situation**
In general bank lending decisions are based on an assessment of a combination of factors, the relative importance of each of these varying according to the circumstances. This situational approach has been developed over many years. It has proved effective in reducing risk while taking on profitable business, but has the big disadvantage that it is costly in staff time.

Because of this drawback banks have begun to make more use of other methods which take a narrower view. An appreciation of the broad view remains important to bankers even when narrow assessment criteria are applied, if only to make lenders aware of the kinds of information they are choosing to ignore.

Each of these approaches may be valid in some circumstances. The guidelines which bankers adopt relate to a broad situational view but they can, of course, be modified.

GUIDELINES FOR MAKING LENDING DECISIONS

6.   The following sections of the chapter look at the main factors which banks take into account when making lending decisions based on an assessment of the overall situation. A number of mnemonics (or memory tricks) have been devised as guides for bankers; here the sections deal with:-

    Purpose;
    Amount;
    Period;
    Expertise;
    Repayments;
    Security.

PAPERS helps you to remember this list. There are other variations on this theme, for example PARSER (Person, Amount, Repayments, Security, Expediency, Remuneration) and CAMPARI (Character, Ability, Margin, Purpose, Amount, Repayment, Insurance).

There is no particular right or wrong order to these points though there is something to be said for dealing with security last since this should become a consideration when all the other aspects have been dealt with. The best advice is to stick to the mnemonic you find easiest to remember, specially if it is one you have come across in your own bank.

The points covered are guidelines in the sense that they guide the banker towards the questions which need to be asked. It is the answers which influence the decision-making process.

PURPOSE

7.   In some circumstances lenders provide money without knowing or seeking to know how the money

is to be used. This frequently applies where borrowing is for general expenditure rather than for one specific purpose, as for example in shopping with a credit card. A business using an overdraft may also spend money without the bank knowing what is being paid for.

Most banks would see these examples as exceptions to the general principle that lending should only be for purposes which the bank knows about and approves. If a customer wants to borrow a substantial amount of money (and what this means depends on the financial standing of the customer) the bank will consider it reasonable to ask why the money is needed. The question has to be considered for a number of reasons.

1. The bank is an adviser.
    Although a customer may see the bank purely as a supplier of funds from the bank's point of view this undervalues the bank's role. Banks deal in financial services including giving advice. If a bank looks at a particular proposal from a customer it may be able to suggest ways in which the purpose can be achieved more easily. What a customer asks for and what is needed are not necessarily the same thing; helping to match lending to the customer's real needs is part of the service the bank provides.
2. The bank is concerned about risk.
    One reason for a business failing to repay a loan is that the money has been badly used. If a bank has the opportunity to see that this is going to happen it can avoid lending, which protects the bank from loss and helps the customer. Knowing the purpose for which a loan is required gives the lender a better chance of judging the level of risk.
3. The purpose of borrowing may be undesirable.
    Inevitably when a bank lends money it becomes associated with what the borrower does with the money. Clearly banks should not lend for purposes which they know to be illegal, but care should also be taken about lending which may lead to adverse publicity. Criticism may arise for political reasons, for example lending to governments which are known to be repressive,

or for moral reasons, for example financing pornographic films. It could be argued that a borrower can give false reasons for wanting money, but by asking questions the banker may identify inconsistencies which will lead to the lending being refused.

Usually the purpose for which borrowing is required does not present a problem to the lending banker, but a full analysis of the situation should include consideration of why the money is needed.

AMOUNT

8. A number of questions need to be asked about the amount the borrower requires.

    1. Is it too much?
        This is perhaps the most obvious question. Customers may feel that obtaining a loan involves a kind of haggling process, by which asking for more than is needed may lead to an agreement by the bank to lend the amount required. There is some truth in this, but competent and experienced lending staff should not be misled by the 'haggler'. If a customer cannot justify borrowing the amount asked for, simply offering a little less is not a sensible alternative. If, however, a customer includes in estimated figures a sum for contingencies or emergencies this will be seen as a sign of careful planning.

    2. Is it too little?
        This less obvious question is probably more important than the first. Understanding how the money is to be used, for example by seeing detailed costings, helps the lender to judge whether anything important has been missed out. If too many items have been ignored the customer's financial capability may be suspect.
        Lenders also need to be aware of the problems they face if they do lend too little. If a business has borrowed £10,000 but needs another £2,000 to keep going because it borrowed too little in the first place the bank will need to spend far more time than it intended in analysing the situation again; in the end there may be little choice but to lend more to avoid losing money on the original loan. If the lender had realised at the outset that £12,000 would be needed a

decision could have been made on that basis.

3. How does the loan compare with the borrower's contribution?

When a bank lends money it can lend the whole amount the customer is going to spend, but in general banks prefer to see some contribution from the borrower. This suggests that the customer has been able to save up some of the money needed, a useful indication of an ability to make repayments. When a business borrows money the funds which the owners put in, the capital resources, are particularly important because they mean that the bank is not taking on all the risk of loss if the business does badly. Bankers often feel that in business lending the owners should put in at least as much money as the bank, but this idea of a 1:1 ratio of invested money and borrowed money is not an absolute rule to follow in all cases.

A lender cannot have a preconceived idea of what is the right amount for the potential customer to borrow. Any evidence the customer can produce to show what his or her needs are will help the lender to come to some reasoned conclusions. Asking the right questions also improves the quality of the decision which is finally reached, and it is in this area that banks can reduce the risks that they take.

PERIOD

9.   The period over which money is lent must depend on the situation. In general banks have traditionally preferred to lend for the shortest possible periods, partly because much of the money which they have available to lend is money which depositors can ask for at short notice. In other words banks borrow short-term so it is safer for them to lend short-term. By borrowing short and lending long the potential for profit is greater but this is because the risk is greater.

The changing banking environment means that banks are now prepared to lend for much longer periods, including lending for house purchase for which the usual period is twenty five years. Business lending may also be for periods as long as this, although as long-term business loans have become more common banks have tried to make sure that more

of the money they take as deposits is on a long-term basis.

Two major factors influence banks in judging what is an appropriate period for lending, the purpose and the source of repayments, both considered in other sections of the chapter.

1. **Purpose**

If the lending is for general expenditure banks still prefer to keep to the policy of lending short-term. If the money is to be used to buy major assets the maximum period will usually be related to the useful working life of the assets. If a machine will last five years a ten year loan to buy it will not make sense; this is not because the machine will be security for the loan but because after five years the business will need to buy a new machine and may have to borrow again while still repaying the old debt. If finance costs build up in this way the business will be harmed.

2. **Repayments**

If a borrower can provide evidence of where repayments are coming from and when the money will be available the lender can use this information to judge how long to lend for.

The period which the potential borrower thinks is appropriate may not seem satisfactory to the bank because it is:-

a) too short, causing difficulty in making repayments *or*

b) too long, adding to the cost for the borrower and the risk for the lender.

The bank can therefore offer to lend over a different period from that suggested by the customer, just as the amount offered may differ from what the customer has requested.

EXPERTISE

10.   This aspect of assessing a lending proposition is the most difficult and important. It is concerned with the characteristics of the customer and any judgement is therefore based on subjective factors. The leading considerations are often summarised as the three Cs.

1. **Character**

Essentially a lender has to feel that the customer can be trusted. Few people have the skill to judge someone's honesty in the course of a short interview, and there is a danger that unconscious prejudices may have a stronger influence than lending staff themselves realise.

2. **Commitment**

Bad debts do not arise simply because customers are dishonest; in fact such cases are rare though often involving spectacularly large amounts of money. A more common problem is the well-intentioned borrower who lacks the motivation to cope with the borrowing. For a business borrower the lack of commitment may be reflected in the business itself performing badly. Customers who do not have the right kind of commitment are likely to have little or no money of their own to put towards the purpose for which they want to borrow.

3. **Capability**

An individual whose finances are well organised and who approaches the bank with a clearly thought out proposal incorporating well-presented facts and figures will come across as being capable of taking on a loan and repaying it. Further evidence of capability comes from the borrower's past record; if loans have been successfully repaid in the past this makes the bank more willing to lend in the future (a policy which might penalise people who have managed their money carefully in the past in order to avoid borrowing).

For business borrowers the question of capability is more complex because the lender needs to be satisfied that the business has:-

a) the right technical skills for the particular industry;
b) the managerial skills to make the business efficient;
c) the financial skills to cope with borrowing.

Many businesses are set up by people who have great technical expertise but little knowledge of management or finance. In deciding whether to lend the banker is trying to judge whether the business has, or can acquire, the range of skills needed, so that it will succeed. There are some clues such

as the customer's own awareness of weaknesses and problems, but again judgement is needed.

The difficulty of judging what people are like by means of an interview, which is costly in staff time, has led banks to look for ways of assessing people by other means. For most personal lending and some business lending credit scoring systems (considered in Chapter 12) are now widely used. These allocate scores to particular pieces of factual information about the customer in order to come to an overall score which determines whether a loan is agreed or not.

The importance of assessing what a borrower is like means that banks will continue to explore ways of improving the quality of the judgements they make about the whole range of personal factors affecting repayment.

REPAYMENTS

11.   Risk in lending arises because repayment is not completely certain. The more certainty the bank has that repayments will be made the more willing the bank will be to lend.

Sources of repayment can be considered in three basic categories.

1. **Regular income**

For an individual regular earnings from a job with a high level of job security would be considered ideal. Even in these cases death or prolonged illness could prevent the regular repayments from being made, but insurance can be taken out to cope with these rare possibilities. High levels of unemployment have also led to the idea of insuring loans against job loss; if the borrower is made redundant repayments can be made under an insurance policy until another job is found.

For a business regular income comes from cash the business makes from trading. Insuring against the loss of such income because of fire or some other specific events is possible, but if the business simply starts to do badly no insurance can cover the loss. This means that the lender's assessment has to be fairly thorough. How banks judge businesses is considered in more detail in Chapters 13 and 14.

2. **A lump sum**

    If a potential borrower is expecting to receive a particular sum of money and intends to use that money to repay the borrowing the bank will want to know:-

    a) how certain it is that the money will be received;

    b) what will happen if the money is not received.

    If there is a high degree of certainty, as for example when a customer has sold a house and contracts have already been exchanged, the bank will usually be quite willing to lend. If there is some doubt the bank will need to be reassured that there are alternative sources of repayment available.

3. **Irregular income**

    Banks are less keen to rely on irregular payments to repay a loan. The uncertainty adds to the risk. There is also the disadvantage that the bank will find it hard to check whether the borrower is having difficulty in repaying if there are no clearly agreed repayment amounts or repayment dates.

Banks can take a number of measures to improve the likelihood of getting repayments. The most important of these is to arrange for funds to be sent direct to the bank rather than passing through the customer's hands first. In the case of a personal borrower this would usually mean making sure that the customer's salary is paid directly into a current account with the bank.

SECURITY

12. In using the mnemonic PAPERS to look at lending, the last item on the list is security. This may be an appropriate place to consider security because it has traditionally been felt by bankers that they should only consider security once they have established that they are happy to lend.

Taking security simply means acquiring a claim to an asset or assets so that if repayment is not made as planned the assets taken as security can be used to obtain repayment. The chapter on security (Chapter 15) looks at the characteristics of good security and explains the most commonly used kinds of security.

In making a decision about lending the availability of some kind of security is a reassuring factor but lenders should be cautious not to allow this to influence them too heavily. If too many other factors suggest that it is unwise to lend the proposition should be declined even if security is good. Getting money back by using (or, as it is more commonly called, realising) security should be a last resort. To enter into lending expecting to have to realise the security is a dangerous policy because:-

a) realising security is time-consuming and expensive;

b) there may be adverse publicity affecting the bank's reputation;

c) the customer's interests are rarely well-served;

d) there may be legal technicalities preventing successful realisation.

It may be useful to ask about security even if the bank is willing to lend unsecured. If the customer has suitable assets to offer as security this can reduce the risk for the bank and may mean that the customer will be charged a lower rate of interest.

For small-scale lending taking security is often not appropriate because the cost of making the arrangements may be too high in relation to the amount being borrowed. Personal loans, for which repayment is to come from regular income, are normally unsecured because they are mostly for fairly small amounts and over fairly short periods.

OTHER FACTORS INFLUENCING LENDING

13. The key factors outlined in the preceding sections are those which banks look at in order to assess the risk associated with a particular borrowing proposition.

There are a number of other considerations which may influence the final decision about lending, mainly relating to the needs and interests of the bank.

1. **Factors discouraging lending**

    a) *Exposure*

    The lending may seem acceptable except that it is to an industry or to a country to which the bank does not want to lend because it is already lending too much.

    b) *Government policy*

    Government restrictions, for example in the form of directives from the Bank of England, may mean that a loan is not agreed (though currently such directives are not in use).

c) *Competition*

If other lenders are charging very low rates for similar lending the interest the customer expects to pay may be too low to justify lending. Here an outright refusal to lend may be less appropriate than advice to try elsewhere.

d) *Split banking arrangements*

If a customer is using a number of different banks to help to arrange finance, as many businesses do, the risk is greater because of the lack of knowledge about problems and the lack of control if things go wrong.

2. **Factors encouraging lending**

a) *Connections*

If the borrower has links through work or family with other important customers the bank will be more willing to lend.

b) *Income for the bank*

If the lending is of a type for which high income can be obtained at low risk this will encourage the bank to lend.

c) *Government policy*

In the past government has specifically encouraged banks to direct their lending towards certain industries, particularly export related business.

RE-SHAPING LENDING PROPOSITIONS

14.   One of the most important principles in lending is that the bank has an advisory role. The service which a bank sells to its borrowing customers is not simply a loan, but advice about borrowing.

In some cases the advice will be to abandon the project for which the loan was required. The banker may identify problems which the customer has not seen and should help the customer to avoid taking on financial commitments which will prove to be a burden. In other cases bankers will need to suggest that the customer looks elsewhere for the funds that are needed, sometimes specifically suggesting one of the bank's own subsidiaries.

If the bank is willing to lend it should do so in a way which it sees as being most suitable for the customer's needs. This may mean suggesting a different amount, a different period or a different source of repayment from that suggested by the customer. If such a re-shaping of the borrower's

proposition does seem necessary the lender should explain why a different approach is suitable. A final decision must be reached by agreement. There is a danger that banks may be seen as patronising if they assume that they know what is in the customer's best interests. On the other hand to fail to suggest ways of improving a lending proposition where improvements are needed is to provide an inadequate service.

SUMMARY

15. a)   Net interest income (the interest from lending minus the interest paid on deposits) is the main source of income for most banks. Lending therefore remains an essential activity even though fee income from other services is becoming more important than ever.

b)   All lending involves risk. High profit is usually associated with high risk but banks are experienced in assessing whether risks in lending are acceptable to them.

c)   Major banks adopt a range of approaches to reducing risk, of which one of the most important is to spread risk across a range of industries and countries.

d)   When banks look at the overall situation in deciding whether to lend they need to consider:-
   Purpose;
   Amount;
   Period;
   Expertise;
   Repayments;
   Security.

e)   Banks are concerned to avoid lending for undesirable purposes, but also need to balance their customers' requirements with their own concern to reduce risk.

f)   Although customers may ask to borrow more than they need banks must also be aware of the problems which arise if a customer borrows too little.

g)   The period of borrowing should be closely related to the purpose of the loan and the source of repayments.

h)   Judging the customer is often the most difficult aspect of a lending decision. The

key considerations are the customer's:-
Character;
Commitment;
Capability.

i) Repayments may come from a known regular income or from an expected lump sum. The bank will be less willing to lend if repayment is uncertain or expected at irregular intervals.

j) Security should only be considered if the other factors favour lending. Assets taken as security are available for use as a last resort if repayment is not made.

k) A number of factors may influence a bank's decision about lending. These include supporting factors like family connections. The level of interest which can be charged also needs to be considered.

STUDENT SELF-TESTING

Self Review Questions

1. What is net interest income? (2)

2. Give an example of a situation where insurance can be used to reduce risk in lending. (4)

3. What is a lending limit? (4)

4. What is country exposure? (4)

5. Give an example of a purpose for which a bank would not be willing to lend money. (7)

6. What problems may arise if a customer borrows too little money? (8)

7. When lending for business purposes what kind of skills apart from financial skills should a lender look for in a potential customer? (10)

8. What disadvantages are there in agreeing to a loan which is to be repaid in irregular instalments? (11)

9. Why is it dangerous to lend money expecting to obtain repayment by realising security? (12)

10. In what ways could competition discourage a bank from lending? (13)

Exercises (answers begin page 330)

A1. How can banks reduce the risk involved in lending? Do measures to reduce risk always lead to a corresponding reduction in profit?

A2. Customer A asks for an overdraft of £500 for 2 months. Customer B wants a similar overdraft for 6 months. They have the same incomes and financial commitments.
To what extent does a difference in the period of borrowing affect the level of risk? Can or should the bank compensate for any extra risk?

A3. What do you consider to be the personal qualities of an ideal borrower?

A4. 'The period for which a bank agrees to lend money must be related to the purpose of the borrowing and the source of repayments.' Justify this statement.

12. Personal Lending

INTRODUCTION

1. This chapter looks at credit scoring as an alternative to traditional loan assessment and then goes on to consider the different kinds of lending which are commonly provided for personal borrowers. These include:-

a) overdrafts;

b) personal loans;

c) revolving credit accounts;

d) budget accounts;

e) credit cards;

f) mortgages.

Attention is also given to the Consumer Credit Act 1974 and how it has affected lending to personal customers.

APPLYING GENERAL PRINCIPLES

2. In providing loans to personal customers the bank's aim is to make profit. To lend too incautiously will mean losses from bad debts. To be too cautious will mean missed opportunities for profitable business. The general principles described in Chapter 11 are intended to help lenders to distinguish between loans which are likely to be repaid and loans which may become bad debts.

The approach to lending using these general principles is one which takes lending staff a lot of time because the kind of questions raised are often open-ended, with no fixed right answers. A customer's ability to repay is a matter of judgement, not fact, and applying judgement requires careful thought. Such an approach is probably only justified when the circumstances are in some way unusual, a loan for a very large amount of money or a loan about which the customer is actively seeking advice.

Increasing competition has meant that the use of formal interviews to discuss personal lending has been considerably reduced. Major factors which have brought about this change include:-

a) the bank's need to save on staff time;

b) the customer's desire to obtain funds with the minimum delay;

c) the customer's preference for not discussing the purpose of the loan;

d) the availability of other lenders willing to lend without an interview;

e) the development of credit scoring.

General principles remain important but the cost of obtaining information about all the relevant aspects of an intending borrower can be very high. By standardising the questions to be asked the bank can achieve much cheaper coverage of most of the elements which an experienced lender would have discussed in an interview.

CREDIT SCORING

3. Credit scoring is a method of allocating scores to specific facts about a customer in order to decide whether to lend. It is based on the principle that statistics about past borrowers and bad debts can be used as a guide to the future.

Personal customers who want to borrow money are usually asked to fill in a loan application form. The questions cover a variety of facts, each of which in the past has been considered as a way of differentiating between good borrowers and bad borrowers For example house owners are generally considered more likely to repay loans than tenants, so customers stating in their loan application that they own their own home get a better score than tenants.

Different credit scoring systems work in slightly different ways. Commonly answers which are seen as favourable are awarded high points scores. If enough points are awarded in total when the loan application is assessed the loan will be agreed. (Conversely some systems use high scores as penalty points, giving them for unfavourable answers, and a low total is needed in order to obtain a loan.)

Calculating the score is a purely mechanical process which can be carried out by a junior member of staff. The process can also be automated, which means a decision can be obtained by keying the answers into the bank's computer system; this can be done by a member of the bank's staff, but it is also possible for customers using sophisticated automated teller machines to feed in information and get a decision directly.

JUDGEMENT IN CREDIT SCORING

4. The fact that credit scoring can be operated by junior staff or even by customers themselves helps to achieve the aim of reducing staff costs, but it does not necessarily make lending decisions more

objective. Judgement still has a key part to play. What is different is that the judgement is made at a higher level in the organisation in:-

a) setting up the credit-scoring system;

b) deciding which questions are the significant ones to ask;

c) allocating scores to different answers;

d) determining the level of score at which a loan is agreed.

There is also some limited scope for judgement at branch level over customers whose scores are near to the borderline. A manager may occasionally decide to lend to a customer who does not have a good enough score. This is a practice which head-office decision-makers tend to oppose because it means that when total bad debt figures are produced they will not reflect how the credit-scoring system has worked.

The lack of opportunity for staff within branches to use their own judgement in lending decisions does have two important disadvantages:-

a) jobs may become more routine and less motivating;

b) skills in judgement and decision-making are not developed (though they may be needed by staff who go on to make commercial loans, loans to business customers).

CREDIT SCORING ASSESSED

5. It is estimated that around three quarters of lending decisions are now based on some form of credit scoring. This suggests that there are considerable advantages in using such systems. However there are possible disadvantages, and these should not be ignored.

Advantages and disadvantages of credit scoring

Advantages for the Bank

1. There can be cost saving (through reduced staff time and use of lower paid staff);

2. Opportunities for the use of new technology are improved;

3. There is scope for improving market share (by easing score requirements);

4. Bad debts can be reduced (by demanding better scores);

5. A quicker service is offered to customers;

6. The bank increases its capacity to deal with more loans;

7. More time can be devoted to difficult, border-line decisions.

Advantages for the Customer

1. Decision-making is speeded up;

2. There is less requirement to explain why money is needed;

3. In theory credit scoring gives a more consistent approach (with all branches using the same system).

Disadvantages for the Bank

1. Initial costs of setting up the system are high;

2. There may be some de-motivation of staff;

3. Opportunities for staff to develop as experienced lenders may be reduced;

4. There is a greater possibility of customers cheating by giving false information.

Disadvantages for the Customer

1. The system may be inflexible (with little scope for poor scorers to obtain any credit);

2. There is a possibility of discrimination (for example against women because in general they are less likely to have a long record of permanent full-time employment than men);

3. The service may be very impersonal.

On balance cost advantages mean that credit scoring is here to stay but the Office of Fair Trading and the Equal Opportunities Commission have taken a close interest in how credit scoring is used to make sure that customers' interests are not harmed.

THE USES OF CREDIT SCORING

6. The preceding sections have concentrated on the use of credit scoring for making decisions about loans to personal customers. This is by far the most important area in which credit scoring is used. It is not only banks but finance houses and credit reference agencies which use the technique for that purpose.

In addition some banks use credit scoring for assessing potential new customers. When an account-opening form is completed the facts recorded can be scored in just the same way as facts on a loan application form. If there are too many unfavourable answers the account will not be opened. Midland Bank was the first major bank to adopt this policy, mainly because it introduced free banking ahead of its competitors and wanted to avoid taking all of their worst accounts. If a customer who has completed a credit-scored account-opening form later wants to borrow the decision can be based on the original score, though some banks prefer to use a completely separate credit-scoring system for loan decisions.

The techniques of credit scoring are also being developed for use in lending to business customers, but the problems are greater. With personal customers statistical analysis of key information can give fairly reliable guidance about future personal customers; with business customers there is less data to work on and more variables to consider. Credit scoring therefore remains predominantly a risk-assessment technique applied to personal lending.

PERSONAL BORROWING NEEDS

7.   Much personal borrowing is to acquire items which in a business context would be considered as fixed assets. The major item for many borrowers is a house. Other important categories are cars, 'white goods' (such as freezers and washing machines) and 'brown goods' (such as television and audio equipment). Furnishings and repairs and decoration are also significant areas for which borrowed funds are often required. All of these are categories for which banks have traditionally always been quite keen to lend.

More recently consumers have also taken loans for a number of purposes which banks would, in the past, have seen as less acceptable. These include investing in shares, particularly the privatisation issues. Customers can also borrow funds to repay previous borrowing. The extent to which this change has occurred is very hard to measure because so much lending is now agreed without knowing what it is for. Credit scoring has contributed to this lack of concern among bankers about how money is to be used, but new forms of lending have also made it impossible for banks to keep track of their customers' use of borrowed funds.

Banks see their customers as having a need for flexibility in arranging borrowing. This has led towards:-

a)   less use of formal interviews;

b)   quicker decision-making;

c)   wider choice of forms of borrowing;

d)   less restriction on borrowing purpose;

e)   longer periods of lending available;

f)   more 'revolving' facilities with no set repayment date.

These developments reduce the control which banks have over their lending but customers' needs are met more effectively. There are now a variety of forms of borrowing which personal customers can choose, and the following sections of the chapter look at the most important of these assessing their advantages and disadvantages to both bank and customer.

OVERDRAFTS

8.   As explained in Chapter 6 overdrafts are the most flexible of the traditional forms of lending which banks provide.

An overdraft is an agreement to allow a customer to write cheques on a current account when there is no longer any money in the account, up to an agreed sum, the overdraft limit, and for a set period of time. The cheques are debited to the account when they are presented so that the balance on the account becomes a negative balance, representing the amount of money owed to the bank by the customer. Such agreements for personal customers are nearly always informal, arranged by letter or telephone with no loan documentation to complete (and under the Consumer Credit Act 1974 there are special exemptions from the normal rules about completing written agreements).

In some cases customers make no arrangement to overdraw and it is when a cheque is presented for payment that the bank has to make a decision about whether to lend. Sometimes the bank will be aware of the customer's regular need to overdraw and will have set a limit without reference to the customer (often called a 'notional limit' and shown in the bank's records as an odd amount e.g. £99 rather than the £100 which a customer might have asked for). If there is no agreed limit or notional limit the bank may create a new overdraft by paying the cheque, or the cheque may be returned unpaid.

Overdrafts have generally been seen as a cheap form of borrowing because:-

a)   the interest rate is usually only a few percent above the bank's base rate;

b)   interest is only paid on the amount actually used;

c)   arrangement fees are usually fairly small.

Curiously the introduction of 'free banking' has made overdrafts far less attractive. 'Free banking' means that no bank charges are incurred if the account is kept in credit. By taking an overdraft a customer may find that bank charges are levied for the operation of the account for the whole of the charging period, possibly three months, and the cost of these charges on top of the overdraft interest may make the borrowing very expensive. In addition many banks have introduced tougher policies towards customers taking unarranged overdrafts, charging interest at far higher rates.

Advantages and disadvantages of overdrafts

Advantages for the Bank
1. Charging for overdrafts can be easily automated (with the limit and interest rate keyed into the computer).
2. The perecentage charged over base rate can be related to risk.
3. A minimum rate can be set in case base rates fall very low (e.g. 3% over base, minimum 6%).

Advantages for the Customer
1. Interest is paid only on money used.
2. No formal documentation needs to be completed.
3. Arrangements can be made easily, e.g. by telephone.

Disadvantages for the Bank
1. Control of borrowing is difficult because there are no regular repayments.
2. Credit scoring cannot usually be applied because there is no formal loan application.
3. There are few opportunities to sell other services.
4. Income may fall if interest rates go down.

Disadvantages for the Customer
1. Heavy bank charges may be incurred.
2. Accidental overdrafts may be charged at very high interest rates.
3. Arrangement fees are often charged (so there is a cost even if no borrowing is taken).
4. Interest rates may rise adding to the cost.
5. One year is the usual maximum period, though this can be extended.

PERSONAL LOANS

9. A personal loan is a structured loan available only for personal borrowing. All retail banks offer loans of this type. The customer borrows an agreed sum and pays it back in regular instalments including interest at a rate which is fixed at the time the loan is arranged. There are rarely any separate arrangement fees or other costs, though banks often quote repayment figures which include premiums for insurance to cover sickness or loss of job.

Personal loans are promoted in a variety of forms often directed at different market segments (an idea explained in Chapter 10). Common examples include car loans and home improvement loans, though some banks emphasise more explicitly that personal loans are for any purpose the customer chooses.

Advantages and disadvantages of personal loans

Advantages for the Bank
1. Quotations can be provided easily (from standard tables of repayments).
2. Decisions can be credit scored from application forms.
3. Procedures for opening the account and recording details on computer are straightforward.
4. Repayments can be automated (from the customer's current account).
5. Monitoring the loan is easy.
6. Opportunities arise for selling other services, in particular insurance.

Advantages for the Customer
1. Arrangements are easy.
2. Repayments are known in advance which helps with budgeting.
3. There are no cost increases even if other interest rates rise.

Disadvantages for the Bank
1. Rates charged are the same irrespective of the credit-worthiness of the customer.
2. Customers with personal loans cannot be charged more if there is a rise in interest rates.

Disadvantages for the Customer
1. If interest rates fall it may be difficult to switch to cheaper borrowing.

REVOLVING CREDIT ACCOUNTS

10.   A revolving credit account is an account which provides the opportunity for borrowing, but like a current account may be operated with a credit balance. Most of the major banks provide revolving credit accounts. The following list outlines the usual features which they have.

Features of revolving credit accounts

1.   The customer agrees to make regular monthly payments (usually from £10 to £50).

2.   A credit limit is agreed (normally 25 or 30 times the monthly payment).

3.   A cheque book is issued and cheques can be drawn up to the agreed limit.

4.   A cheque guarantee card and cash dispenser card may also be provided.

5.   Interest is charged on any borrowing at an agreed rate (and rate changes are usually announced in the press).

6.   Interest is paid on any credit balances (though at lower rates than the debit interest, and often below what is offered on deposit accounts).

7.   Insurance is usually offered to pay off the debt in the event of death, or to meet repayments if the borrower is ill or made redundant.

Many banks require the holder of a revolving credit account to have a current account as well, but others, for example the Co-operative Bank, promote their account as a second account to attract customers whose main account is with another bank.

Advantages and disadvantages of revolving credit accounts

Advantages for the Bank

1.   Credit scoring can be applied when a customer applies for the account.

2.   Payments into the account can be automated.

3.   Monitoring the account is easy.

4.   Customers who bank with competitors may be attracted.

5.   Other services such as insurance can be sold.

6.   Interest rates can be adjusted to encourage either more saving or more borrowing.

Advantages for the Customer

1.   Most services provided with a current account are available.

2.   Borrowing is very flexible.

3.   Interest is paid on credit balances.

Disadvantages for the Bank

1.   Opening the account is costly compared to loans because of the issue of cheque books and plastic cards.

2.   The account is unlikely to attract high levels of deposits.

3.   Borrowing will be on a small scale too so interest earned will not be very high in total.

Disadvantages for the Customer

1.   Borrowing may be quite expensive.

2.   If the credit limit is fully used repayment may take a very long time.

BUDGET ACCOUNTS

11.   Many banks do not offer a budget account as a separate product from their revolving credit account. The aim of a budget account is to help customers to spread the cost of known commitments such as major bills evenly through the year. A revolving credit account can be used for that purpose but budget accounts operate specifically on an annual basis.

Features of budget accounts

1.   An applicant for a budget account completes a form detailing expected bills for the coming year.

2.   The bank makes a charge for setting up and operating the budget account, usually a percentage of the total bills.

3.   No other charges are incurred and no interest is paid when the account becomes overdrawn.

4.   A cheque book is issued to the customer and cheques can be written for the purposes agreed in the original schedule of bills.

5.   Payments into the account are calculated as a twelfth of the total bills including the bank's charge.

6.   The monthly payments are made from the customer's current account.

7. At the end of the year a new account can be arranged starting with the closing balance on the old account if this is in credit.

This type of account is most useful for people who find it difficult to organise their finances. One of the main advantages of applying for the account is that the customer has to think carefully about what bills are likely in the year ahead.

Advantages and disadvantages of budget accounts

Advantages for the Bank

1. The fixed charge provides income even if no borrowing is taken.
2. Credit scoring can be applied when the account is opened.
3. Payments into the account are automated.
4. Monitoring is easy.

Advantages for the Customer

1. Use of the account helps with financial planning.
2. Money is available to pay bills when they fall due.
3. Spending on bills is separated from other spending, which means that surplus income is identified.

Disadvantages for the Bank

1. Opening the account may be expensive, particularly if it is only operated for one year.
2. No interest is earned even if the level of borrowing is high (though if borrowing is far above the amount foreseen in the schedule of bills the bank may make an additional charge).

Disadvantages for the Customer

1. There may be a minimum charge which is expensive if only a few bills are involved.
2. If the account is overdrawn at the end of the year the debt may have to be repaid straightaway.

CREDIT CARDS

12. Credit cards have now become one of the most familiar forms of borrowing. By the end of 1984 over seven million people had Access cards and about the same number had Barclaycards; in all nearly twenty five million credit cards of various kinds had been issued in the United Kingdom and the number is growing.

Credit cards are rather different from the forms of borrowing described in the preceding sections because:-

a) they represent a special method of making payment as well as a form of borrowing;

b) they are provided by centralised organisations rather than issued through the branch network;

c) they can be used internationally (see Chapter 19).

Features of credit cards

1. The customer is set a limit when the card is issued (and this can be increased by the credit card company).
2. Spending using the credit card is recorded by the credit card company which sends out a monthly bill.
3. Borrowing is interest-free if repayment is made in full by a date specified on the monthly statement.
4. A minimum repayment is required from the customer each month, usually a set percentage of the amount owed.
5. When interest is incurred the rate is determined by the credit card company (with changes announced in the press).
6. On some cards interest is paid on credit balances.

Advantages and disadvantages of credit cards

Advantages for the Bank

1. Interest rates are high (and the high rates do not seem to put off borrowers).
2. Other income is obtained in the form of commission from businesses which accept the credit card (at rates negotiated with the credit card company).
3. There are good opportunities for increasing automation and reducing paperwork.

Advantages for the Customer

1. Borrowing can be used to obtain cash from banks or cash dispensers as well as for buying goods and services.

2. As a method of payment credit cards are often quicker and easier than cheques.

3. Interest charges can be avoided by repaying in full when the statement is received.

Disadvantages for the Bank

1. There may be some loss of contact between branches and their customers.

2. High interest rates have attracted adverse publicity.

Disadvantages for the Customer

1. Not all shops accept all credit cards.

2. Charges are specially high for drawing cash because there is no free credit period.

Note that some cards like American Express or Diners Club are more strictly described as charge cards or courtesy cards because they are intended as a means of payment and do not provide extended credit. They are not therefore a form of personal borrowing.

Many store credit cards operate in the same way as bank credit cards, and they are often run by the credit card departments of banks. Advantages and disadvantages are therefore similar except that the stores have the important additional advantage that they can improve customer loyalty by providing their own in-house card. Other store credit cards are similar to the banks' revolving credit accounts except that payments are made by card rather than by cheque.

GOLD CARDS

13. One important development of the idea of the credit card is the gold card or premier card. As with other lending products different brand names apply but the basic idea has been adopted by all the leading banks and some of their non-bank competitors.

Features of gold cards

1. They are only offered to customers with a high income, usually £20,000 a year or more.

2. A joining fee is charged, which may be as much as £20.

3. An annual subscription is charged, up to £60.

4. The card can be used to guarantee cheques for amounts above the usual £50 limit, in some cases for as much as £350.

5. Card holders are entitled to an automatic overdraft, usually of about £10,000.

6. Card holders are normally provided with automatic personal accident insurance.

These cards are important as status symbols as well as providing a range of financial services. As a form of borrowing they have the disadvantages of other credit cards plus additional costs, though from a bank's point of view they have the special advantage of helping to identify a particular segment of the market, a segment which is likely to include people willing to spend a lot for good services.

MORTGAGES

14. In common usage banks, like building societies, are referred to as providers of mortgages for personal customers. Strictly speaking the service which a bank provides to a house buyer is a house purchase loan. The mortgage is the security which the borrower gives to the bank. (See Chapter 16 for a more detailed explanation.)

Features of house purchase loans

1. Borrowing is not usually for the full price of the property so the borrower needs to provide a deposit.

2. The maximum amount lent will usually depend on the borrower's income, for example three times annual salary.

3. Before lending the bank will obtain a valuation of the property to be purchased and will only lend a proportion of that amount.

4. Some banks impose a minimum of £15,000, originally introduced in order to ensure that loans were outside the terms of the Consumer Credit Act.

5. Loans are usually for 20 or 25 years, though shorter periods are possible.

6. The borrower makes regular monthly payments.

7. Repayments may be:-
    a) spread over the period of the loan (a *repayment mortgage*, in which case the monthly payments are partly interest and partly capital) *or*
    b) in a lump sum at the end of the period from the proceeds of an endowment insurance policy (an *endowment mortgage*, in

which case the monthly payments are entirely of interest).

8. The borrower will need to take out life insurance to cover the loan, usually a relatively cheap mortgage protection policy for a repayment mortgage or a more expensive endowment policy for an endowment mortgage.

9. Interest rates are usually more closely linked to building society rates than to the bank's own base rate.

10. Borrowers are able to obtain tax relief on the interest which they pay for a house purchase loan of up to £30,000, reducing the cost of borrowing considerably.

A less common alternative is a pension mortgage. This is repaid from an insurance policy, but is only available to people who have income which is not covered by a pension scheme. Pension mortgages offer extra tax benefits and recent legislation is expected to increase their popularity.

Advantages and disadvantages of house purchase loans

Advantages for the Bank

1. House owners are considered good customers.

2. The customer is tied to the bank for a long time.

3. The bank can determine its interest rate for mortgages separately from its base rate for other lending.

4. There are excellent opportunities for selling other services.

Advantages for the Customer

1. A house is a very good form of investment, particularly with tax relief on mortgage interest for borrowing up to £30,000.

2. Sometimes there is a choice of fixed or variable interest rates.

3. Special low interest offers are sometimes provided for new house owners.

Disadvantages for the Bank

1. Arranging a house purchase loan is complex and time-consuming.

2. Credit scoring applicants is not always possible.

Disadvantages for the Customer

1. Bank interest rates are sometimes higher than building society interest rates.

2. Building societies are more experienced mortgage lenders than banks.

In general the introduction of house purchase loans by banks has improved choice for customers. Previously building societies had by far the biggest share of the market. Now a variety of different institutions including new specialist mortgage lenders are competing.

THE CONSUMER CREDIT ACT

15. An important influence on much bank lending to personal customers has been the Consumer Credit Act 1974. The Consumer Credit Act applies to any individual; only corporate customers, companies, are excluded from the Act's definition of a consumer. Note that in this chapter the term personal customer has been used to refer to customers using bank accounts for personal rather than business purposes. The Consumer Credit Act definition is much wider, including sole traders and partnerships.

The main provisions of the Consumer Credit Act 1974 deal with:-

a) licensing;

b) seeking business;

c) different categories of lending agreements and the rules that apply to them.

Because of the complexity of the Act it was introduced in stages and only finally came into force in 1985. The Director General of Fair Trading is responsible for administering the Act, and booklets and leaflets dealing with many aspects of the legislation have been published by the Office of Fair Trading. At local level trading standards officers are responsible for looking into breaches of the law.

LICENSING UNDER THE CONSUMER CREDIT ACT

16. It is a criminal offence to arrange or provide credit without a licence issued under the Consumer Credit Act 1974. Licences cover various types of credit business such as credit reference agencies and debt counsellors as well as providers of credit. Shops which introduce customers to a finance house to help them to pay for major purchases also need to be licensed. Banks are licensed as providers of credit

but they also need to be aware that many of their business customers need licences. When opening a new account for a business checking that a Consumer Credit licence has been obtained is a sensible precaution.

Note that although banks answer status enquiries about their customers they have not registered as credit reference agencies on the grounds that they do not collect information in order to provide references.

SEEKING BUSINESS UNDER THE CONSUMER CREDIT ACT

17.   Part of the purpose of the Consumer Credit Act was to prevent people from being persuaded to enter into credit agreements which were not in their best interests. To achieve this aim the Act brought in restrictions in three main areas.

1.   **Advertising**
     If advertisements give any details of credit terms they must include the Annual Percentage Rate (A.P.R.). The purpose of this is to make it possible for consumers to compare different credit offers.

2.   **Canvassing**
     It is now illegal to go to people's homes uninvited or to approach them in the street to offer them credit. Where a credit agreement is signed at home, for example following a meeting with an invited salesman, the customer has the additional right to a cooling-off period during which the agreement can be cancelled.
     Approaches to customers at their trade premises are permitted, and overdrafts offered to existing customers are also treated as permissible.

3.   **Minors**
     It is illegal to send out any offer of credit to anyone under 18, a further, more specific limitation on canvassing.

TYPES OF AGREEMENT UNDER THE CONSUMER CREDIT ACT

18.   The Consumer Credit Act distinguishes between about 15 different types of agreement which banks can enter into with customers. In practice most banks do not have as many as 15 different agreement forms, but all the banks have found that the

range of documentation needed is far wider than before the Act came into force.

The most important category is the regulated agreement, but this is sub-divided. Differences arise according to whether the signing takes place at the bank, whether security is given and whether land forms part of the security.

Regulated Agreements

An agreement to provide credit counts as a regulated agreement if:-

a)   the borrower is an individual or group of individuals (i.e. not a company);

b)   the amount is below £15,000;

c)   the loan is not used to finance international trade;

d)   the lending is not mortgage lending by a specialist lender.

This means that most bank loans and overdrafts are regulated agreements, but overdrafts are a special case because they are exempted from the rule that regulated agreements have to take the form of a standard signed document. Loan agreements do have to be in a prescribed form.

Cancellable Agreements

A cancellable agreement is a regulated agreement which is not signed by all the customers on the bank's premises. It gives the customer a cooling-off period in which to cancel the agreement, though with bank lending this is very unlikely to occur and most banks lend without waiting for the cancellation period to expire.

OTHER REQUIREMENTS OF THE ACT

19.   The Consumer Credit Act imposes precise requirements on lenders after a credit agreement has been entered into as well as at the time of making the agreement.

1.   **Information**
     Although banks are not legally obliged to provide statements for loan accounts the Act does require statements to be sent to customers with overdrafts. Where the account is a joint account copies must be sent to each account holder unless they have signed a 'dispensing notice' agreeing to share a statement.

If a customer asks for information about the terms or amount of any outstanding borrowing this must be provided (though banks would expect to do this anyway). In addition if someone else has given security for the customer's debt that person is entitled to be told how much is owed.

2. **Liability for goods and services**
   Where a customer has used credit to buy goods or services and the supplier is in breach of contract, for example because the goods are faulty, the customer can usually claim against the provider of credit. From a bank's point of view this is most likely to occur with credit card purchases.

3. **Default**
   If a borrower fails to repay under a regulated agreement the lender must issue a 'default notice' in a prescribed wording before taking any legal proceedings.

These requirements are intended to give extra protection to borrowers. In general banks have found that they add to the administrative costs of providing finance and therefore harm rather than help bank customers.

SUMMARY

20. a) The use of formal interviews to help make decisions about lending to personal customers has been reduced because of a number of factors, in particular the need to save on expensive staff time.

b) Credit scoring, allocating scores to facts about a customer in order to rate their overall credit-worthiness, has become an important way of making lending decisions. Credit scoring systems are based on the judgements of the people setting up the system rather than on the judgements of branch staff, and this helps to standardise and speed up the decision-making process.

c) There are disadvantages in using credit scoring including the cost of establishing a system and the reduced opportunities for motivating staff and developing their skill as lenders.

d) Credit scoring can be used for making decisions about whether to open accounts for customers and, to a limited extent, for assessing business lending.

e) Because of the changing banking environment new lending services have been created but traditional forms of lending like the overdraft are still offered to customers.

f) Overdrafts provide flexible variable rate borrowing, but can prove expensive if taking an overdraft also means incurring bank charges.

g) Personal loans are structured, fixed rate loans which are ideal for budgeted expenditure, but may tie the borrower to high rates if interest rates in general come down.

h) Revolving credit accounts are based on regular payments into an account from which borrowing can be taken up to an agreed limit, usually a multiple of the monthly payment. The account can be used for saving too, because interest is paid on credit balances.

i) Budget accounts are intended to help customers with their financial planning. Regular payments are made into an account in order to cover the expected bills for the year, and usually a service charge is made instead of charging interest for the periods when the account becomes overdrawn.

j) Credit cards provide a method of payment as well as a form of borrowing. The interest charges are quite high if borrowing is taken, but a period of interest-free credit is available.

k) Gold cards are status symbol credit cards for high earners. They offer financial services including automatic entitlement to an overdraft in addition to the benefits of ordinary credit cards.

l) Mortgages, or more accurately house purchase loans, are offered by banks in competition with building societies. The two major alternatives are repayment mortgages and endowment mortgages.

m) The Consumer Credit Act 1974, which finally came fully into force in 1985, is a major influence on lending to personal customers. Its main provisions deal with licensing, seeking credit business and different categories of lending agreements.

n) One of the most important concepts in the Consumer Credit Act is the regulated agreement. Agreements to provide credit to private individuals of amounts up to £15,000 are normally regulated agreements, which give the borrower or borrowers rights which are not available to borrowers in unregulated agreements.

o) When a regulated agreement is in force lenders have certain obligations to provide information and to follow clearly laid down procedures in the event of a default. The lender may also incur liability for goods or services acquired on credit.

STUDENT SELF-TESTING

Self Review Questions

1. State three of the factors which have reduced the use of formal interviews in making decisions about personal lending. (2)

2. What are the main disadvantages for customers of using credit scoring? (5)

3. For what purposes is credit scoring used apart from deciding about credit for personal customers? (6)

4. What are the main disadvantages for customers of using an overdraft? (8)

5. What advantages are there for customers in using a personal loan? (9)

6. What are the main differences between a revolving credit account and a budget account? (10,11)

7. What makes a gold card different from an ordinary credit card? (12,13)

8. What are the main differences between a repayment mortgage and an endowment mortgage? (14)

9. What restrictions on canvassing are imposed under the Consumer Credit Act? (17)

10. In what circumstances is a loan a regulated agreement under the Consumer Credit Act? (18)

Exercises (answers begin page 332)

A1. Compare and contrast the advantages and disadvantages of overdrafts, revolving credit accounts and budget accounts.

A2. 'With credit scoring we can decide on the level of bad debt we want, which does not mean the lowest possible level.' Comment on this statement.

A3. Personal loans and overdrafts remain the most important forms of lending provided by branch bankers for individual customers. In what circumstances would each be most appropriate?

A4. How would you establish whether an agreement to lend money was a regulated agreement under the Consumer Credit Act, and why would this matter?

13. Commercial Lending

INTRODUCTION

1. This chapter considers how personal lending and commercial lending differ and looks at the extra difficulties of assessing risk in commercial lending. There is an introduction to some of the main reasons for businesses to borrow. These include:-

a) trading finance;

b) purchases of fixed assets;

c) acquisitions or takeovers of businesses.

The chapter ends with a review of some of the legal constraints on lending followed by an assessment of the main forms of business borrowing, overdrafts and loans.

PERSONAL LENDING AND COMMERCIAL LENDING

2. Commercial lending, lending to a business, is often very different from lending to a personal customer. The main reason for this difference is that the risk of not being repaid has an added dimension. In both cases there is risk concerning the character, commitment and capability of the person borrowing the money, but in commercial lending there are additional risks associated with the business. A highly capable person may do badly in business because of factors which no-one could reasonably have expected. From the bank's point of view such unexpected problems may result in a bad debt.

The risk connected with lending to business depends on an enormous number of factors. For any particular type of business the risk of failure is affected by:-

a) the state of the economy;

b) trends in demand for the product or service provided;

c) competition with other suppliers;

d) competition from substitute products or services;

e) technological changes.

In addition for an individual business the risk of failure will be increased if:-

a) financial resources are too limited;

b) suitable labour and equipment are not available;

c) raw materials or other supplies are difficult to obtain;

d) technical skills are lacking;

e) marketing skills are lacking;

f) managerial skills are lacking.

In personal lending a banker only needs to assess the borrower, and can therefore use the technique of credit scoring to sum up what the borrower is like. In commercial lending the lender needs to take a view about the kind of business the customer is involved in and needs to judge whether the customer has enough of all the necessary skills and resources to make the risk acceptably low. Although the relative risks of different types of business can be assessed, and perhaps allocated a score on the basis of past lending statistics, scoring skills and resources is much more of a problem. Formal interviews therefore remain an important method of making commercial lending decisions.

Personal lending also tends to differ from commercial lending because commercial lending is often:-

a) for larger amounts of money;

b) for longer periods;

c) intended for a specific purpose agreed between bank and customer.

There are exceptions to this general pattern. For example in personal lending house purchase loans meet all three of these criteria more commonly associated with business lending, while a sole trader may take a short-term overdraft of an amount far smaller than many personal loans. Nevertheless the largest loans which banks provide are certainly those for commercial purposes.

PURPOSES OF BORROWING

3. The uses to which a business can put borrowed money are even more varied than the uses personal customers find for their loans. Grouping these business purposes into broad categories can help to explain how banks look at business lending. Such categories are arbitrary because businesses themselves do not have to categorise their decisions about spending or borrowing in this way, but they may be relevant to banks because lenders do not ask exactly the same questions in all circumstances.

In the following sections of this chapter each of the categories listed below is described in more detail.

Later chapters include case study examples which illustrate some of these kinds of situation.

1. Borrowing to provide additional finance for normal trading.
2. Borrowing to purchase fixed assets to use in the business.
3. Borrowing to acquire or takeover a business.

WORKING CAPITAL

4. Working capital is the capital used in the day-to-day running of a business. It finances the assets which are continuously changing as the business operates, in particular the stock and debtors.

Working capital is calculated as current assets minus current liabilities. In some cases, particularly for businesses which have far more creditors than debtors, the calculation can show a negative figure (as in the example of A Grocer Ltd shown below). This means that the owners of the business are not providing working capital but are relying on the creditors to finance day-to-day transactions. Where, as is more common, the figure is positive (as in the example of A Trader Ltd) this indicates that the owners are providing working capital in addition to the capital needed to finance the fixed assets.

Example		
	A Grocer Ltd	A Trader Ltd
	£	£
Capital	10000	10000
Fixed Assets	12000	3000
Stock	4000	4000
Debtors	1000	3000
Cash	2000	2000
Creditors	(9000)	(2000)
	10000	10000
Working Capital	(2000)	7000

The example of a grocer is used to illustrate a business with negative working capital because few of a grocer's sales will be on credit (so there will be a low figure for debtors) but stocks will often be bought on credit from wholesalers. For most businesses it would be considered highly risky to be in this position because if the creditors demand cash the business will face liquidation. Even for the grocer here the position looks bad because stocks are far lower than the amount owed to creditors, which would not normally be the case.

TRADING FINANCE

5. It is important to recognise that although bankers and their customers do speak of lending for working capital this is not strictly accurate. If a bank provides money it is rather like the creditors providing money. If in the above example of the grocer the word 'Bank' replaced the word 'Creditors', this would show the bank financing the day-to-day running of the business. The more the bank lends, the lower the figure for working capital. A more accurate term for such lending might be TRADING FINANCE since the loan acts as a substitute for working capital rather than providing working capital.

If a bank is asked to provide trading finance this in itself does not explain why borrowing is needed. The bank should ask for further information about the purpose of the borrowing. Two of the most likely reasons for needing trading finance are:-

a) expansion of the business;

b) a temporary shortage of cash.

These are considered in the next two sections.

EXPANSION

6. If a business grows it is likely to need more capital. One of the most common ways to acquire this capital is to make profit and keep the profit in the business, but if expansion is rapid the capital may be needed before enough profit has been made. Even if all the fixed assets of the business, like equipment and premises, are adequate to cope with a higher level of sales turnover more working capital will be needed (except for those fortunate businesses which are financed by creditors). Roughly speaking if sales go up by 50% a business will have 50% more debts outstanding (unless the increase in turnover comes from extra selling for cash). Similarly more supplies will need to be bought so creditors will go up by about 50% and holdings of stock will need to be roughly 50% higher.

In our example of A Trader Ltd this would give the following figures before and after a 50% increase in turnover.

	Before £	After £
Capital	10000	10000
Fixed Assets	3000	3000
Stock	4000	6000
Debtors	3000	4500
Cash	2000	(500)
Creditors	(2000)	(3000)
	10000	10000

The capital and fixed assets remain unchanged. In order to finance the extra stock and debtors more cash is needed amounting to £3,500. £1,000 of this comes from the increased creditors and £2,000 comes from the cash which the business already had but this leaves a shortfall of £500. The balance sheet shows this as a negative figure; the implication is that the company would have to borrow £500. Of course, in practice a 50% increase in turnover would not happen overnight. Profit made as sales increased would reduce the need to borrow. The more quickly expansion takes place the more likely there is to be a need for borrowing.

A business which expands rapidly without having enough of its own capital to finance the expansion is described as OVER-TRADING. If a bank provides finance but does not make sure that expansion is slowed down the business's borrowing needs may get bigger and bigger until it is forced into liquidation.

TEMPORARY CASH SHORTAGES

7.   Some business borrowing for trading purposes is intended to even out irregularities in the flow of money through the business. One of the major payments for many businesses is an annual payment of tax; some businesses will borrow to pay this and repay the borrowing from income over the next few months. Many businesses operate on a seasonal cycle; toy shops, for example, stock up as fully as possible before Christmas and may pay for the stock with a 'stocking loan' from a bank, relying on the income from Christmas sales to repay the debt.

Bankers lending to businesses to meet temporary cash shortages of this kind need to be cautious about the reasons for the cash shortage. If a business is making losses this will appear as a reduction of working capital well before formal audited profit and loss accounts are produced. To lend when a cash shortage is permanent rather than temporary creates a problem for the bank without really solving the problem for the customer.

PURCHASING FIXED ASSETS

8.   When a business needs to acquire substantial assets like machinery or premises the profit which those assets will help to earn will not be made straightaway. In some cases it may take many years of trading to get back the cost of a major purchase. Businesses which have not already built up surplus cash therefore turn to outside sources of finance when they want to buy fixed assets.

As a general principle banks are willing to lend money for the purchase of fixed assets provided:-

a)   the borrower can show fairly convincingly that the assets to be acquired will benefit the business;

b)   the borrower is contributing a reasonable proportion of the purchase price;

c)   the period of the loan is no greater than the working life of the asset.

Demonstrating that the asset to be purchased will be of value to the business means having a clear plan of how the business is expected to develop. Ideally this will include costings for the new asset and projections of expected cost savings or additional sales income which will arise as a result of the purchase.

The amount which a bank will expect the borrower to provide depends on the circumstances. In some cases the borrower will be required to contribute as much as 50% of the purchase price but more commonly the bank will lend more. There is no simple rule to determine the level of lending to which the bank can agree. In general the more the borrower is contributing the more willing the bank will be to lend, but the borrower's contribution may take two forms:-

a)   cash to be spent on the fixed assets *or*

b)   funds already invested in the business as a whole.

In the examples below extremes of these two cases are shown. A borrower wants to buy new machinery costing £5,000. In the first case half of this will come from the company's own cash. In the second case the high level of capital means that the bank will lend the full £5,000.

	A Ltd £	B Ltd £
Capital	7000	17000
Fixed Assets	1000	9000
Stock	2500	6000
Debtors	1500	4500
Cash	3000	500
Creditors	(1000)	(3000)
	7000	17000

In practice decisions would rarely be based on consideration of just one balance sheet, but if information about the management and profitability of each of these companies was favourable lending for new machinery would not present any problem.

PROBLEMS OVER FIXED ASSETS

9.   There are a number of difficulties for banks when lending money to purchase fixed assets, as in any other kind of lending. The following list covers some of the main aspects to which attention needs to be given.

1. **Unsuitable assets**
    If the business finds that the assets are not what was really needed (for example premises in the wrong place or machines which are obsolete) far less income may be produced than was originally expected. This would lead to difficulty in making repayments. The lender therefore needs to consider carefully the assets to be acquired to see how well they fit in with the needs of the business.

2. **Assets with a short life**
    When banks agree to lend for fixed assets they usually expect the period of the loan to be shorter than the useful working life of the assets bought. If this turns out not to be the case the customer will want to borrow money for replacement assets while still paying off the previous loan.

3. **Weakening of financial structure**
    Amounts borrowed for fixed assets may be quite large, and when a business borrows a sum of money which is large in relation to the total size of the business this makes the business weaker, in the sense that there is an increased risk of the business going

into liquidation if circumstances are unfavourable. Before taking on the borrowing the business did not have the obligation to pay interest and make repayments of capital; after borrowing these payments may use up all the available profit or more, eating into the capital of the business.

4. **Changes in trading**
    Very often the purpose of investing in new fixed assets is to expand the business. This means that more selling takes place, which in turn implies that more working capital will be needed (as explained earlier in the chapter). Failure to allow for this in planning purchases of fixed assets is a common error, and a very dangerous one.

The problems which may arise for banks when they lend for the purchase of fixed assets are often the result of inadequate analysis of the implications for the business of taking on more debt. Part of the role of the banker is to provide good advice for customers, for example about the need to allow for extra working capital when considering an expansion of the business.

TAKEOVERS AND ACQUISITIONS

10.   A decision to buy a whole business needs even more careful consideration than a purchase of fixed assets. Banks are often approached by customers for finance to help in acquiring a business, sometimes for a business in which the buyer is already working (as for example in a management buyout) but more often where the buyer is an outsider and does not have detailed knowledge of how the business has been run in the past. Such requests may have to be refused because the purchase would not be in the customer's best interests. Taking over an unprofitable business or an unfamiliar business can turn out to be a very expensive mistake.

Some of the problems which arise from buying a business are the same as those associated with acquiring fixed assets. A major additional problem is the lack of management expertise needed to cope with the new business because the buyer has:-

a)   only run smaller businesses before;

b)   never worked in the industry concerned;

c)   not had full responsibility for all decision-making before;

d)   had little previous business experience at all.

For these and many other possible reasons a new owner of a business may find that he or she lacks some of the skills needed. Only if these missing skills can be quickly developed or bought in is it wise for the customer to go ahead with the proposed acquisition.

When a purchase of a business does take place it can take the form of:-

a) purchase of all the assets of the business *or*

b) purchase of a controlling shareholding (over 50% of the shares) where the business to be bought is a company.

In the first case care must be taken to establish clearly what the various assets are, and how the liabilities of the business are to be dealt with. For a small business run by a sole trader the liabilities are personal and cannot be transferred easily just by selling the business (because the creditors will not be happy to be owed money by a newcomer who may be a complete stranger), so it is usually sensible for all liabilities to be paid off when the purchase takes place. Valuation of stock may also be a difficulty because any agreement in advance about the price for the stock may be disadvantageous to the buyer; until the business changes hands the original owner can continue to sell stock, often disposing of quite a lot of it by holding a 'closing down' sale.

Where a company is purchased some of these difficulties are avoided because the company has its own legal identity and can continue to owe money and be owed money even if the owners change. There is just as much difficulty in determining the price at which the business should be sold. Even for takeovers of companies quoted on the stock market this is a matter of dispute and disagreement (though such large-scale mergers and takeovers are beyond the scope of this text).

PRICING OF ACQUISITIONS

11.   Even if a customer can demonstrate to the bank that buying a particular business makes sense, judging how much to pay is a very difficult matter. Simply estimating values for each of the assets is not usually considered an adequate approach because:-

a) accurate valuations are impossible;

b) the business as a going concern should be worth more than its assets.

Approximate valuations of the assets will usually be produced, based either on the seller's most recent balance sheet or on the buyer's estimates, but because the business is operating and making (or capable of making) profits the price for the business will usually be higher than for a collection of similar assets not actively being used. The difference between the book value of the assets (the asset values shown on paper, as in the books of the business) and the total price paid for the business is referred to as *goodwill*.

The problem of pricing an acquisition can therefore be seen as a question of valuing goodwill. The term goodwill arises from the view that an established business can expect its regular customers to keep coming back, because they feel goodwill towards the business. How valuable this is may be judged by the profit the business is making. No clear rules are possible but to pay the equivalent of three, four or five years' net profit as goodwill might be considered reasonable for the type of business which would expect to have repeat orders or a regular clientele.

Conversely if a business is making losses it might be unwise to pay anything for goodwill, and in some cases businesses can be bought at a discount, a price below the book value of the separate assets. In such cases the buyer can make a return on the investment most quickly and easily by selling off the assets. This is known as asset-stripping (though very often asset-stripping takes more complicated forms).

Banks are more willing to provide funds for the development of profitable businesses than to assist in the closing down of unprofitable ones. One of the factors which banks consider when lending for the purchase of businesses is what prospects the business has of making profit in the future.

Note that because payments for goodwill are a form of premium charged when a business is sold, if the word 'goodwill' appears in a set of accounts it means that the business has been bought at some time in the past. Once the sale has taken place the goodwill is no longer of any value and the entry in the accounts should be written down in the same way that fixed assets are depreciated, deducting a proportion of the amount from profit each year until it has all gone.

LEGAL CONSTRAINTS ON LENDING

12.   Whatever the purpose of commercial borrowing banks need to consider possible legal problems.

For sole traders and partnerships this means complying with the requirements of the Consumer Credit Act (described in more detail in Chapter 12). As with any other personal borrowing loans below £15,000 (except those for the finance of international trade) are regulated agreements under the Act.

For corporate customers the legal constraints are rather different. The bank will have a copy of the company's memorandum and articles of association and will therefore have access to information about the company's objects clause and the powers of the directors. Care must be taken to ensure that borrowing is not outside the powers of the directors or the company. The following case study illustrates some of the problems which can arise if banks do not take sufficient care.

CASE STUDY: PYROGEN PRODUCTS

13. Read the following case study and attempt the questions which follow before going on to look at the suggested solution.

Pyrogen Products Ltd

Last year your manager granted a loan of £25,000 to Pyrogen Products Ltd to be repaid as a lump sum on the 14th of last month. The money was to finance research by the company, a manufacturer of fire extinguishers, into solar heating panels. At the repayment date the company's current account stood at £1,768 and there was a further £24,000 in a deposit account. Because no instructions had been received about repayment the manager wrote to the company asking for authorisation to transfer funds to clear the loan. The managing director who had previously been on very good terms with your manager wrote a very aggressive letter of reply, refusing to pay on the grounds that:-

a) *the finance director who had negotiated the loan had exceeded his authority;*

b) *the purpose of the loan was outside the terms of the company's objects clause.*

You are able to confirm from the bank's copy of the company's memorandum and articles that there is no specific reference to solar heating in the company's objects clause. In addition you read the articles and come across the following clause.

Extract from the Articles of Association

'. . . any borrowing in excess of £5,000 by or on behalf of the company requires the formal approval of the board of directors.'

Your manager comments that the bank may have some protection from the European Communities Act or from the rule in Turquand's case.

Extract from the European Communities Act 1972 section 9(i)

'In favour of a person dealing with a company in good faith, any transaction decided on by the directors shall be deemed to be one which it is within the capacity of the company to enter into . . . and a party to a transaction so decided on shall not be bound to enquire as to the capacity of the company so to enter into it . . . and shall be presumed to have acted in good faith unless the contrary is proved.'

Royal British Bank v. Turquand (1856)

Facts

A company of which Turquand was the manager borrowed money but did not obtain the approval of the shareholders in general meeting as the company's internal rules required. The bank sued to get its money back.

Judgement

Where the company's internal rules make provision for action such as borrowing an outsider (in this case the bank) can assume that any necessary formalities have been correctly carried out.

Required:

Your answers to the following questions.

1. What does the managing director mean by saying that the borrowing was outside the terms of the company's objects clause?

2. What is the significance of the fact that the finance director had not been authorised to negotiate the loan?

3. Does the European Communities Act help the bank here?

4. Can the rule in Turquand's case help the bank here?

5. How could the problem have been avoided?

6. In what way has the relationship between the bank and the company been changed by the conflict over this loan?

SUGGESTED SOLUTION: PYROGEN PRODUCTS

14.   Do not read this section until you have made your own attempt to answer the questions.

1.   What does the managing director mean by saying that the borrowing was outside the terms of the company's objects clause?

What the managing director means is that the borrowing was 'ultra vires' the company, outside the powers of the company, and therefore an unenforceable contract. If the claim is correct the bank will not be able to get its money back from the company, though it may have a claim against the finance director if he can be contacted.

Whether a court of law would agree that the purpose of the borrowing was 'ultra vires' the company is not certain. Objects clauses are usually worded very broadly and for a company already involved in manufacturing the clause may well include terms general enough to allow for research into other fields. The doubt about this might be resolved by referring to specialist lawyers or the matter might need to be taken to court.

2.   What is the significance of the fact that the finance director had not been authorised to negotiate the loan?

If the finance director was not authorised to negotiate the loan the likelihood of the bank making a successful claim against the company is further reduced. The fact that the director appears to have acted without the knowledge or approval of his colleagues means that the borrowing may have been arranged fraudulently, in which case the bank's position will be very weak; the director concerned may have disappeared with the money.

3.   Does the European Communities Act help the bank here?

Although, as the extract from the European Communities Act shows, as a general principle outsiders can enter into contracts with companies without knowledge of their powers, banks are in a weaker position because they do normally have a copy of the memorandum and articles of associa-

tion. It therefore seems unlikely that they could claim not to know what powers a company has, though case law has not made this clear. Only a change in the law on the 'ultra vires' rule will give banks certain protection.

4.   Can the rule in Turquand's case help the bank here?

In a sense the rule in Turquand's case does help the bank because it deals with the fact that the finance director did not have formal approval from the board. Under the rule in Turquand's case the bank is entitled to assume that this approval had been obtained. The bank cannot suffer loss merely because the internal requirements of the company had not been carried out. However the main risk to the bank arises from the fact that the borrowing was 'ultra vires' the company, not from the failure to obtain board approval. Ultimately Turquand's case may therefore be irrelevant.

5.   How could the problem have been avoided?

The problem could have been avoided by better communication. When the borrowing was arranged this should not have been done simply on the basis of discussion with one member of the company's board. Formal confirmation should have been obtained in writing from the company.

In addition the company's memorandum and articles should have been consulted, particularly as this borrowing was known to be for a purpose rather different from the company's previous field of activity.

Note that it would not have been acceptable to transfer the funds from the company's deposit account without the company's approval until the company had been informed that it had defaulted on the loan. The bank might have become liable for any losses incurred if it had carried out such a transfer and then refused to make other payments.

6.   In what way has the relationship between the bank and the company been changed by the conflict over this loan?

A matter of great concern to the bank here is that a previously good bank-customer relationship is now threatened. The managing director has adopted an aggressive tone which suggests that future dealings will be difficult. Selling the bank's services will now be a problem and getting back the money owed may require legal action which will certainly make matters worse.

The apparent problem in this case study is the managing director's refusal to pay back the money borrowed. Underlying this are problems over the banker-customer relationship and two separate legal problems, the question of whether the borrowing is 'ultra vires' the company and the question of whether the finance director had the power to arrange the loan. Of the legal problems the first is the more serious, but the company does not necessarily have a very strong case. The current rules on 'ultra vires' actions by companies are expected to be changed by the end of the 1980s, and problems of this type will no longer arise.

Behind the two legal problems is the more basic problem of why the manager lent money without checking on the information that he needed. This case illustrates the risks which lenders can run if they do not appreciate the difficulties in lending to companies.

BASIC FORMS OF LENDING

15.   Although the purposes for which businesses borrow may differ from the purposes for which individuals borrow the main forms of lending which banks offer to business customers are similar to those offered to personal customers. The remaining sections of this chapter deal with these basic forms of lending:-

a)   overdrafts;

b)   loans (at fixed interest rates or at variable interest rates).

Just as there are more specialised forms of lending which have been developed to meet the needs of personal customers, so there are specialist forms of finance for business. These are considered in the next chapter.

OVERDRAFTS

16.   Business overdrafts, like personal overdrafts, enable the customer to write cheques on a current account while the balance falls below nil. A limit is agreed for a fixed period, though for businesses

the time scale may be longer than for individuals; overdraft limits are often renewed every year making the borrowing agreement more or less permanent. This is only a cause for concern if the balance never becomes positive. A large overdraft which regularly swings back into credit is considered healthy from a bank's point of view because it shows that the business is making enough money to keep repaying the money used.

Banks can usually get a fairly clear view of how an overdraft is operating by looking at computer records of maximum and minimum figures, for example on a monthly basis. The following examples illustrate the difference between a healthy swing and a potential problem.

Example: D Ltd		
Agreed limit − £15,000 for six months		
	Maximum	Minimum
5 months ago	14205	1071
4 months ago	9788	202
3 months ago	9941	527 CR
2 months ago	11006	1104
1 month ago	9083	1066 CR
This month	8186	2113 CR

Example: E Ltd		
Agreed limit − £15,000 for six months		
	Maximum	Minimum
5 months ago	14111	2003
4 months ago	11016	2481
3 months ago	9902	2779
2 months ago	12114	3116
1 month ago	14909	2030
This month	15865	4005

D Ltd has a healthy swing from overdraft into credit. Points to note are:-

a)   the overdraft limit is not exceeded;

b)   the maximum figures are lower in more recent months;

c)   credit balances are higher in more recent months.

There does seem to be a need for the overdraft to be continued, but probably at a lower level than the £15,000 previously agreed.

For E Ltd the profile is rather less acceptable to the bank because:-

a) the overdraft limit has been exceeded;

b) the maximum figures are higher in more recent months;

c) the account never swings into credit;

d) the lowest level of borrowing is over £2,000.

The figure of £2,000 identified as permanent borrowing by E Ltd is often referred to as 'hard core' borrowing because even when the company pays in money this part of the borrowing is not repaid. Generally banks prefer to see this kind of long-term lending as a loan (with at least some proposals for gradual repayment) rather than as part of an overdraft.

LOANS

17.   If personal customers want to borrow money, except in the very short term, they will usually be offered a personal loan, a structured loan at a fixed rate of interest. Banks offer similar loans to businesses, often referring to them as business loans. They have the same advantages and disadvantages as personal loans (see Chapter 12), in particular helping a business to budget fairly accurately.

Because business needs are often different from the needs of personal customers banks also provide alternative forms of loan.

1. **Loan accounts**
   The normal form of loan account which banks provide for businesses (and occasionally for personal customers) is an account on which interest is charged at a rate linked to the bank's base rate, a variable rate. The borrower pays interest on the whole amount of the loan, which is created by crediting the customer's current account. Repayments are often made monthly but there is no requirement to stick to a rigid pattern of equal payments as there is with a structured loan.

2. **Other variable rate loans**
   Although the bank's base rate is an important rate for determining other interest rates it does not usually affect the largest loans. For major business lending interest is often charged at a rate linked to rates in the money markets, using LIBOR (London InterBank Offered Rate) as a guideline. The basic principle is the same but rates move more often in the money markets, so this kind of borrowing suits customers if interest rates are falling because the benefit of lower rates is obtained more quickly.

3. **Loans with fixed or variable rates**
   Because of the risk to a business of becoming locked into a form of interest rate which turns out to be unsuitable some banks provide long-term loans which allow for changes in interest rate structure at intervals. For example a loan over twenty five years might include the right for the borrower to decide every five years about whether to borrow at a fixed rate or a variable rate. Each decision would determine the cost of the borrowing over the next five years but not for the whole period of the loan.

Note that it is also possible for borrowers who have long-term loans to change from fixed interest to variable interest (or vice versa) by means of an interest rate swap (described in Chapter 23). The aim of such swaps is to enable borrowers to get the kind of interest rate structure they want more cheaply than by borrowing directly in the preferred form.

SUMMARY

18. a) Commercial lending has to allow for risks associated with each particular type of business and for risks caused by weaknesses of the actual business such as a lack of some of the skills or resources needed for success.

b) Businesses borrow for a number of reasons. Three important broad categories are:-
1. for working capital;
2. to purchase fixed assets;
3. to acquire a new business.

c) Finance for working capital, more accurately referred to as trading finance, is needed most when a business expands, increasing its turnover so that more debtors and stocks need to be financed. There may also be a need for trading finance to cover seasonal or other temporary shortages of cash.

d) Loans are often made for purchases of fixed assets provided the borrower contributes part of the purchase price and the period of the loan is no longer than the working life of the asset.

e) Problems may arise when lending for the purchase of fixed assets. One of the most important for lenders to be aware of is the likely need for extra working capital if assets are acquired in order to increase turnover.

f) When a new business is bought the buyer needs to have all the skills to operate it. The bank may turn down a credit-worthy customer if the business problems do not seem to be ones the customer can deal with.

g) Acquisitions of existing businesses may be by purchase of the business assets. In the case of companies an alternative is to purchase a controlling shareholding.

h) Pricing is one of the difficulties in acquiring a business. A price needs to be put on the goodwill, the benefit a buyer obtains from purchasing a going concern rather than just the separate assets which the business uses.

i) Commercial lending to sole traders and partnerships comes under the Consumer Credit Act, but loans to companies face different legal constraints. In particular there are dangers in lending without being fully aware of the significance of the Memorandum and Articles of Association (though this 'ultra vires' rule is likely to be ended).

j) Companies may borrow by overdraft, and this often provides a long-term form of finance because the overdraft limit is renewed each year. Care needs to be taken to avoid a build-up of hard-core borrowing.

k) Loans for businesses take a variety of forms including structured, fixed-interest loans (like personal loans) and variable rate loans with interest linked to the bank's base rate or to money market rates. Some long-term loans combine features of both by giving the borrower a choice at intervals of whether to borrow at a fixed rate or a variable rate.

STUDENT SELF-TESTING

Self Review Questions

1. Why is it difficult to apply credit scoring to commercial lending? (2)

2. Why do some businesses have negative working capital even though they are trading profitably? (4)

3. Why do businesses usually need more working capital if they expand? (6)

4. Why is a purchase of fixed assets often associated with a need for more working capital? (9)

5. Why is it difficult for a buyer to take over the liabilities of a sole trader's business? (10)

6. What is goodwill? (11)

7. What can you assume about a business which shows goodwill as an item in its balance sheet? (11)

8. What is the rule in Turquand's case? (13,14)

9. What is 'hard core' borrowing? (16)

10. Why would a borrower want to be able to choose at intervals whether to pay interest at a fixed rate or a variable rate? (17)

Exercises (answers begin page 333)

A1. What is working capital? Explain why increasing turnover can lead to a need for extra working capital, illustrating your answer with appropriate figures.

A2. The current balance sheet of Growers Ltd is shown below. The company is planning to spend £5,000 on new equipment, and wants some idea of how this will affect the balance sheet. Answer the questions which follow.

Balance Sheet of Growers Ltd today

	£
Fixed Assets	20000
Current Assets	8000
Current Liabilities	(7000)
	21000
Capital	
Shares	10000
Reserves	8000
Long-term Liabilities	3000
	21000

144

1.   Draw up the new balance sheet of the company on the assumption that the spending is financed by means of a loan account.

2.   Add a further column to the balance sheet to show the effect if the spending is financed by an overdraft.

3.   Calculate the current ratio (current assets: current liabilities) for each of the two new sets of figures.

4.   What do the figures tell you about the two different methods of financing?

A3.   Lowbourne Ltd, a customer at your branch, is requesting a loan of £20,000 to buy new machinery costing £30,000. The company has £10,000 in a deposit account to put towards the purchase. Your manager tells you that he thinks the company is asking for too little. Why do you think he said this, and how could you check whether you agree?

A4.   What is the 'ultra vires' doctrine, and in what circumstances does it pose problems for banks lending money?

14. Forms of Finance

INTRODUCTION

1. This chapter looks at alternatives to loans and overdrafts which banks can offer to business customers. Most of these other forms of finance are not directly offered by bank branches, but are provided by subsidiary companies or through head office departments.

Some of these forms of finance are loans of a kind but many of them are rather different from ordinary lending. The legal relationship of bank and customer is not necessarily a straightforward one of debtor and creditor.

The chapter deals with:-

    a) leasing;

    b) hire purchase;

    c) factoring;

    d) discounting bills of exchange;

    e) acceptance credits;

    f) issuing securities;

    g) venture capital.

Each of these terms is explained and the advantages and disadvantages of each form of finance are considered.

LIMITS ON BRANCH LENDING

2. When banks are approached by businesses for financial assistance this is usually done at branch level. Only the largest companies approach banks directly at the head office level or are regularly contacted directly by head office representatives. Branch managers therefore operate as financial general practitioners who can:-

    a) offer solutions to customers' problems if they are not too large or difficult;

    b) refer customers to appropriate specialists where greater expertise is needed.

Note that because of the rules on polarisation in the Financial Services Act (see Chapter 7) the role of managers may change because most of the major banks have opted to turn branches into sales operations rather than impartial advice centres. Such changes do not prevent managers from referring customers to their own bank's subsidiaries (though if branches refer customers in this way branch staff cannot encourage customers to take up the recommendations of the specialists).

Some referred cases are simply customers whose borrowing requirements are greater than the manager's discretionary limit. A decision then has to be made at a higher level. In other cases the branch manager decides that the forms of finance available through the branch like an overdraft or a loan are not really suitable for the customer's needs. The customer may have realised this before approaching the bank, but more commonly it is the manager's decision to decline a request for conventional bank lending which leads to a referral to a specialist provider of finance.

SOURCES OF SPECIALIST FINANCE

3. Small banks or banks which deal only with retail banking may lose business if their customers need specialist forms of finance which they are unable to provide. The big clearing banks have overcome this problem by developing or acquiring the specialist skills. The staff with the right expertise are employed by the bank, but because few of them are needed in comparison to the number of branches they are grouped together in specialist units.

Banks are likely to organise these specialists in units within the main bank if all or most of their business comes through the branch network. In many fields the specialists have clients or customers in their own right and exist comfortably as separate, fairly independently run subsidiary companies. Finance houses, for example, are well established as separate financial intermediaries and attract their own business as well as dealing with customers referred by branch managers. Similarly merchant bank subsidiaries may have their own clients apart from customers of the parent bank.

An important aspect of the expertise of specialist lenders is that they are familiar with types of risk with which branch managers do not usually deal.

LEASING

4. Leasing is a form of finance associated with purchases of fixed assets such as plant and machinery, from typewriters to jumbo jets. Generally premises are not covered by bank leasing because property can be rented if a business does not want to own property outright. In the context of banking

the term leasing refers to finance leasing as explained below.

Note on Terminology

Finance Leasing

A finance lease is an agreement between a leasing company and a user of a fixed asset designed to cover the whole of the useful life of the asset purchased from new. The user has most of the benefits of owning the asset without having to pay out the full cost at the outset. It is therefore similar to buying the asset with a loan and paying back the loan in instalments.

This is rather different from ordinary, short-term leasing or hire of equipment offered by specialist hire companies rather than finance companies. Users of the equipment do not obtain new equipment and the hire company has to allow in its charges for the fact that the equipment may lie idle for long periods.

Leasing is a service provided by most finance houses. Where a customer of a bank wants to purchase fixed assets and a bank loan does not seem appropriate the branch manager may call in the local finance house manager. The finance house can then buy the asset the customer wants, lease it to the customer and collect instalments which cover the cost of the asset plus interest. Once enough payments have been made to cover the costs of the finance house it is usually possible for the customer to continue to lease the equipment at a nominal charge. Leasing may be a useful form of financing for the customer because:-

a) bank borrowing is not available,

b) bank borrowing is more expensive *or*

c) bank borrowing is needed for other purposes.

Before the Finance Act 1984 tax benefits were seen as the main reason for choosing leasing as a form of finance. Companies which did not expect to pay any Corporation Tax (because they had made losses or had entitlements to tax reliefs as great as their total profit) could pay very low leasing payments because the leasing company could take advantage of the tax relief in the form of capital allowances for purchases of new equipment. In 1984 these capital allowances (which in some cases meant that the full cost of equipment could be deducted from the bank's taxable profit) were abolished and replaced by writing down allowances of 25%. There is still therefore some tax benefit for companies using leasing but other factors now have a stronger influence on the choice between buying and leasing.

LEASING ASSESSED

5.   The fact that the leasing industry did not collapse in 1984, as some people had expected, following the changes in tax regulations, indicates that leasing has considerable advantages. These are summarised below together with the main disadvantages.

Advantages and disadvantages of leasing

Advantages for the Bank

1.   Leasing charges are a source of profit for the bank.

2.   The purchase of new equipment to lease to customers allows the bank to claim writing down allowances which reduce the bank's tax bill.

3.   The bank does not have to turn away customers just because a loan cannot be offered.

Advantages for the Customer

1.   The costs of leasing are low because the lessor (the bank) has the tax benefits.

2.   The cost of an asset can be spread over most of its useful life.

3.   Access to bank borrowing for other purposes is not restricted by entering into a leasing contract.

4.   After the primary period of the lease which pays back the finance company the customer may be able to continue using the equipment at a nominal cost.

Disadvantages for the Bank

1.   Customers may be unhappy at using an unfamiliar form of finance.

2.   Disposing of assets at the end of the leasing period may be difficult if the customer does not want them.

Disadvantages for the Customer

1.   A leased asset does not become the outright property of the company using it.

HIRE PURCHASE

6.   Although hire purchase is often associated with consumer finance for buying household goods, businesses also use hire purchase as a way of financing the acquisition of fixed assets by payment in instalments. The kind of assets bought are those which could be covered by a finance lease.

Hire purchase, like leasing, is commonly provided by finance houses, but unlike leasing acquiring assets on hire purchase does give the user outright ownership once all the payments have been made.

This difference between leasing and hire purchase has some important implications.

1.   The user, rather than the finance house, is entitled to the writing down allowance, so it is most suitable for companies which pay tax.

2.   Because the finance house has no tax benefit the instalments are higher than for a finance lease.

3.   At the end of the period of regular payments no further money needs to be paid and the user can sell the asset or continue to use it.

Note that customers using hire purchase are usually required to pay 20 to 25% of the cost of any asset from their own resources, rather than having the 100% finance which is available with leasing. This requirement reflects in part the greater risk to the finance house because it does not maintain ownership of the asset.

HIRE PURCHASE ASSESSED

7.   As the following table indicates some of the advantages and disadvantages of hire purchase are similar to those for leasing, and the service is often provided by the same division or subsidiary of the bank.

Advantages and disadvantages of hire purchase

Advantages for the Bank

1.   Interest charges add to the bank's profit.

2.   The revenue is usually greater than for an equivalent bank loan.

Advantages for the Customer

1.   The cost of an asset may be spread over its useful life.

2.   The purchaser retains the benefit of the writing down allowance.

3.   The V.A.T. paid on the purchase can be deducted immediately from any V.A.T. owed to H.M. Customs and Excise (even though the full purchase price is paid in instalments).

Disadvantages for the Bank

1.   The customer obtains rights over the asset before paying for it in full.

Disadvantages for the Customer

1.   There is usually a requirement to pay a deposit of 20 to 25% of the cost of the asset acquired.

FACTORING

8.   Another of the forms of finance associated with particular assets is factoring. The assets in question are the debts of the business.

Companies which offer debt factoring (known as factor companies or factoring companies) provide a range of services for their clients. Some factor companies are independent, but many of the largest are subsidiaries of banks. The range of services is outlined below.

1.   At the simplest level factor companies operate a sales ledger service, keeping accounts for debtors and dealing with the routine administration of sending out statements and reminder notes.

2.   The sales ledger service may also include credit control work, assessing potential customers (people who want to buy from the factor company's client) and allocating or reviewing credit limits (limits on the value of goods or services to be sold to each customer).

3.   For businesses which want to use their debtors as a source of finance factor companies can provide loans against the debts. The factor company usually lends 75 to 80% of the value of invoices which the client company provides. These invoices show that goods or services have been supplied by the client company but payment by the debtors has to be made to the factor company. The factor company then collects the money from the debtors and pays over the remaining portion of the money less the charges for the service and less any bad debts.

4. Some clients prefer a service which removes the risk of losses from bad debts. They can choose non-recourse factoring which means that the factor company buys the debtors but does not deduct any bad debts when settling up. The client can only sell to customers approved by the factor company.

The sales ledger service is not a source of finance at all but factoring is generally seen as a source of finance because it offers the possibility of raising money. One of the drawbacks of factoring is that it does not have a very positive image. If a company uses factoring it may be seen as being in financial difficulties, selling its debts because it cannot raise money in any other way. Because this misconception is quite common factor companies also offer their customers confidential factoring, which means that invoices do not name the factor company. The risk to the factor company is much greater because repayment of the money advanced goes direct to the client, who has to be trusted to use the money to repay the factor company.

The ideal customer for factoring is a business which:-

a) sells to a fairly small number of customers with none taking too high a proportion of the sales;

b) deals in invoices of at least £500 a time;

c) has a turnover of £1 million a year or more.

Factoring can also be used by exporters, using the invoices which they send to their customers abroad. (See Chapter 22.)

FACTORING ASSESSED

9. The following table compares advantages and disadvantages of factoring.

Advantages and disadvantages of factoring

Advantages for the Bank

1. Profit can be made from the accounting services offered.

2. Interest charges are often above those on overdrafts.

3. The bank's factor company can build up a detailed data bank of information about the creditworthiness of companies with which its clients have dealings.

Advantages for the Customer

1. The accounting services can save on staff time.

2. Immediate cash is available so there is no need to wait for debtors to pay.

3. Non-recourse finance is available giving protection against bad debts.

4. Bad debts may be avoided by following the recommendations of the factor company about which people to offer credit to.

Disadvantages for the Bank

1. Factoring has an unfavourable image.

2. Non-recourse factoring gives the bank's factoring company the risk of bad debts.

Disadvantages for the Customer

1. The service is only available for customers which sell on credit for fairly large amounts at a time.

2. Businesses may be unable to use the service because their total turnover is too small.

3. The customer usually has to let the factor company deal with all invoices. and cannot choose which ones to sell.

4. The cost is usually higher than for an overdraft.

5. Non-recourse and confidential factoring are even more expensive.

6. Businesses using factoring may become more remote from their own customers than they would be if they dealt with collecting payments themselves.

DISCOUNTING BILLS OF EXCHANGE

10. Discounting as a form of finance has some similarities with factoring except that instead of being based on debts which are evidenced by invoices the documents used in discounting are bills of exchange. These represent trade debts which have been legally acknowledged.

Note on Terminology

A bill of exchange is defined in the Bills of Exchange Act (1882) as 'an unconditional order in writing, addressed by one person to another, signed by the person giving it, requiring the person to whom it is addressed to pay on demand or at a fixed or determinable future time, a sum certain in money to or to the order of a specified person, or to bearer'.

The following example shows what a bill of exchange might look like. Wording and layout do vary but the elements included in the definition can be seen in this illustration.

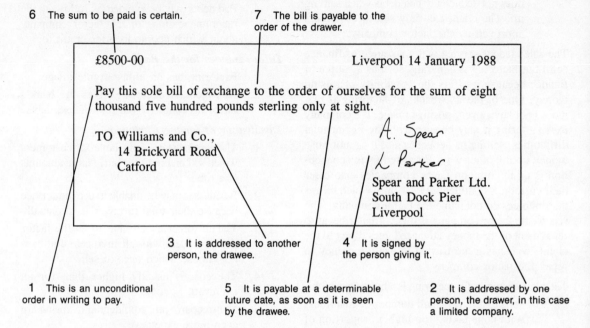

6 The sum to be paid is certain.

7 The bill is payable to the order of the drawer.

£8500-00   Liverpool 14 January 1988

Pay this sole bill of exchange to the order of ourselves for the sum of eight thousand five hundred pounds sterling only at sight.

TO Williams and Co.,
14 Brickyard Road
Catford

A. Spear

L Parker

Spear and Parker Ltd.
South Dock Pier
Liverpool

3 It is addressed to another person, the drawee.

4 It is signed by the person giving it.

1 This is an unconditional order in writing to pay.

5 It is payable at a determinable future date, as soon as it is seen by the drawee.

2 It is addressed by one person, the drawer, in this case a limited company.

Once the person to whom the bill is addressed, the drawee, has seen it it must be either:

a) paid (if it is a sight bill) *or*

b) accepted (if it is a term bill).

The example here is of a sight bill because it states on it that payment is to be made simply 'at sight'.

Finance by means of discounting uses accepted bills, term bills which the drawee has signed. These differ from the example shown because the date for payment is in the future, often a specified number of days after sight, for example at thirty days sight. (See Chapter 21 for an illustration of a term bill.) The drawee, the person to whom the bill is addressed will sign the bill when it is presented, and this signature is known as an acceptance. The acceptance is a legally binding commitment to pay the bill on the due date. It is this legal promise which makes the bill a valuable document if the drawee is a financially sound business. Because of the seriousness of defaulting on a bill of exchange payment is only likely to be refused if the drawee is insolvent. By waiting until the due date the drawer is almost certain to get the money owed.

If, however, the drawer wants the money earlier the document can be sold at a discount to anyone willing to buy it. In practice this usually means the drawer's bank.

The drawer cannot expect to get the full face value of the bill because the buyer will have to wait to get the money from the drawee. In effect the money paid by the buyer is like a loan for the period from the purchase until the maturity date of the bill. The amount of the discount is therefore equivalent to the interest on the amount paid.

DISCOUNTING ASSESSED

11. **Advantages and disadvantages of discounting bills**

Advantages for the Bank

1. Discounting can be arranged by the bank itself rather than through a subsidiary.

2. Profits are made from the discounting fee at fairly low risk.

3. There is recourse to the customer if the acceptor of the bill fails to pay.

4. If the bank needs cash it may be possible to re-discount the bill to another buyer.

Advantages for the Customer

1. Cash is obtained immediately instead of waiting for the bill to mature.
2. Charges are comparable to overdraft interest.
3. The customer selects which bills to offer for sale.

Disadvantages for the Bank

1. Care needs to be taken that the acceptor is financially sound.
2. There is a slight risk of non-payment on the due date.
3. Bills drawn and accepted by private companies may not be resaleable.

Disadvantages for the Customer

1. The service is only available for genuine trade transactions, and in many trades bills of exchange are not used.
2. Banks may be reluctant to deal with bills for very small amounts.

ACCEPTANCE CREDITS

12. To provide finance on a larger scale, commonly for amounts of £20 million or more, for major companies, banks can undertake to accept a customer's bills of exchange. Although such bills usually state on them the trade or transaction to which they relate they are not a means of payment between traders but simply a means of raising finance.

The bills used are similar in form to other bills of exchange except that it is the customer's bank which is named as the drawee and which accepts the bills, promising to pay them at the due date. They are usually in round amounts, perhaps £500,000 or £1 million, and the bank agrees with the customer a limit, like an overdraft limit, on the maximum value of bills which can be outstanding at any one time. The bills are normally drawn for 30, 60 or 90 days. The name 'acceptances' or 'bankers acceptances' is applied to them once the bank has added its signature as acceptor. These are the kind of bills referred to in the money markets as commercial bills.

The interest charged is calculated in the same way as on bills of exchange which the bank discounts except that the buyers of the bills (who obtain the interest in the form of the discount) are usually banks or discount houses dealing in the money markets rather than the customer's own bank. This means that the interest, which determines the price, is linked to money market rates rather than the bank's base rate. For major companies one of the advantages of acceptance credits is that money market rates are often lower than overdraft rates linked to base rate. Company treasurers will often have both sources of borrowing available and will simply use whichever happens to be cheaper when the funds are needed.

ACCEPTANCE CREDITS ASSESSED

13. Although acceptance credits are not available for small businesses because the cost of setting up a programme is too high to justify small-scale borrowing there are important advantages for companies which can use this method of raising money, as the table shows.

Advantages and disadvantages of acceptance credits

Advantages for the Bank

1. Profit is made from fees for arranging an acceptance credit programme.
2. Other banks or discount houses usually provide funds by buying bills the bank has accepted.
3. The bank has recourse to the customer when the bills become due for payment.

Advantages for the Customer

1. The costs may be less than for an overdraft.
2. Using acceptance credits as well as an overdraft gives the company a choice of types of interest rate.
3. The company gets its name known in the money markets, which may help with future borrowing arrangements.

Disadvantages for the Bank

1. The bank takes on a commitment to pay when it accepts a bill of exchange.

Disadvantages for the Customer

1. Small-scale borrowing is not available.
2. Arrangement fees need to be paid even if the borrowing is not used.

ISSUING SECURITIES

14.   As explained in Chapter 2 many businesses raise money directly from investors rather than using a bank or other financial institution as an intermediary. Nevertheless banks still have a role to play because they have the expertise to negotiate between suppliers of funds and users of funds. This role may involve:-

a)   assessing the user's needs;

b)   advising on possible sources of funding;

c)   recommending the best possibilities;

d)   arranging for documentation to be prepared;

e)   making sure all legal formalities are carried out;

f)   helping to find buyers for the securities issued;

g)   underwriting the issue, guaranteeing that the user will get the funds needed;

h)   dealing with interest payments or dividends after the securities have been placed with investors.

It is in providing an underwriting service that the bank itself has a potential liability to provide funds. With some forms of security, for example the relatively new sterling commercial paper market (documents issued by major companies for periods of up to about a year, usually for amounts between £20 million and £120 million in £½ million denominations) banks have often become major holders of the documents because they have not found enough other buyers.

Issuing securities, in whatever form from short-term commercial paper to permanent capital in the form of shares, is an investment banking service, and therefore more likely to be handled by a merchant banking subsidiary than by a commercial bank.

SECURITIES ISSUES ASSESSED

15.   The issue of securities is a service which banks provide for public companies rather than for private companies because of the legal restrictions on approaching investors to put funds into private companies. The advantages and disadvantages for customers in the table below are therefore those affecting public companies.

Advantages and disadvantages of issuing securities

Advantages for the Bank

1.   There is an opportunity to earn fees from the work involved.

2.   The bank can diversify away from the declining market for straightforward lending to major companies.

3.   Relationships can be established with major companies which are not already account-holding customers.

Advantages for the Customer

1.   The company has direct access to investors' money.

2.   Costs of obtaining funds are usually lower than borrowing.

3.   There is a wide choice of forms of security to issue, including permanent capital.

Disadvantages for the Bank

1.   Income is lower than for lending similar sums.

2.   Borrowing customers often develop a close relationship with their bank but companies are more likely to shop around for a bank to issue securities.

Disadvantages for the Customer

1.   A weaker relationship with account-holding banks may be a disadvantage when loans are needed.

2.   Early repayment may be more difficult with many securities than it is with borrowing.

On balance there are probably stronger advantages for customers than disadvantages, which is why more companies are making use of the securities markets and relying less on bank lending.

VENTURE CAPITAL

16.   Where companies want to raise finance but are not in a strong position to borrow money, for example because their existing level of borrowing is already high, new share capital is needed. For companies quoted on the stock market or large enough to issue shares on the Unlisted Securities Market the general public can be asked to invest. For smaller companies the traditional source of new share capital has been friends and relatives.

During the 1980s banks began to offer funds in the form of share capital to companies which they believed would grow big enough for a public flotation. This share capital for new or expanding businesses is often referred to as 'risk capital', emphasising the risk involved in any investment in shares, or 'seedcorn capital' suggesting the idea that it will lead to growth. Government encouragement has been given to individuals to provide venture capital by legislation, for example by the introduction of the Business Expansion Scheme which gives substantial tax benefits to investors in companies with which they have no direct connection.

Banks are usually fairly selective about the businesses to which they offer venture capital. Where normal lending seems appropriate instead venture capital will not be provided, and for some businesses the offer of venture capital is linked to other loans as part of a complete financing package. Some venture capital deals also give the bank some control over company management by means of a seat on the Board of Directors. Venture capital is often associated with lending to new technology industries, but banks do not impose any restriction on the type of business. The factors which banks are looking for in providing investment rather than loans are growth prospects, possible future dividends and a likelihood that the shares acquired will eventually become marketable.

VENTURE CAPITAL ASSESSED

17.   Providing venture capital is unlikely to become a major part of any bank's product range because the numbers of businesses for which it would be a suitable service are limited. It also involves special risks which are less familiar to bankers than the risks in providing loans. However by including venture capital as an option available to customers banks are able to meet the needs of businesses which might otherwise have had to turn to non-bank competitors for finance.

Advantages and disadvantages of venture capital

Advantages for the Bank
1.   Offering venture capital helps to provide a more complete product range.
2.   A return may be earned in the form of dividends on the shares acquired.

3.   There may be substantial capital gains if the company concerned is floated on the Unlisted Securities Market.
4.   Providing venture capital may create a very strong relationship between bank and customer.

Advantages for the Customer
1.   There is no need to pay interest on the funds obtained.
2.   Dividends only need to be paid if profits are made.
3.   Loans may be available in addition to any venture capital.

Disadvantages for the Bank
1.   There may be long delays in obtaining any return on the investment.
2.   Risks of loss are high.

Disadvantages for the Customer
1.   There may be some loss of control over the business.

SUMMARY

18. a)   Branches of banks do not have expertise in all fields of finance, so branch managers act as financial general practitioners referring customers to specialists where appropriate (though this role may now be changing as banks choose whether branch staff should be independent advisers or salesmen of the bank's own products).

b)   Many of the specialist forms of finance are provided through subsidiary companies owned by banks.

c)   Leasing enables businesses to obtain the use of fixed assets without becoming the owners of them. Finance leases can spread the cost of the asset just as a loan could, but the cost may be lower, partly because of tax benefits available to the leasing company.

d)   Hire purchase is also used for acquiring fixed assets but it is more suitable for businesses which have some funds to provide as a deposit and which have taxable profits from which writing down allowances can be deducted.

e)   Factoring provides a form of finance based on selling debts. The client of a factor company can obtain advances against invoices for goods being sold on credit provided the invoice amounts and total turnover are large enough.

f)   For businesses which use bills of exchange in their trade it is possible to raise money by selling an accepted bill of exchange, a promise to pay a sum owed at a future date. The buyer of the bill, usually the bank which has an account for the seller, takes the bill at a discount which is equivalent to the interest on the amount paid out for the period until the bill matures.

g)   On a larger scale bills of exchange can be used by businesses to raise funds in the money markets, often as an alternative to large-scale borrowing on overdraft. An overdraft would mean paying interest linked to the bank's base rate, but using an acceptance credit allows borrowing at rates linked to money market rates.

h)   Banks can also help businesses to obtain finance by arranging the issue of securities. In some cases the banks also underwrite issues, which means that they guarantee to provide the money the customer wants even if no other buyers can be found. Major companies often choose to issue securities rather than taking bank borrowing because of lower costs.

i)   For smaller, growing businesses banks can provide venture capital, cash used to acquire shares in the business. The return to the bank may come in the form of dividends (though dividend payments are likely to be very low in the early stages) or in the longer term from a sale of the shares if the company is able to obtain a quotation, for example on the Unlisted Securities Market.

STUDENT SELF-TESTING

Self Review Questions

1.   What is the difference between finance leasing and ordinary leasing? (4)

2.   What is a writing-down allowance? (4)

3.   What are the main differences between hire purchase and leasing? (6)

4.   What are the advantages for customers of using hire purchase? (7)

5.   What is non-recourse factoring? (8)

6.   What are the disadvantages for customers of using factoring? (9)

7.   Why is an accepted bill of exchange more valuable than an unaccepted bill? (10)

8.   What is an acceptance credit? (12)

9.   What are the main advantages for customers of raising money by issuing securities? (15)

10.   What are the advantages for banks of providing venture capital for customers? (17)

Exercises (answers begin page 334)

A1.   Compare and contrast leasing and hire purchase as forms of finance for purchasing fixed assets.

A2.   What is factoring, and in what circumstances would it be a suitable form of financing?

A3.   Major companies might choose to raise money by using acceptance credits or by issuing securities. What are the relative advantages and disadvantages of each?

A4.   What is venture capital? How do banks get their money back if they provide finance in this form?

15. Balance Sheets and Company Accounts

INTRODUCTION

1. This chapter deals with the assessment of businesses using financial data which is normally available to banks when making lending decisions.

The data may take the form of:-
   a) balance sheets;
   b) profit statements;
   c) funds flow statements;
   d) management accounts.

Each of these types of accounting information is examined in turn with illustrative case studies to show how different interpretations can be reached. The chapter ends by bringing together some of the ideas to show how they are interconnnected, since in practice banks do not choose just one form of information on which to base a decision; all possible data needs to be taken into account.

ASSESSING BUSINESSES

2. In looking at any lending proposition a number of factors have to be weighed up, as described in Chapter 11. When lending to a business the financial data which the business is able to provide about its operations gives many valuable clues to the intending lender, but it is important to recognise that the figures are not of much use on their own (which is why each of the case studies in this chapter contains at least some background information on the business concerned). The lender must understand what the business does in order to make sense of the figures.

For branch managers discussions with the borrower or, ideally, a visit to the customer's premises can be very helpful in getting to know the business. How the business presents itself to the outside world is a useful indicator of whether the borrower is likely to make good use of any funds lent. Lending is a matter of judgement so feelings about the customer may be as important as factual evidence.

For lenders at head offices dealing with applications from branches (and for students tackling lending case studies) background information has to be summed up briefly. Sometimes, as in some of the examples

in this chapter, the details may seem inadequate, and the lender will need to ask for further facts.

Note that although all businesses which want to borrow will be able to provide financial information for the bank to analyse, in general companies provide more complete and more varied financial reports than partnerships or sole traders. This chapter therefore concentrates on company accounts.

USING COMPANY ACCOUNTS

3. When looking at any accounting data provided by a company it is useful to have in mind a checklist of key questions. The following list indicates some of the most important considerations.

   1. What does the company do?
      This is a starting point because it is in the light of knowledge of what the company does that the figures begin to make sense.

   2. How reliable are the figures?
      When dealing with formally produced annual accounts of companies banks have some reassurance that the figures are fairly reliable because the accounts are audited, checked by professional accountants. If they find that the figures are misleading because of the accounting methods used or because of any errors or omissions their qualifying comments will be added to the accounts. Interim figures or figures produced by the company's management for its own purposes may be more up-to-date but will not be completely reliable. Any analysis which a banker carries out on such unaudited figures needs to be treated cautiously.

   3. Who owns and runs the company?
      With smaller companies, as with sole traders and most partnerships, the answers to these two questions are often the same, and banks lending to one or two man companies will usually make sure that the directors are personally committed to repaying any borrowing. For larger companies the distinction between owners and managers may be important because if good managers leave, then the company needs to find suitable replacements. Any lender needs to be sure that the company has enough capable people to keep going. Some major public companies have achieved

success largely on the basis of one leading personality, but investing in such companies is clearly more of a risk than opting for a company with a wide range of management talent.

4.   How profitable is the company?
Various measures of profitability, profit ratios, are available and can be used to make comparisons from year to year, or with other businesses. Some of these are described later in the chapter.

5.   How liquid is the company?
Again ratios can be used to assess whether a business seems capable of meeting its debts when they fall due.

6.   How big is the company?
Company size can be measured in several ways, including the number of employees and the total turnover per annum. Perhaps the most usual measure is the amount of capital employed in the business. This is defined simply as the shareholders' stake plus any long-term borrowing.
Underlying this simple definition are a number of difficulties which make the exact calculation of a figure for capital employed something of a problem.
a)   Shareholders' stake, consisting of issued share capital plus all reserves including profit retained in the business, may need to be adjusted to allow for the fact that assets like goodwill have no real value or that other assets like property are undervalued.
b)   Long-term borrowing is usually clearly shown in company balance sheets but may be hidden as a 'hard core' overdraft (described in Chapter 13).
c)   Capital employed is constantly changing because it increases as profit is made. When dealing with annual accounts an average figure for the year is often used.

7.   How dependent is the company on borrowing?
The extent to which a bank is prepared to advance money to a creditworthy company is related to the level of borrowing which the business has already taken. A company which is heavily dependent on loans may be advised by its bank to raise further

money from shareholders rather than incurring heavier debts and a heavier burden of interest to pay.

8.   How good are company prospects?
One of the reasons for looking at company accounts is to judge what the future will be by looking at trends established over the past few years. The accounts may point towards future progress and prosperity or they may highlight specific problems which need to be tackled. As with all of the questions in this list any numerical information needs to be interpreted in the light of wider knowledge about the business.

WHAT BALANCE SHEETS SHOW

4.   A balance sheet is a picture of a business at a point in time. Because businesses are dynamic, changing all the time, any snapshot can be misleading. Although a single static picture may give enough information to judge that a business is doing well or badly (as in the case study which follows) more often additional information is needed.

The balance sheet summarises assets and liabilities. To some extent these can be modified so that they look their best on the date when the balance sheet is to be produced. This kind of adjustment to accounting figures is known as 'window-dressing'. The scope for such changes is limited but lenders should be aware that it happens, usually within the rules laid down by the law and the accounting professional bodies.

For any business with seasonal variations the choice of the balance sheet date can be an important way of planning what the business will look like. Anything special about the time of year could mislead the unwary lender, but where possible banks look at a series of balance sheets to see what changes are taking place and the whole series will be subject to the same seasonal factors.

Measuring the strengths and weaknesses of balance sheets depends on judgement, but lenders can make use of simple ratios. These cannot give clear answers to how well a business is doing, but they can raise questions.

Among the most important ratios are:-

1.   **Current Ratio**
This is the ratio of current assets to current liabilities, usually expressed as a ratio to

one. For example if current assets of a business are £2,424 and current liabilities are £1,212 the current ratio of the business would be 2:1. This is sometimes seen as the ideal ratio, but each business has to have a current ratio to meet its own needs. Changes in the ratio are more significant than the actual figure.

2. **Acid Test Ratio**
   This ratio compares current liabilities with the liquid assets of a business, and that means the current assets excluding any stock (which may be difficult to sell) plus any other liquid assets like quoted investments. It is sometimes claimed that an ideal ratio is 1:1 because this shows that all short term debts can be met in the foreseeable future, but again the needs of each business are different so there is no such thing as the right figure.

3. **Gearing Ratio**
   The gearing ratio is the ratio of borrowed funds in a business to the total invested funds. If a business has a bank loan of £15,000 and shareholders' capital including reserves and retained profit of £45,000 giving a total investment of £60,000 the gearing is 0.25:1. In other words a quarter of the capital employed is borrowed. Generally such calculations ignore short-term borrowing.

The first two of these ratios are liquidity ratios (and the acid-test ratio is sometimes referred to as *the* liquidity ratio). The gearing ratio is only one of a number of ways of showing how important borrowing is to the business by comparing borrowing to shareholders' funds.

Note that the balance sheet does not indicate profitability so no profit ratios can be based on balance sheet figures.

CASE STUDY: POSSUM LTD

5. *Possum Ltd is a small company which produces small furry toys such as teddy bears, in a ground floor leasehold shop unit in the main street in Gloucester.*

The shop is managed by Ann Miles, who is employed by the company at a wage of £95 gross a week. She is mainly engaged in the craftwork of producing the toys, using a variety of materials and a range of

standard patterns. She also has time to serve in the shop. At busier periods, holidays and weekends, the directors help out too, but both of them have other interests. They do each manage to spend a couple of days a week at the shop to check on the ordering of materials and keeping the accounts up-to-date.

The company has been in account with you since it was formed five years ago and at that time the two directors each put in £1,200 with the rest of the share capital provided by a relative of one of them.

Your manager has asked you to review the position of the business on the basis of the latest balance sheet.

Balance Sheet of Possum Ltd as at the end of last month

Fixed Assets	At Cost	Depreciation to date	Net
Leasehold Property	30000	24000	6000
Machinery	4500	1500	3000
Fixtures and Fittings	4000	600	3400
	38500	26100	12400

Current Assets

Stock/Work in			
Progress	1220		
Finished Goods	2315	3535	
Debtors		110	
Cash		25	3670
			16070

financed by:

Capital

Ordinary Shares	3000		
Retained Profits	345	3345	
Preference Shares		500	3845

Longterm liabilities

Bank Loan	4500

Current liabilities

Creditors	4325	
Bank	2885	
Electricity due	515	7725
		16070

Notes

a) *Depreciation has been charged on leasehold property at 20% per annum (for the five-year lease), on machinery at 12% per*

annum and on fixtures and fittings at 12%
per annum.

b) The preference shares are held by the
relative who also owns 20% of the ordinary
share capital.

c) The bank loan is secured by a mortgage of
one of the directors' houses and was agreed
ten months ago, repayable over 5 years.
(See Chapter 16 for more information about
security.)

d) The bank agreed an overdraft limit of
£2,500 for 12 months when the loan was
taken.

Required:

Your comments to the manager on the position of
the business.

SUGGESTED SOLUTION: POSSUM LTD

6.   There are a number of ways of approaching a
question which looks at a single balance sheet or
set of balance sheets. One way is to consider the
same kind of isues which would need to be tackled
in dealing with a complete set of accounts (as in Case
Study: Medequip Ltd, later in the chapter), though
in many areas the information will be incomplete
or inconclusive.

A simpler approach is to look at the balance sheet
item by item (an approach which is suitable here but
which might be ruled out as too long or time-
consuming if a mass of other information also had
to be taken into account).

1.   Fixed Assets
The rate of depreciation on the leasehold
property indicates that the lease is now very
near to expiry, and an important question
to ask is whether the company is entitled
to renew it. If not the company may be
forced to cease trading unless new premises
can be found quickly.

Both the machinery and fixtures and fittings
will have fallen in value since they were
bought and the depreciation charged may
not be enough to reflect the real loss of value
if the equipment had to be sold.

2.   Current Assets
The value of work-in-progress seems
exceptionally high for hand-made craft
goods. £1,210 must be the equivalent of
quite a lot of partly completed teddy bears.

The full total of stock, including finished
goods, is also high, particularly when
compared to the size of the business, since
it is more than the shareholders' stake in
the business of £3,345.

The debtors figure is not very great, though
there seems no reason to have debtors at
all in this kind of trade.

The low cash figure is not a problem in itself
though the very low total for liquid assets
does look dangerous for the business. The
acid-test ratio is an extraordinarily low
0.02:1, since the company has virtually no
liquid assets.

3.   Capital
The original investment of £3,000 in
ordinary shares and £500 in preference
shares has hardly increased in the five years
of trading, with total retained profits the
equivalent of less than £70 a year, which
is below 2% per annum return on the initial capital.

4.   Long-term liabilities
The bank loan of £4,500 will require
repayments of £900 a year. Even if it was
interest-free this would be a level of
payments which the business does not seem
able to meet. It appears likely that the
business has deteriorated rapidly since the
loan was agreed since figures like the recent
balance sheet would not have justified
lending.

5.   Current liabilities
The creditors outweigh the current assets
by nearly 1.2:1, which means that even if
all the stock could be turned into cash quickly the business could still not pay off its
debts.

In addition the bank is owed over £2,500,
so the company has exceeded its agreed
limit, and shows no capacity to repay the
extra borrowing, let alone the original
amount, even though the period for which
the overdraft was agreed is nearing its end.

The fact that money is owed for electricity
is not in itself a problem (because the bill
may have been received just before the
balance sheet date) but the amount is high
in comparison to the company's liquid
assets, and credit which the company might
have used is already overstretched.

6. Summary
In all items in the balance sheet there is evidence of a business in difficulties. Each, on its own, could be coped with, but the sum of all of these difficulties means that the company is in a very poor state, with liquidation likely in the near future unless a dramatic improvement has taken place since these figures were produced.

Liabilities far exceed the capital of the business, and the bank's stake is far greater than that of the shareholders. The low total for retained profit suggests that profitability is poor (though the directors may deliberately draw out most of the profit). Worst of all the liquidity of the business makes it unlikely to survive. The current ratio of less than 0.5:1 is low but the situation is far worse than this suggests because almost all the current assets are in the form of stock which may be unsaleable. Working capital is negative and the debts to the bank impose an enormous commitment just in terms of interest to be paid.

Further lending would seem extremely unwise even though the bank does have some security. The directors do not appear to have any great commitment to the success of the business and the bank should take action as soon as possible to get its money back.

WHAT PROFIT STATEMENTS SHOW

7.   A profit statement or profit and loss account is the formal end-of-year accounting procedure for showing the calculation of profit, which is generally considered to be an important measure of business efficiency. The figures that go into the profit and loss account come mainly from the factual records of the company's spending during the year, but partly from estimates produced at the end of the year in respect of less certain information like the value of stock and the depreciation of fixed assets.

When companies present their profit figures to shareholders much of the detail is left out. In some cases little more than turnover and profit are shown. Banks may be able to see rather more of the information if they are being asked to lend money. Key figures to look for are:-

1.   **Net Profit**
The most important of the figures is the net profit. Net profit is the amount left from sales income after all running expenses have been deducted. The net profit is available to:-
a) pay taxes;
b) pay dividends to shareholders;
c) retain in the business to help the company grow.

2.   **Retained Cash Flow**
Retained cash flow is the cash earned by the business and not spent. It is sales income minus the cash expenses. A fairly good estimate of the figure can be obtained by adding the depreciation to the net profit.

3.   **Gross Profit**
Gross profit is the sales income minus the costs of providing the goods to be sold. This profit figure, before deduction of the running expenses, indicates the mark-up on the goods.

4.   **Manufacturing Profit**
For businesses which make goods the value of goods produced minus the costs of production gives an estimate of the manufacturing profit, but it is only when sales take place and gross profit can be calculated that the value of such estimates becomes clear.

The net profit and gross profit are commonly compared to the sales turnover as percentages, and changes in the percentages (also known as NET PROFIT MARGIN and GROSS PROFIT MARGIN) indicate changes in how the business is operating. A reduction in gross profit percentage, for example, means that margins are being reduced, possibly:-
a) a deliberate policy to increase sales *or*
b) a sign of problems because of reduced competitiveness.

If the gross profit ratio is unchanged but the net profit ratio has fallen this indicates that the running expenses have increased more rapidly than sales income, a potential source of problems.

A ratio which is often considered the most important of all is the Return On Capital Employed (R.O.C.E.) which is the net profit as a percentage of the capital employed. This is seen as important because in theory it is comparable to an interest rate on the funds invested in a business (though in practice the difficulty of being objective about the value of profit or of capital means that it may be misleading to compare the figure for one business with that for a completely different kind of business).

No profit ratio can be considered the right figure to aim for. Ratios have meaning in comparison to other figures, for example from previous years. In the case study which follows the comparison is with other businesses. Differences between the profit and loss accounts of the businesses suggest areas which need attention.

CASE STUDY: ACTION FASTENERS LTD

8. *The following figures show the sales revenue and expenses of three similar businesses manufacturing metal fasteners for the clothing industry. All are customers at your branch. Action Fasteners Ltd wishes to borrow from you and you are satisfied with the state of the company's balance sheet.*

	Action Fasteners Ltd	Buckles Ltd	Clips Ltd
	£	£	£
Sales	2104	2746	2081
Expenses			
Labour	400	384	312
Materials	420	666	416
Variable Overheads	252	328	250
Fixed Overheads	358	328	290
Marketing	190	326	313
Administration/ Finance	316	330	248
Net Profit before tax	168	384	252
Capital Employed	2224	1490	1241

Required:-
Your answers to the following questions.

1. Is Action Fasteners Ltd as successful as its competitors?

2. How do the costs of the three companies compare?

3. What policy changes might Action Fasteners Ltd be asked to consider before you agreed to any further borrowing?

SUGGESTED SOLUTION: ACTION FASTENERS LTD

9. The main difficulty in comparing the three businesses here is that they are all slightly different in size and in the pattern of their expenses. To begin with it is clear that Action Fasteners Ltd has a smaller net profit figure than its competitors, but the significance of this can be established by looking at a comparison between the rates of profit.

	AF Ltd	B Ltd	C Ltd
Net Profit/Sales	8%	14%	12%
Net Profit/ Capital Employed	8%	26%	20%

1. These figures highlight the relative weakness of Action Fasteners Ltd. The poorer rate of profit is one simple way of indicating that the company has a problem in comparison to its competitors, and this may be a matter of costs.

2. To analyse more fully where the costs of Action Fasteners Ltd differ from those of the other companies it helps to treat all of the costs as percentages of the turnover. This gives the table below.

From these figures it is clear that Action Fasteners Ltd has substantially higher labour costs than the other companies and spends far less on marketing. This does not imply that Action Fasteners Ltd is wrong in its policies; the purpose of the comparison is to raise questions for the bank to investigate rather than to answer them.

3. This means that Action Fasteners Ltd might be asked to consider giving greater

	Action Fasteners Ltd		Buckles Ltd		Clips Ltd	
Sales	2104	100%	2746	100%	2081	100%
Expenses						
Labour	400	19%	384	14%	312	15%
Materials	420	20%	666	24%	416	20%
Variable Overheads	252	12%	328	12%	250	12%
Fixed Overheads	358	17%	328	12%	290	14%
Marketing	190	9%	326	12%	313	15%
Administration/Finance	316	15%	330	12%	248	12%

emphasis to marketing and the reduction of spending on labour. Asking the directors of the company about these issues is important because:-

a) it shows that the bank is trying to understand the company's problems;

b) there may be good reasons for the difference from the other two companies;

c) the proposed borrowing may be connected with these cost problems. For example acquiring labour-saving machinery might be seen as an attempt to tackle one of the problems here; given enough other favourable factors a loan could be offered for that purpose, though some review of the company's approach to marketing might also be desirable.

WHAT FUNDS FLOW STATEMENTS SHOW

10. A funds flow statement shows what has happened to funds coming into a business or leaving a business over a period of time, usually one year. In general terms funds flow statements are produced by comparing the position of the business at two points in time, two balance sheet dates. Adjustments can then be made for changes which are not evident from the balance sheets themselves.

The formal name for a funds flow statement is a statement of sources and applications of funds, and this describes how a funds flow statement is divided up. Some funds flow statements deal with cash. Others treat working capital as the funds of the business.

Funds flow statements now regularly appear in the published accounts of companies. They can also be used as a forecasting tool because they can be drawn up to show changes between a present or recent balance sheet and the position the business is expected to be in at some point in the future.

Funds flow statements are usually divided into three sections:-

a) sources of funds;

b) applications of funds;

c) the change in funds.

The change in funds is the difference between the sources and applications, and for funds flow statements dealing with working capital this third section is sometimes analysed into its component parts.

CASE STUDY: GROWMOOR LTD

11. This case study looks at an example of a funds flow statement and asks what it can tell the intending lender.

Statement of Sources and Applications of Funds of Growmoor Ltd for the period 1 January 1987 to 31 December 1987			
	£ 000s	£ 000s	£ 000s
Sources of Funds			
Contribution from Trading			
Retained Profit	15		
Depreciation	28	43	
Sale of Investments		125	168
Applications of Funds			
Purchase of Fixed Assets		118	
Loan Repayments		17	135
Excess of sources over applications			33
Changes in Working Capital			
Working Capital at 1 January			215
Working Capital at 31 December			248
Increase in funds			33

Required:-

Your comments about what this statement tells you about the operations of Growmoor Ltd during 1987.

SUGGESTED SOLUTION: GROWMOOR LTD

12.   This funds flow statement shows that the business made a trading profit of at least £15,000 during 1987. How good this is can only be judged in the light of other information, for example on sales turnover or capital employed. The actual profit figure may have been higher because some of the profit could have been paid out as tax or dividends. These items would normally appear as applications of funds with the profit figure in the sources correspondingly higher (shown as net profit rather than retained profit).

Retained cash flow from normal trading, often described in funds flow statements as contribution from trading, amounted to £43,000 but the total of working capital rose by less than this because of the heavy spending on fixed assets which used up most of the income from selling investments.

Because loan repayments of £17,000 were made during the year the profit of £43,000 was not all available to increase working capital.

Note that usually more detailed analysis is possible because other information is accessible. The balance sheets at the beginning and end of the year can be very helpful in judging how important the movements of funds are in relation to the size of the business. In this particular statement there is also no analysis of the changes within the working capital to show what form the increase of £33,000 has taken.

Note that the amount by which the sources exceeds the applications is the same as the change in funds from the beginning of the year to the end. If applications had been greater than sources this would have been reflected in a fall in funds.

MANAGEMENT ACCOUNTS

13.   Management accounts are accounts produced to help the management of a company in its decision-making. They therefore emphasise what is happening in the business or what is going to happen, in contrast to financial accounts which report what has happened in the past.

Management accounts take a number of different forms. Three kinds of management accounting information which banks find specially useful are:-

a)   working capital analysis;

b)   cash forecasts;

c)   investment appraisal.

In each case the purpose of the information is to help in making good decisions. Absolute accuracy is therefore not as important as it is for financial accounts which have to be presented to other people, notably the shareholders. Banks, in using management accounts from their customers are therefore in a privileged position of seeing internal information not usually disclosed to outsiders or even to the owners of the business.

WORKING CAPITAL ANALYSIS

14.   Because working capital represents the funds used in the day-to-day running of a business it is important for management to keep close control of how the working capital is used. To have too much money tied up in slow-selling stock or slow-paying debtors is inefficient.

It is also through changes in working capital that profit or loss is first noticeable. Unless extra funds are brought in from outside the business any increase in working capital must be the result of selling at a profit. Equally if a business trades at a loss the working capital will fall.

Banks lending to businesses are increasingly concerned to monitor progress on a regular basis rather than waiting until a problem has built up before taking any action. (See Chapter 17 for more on control of lending.) It is now quite usual for the borrower to be asked to provide figures each month from the company's internal records for:-

a)   stock and work-in-progress;

b)   debtors;

c)   cash and bank;

d)   creditors.

In some cases fairly specific terms and conditions will be applied to make sure that the borrower keeps a firm control over working capital. (See Case Study: Xenon Ltd in Chapter 17.)

CASH FORECASTS

15.   A cash forecast or cash budget is a summary of expected cash receipts and payments over a future period. Many businesses, as a matter of routine, produce cash budgets every six months for the year

ahead. Others take a longer term view than this but also draw up more detailed short-term cash budgets.

Most businesses approaching a bank for funds would expect to be asked for a cash budget to show what revenue will be created if the loan is agreed. This provides evidence of a certain amount of planning and forethought, but since the figures are only estimated they cannot prove that the business will be able to repay the loan.

(For an example of a cash budget and how it might be interpreted by the bank see Case Study: Burnett Ltd in Chapter 17.)

INVESTMENT APPRAISAL

16.   When major new fixed assets are being purchased the aim of the business is usually to obtain a return on the funds invested. Various techniques are available for measuring the return or for comparing different investment choices. Although these techniques are beyond the scope of this text bank staff should be aware that such techniques exist. The least sophisticated are based simply on estimates of cash flows, rather like a fairly specific form of cash budget. Others make use of the idea that money earned now is worth more than the same amount earned in the future, and adjust expected cash flows to allow for this principle, by a process known as 'discounting'. The most sophisticated methods try to assess risk by using estimates of the probability of different outcomes, and are often so complex to calculate that computers need to be used.

INTERPRETING A SET OF ACCOUNTS

17.   Whether a bank is faced with management accounts or only with a set of financial accounts, in order to come to a balanced view of the business it is important to adopt a systematic approach. There is not one right or wrong order in which to deal with the important elements of an assessment of a set of accounts but by being consistent the likelihood of omitting anything essential is reduced.

Banks recognise this by using standard forms for reports on lending propositions. For students it is necessary to remember what to include and a standardised approach helps the memory.

The following summary is a suggested structure for analysing accounting information for lending purposes.

1.   Background
This may cover any of the general information about what kind of business is involved, what kind of past record it has and what needs it is likely to have.

2.   Capital
Particular points to look for are the gearing of the business (the ratio of borrowed funds to permanent capital) and any hidden reserves (where assets are undervalued so that the real value of the owners' investment in the business is hidden).

3.   Profit
The key consideration here is the trend of the profit ratios and what factors have affected this in the past.

4.   Liquidity
If a profitable business is becoming illiquid, for example by overtrading, lending will not solve the problem, so although there is no right level for a company's liquidity lenders should look out for any evidence of a worsening situation.

5.   The current position
Any financial accounts are, by their nature, out of date and even management accounts may not be completely up to date, so it is important for lenders to know whether any significant changes have taken place since the accounting information was produced. This may be evident from information available, but often the lender will need to ask about the current position.

6.   The proposition
The basic analysis of any proposition can follow the pattern of the PAPERS mnemonic (described in Chapter 11) or any similar structured approach.

7.   Other information
In any lending situation the facts will lead the lender to particular questions and lines of inquiry. In some cases relevant data will be given but often, as in judging the current position, it will be necessary to ask for more details.

8.   Conclusion
The conclusion of any analysis of accounting information should include a summary of positive and negative findings so that

these can be weighed against one another to reach a balanced view.

9. Recommendations
Usually some kind of judgement will need to be made about whether to lend or not. This decision must be made if it asked for, but conditions can be attached to any agreement to lend. (Many lending case studies are designed to be open-ended with no clear right or wrong answer; it is the quality of the argument which is important.)

Important DOs and DON'Ts

DO use language carefully and avoid overstating your case.
DO look for comparisons between figures.
DO allow for non-accounting information.

DON'T assume that only one interpretation is possible.
DON'T state obvious facts without comment or explanation.
DON'T assume that no other information is available.
DON'T forget to consider Purpose, Amount, Period, Expertise, Repayments and Security.

CASE STUDY: MEDEQUIP LTD

18. *Medequip Ltd is a well-established company which has been in account since 1961. It specialises in manufacturing and fitting equipment for hospitals and has gained a good reputation with local health authorities in the south-east of the country since commencing trading. The company's products are mostly one-off designs to fit existing hospital sites.*

The most recent expansion was into Hampshire, a development made possible by the move to larger premises in 1981, financed by a bank loan successfully repaid over five years. Since then there has been no borrowing on the account, and the present balance is £4898.24 credit.

The bank has recently been approached by the managing director to request assistance with a new project involving a contract with Suffolk County Council. The bank has already seen evidence of the contract which seemed highly satisfactory except for penalty payments of £1,500 a day for any delay beyond the agreed completion date for the work. Now the company have been in touch again to say that

the contract has been re-negotiated to give an extra two months to complete the work. In addition the penalty payments have been reduced to £800 a day.

The sum requested is £50,000 over two years to pay for the initial planning work and the raw materials. The company will find the rest of the costs for the project, about £80,000, mostly for wages. The council will be paying £200,000 when the contract is completed and repayment will therefore be made in one lump sum at the end rather than in regular instalments.

Required:-
Your assessment of the present state of the business and your response to this request. (See the balance sheets opposite.)

SUGGESTED SOLUTION: MEDEQUIP LTD

19. The information available for this case study consists of text describing the business and three years accounts in the summary format which banks commonly use (sometimes referred to as a balance sheet carding, because the information is arranged in a standard layout on a bank record card). The company would not present its own accounts in this format. It is because of the standard layout that some sections of the accounts show figures of nil.

The following analysis is not a model answer, because there can be no one right answer to a question which is a matter of judgement. If you have tackled the question before reading this solution you should pay particular attention to any areas mentioned here which you have omitted, but do not assume that if you disagree with some of the views here you are necessarily wrong.

a) The background to this business is encouraging because:-
   1. the company has been known to the bank for a long time;
   2. the company apparently has a good reputation;
   3. previous borrowing for a similar purpose was successfully repaid.

b) The capital position of the business looks strong because:-
   1. in absolute terms capital employed has been rising (and faster than inflation);
   2. gearing presents no problem as there is currently no borrowing;

The following figures show the bank's summary of the company's accounts for the last three years.

CUSTOMER Medequip Limited		
BALANCE SHEET ANALYSIS Date: December 31st		
Year	**1985**	**1986**	**1987**

	1985	1986	1987
	£	£	£
Share Capital	135000	135000	135000
Retained Profits	57261	61832	68034
Other Reserves	15000	15000	15000
(Sub-total)	207261	211832	218034
Debentures	0	0	0
Other loans (over one year)	0	0	0
CAPITAL EMPLOYED	207261	211832	218034
FIXED ASSETS			
Premises	112000	112000	112000
Plant	59560	56560	53060
Vehicles	21990	22470	23950
Fittings	0	0	0
Other:	0	0	0
(Sub-total)	193550	191030	189010
CURRENT ASSETS			
Stock	10657	15988	19469
Debtors	14212	18522	21498
Other: *Work in Progress*	29886	32223	38256
Cash	3552	3110	3899
(Sub-total)	58307	69843	83122
CURRENT LIABILITIES			
Creditors	19066	23001	26958
Tax due	12030	12540	13640
Dividend due	13500	13500	13500
Other	0	0	0
Overdrafts/Loans	0	0	0
(Sub-total)	44596	49041	54098
NET ASSETS	207261	211832	218034
Profit and Loss (figures for one year)			
Turnover	408500	422750	455200
Gross Profit	95251	96688	100021
Pre-tax Profit	29729	30611	33342
− taxation	12030	12540	13640
− dividend	13500	13500	13500
Net Profit	4199	4571	6202
Depreciation	7700	8100	8700
Retained Cash Flow	11899	12671	14902

3. the capital employed is far larger than the proposed loan;

4. continuing profits at the present rate will improve the capital position quite quickly;

5. the premises show no change in value over the three years so there may be a hidden reserve.

c) Profitability of the business seems to be good. Evidence for this includes:-

1. in absolute terms more profit (gross and net) is being made each year;

2. net profit as a percentage of sales is rising each year (1985 1.02%, 1986 1.08%, 1987 1.36%);

3. the return on capital employed is rising each year (1985 2.03%, 1986 2.15%, 1987 2.84%);

4. retained cash flow is similarly rising so cash to repay the borrowing is being generated.

On the other hand there are some less favourable factors:-

1. the gross profit ratio has been reduced a little each year possibly to keep the business competitive;

2. two years retained cash flow does not seem enough to meet the cost of the borrowing of £50,000, so if the project is unprofitable the business will be in difficulty over repayments.

d) Liquidity of the business is reasonably good. Key factors here are that:-

1. the current assets are greater than the current liabilities each year;

2. this margin, the amount of working capital, is increasing each year.

In contrast to this a possible cause for concern is the fact that a high proportion of the current assets is in the form of stock and work-in-progress. This means that:-

1. highly liquid assets are less than current liabilities;

2. even in the best year liquid assets cover less than half the current liabilities, an acid-test ratio of 0.47:1.

This apparent lack of liquidity does not seem to be a serious problem because the business has not needed to borrow (and the acid-test ratio has been improving).

e) Little is known about the current position except that the bank balance is greater than shown in the balance sheet.

Other information would be required, particularly working capital figures, but it is important to remember that the borrowing may alter some aspects of the business in any case so a record of what has happened will not give a complete picture.

f) The proposition is not simply a continuation of the business as before, though the change is not as dramatic as a take-over or an acquisition. Here a new contract is being undertaken over a period of two years. The value is £200,000, equivalent to £100,000 a year, over a fifth of the company's current turnover. With such a large contract it is important to consider:-

1. whether this work will be in addition to normal trade *or*

2. whether other business will be affected (leading to some loss of normal profit).

It is also appropriate to consider a checklist for assessing lending (such as the PAPERS mnemonic described in Chapter 11). There are no serious problems about any of the key issues here but a number of questions might be asked. A full answer would include discussion, for example, of the kind of security which might be taken, but since security is the subject of the next chapter it is sufficient to state here that adequate security is available.

g) The most important additional information that a bank would hope to see in a situation like this is a cash flow forecast covering the period of the loan. This would show changes in the other business of the company as well as the expected costs and revenue from the new contract.

h) In conclusion it seems that the business is in a healthy position. The considerable strengths of the proposition do outweigh the drawbacks, but there is still some risk to the customer and therefore to the bank. The county council might fail to pay for the work done or exceptional delays might lead to penalty payments, but both of these are probably fairly unlikely.

i) The wording of the case study specifically requires a response to the request for borrowing. This does not have to be unconditional, but any conditions should be clearly spelt out. It would be possible to argue here that the loan should be agreed, provided that adequate security was arranged first. A more cautious lender might only agree if the county council would consent to making payment in stages rather than in one lump sum at the end of the two years. This would reduce the total amount of borrowing needed.

DIFFERENT TYPES OF BUSINESS

20. Because accounting information is only a part of what a bank needs to consider in making a lending decision there is no such thing as a perfect set of accounts for the lender. Lenders need to recognise that different types of business operate in different ways.

A jeweller would expect to have a high value of stock in comparison to annual sales; a fishmonger or greengrocer would hold relatively little stock in relation to turnover. Service industries do not have any stock while manufacturing businesses need stocks of raw materials and work-in-progress as well as stocks of finished goods available for sale. These kinds of difference indicate that any calculations or ratios based on stock and how quickly it is sold will be of no value to a lender who does not appreciate what kind of business wants to borrow money.

Similar illustrations could show that ratios of current assets to current liabilities do not conform to any set pattern for all businesses. The view that current assets should always exceed current liabilities in order for a business to feel safe that it can pay its debts ignores the real situation in which many businesses find themselves.

Capital ratios, for example the gearing ratio comparing borrowing to invested capital, can be a useful guide for assessing businesses of all types, but even capital ratios vary significantly between industries.

SUMMARY

21. a) In assessing a business a lender needs to understand what the business does and how it operates before accounting information about it can make sense.

b) A number of key factors need to be considered when looking at any accounting data. These include:-
   1. what the business does;
   2. the reliability of the figures;
   3. the ownership and management of the business.

c) Within the accounting data the most important considerations for lenders are:-
   1. profitability;
   2. liquidity;
   3. capital and borrowing.

d) Balance sheets summarise assets and liabilities at a fixed point in time. This chosen time may not be typical of the normal operations of the business.

e) Ratios indicating the liquidity and the gearing of the business can be calculated on the basis of balance sheet information, but they are most useful when they can be used to make comparisons from year to year to identify trends.

f) Profit and loss accounts or profit statements are usually seen as a measure of business efficiency, though accountants do have some discretion about what figures to include. Key figures to note are the gross profit, net profit and retained cash flow. Ratios based on profit related to sales can be used to compare businesses or identify trends in a business.

g) Profit can also be related to the capital employed in a business. This Return On Capital Employed (R.O.C.E.) is often considered the most important of all ratios.

h) Funds flow statements, more correctly known as statements of sources and applications of funds, show what has happened to the funds coming into and going out of a business over a period of time.

i) Management accounts are accounts produced by businesses for internal use rather than to show to other people. Banks often have access to this inside information, particularly in the form of:-
   1. working capital analysis;
   2. cash forecasts;
   3. investment appraisal.

j) In interpreting any set of accounts a standardised approach is useful because it helps to make sure that key points are not missed out. Valuable DOs and DON'Ts include:

1. DO avoid overstating opinions;
2. DON'T state obvious facts without comment or explanation;
3. DON'T assume that no other information can be obtained.

k) Different businesses operate in different ways and their accounts therefore differ too. Do not expect standard ratios to apply to all businesses.

STUDENT SELF-TESTING

Self Review Questions

1. What are the advantages and disadvantages of using unaudited figures when assessing businesses? (3)

2. What is capital employed? (3)

3. What is the difference between the current ratio and the acid-test ratio? (4)

4. What is retained cash flow? (7)

5. Why is R.O.C.E. considered to be so important? (7)

6. What three sections normally form a funds flow statement? (10)

7. What is the contribution from trading shown in a funds flow statement? (12)

8. How are changes in working capital a guide to profitability? (14)

9. What is a cash budget? (15)

10. Is there a problem for a business if current liabilities exceed current assets? (20)

Exercises (answers begin page 335)

A1. 'A balance sheet is an inadequate basis for deciding whether to lend to a business.' Discuss.

A2. What ratios are most commonly used to assess the profitability of businesses? How suitable are they?

A3. The following balance sheets represent two businesses, one a finance company and the other a manufacturer. Which do you think is which? List the evidence which you have used to come to this decision.

	Company A	Company B
Fixed Assets	2080	13
Stock	485	0
Debtors	405	2696
Other Assets	560	821
	3530	3530
Capital	2400	800
Long-term liabilities	650	1090
Current liabilities	480	1640
	3530	3530

A4. Compare the two main ratios for analysing liquidity. What are the relative strengths and weaknesses of each?

16. Security for lending

INTRODUCTION

1. This chapter looks at why banks take security when lending and at the characteristics of good security. The main part of the chapter deals with the most important forms of security:-

a) guarantees;

b) stocks and shares;

c) life policies;

d) land;

e) mortgage debentures.

Each of these is assessed to show how well it matches up to the criteria for good security. Some of the other less widely used forms of security are also briefly considered.

THE NEED FOR SECURITY

2. As explained in Chapter 11 all lending involves risk, and the basic risk to the bank is that the borrowing will not be repaid. This risk can be reduced, though never entirely removed, by taking security.

Taking security means arranging to obtain control over assets which can be turned into cash to repay the borrowing if the borrower fails to repay. This extra protection seems at first sight such a good idea that banks might be expected to lend only if security is taken. In practice a lot of lending is unsecured. It is therefore useful to consider what advantages and disadvantages there are in taking security.

Advantages and disadvantages of taking security for lending

Advantages for the Bank

1. There is a greater likelihood of getting back the money lent.

2. The reduction in losses from bad debts means greater profits.

Advantages for the Customer

1. Offering security can be a way of paying a lower rate of interest.

2. In some cases borrowing is only agreed when security is provided.

Disadvantages for the Bank

1. Taking security can be a time-consuming and therefore costly process.

2. Paperwork may be very complicated, particularly for regulated agreements under the Consumer Credit Act.

3. Even if security is taken repayment is not certain because there are often legal problems over getting money from the security.

4. Customers may resent having to provide security.

Disadvantages for the Customer

1. Having to give security may seem like a threat.

2. The cost of arranging the security may be very high, and it is the customer who has to pay.

Taking security is therefore not a requirement for all lending, but a factor to be weighed up along with all the others when making a lending decision.

THE PRINCIPLES OF GOOD SECURITY

3. Taking security means acquiring rights over assets. Some assets are more suitable than others. In general the kind of qualities that are desirable in assets taken as security can be summed up in the mnemonic 'Security is for EVER'.

Assets should be:-

a) Easy to value;

b) Valuable;

c) Easy to charge;

d) Realisable.

1. **Easy to value**
   One of the first steps in taking any security is to look at the assets available as security to see what they are worth. Some assets are very easy to put a value to, for example quoted stocks and shares, because the prices at which they are bought and sold are published each day. Valuing the stock of a business is much more difficult.

2. **Valuable**
   Clearly any asset used as security must have value. Ideally security should rise in value, because the risk involved in lending increases with time so it is sensible for

greater security to be available to correspond to the greater risk. Houses tend to rise in value faster than the rate of inflation but perhaps even better from this point of view are endowment insurance policies which become more valuable as more premiums are paid.

3. **Easy to charge**
   One of the disadvantages of taking security is that it can be costly to take a charge (which means to turn an asset into security). The simpler the process the cheaper it will be. Charges over land are often quite complicated. In contrast getting a guarantee signed is very simple.

4. **Realisable**
   Although banks do not usually take security expecting to have to realise it (which means to use it to get back their money) being able to convert the assets into cash is essential. The best forms of security are those which are most free from legal problems or other difficulties in getting back the money owed.

These four criteria can be applied to any asset to see whether it is suitable as security. Most will be less than ideal in some respects but the assets commonly taken as security by banks do meet some of the requirements fairly well. There is one other consideration which helps to make some assets more widely used than others, their availability. Banks often have little choice about what security to take and simply accept whatever the customer can provide.

TYPES OF CHARGE

4.   When any assets are taken as security agreement needs to be reached about:-

a)   which assets are included;

b)   the circumstances in which the lender can dispose of the assets;

c)   the circumstances in which the borrower can regain full control of the assets.

A general term to describe such an agreement is a *charge*. Charges can be created orally, by what is said rather than by anything written, but normal banking practice is for a charge to be in writing, mainly because a signed document is convincing evidence in a court of law. The wording which banks use in their standard charge forms is designed to give the bank as much protection as possible from the legal loopholes which customers in the past have used to prevent banks from getting their money back.

The strongest kind of charge is known as a *legal charge*. In general this means that the lender has carried out all the formalities necessary to obtain complete control over the asset charged. The asset can then be sold without reference to the borrower if the loan is not repaid.

Any charge which does not give this complete control and power of sale is described as an *equitable charge*. A charge given orally is almost always an equitable charge.

Most charges which banks take are *fixed charges* because they relate to a specific asset or a number of assets. For example a mortgage of someone's house is a fixed charge because the house in question is identified. If the customer moves house the mortgage has to be released so that the property can be sold and the bank may ask for a new charge over the new property.

Charges which cover a category of assets are usually *floating charges*. Charges of this type enable the customer to buy and sell the assets charged without having to arrange for the charge to be released each time an asset is sold.

Often security is given by the customer borrowing the money, for example where a company mortgages its premises. This is known as *direct security*. If the borrower has no suitable assets to charge someone else may give security. This *third-party security* can be by means of a guarantee or by a charge over any assets owned by the third party. Directors of small companies are frequently required to provide third-party security for loans to their companies, and relatives often provide third-party security for personal borrowers.

THE TERMINOLOGY OF SECURITY

5.   Charges over different assets are often described by more specific names rather than by the general term charge. A guarantee is something of an exception because it does not relate to any identifiable assets but depends on the financial standing of the person giving the guarantee and is therefore not a charge at all.

The names commonly applied to the other main forms of security are summarised below.

1. Charges over stocks and shares are known as mortgages (legal or equitable).

2. Charges over life insurance policies are known as assignments (legal or equitable).

3. Charges over land are known as mortgages (legal or equitable).

4. Charges over the whole range of a company's assets are known as mortgage debentures (and usually include a fixed charge over some assets and a floating charge over the rest).

The charge forms which banks use for legal charges may include the words 'legal charge' or may use the more precise terms listed. Where banks choose to take equitable charges the document most commonly used is a memorandum of deposit. Different documents are used for the different types of asset though they are similar in effect.

Coutts and Co. v. Browne-Lecky and others (1947)

Facts

B-L had borrowed money and the other defendants had guaranteed the loan. The bank sued for repayment.

Judgement

The court held that because B-L was a minor the borrowing could not be legally enforced and therefore the guarantee could not be enforced either.

GUARANTEES

6. A guarantee is a promise by a third party to repay the lender if the borrower fails to pay. It could be summed up as being a statement by the guarantor to the lender saying:-

"I will pay you what you are owed if the borrower does not pay."

One weakness of this from the lender's point of view is that if the borrower can show that no money is owed the guarantee may be of no value. This is a problem which used to arise when lending to minors because they were not legally obliged to repay money lent to them. The MINORS' CONTRACTS ACT 1987 has altered the position so that a guarantee relating to a debt owed by a minor is not invalid merely because the debt is unenforceable. The leading case illustrating the principle that in general a guarantee is only valid for a valid debt is the Browne-Lecky case. This illustrates the idea that a guarantee is less effective than an indemnity though the change in the law means that a decision today on similar facts would give the lender better protection.

Similar problems can arise if the borrower is a limited company acting 'ultra vires'. (See Chapter 13.)

A bank is in a stronger position if it takes an indemnity. This is, in effect, a statement by the indemnifier to the lender saying:-

"I will make sure you get your money back."

This means that even if the borrower can escape from legal liability the person giving the security cannot escape. Following the Browne-Lecky case it has become normal practice to include an indemnity clause in the standard form that banks use when taking a guarantee. This can be seen in clause 14 of the specimen which follows.

Note that students who go on to take the Chartered Institute of Bankers Stage 2 examinations will need to be familiar with all of the clauses of standard security forms used by their own banks.

SPECIMEN *(by kind permission of TSB England and Wales plc)*

TSB England & Wales plc

Guarantee
by person(s) or a body corporate - for both limited and unlimited guarantees

THIS GUARANTEE is given the _____ day of _____ 19____

BY
Full Name

Address

Full Name

Address

Full Name

Address

("the Guarantor")
FOR
Full Name

Address

Full Name

Address

("the Principal")
IN FAVOUR OF
TSB ENGLAND & WALES PLC
("the Bank")

NOW IT IS HEREBY AGREED AND DECLARED as follows:-

Definitions

1   In this Guarantee unless the context otherwise requires:-

   "Bank" includes its successors and assigns;

   "Guarantor" includes his personal representatives;

   "Guarantor's Liabilities" means all moneys for which the Guarantor is liable under Clause 14 hereof and any and every part thereof;

   "Guarantee Limit" means the sum (if any) specified in the Schedule hereto;

   "Liabilities" means the Guarantor's Liabilities and the Principal's Liabilities and any and every part thereof;

   "Principal's Liabilities" means all moneys, liabilities, costs and expenses now or hereafter due, owing or incurred by the Principal (whether alone or jointly with any other person) to the Bank (including any such as are referred to in Clause 6 hereof but excluding any arising under a regulated agreement) upon whatever account or accounts or otherwise howsoever and whether actually or contingently and whether presently or in the future and whether as a principal, surety or otherwise together with all interest, discount, commission or other charges computed and compounded in accordance with the terms (if any) agreed from time to time between the Principal and the Bank and subject thereto according to the usual mode of the Bank after as well as before demand or judgement. The expression the "Principal's Liabilities" includes any and every part thereof;

   "person" includes a partnership and an unincorporated association;

   "Principal" includes his personal representatives;

   "regulated agreement" means a regulated agreement within the meaning of the Consumer Credit Act 1974 and any agreement which if it had been modified by virtue of being secured or further secured by this Guarantee would have become a regulated modifying agreement within the meaning of that Act

   and reference to any statutory provision shall be deemed to include reference to any statutory modification or re-enactment thereof for the time being in force.

Registered Office: 60 Lombard Street, London EC3V 9EA. Registered in England and Wales: Number 1089268   EW-XX-1411-0086

Page One

172

SPECIMEN *(by kind permission of TSB England and Wales plc)*

Consideration

2   In consideration of the Bank granting or continuing to grant to the Principal time, credit or banking facilities the Guarantor hereby undertakes to and agrees with the Bank as set out in this Guarantee.

Guarantee

3   The Guarantor hereby guarantees due payment to the Bank of the Principal's Liabilities on demand being made on the Guarantor by the Bank.

Guarantee Limit

4   If a Guarantee Limit is specified in the Schedule hereto the total sum recoverable from the Guarantor hereunder, notwithstanding the provisions of Clauses 3, 5, and 14 hereof, shall be the amount of the Guarantee Limit together with

(1)   interest on the amount of the Guarantee Limit or such lesser sum as may be due and owing and charges accruing to the Bank from the Principal whether before or after the date of demand or of expiry of any notice given under Clause 6 hereof and not debited to the Principal's account at such date;

(2)   all costs and expenses recoverable from the Principal and not debited to the Principal's account at such date, and

(3)   all sums payable under Clause 10 hereof.

Continuation of Security

5   Subject to Clause 6 hereof, this security shall remain in full force and effect as a continuing security until the Bank discharges this security, shall not be determined by the death or disability of the Guarantor, and shall be in addition to and shall be independent of every other security which the Bank may at any time hold for the Principal's Liabilities.

6   This security may be determined as a continuing security at the expiration of not less than three months written notice given to the Bank by the Guarantor and the Principal's Liabilities hereby secured shall be fixed at the amount thereof outstanding on the date of expiry of such notice together with any of the Principal's Liabilities which are then unascertained or contingent and any interest, costs and expenses in respect of the foregoing. Without prejudice to Clause 19(2) hereof, any such notice shall, if the Guarantor comprises more than one person, be given by every such person. The Bank may, during the period of any such notice, fulfil any requirement of the Principal based on agreements expressed or implied prior to receipt by the Bank of such notice and the Bank may afford the Principal such further accommodation as the Bank would have done had it not received such notice and any moneys or liabilities thereby due or incurred by the Principal to the Bank and not paid or discharged before expiry of such notice shall form part of the Principal's Liabilities.

Dealings with Third Parties

7   The Bank may in its discretion grant time or other indulgence to or make any other arrangement, variation or release with:-

(1)   the Principal or any other person or persons not party hereto or

(2)   where there are two or more persons comprised in the expression the "Guarantor", any such persons

in respect of the Liabilities or any other security therefor without prejudice either to this security or to the liability of the Principal or the Guarantor or (in a a case falling within sub-clause (2) of this Clause) of other persons comprised in such expression for the Liabilities.

Breaking Accounts

8   If the Bank receives notice of any subsequent charge or other interest affecting any security which it holds for the Liabilities (whether such security was given by the Guarantor or otherwise) or on the expiry of a notice given to the Bank under Clause 6 hereof or in the event of the Bank making a demand hereunder the Bank may open a new account or accounts for the Principal in its books and credit all payments by or to the credit of the Principal to such new account or accounts. If the Bank does not open a new account then, in any case where there is an overdraft or similar account, as from the time of receipt of such notice, such expiration or such demand all moneys credited to such overdraft or similar account shall

(1)   where notice of a subsequent charge or interest has been received, unless and until the Bank agrees its priority in respect of the Liabilities due, owing or incurred subsequent to receipt of such notice with the subsequent chargee or person entitled to such other interest or

(2)   in any other case, unless and until the Bank otherwise agrees in writing

be treated as having been credited to a new account of the Principal opened on the date of receipt of such notice and not as having been applied in reduction of the Liabilities.

Transfer of Credit Balances

9   The Bank shall be entitled to set off against any sums standing to the credit of any account of the Guarantor with the Bank (whether current or otherwise or subject to notice or not) the liability of the Guarantor to the Bank hereunder.

Costs

10   The Guarantor will pay the Bank on demand all costs, charges and expenses incurred by the Bank in connection with the recovery or attempted recovery by the Bank of moneys due to the Bank hereunder whether or not such costs, charges, expenses and moneys or part thereof would be allowable upon a party and party or solicitor and own client taxation by the Court.

Suspense accounts

11   All moneys paid to or received, recovered or realised by the Bank (whether or not as a result of the exercise of its rights under this Guarantee) may in the discretion of the Bank be credited to any suspense or impersonal account and may be held in such account for so long as the Bank may think fit pending the application from time to time (which the Bank shall be entitled to do at its discretion) of such moneys and the accrued interest thereon (at the rate, if any, agreed in writing between the Guarantor and the Bank) in or towards the discharge of the Liabilities.

Warranties

12   The Guarantor hereby warrants that the Guarantor has not taken and will not take from the Principal without the consent in writing of the Bank any security from the Principal in respect of the Guarantor's liability hereunder and the benefit of any security so taken shall be held in trust as a security to the Bank for the fulfilment of the obligations of the Guarantor hereunder and shall forthwith be deposited with the Bank for that purpose.

Principal's Insolvency

13   If the Principal is adjudicated bankrupt, is wound up, goes into liquidation or makes any composition or arrangement with the Principal's creditors then:-

(1)   until the Bank has received one hundred pence in the pound in respect of the Liabilities the Guarantor shall not (a) be subrogated to the Bank in respect of, share in or otherwise have the benefit of any claim of the Bank arising out of or in connection with the Liabilities or any related security (b) be entitled to any other right of a surety discharging its liability against the Bank or any other person (c) make any claim or file any proof in such bankruptcy, winding-up or liquidation or enter into any such composition or arrangement (whether on account of moneys received or recovered by the Bank hereunder or under any related security or otherwise) or (d) exercise or claim any set-off or counter-claim against the Principal (whether on account of moneys received or recovered by the Bank hereunder or under any related security or otherwise) or do any other act or thing which would or might diminish the assets of the Principal available for distribution among the Principal's other creditors and

SPECIMEN *(by kind permission of TSB England and Wales plc)*

(2) neither the existence of this Guarantee nor any moneys received or recovered by the Bank hereunder or under any related security shall impair the right of the Bank to claim or prove in such bankruptcy, winding-up or liquidation or enter into any such composition or arrangement for the total amount of the Principal's Liabilities.

Liabilities unenforceable against Principal

14 If the Bank is unable to receive any moneys from the Principal as a result of any agreement or purported agreement between the Bank and the Principal proving to have become void, voidable or unenforceable for any reason whatsoever, whether or not known to the Bank and including, without limitation:-

(1) any legal limitation, disability or want of capacity on the part of the Principal

(2) any want of authority or capacity of any person acting or purporting to act on behalf of the Principal

(3) any event or circumstance entitling the Principal to plead frustration, force majeure or the like or

(4) the effect of any law, order, regulation, decree or similar instrument

the Guarantor shall be liable as sole or principal debtor for such moneys and will indemnify the Bank against all loss and damage which the Bank may sustain by reason of such voidness, voidability or unenforceability.

Exercise of Remedies

15 The Bank shall be entitled to exercise all or any of its rights and remedies in respect of the Liabilities (whether under this Guarantee or otherwise) in such manner and at such times as it may at its sole discretion decide including, without limitation, its right to enforce this Guarantee without first taking action or obtaining judgement against the Principal in any court, making or filing any claim in a bankruptcy or liquidation of the Principal or making demand of the Principal for the Liabilities.

Retention of Security

16 If

(1) any release, settlement, discharge or arrangement is given or entered into by the Bank to or with the Principal or one or more of the persons comprising the Guarantor (if more than one) in reliance upon or as a result of any settlement, security, assurance, covenant, contract, payment or other act or instrument made, given or done by the Principal or such one or more of the persons comprising the Guarantor or any other person and

(2) any such settlement, security, assurance, covenant, contract, payment or other act or instrument is subsequently avoided, impaired or otherwise affected by reason of any provision of law relating to bankruptcy, insolvency or liquidation

the Bank shall be entitled to recover from the Guarantor or the other persons comprising the Guarantor to the full extent of this Guarantee the value or amount of any such settlement, security, assurance, covenant, contract, payment or other act or instrument as if such release, settlement, discharge or arrangement had never been given or entered into.

17 The Bank shall be under no obligation at any time to return this Guarantee to the Guarantor and, for the purposes of Clause 16 hereof, the Bank shall be entitled (notwithstanding any release, settlement, discharge or other arrangement given or entered into by the Bank to or with the Principal or any one or more of the persons comprising the Guarantor (if more than one)) to retain any security related to this Guarantee for

six months after the Liabilities have been fully and finally discharged but if during such period either the Principal or any one or more of the persons comprising the Guarantor (if more than one) commits an act of bankruptcy or a petition is presented for, or the Principal or such one or more of the persons comprising the Guarantor takes action for, the purpose of the bankruptcy, winding-up or liquidation of the Principal or (as the case may be) such one or more of the persons comprising the Guarantor, the Bank may retain any such related security for such further period as it shall think fit.

Changes in Bank or Principal

18 This Guarantee shall remain in full force and effect as a continuing security notwithstanding any change

(1) in the name of the Bank or any change in the constitution of the Bank, its successors or assigns or any change in the custodian trustees of the Bank or

(2) if the Principal is an unincorporated body, committee, partnership, trustees or debtors on joint account, in the persons comprised in the term the ''Principal'' whether by death, retirement, change, accession, addition or otherwise howsoever.

Joint Parties

19 (1) If there are two or more persons comprised in the expression the ''Principal'' such expression shall be deemed to include all or any or each of such persons.

(2) If there are two or more persons comprised in the expression the ''Guarantor'' such persons shall be bound hereby as joint and several obligors and such expression when used in this Guarantee shall be deemed to include all or any or each of such persons. None of such persons shall be released from liability hereunder by reason of this Guarantee ceasing to be binding (for whatever reason) as a continuing security on any other or others of them.

Notices

20 Any demand or notice to be served on the Guarantor hereunder shall be made in writing signed by any manager or officer of the Bank or of any branch thereof and may be served on the Guarantor (without in any way preventing the Bank from serving the same in any other manner) either personally or by post. A demand or notice served by post may be addressed to the Guarantor at the Guarantor's address or place of business last known to the Bank or if the Guarantor is a company at its registered office and a demand or notice so addressed and posted first class postage prepaid shall be deemed to have been made or given at noon of the second day following the day of posting and shall be effective notwithstanding that it may be undelivered or returned undelivered. If the expression the ''Guarantor'' includes more than one person a demand or notice served on any one of them shall be deemed a sufficient service on all of them. A certificate by any manager or officer of the Bank or of any branch thereof as to the amount of the Liabilities shall, save in the case of a manifest error, be conclusive evidence for all purposes against the Guarantor. Any notice to be given to the Bank shall be addressed to the Bank at the address shown hereon as the Bank's address for notices or such other address as the Bank may notify to the Guarantor from time to time.

Construction

21 The headings in this Guarantee shall be ignored in construing the same. This Guarantee shall be governed by and construed in accordance with English law.

IN WITNESS whereof this Guarantee has been executed by the Guarantor the day and year first above written.

The Schedule (The Guarantee Limit)

There is **NO GUARANTEE LIMIT** under this Guarantee

or

The **GUARANTEE LIMIT** under this Guarantee is £

(pounds)

Page Three

174

SPECIMEN *(by kind permission of TSB England and Wales plc)*

The Common Seal of _____

_____

was hereunto affixed pursuant to a Resolution of

the Board of Directors dated _____

in the presence of:-
Director

Secretary

Signed by the above-named

Guarantor's Signature

in the presence of:
Witness's Signature

Witness's Name

Address

Occupation

Signed by the above-named

Guarantor's Signature

in the presence of:
Witness's Signature

Witness's Name

Address

Occupation

Signed by the above-named

Guarantor's Signature

in the presence of:
Witness's Signature

Witness's Name

Address

Occupation

I/Each of us/the above Company hereby acknowledge receipt of a copy of the above guarantee.

Branch

Account

Bank's address for notices

GUARANTEES ASSESSED

7.   This section summarises the advantages and disadvantages of bank guarantees as a form of security.

Advantages of guarantees as security

1.   Guarantees are a very easy form of security to take.
2.   The method of valuation is very straightforward, involving only a regular status enquiry on the guarantor.
3.   If the guarantee is unlimited the value of the security will exactly cover the amount of the debt.
4.   Because guarantees are always provided by a third party, if the borrower becomes bankrupt the Trustee in Bankruptcy cannot have a claim on the security (an advantage shared by all third party security).

Disadvantages of guarantees as security

1.   Guarantors never expect to have to pay up and are likely to resist any claim for payment.
2.   The guarantor might be a valued customer whom the bank does not want to upset.
3.   The guarantor might become insolvent without the bank knowing.
4.   Legal objections are often raised by guarantors, for example claiming that the form was only signed as a result of undue influence. If a close relative of the customer was persuaded to sign a guarantee without obtaining separate legal advice about the significance of the form the court might uphold such a claim and therefore stop the bank from getting its money.

To sum up guarantees are easy to value and easy to take as security but they can be very difficult to realise.

STOCKS AND SHARES

8.   Many people who want to borrow money are able to offer stocks and shares as security, and this may become increasingly true as more people become share owners.

A bank can obtain an effective charge over stocks and shares in a variety of ways. The most simple is a verbal agreement . The case of Harrold v. Plenty shows that this is enough to create an effective charge.

Harrold v. Plenty (1909)

Facts

H. lent money to P. who handed over a share certificate as security.

Judgement

By giving the share certificate as security an equitable mortgage was created.

The evidence of a bank's record of what was agreed at an interview with the customer could be adequate to persuade a court of law that a valid charge had been created. However it is much safer for the bank to get a charge form signed. Very often, for stocks and shares, the charge form used is a *memorandum of deposit* which creates an equitable charge. This type of charge form is illustrated opposite.

To create a legal charge the stocks or shares need to be transferred into the name of the bank or, more commonly, its nominee company (a specialist company owned by the bank for the purpose of looking after other people's shareholdings). The transfer is carried out by getting the customer to complete a mortgage form which is then registered with the company. This gives the bank the power to sell the shares when it wants to, and, incidentally, means that any dividends or other communications from the company about such matters as rights issues (see Chapter 2) will go to the nominee company and have to be redirected to the customer.

SPECIMEN *(by kind permission of National Westminster Bank plc)*

NWB1026 (Revised February 1982) **Memorandum of Deposit of Stocks Shares etc** - Unscheduled by person(s) or Company

To **National Westminster Bank PLC**

1 In consideration of **National Westminster Bank PLC** (the Bank) giving time credit banking facilities or other accommodation to

(the Mortgagor)
the Mortgagor charges all stocks shares bonds receipts or other property and/or the proceeds of sale thereof (collectively called the Securities) and documents evidencing the Mortgagor's title thereto now or hereafter deposited with the Bank or transferred to the Bank or its nominees by the Mortgagor as a continuing security to the Bank for the discharge on demand of:

(i)   all present and/or future indebtedness of the Mortgagor to the Bank on any current and/or other account with interest and bank charges and

(ii)   all other liabilities whatsoever of the Mortgagor to the Bank present future actual and/or contingent and

(iii)   all costs charges and expenses howsoever incurred by the Bank in relation to this Charge and such indebtedness and/or liabilities on a full indemnity basis

and for the payment of interest on the foregoing day by day from demand until full discharge such interest to be chargeable at the rate of interest payable or deemed to be payable by the Mortgagor (whether before or after judgment) as calculated and compounded in accordance with the practice of the Bank from time to time.

2 The charge shall include all dividends or interest hereafter paid on the Securities and all rights moneys or property accruing or offered at any time by way of redemption bonus splitting preference option or otherwise to or in respect of the Securities and the Mortgagor undertakes to lodge with the Bank on receipt all such dividends and interest and all documents hereafter received by the Mortgagor in relation to any such rights moneys or property.

3 Where the Mortgagor includes more than one person this Charge shall be construed as referring to all or any one or more of those persons and the obligations of the Mortgagor shall be joint and several.

4 The Mortgagor will at the request of the Bank execute legal transfers of the Securities to the Bank or its nominees or otherwise as the Bank directs but in the event of any such transfer being effected neither the Bank nor its nominees shall be liable for any loss occasioned by any exercise or non-exercise of rights attached to such transferred securities or by any failure to forward or report to the Mortgagor any notice or other communication received in respect of such transferred securities.

5 The Bank shall have a power of sale over the Securities which shall be exercisable at any time after demand and the Bank is hereby authorised to give a good discharge for any moneys received by the Bank in exercise of such power of sale and for any moneys received in respect of the Securities at any time during the subsistence of this Charge.

6 In case the Mortgagor shall have more than one account with the Bank it shall be lawful for the Bank at any time and without any prior notice forthwith to transfer all or any part of any balance standing to the credit of any such account to any other such account which may be in debit but the Bank shall notify the Mortgagor of the transfer having been made.

7 None of the persons included in the expression 'the Mortgagor' shall be entitled to any of the rights or remedies legal or equitable of a surety as regards the indebtedness or liabilities of any of the other persons included in the expression 'the Mortgagor'.

8 The Mortgagor declares that the Securities are in the Mortgagor's beneficial ownership and are not held as trustee or subject to the rights of any third parties.

9 All Securities hereafter deposited with the Bank by the Mortgagor for safe custody shall be subject to this Charge unless excluded herefrom by express reference thereto in any receipt or acknowledgment issued by the Bank at the time of the deposit.

Page One

SPECIMEN *(by kind permission of National Westminster Bank plc)*

10 If the Bank receives or is deemed to be affected by notice whether actual or constructive of any subsequent charge or other interest affecting any of the Securities and/or the proceeds of sale thereof the Bank may open a new account or accounts with any person for whose liabilities this Charge is available as security. If the Bank does not open a new account it shall nevertheless be treated as if it had done so at the time when it received or was deemed to have received notice and as from that time all payments made to the Bank shall be credited or be treated as having been credited to the new account and shall not operate to reduce the amount for which this Charge is security.

11 A demand or notice hereunder shall be in writing signed by an officer or agent of the Bank and may be served on the Mortgagor either by hand or by post. In the case of a company service by hand may be made either by delivering the same to any officer of the company at any place or leaving the same addressed to the company at its registered office or a place of business last known to the Bank. A demand or notice by post may be addressed to the Mortgagor at the registered office or address or place of business last known to the Bank and shall be deemed to have been received on the day following the day on which it was posted and shall be effective notwithstanding it be returned undelivered and notwithstanding the death of the Mortgagor.

If given by a Company add 'Signed by

Director(s) of

acting for and on behalf of the Company by virtue of a Resolution of the Directors passed the day of 19

Dated this   day of

One thousand nine hundred and

Signed by the above-named

*

in the presence of:

Signature of Witness _____

* Insert name of Chargor

Name in full (in Block Letters) _____

Address _____

_____

Occupation _____

Signed by the above-named

*

in the presence of:

Signature of Witness _____

Name in full (in Block Letters) _____

Address _____

_____

Occupation _____

If executed by a Company the acknowledgment should be signed by a Director or by the Company Secretary

I/We acknowledge receipt of a completed copy of this document _____

_____ Signature(s)

NWB1026 Rev Feb 82-1

SPECIMEN

(by kind permission of National Westminster Bank plc)

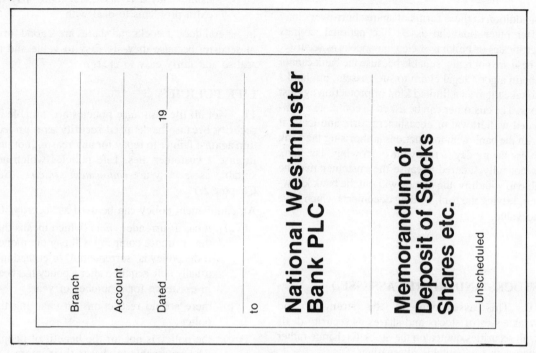

Branch _____

Account _____

Dated _____ 19___

to

National Westminster Bank PLC

Memorandum of Deposit of Stocks Shares etc.

—Unscheduled

Page Three

TYPES OF STOCKS AND SHARES

9.   Stocks and shares can take many forms. The ones most commonly used as security for loans are fully-paid shares or government stocks quoted on the Stock Exchange. A number of other categories of shares might be offered as security but most have major drawbacks.

1.   Partly-paid shares
Partly-paid shares are not very suitable as security because if the shareholder fails to make further payments when they are due the shares may be forfeited making the security worthless. If the bank takes a legal charge the risk is even greater because the bank itself will be liable to the company for the unpaid instalment.

2.   Foreign shares
Although some foreign shares have the advantage of being 'bearer' documents, which means the bank can obtain a full legal mortgage simply by having possession of the share certificate without getting a charge form completed, foreign shares are often more difficult to realise than shares quoted in the United Kingdom. They are subject to foreign laws which may be rather different from English law and there is also greater difficulty in valuing foreign shares because prices are normally quoted in foreign currencies.

3.   Shares in private companies
The most important problem for a bank if it takes shares in a private company as security is that there may be no-one who wants to buy the shares. It is also difficult to obtain a valuation of the shares except by going back to basic accounting principles and looking at all the assets and liabilities

of the business. Even this approach to valuation may be of little help because there is no established market in which to find a buyer.

In addition to these forms of shares borrowers may offer other financial assets like national savings certificates or building society passbooks as security. These are not really suitable because the bank cannot obtain a good legal claim to such assets, but banks do take them as a limited kind of protection against loss. The customer can be asked to complete an undated withdrawal or encashment form and leave it with the bank with instructions authorising the bank to use the money to repay the borrowing. The bank is not fully secured because the customer may be able to withdraw the money without the bank knowing, leaving the bank holding documents which have no value.

STOCKS AND SHARES ASSESSED

10. This assessment of the strengths and weaknesses of stocks and shares as security deals with securities quoted on the Stock Exchange rather than with less suitable alternatives.

Advantages of stocks and shares as security

1. Obtaining a valuation is very easy because up-to-date prices are publicly available.
2. For the ordinary shares of companies there is a tendency for values to increase (since shareholders get part of their return in the form of capital growth as the company expands).
3. It is fairly easy to take a charge over stocks and shares, particularly an equitable charge by means of a memorandum of deposit.
4. Realising quoted shares is straightforward because there is a market through which they can be sold.

Disadvantages of stocks and shares as security

1. The value may fluctuate enormously (so banks try to make sure that there is a wide margin between the value of the security and the amount lent).
2. Shares in any one company may do very badly (so banks prefer to take shares from a range of companies).

3. Taking legal mortgages over many different shareholdings requires a lot of paperwork.
4. If a company restructures its shares, for example by a rights issue, there may be extra problems to deal with.

In general quoted stocks and shares are a good form of security because they are easy to value and to realise and fairly easy to charge.

LIFE POLICIES

11. Not all life insurance policies are suitable as security because banks need security as a protection against failure to repay for any reason, not just in case a customer dies. Life policies which are suitable as security are *endowment policies*. (See Chapter 2.)

An endowment policy can be used as security if:-

a) it has a surrender value (which means that the insurance company will pay out money if the policy is 'surrendered' or cashed in), usually only acquired after a policy has been in existence for a number of years;

b) there are no restrictions on charging the policy;

c) the policy is not for the benefit of people who are unable to charge their interest in it, for example young children.

Normally a bank will only be interested in taking such a policy as security if:-

a) the surrender value is near to or above the amount borrowed;

b) the insurance company is considered reputable;

c) the policy comes under English law.

If a policy is offered as security and considered acceptable the bank will arrange for the policyholder (and, if necessary, any other beneficiaries named in the policy) to complete a form assigning the rights under the policy to the bank. See the specimen charge form opposite.

SPECIMEN *(by kind permission of Royal Bank of Scotland plc)*

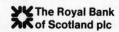 **The Royal Bank of Scotland plc**

Assignment of Life Policy
Secs 15

THIS IS AN IMPORTANT DOCUMENT. SIGN ONLY IF YOU WANT TO BE LEGALLY BOUND. YOU ARE RECOMMENDED TO TAKE INDEPENDENT LEGAL ADVICE BEFORE SIGNING.

Date: 19

Definitions

Mortgagor:

Bank: The Royal Bank of Scotland plc

Interest: Interest at the rate stipulated by the Bank from time to time or in the absence of a stipulation the rate of   %
                             per annum above the Bank's fluctuating Base Rate

Policy: Name of Insurer:

                             Policy Number:

                             Date:

                             Sum Assured:

                             Name(s) of Assured:

Mortgagor's Obligations: All the Mortgagor's liabilities to the Bank of any kind (whether present or future actual or contingent and whether
                             incurred alone or jointly with another) including banking charges and commission

Expenses: All expenses (on a full indemnity basis) incurred by the Bank at any time in connection with the Policy or the
                             Mortgagor's Obligations or in taking perfecting enforcing or exercising any power under this deed with Interest from
                             the date they are incurred

Charge

1   The Mortgagor covenants to discharge on demand the Mortgagor's Obligations together with Interest to the date of discharge and
        Expenses and as a continuing security for such discharge and as beneficial owner assigns to the Bank the Policy and all money that may
        become payable under the Policy

        Provided That the Bank will reassign the Policy to the Mortgagor upon discharge of the Mortgagor's Obligations Interest and Expenses

Maintenance of Policy

2.1   The Mortgagor will comply with the terms of the Policy and punctually pay all premiums due under the Policy and on request by the Bank
        produce the premium receipts to the Bank

2.2   If there is any default by the Mortgagor under Clause 2.1 the Bank may take any action or make any payments necessary to maintain the
        Policy or obtain a substituted policy

Restriction on Charging

3   The Mortgagor will not without the Bank's prior written consent create or permit to arise any mortgage charge or lien on the Policy

Powers of the Bank

4.1   Section 103 of the Law of Property Act 1925 shall not apply and the Bank may exercise its power of sale and other powers under that or
        any other Act or this deed at any time after the date of this deed

4.2   The Bank may without restriction sell or surrender the Policy or convert it into a paid up Policy and/or exercise any rights conferred by the
        Policy

4.3   Section 93 of the Law of Property Act 1925 shall not apply to this deed

Page One

SPECIMEN *(by kind permission of Royal Bank of Scotland plc)*

Power of Attorney

5   The Mortgagor hereby irrevocably appoints the Bank to be the Attorney of the Mortgagor (with full power of substitution and delegation) in the Mortgagor's name and on the Mortgagor's behalf and as the Mortgagor's act and deed to sign or execute all deeds instruments and documents which may be required by the Bank pursuant to this deed or the exercise of any of its powers

Appropriation

6.1   Subject to Clause 6.2 the Bank may appropriate all payments received for the account of the Mortgagor in reduction of any part of the Mortgagor's Obligations as the Bank decides

6.2   The Bank may open a new account or accounts upon the Bank receiving actual or constructive notice of any charge or interest affecting the Policy and whether or not the Bank opens any such account no payment received by the Bank for the account of the Mortgagor after receiving such notice shall (if followed by any payment out of or debit to the Mortgagor's account) be appropriated towards or have the effect of discharging any part of the Mortgagor's Obligations outstanding at the time of receiving such notice

Preservation of other Security and Rights and Further Assurance

7.1   This deed is in addition to all other security present or future held by the Bank for the Mortgagor's Obligations and shall not merge with or prejudice such other security or any contractual or legal rights of the Bank

7.2   The Mortgagor will at the Mortgagor's own cost at the Bank's request execute any deed or document and take any action required by the Bank to perfect this security or further to secure on the Policy the Mortgagor's Obligations

Notices

8.1   Any notice or demand by the Bank may be sent by post or telex or delivered to the Mortgagor at the above address or the Mortgagor's address last known to the Bank or if the Mortgagor is a company may be served personally on any director or the secretary of the Mortgagor

8.2   A notice or demand by the Bank by post shall be deemed served on the day after posting

8.3   A notice or demand by the Bank by telex shall be deemed served at the time of sending

Governing Law

9   This deed shall be governed by and construed in accordance with the laws of England

Interpretation

10.1   The expressions 'Mortgagor' and 'Bank' where the context admits include their respective successors in title and assigns

10.2   If two or more persons are included in the expression 'Mortgagor' then the use in this deed of the word 'Mortgagor' shall be deemed to refer to such persons both together and separately and the Mortgagor's Obligations shall be their joint and several obligations and each of them shall be primarily liable by way of indemnity for the liabilities to the Bank of the other or others of them

10.3   The expression 'Policy' shall include any policy substituted for any policy charged by this deed

10.4   If the expression 'Policy' includes more than one policy then the use in this deed of the word 'Policy' shall be deemed to refer to such policies both together and separately

10.5   Interest will be calculated both before and after demand or judgment on a daily basis and compounded quarterly on such days as the Bank may select but after a demand Interest will also be calculated on the Mortgagor's Obligations together with accrued Interest as at the date of the demand

In Witness whereof this deed has been duly executed

Signed Sealed and **Delivered** (SEAL)	**Signed Sealed** and **Delivered** (SEAL)
by the first named Mortgagor	by the second named Mortgagor
in the presence of:—	in the presence of:—
Witness' name in full	Witness' Name in full
Signature	Signature
Address	Address
Occupation	Occupation

Page Two

SPECIMEN *(by kind permission of Royal Bank of Scotland plc)*

The Common Seal of the Mortgagor
was affixed in the presence of:—

Director   Secretary

Page Three

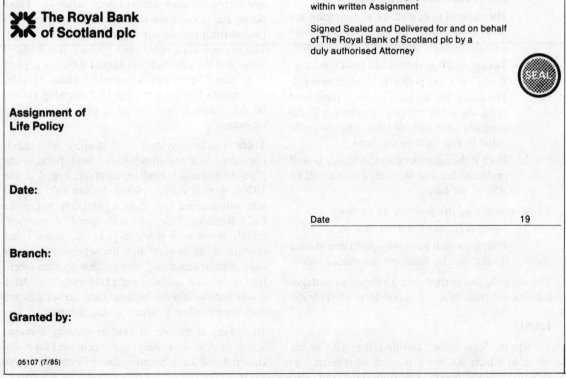

The Royal Bank of Scotland plc releases and re-assigns to the within named Mortgagor the Policy comprised in the within written Assignment

Signed Sealed and Delivered for and on behalf of The Royal Bank of Scotland plc by a duly authorised Attorney

**Assignment of
Life Policy**

Date:

Date   19

Branch:

Granted by:

05107 (7/85)

Page Four

To complete a legal assignment of a life policy the bank also has to contact the life insurance company and receive acknowledgement from it of the bank's interest in the policy. This prevents the company from paying out under the policy to anyone other than the bank, unless the bank first releases its charge.

LIFE POLICIES ASSESSED

12.   Life policies are one of the best forms of security available to banks and might be more widely used except that:-

a) many borrowers do not have endowment insurance;

b) endowment policy holders often have their policies assigned to building societies in connection with their mortgages;

c) insurance companies themselves are often willing to provide loans on very good terms to their policy holders.

Advantages of life policies as security

1. Endowment policies are very easy to value. The surrender value may be shown on the policy, but if it is not shown the company will provide the figure if asked.

2. The value of policies rises as premiums are paid. Banks can often make the payments directly from the customer's bank account.

3. Taking a charge over a life policy is easy.

4. Realising a life policy is straightforward. The policy and the bank's charge form need to be sent to the company together with the company's encashment form. The surrender value is then sent to the bank.

5. Even if the customer dies the lender is well protected because the sum insured will be sent to the bank.

Disadvantages of life policies as security

1. Some policies cannot be charged.

2. Policies which have only just been started do not usually have any surrender value.

The advantages clearly outweigh the disadvantages making life policies a very good form of security.

LAND

13.   In the legal sense, and therefore also in the sense in which the word is used in referring to security, 'land' means not only land but also buildings on the land. This is an important principle because buildings are often more valuable than the land they are built on.

The law dealing with land is far more complicated than the law covering other forms of bank security. The distinction between legal and equitable charges applies to land as it does to stocks and shares or to life polices, but in addition land is divided into two categories:-

a) registered land;

b) unregistered land.

Procedures for dealing with the two categories are quite different.

Owners of registered land have a single document as evidence that they own a piece of land. This is known as a *land certificate* and is issued by the Land Registry, a government agency which operates from a number of regional offices. Each Land Registry office keeps a register of the details of properties within the area which it covers. Each registered property is allocated a specific reference number and a new certificate is produced each time a registered property changes hands.

Owners of unregistered land have a series of *deeds and documents* as evidence of their ownership. These deeds and documents show how the property has passed from one owner to another over the years. The earliest documents may go back hundreds of years and the complete set should have no gaps to it so that it provides a complete chain of title. This means that each change of ownership should be documented, whether as a gift, a sale or an inheritance.

There are two systems for dealing with land, registered land and unregistered land, because the plans to introduce land registration, begun in the 1920s, were never completed. Before 1925 all land was unregistered and when registrations began the Land Registry dealt only with specified counties, mostly those with dense population. Some other counties were brought into the scheme but others have remained excluded. Even within counties where land registration operates some land owners still have deeds and documents because land certificates are only issued when property changes hands.

In looking at the use of land as security it makes sense to deal separately with registered land and unregistered land because the differences are so great.

CHARGES OVER REGISTERED LAND

14.   Ownership of registered land is recorded in a formal register and each separately owned piece of registered land has its own registration number. In addition the Land Registry (which deals only with registered land) keeps records of charges over the land and issues charge certificates to people who have taken charges, including banks which have lent money against mortgages. A charge certificate is similar to a land certificate but with a different cover, and with the charge form signed by the owner of the property sewn into the document.

The registered number of a property must be known in order to find out what charges have been registered and the information is not publicly available. Owners of property and owners of charges can inspect the register but others can only do so with permission (so when a bank wants to check the register before taking a charge it has to get the owner's authority).

It is possible to obtain an equitable charge over registered land simply by holding the land certificate. A slightly better form of security is to hold the certificate together with a completed legal mortgage form (see specimen below). Either of these options saves on the fees which the Land Registry requires for registering charges. The main disadvantage is that the bank cannot get its money back by selling the property unless the charge has been registered.

A legal charge is one which is registered by sending the land certificate and the completed legal mortgage form to the Land Registry. The bank as mortgagee then receives a charge certificate.

If a customer has already mortgaged property to another lender, for example a building society, the bank can still take a mortgage using exactly the same form but it will be a second mortgage rather than a first mortgage. This means that if the property is sold to pay off the borrower's debts the bank will be second in the queue of people to receive a share of the sale proceeds. When taking a second mortgage the bank will not have the land certificate (which will be at the Land Registry) but will send off its completed mortgage form and obtain a charge certificate. This will show the bank's charge and the prior charge to the building society.

Note that second mortgages of stocks and shares and life policies are also possible but are much rarer. Second mortgages of land are quite common because property is often of high value in relationship to a customer's borrowing. Further mortgages following on from a second mortgage are quite possible but few lenders would be interested in taking a fourth or fifth mortgage.

CHARGES OVER UNREGISTERED LAND

15.   Although there is no system of recording all unregistered land and who owns it there is a register of charges over unregistered land. This is kept at the Land Charges Registry, a separate organisation from the Land Registry. The Land Charges Registry keeps records in alphabetical order so it is only possible to find out what charges have been taken if the name of the owner of the property is known.

As with registered land it is possible to take a first charge or a subsequent charge and where several charges have been taken there are legal rules for determining the order of priority.

To take a first legal charge of unregistered land it is necessary to obtain the deeds and documents (checking that there is a good chain of title). Then the borrower completes a legal mortgage form (which is the same as the form used for registered land). No registration is required provided the bank keeps the deeds. For a second or any subsequent mortgage a mortgage form needs to be completed. Then the charge should be registered at the Land Charges Registry to make sure that no other charge can obtain priority (which would reduce the bank's chances of getting its money back). When taking a second mortgage the deeds are not available because they are held by the first mortgagee. If the property is sold it will be the first mortgagee who receives the sale proceeds, so the second mortgagee will give notice to the first mortgagee so that surplus money can be passed on rather than given back to the mortgagor.

An equitable first mortgage can be obtained simply by possession of the deeds, though a memorandum of deposit would usually be completed. An equitable second mortgage is created if the second mortgagee does not complete all the formalities for a full legal mortgage.

SPECIMEN *(by kind permission of Standard Chartered Bank plc)*

FM 4941 (1/85)

LEGAL MORTGAGE OF FREEHOLDS AND LEASEHOLDS
(by one or more persons or a limited company)

THIS LEGAL CHARGE made the ....day of ....19 ....

between ....

....

....

....

(hereinafter called "the Mortgagor" which expression shall include and extend to persons deriving title under the Mortgagor) of the one part and STANDARD CHARTERED BANK (hereinafter called "the Bank" which expression shall include and extend to its successors and assigns) of the other part

WITNESSETH as follows:-

1. In consideration of the Bank granting or continuing banking facilities or other accommodation for as long as the Bank may think fit to the Mortgagor or to third parties guaranteed by the Mortgagor or guaranteeing banking facilities or other accommodation at the Mortgagor's request at any other bank on the Mortgagor's account or on that of third parties the Mortgagor hereby covenants with the Bank that the Mortgagor will on demand pay to the Bank all sums of money which now are or at any time or times hereafter may become due or owing or may be accruing or becoming due to the Bank by the Mortgagor either alone or jointly with any other person or persons company or companies on any account or in respect of any liability whatsoever whether actual or contingent and whether in the character of principal debtor or guarantor or surety or otherwise together with in all cases interest and all other banking charges and so that interest shall be computed (as well after as before any demand or judgement) according to the usual mode of the Bank in dealing with current accounts.

2. The Mortgagor as beneficial owner hereby charges by way of legal mortgage ALL AND SINGULAR the property mentioned or described in the schedule hereto (hereinafter called "the Mortgaged Property") with the payment to the Bank of the principal money interest and other monies hereby covenanted to be paid or intended to be hereby secured and it is hereby declared that the interest of the Mortgagor in the Mortgaged Property is as stated in the schedule hereto and that the Mortgaged Property is free from all charges and encumbrances.

3. On or after repayment to the Bank of the monies hereby secured the Bank will at the request and cost of the Mortgagor discharge this security.

4. THE MORTGAGOR HEREBY FURTHER COVENANTS WITH THE BANK:-

    (a) To keep the Mortgaged Property and the buildings now or for the time being comprised in this security in good and substantial repair and condition

    (b) To keep the aforesaid buildings insured in the joint names of the Mortgagor and the Bank or with the interest of the Bank endorsed or noted on the policies in such manner as the Bank may require against loss or damage by fire and such other risks as the Bank shall from time to time consider necessary to the full value thereof or as the Bank shall decide in an insurance office approved by the Bank

    (c) Punctually to pay all premiums for keeping the aforesaid insurance on foot and on demand to lodge the policies and premium receipts with the Bank

    (d) Duly and punctually to pay all rates rents taxes and other outgoings in respect of the Mortgaged Property

    (e) (i) Not to cut remove maim or injure the Mortgaged Property nor

        (ii) to make any alterations improvements or additions thereto without the prior written consent of the Bank

    (f) To comply in all respects with the terms of provisions of the Town and Country Planning Acts and in particular not to change the present use of the Mortgaged Property without the prior written consent of the Bank.

    AND in case of default by the Mortgagor in the performance of any of the covenants in relation to the Mortgaged Property it shall be lawful for but not obligatory upon the Bank to do whatever may be necessary to make good such default and all sums expended by the Bank in that behalf shall be added to the monies hereby secured and bear interest accordingly and for the aforesaid purposes the Mortgagor will permit the Bank to enter upon the Mortgaged Property to effect such repairs as the Bank may consider necessary without thereby becoming liable as mortgagee in possession and the Bank may effect insurances in such amounts and against

Page One

SPECIMEN *(by kind permission of Standard Chartered Bank plc)*

such risks as the Bank shall decide and all monies received on any insurance of the Mortgaged Property whether effected by the Mortgagor or by the Bank and whether or not such insurance is one for the maintenance of which the Mortgagor is liable hereunder shall be applied towards making good the loss or damage in respect of which the monies are received or towards the discharge of the monies hereby secured as shall be required by the Bank.

5.   IT IS HEREBY AGREED AND DECLARED as follows:-

(a)   At any time after notice demanding payment of any monies hereby secured shall have been served by the Bank on the Mortgagor the Bank may forthwith without any further demand or notice enforce this security and exercise the powers conferred by Section 101 of the Law of Property Act 1925 (the Act) as varied or extended by this deed and in the exercise of the statutory power of sale the Bank shall be free from the restrictions imposed by Section 103 of the Act

(b)   At any time after the power of sale may be exercisable the Bank may by writing under the hand of any manager of the Bank appoint any person or persons (including a manager or other official of the Bank) to be a Receiver of the Mortgaged Property and may similarly remove any Receiver and appoint another in his stead and every Receiver so appointed shall be the agent of the Mortgagor and the Mortgagor shall be solely responsible for his acts or defaults and for his remuneration.

(c)   The powers conferred on mortgagees or receivers by the Act shall apply to this security except in so far as they are expressly or impliedly excluded and where there is any ambiguity or conflict between the powers contained in the Act and those contained in this security the terms of this security shall prevail

(d)   The statutory power of leasing or agreeing to lease and of accepting or agreeing to accept surrenders of leases and tenancies shall not be exercised without the Bank's previous consent in writing and no restriction on the consolidation of mortgages shall apply to this security

(e)   The Mortgagor shall at any time at the request of the Bank but at the cost of the Mortgagor execute or obtain the execution of any other or further mortgage charge or other document which the Bank may in its discretion think requisite or necessary for completing perfecting or giving effect to the security hereby intended to be given

(f)   The Mortgagor will bear and pay all legal charges and costs (on a full indemnity basis) and expenses incurred or to be incurred by the Bank in respect of any matter arising under or connected with this mortgage for the enforcement thereof or any other or further mortgage charge or other document and in case of default by the Mortgagor of the foregoing all sums expended by the Bank shall be added to the monies hereby secured and bear interest accordingly

(g)   During the continuance of this security no persons shall be registered under the Land Registration Act 1925 or any similar statutory provision as proprietor of the Mortgaged Property or any part thereof without the consent in writing of the Bank and the costs incurred by the Bank of lodging from time to time a caution against such registration shall be deemed to be costs properly incurred by the Bank under this security

(h)   In addition to all other protection afforded by law every purchaser or third party dealing with the Bank or any Receiver appointed by the Bank shall be entitled and bound to assume without enquiry that some monies are owing on the security hereof and have become payable and a notice in accordance with the provisions of clause 5(a) has been served

(i)   The Mortgagor hereby irrevocably appoints the Bank and any person nominated in writing under the hand of any manager of the Bank including every Receiver appointed hereunder to be the attorney of the Mortgagor in the name and on behalf of the Mortgagor and as the Mortgagor's act and deed to execute seal and deliver and otherwise perfect any deed assurance or instrument which may be required or deemed proper to fulfil any purpose of the security hereby intended to be given and generally to use the name of the Mortgagor in the exercise of all or any of the powers hereby conferred on the Bank or any Receiver appointed by it.

6.   This security shall not be considered as satisfied or discharged by any intermediate payment or satisfaction of the whole or any part of the monies hereby secured but shall constitute and be a continuing security to the Bank notwithstanding any settlement of account or any other matter or thing whatsoever.

7.   This security shall be in addition to and is not to prejudice or be prejudiced by any other security whether by way of mortgage charge lien or otherwise which the Bank may now or at any time hereafter have or hold for all or any of the monies hereby secured.

8.   In the event of the Bank receiving notice that the Mortgagor has encumbered or disposed of the equity of redemption or any part thereof the Bank may forthwith open a new or separate account with the Mortgagor and if the Bank does not open a new or separate account the Bank shall nevertheless be treated as if it had done so at the time of receipt of such notice and as from that time all monies paid by the Mortgagor shall be credited or be treated as having been credited to

Page Two

SPECIMEN *(by kind permission of Standard Chartered Bank plc)*

the new or separate account and shall not operate to reduce the amount due to the Bank by the Mortgagor at the time of receipt of such notice and furthermore the Bank may forthwith discontinue any guarantee or any other facility given or granted on the account of the Mortgagor.

9. Any notice or demand by the Bank shall be in writing signed by an officer of the bank and may be served by delivering the same to the Mortgagor or by post addressed to the Mortgagor at the address last known to the Bank a demand or notice so addressed and posted shall be deemed to have been served at the expiration of forty-eight hours after it has been posted and shall be effective notwithstanding that it be returned undelivered.

10. This security shall remain valid and binding for all purposes notwithstanding any change by amalgamation consolidation or otherwise which may be made in the constitution of the company by which the business of the Bank may from time to time be carried on and shall be available to the company carrying on that business for the time being.

11. Where this Deed is executed by more than one party of the one part their liability hereunder shall be joint and several and every convenant and agreement shall be construed accordingly and all references to the Mortgagor herein contained shall where the context requires or admits be construed as references to all or any of the parties of the one part and no one of them shall be nor shall this security be released or discharged by death or the death release or discharge of any other of them.

IN WITNESS whereof the Mortgagor has hereunto set his/their hand(s) and seal(s)/caused its Common Seal to be hereunto affixed the day and year first above written.

The SCHEDULE above referred to:

All the property comprised in the following deeds and documents or to which the same or any of them relate	Description and Location of the Mortgaged Property	Mortgagor's Interest in the Mortgaged Property (if leasehold state term and date of commencement)

Page Three

SPECIMEN *(by kind permission of Standard Chartered Bank plc)*

Signed Sealed and Delivered
by the above-named

.... ⎫
                                    ⎬   ....   ◯
                                    ⎭

in the presence of

Witness ....

Address ....

Address ....

Signed Sealed and Delivered
by the above-named

.... ⎫
                                    ⎬   ....   ◯
                                    ⎭

in the presence of

Witness ....

Address ....

Address ....

The Common Seal of

....

was hereunto affixed pursuant to a resolution of the Directors dated the......................

day of .... 19 .... in the presence of

.... Director

.... Director
Secretary

"It was resolved that the Common Seal of the Company be affixed to the Legal Mortgage in favour of Standard Chartered Bank which was produced to the Board and approved and on which document a certified copy of this resolution shall be inscribed".

The above is certified to be a true extract from the Minutes of the Board of Directors.

.... Secretary

DISCHARGE

STANDARD CHARTERED BANK hereby acknowledge that

.... has paid to the Bank

all monies secured by the within-written mortgage which security is accordingly discharged.

IN WITNESS whereof the Common Seal of the Bank has been hereunto affixed this

.... day of .... 19 ......

The Common Seal of STANDARD CHARTERED BANK
was hereunto affixed in the presence of:

.... Director

.... Secretary

Page Four

LAND ASSESSED

16.   This summary of the advantages and disadvantages of land as security concentrates on its general features though some of the factors only apply to registered land or to unregistered land.

Advantages of land as security

1.   Property values tend to rise faster than inflation;.
2.   There is always a market for land because it is limited in supply.
3.   The value of domestic property is usually fairly easy to estimate.
4.   For registered land there is only one document of title, the land certificate.

Disadvantages of land as security

1.   Realising the security may be a very slow process.
2.   The paperwork in taking the security may be complex, particularly for unregistered land.
3.   The costs of taking the security are high, specially for registered land.
4.   Valuation of factories and other industrial premises may be very difficult, which may mean a professional valuer will have to be called in, adding to the cost.
5.   Property values may fall.

Overall property is quite good as security because it usually rises in value, but it is difficult and expensive to deal with.

MORTGAGE DEBENTURES

17.   A mortgage debenture is an unusual form of security because it can only be given by companies. It is a charge created by a company over its assets in general.

A general charge is often referred to as a floating charge, but mortgage debenture charge forms may also include fixed charges over some assets as in clause 3 of the specimen below. Typically these fixed or specific charges relate to property and to debts owed to the company.

The floating charge is a means of taking as security assets which cannot easily be charged by a fixed charge, for example the stock which a company buys and sells; to carry out the procedures for releasing security each time a sale took place would be quite impracticable.

If a company gets into financial difficulties so that the bank wants to realise the security the assets covered by fixed charges can be realised just as though separate charge forms had been completed. Before any money can be obtained from the assets covered by the floating charge the charge needs to be 'crystallised' which usually means that an act of default has occurred as laid down in clause 6 of the specimen. At this stage the bank can appoint an administrative receiver (see Chapter 9). The administrative receiver can then arrange to sell the company's assets to repay the bank.

One of the weaknesses of a floating charge is that if the company is put into liquidation any sale proceeds from the assets covered by the floating charge must be used first to pay the debts owed to certain other people, defined in law as *preferential creditors*. The Companies Act 1985 lays down which claims against a company are preferential, taking preference over floating charge holders as well as unsecured creditors. Unpaid taxes and unpaid wages, within certain limits and restrictions, are the main preferential claims. Any assets covered by a fixed charge can be sold for the benefit of the mortgagee regardless of any preferential claims, which is one of the reasons why banks try to include as many assets as possible under the fixed charge when taking a mortgage debenture. (See section 3 of the specimen form which refers to specific charges over stocks and shares, sub-section d, and over debts, sub-section e.)

SPECIMEN *(by kind permission of TSB England and Wales plc)*

TSB England & Wales plc

Mortgage Debenture

THIS MORTGAGE DEBENTURE made the ⌊_____⌋ day of _____ 19 ⌊___⌋

BETWEEN
(1)

_____ LIMITED ⌋
Registered Number

⌊_____⌋ whose registered office is at
Address

⌊_____⌋

("the Company") and
(2) TSB ENGLAND & WALES PLC
("the Bank")

WITNESSES and it is hereby agreed and declared as follows:-

1   The Company hereby covenants with the Bank to pay or discharge to the Bank on demand being made by the Bank all moneys and liabilities which shall for the time being be due owing or incurred to the Bank by the Company (whether actually or contingently and whether solely or jointly with any other person firm or corporation and whether as principal or surety or otherwise and in whatever style or name and upon whatever account or accounts or otherwise howsoever) together with all interest discount commission or other lawful charges computed and compounded in accordance with the terms for the time being and from time to time agreed between the Company and the Bank relating thereto (if any) and subject to any such terms computed and compounded according to the usual mode of the Bank as well after as before any demand or judgement obtained all of which are hereinafter referred to as "the Liabilities".

2   This Mortgage Debenture shall be security for the payment and discharge to the Bank on demand by the Bank of the Liabilities.

3   The Company as beneficial owner hereby charges in favour of the Bank with the payment or discharge of the Liabilities:-

(a)   by way of legal mortgage all the freehold and leasehold property of the Company the title to which has been registered at HM Land Registry and which has been described in the Schedule hereto

(b)   by way of legal mortgage all other freehold and leasehold property of the Company now vested in it whether or not registered at HM Land Registry

(c)   by way of specific equitable charge all future freehold and leasehold property belonging to the Company during the continuance of this security

(d)   by way of specific charge all stocks, shares and/or other securities now and at any time during the continuance of this security belonging to the Company in any of its subsidiary companies (which expression shall for the purposes of this Mortgage Debenture have the meaning given in Section 154 of the Companies Act 1948)

(e)   by way of specific charge all book and other debts now and from time to time due or owing to the Company so that all moneys which it may receive in respect thereof are to be paid into the Company's account with the Bank

(f)   by way of floating charge its undertaking and all its assets and rights (other than those charged under paragraphs (a)-(e) of this clause) whatsoever and wheresoever present and future including building and trade fixtures fixed plant and machinery

(g)   by way of assignment its goodwill subject to redemption on discharge of the Liabilities.

The property charged under paragraphs (a)-(g) of this clause shall hereinafter be called "the assets".

4   The Company shall not except with the prior written consent of the Bank (a) create or permit to subsist any mortgage charge lien pledge or other security over the assets or any of them ranking in priority to or *pari passu* with the charge hereby created or (b) part with, sell or dispose of the whole or (except in the ordinary course of the Company's business and for the purpose of carrying on the same) any part of the assets or (c) enter into any arrangements to sell, factor, discount, assign or deal with any of its book or other debts or securities for money (i) with any person or company not obliged to the Company in relation to such debts or securities and (ii) with any person or company obliged to the Company in relation to such debts or securities save insofar as the same may be necessary in the ordinary course of getting in and realising such debts or securities.

5   (a)   The Company hereby covenants with the Bank that until this Mortgage Debenture is discharged the Company will:-

(i)   keep all buildings forming part of the assets and all fixtures fittings plant and machinery thereon and therein in good repair and will insure and keep insured the same against loss and damage by fire and such other risks as the Bank may from time to time stipulate in the full replacement value thereof with insurers approved by the Bank and if so required by the Bank in writing in the joint names of the Company and the Bank. If no such requirement is made by the Bank the Company will unless the Bank shall otherwise expressly agree in writing procure that the interest of the Bank is noted on the policy or policies of such insurance. The Company will duly pay all premiums and other moneys necessary for effecting and keeping up such insurance as and when the same become due and will on demand produce to the Bank the policy or policies of such insurance and the receipt for every such payment. All moneys

Registered Office: 60 Lombard Street, London EC3V 9EA. Registered in England and Wales: Number 1089268

EW-XX-1288-0086

SPECIMEN *(by kind permission of TSB England and Wales plc)*

to be received by virtue of any insurance whatsoever on the said buildings fixtures fittings plant and machinery (whether effected or maintained by the Company under the obligations contained in this paragraph (a)(i) or otherwise) shall (without prejudice to any obligation having priority to the obligations hereby imposed) be paid to the Bank (and if not paid directly to the Bank by the insurers then the Company shall hold the same in trust for the Bank and shall account to the Bank accordingly) and shall at the option of the Bank be applied in making good or in recouping expenditure incurred in making good the loss or damage in respect of which the same was received or in discharge or reduction of the Liabilities;

(ii) not without the prior written consent of the Bank (which shall not be withheld except for the purpose of protecting this security) make or suffer to be made any alterations in or additions to or removals from any building forming part of, or carry out or suffer to be carried out any development on, or change or suffer to be changed the user of any of the property referred to in Clause 3(a), (b) and (c) or (except for the purpose of effecting necessary repairs thereto or of replacing the same with new or improved models or substitutes) remove any of the machinery, utensils, chattels and things belonging to or in use by the Company and whenever any of the same are destroyed, injured or deteriorate forthwith repair, replace and make good the same;

(iii) observe and perform all the requirements and regulations of the local and other competent authorities concerning any of the assets and within seven days of the receipt by the Company of any notice order or proposal made given or issued by any such authority and concerning any of the assets to give full particulars thereof to the Bank and forthwith and at the cost of the Company take all reasonable and necessary steps to comply with the same or (if the Bank so requires) to make or join with the Bank in making such objections or representations in respect of the same as the Bank may desire;

(iv) observe and perform all covenants stipulations and conditions to which any of the assets or the user thereof is now or may hereafter be subjected and (if the Bank so requires) produce to the Bank evidence sufficient to satisfy the Bank that such covenants stipulations and conditions have been observed and performed;

(v) not without first obtaining the written consent of the Bank grant or agree to grant any licence or tenancy affecting any part of the assets nor exercise the powers of leasing or agreeing to lease or of accepting or agreeing to accept surrenders conferred by sections 99 and 100 of the Law of Property Act 1925;

(vi) procure that no person other than the Company shall be registered under the Land Registration Acts 1925 to 1971 as proprietor of any freehold or leasehold land comprised in the assets or any part thereof without the consent in writing of the Bank and the costs incurred by the Bank in lodging from time to time a caution against registration of the said land shall be deemed to be costs properly incurred by it hereunder and shall be repaid by the Company on demand and until repayment shall form part of the Liabilities and be secured hereunder accordingly;

(vii) procure that no person or persons is or are entitled to any right which might affect the value of any of the assets hereby charged (unless such entitlement exists at the date hereof or exists at the time of the acquisition by the Company of the relevant asset) without the prior consent in writing of the Bank;

(viii) carry on and conduct its business in a proper and efficient manner and not without obtaining the previous written consent of the Bank make any substantial alteration in the nature of that business;

(ix) not without the written consent of the Bank, which the Bank shall be entitled at its sole discretion to withhold, to enter into or offer to enter into any contract for the purchase of any goods or chattels which delays or purports to delay the passing to the Company of the property in any such goods or chattels until a time beyond the delivery to the Company of the same;

(x) furnish to the Bank copies of the trading and profit and loss accounts and audited balance sheet in respect of the financial year of the Company and of every subsidiary thereof (together with any consolidated accounts prepared in respect of the Company or any subsidiary thereof) forthwith upon the same becoming available and not in any event later than the expiration of six months from the end of each financial year and also from time to time such other information respecting the affairs of the Company or any such subsidiary as the Bank may reasonably require;

(b) In the event that the Company shall at any time or times commit any breach of any of the covenants contained in Clause 5(a) the Company shall keep the Bank indemnified against such breach and without prejudice to such indemnity and to any other rights and remedies which it may have the Bank may (but shall not be obliged to) for the purpose of ensuring that so far as practicable such covenant is fulfilled take such action (with power to enter upon any property comprised in the assets without thereby becoming a mortgagee in possession) and/or pay to such person or persons such amount or amounts as the Bank shall deem proper and all moneys expended by the Bank in so doing shall be deemed to be properly paid by the Bank and shall be repaid by the Company on demand and until repayment shall form part of the Liabilities and be secured hereunder accordingly.

6   The security constituted by this Mortgage Debenture shall become enforceable in the event that:-

(a) any of the Liabilities hereby secured remain unpaid or discharged when the same ought to be paid and discharged by the Company; or

(b) there is a breach by the Company of the terms and conditions of this Mortgage Debenture; or

(c) the Company is ordered or resolves to be wound up; or

(d) the Company enters into any composition or arrangement for the benefit of creditors; or

(e) any distress or execution is levied or threatened against any of the assets; or

(f) the Company is unable to pay its debts whether within the meaning of Section 223 of the Companies Act 1948 or not; or

(g) the Company certifies that it is unable to pay its debts as and when they fall due; or

(h) any loan debt guarantee or other obligation constituting indebtedness of the Company shall become due or shall be capable of being declared due prior to its stated maturity or shall not be paid at maturity or if the Company is in breach of or in default under any agreement pursuant to which any such indebtedness was incurred; or

(i) the Company shall suspend or threaten to suspend its operations, or if all or a substantial part of the assets of the Company shall be expropriated by any governmental or other authority or if the Company shall transfer or dispose of all or a substantial part of the assets; or

(j) an encumbrancer shall take possession or a receiver shall be appointed or any secured creditor of the Company shall seek to enforce its security in respect of all or any substantial part of the assets;

but any third party or purchaser shall in relation to any such enforcement be entitled to assume that one or more of such events has occured.

Page Two

SPECIMEN *(by kind permission of TSB England and Wales plc)*

7   (a)   At any time after the occurrence of any of the events specified in Clause 6 above or after any of the Liabilities shall have become immediately payable the Bank may from time to time appoint under seal or under the hand of a duly authorised officer of the Bank any person or persons to be a Receiver and Manager or Receivers and Managers (hereinafter called 'the Receiver' which expression shall where the context so admits include the plural and any substituted receiver and manager or receivers and managers) of the assets or any part or parts thereof and may from time to time under seal or under hand of a duly authorised officer of the Bank remove any one or more Receiver or Receivers so appointed and may so appoint another or others in his/their stead.

   (b)   The foregoing powers of appointment of the Receiver shall be in addition to and not to the prejudice of all statutory and other powers of the Bank under the Law of Property Act 1925 (and so that any statutory power of sale shall be exercisable without the restrictions contained in sections 103 and 109 of that Act) or otherwise and so that such powers shall be and remain exercisable by the Bank in respect of any part of the assets in respect of which no appointment of a Receiver by the Bank shall from time to time be subsisting and notwithstanding that an appointment under the powers of sub-clause (a) of this Clause shall have subsisted and been withdrawn in respect of that part of the assets or shall be subsisting in respect of any other part of the assets.

   (c)   A Receiver so appointed shall be the agent of the Company and the Company shall be solely responsible for his acts defaults and remuneration.

   (d)   A Receiver so appointed shall have and be entitled to exercise all powers conferred by the Law of Property Act 1925 in the same way as if the Receiver had been duly appointed thereunder and shall furthermore but without limiting any powers hereinbefore referred to have power:-

   (i)   to take possession of collect and get in the property in respect of which he is appointed or any part thereof and for that purpose to take any proceedings in the name of the Company or otherwise as may seem expedient;

   (ii)   to carry on or manage or develop or diversify the business of the Company and for that purpose to raise money on any part of the assets in priority to this security or otherwise;

   (iii)   to sell or concur in selling let or concur in letting and to accept surrenders of leases of any part of the assets in such manner and generally on such terms and conditions as he thinks fit and to carry any such sale letting or surrender into effect by conveying leasing letting or accepting surrenders in the name of or on behalf of the Company or otherwise. Any such sale may be for cash debentures or other obligations shares stock or other valuable consideration and may be payable in a lump sum or by instalments spread over such period as the Bank shall think fit and so that any consideration or part thereof received in a form other than cash shall *ipso facto* forthwith on receipt be and become charged with the payment of all the moneys hereby secured as though it had been included in the charge hereby created and formed part of the assets so charged; plant machinery and other fixtures may be severed and sold separately from the premises containing them without the consent of the Company being obtained thereto;

   (iv)   to make any arrangement or compromise which he or the Bank may think expedient;

   (v)   to make and effect any repairs renewals and improvements of the Company's plant machinery and effects which he or the Bank may think expedient and to maintain or renew any insurances;

   (vi)   to make calls conditionally or unconditionally on the members of the Company in respect of the uncalled capital with such and the same powers for the purpose of enforcing payment of any calls so made as are by the Articles of Association of the Company conferred on the Directors thereof in respect of calls authorised to be made by them in the names of the Directors or in that of the Company or otherwise and to the exclusion of the Directors' power in that behalf;

   (vii)   to appoint managers officers servants workmen and agents for the aforesaid purposes at such salaries and for such periods as he may determine;

   (viii)   to do all such other acts and things as may be considered to be incidental or conducive to any of the matters or powers aforesaid and which the Receiver lawfully may or can do as agent for the Company.

   (e)   All monies received by any Receiver shall be applied by him for the following purposes subject to the claims of secured and unsecured creditors (if any) ranking in priority to or *pari passu* with the charge hereby constituted and in the following order:-

   (i)   in payment of all costs charges and expenses of and incidental to the appointment of any Receiver and the exercise of all or any of the powers aforesaid and of all outgoings properly paid by any Receiver;

   (ii)   in payment of remuneration to any Receiver at such rate as may be agreed between him and the Bank;

   (iii)   in or towards the payment to the Bank of all monies hereby secured and the discharge in favour of the Bank of all liabilities hereby secured;

   (iv)   any surplus shall be paid to the Company or other the person entitled thereto.

   (f)   The Bank shall not nor shall any Receiver or Receivers appointed hereunder be liable to account as mortgagee or mortgagees in possession in respect of the assets or any part thereof nor be liable for any loss upon realisation or collection of the assets or any part thereof for which a mortgagee in possession might as such be liable and all costs charges and expenses incurred by the Bank or any Receiver appointed hereunder (including the costs of any proceedings to enforce the security hereby given) shall be repaid by the Company on demand and until repayment shall form part of the Liabilities and be secured hereunder accordingly.

   (g)   The Company hereby agrees to indemnify and hold harmless any Receiver appointed hereunder from and against all actions, claims, expenses, demands and liabilities whether arising out of contract or in tort or in any other way incurred or which may at any time be incurred by him or by any manager, agent, officer, servant or workman for whose debt, default or miscarriage he may be answerable for anything done or omitted to be done in the exercise or purported exercise of his powers under this Mortgage Debenture or under any appointment duly made under the provisions of this Clause.

8   The Company hereby irrevocably appoints the Bank and any Receiver appointed by the Bank jointly and also severally the Attorney and Attorneys of the Company for the Company in its name and on its behalf and as its act and deed or otherwise to seal and deliver and otherwise perfect any deed assurance agreement instrument or act which may be required or may be deemed proper for any of the purposes aforesaid.

9   The restriction on consolidation contained in Section 93 of the Law of Property Act 1925 shall not apply to this security.

10   (a)   The Company hereby warrants to the Bank that there are not now and will not during the continuance of this security without the prior written consent of the Bank first had and obtained be any prior incumbrances on any of the assets.

   (b)   At any time after this security becomes enforceable or after any powers conferred by any incumbrance having priority to this security become exercisable the Bank may redeem such or any other prior incumbrance or procure

Page Three

SPECIMEN *(by kind permission of TSB England and Wales plc)*

the transfer thereof to the Bank and may settle and pass the accounts of the incumbrancer and any account so settled and passed shall be conclusive and binding on the Company and all moneys paid by the Bank to the incumbrancer in accordance with such accounts shall be deemed to be properly paid by the Bank and shall be paid by the Company to the Bank on demand and until repayment shall form part of the Liabilities and be secured hereunder accordingly.

11   All moneys received recovered or realised by the Bank under this security may in the sole discretion of the Bank be credited to any suspense or impersonal account and may be held in such account for so long as the Bank may think fit pending their application from time to time (as the Bank shall be entitled to do in its discretion) in or towards the discharge of any of the Liabilities hereby secured which shall from time to time become due.

12   (a)   This security shall constitute and be a continuing security notwithstanding any settlement of account or other matter or thing whatsoever and in particular (but without prejudice to the generality of the foregoing) shall not be considered satisfied by any intermediate repayment or satisfaction of the Liabilities or any part thereof and shall continue in full force and effect until final repayment in full and total satisfaction of the Liabilities.

(b)   This security shall remain in full force and effect unless and until the Bank discharges this security by endorsing the receipt hereon.

13   The Company will deposit with the Bank all deeds and documents of title relating to the property referred to in Clause 3(a), (b) and (c) and will forthwith on being required from time to time by notice in writing by the Bank so to do at the cost and expense of the Company execute and sign and do all documents deeds and things which shall be necessary to create a formal charge by way of legal mortgage or sub-mortgage in favour of the Bank of all or such parts of the assets as shall be specified in the said notice to further secure the payment and discharge of the Liabilities or any part thereof.

14   If the Bank so requires the Company will deposit with the Bank and the Bank during the continuance of this security shall be entitled to hold all deeds and documents of title relating to the assets or any part therof (and the insurance policies thereon) unless the same relate to or are comprised in any security ranking in priority hereto and are in the possession of the prior mortgagee or chargee.

15   This security shall be in addition to and shall not operate so as in any way to prejudice or affect any other security which the Bank may hold for or any right which it may have in respect of the Liabilities or any part thereof whether from the Company or any other person not party hereto and further the Bank shall have full power at its discretion to give time for payment to or make any other arrangement with any such other person without prejudice to the liability of the Company hereunder.

16   If the Bank receives notice of any subsequent charge or other interest affecting any part of the assets the Bank may open a new account or accounts with the Company. If the Bank does not open a new account it shall nevertheless unless it gives

express written notice to the contrary to the Company be treated as if it had done so at the time when it received notice and as from that time all payments made by the Company to the Bank shall be credited or be treated as having been credited to the new account and shall not operate to reduce the amount due from the Company to the Bank at the time when it received the notice.

17   In case the Company shall have more than one account with the Bank it shall be lawful for the Bank at any time and without any prior notice forthwith to transfer all or any part of any balance standing to the credit of any such account to any other such account which may be in debit but the Bank shall notify the Company of the transfer having been made.

18   All costs charges and expenses incurred hereunder by the Bank including (without prejudice to the generality of the foregoing) all moneys expended by the Bank under Clauses 5(b), 7(f) and 10(b) hereof and all other moneys paid by the Bank in perfecting preserving discharging or otherwise in connection with this security and all costs of the Bank of all proceedings for enforcement of the security hereby constituted or for obtaining payment of the Liabilities or any part thereof (whether or not such costs charges expenses and moneys or part thereof would be allowable upon a party and party or solicitor and own client taxation by the Court) shall be recoverable from the Company as a debt and may be debited to any account of the Company and shall bear interest accordingly and shall form part of the Liabilities and be secured hereunder accordingly and the charge hereby conferred shall be in addition and without prejudice to any and every other remedy lien or security which the Bank may have or but for the said charge would have for the Liabilities or any part thereof.

19   A demand or notice hereunder shall be in writing signed by an officer of the Bank and may be served on the Company (without in any way preventing the Bank from serving the same in any other manner) either personally or by post. A demand or notice served by post may be addressed to the Company at its registered office or at its address last known to the Bank and a demand or notice so addressed and posted first class postage prepaid shall be deemed to have been made or given at noon on the second day following the day of posting and shall be effective notwithstanding that it be returned undelivered. Any notice to be given to the Bank shall be addressed to the Bank at the address shown hereon as the Bank's address for notices or such other address as the Bank may notify to the Company from time to time.

20   In respect of any freehold or leasehold property hereby charged the title to which is registered at HM Land Registry it is hereby certified that the charge created by this Mortgage Debenture does not contravene any of the provisions of the memorandum and articles of association of the Company.

21   Where the context so admits the expression the "Company" shall include its successors and permitted assigns and the "Bank" shall include its successors and assigns and any reference herein to a person if the context so admits apply also to a company, partnership or unincorporated association and any reference herein to any statutory provision shall be deemed to include reference to any statutory modification or re-enactment thereof for the time being in force.

SPECIMEN *(by kind permission of TSB England and Wales plc)*

The Schedule

All the property comprised in the undermentioned title(s) at HM Land Registry

Title No.	County and District or London Borough	Short description of Property

IN WITNESS whereof the Company has caused its Common Seal to be hereunto affixed the day and year first above written

The Common Seal of _____

_____ LIMITED

was hereunto affixed pursuant to a Resolution of the Board of Directors in the presence of:-

Director

_____

Secretary

_____

Page Five

SPECIMEN *(by kind permission of TSB England and Wales plc)*

Certificate of the Registration of a Mortgage or Charge

I HEREBY CERTIFY that a mortgage or charge dated the ⎿_____⏌ and created by

⎿_____⏌
                                                                    Date

was registered pursuant to section 395 of the Companies Act 1985 on the ⎿_____⏌
                              Date   No.

given under my hand at Cardiff the ⎿_____⏌ ⎿_____⏌
Assistant Registrar of Companies

⎿_____⏌

N.B. When this Mortgage Debenture is returned by the Registrar the above should be completed in identical terms to the Registrar's Certificate. The Registrar's Certificate should also be attached to this Mortgage Debenture.

Receipt

TSB England & Wales plc hereby acknowledge that they have received the balance of the moneys (including interest and costs) secured by the within-written Deed payment having been made by

⎿_____⏌

In witness whereof a duly authorised attorney of
the Bank has hereunto set his hand and seal this
Date

⎿_____⏌

SIGNED, SEALED AND DELIVERED by

Attorney's Full Name (BLOCK CAPITALS)   Attorney's Signature

⎿_____⏌ ⎿_____ SEAL ⏌

as attorney duly authorised by deed
for and on behalf of TSB England & Wales plc
in the presence of:

Witness's Signature
⎿_____⏌
Name
⎿_____⏌
Address
⎿_____⏌
⎿_____⏌
Occupation
⎿_____⏌

Branch   Bank's address for notices
⎿_____⏌
Account
⎿_____⏌

⎿_____⏌

FLOATING CHARGES ASSESSED

18.   If assets are covered by the fixed charge within a mortgage debenture the security is no different from a charge over those assets using a specific charge form, provided all the required formalities are completed.

The floating charge within a mortgage debenture has rather different qualities. Note that most floating charges are given by companies, though there is a much rarer form of floating charge, an Agricultural Charge, which can be given as security by farmers provided they are not companies.

Advantages of floating charges as security

1.   The lender can take a charge over assets which would otherwise be difficult to charge.
2.   The procedure for taking the charge is straightforward.

Disadvantages of floating charges as security

1.   Putting a value on all the assets may be very difficult.
2.   If the security needs to be realised many of the assets may have disappeared or fallen in value.
3.   Realising the security will usually mean appointing a receiver whose costs will reduce the value of the sale proceeds.
4.   The charge may not be valid if the business was insolvent when the security was given.
5.   A business which agrees to give a floating charge to a lender is often seen as being in financial difficulties, and the adverse publicity could add to the problems the business faces.

The disadvantages listed here indicate that floating charges are not an ideal form of security though they may be a useful supplement to other security, for example property covered by a fixed charge.

OTHER FORMS OF SECURITY

19.   Apart from the very common types of security, guarantees, stocks and shares, life policies and land, a number of other forms of security are available to lenders. The following list comments briefly on some of those used by banks.

1.   **Debts**
In the section dealing with mortgage debentures it was explained that a fixed charge over debts is commonly included. Businesses for which debtors are a major asset can use the debts as a form of security. In some cases a range of debts are charged (just as debts can be sold to factor companies as described in Chapter 14). If only one single debt is charged, for example the proceeds from a major contract, even better security can be obtained by giving notice to the debtor of the assignment of the debt. This ensures that the borrower cannot prevent payment from being sent to the bank.

2.   **Bills of Exchange**
In a sense bills of exchange form security for a bank when it lends money by discounting bills. This was described in Chapter 14.

3.   **Ships**
A mortgage can be taken over a ship (or even a share in a ship) just as it can over land. The charge can be registered at the port of registration of the vessel preventing it from being mortgaged or sold to anyone else while it is charged to a lender.

4.   **Goods**
Importers of goods are sometimes lent money in the form of a produce advance which is a loan using the goods themselves as security. The sale proceeds of the goods are then used to repay the borrowing. (See Chapters 17 and 22.)

5.   **Legacies**
If a customer is expecting to receive a substantial sum of money which has been left in a will but is not payable to the customer immediately, the bank may lend money using the customer's interest in the will as security. The testator must have already died and probate must have been granted, so that the assets are held in trust. The customer is said to have a *reversionary interest* because the assets revert to, or pass to, him or her at a future date. It is this reversionary interest which is charged to the bank. This form of security is complex and not widely used because of the problems which can arise.

6. **Solicitors' Undertakings**

Where the legal aspects of security arrangements are being dealt with by solicitors, documents of title relating to assets charged or to be charged to the bank may be held by the solicitors for some time, particularly when dealing with land. A solicitor's undertaking provides the bank with a formal promise backed up by the Law Society that the assets will not be released to anyone else without the bank's approval. The solicitors involved will often be those chosen by the bank's customer rather than by the bank itself so a status enquiry to check on the solicitors may be needed. Now that licensed conveyancers can deal with property transactions banks can also expect to be offered undertakings by conveyancers. These will not have the backing of the Law Society but conveyancers may have insurance cover to enable them to pay out if any claim is made against them.

Solicitors' undertakings are a very frequently used form of bank security but they are usually only taken as a temporary measure while other security is being arranged or released.

TAKING SECURITY

20.   Whatever form of security a bank wants to take there are a number of steps which are normally required.

1. Carrying out a valuation (for example looking up share prices).

2. Checking that there are no restrictions on taking a charge and no prior charges affecting the assets to be taken as security (for example making an official search at the Land Charges Registry before taking a mortgage of unregistered land).

3. Obtaining documents of title if they are available (for example the original of a life insurance policy).

4. Arranging completion of the bank's charge form, preferably at the bank or at the office of a solicitor known to the bank.

5. Registering the charge (for example at the Land Registry when taking a mortgage of registered land). Note that many of the charges which companies give also need to

be registered at Companies House in order to give the lender valid security.

Not all of these steps are needed for all kinds of security, and for most kinds of security some other factors also need to be taken into consideration. Banks produce *progress sheets* for all the major types of security; these outline the steps to be taken in each case and act as a checklist to tick off as progress is made. One of the tasks of a security clerk is to make sure that all of the necessary steps are taken in the right order and with the minimum of delay.

RELEASING SECURITY

21.   Security is released when it is no longer needed. This is usually because the customer has repaid the money borrowed and is not expected to take further borrowing in the near future. In other cases the customer may need the assets which were charged to the bank but has been able to provide alternative security for the borrowing.

The process of releasing security is usually a reversal of the steps taken in creating the security. Where charges have been registered notice has to be given of the release of the security. The bank's charge form can often be kept by the bank with other lapsed papers, available for future reference, but in some cases the document becomes part of the official chain of title of the asset charged and has to be given back to the customer. This applies to legal mortgages of unregistered land and to legal assignments of life policies.

REALISING SECURITY

22.   A lender realises security when the borrower fails to repay. Realisation is simply the process of converting the security into money to pay off the debt, but this simple idea may be very complicated in practice for a number of reasons.

1. The borrower may be entitled to notice or extra time before the assets can be disposed of. Where possible bank charge forms remove such rights from customers, but regulated agreements under the Consumer Credit Act still require a formal default notice before any security can be realised.

2. There may be limitations on the lender's powers to realise the security. A full legal mortgage gives the mortgagee the power to sell the assets mortgaged (as well as other

less useful legal rights such as the power to retain the asset or to sue for the debt) but the rights of an equitable mortgagee are less useful for a bank trying to get its money back; it is usually necessary to apply for a court order before a sale can take place, and that means there is delay in getting repayment.

3. There may be a legal dispute about the validity of the security. Borrowers often try to claim that the security cannot be enforced and the case law about security demonstrates how wide a range of reasons customers can discover for not repaying.

When security is realised the amount obtained is unlikely to be exactly the amount owed. If there is a shortfall the proceeds are often credited to a realised security account, rather than the customer's account, while steps are taken to get money back in other ways. This is particularly important where the security was given by a third party because a claim against the customer for the full amount can still be made (which can be very valuable where the borrower is insolvent and only pays creditors part of what is owed − see Chapter 8).

If the money obtained from realising security is greater than the amount owed the bank cannot make a profit from it but must release the surplus. Care has to be taken that it is paid out to the right person. For example a trustee in bankruptcy may have the first claim on it, in which case paying it to the customer would not release the bank from liability. Similarly the bank may have received notice of a second charge over the asset which means that after the bank has cleared its debt any surplus should go to the second mortgagee to repay the debt secured by the second mortgage.

SUMMARY

23. a) Taking security when lending is a way of reducing risk, usually by obtaining control over assets which can be turned into cash if the money lent is not repaid.

b) The basic principles of good security are that it should be:-
   1. easy to value;
   2. valuable;
   3. easy to charge;
   4. realisable.

c) Charges over assets may be:-
   1. legal (giving full control and the power to sell the asset charged), *or*
   2. equitable (a term which covers a range of less complete forms of control).

d) Most charges which banks take are fixed charges relating to specific assets. Some charges are floating charges covering a category of assets.

e) Guarantees used by banks are technically indemnities rather than guarantees in the strict legal sense because they enable the bank to have valid security even if the debt is unenforceable. The main advantage of guarantees as security is that they are easy to take.

f) Mortgages can be taken of stocks and shares, but there are dangers in charging stocks and shares which are not quoted on the Stock Exchange. The main drawback of any shares taken as security is that they may fluctuate enormously in value.

g) Endowment life insurance policies can be assigned to banks as security. Provided there are no obstacles to taking a valid charge a life policy is an excellent form of security meeting all the criteria for good security.

h) Land is often taken as security but the relevant law is very complex which can make taking the security and realising it a difficult process. Different rules apply to registered land and unregistered land.

i) With registered land the owner has a land certificate. A lender taking a charge obtains a similar document called a charge certificate. Land certificates and charge certificates are issued by the Land Registry (which deals only with registered land). Records kept by the Land Registry are based on reference numbers allocated to each property on the register.

j) With unregistered land the owner has deeds and documents. A lender taking a first legal mortgage normally holds the deeds and a completed mortgage form. A second or subsequent mortgagee only has a charge form, but can register the charge at the Land Charges Registry. This is quite separate from the Land Registry and keeps records based on the names of the owners of the land against which any charge is recorded.

k) The main advantage of land as security is that it tends to rise in value faster than inflation. The main disadvantages are the cost and complexity of taking the security.

l) Mortgage debentures, or fixed and floating charges, are a form of security given only by companies. The fixed charge gives the lender priority over preferential creditors in getting money back but the floating charge ranks after preferential claims if the company is put into liquidation.

m) Other forms of security include:-
   1. Debts;
   2. Bills of Exchange;
   3. Ships;
   4. Goods;
   5. Legacies;
   6. Solicitors' undertakings.

n) Many of the steps in taking security are common to most forms of security. These include:-
   1. Valuation;
   2. Searches;
   3. Obtaining any documents of title to the assets;
   4. Completing the charge form;
   5. Registration of the security.

o) Release of security is, in most cases, a reversal of the steps taken to complete the security. Realising security may be more complicated because it may be necessary to apply to a court of law for permission to dispose of assets charged, particularly where an equitable charge has been taken. Care must be taken in dealing with any surplus money.

STUDENT SELF-TESTING

Self Review Questions

1. What does the term 'a charge' mean? (4)

2. What is the difference between an indemnity and a guarantee? (6)

3. What principle is illustrated by the case of Coutts and Co. v. Browne Lecky and others? (6)

4. Why are shares in private companies not very suitable as security? (9)

5. What are the advantages of taking stocks and shares as security? (10)

6. What is a surrender value? (11)

7. Why are life policies not used more widely as security for bank lending? (12)

8. What are the main differences between registered and unregistered land? (13)

9. What is a mortgage debenture? (17)

10. What are the disadvantages of floating charges? (18)

Exercises (answers begin page 336)

A1. What are the key factors to look for in good security? Explain each by reference to specific forms of security.

A2. Distinguish between a charge, a legal mortgage and an equitable mortgage.

A3. To what extent do stocks and shares meet the requirements of good security?

A4. 'Life policies are ideal security.' To what extent do you agree with this statement?

17. Lending Situations

INTRODUCTION

1. This chapter looks at a number of lending situations by means of case studies. Students should write their own answers to the questions set before going on to read the suggested solutions for each case study.

The main themes linking the case studies are:-

a) the control of lending;

b) the recovery of lending;

c) security-based lending;

d) variations between industries.

CONTROL OF LENDING

2. The most simple method by which a bank can control lending is to set a date for repayment of the borrowing and make a diary note to check that repayment has been made. For some kinds of lending this kind of control system of checking on the final outcome is quite adequate. For short-term loans repaid in a lump sum, for example from a sale of a house or stocks and shares, the diary note or a computerised equivalent of it is the most appropriate form of control. If repayment has been made little further action is required, but if the loan has not been cleared other measures need to be taken. This may mean contacting the people who should have sent the money. Asking the customer for any news may also be a sensible step.

With structured lending requiring regular repayment in instalments checking the balance on the loan after each payment date would be very time-consuming. Two useful solutions to the problem of how to maintain control in these circumstances are:-

a) to program the computer to provide a print-out of any late payments *or*

b) to make sure payments are made by standing order from a current account.

Both of these are preferable to simply waiting until the final payment is due to see whether anything has gone wrong because it is easier to take corrective action the earlier a problem is identified. If, as is most common, payments are from a current account the first warning sign of possible problems in repaying the loan is that the current account becomes overdrawn. This will be identified immediately by a computer analysis of unarranged overdrafts. The customer can then be invited to discuss what has gone wrong and why. The answers will determine what further action the bank should take.

With more complex business lending the bank may want to check fairly frequently what is happening to the financial position of the business. In some cases, such as building projects, the most straightforward way of checking is to go and see how work is progressing, but the most common form of control is to ask for regular management accounting information. Lenders do therefore need to understand what the figures mean so that they can see problems as they arise and discuss with customers the steps that they might take.

The first of the case studies which follows deals with a lump sum repayment and the second with conditions imposed by a bank based on management accounting information.

CASE STUDY: BOB BURTON

3. *Some while ago your branch received a letter from solicitors Hassell and Strife regarding your customer Bob Burton. The letter stated that by the 14th March they would be forwarding to you a sum in the region of £89,000 representing the sale proceeds of his late mother's house. In anticipation of this your manager lent Bob £10,000 to buy a new car.*

On the 15th March a note in the branch diary reminds you to check the balances on Bob's two accounts and you find that the loan account balance is still at £10,000 and the current account balance is £459.60. Your first step is to see whether the funds have been received that day by post.

Required:
Your comments on what action should be taken:-

1. if you find that a draft for £89,500 has been received from Hassell and Strife;

2. if no funds have been received.

SUGGESTED SOLUTION: BOB BURTON

4. This case is concerned with the repayment of a loan from an expected lump sum. Both possibilities are fairly straightforward.

1. If the payment from Hassell and Strife has been received the control system for making sure the loan is repaid is almost complete.

A few further practical steps are still needed. The bank should:-
a)   send a letter of acknowledgement to the solicitors;
b)   pass credit entries for £10,000 plus any interest to Bob's loan account, closing the account, and for the rest to his current account;
c)   notify Bob of the action you have taken;
d)   invite him to come and discuss with the manager his plans for investing the money (if this has not already been done).

2.   If no funds have been received the diary system reminding the branch to follow up the matter has shown its importance. The best approach may be to telephone the solicitors to check whether there is any news. A likely response is that there has been some delay in the paperwork. If this is the case you should:-
a)   record what the solicitors have said;
b)   diarise to check on the money again after an appropriate time;
c)   if the delay is likely to be a long one notify Bob.

If the funds should have been sent but have been overlooked your phone call may avoid some delay. Once the money is received the steps outlined in 1. above should be carried out.

CASE STUDY: XENON LTD

5.   *Xenon Ltd has a borrowing limit of £22,500 which is due for review this month. £4,500 of the borrowing is covered by a fully supported guarantee. It has been agreed that the further borrowing, up to £18,000, should not exceed 50% of current assets. The last six months figures are as follows:-*

Months ago	5	4	3	2	1	This month
Debtors	8420	9744	10446	7326	9544	5976
Stock:						
– unfinished	6722	7500	8338	11428	11762	13310
– finished	14168	15446	15914	17102	17294	17012
Total	29310	32690	34698	35856	38600	36298
Overdraft	16520	19078	21446	20636	22340	20450

Required:
Your answers to the following questions.

1.   Have the overdraft agreement requirements been met?

2.   Given that you have no information about the creditors figures what effect do you think the changes shown here might have had on working capital, and why?

3.   How well do you think the business is doing, judging by the limited information provided?

SUGGESTED SOLUTION: XENON LTD

6.   The main difficulty about this exercise is that the information is incomplete so some intelligent guesswork is needed. For example it seems reasonable to assume that the unfinished stock is partly of raw materials being bought on credit, so a rise in the figure suggests a rise in creditors.

1.   The following table of figures shows that for each of the six months in question the percentage of unsecured borrowing to current assets has remained below 50%, reaching 49% at its highest three months ago. The bank's requirement has therefore been met.

Months ago	5	4	3	2	1	This month
Current Assets	29310	32690	34698	35856	38600	36298
Overdraft	16520	19078	21446	20636	22340	20450
Unsecured borrowing	12020	14578	16946	16136	17840	15950
Unsecured borrowing figures shown as percentages of total current assets						
	41%	46%	49%	45%	46%	44%

2.   As the figure for the unfinished stock has been rising there is a likelihood that creditors have also been going up. The rise in current assets over the six months is £(36298 − 29310) = £6988 and the overdraft has risen by £(20450 − 16520) = £3930, a difference of £3058.

If creditors have risen by £3058 or more the working capital will be lower now than it was six months ago. The rise in unfinished stock is well above that figure. This makes a reduction in working capital seem likely.

3.   The business does not seem to be doing particularly well because:-
a)   the decline in debtors suggests that sales may be falling;
b)   the increases in stock suggest that goods are being half-finished or finished and left unsold;
c)   the rising overdraft suggests that extra spending is taking place without adding to revenue.

The overdraft ought to have been reducing by this stage if it was agreed for six months.

RECOVERY OF LENDING

7.   If a customer fails to make repayment at the due date the bank has to consider what steps need to be taken to recover the debt. Ideally the bank likes the customer to make the first move if any problem has occurred. For example a personal customer who is made redundant will have difficulty in paying back any loan, but an approach to the bank is likely to get a more sympathetic response than ignoring the problem and hoping it will go away.

If it is the bank which has to take the first step to recover a debt the customer will be seen in an unfavourable light, though this may be a minor matter if repayment is made soon. Banks usually have a series of letters to send out to customers owing money.

1.   The first and mildest reminder may be to send out a statement of the account or a brief note asking whether payment has been overlooked.

2.   If there is no response this may be followed up by a request for the customer to contact the branch to discuss the matter.

3.   Further letters may take a stronger line insisting on an immediate reply.

4.   If these are ignored a last resort is to threaten legal action, though this should rarely be needed.

5.   Finally if the customer has disappeared or refuses to have any contact with the bank the debt may be put in the hands of professional debt collectors.

For loans which are regulated agreements under the terms of the Consumer Credit Act 1974, before legal proceedings can be taken against the borrower a default notice must be issued. This gives the customer the opportunity to put things right and gives extra time to pay.

For business customers recovery of loans may depend on getting the business to change the way in which it operates. If management accounts highlight fundamental problems such as rising costs and falling sales new policies may need to be introduced. Failure to adapt will lead to liquidation and recovery of the debt may then depend on any security that was taken. If a business does go into liquidation the procedure for the bank is to make a formal claim for repayment from the liquidator. This is known as submitting a 'proof' or 'proving' the debt. If the 'proof' is accepted the bank will be entitled to a proportion of the money raised from selling the assets of the business but will not expect to be repaid in full. The same kind of approach applies in the event of a personal bankruptcy.

Any direct security (provided by a borrower before going into liquidation) reduces the amount which can be claimed from the liquidator. Note that having third-party security is a great advantage (as explained in Chapter 16) because a claim for the full debt can be made to the liquidator and a similar claim can be made on the surety, the person providing the security. This gives the bank an increased chance of getting full repayment (though if the bank receives more than it is owed it cannot keep the extra money).

Recovering debts by realising security is a very specialised field for which the banks have their own experts. Branch bankers are unlikely to be directly involved. Students should appreciate that lenders try to avoid having to rely on security except in those rare cases considered in the next part of the chapter where assets are taken as security with the intention of selling them to repay the borrowing.

SECURITY-BASED LENDING

8.   In some cases customers have assets to sell and are able to offer those assets as security for borrowing until the point when the sale takes place. Sale proceeds can then be used to repay the borrowing.

This kind of lending is rather an exception to the general principle that the security for a loan should be one of the last considerations after it has already been decided that the proposal is a good one.

The two main forms of security-based lending which banks regularly handle are:-
   a)   produce advances;
   b)   bridging loans.

PRODUCE ADVANCES

9.   In general terms a produce loan is a loan made to purchase stock and repaid when the stock is sold.

Produce loans are most commonly offered to importers who deal in the kind of commodities traded in the London commodity markets, basic foodstuffs like sugar, wheat or tea and other raw materials like cotton or metals. Similar loans can be provided for any trader provided that:-
   a)   there are well established markets for the goods so that buyers can always be found fairly quickly;
   b)   the amounts involved are large enough to justify the extra work the lender needs to carry out to take the goods as security.

The basic questions which a bank needs to consider before agreeing to a produce advance are:-
   1.   What type of goods are being offered as security?
        Are they perishable?
        Are they easily saleable?
   2.   How reliable is the customer?
        Would you be prepared to lend unsecured?
   3.   Are there any other claims over the goods which might reduce the effectiveness of the bank's security, for example retention clauses by which the original producer of the goods retains ownership until full payment has been received.

The main steps to take in completing a produce advance are:-
   a)   Valuation. The bank can obtain a good margin by lending 90% of the value or less.

   b)   Obtaining good title, which can be by a variety of methods. One of the documents commonly used is letter of pledge.
   c)   Checking insurance cover which is usually the customer's responsibility under a letter of pledge.
   d)   Carrying out a status inquiry on the ultimate buyer.

See also Chapter 22 on finance for importers.

BRIDGING LOANS

10.   The term bridging loan can be applied to any form of lending where a major purchase is made before a major sale. The sale proceeds are needed to pay for the purchase so the loan is provided to bridge the gap between the two transactions. In a narrower sense the term bridging loan refers to a loan to buy one house before selling another because this is the most common situation in which bridging finance is needed. Building societies are rarely willing to allow a customer loans for two properties at the same time so when the purchase takes place before the sale it is usually a bank which provides the bridging finance.

When a bank provides a bridging loan for a customer moving house the basic minimum requirement is a charge over the house to be sold. Very often a charge will also be taken over the new house. All of the legal paperwork will be dealt with by solicitors and they will provide security in the form of a solicitors' undertaking to protect the bank's position. The undertaking will confirm that:-
   a)   if a sale takes place the sale proceeds will be sent to the bank;
   b)   if no sale goes through the deeds or land certificate will be held to the bank's order (and therefore not released to anyone else without the bank's permission);
   c)   if necessary any sale proceeds will go towards the purchase of the new property and those deeds will be held to the bank's order.
        (See Chapter 16 on the distinction between deeds and a land certificate.)

Because the bank expects to get its money back from the sale of the property the main danger to the bank is that the property will prove difficult to sell. An initial valuation is particularly important but evidence that contracts have been exchanged for the sale can make this kind of lending very safe. An offer to buy (or sell) a property can be withdrawn at any time up to the moment when contracts have been exchanged; from that point the buyer is committed to paying for the property on an agreed completion date, usually a few weeks later. Little apart from bankruptcy will prevent the transaction going ahead.

If contracts have been exchanged the period of the loan is known at the outset, and it is usually a fairly short period so that even though the amount borrowed may be many thousands of pounds the total interest charge should not be unmanageable.

An 'open-ended bridger' where contracts for the sale of the first property have not been exchanged is much more risky for bank and customer because if the intending buyer changes his mind there may be a long delay before another buyer is found. This could mean paying interest on a very large sum for a considerable period of time. Attracting another buyer might mean cutting the selling price which could leave the customer short of money to repay the bank. Banks do lend in these circumstances but only where there are special reasons for doing so, for example where a customer's employer is willing to pay all the interest charges.

CASE STUDY: MARY DEAKIN

11.   *Mary Deakin has come into the branch to explain that she is moving house shortly because she has just changed her job. The house she wants to buy is on the market at £47,000 and her offer of £45,000 has just been accepted. She has had a full survey carried out and this shows that there are no major problems. Her building society has agreed a mortgage of £30,000.*

She has had an offer of £36,000 for her present house on which there is a building society mortgage of £16,000. She now needs a loan to cover the period between the purchase of her new house and the sale of her old house.

Required:
You comments on how much Ms. Deakin needs to borrow and what questions you would need to ask her before agreeing to lend.

SUGGESTED SOLUTION: MARY DEAKIN

12.   This apparently simple question hides a complicated situation to which there may be more

than one solution. Essentially the bank is being requested to provide bridging finance to cover, or bridge, the period during which Ms. Deakin will own the new house but will not have received the sale proceeds of the old house. If contracts have been exchanged on both properties the period of the loan will be known; if contracts have not been exchanged for the sale of the old property the situation is less certain and the bank may prefer not to lend.

One reason that banks are often asked for bridging loans is that building societies are not normally prepared to lend a customer money for two properties at the same time. Until the first is sold the loan for the new property will not be made available.

Option A

The bank can provide a bridging advance of £45,000 until the original house is sold. At that time the old mortgage will be paid off from the £36,000 received and the remaining £20,000, the owner's equity or stake in the property, can be paid to the bank. The customer will also receive the £30,000 mortgage money from the building society which will clear the bank loan leaving £5,000 to pay for legal and moving expenses.

Option B

The bank can take over the mortgage on the old property so that the building society will provide the new mortgage of £30,000 straightaway. To pay off the old mortgage will take £16,000, and a further £15,000 will be needed to buy the new property so the total amount the bank will lend will be £31,000. When the property is sold for £36,000 the surplus of £5,000 will be available as it was in option A.

Option B with a total debt of £31,000 is cheaper for the customer than borrowing £45,000.

Since banks are now competing in the market for house loans it is also possible that the bank manager would try to persuade Ms. Deakin to take a bank mortgage for the new property rather than a building society mortgage, particularly if there was a likelihood of selling an endowment policy at the same time.

There are a number of key questions to raise here:-

a)   Which building society provided the original mortgage?

b)   Which building society is providing the new mortgage?

c) When is exchange of contracts for each property?

d) What are the addresses of the two properties?

e) Which solicitors are acting in the two transactions?

VARIATIONS BETWEEN INDUSTRIES

13.   One of the fascinations of banking is that bankers come into contact with all kinds of businesses because almost all businesses need bank accounts. Most kinds of business also need to borrow from time to time. Bank staff who make lending decisions have to be sensitive to the differences between industries and have to get to know how their customers operate. Each business needs to be judged on its own merits because as Chapter 15 showed set formulae and rules about lending can often be misleading.

The differences between businesses and industries can arise for a variety of reasons. The following list suggests some of the most important factors.

1.   **Time scale**
   The time scale of an industry may be affected by production time or by distribution time. Farming, for example, operates on a very long time scale with growing periods for crops of many months. Most income is generated at set harvest times so there are strong seasonal variations in most farmers' cash needs. In contrast selling fresh farm produce needs to be a short process because stock cannot be kept for more than a few days.

2.   **Capital requirements**
   Industries have different needs for capital. Manufacturers of hand-made craft goods will require far less capital to pay for equipment than manufacturers in high technology industries where replacement equipment is needed frequently in order to keep up-to-date.

3.   **Competition**
   Although all businesses face some kind of competition, the strength of competition can make some industries different from others because more competitive industries are more likely to incur higher levels of spending on marketing and on keeping up-to-date.

These broad areas of difference between different industries provide a general framework from which lenders can begin to understand the background to business customers which want to borrow. It is important to recognise too that within any industry there are enormous variations between individual businesses, most obviously in size but also in such other respects as:-

a) the personalities of the leading decision makers;

b) the market segments at which the business is aiming;

c) the extent to which new technology is used.

CASE STUDY: BURNETT LTD

14.   *Read the following case study and answer the questions which follow.*

Amounts in £ thousands

MONTHS	1	2	3	4	5	6
Opening Cash	45	(35)	(52)	(69)	(16)	(33)
+ Receipts	–	–	–	70	–	140
Sub-total	45	(35)	(52)	1	(16)	107
Payments	80	17	17	17	17	17
Closing Cash	(35)	(52)	(69)	(16)	(33)	90

These figures represent the expected cash flow for Burnett Ltd, a firm of local builders, over the next six months. On the basis of these figures you have agreed to a £70,000 overdraft for six months. Each month you will be able to check that the balance is roughly in line with the figures shown here. The company is involved in a project to build six houses which should sell for £35,000 each. Two will be completed and sold by the end of the fourth month and the rest by the end of the sixth month. Expenses paid by the company will be a regular £17,000 a month. Note that the company will be putting in £45,000 of its own money towards the initial purchase of the building land, and expects to end up with £90,000 in cash.

The manager has already seen a more detailed analysis of the payments to be made and considers the estimates to be reasonable.

Required:
Your answers to the following questions.

1.   What is the maximum level of borrowing you would expect if the first two houses are sold in month three?

2. What problem will arise if the two houses are not sold until month five?

3. Why would the manager have looked at the more detailed costings when he is not an expert on building?

4. If a similar cash forecast had been produced by a retail shop what would your reaction have been, and why?

SUGGESTED SOLUTION: BURNETT LTD

15. The cash flow figures on which the questions are based are only a forecast so any calculations can only be estimates.

1. If £70,000 is received in month 3 instead of month 4 the balance at the end of the month will be £1,000 credit. Month 4 will still end at £16,000 overdrawn so the largest overdraft will be in month 2, £52,000.

2. If the first two houses are not sold until month 5 the overdraft needed at the end of month 4 will be £86,000, £70,000 higher than the estimate. This exceeds the agreed overdraft limit and is very high in comparison to the amount the company is putting in.

3. Even if the manager does not know in detail what different building materials cost he may notice something missed out, like legal costs. The care with which the figures have been produced will also be a factor in deciding whether to lend because it is an indicator of the professionalism of the company.

4. It would certainly be astonishing to see a retailer with a cash flow like this with no sales at all in four out of the six months of trading. The figures clearly point to a business which produces large items and only needs irregular sales.

SUMMARY

16. a) Control of lending at its simplest means checking that repayment has been made at the due date. With more complex business lending the bank may make regular checks on the financial position of the borrower.

b) Banks prefer customers to make contact if they have difficulty in repaying borrowing.

Banks themselves have a range of approaches to slow payers from reminders to threats of legal action.

c) If a business customer has difficulty in repaying it may be necessary to make changes in the way the business operates. If the business does not improve and has to go into liquidation recovery of the debt may depend on realising any security.

d) Other things being equal a debt secured by third-party security is more likely to be repaid in full because separate claims can be made against the borrower's assets and against the surety's assets.

e) Some lending is specifically related to security. Important examples are:-
1. produce advances where the security is in the form of goods, often basic commodities;
2. bridging advances where a loan is provided to help buy one house pending receipt of sale proceeds of the previous house.

f) Major differences between the financial needs of industries arise from a number of factors including:-
1. time scale;
2. capital requirements;
3. competition.

STUDENT SELF-TESTING

This chapter has no short answer questions because it is based on case studies. It is particularly important for students to tackle as many of the longer questions from this chapter as possible.

Exercises (answers begin page 337)

A1. Wainwright and Son is a firm of builders which has banked with you for many years. The firm specialises in repairing and replacing traditional wooden doors, doorframes and window-frames. In spite of the growth in demand for plastic frames the business has been steadily successful and the partners have built up healthy credit balances.

They have recently been offered a contract by the local council to refit all the frames on a group of twenty houses on which renovations have begun recently. The total value of the contract will be £48,000 and should provide them with a steady flow of work for the next 4 months without preventing them from carrying on their normal trade. The main problem is that they will have to pay for all the materials themselves and will only get any money when the contract is completed. Material costs will be in the region of £9,000. They can provide £3,000 from their own resources while continuing to pay the workforce, and they therefore wish to borrow £6,000.

1. What further information would the bank require before agreeing to lend?

2. What possible problems do you foresee if the bank does lend in these circumstances?

A2. Peter and Jane Blackstock have been running a small shop in Beverley for the past five years, selling and repairing bicycles. They are thinking of taking over an additional shop in Driffield and have come to ask whether the bank can help. The Blackstocks have saved up £11,000 in the five years during which they have been trading and this sum is in a deposit account at your branch. They have a house worth £40,000 purchased four years ago with a building society mortgage of £30,000.

They have sent in to the bank the last year's accounts of the shop they are hoping to buy. The shop sells toys and sports goods and the Blackstocks are intending to continue in this line of business as well as using the site as an additional outlet for sales of bicycles. The proposed purchase price of the business is £95,000 including small freehold premises valued at about £60,000.

1. List the questions you would expect the manager to ask the Blackstocks when they come in to see him.

2. What other factors would be important in reaching a decision about whether to lend, assuming satisfactory answers were given to all the questions raised?

A3. Gareth Atkinson, the son of one of your wealthy customers, opened an account last September when he started a course at Manchester University. You have just received an urgent phone call from him saying that it is now three weeks into the new term and he has not yet received his grant cheque. He would like an overdraft of £200 until his money arrives.

1. What information would the manager need to check before agreeing to this request?

2. From the information given what factors do you consider to support the decision to lend.

A4. 'Lending is easy. Control and recovery of lending are difficult.' To what extent do you agree with this statement?

18. The Background to International Banking

INTRODUCTION

1. This chapter looks at the involvement of United Kingdom banks in foreign business in the past and how the traditional role has changed. There has been rapid growth in many areas of international banking and there are a number of key issues which present particular problems. The most widely reported of these is the problem of international debt with some countries facing severe difficulty in repaying money borrowed from international banks.

The chapter consists of two parts, the first looking at the historical perspective and the second at the broad outline of current problems, some aspects of which will be examined in more detail in later chapters.

THE PURPOSE OF A HISTORICAL PERSPECTIVE

2. The following very brief summary of some of the important stages in the history of international banking covers the period from the Middle Ages to the 1980s. This field provides scope for much more detailed analysis but the aim here is to show how major United Kingdom banks have become so involved in international banking.

THE MIDDLE AGES

3. In the early Middle Ages the largely agricultural economy of Western Europe had little need for professional banking services but international trade did begin to grow, particularly from the tenth to the twelfth century, as the peoples of Europe tried to improve their living standards by acquiring goods not immediately available from their own communities. At this time precious metals, often but by no means always in the form of coins, provided an internationally acceptable means of exchange. The need for banking services arose where large sums of money were needed in distant locations, partly for trade but more particularly for war; a king who could not pay his army because his cash was not readily to hand would not retain much support. This gave scope for wealthy merchants who traded in many parts of the known world to provide cash where it was needed in return for promises of payment with interest at a later date or in a different place. Because of the importance of the Mediterranean as a meeting place for different cultures many of the leading merchants were from Italy, in particular from the trading centres of the region of Lombardy. Their trading empires were vast, stretching far beyond the Mediterranean coast into Africa, the Arab world of the Middle East, the kingdoms and principalities of central Europe and, of course, to England, where their former presence is reflected today in the name of Lombard Street in the City of London.

EUROPE AND THE WIDER WORLD

4. The fifteenth and sixteenth centuries were a period of an expansion of the horizons of Western Europe as exploration led to new trading links with Africa, Asia and the Americas. The financing of expeditions required wealth and although this came largely from the rulers of countries, princes and kings who were able to raise money from their subjects, the growing class of merchants was also able to participate in these ventures. The profit from trade and the access to valuable resources from abroad led the major European countries into a race to acquire overseas territories. The Spanish and Portuguese were quick to divide up South America between them since the mineral resources, in particular silver, were of immense value. Britain and France became major rivals in North America and the Far East, and Britain was the more successful of the two in building an empire, partly because of the special advantages of London, which provided an ideal base for organising and financing expeditions because it was both a major port and the centre of government. Through the seventeenth and eighteenth centuries (while wars within Europe took up more of the resources of many of Britain's rivals) companies set up by royal charter or joint-stock companies in which the wealthy could participate by purchasing a 'share', an entitlement to part of the proceeds, were able to take advantage of Britain's growing influence in the world to sell British goods and buy foreign materials.

THE NINETEENTH CENTURY

5.   Until the nineteenth century the financiers who had supported the expansion of trade were not usually bankers in the sense that we use the term today since they did not specialise in financial services. They were landowners receiving rents or merchants making money from trade, and it was the wealth they had accumulated which enabled them to put money into new ventures.

In the nineteenth century local banks began to appear as society moved towards an economy based on paid employment and people at all levels of society became familiar with cash as a means of exchange and savings as a way of deferring spending. At the international level the significance of this development was that funds collected through the British banking network were available to invest in major capital projects, partly within this country on metalled roads, on railways and on canals, but also on similar investment overseas, in North and South America and in Asia. Specialist financial skills came to be needed to deal with these more complex projects abroad and this need led to the development of British overseas banks, a type of institution which has now faded from prominence (see Chapter 1). At this stage banks played an active part in raising funds from domestic markets to lend to companies set up to make money from capital projects abroad or to lend to governments trying to encourage a modernisation of their industry.

LONDON AS A FINANCIAL CENTRE

6.   The mergers in domestic banks in the 1950s and 1960s left British retail banking dominated by the big four, Barclays, Lloyds, Midland and National Westminster. In international business the dominance was less pronounced. Both Barclays and Lloyds had their own subsidiaries with extensive overseas interests and Midland and National Westminster were building up international links but many other British banks had international reputations in their own specialist fields. Well before the clearing bank mergers London had gained the status of a major international financial centre. The following table highlights the main reasons for London's importance at the end of the Second World War.

Factors making London an international financial centre (1945)

1.   The presence of a strong domestic banking system (soon to be dominated by the big four);

2.   The existence of a number of British overseas banks;

3.   The international role of leading merchant banks;

4.   The role of Lloyds of London as an international centre for the insurance industry;

5.   The presence of a major shipping exchange for buying, selling and chartering ships;

6.   The development of a well-organised stock market;

7.   The importance of sterling as an international currency because of Britain's extensive trading links;

8.   The stability of Britain's political system and the country's influence in world affairs following the Second World War.

THE CHANGING ROLE OF LONDON

7.   Since the end of the Second World War the international financial markets have changed considerably and the rate of change has increased dramatically in the last few years. International finance has moved away from bank lending towards direct financing with investors buying securities issued by the users of funds as described in Chapter 2. Banks have an increasing role as arrangers or negotiators of securities issues rather than as straightforward deposit-taking intermediaries.

For the major United Kingdom clearing banks the changes in the general pattern of international business have been reflected in some internal re-organisation. Both Lloyds Bank and Barclays Bank have merged their international banking subsidiaries into the main bank to provide greater integration and most of the leading British banks have carried out some organisational changes in their securities business to deal more effectively with the changed and changing environment.

The banking industry has combined international business with domestic business since it first began. Although some United Kingdom banks have sometimes treated the two areas as separate, during the last few years the scope for growth in international business persuaded the leading banks to concentrate far more on foreign business. This became a major source of profit rather than a just a fringe activity, though during 1987 the losses reported by some of the largest banks as a result of writing off bad debts abroad have put this expansion into a new perspective. Irrespective of any fears about the risks of international banking British bankers cannot escape the fact that the industry has become international. Britain's valuable invisible earnings from banking can only be maintained if London continues in its role as a leading international financial centre.

Factors making London an international financial centre (today)

1. The presence of a strong domestic banking system (with increasing competition from the building societies);

2. The strong foreign exchange market (estimated as handling a third of world foreign exchange turnover in 1984);

3. The extensive and growing representation of foreign banks (numbering approximately 400 by the end of 1985);

4. The high level of international lending carried out;

5. The high level of securities business, particularly in Eurocurrencies (described in Chapter 23);

6. The continuing strength of shipping and insurance;

7. The opportunities for foreign businesses to act as securities dealers on the United Kingdom stock exchange;

8. Britain's position in the time zone between Tokyo and New York, the other two leading financial centres;

9. Continuing political stability (in spite of uncertainty about the value of sterling because it can be so severely affected by oil prices).

The changes that have already taken place in banking, including the changes in the United Kingdom stock market known as the Big Bang (described in Chapter 2) mean that London's prominence in international finance is now based on rather different factors from those which mattered most in 1945.

FOREIGN AND INTERNATIONAL BANKING

8. In looking at the history of banking it is clear that there is great overlap between different areas of banking business. Some people have attempted to distinguish between foreign services and international services but the borderline is far from clear. In general terms foreign business usually means the work done by the domestic branch network including the provision of travel facilities and the whole range of methods for making and receiving foreign payments. International banking is the more specialised work carried out in departments or head offices providing services for major international customers, multinational companies, international agencies or foreign governments.

Any bank which has a substantial domestic business is likely to be called on to provide foreign services for customers who are importers, exporters or simply holiday-makers. The next section of this chapter looks at the implications for major banks of changes in foreign business.

The decision to enter into international banking is a more difficult one to make. The big four have become heavily committed to international banking because of their past history. Other United Kingdom clearing banks like Trustee Savings Bank and Co-operative Bank have a far smaller commitment and may well choose to keep to a more restricted role having seen the losses incurred by some of their larger competitors. In theory risk in international banking need not be any greater than risk in domestic banking and a wider spread of lending should reduce risk (avoiding putting all the eggs in one basket). Practical experience suggests a slightly different outlook.

In any case to take advantage of the opportunities in international banking may require a substantial capital base. The major players in the field are enormous Japanese and American banks which make most British banks seem fairly small. One of the current issues for United Kingdom banks is whether they are big enough in international terms. Even the biggest of the British merchant banks have been considering links with larger foreign banks to obtain enough capital to remain competitive. The question of scale is considered later in the chapter.

FOREIGN BUSINESS

9.   The United Kingdom high street banks have large branch networks in comparison to their foreign competitors operating in this country, but as the provision of banking services becomes more automated these large networks can have their disadvantages (as discussed in Chapter 6). Competitors which do not have numerous branches can often provide competing services more cheaply through different distribution channels. This has forced large banks to look for more, and more profitable, ways of using their branches. One of the possible directions for change is a greater involvement in travel and tourism. Bank branches could become places for obtaining details of holiday flights, accomodation locally or abroad and a whole range of other information. The essential requirements of a shop front which can be used to welcome customers and a computer network which can distribute the information and transmit messages are already there in the bank branches.

Midland Bank with its shareholding in Thomas Cook already has a susbstantial interest in the travel industry (in spite of the rumours during 1987 that it might sell the business to cover its losses on foreign debts). The other banks as providers of travel cheques, currency and holiday insurance are also competitors in the field to a lesser extent. There is no certainty that banks will develop further in this direction but it remains a clear possibility.

The provision of services for importers and exporters is already well established and there is less scope for further development on a large scale. Nevertheless conditions are constantly changing and the banks need to be highly adaptive to remain competitive. Some examples of the changes taking place are described in the chapters which follow.

INTERNATIONAL BUSINESS

10.   The motivation to expand international banking services is rather different from the pressures encouraging banks to expand or adapt their foreign services. Instead of having the facilities and trying to find the best use for them, in international finance

the environment is more aggressive. Large scale foreign competition means that banks have to try to offer a full range of international services in order to compete at the top level. The alternative, chosen by many smaller banks, is to specialise in one or two aspects of international finance so that business is maintained because of a good reputation rather than because of a broad relationship with clients. For the big banks like the United Kingdom big four establishing a relationship is important because no large organisation can have a reputation for being the best in everything, but customers may be happy to use a bank they do not see as the best if it gives good service over a wide range of activities.

INTERNATIONAL DEBT PROBLEMS

11.   One of the most serious issues for banks internationally since the 1970s has been the difficulty faced by many countries in repaying borrowed money. In the early 1970s oil prices rose very suddenly as the oil producing countries realised how dependent the rest of the world had become on this scarce commodity.

From the point of view of the United Kingdom the price rises had a double-edged effect. They were a benefit because it became well worth while to invest in the expensive technology to extract oil from the North Sea, an investment which would not have been worthwhile if oil prices had remained low. At the same time the price rises were a drawback because much of the oil used in Britain is imported, which caused generally higher prices because almost all goods and services are affected by the cost of oil through its direct effect on transport costs. High prices became increasingly useful as the United Kingdom increased its level of oil exports.

In contrast to this the poorer countries with no oil of their own were forced to pay much more than before which meant that they needed to export more of their own goods in order to pay for the same quantities of imported oil. For countries which were already in debt the exports which would have earned money to pay interest and repay international borrowing were no longer enough.

Banks which had lent money to poorer oil importing countries found that the borrowers could not repay their debts. This has led to a number of measures designed to prevent the problem of bad debts from harming the world's banking system, which could collapse if confidence in banks disappeared. The banks themselves cannot fully escape from the consequences of the loans they offered in the past. During 1987 many leading American and British banks announced record levels of provisions for bad debts, mostly relating to loans to countries which are having difficulty in paying because of their lack of foreign exchange.

When the problems first appeared banks lent new money to pay off existing debts, which is known as 'rolling over' the loans. In many cases they charged more interest because the borrowing was seen as more risky than usual. Later banks accepted that this made the problem worse rather than better, and a new policy of re-scheduling debts became more widespread. The term 're-scheduling' simply means a re-arrangement of the terms of the original loan, usually to give the borrowing country more time to pay. Variations on this idea have also been suggested, among the most well known being the Baker plan put forward in October 1985 with the aim of involving lenders, borrowers and the International Monetary Fund in talks designed to improve economic performance in the borrowing countries; stronger economies should be better able to repay their debts.

BRITISH BANKS AND DEBT PROBLEMS

12.   These repayment problems faced by many poor countries are often described as the *international debt crisis*, but in the usual sense of the word crisis, meaning a sudden emergency, this is not a particularly accurate description since the problem is a long-term one (which became more noticeable when oil prices rose but which does not have one single cause). Debt will remain an issue of current concern for many years. The Baker plan, for example, was not just intended to deal with countries which cannot afford the price of oil; oil prices had fallen since the problem of debt first appeared and by 1985 some of the oil producers were in difficulties. The countries specifically covered by the Baker plan included seven net exporters of oil, among them Mexico, Peru and Venezuela, but the list of problem debtors is constantly changing, affected both by internal politics and by the world economic climate. Banks have at least learned the lesson that countries, just like businesses, can get into financial difficulties and prove unable to pay back borrowed money.

For the British banks which have lent heavily to debtor countries the result has been bad debt provisions of such a size that overall losses have been recorded. Lloyds Bank, for example, announced a pre-tax loss of £697 million for the first half of 1987 as a result of charging £1,066 million to its profit and loss account for bad debts provisions relating to countries experiencing repayment difficulties. For Midland Bank the effects seem even more dramatic. When it announced its provision for bad debts it also announced that:-

a)   it wanted to raise an extra £700 million by a rights issue;

b)   three of the bank's subsidiaries, Clydesdale Bank, Northern Bank and Northern Bank (Ireland) were to be sold to National Australia Bank for £400 million.

The fact that such heavy provisions have now been made shows that the banks have recognised the extent of the problem.

INTERNATIONAL BANKING AND 'SECURITISATION'

13.   Another of the major concerns for leading international bankers has been the trend towards securitisation of debt (as described in Chapter 2). Major business customers have chosen more and more to issue securities rather than take loans from banks. Large scale bank lending had been largely directed at the major companies in the developed world and they had seemed a safe source of profit in comparison to loans to underdeveloped countries hit by the oil crisis. Now investors have begun to believe that placing their money directly with multinational businesses is just as safe as depositing it with a bank. The role of the bank as intermediary no longer seems as important as it once did, and both investors and companies (using invested funds rather than a bank loan) can gain by cutting out the middle man. The investor cannot get money back from the company (which would of course be possible with a bank account) but provided there is an active market in the securities the investor has bought it is always possible to sell. The main risk to the investor is that prices can fluctuate so there could be a considerable loss of capital.

During the 1980s there has been a very significant increase in the number of companies raising money by isssuing securities rather than by borrowing. This securitisation means a major change in the role of banks dealing with largescale finance for international customers. Bankers are increasingly adopting the role of advisers and arrangers of finance rather than providers of loans. Their income will come more and more from the services they provide and rather less from the interest on money lent out (as shown in Chapter 11). Smaller scale lending to individuals and businesses through the branch network is not likely to be affected by securitisation but adjusting to the changing pattern of international financial requirements will be important to all banks which aim to operate internationally.

FOREIGN DOMINANCE OF INTERNATIONAL BANKING

14.   The major banks in the world are competing against one another in an increasingly tough environment. In many countries a process of deregulation is taking place, removing restrictions and regulations which helped to protect local banks from foreign competition. Even in the already fairly liberal environment of London, where foreign banks had been accepted for a long time, there are new opportunities for outside financial institutions to participate, for example in the Stock Exchange where Nomura Securities, a Japanese owned business, became the first foreign member in 1986. American banks also strengthened their presence by acquisitions of stock-broking or stock-jobbing firms before the Big Bang. This foreign expansion helps to strengthen London's claim to be a leading international financial centre but it may leave the British banks as minor participants in their home market unless they react effectively to the challenge.

In world terms banking is dominated by the Japanese. A regular survey by 'The Banker' magazine lists the world's leading banks in order of total assets (measured in United States dollars). The following list shows the banks which they placed as the top ten in July 1987.

1.	Dai-Ichi Kangyo Bank	Japan
2.	Fuji Bank	Japan
3.	Sumitomo Bank	Japan
4.	Mitsubishi Bank	Japan
5.	Sanwa Bank	Japan
6.	Citicorp	United States
7.	Norinchukin Bank	Japan
8.	Industrial Bank of Japan	Japan
9.	Credit Agricole	France
10.	Banque Nationale de Paris	France

One of the reasons for the dominance of the Japanese in such a list is that the yen is a very strong currency in relation to the dollar so that the assets of Japanese banks appear particularly valuable in dollar terms. Even allowing for this the fact that Japan has 7 banks in the world's top ten (and over 20 in the world's top fifty) indicates the enormous strength of the Japanese banking industry.

In a less international market these rankings would be of little significance to British banks, but with improved technology major foreign banks can sell their services just as easily here as anywhere else in the world. The sheer size of the Japanese banks means that they they have the capacity to undercut competitors to win market share and to make mistakes in their lending without risk of serious harm.

The dominance of Japan, and currently to a lesser extent the United States, is a clear reflection of the economic importance of the two countries in world affairs. The United States is the largest single market for goods and services in the world and Japan is now in second place. Japan also ranks second only to the United States in terms of the size of its stock market, and in 1986 Japan became the world's leading creditor nation, lending more money abroad than even the United States. This enormous power concentrated in just two countries makes it difficult for the banks of other less influential countries to compete on equal terms.

BRITISH BANKS ON THE WORLD STAGE

15.   The largest of Britain's banks are big enough to be true participants in international markets. National Westminster and Barclays were ranked 17th and 18th repectively in the Banker's 1987 table and in some years with a stronger pound they have ranked among the world's top ten. Midland and Lloyds both appeared in the top fifty in 1987 but there are then few other British banks of substantial size in world terms. Only one other, Standard Chartered, was rated in the top 100. Other leading European countries like France and Germany have twice as many banks big enough to be in the top 100.

The big four have tried to maintain their international stature by matching their foreign competitors in developing into new areas of business. Both Barclays and National Westminster acquired members of the Stock Exchange in order to become more fully involved in the securities industry and both have also developed securities businesses in the other leading financial centres, New York and Tokyo. As de-regulation makes other foreign markets more open British banks will enter the markets along with the leading Japanese and American banks. A continuing expansion of activities may be the only way to ensure that the leading United Kingdom banks remain truly international. The unsuccessful attempt by Lloyds Bank to take over Standard Chartered during 1986 is also an indication of how increased size is perceived as an important factor in remaining competitive in what is now a global market.

SUMMARY

16. a)   The involvement of banks in foreign business has a very long history and is closely tied to the history of world trade.

b)   Britain's importance in world affairs helped the trading businesses and banks of the United Kingdom to develop strong international interests.

c)   London acquired a major role as an international financial centre. This has continued into the twentieth century and although the role continues to change as the pattern of world trade and international finance changes there are still good reasons for London's international importance.

d)   The major United Kingdom banks are involved in both foreign business and international business. The distinction between these two fields is not clear cut though foreign services are usually seen as those provided by banks through the branch network while international services are those provided for major customers through head offices or specialist departments.

e)   Involvement in international banking is difficult for small banks. The biggest United Kingdom banks are large enough to be fully international but smaller British commercial banks are more likely to provide only foreign services.

f)   Foreign business is an area of potential development for many banks as there is scope for increasing links with the travel industry (as Midland Bank has done through its ownership of the Thomas Cook travel agents).

g)   International business presents some serious problems for banks.
   1.   The international debt crisis has led to many banks writing off large sums of money lent to countries which cannot afford to repay.
   2.   The trend towards the securitisation of debt has meant that there is far less opportunity to provide loans to major companies; instead banks are having to arrange finance by issues of securities with fee income rather than income from interest.

h)   The de-regulation of financial markets all over the world gives greater scope for international banks, but it is the largest which will be in the best position to benefit from the changes taking place. Major foreign banks, particularly from Japan and the United States, will provide tough competition for British banks wherever they operate, even in the United Kingdom.

STUDENT SELF-TESTING

Self Review Questions

1.   Why was London a major financial centre in 1945? (6)

2.   What factors make London an international financial centre today? (7)

3.   What is the difference between foreign business and international business in banking? (8)

4.   How might banks in the future play a greater role in travel and tourism? (9 + your own ideas)

5.   What was the aim of the Baker plan? (11)

6.   What is the international debt crisis? (12)

7.   What is securitisation? (13)

8.   What effect does securitisation have on banks? (13)

9.   How many of the 1987 top ten banks (according to the Banker magazine) were Japanese? (14)

10.   Where was the highest ranking British bank in the Banker's 1987 world rankings? (15)

Exercises (answers begin page 338)

A1. How has the role of London as a financial centre changed since the Second World War?

A2. Does the international debt crisis really affect the United Kingdom clearing banks with their strong domestic branch networks?

A3. To what extent is it possible to distinguish between foreign banking services and international banking services?

A4. Can United Kingdom banks claim to be truly international?

19. Travel Facilities

INTRODUCTION

1. In the previous chapter dealing with the background to foreign business and areas of current concern the potential for expansion of travel business in banking was commented on. In this chapter the subject is the present state of banking services in the field of travel.

The first part of the chapter looks at the banks' involvement in the provision of travel facilities, referring to competitors as well as the banks themselves. This is followed by an examination of specific services and how they are operated.

The main services described are:-
   a) foreign currency;
   b) travel cheques;
   c) credit open facilities;
   d) travellers' letters of credit;
   e) eurocheques;
   f) credit cards.

THE BANKS AND THEIR COMPETITORS

2. Banks have dealt with the financial aspects of travel for many years. They have had a dominant position in the market for a number of reasons. Banks have had the facilities for safeguarding cash so it is natural that they should deal in foreign currencies as well as sterling. Before 1979 the banks had the added advantage that only authorised institutions were permitted to issue currency to the public; banks were the major authorised institutions. Banks were also in a strong position to issue travel cheques since these need to bear the name of an organisation which is seen as financially undoubted by anyone to whom the cheques are offered for encashment or as a means of payment. Some of the banks' advantages remain but the increasingly competitive financial services industry has meant the threat of new entrants into travel facilities business, which now involves not only banks and travel agents but also money shops, the Post Office and, to an increasing extent, building societies.

At the same time providers of travel services have been trying to broaden their range of products. Major travel companies like Thomas Cook (widely acknowledged as the 'inventor' of travel cheques and now a subsidiary company of Midland Bank) and American Express can provide a full range of financial services to meet the needs of travellers. Smaller travel firms are equally willing to make at least some financial arrangements, for example to act as insurance brokers, selling a suitable policy to cover accident, theft or injury while abroad and collecting the appropriate premium.

The exchange of currency and travel cheques is often referred to as 'bureau de change' business. In large cities some businesses operate purely as 'bureaux de change' in competition with the banks, but they generally charge higher commissions than banks and have a wider spread between buying and selling prices. It is their convenient location and long opening hours which attract customers.

FOREIGN CURRENCY

3. The most basic of the travel facilities offered by all banks is the exchange of foreign currency, which in this context means notes and coins.

Not all foreign currencies can be bought or sold through the banks because the governments of some countries do not permit the import or export of the notes and coins which they issue. This is generally the case in Eastern Europe. There is also a very limited market for the currency of many of the poorer countries which have little foreign trade or tourism, and banks may not be able to quote buying or selling prices in these cases.

For the major currencies banks do buy and sell regularly. Larger branches of the commercial banks keep a stock of each widely traded currency and can meet requests for small amounts on demand. Smaller branches can supply customers by ordering currency from the bank's central department, so customers may have to give a few days' notice.

BUYING AND SELLING RATES

4. So that customers know the buying and selling prices (or rates) for currency bank branches normally display an up-to-date list which shows two prices for each currency traded.

Example		
Currency	*Bank Sells*	*Bank Buys*
Austria	20.5	21.5
Belgium	60.0	62.0
Canada	1.95	1.99

Here, for example, if a customer wishes to buy £100 worth of Belgian Francs the rate at which the bank will sell to the customer is 60 Francs to the pound. The customer will therefore receive 6000 Francs or possibly a little less if commission is charged. Most banks now charge a fixed sum of 50p or £1 per transaction, though some charge on a percentage basis which can make larger deals rather expensive for the customer.

In contrast to this if a Belgian tourist or a customer returning from Belgium calls at the bank with 6000 Belgian Francs to change the bank will not pay out as much as £100. If the bank did pay £100 or more it could be worthwhile for people to buy currency simply in order to change it back at a profit. Instead, of course, it is the bank which stands to make a profit. By buying 6000 Francs at 62 to the pound the bank pays out £(6000 ÷ 62) = £96.77 and receives in return currency which it can sell to another customer for £100. This profit of £3.23 arises from the difference between the buying and selling rates, which is often referred to as the margin or spread. In addition the bank will probably take a commission from the customer, which makes it even less likely that the customer can gain from speculating by buying currency and selling it back. Even though the rates change frequently it would need a substantial movement before the bank's buy-ing price for foreign notes would fall below a previous day's selling price.

CHANGING CURRENCY

5. When changing currency the branch foreign clerk carrying out the transaction will usually complete an exchange slip showing the details. This provides a record for the customer and helps the bank to trace any errors. In its simplest form this may consist of no more than a printout from a calculator, but some banks still use the more traditional and more formal system of producing a document which can be processed along with other entries dealing with changes in the cash held by the branch.

An example of this kind of form is shown below.

Here the customer will be asked to fill in his or her name and address and the cashier will then pay out £100.42 in exchange for the 6000 Belgian Francs and 100 Austrian Schillings.

From the bank's point of view the form here is a debit entry and instead of being cashed the slip could be credited to a customer's account.

If a customer wishes to change coins rather than notes the bank will offer a much less favourable rate or will advise the customer to keep the coins for use on future trips abroad because the cost of handling

Example

Commercial Bank Ltd   Colchester Branch

Foreign Currency Bought

Quantity	Currency	Rate	Commission		Net
6000	BELGIUM	62	96.77	0.50	96.27
100	AUSTRIA	21.5	4.65	0.50	4.15

DR. FOREIGN TILL ACCOUNT
ACCOUNT NO. 56712356   £100.42

Customer Name

                                                      Address (local)

coins is much greater than the cost of handling notes. The foreign clerk also has to be aware of any special restrictions or regulations concerning the denominations of notes which can be brought out of or taken into certain countries. The basically simple process of exchange is therefore more complicated than it may first appear.

THE FLOW OF CURRENCY

6.   Just as with transactions in sterling it is unlikely that the amount of a currency going out to customers will be matched exactly by the currency coming in from customers. At branch level this problem is solved by buying in currency from the bank's currency trading department or selling surplus currency to it. For a branch which operates a foreign till dealings with the department may be frequent as the branch buys or sells to comply with limits on how great a value of currency can be held at any one time. Rates used between branch and head office will not be the rates quoted to customers, but special rates agreed for each transaction.

From the bank's point of view imbalances in the flow of a particular currency will be dealt with by importing or exporting the money, an expensive business which justifies the often wide gap between buying and selling rates. So Spanish currency is likely to be imported because there is great demand from British holidaymakers heading for the sun, while Japanese currency is more likely to be exported as Japanese tourists to Britain are generally more numerous than Britons visiting Japan, and British banks would therefore expect to end up with more yen notes than their customers would want to buy.

TRAVEL CHEQUES

7.   For travellers carrying large amounts of cash while abroad there is a serious risk that the money will be lost or stolen. There are a number of ways of reducing this risk apart from the obvious safety precaution of not keeping all the money in one pocket. One of the first ideas for helping to make travellers' money more secure was the travellers' cheque scheme. Travellers' cheques, now more commonly referred to as travel cheques, are designed to ensure that only the rightful owner can obtain cash. Travel cheques are similar in appearance to other cheques except that they are usually for convenient round sums of money (pre-printed onto the travel cheque) and are signed by the holder, the

traveller, when they are issued. This signature can then be compared with the signature of whoever tries to cash the cheque which means that only the true holder or a skilful forger will be able to get money for it.

British travellers abroad can choose between sterling travel cheques or travel cheques in the currency of the country to be visited. In either case payment is made in advance but by buying currency travel cheques the amount of currency to be obtained is fixed in advance. Subsequent changes in the exchange rate will not make any difference. Sterling travel cheques are converted at the time of encashment and the rate will vary from day to day.

SUPPLIERS OF TRAVEL CHEQUES

8.   Travellers can obtain travel cheques from a variety of sources. Travel agents may well supply them as part of their travel service, some building societies now provide them and they are also available from major Post Offices. However these suppliers are not usually the issuers of the travel cheques. A small travel firm or a provincial building society is not likely to have a good enough financial standing abroad to make travel cheques in its own name acceptable. The market as far as issuers is concerned is therefore dominated by famous names. Thomas Cook travel cheques and American Express travel cheques are acceptable worldwide and both companies issue them in currencies of most major trading countries. It is also possible to obtain travel cheques denominated in European Currency Units (ECUs) which are more stable in value than an individual national currency and give the holder a choice of currencies to draw depending on the country being visited. (A fuller explanation of the nature of ECUs is included in Chapter 23).

Even though many British banks are internationally known they cannot claim such widespread recognition as their travel business rivals and most of them issue travel cheques in a smaller range of currencies. If a customer requires travel cheques in a currency for which the bank does not offer its own cheques this simply places the bank in the position of most other suppliers; it will supply travel cheques issued by someone else, either one of the big names or a major bank in the appropriate country. Where a foreign bank is used the United Kingdom bank would choose a *correspondent bank* with which the British bank already has links. Correspondent banks would usually operate accounts for one another in order to make payments abroad (as described in Chapter 21) and may offer a number of other services. The use of a local correspondent bank for the issue of travel cheques should mean that the traveller has no difficulty in getting the cheques exchanged.

TRAVEL CHEQUES ASSESSED

9.   The following table summarises the major advantages and disadvantages of using travel cheques. Note that the ease of obtaining refunds and the speed at which this can be done depends on the issuer. American Express with an international network of offices has a reputation for rapid refunds which British banks cannot usually match.

Advantages and disadvantages of travel cheques

Advantages
1.   They are available in sterling or in currency.
2.   They are safer than handling cash.
3.   Refunds are available if they are stolen.
4.   They may be accepted by hotels and some shops in payment for goods.

Disadvantages
1.   Payment must be made in advance.
2.   Commission charges add to the cost.
3.   Serial numbers need to be recorded in order to obtain refunds.
4.   They are not *widely* accepted as payment for goods and services.

ALTERNATIVES TO TRAVEL CHEQUES

10.   Travel cheques are primarily a means of obtaining cash while abroad but also, directly or indirectly, provide access to goods and services. They can also be used in the United Kingdom, but this chapter deals with banking services intended for use abroad, so the alternatives considered here are those which can be used in other countries.

Alternative banking facilities which simply offer a way of drawing cash while abroad are credit open arrangements and travellers' letters of credit.

More recently developed facilities which can be used more widely to obtain goods and services are eurocheques and credit cards.

CREDIT OPEN ARRANGEMENTS

11.   An open credit or credit open facility is simply an arrangement by which a customer of one branch can cash personal cheques up to an agreed limit at another branch or a branch of another bank. Such arrangements can be made internationally so that a customer abroad can go to a foreign bank to withdraw money. The customer's bank will have already specified how much can be drawn out, either in total or during a given time, for example an amount per week.

This kind of arrangement may be suitable for someone visiting a specific place rather than travelling round but does not really allow for any unexpected problems which might make it more convenient to draw cash somewhere else. Because of this inflexibility it is now becoming a rare method of obtaining cash abroad.

TRAVELLERS' LETTERS OF CREDIT

12.   A travellers' letter of credit, like a credit open facility, is pre-arranged to enable the traveller to draw out money, in this case from a range of possible banks. The traveller needs both a letter of credit which will specify the limit on the amount to be withdrawn and a document confirming signature, the equivalent of the holder's signature on a travel cheque.

This method of obtaining cash is now very unusual because of the range of rather more straightforward alternatives including travel cheques. Because of its rarity it has come to be seen as a fairly unacceptable method of drawing money. A paying bank which is offered a traveller's letter of credit is likely to view it with considerable suspicion and may decline to pay out even if the documentation is perfectly valid.

EUROCHEQUES

13.   The Eurocheque scheme is an agreement between banks of most European countries to cash cheques drawn on other participating banks provided certain conditions are met. Originally the British banks were involved in the scheme simply by issuing ordinary cheque guarantee cards which could be used with a standard cheque book. The procedure for the customer wishing to cash a cheque was the same abroad as in the United Kingdom. Banks of

all other countries in the Eurocheque scheme provided customers with distinctive Eurocheques of a uniform design recognisable to all participating banks and eventually the British banks, partly because of the extensive fraudulent use abroad of stolen cheque cards, adopted the same approach. The major clearing banks phased in the new system between 1984 and 1986 and now customers wishing to cash cheques under the Eurocheque scheme must have a special Eurocheque guarantee card and a supply of uniform Eurocheques, making the scheme less open to fraud but also less convenient, although no new account is needed since the Eurocheques can be drawn on an ordinary current account. The new system also gave the banks the opportunity to bring in a charge for issuing the card, again bringing British banks more into line with continental banks, many of which had been charging for domestic cheque guarantee cards for years.

Eurocheques backed by the Eurocheque guarantee card can also be used to buy goods and services abroad and are acceptable in many shops and hotels. From the recipient's point of view the cheques represent guaranteed payments and can be credited to a bank account just like cheques drawn on local banks. Although the number of countries involved in the scheme has grown these are all in or around Europe. There seems no prospect of other major countries such as Japan and the United States joining the scheme in the near future because their banking systems are in some ways very different from their European counterparts.

CREDIT CARDS

14.   As explained in Chapter 12 credit cards have become an increasingly important form of lending to personal customers. For customers travelling abroad the fact that the major credit cards available in the United Kingdom belong to wider international groups makes them a very valuable means of payment. Access as part of the Master Card group and Trustcard and Barclaycard as part of the Visa group are accepted in all Western countries and in a very large number of less developed countries, at least in the commercial and tourist areas.

Although exact procedures for making payment may vary slightly from place to place, some being more advanced in the use of electronic card readers or online verification of limits than others, essentially all that is required is a signature to confirm the owner's identity or the equivalent of a signature in the form of a keyed-in Personal Identification Number.

In some countries, notably the United States, credit cards are sometimes seen as more acceptable than cash or travel cheques, but even where this is not the case the credit card is a useful piece of equipment for the traveller because it provides spending power without tying up money beforehand, and can be a good back-up if any unexpected expenditure is incurred. The usual terms apply, allowing a period of interest free credit if the bill is settled in full by the due date, and where purchases have been made in foreign currency the amount to be paid will be converted into sterling by the credit card company with details of the rate shown on the customer's statement.

OTHER SERVICES FOR TRAVELLERS

15.   The banks' involvement in providing customers with the means to obtain goods and services abroad has led to a number of connected services, a small part of a bank's overall product range but significant because such services indicate the concern to maintain diversity, to offer something of everything and to treat the relationship with the customer as a broad relationship rather than offering to meet only one single need at a time.

Traditionally one of the first services with which a would-be traveller might seek the bank's assistance was in obtaining a passport or visas. This service, now little used and little promoted, involved dealing with corespondence between customer and passport office, acting, in effect, as little more than a post box. For a customer to use an intermediary in this way rather than to apply direct is clearly costly in staff time so that a realistic charge for the service would deter most potential users.

Similarly fading away from the product range of some banks is the provision of bail bonds. In some countries relatively minor motoring offences can result in a traveller's car being impounded or the motorist himself being arrested to ensure that fines or legal costs do not go unpaid. Because of this visitors to, for example, Spain are recommended to take with them a document to the local police or courts guaranteeing the payment of any sums due. These bail bonds are available from banks, but the major share of the market is taken by the motoring organisations which are better placed to provide a full package of services for the motorist abroad.

The most important of the subsidiary services which banks offer to travellers is travel insurance. Here the competition from motoring organisations and travel agents is fierce but the banks are better placed to combat it, partly because customers are likely to come to the bank for foreign currency, but also because the banks are very experienced in insurance. All the major banks have large insurance broking subsidiaries which can get good deals from insurers and therefore offer customers a good policy. Some banks are also starting to act as insurers, or under-writers, selling their own policies rather than just earning commission by selling policies underwritten by insurance companies.

scheme is limited in scope but is very well known within the participating countries. The cheques and cheque guarantee cards used are of a uniform design.

h) Credit cards can also be used abroad to purchase goods and services. The credit card company deals with the conversion of foreign currency to sterling so that from the customer's point of view the transaction is as simple as a credit card payment in this country.

i) Banks also offer travel facilities which are less directly concerned with obtaining cash or making payments. Obtaining passports and issuing bail bonds are not widely promoted but travel insurance is still important.

SUMMARY

16. a) Banks have had a tradition of providing services for customers travelling abroad.

b) The buying and selling of foreign currency notes and coin is a basic part of this range of services.

c) Banks can earn money both from commission on currency deals and from the margin or spread, the difference between buying and selling prices.

d) To provide holidaymakers with the money they want to take with them British banks have to buy in currency from countries popular with British tourists.

e) Travel cheques provide a safer alternative to carrying large quantities of cash while abroad and are available in most major currencies. However there are certain disadvantages to using travel cheques, in particular the need to pay out all the money in advance.

f) Credit open facilities abroad and travellers' letters of credit provide alternative ways for customers to draw cash while outside the United Kingdom but the limitations of these services mean that they are not now widely used.

g) The Eurocheque scheme is an increasingly accepted way of obtaining cash or buying goods and services while abroad. The

STUDENT SELF-TESTING

Self Review Questions

1. Which is higher and why, the rate at which a bank sells foreign currency or the rate at which it buys? (4)

2. What information is recorded on a foreign currency exchange slip? (5)

3. If a branch holds more of a particular currency than it needs what does it do? (6)

4. If a bank holds more of a particular currency than it needs what does it do? (6)

5. Who are the banks' main competitors in supplying and issuing travel cheques? (8)

6. What are the advantages and disadvantages of using travel cheques? (9)

7. What are the disadvantages of using credit open facilities and travellers' letters of credit? (11,12)

8. What is the uniform Eurocheque scheme and how does it work? (13)

9. a) Which international credit card group does Access belong to?
   b) Which international credit card group does Barclaycard belong to? (14)

10. What makes travel insurance a more successful service for banks than bail bonds or issuing passports? (15)

Exercises (answers begin page 339)

A1. Read the following table of rates and answer the questions.

Foreign Notes Rates

Currency	Bank sells	Bank buys
Malta	0.52	0.54
Netherlands	3.21	3.24
Norway	10.45	10.49

Base your answers on the above rates.

1. A customer comes in to change 400 Norwegian Kroner in 100 Kroner notes and 600 Dutch Guilder in 10 Guilder notes. As an inexperienced foreign clerk what do you need to check? Assuming there are no problems how much does the customer receive in sterling if the bank charges a flat £1 commission per transaction?

2. Is a Maltese pound worth more or less than a pound sterling? Ignoring commission how much profit would the bank make by buying a thousand Maltese pounds from one customer and then selling them to another?

A2. Read the following table of rates and answer the questions.

Foreign Notes Rates

Currency	Bank sells	Bank buys
Denmark	10.78	10.82
France	9.30	9.33
Germany	2.82	2.84

Base your answers on the above rate sheet.

1. A customer has thirty Deutsche Marks and ninety French Francs. For which currency does the bank pay out most sterling?

2. What is the total bill for a customer wanting to buy 500 French Francs and 800 Danish Kroner, including £1 commission for each transaction?

A3. What two methods of payment apart from cash would you recommend most strongly to a customer going on a motoring holiday in the United States? Give reasons for your suggestions.

A4. A customer of yours is taking a cycling trip round Belgium, Holland and France. Why would you not recommend a credit open facility or travellers' letter of credit and what alternatives would you suggest?

20. Foreign Exchange

INTRODUCTION

1.   This chapter deals with foreign exchange in a broader sense than in the last chapter. Here foreign exchange means not just notes and coins, but also bank balances which represent a far larger proportion of the total amount of money in circulation.

Even if people never travelled abroad and therefore never needed the notes and coins of other countries there would be an enormous need for foreign currency in this broader sense because countries take part in international trade. If a French car manufacturer sells vehicles in Britain the buyers will want to pay in sterling and the seller will probably want to receive French francs. These trading needs mean that buying and selling of currencies takes place continuously and it is banks which make sure it is always possible for an exporter to sell foreign currency which has been received or for an importer to buy the currency needed to pay for goods from abroad.

The chapter covers the way in which changes in exchange rates represent a risk for international traders, how exchange rates are determined and how forward contracts can be used to reduce exchange risk. The chapter also includes a section on how the financial press writes about foreign exchange.

THE EXTENT OF FOREIGN TRADE

2.   The United Kingdom has traditionally been more concerned with the need for foreign exchange than many other countries because:-

a)   self-sufficiency is difficult to achieve in such a small country so imports are very important;

b)   exports are essential to pay for imported necessities;

c)   as an island Britain has developed an extensive merchant navy serving the trading needs of other countries.

The entry of the United Kingdom into the European Economic Community in 1972 changed the pattern of British trade but not its importance. By 1986 trade with other members of the European Community amounted to 53% of imports (£43 billion) and 48% of exports (nearly £35 billion). For 1986 total imports were £81 billion and total exports nearly £73 billion.

Note that the government statistics quoted here are subject to revision as further information comes to light. They do, however, give a good indication of the overall volume of trade and the imbalance between imports and exports.

RISKS IN FOREIGN TRADE

3.   The overall trade figures cover transactions ranging from huge contracts for expensive machines and equipment to the kind of deals undertaken by small businesses going into exporting or importing for the first time. One common factor is that in all cases the normal business risks of dealing with other people are increased in a number of ways. Very often foreign trade involves:-

a)   communicating in foreign languages;

b)   coping with different trade practices;

c)   complying with foreign laws and regulations;

d)   acting on more limited information about the people abroad than about suppliers or customers locally;

In addition to this one of the parties involved will incur some exchange risk unless both parties deal in the same currency. Although banks can give advice which will help importers or exporters to cope with or reduce some of the other risks of international trade it is in dealing with exchange risk that banks can be of most value to their customers.

EXCHANGE RISK

4.   The concept of exchange risk is a fairly simple one (though see Chapter 23 for a more detailed explanation of different forms it can take). In any international trade deal one of the parties will need to change foreign currency, and risk arises because exchange rates are not fixed but vary from day to day.

If, for example, an exporter is selling to a Swedish customer he will probably have to quote a price in Swedish kroner. If the exchange rate alters after the contract has been agreed the kroner he receives may be worth less than originally expected and the deal may prove unprofitable.

Exchange risk, the risk that exchange rate movements will alter affecting the value of a transaction,

---

Example

At the time of the contract £1 = Sw. Kr. 10

Cost of goods	£5000
Intended profit	£ 500
	£5500

Selling price agreed as Sw. Kr. 55000

At the time of payment £1 = Sw. Kr. 11

Sterling received (ignoring commission and the cost of sending the payment) is only £5000.

The transaction would therefore leave no profit at all.

---

has made this deal unprofitable. At any rate of more than 11 kroner to the pound the result would have been a loss.

Corresponding to the risk of loss is the opportunity for extra profit. If the exchange rate had moved the other way the Sw.Kr. 55000 could have been worth a lot more than £5500. Avoiding the risk of loss usually implies also losing the opportunity for this kind of gain, as explained later in the chapter.

THE DETERMINANTS OF EXCHANGE RATES

5.   Because the exchange rate on any import or export transaction can make a difference to the profit on the deal it would clearly be extremely useful for business people to know what exchange rates will be in the future. Unfortunately such forecasting is extremely difficult.

Exchange rates are determined by a market mechanism controlled by supply and demand. If in general more people want to buy a currency than to sell it the price will rise until it becomes so expensive that some buyers are put off and more sellers are attracted into the market. The price therefore reaches an equilibrium or balance between what buyers will pay and what sellers are willing to accept. (This equilibrium value is not constant but changes all the time because the beliefs and aims of buyers and sellers are constantly changing.)

To understand how price is determined therefore means going back to the question of why there are sellers and buyers.

For any currency there could be an increase in the number of sellers for any of the following reasons, separately or in combination.

1.   The economy might be doing badly so that the currency is expected to fall in value.

2.   A cut in interest rates might have made the currency a less attractive investment.

3.   More foreign imports might be coming into the country so more foreign currency would need to be bought to pay for them.

4.   Alternative currencies might have become more attractive because of better interest rates or better economic performance.

Similarly there could be an increase in the number of buyers of a country's currency for a variety of reasons. These include the following factors.

1.   The economy might have shown exceptional growth so that the currency is expected to rise in value.

2.   The currency might seem a more attractive investment because of higher interest rates.

3.   An increase in exporting could mean that more foreign importers need to buy the currency.

4.   The currency might be unusually attractive as an investment because it seems under-valued in relation to other currencies.

It is the balance between these ever changing factors which decides whether supply exceeds demand, leading to a fall in price, or whether there are more buyers so that prices rise.

SPOT RATES AND FORWARD RATES

6.   Most of the buyers and sellers of currency are reacting to changes in the kind of factors outlined above. Their decisions about whether to buy or to sell are ones which they want to carry out straightaway which means that they want to agree a price for the currency in which they want to trade as soon as possible.

This kind of rate offered by a foreign exchange dealer on the spot, usually over the telephone, is referred to as a spot rate. It does not imply that the currency to be bought or sold will change hands immediately since exchange dealing procedures are not instantaneous. Anyone buying or selling currency is quoted a *value date* for the transaction, a date on which the currency will be confirmed as available for use, and generally for spot rate transactions this value date will be two working days from the day the rate is agreed.

In some cases customers know what currency they will need to buy or sell in the future and are able to make arrangements in advance, often as a way of avoiding exchange risk. Such advance agreements about purchases or sales of currency are known as forward foreign exchange contracts or forward contracts for short. The customer does not have to pay at the time of arranging the contract but is committed to dealing at the agreed rate. This rate will not normally be the same as the spot rate when the deal is made but will be at a special forward rate.

There is some risk from the bank's point of view in entering into a forward contract with a customer because if a customer promises to sell a certain amount of currency but fails to do so (for example because of insolvency) this may leave the bank having to buy the currency at the spot rate. Since rates change all the time the spot rate at the date arranged for the forward contract may be very different from the contracted rate and the bank could make a loss. Because of this risk banks only arrange forward contracts for creditworthy customers.

PREMIUMS AND DISCOUNTS

7.   Normally forward exchange rates are quoted for 1 month, 3 months and 6 months ahead but different periods can be arranged if required. The way in which rates are quoted is in the form of a premium or discount compared to the spot rate. The following table gives an example of the kind of information provided, showing spot rates followed by forward rates. The forward premiums and discounts represent small variations from the spot rate and *may* be shown in smaller units of currency, for example cents rather than dollars.

	Bank sells	Bank buys
United States Dollars	1.4370	1.4380
1 month premium	0.65c	0.61c
3 month premium	1.85c	1.80c
Portuguese Escudos	208.44	209.30
1 month discount	45c	115c
3 month discount	190c	340c

The rate of exchange is in a sense the reverse of a price. A shopkeeper selling goods at 2 for £1 might buy them at 3 for £1, a higher rate and therefore a lower price.

The terms premium and discount refer to price so the U.S. dollars quoted at a premium have a forward price which is higher than the current price. This makes the forward rate lower than the current rate. To calculate the forward rate premiums are therefore deducted and conversely discounts are added on. For example the rate for the bank to sell dollars for a contract in a months's time is 1.4370 minus 0.0065 = 1.4305. (Note that the premiums are shown here in cents rather than dollars so care needs to be taken in calculating the addition of the premium.) The table could therefore be re-written as follows (though this is not the way in which forward rates are normally presented).

	Bank sells	Bank buys
United States Dollars (spot)	1.4370	1.4380
1 month	1.4305	1.4319
3 month	1.4185	1.4200
Portuguese Escudos (spot)	208.44	209.30
1 month	208.89	210.45
3 month	210.34	212.70

When a customer makes a forward contract this is based on the appropriate forward discount or premium quoted by foreign exchange dealers. As explained later in the chapter the figures that they use are related to differences in interest rates.

In some cases forward rates are quoted at par, which means that the forward rate is the same as the spot rate when the contract is arranged, but this is fairly uncommon.

AVOIDING EXCHANGE RISK

8.   Because forward contracts can be arranged in advance of when a currency transaction is to take place they can be used to avoid exchange risk and this is the basic purpose of entering into a forward contract. For an exporter, for example, a set amount of currency due to be received from a foreign buyer will have a known value in sterling as soon as a

forward contract is arranged. Even if exchange rates alter there is no risk of ending up with less pounds than expected (though also no possibility of the extra profit from a favourable movement in the rates). Most businesses prefer to remove uncertainty as far as possible so forward contracts are widely used.

Where an exchange of currency is to take place at a known date in the future, for example because it is the maturity date for a bill of exchange, a forward contract can be arranged for that fixed date. Quite often such precise timing is not possible; an exporter may be kept waiting for money due and can only judge approximately when it will arrive. In such circumstances an *option forward contract* is more appropriate than a *fixed forward contract*. An option forward contract sets a range of dates during which the contract can be completed, for example between three months and six months from when the contract is made. The exchange rate for the contract will normally be the rate for the beginning of the option period or the end of the option period, according to which is more favourable to the bank.

For most customers forward exchange contracts are a convenient and cheap means of avoiding or reducing exchange risk. Alternatives include:-

a) operating a currency account (suitable where both income and costs are in the same foreign currency);

b) invoicing in sterling (possible only where the foreign buyer is agreeable since it means the exchange risk is transferred from the United Kingdom exporter to the buyer);

c) buying a currency option (which is more expensive than a forward contract but gives the customer the choice of whether to complete the deal or not, so that he is not tied to an exchange rate which turns out to be less satisfactory than the spot rate when the transaction is completed − extra profit remains a possibility). Note that options (strictly known as true or pure currency options) should not be confused with option forward contracts.

INTEREST RATES AND EXCHANGE RATES

9. When banks or other currency dealers quote rates for forward contracts they do not use guesswork to decide what premium or discount to offer. The premium or discount for a particular currency is not intended to be an assessment of the future price of the currency (even though bank customers may tend to see it in that way).

In fact the premium or discount represents an adjustment based on the difference between the interest rates in the two countries concerned. A premium for the sterling-dollar rate as shown in the example earlier in the chapter means that interest rates in the United Kingdom are higher than interest rates in the United States. When this is the case the pound is described as being a weaker currency than the dollar; investors or speculators will only buy pounds because of the higher interest rate.

Strong currencies, generally those of successful exporting countries, are ones which do not need the support of high interest rates. Speculators will buy strong currencies even if the interest is low because such currencies tend to rise in value. (See also the section of this chapter which deals with terminology used in press reports.)

Example

A British investor puts money into a U.S. dollar account at 4% per annum, a lower interest rate than the 9% per annum available on a deposit account in sterling, because of the expectation of getting more pounds to the dollar when changing the money back.

Twelve months later the currency is changed back and the exchange rate is such that the number of pounds obtained more than makes up for the interest lost because of the 5% difference in interest rates. There is, of course, a risk that exchange rates may not have moved as expected and the speculator may lose money.

If in this example the investor wanted to arrange a forward contract to change the dollars back to pounds the premium for the forward contract would be equivalent to an interest rate of 5%, the difference between rates in the United States and the United Kingdom.

It is differences in interest rates between countries which determine the size of exchange rate discounts and premiums. In general terms therefore the currency in which an investment is made should make no difference to an investor if a forward contract is used to convert the currency back, because the premium or discount will exactly counteract the gain or loss from the difference in interest rates. In practice small losses are likely because of the dealing costs of converting the currency twice.

This direct link between interest rates and forward exchange rates means that there is a tendency for the influences on exchange rates to also affect interest rates. If there are more sellers of pounds than buyers a short-term measure which the Bank of England can adopt is to buy pounds to even up the supply and the demand. Because the country's currency reserves are limited this process cannot be continued indefinitely. In the longer term an increase in interest rates can make the pound more attractive as an investment, though the solution which governments prefer to achieve is an improvement in economic performance so that the currency becomes attractive without having to pay higher interest rates.

GOVERNMENT POLICY ON EXCHANGE RATES

10. Governments may specifically identify exchange rates as a target of economic policy and take measures to maintain stability because this helps both export and import businesses to plan sensibly. More commonly interest rates are adopted as a target of government policy with the aim of keeping interest reasonably low. This is intended to ensure that the cost of investment will not deter businesses from developing new ideas. Because interest rates and exchange rates are connected a policy of keeping interest rates low may lead to unacceptable fluctuations in exchange rates, while a policy of stable exchange rates may create very high interest rates from time to time. The government's role is therefore something of a juggling act with different kinds of adjustment needed as different problems occur in the economy.

FACTORS OUTSIDE GOVERNMENT CONTROL

11. Although the government has considerable influence over the economy there are many areas where this influence is very indirect or where outside pressures are more important. Key factors having a bearing on exchange rates but over which the government does not have direct control are:-

a) foreign investment (which may be influenced strongly by the policies of foreign governments or by the attitudes of speculators);

b) the economic performance of trading partners or competitors of the United Kingdom;

c) world oil prices (determined largely by the governments of the leading countries of O.P.E.C, the Organisation of Petroleum Exporting Countries);

d) the balance of trade (which government can influence by encouraging exports or by trying to reduce spending power so that less goods are imported);

e) the mineral resources of the country, for example access to oil reserves the presence of which is purely a matter of chance not government action;

f) the capacity of the country's workforce to produce competitive goods and services (influenced by government policy on education and training but more influenced by management skills).

Information about all of these issues and about political decisions affecting exchange rates is constantly being monitored by foreign exchange dealers so rates are changing all the time. Whenever a buyer or seller of currency wants to deal a price is available based on the market's assessment of all the latest relevant news.

THE SIZE OF THE FOREIGN EXCHANGE MARKETS

12. Foreign exchange is bought and sold continuously but many of the transactions which take place are purely financial and do not relate to trade in goods or services. This is because dealers in foreign currencies are always looking for opportunities to make a profit from any misalignment of rates or any future change in rates which other dealers have not predicted. Even very tiny differences in rates can be worth acting on because the amounts of money traded are so large.

This constant buying and selling makes it very difficult to measure the volume of trade in currencies. Estimates are made on the basis of statistics collected by central banks which supervise the banking system in each country.

The following table gives some idea of the scale of operations.

Foreign exchange market	Value of transactions in U.S. $ per day	Percentage of world turnover
London	90 billion	25-35%
New York	50 billion	about 20%
Tokyo	48 billion	about 20%

The percentages of world turnover can only be estimates because of the lack of data. Figures shown here are based on surveys early in 1987 by the central banks of the three countries. It is significant that the total turnover in London alone is in the region of ten times the total volume of world trade. The strength of London as the leading centre for foreign exchange business can benefit United Kingdom trade, but it does present some problems for British governments because the pound is always likely to be affected by speculation.

PRESS REPORTS ON FOREIGN EXCHANGE

13.   Leading newspapers include regular reports on changes in the foreign exchange markets. The language used by financial journalists is a special jargon which bank staff should understand. The following list of commonly used terms should prove helpful.

1.   **To harden** − to rise in price.
e.g. 'short-term rates hardened' means that interest rates for borrowing short-term became higher.

2.   **Pressure** − selling, often by speculators.
e.g. 'there was strong pressure against the pound' means that people wanting to sell pounds for foreign currency out-numbered buyers of pounds, which leads to a fall in the value of the pound.

3.   **To soften** − to fall in price.
e.g. 'there was some softening of the pound' means that the pound fell in price, so pounds could be bought with smaller amounts of foreign currency.

4.   **Strong** − tending to rise in price.
e.g. 'a strong pound caused problems for exporters' means that it became harder for British exporters to sell because prices charged to foreign customers became higher.

5.   **Support** − government intervention to control the exchange rate, usually to stop the currency from falling in value.
e.g. 'Bank of England support was needed to counteract pressure on the pound' means that the Bank of England bought pounds (using the country's reserves of foreign currency) so that the selling of pounds would not lead to a fall in the price of the pound.

6.   **Weak** − tending to fall in price.
e.g. 'a weak peseta encouraged the Spanish tourist industry' means that people were more likely to go to Spain on holiday because their own money would buy more Spanish currency.

A PRESS REPORT INTERPRETED

14.   *In early trading the pound strengthened against the Deutschemark but following the latest trade figures pressure on the pound mounted as commentators anticipated an announcement on base rates. Bank of England support reversed early falls in the rate for the dollar but the pound ended weaker against most other currencies.*

Key points to note about the above report are:

1.   The rates at which deals are done vary throughout the day. At branch level a rate for the day may be more usual but if very large amounts are traded or if a currency has changed in value more than usual the rates quoted early in the day by head office may need to be amended.

2.   Government statistics on major aspects of the economy (like the figures on the balance of trade referred to above or the figures on money supply or unemployment) all have an influence on the rates quoted in the foreign exchange market. Statistics produced by foreign governments will also have an influence.

3.   The reference to base rates indicates the very close link between foreign exchange and interest rates discussed earlier in the chapter.

4.   Because of the importance of the U.S. dollar as an international currency the rate for the dollar is frequently given special attention.

Note that if the pound rises in value in relation to the dollar (for example because the Bank of England sells dollars for pounds) this does not necessarily mean that it rises in relation to all other currencies.

Most reports on the foreign exchange markets quote the rate for the dollar. It is also quite common to include the figure for the pound's value against a trade-weighted index of currencies (often referred to as a 'basket of currencies'). This gives a better indication of how well the pound is performing if the value of the dollar is unusual for any reason.

SUMMARY

15. a) Foreign exchange transactions mostly take place between banks and do not involve cash.

b) In the United Kingdom the importance of foreign exchange is greater than in many other countries because of our dependence on international trade.

c) Trade with other countries involves specific extra risks apart from those incurred by all businesses. One of the most important of these risks is exchange risk, the risk that expected income or expected costs will be altered because of a change in exchange rates.

d) Exchange rates are determined by a broad range of economic factors but the basic mechanism of the foreign exchange markets is based on the fundamental principle of supply and demand.

e) Forward exchange rates enable a customer of a bank to fix in advance the income or cost of a particular future transaction. Forward rates are normally shown as premiums or discounts related to the spot, or current, rate. To calculate the forward rate *premiums are taken off the spot rate and discounts are added on*. The size of discount or premium is related to the difference in interest rates in the two countries concerned.

f) The government tries to control exchange rates and interest rates because of their effect on economic performance. However many important influences on exchange rates cannot be controlled by the government of one country alone.

g) The United Kingdom has the largest foreign exchange market in the world, based in London.

h) Financial journalists who write about the foreign exchange markets have their own jargon for describing what is happening. A knowledge of this terminology is important to bankers.

STUDENT SELF-TESTING

Self Review Questions

1. How important is the EEC in United Kingdom trade? (2)

2. What factors make foreign trade more risky than business within this country? (3)

3. Explain the term 'exchange risk'. (4)

4. Foreign exchange rates are determined by supply and demand, but what affects the demand for a currency? (5)

5. What is a forward exchange contract and why would it be used? (6)

6. If a currency is quoted at a premium what does this mean? (7,8)

7. What is the connection between interest rates and forward exchange rates? (9)

8. Why do governments try to influence exchange rates? (10)

9. Why is it difficult to measure the size of the foreign exchange market? (12)

10. How does a strong pound differ from a weak pound? (13)

Exercises (answers begin page 340)

A1. Read this passage and answer the questions which follow.

The French franc strengthened on the foreign exchanges yesterday following the announcement of a major austerity package by the new French government. This rise meant that the pound's trade weighted value fell slightly.

The pound's rate against the dollar was little changed on the day in spite of some early selling, because of pressure on the dollar during late trading.

1.   Why should the French government's announcement have led to a change in the exchange rate for the franc?

2.   If the franc changes in value why does this affect the pound?

3.   What is 'pressure on the dollar'?

4.   In the reference to 'early selling', what was being sold?

A2.   What is exchange risk and why does it matter? By what methods can an exporter reduce or remove exchange risk?

A3.   What influences are there on exchange rates, and to what extent can these be controlled by government?

A4.   If the Japanese yen is at a premium to the pound in the forward exchange market what does this tell you about interest rates in Japan and the United Kingdom? What relationship is there between the premium and the difference in interest rates?

21. Payments Abroad

INTRODUCTION

1. This chapter looks at the methods which are available for making payments to other countries. Banks have a major role both in sending payments and in dealing with payments received for customers.

The three basic methods of payment which banks offer to their customers are:-

a) mail transfers;

b) urgent transfers;

c) drafts.

After considering these three methods the chapter deals with secondary methods of settling international debts. The most important of these are collections and documentary credits.

THE CURRENCY IN WHICH PAYMENTS ARE MADE

2. If a person in England wants to pay money to someone in France it is most likely that the Englishman will have pounds but the Frenchman will want francs. To make a payment abroad a choice has to be made about which currency to use. In our case it will normally be francs or pounds, but a currency of a third country might also be used.

Apart from a relatively small amount of money in the form of notes and coins, pounds are kept in bank accounts in the United Kingdom. A payment abroad in pounds therefore simply means transferring ownership of money in a bank account, probably in London, to a foreign bank for the benefit of its customer.

To make a payment in francs would require the purchase of francs held in a bank in France. Once purchased they can easily be sent through the French banking system to credit the account of the person who is to receive payment.

THE PAYMENT AS A MESSAGE

3. Since payments abroad do not involve the physical transfer of money, payment depends upon messages sent through the banking system. Our example of a payment from the United Kingdom to France can be represented by the following diagram.

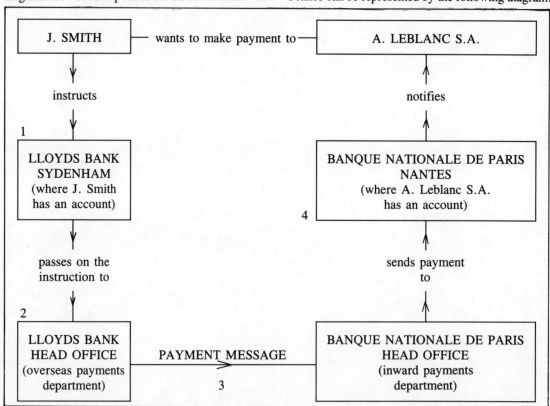

The stages of the procedure are as follows.

1. J Smith instructs his branch of Lloyds bank to make payment and his account is debited with the amount and any costs.

2. Instructions are then passed to the head office.

3. A message is sent to the appropriate French bank, in this case Banque Nationale de Paris. (If Lloyds does not have any connection with the French bank, perhaps because it is a very small bank, the message will go to a major bank asking them to make payment to the other bank.)

4. The French bank pays the money to its customer.

STERLING PAYMENT MESSAGES

4. If a payment abroad is to be made in sterling Smith can be debited and the money can be credited to a sterling account in the name of Banque Nationale de Paris.

The message to be sent will then tell the head office of Banque Nationale de Paris that money has been credited to its sterling account with Lloyds bank in London. In addition details will be provided of:-

a) who has sent the money;

b) who is to receive the payment (the beneficiary);

c) the details of the beneficiary's bank account if known;

d) any relevant reference numbers, e.g. for invoices;

e) the amount of the payment;

f) how the banks' charges are to be dealt with.

The message will also require a verification code. The French bank will not act on any message about a payment for a customer unless it is convinced that the message is genuine.

In spite of all the details needed the essence of the message is very simple. It states *WE HAVE CREDITED YOUR STERLING ACCOUNT WITH US – PLEASE PAY YOUR CUSTOMER*. From the point of view of the United Kingdom bank this type of sterling account held in the name of a foreign bank is known as a 'vostro' account (which means 'your account' as in the message).

When a message like this is received the French bank will contact its customer to tell him and to ask for his instructions. If he operates an account in pounds through Banque Nationale de Paris he may ask for the money to be kept in sterling. This will require an entry in the French bank's records to show that some of the pounds they hold are held on behalf of the customer. More commonly the recipient of a payment from abroad will want the money converted. Leblanc will be able to get his bank to sell the pounds for francs at the going rate and have the sum credited to his account.

CURRENCY PAYMENT MESSAGES

5. If Smith knows that Leblanc wants to be paid in francs it is equally possible for the payment to be sent in French francs rather than pounds. This requires a different procedure and a rather different message.

Lloyds would instruct the French bank to debit the French franc account which they have in the name of Lloyds bank. Other information would be the same, and again a verification code would be needed but the basic message would be *PLEASE DEBIT OUR FRENCH FRANC ACCOUNT WITH YOU AND PAY THE MONEY TO YOUR CUSTOMER*. From the point of view of the United Kingdom bank this type of foreign currency account held abroad is known as a 'nostro' account (which means 'our account').

In this case Banque Nationale de Paris would notify Leblanc but he would not have the choice of keeping the money in sterling. The exchange of sterling into francs would have already taken place, based on the rate in London at the time Smith's account was debited to make the payment.

If a different currency had been used the process of sending messages would have been more complicated. For example a payment to Leblanc in France in U.S. dollars would have meant that Lloyds would have needed to sent instructions to a bank in the United States to say *DEBIT OUR DOLLAR ACCOUNT AND CREDIT THE DOLLAR ACCOUNT OF B.N.P.* A message would also have been sent to Banque Nationale de Paris to say *WE HAVE ARRANGED FOR YOUR DOLLAR ACCOUNT AT X BANK TO BE CREDITED. PLEASE PAY YOUR CUSTOMER.*

MAIL TRANSFERS

6. Traditionally payment messages could be sent either by airmail or by telex. The airmail method

was slower and cheaper and so suitable where speed was not essential, particularly for smaller payments. The term mail transfer therefore means a non-urgent payment abroad through the banking system.

Today mail transfer payments are made either:-

a) by airmail;

b) by computer message through the SWIFT network.

SWIFT (the Society for Worldwide Interbank Financial Telecommunication) is a computer network linking the banks of all the world's leading trading nations. It was established in 1973 with less than 250 participating banks in just 15 countries. Membership now includes over 1000 banks in over 50 countries and by 1985 the network was handling well over 600,000 transactions a day. The majority of international payments sent from the United Kingdom now go through SWIFT though payments to some minor trading nations still have to use airmail. The term mail transfer is therefore a little misleading though not completely out-of-date.

For the customer sending a payment by mail transfer there is no need to know whether the bank is using airmail or SWIFT. The customer completes a form giving all the details the bank needs. This information is then sent to the bank's head office (often through the bank's own computer network) and then sent on to the foreign bank's head office by the most convenient means.

URGENT TRANSFERS

7.   As the name implies an urgent transfer is used for sending payments abroad as quickly as possible. Speed may be important because the money is needed for some emergency or because the amount involved is very large.

Because of the methods used in the past this type of payment is sometimes referred to as a CT (cable transfer) or TT (telegraphic transfer). Today payments are made either:-

a) by telex;

b) by computer message through SWIFT.

Telex is quicker than airmail. If SWIFT is used, urgent messages are given priority to ensure that an urgent transfer is quicker than a mail transfer. Obtaining priority costs money but the cost is justified if saving time is important.

FOREIGN DRAFTS

8.   Sometimes a customer may want a form of payment which can be sent directly to someone abroad rather than via a bank account. This may be needed, for example, to make a holiday booking or to send an order for a small item to a foreign mail order retailer. In these circumstances a payment by mail transfer or urgent transfer is not appropriate. The alternative is to use a draft.

The basic principle that a payment abroad is a message still applies but in this case the message takes the form of a document rather like a cheque, drawn by one bank on another. In our example Lloyds Bank would write out a draft in French francs payable to Leblanc drawn on the Banque Nationale de Paris or any other correspondent bank (a bank with which Lloyds has an account abroad). This draft would be given to Smith and his account debited with the cost of it (usually roughly similar to a mail transfer). Smith can then send the draft together with any other information, for example an order for goods, by post to Leblanc.

In the meantime Lloyds will send a message to Banque Nationale de Paris to say that a valid draft has been issued. The essential content of this message will be *PLEASE DEBIT OUR FRENCH FRANC ACCOUNT WITH YOU WHEN DRAFT NO. abc IS PRESENTED FOR PAYMENT.* The draft itself is an instruction to pay so this message acts a validation of the document helping to prevent fraud. Leblanc's branch of the bank will not need to know about this message although they may see the draft when it is paid in.

It is also possible for foreign drafts to be issued in sterling but this is now fairly rare because if a sterling payment drawn on the United Kingdom is acceptable to the beneficiary a cheque can be sent instead.

CHOOSING A METHOD OF PAYMENT

9.   The three basic methods of payment are suited to different circumstances. The choice to be made between them will depend on the balance between speed and cost. To get money sent abroad more quickly costs more. This may be of great importance where large sums are concerned because while the message is being processed the money is held by the banking system and the customers do not get paid any interest. If there is no hurry a cheap method can be used.

The foreign draft is likely to be the slowest method for getting money from one bank account to another but may be the best choice where the beneficiary needs to see that payment has been received.

More complex methods of settlement of international debt are possible to protect the interests of the parties concerned but all of them depend on one of the three basic methods of payment for the final transfer of ownership of the money.

BILLS OF EXCHANGE

10.   As described in Chapter 14 a bill of exchange is a document which shows that one person owes money to another and it can be used to make a payment in much the same way as a cheque (which is itself a special form of bill of exchange). Bills of exchange are only used in a limited number of industries within the United Kingdom, but in foreign trade they are much more common. It is therefore important for bankers to know what bills of exchange are and how they are used.

The definition of a bill of exchange (given in Chapter 14) consists of a number of important elements.

1.   The bill must be unconditional, which means it cannot say that payment will be made *if* some event occurs.

2.   The bill must be in writing, though typed documents are now more common and are legally acceptable.

3.   The bill is addressed by one person, the drawer, who prepares the document and signs it.

4.   The person to whom it is addressed is required to pay the amount shown.

5.   The amount must be definite, though it may require some calculation, for example of interest.

6.   The date for payment must be definite, whether as a specific date or a date which can be calculated once the bill has been presented to the drawee.

7.   The person who is to receive the money, the payee, is often the same as the drawer though bills can be made out to other people, for example banks, or to the bearer (which means that whoever has possession of the bill after it has been accepted is entitled to the money).

BILLS OF EXCHANGE ASSESSED

11.   The following table summarises the advantages of using bills of exchange in international trade.

Advantages of using bills of exchange in international trade

For the drawer (the exporter who is to receive the money)

1.   The drawer initiates payment so that it does not get overlooked.

2.   Before documents relating to goods are released the drawee of a bill can be required to pay it *or* accept it (which means signing it to confirm that payment will be made at a future date).

3.   Refusal to pay a bill once it has been accepted is unlikely because it is seen by the business community as a very serious matter affecting the acceptor's credit-worthiness.

4.   Once a bill of exchange has been accepted the acceptor is legally committed to pay even if the drawer has not completed his part of the underlying contract satisfactorily.

5.   As the holder of an accepted bill an exporter has the choice of waiting until the due date to obtain payment or discounting the bill through a bank in order to get money straightaway (as described in Chapter 14).

For the drawee (the importer who is to pay the money)

1.   The exporter is unlikely to send out a bill of exchange for payment until he has completed his side of the contract e.g. shipped the goods that were ordered.

2.   Acceptance or payment of the bill as agreed in the underlying contract may entitle the importer to documents which he needs in order to get hold of the goods which were ordered.

3.   If the bill of exchange is a term bill, not payable immediately, the importer can take a period of credit from the date of acceptance until the date for payment.

The following example shows a bill of exchange used for international trade.

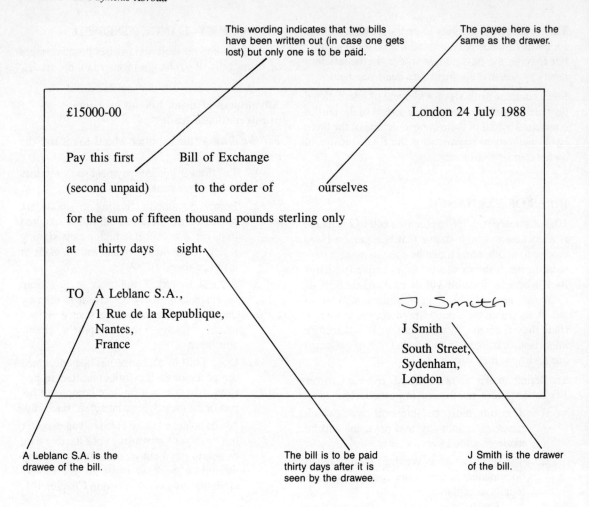

This wording indicates that two bills have been written out (in case one gets lost) but only one is to be paid.

The payee here is the same as the drawer.

£15000-00

London 24 July 1988

Pay this first   Bill of Exchange

(second unpaid)   to the order of   ourselves

for the sum of fifteen thousand pounds sterling only

at   thirty days   sight.

TO   A Leblanc S.A.,
       1 Rue de la Republique,
       Nantes,
       France

J. Smith

J Smith

South Street,
Sydenham,
London

A Leblanc S.A. is the drawee of the bill.

The bill is to be paid thirty days after it is seen by the drawee.

J Smith is the drawer of the bill.

COLLECTIONS

12. One of the situations in which banks are likely to deal with bills of exchange is where an importer has agreed to pay for goods by bill of exchange. Instructions about the documents relating to the goods are given by the exporter to his bank and written into a *collection order* which the bank sends through the banking system. The term collection order is used because the order specifies how the money to be paid is going to be collected.

The collection order covers:-

    a)   what documents are attached;

    b)   who is to pay;

    c)   how much is to be paid;

    d)   a reference number for any queries;

    e)   instructions on the method of payment to be used (mail transfer, urgent transfer or draft);

    f)   how the banks' charges are to be dealt with;

    g)   who is to be consulted in case of difficulties;

    h)   when the documents are to be released (when the bill is accepted or when it is paid).

An example of the kind of form which a customer would need to complete to arrange a collection is shown opposite. It is an exporter who normally gives the instructions about a collection so this is the kind

SPECIMEN *(by kind permission of Royal Bank of Scotland plc)*

The Royal Bank of Scotland plc	Documents for Collection — Instruction and Indemnity

From — Customer's name

Branch reference	Customer's reference

Date

We enclose the following item (please mark X as appropriate)

For collection abroad		For Sale	
For collection in London		For	

Drawer	Amount

Drawee

Date of Bill	Tenor

Mode of Transport and Goods

Drawer's Bankers

(Bills will normally be forwarded to the Bank's own correspondents for presentation through any bankers specified unless instructions to the contrary are given below)

Documents (please state how many of each)

Draft	Invoice	Cons/Cert Invoice	Certificate of Origin	Packing Spec list	Bills of Lading	Air Waybill	Insurance Pol/Cert	Statement	Other Documents			

If drawn under a Letter of Credit or Letter of Authority the instructions sections below need not be completed, but please give details here of the Letter of Credit or Letter of Authority which should be attached

Instructions to Bank (please mark X as appropriate)

Deliver documents against acceptance	Collect all charges from Drawee
When accepted due date to be advised by Cable/Airmail	Collect Correspondent bank Charges only from Drawee
Return accepted draft to us	Collect interest at % pa from date/date of acceptance of draft to approximate date of arrival of funds in London
Deliver documents against payment	Do not waive interest/charges which are for Drawee's account
If unaccepted or unpaid, obtain advice by Cable/Airmail	Arrange for proceeds to be remitted to you by Cable/Airmail at our expense
Protest if unaccepted or unpaid	If existing Local Exchange Control Regulations in the country of payment so require you are authorised to accept payment in local currency and Drawee's undertaking to be responsible for any loss of exchange
Do not protest if unaccepted or unpaid	
If necessary hold for arrival of goods	
If dishonoured store goods and insure them	Any other instructions
If dishonoured store goods in Customs or bonded warehouse and insure but do not pay customs duty without reference to us	
In case of need refer to	

But do not follow his/their instructions without first obtaining our confirmation	
Whose instructions may be followed and to whom all documents may be handed free of payment if required	

It is understood that in respect of this transaction you shall not be liable for any delays, postal losses, or differences in exchange, or for any acts or defaults of your agents or correspondents (including their insolvency) or their employees. This indemnity shall remain in force and effect until final settlement of the transaction. Unless otherwise instructed by me/us, you shall forward all documents by first airmail

Customer's signature

Subject to Uniform Rules for Collections
International Chamber of Commerce Publication No 322
or as amended by any subsequent revision of ICC

For Bank use only	Countersigned
Branch stamp No 7	Manager

03051 (6/85)

of form a United Kingdom exporter would expect to fill in. The form asks for all the information which the bank would include in its own collection order to send on to a bank abroad. (If a collection is sent to this country for payment by a United Kingdom importer the importer's bank will receive a collection order giving all the necessary instructions.)

The procedure for dealing with a collection is represented in the following diagram. (The diagram illustrates a collection with a bill of exchange and documents of title to goods, but not all collections follow this pattern.)

For the importer's bank the process of dealing with a collection creates an unusual relationship with the customer because the bank is acting as agent for the remitting bank (the bank which sends the collection). By internationally agreed rules the bank must do as instructed by the remitting bank even though this may not be in its own customer's best interests.

TYPES OF COLLECTION

13. Collections can be categorised according to what is sent with the collection order.

    1. **Clean Collections**

        A clean collection is a collection order accompanied only by financial documents.

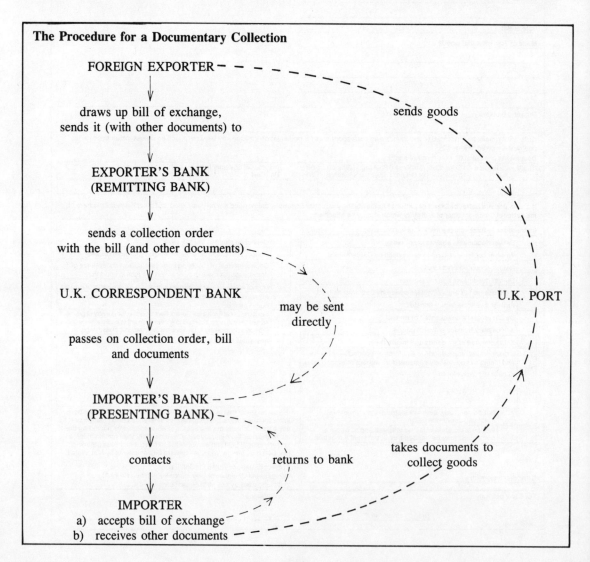

The Procedure for a Documentary Collection

FOREIGN EXPORTER

    draws up bill of exchange,
sends it (with other documents) to

    EXPORTER'S BANK
(REMITTING BANK)

    sends a collection order
with the bill (and other documents)

    U.K. CORRESPONDENT BANK

    passes on collection order, bill
and documents

    IMPORTER'S BANK
(PRESENTING BANK)

    contacts

    IMPORTER
a) accepts bill of exchange
b) receives other documents

sends goods

U.K. PORT

may be sent directly

returns to bank

takes documents to collect goods

This usually means one or more bills of exchange, but the term also applies to some other items for which payment can be requested.

2. **Documentary Collections**

A documentary collection is a collection order accompanied by commercial documents. These are released to the person who is to make payment.

In some cases a documentary collection will have no financial document with it but will simply ask for payment of a stated sum. More commonly the commercial documents are accompanied by a financial document, and it is when the financial document is paid that money will be sent back to the remitting bank by one of the three basic methods.

Note that commercial documents are not necessarily documents of title by which the holder can prove that he has a right to the goods they describe. As explained later in the chapter only *bills of lading* are normally documents of title.

FINANCIAL DOCUMENTS

14. The bill of exchange is the most important type of financial document commonly sent through the international banking system for collection.

An alternative form of financial document (which has become a little more widely used since the ending of Exchange Control regulations in 1979) is the cheque. If a United Kingdom importer sends a payment for goods by cheque then the exporter receiving the cheque will pay it into a bank abroad where it will be processed like any other bill of exchange. It will be sent back to the bank it is drawn on in the United Kingdom together with a collection order specifying how payment is to be made. The cheque itself is a way of settling a bill owed to someone abroad but it does not act as an effective form of payment.

Apart from bills of exchange and cheques the other type of financial document which banks sometimes send for collection is the promissory note.

The payee of the promissory note is Schneider A.G.

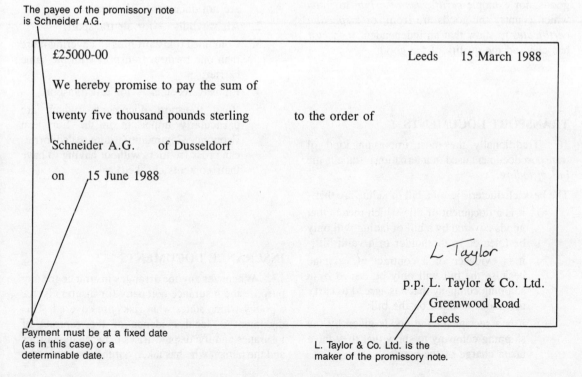

£25000-00   Leeds   15 March 1988

We hereby promise to pay the sum of

twenty five thousand pounds sterling   to the order of

Schneider A.G.   of Dusseldorf

on   15 June 1988

L Taylor

p.p. L. Taylor & Co. Ltd.
Greenwood Road
Leeds

Payment must be at a fixed date (as in this case) or a determinable date.

L. Taylor & Co. Ltd. is the maker of the promissory note.

As the example above illustrates this has some similarities with a bill of exchange but it is the person who is going to pay who draws up the document. The payee will usually hold on to the note until it is near to the payment date (or due date). There is no need to send it any earlier because it does not require any acceptance having already been signed by the person who is to pay. Just before the due date the note is then sent for collection like a bill of exchange.

COMMERCIAL DOCUMENTS

15.   When a contract is drawn up between an importer and an exporter the two parties need to discuss what documentation will be used and to agree about how the documents will be dealt with. The normal minimum requirement is for three basic types of document:-

a)   transport documents;

b)   insurance documents;

c)   invoices.

Other possible requirements which will be seen less often are documents providing evidence about the goods, for example *certificates of origin* to show which country the goods are from, or *inspection certificates* to show that an independent inspector has checked the quality of the goods.

TRANSPORT DOCUMENTS

16.   Traditionally the most important kind of transport document used in international trade is the *bill of lading*.

The basic characteristics of a bill of lading are that:-

a)   it is a document of title which means that goods covered by a bill of lading will only be released to the holder of a valid bill;

b)   it is evidence of a contract of carriage because the bill will only be issued by a shipping company that has agreed to carry the goods detailed on the bill;

c)   it is a receipt for the goods given by the shipping company to show that they have taken charge of the goods.

The idea of issuing a document of title to the goods was an important protection for both importer and exporter because it helped to make sure that the goods did not get into the wrong hands (particularly as goods might be held by a shipping company for a very long time). Today a number of factors make the use of traditional bills of lading less suitable.

1.   The speed at which ships can be loaded and unloaded has increased, for example by the use of containerisation.

2.   More freight is now carried by aircraft, which have never made use of the system of bills of lading.

3.   Shipping documents are beginning to be handled electronically making the old-style pieces of paper unnecessary.

The other forms of transport document which are commonly used act as receipts and evidence of a contract of carriage but are not documents of title. This means that the importer can obtain his goods by producing suitable identification; the actual transport documents are not essential to persuade the carrier to hand over the goods.

The main transport documents are:-

1.   Sea waybills – shipping documents which are not documents of title;

2.   Air waybills – for air transport;

3.   Combined transport bills – covering more than one form of transport with the same carrier;

4.   Railway receipts – for rail transport;

5.   Road transport documents (which are particularly important in the European Economic Community where sealed lorries can cross frontiers without having to have their contents checked).

INSURANCE DOCUMENTS

17.   Whenever anyone arranges insurance for any purpose the insurance company (or insurer) issues a policy which states what risks are covered. This document is legal evidence of the contract of insurance and if a dispute arises between the insurer and the person who has taken out the insurance (the

insured) the courts can refer to the policy to decide what the words mean. In international trade protecting goods while they are being sent from an exporter to an importer includes taking out insurance. Whether it is the responsibility of the exporter or the importer depends upon the terms agreed in the underlying contract between the two parties.

If the exporter is responsible he will obtain a policy and will either:-

a)   send the policy to the importer along with the other documents relating to the goods *or*

b)   keep the policy but send the importer an insurance certificate which shows that the particular goods being sold are covered by the policy.

The second alternative is commonly used by regular exporters because they can take out a policy to cover a number of different contracts.

A bank handling documents would therefore expect to see either an insurance policy or an insurance certificate as evidence that goods had been insured.

INVOICES

18.   For business contracts within one country it is usual for the seller of goods to provide the buyer with an invoice detailing the goods being sold and showing prices and any appropriate reference numbers. This is equally true in international trade. The exporter will produce invoices for the importer. Normally these will be in multiple copies, often six or more, because they will be used in various departments of the importing company. As with other documents the precise requirements will be agreed in advance by the importer and exporter when the contract is made.

BANKS AND THE DOCUMENTS OF INTERNATIONAL TRADE

19.   The documents of international trade described above are, of course, of vital importance to importers and exporters. It is also essential for banks to be familiar with the documents because of their role in international trade. Not only do banks give

advice to their customers about documentation. They are also expected to handle the documents, for example accompanying bills of exchange sent for collection. The inward collections department of a bank must know whether the right documents have been sent with the collection order and even at branch level it is important for the foreign clerk to know what he or she is dealing with. Immediate action is needed if documents are missing or do not relate to the bill they are with.

In general expert knowledge of documents is not needed at branch level as far as collections are concerned because the international rules governing collections do not require banks to check every detail. These international rules, the *Uniform Rules for Collections* drawn up by the International Chamber of Commerce and adopted by banks of most major trading countries emphasise that any bank dealing with a collection is acting as agent for the bank which sent the collection. The implication of this is that with an inward collection the bank is asking its customer to pay but is not acting on behalf of its customer; requests by the customer to ignore the terms of the collection order must be refused.

A more thorough knowledge of documentation is needed when dealing with documentary letters of credit (which are described below). Here the international rules, the *Uniform Customs and Practice* drawn up by the International Chamber of Commerce, do require banks to check carefully that documents produced are exactly as specified in the letter of credit.

DOCUMENTARY CREDITS

20.   Bankers' documentary letters of credit, more commonly referred to simply as documentary credits provide a means by which an exporter can get his money safely before goods sent abroad have been received by the importer. For the exporter this is in effect a guarantee of payment, which is nearly as good as getting paid in advance. For the importer it is better than paying in advance because by specifying the documents which the exporter must produce the importer retains some control over the goods. For example inspection certificates can be requested to try to make sure the quality of goods purchased is acceptable.

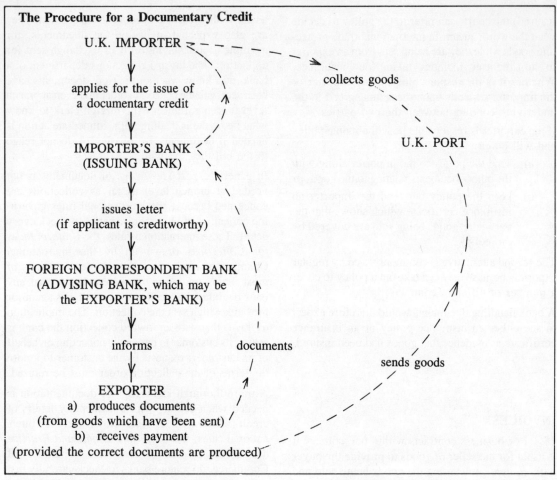

The Procedure for a Documentary Credit

U.K. IMPORTER

applies for the issue of
a documentary credit

IMPORTER'S BANK
(ISSUING BANK)

issues letter
(if applicant is creditworthy)

FOREIGN CORRESPONDENT BANK
(ADVISING BANK, which may be
the EXPORTER'S BANK)

informs   documents

EXPORTER
a)   produces documents
(from goods which have been sent)
b)   receives payment
(provided the correct documents are produced)

collects goods

U.K. PORT

sends goods

Exporters like to arrange payment by documentary credit if they can, because they can be sure of getting their money if they produce the right documents.

The basic steps in making a payment by documentary credit are as follows.

1.   A contract is made between an importer in one country and an exporter in another in which it is agreed that payment will be by documentary credit.

2.   The exporter prepares the goods for export.

3.   The importer arranges the documentary credit by applying to his bank for a letter of credit to be issued.

An example of the kind of form used by a customer to apply for the bank to issue a documentary letter of credit is shown opposite. Note the space left for specifying any documents other than those commonly used.

4.   The importer's bank (the issuing bank) draws up the letter of credit (if it considers the importer creditworthy) including in it details of documents which the exporter will have to produce. The letter is sent to the exporter's bank.

5.   The exporter's bank (the advising bank) advises the exporter that the letter has been received and the exporter then produces the documents to show that the goods have been sent. By producing documents which comply exactly with the terms of the letter of credit the exporter can be sure of payment, guaranteed by the bank which has issued the letter of credit. In some cases the contract between exporter and importer will arrange for a bank in the exporter's country to add its guarantee or confirmation that payment will be made; such a bank is known as a *confirming bank*.

242

SPECIMEN *(by kind permission of TSB England and Wales plc).*

TSB BANK

Application for Documentary Credit

(Send to Foreign Services Department, Administration Centre)

TSB England & Wales plc

Sort Code   Branch

Date

Bank use only
FD/DC/OUT

Dear Sirs

We request you to establish for our account a Documentary Credit in accordance with the details given below.

Please advise the beneficiary by Airmail/SWIFT/Telex*.   Credit to be Irrevocable/Revocable/Transferable*.

Advising bank

Beneficiary (full name and address)

From (applicant) name and address

Amount (figures)   Amount (words)

Terms of draft
At   date/sight
Drawn on

Expiry date

in

Documentation required

Credit to be available for payment/negotiation/acceptance* of drafts accompanied by the following documents:

- Commercial invoices in
- Packing list in
- Certificate of origin in
- Combined transport document

OR

- Full set of clean on board marine Bills of Lading
  - Consigned to order (of)
  - Blank endorsed
  - Marked "Freight Prepaid" (for C&F, CIF shipments)
  - Marked "Freight payable at destination" (for FOB shipments)
  - And "Notify"

OR

- Consignors copy of Airway Bill issued and signed by carriers or their agents evidencing aircraft identification and marked "Freight Paid/Collect*", date of dispatch, bearing this letter of credit number and showing goods consigned to

OR

- Other (please specify)

- Insurance covered by applicant (for FOB, Ex works shipment)

OR

- Insurance policy/certificate* required (for C&I, CIF shipments) in duplicate, for _____% of invoice value, covering Institute Cargo Clauses All Risks, Institute War Clauses and Institute Strikes, Riots and Civil Commotions Clauses.

Additional risks (please specify)

- Other documents (please specify)

Covering shipment/dispatch of goods as below, of _____ origin, to be invoiced FOB / C&F / CIF / (Other) _____ *
From   Transportation to

Transhipment   Partial shipment   Date
allowed / not allowed*   allowed / not allowed*   Shipment to be effected not later than _____

Goods (brief particulars, where possible)

Documents to be presented within _____ days after the date of the shipping documents and in any event within Credit validity.

Charges incurred outside the UK are for our account/beneficiary's account*.

(Delete whichever does not apply)*

EW-XX-1342-0287

Page One

SPECIMEN *(by kind permission of TSB England and Wales plc).*

Special Instructions

Terms and Conditions

In consideration of your establishing a credit (the "Credit") in accordance with this Application, we agree as follows:

1.   that at any time and from time to time after the establishment of the Credit, you may debit to any account or accounts of ours with you or, on demand, we will provide you with, such amount or amounts, at such office or offices of yours as you may require, as will meet disbursements (made or to be made) under the Credit or otherwise in accordance herewith, payments (made or to be made) under any drafts drawn under the Credit and all commissions, charges, interest on overdue payments and expenses in connection with the Credit and so that in any case where any amount so debited or provided as in a currency other than the currency in which the relative disbursement, payment, commission, charges, interest or expenses (the "outgoing") was or is to be made or paid such amount shall be the equivalent of the amount of the outgoing translated at the rate of which you would sell us the currency of the outgoing for the currency in which such amount is so debited or provided in accordance with your usual practices at the time of such debiting or provision together with the amount of your usual charges for procuring the transmission or transfer of the amount of the outgoing in accordance with your usual practices to the place where such outgoing was or is to be made or paid.

2.   that until all our liabilities to you hereunder have been discharged or until all the goods for which payment is made under or by virtue of the Credit (the "Goods") shall have been sold by ourselves or yourselves, the Goods shall be kept fully insured against all usual risks including war risks in a manner satisfactory to you and to lodge with you or or produce to you the policies, if called upon to do so, and if such insurance is not affected or the policies are not so lodged or produced, you may (but shall not be bound to) effect such other or additional insurance as you may see fit at our expense.

3.   that the Goods and all documents and policies relative thereto received by you shall be received by you as pledges, such Goods, documents and policies being pledged to you to secure all our obligations and liabilities present or future ascertained or contingent to you under or arising out of this Application or otherwise and that you shall have full discretion and power of sale over the Goods without notice to us.

4.   to sign, execute and/or deliver any transfer deed or documents which you may require us to sign, execute and/or deliver for perfecting your title to the Goods and/or vesting the same in or delivering the same to any purchaser or purchasers from you.

5.   to procure promptly any necessary import,export or other Licences and to comply with all regulations of any government or other competent authority relating to the Goods any shipment or warehousing of the Goods, the Credit or otherwise in connection therewith or herewith, and to furnish such certificates in that respect as you may at any time require.

6.   that neither you nor any officer, employee, correspondent or agent of yours shall be liable for any action taken or omitted by you or them hereunder or under or in connection with the Credit or the Goods unless directly caused by the gross negligence or wilful misconduct of yourselves, or your officers, employees, correspondents or agents.

7.   that in the event of any amendment to the Credit (including any extension of the expiry date thereof) the terms hereof shall remain in full force and effect and be binding upon us and apply to the Credit as if such amendment had been incorporated in this Application.

8.   that the Credit shall be subject to the Uniform Customs and Practice for Documentary Credits as revised from time to time.

9.   that, if this Application is signed by one individual, the terms "we", "our", "ours", "ourselves", and "us" shall be read throughout as "I", "my", "mine", "myself" and "me", as the case may be or, if this Application is signed by or on behalf of more than one party, the obligations hereunder shall be joint and several.

10.   that this Application shall be governed by and construed in all respects in accordance with the laws of England.

It is hereby agreed that this application and the opening by you of a documentary credit shall be subject in all respects to the terms and conditions set out above. This application consists of _____ page(s).

⌐Till Crossing Stamp

Date

Authorised signature(s)

On behalf of

Branch signature

Page Two

6.   The exporter's bank checks the documents (acting as agent for the importer's bank) and if they are:-

a)   completely correct – payment is made to the exporter and the documents are sent to the importer's bank which will then pay back the exporter's bank;

b)   almost correct – payment can be made to the exporter after taking an indemnity from him by which he promises to repay if the documents are refused;

c)   incorrect – the exporter will have to get new documents or send the wrong documents for collection which will mean a delay in getting paid.

7.   If the documents are correct the importer's bank will pay the exporter's bank as agreed in the letter of credit by one of the three basic methods of payment, draft, mail transfer or urgent transfer. The importer will receive the documents and collect the goods.

The kind of documents used in a documentary credit are generally the same kind of documents used for collections (insurance documents, invoices and transport documents) but a variety of other documents may also be requested.

DOCUMENTARY COLLECTIONS AND DOCUMENTARY CREDITS

21.   Although there are certain similarities between documentary collections and documentary credits there are also important differences. These are summarised in the following table.

Collections	Credits
1. The exporter (principal) requests the bank to handle the collection.	1. The importer (applicant) requests the bank to issue a letter of credit.
2. The exporter controls what banks can do by what is included in the collection order.	2. The importer controls what banks can do by specifying the documents required.
3. For the exporter obtaining payment depends on the importer's ability to pay.	3. For the exporter obtaining payment depends on producing the correct documents and on the credit-worthiness of the bank which has agreed to pay.
4. For the importer getting the documents usually depends on paying or accepting a bill of exchange.	4. For the importer the commitment to pay arises when an application is made. Obtaining the documents requires no further formalities.

THE RANGE OF METHODS OF SETTLEMENT

22.   Students need to pay special attention to collections and documentary credits because they are complicated, but they are only two of the possible choices which importers and exporters can make about the payment terms for settling a debt. The following list shows the options which are available. From the exporter's point of view these are shown in order of decreasing risk, the most 'dangerous' first. The risk increases from an importer's point of view.

1.   Consignment of goods (which means sending them abroad without having a definite sale arranged and waiting for payments as the goods are sold).

2.   Open account trade (which means goods are sent and payment is made at intervals, allowing a period of credit as in much trade within the United Kingdom).

3.   Documents sent direct to the importer with payment to be made when they are received (which gives the exporter no control).

4.   Collections.

5.   Documentary credits.

6.   Payment in advance (which means the exporter gets his money before sending goods, and may have a period of credit during which the money can be used to make or purchase the goods to be exported).

SUMMARY

23. a) Payments abroad consist of messages. These may deal with payments in any currency but the currency used will determine what message is needed because when a currency changes hands it does not move from one country to another; it is simply ownership of the funds which changes.

b) Different payment methods depend on different kinds of message.
1. Mail transfers are messages sent by air-mail or SWIFT to a bank;
2. Urgent transfers are messages sent by telex or SWIFT to a bank;
3. Drafts are messages in the form of documents which can be sent directly to a beneficiary instead of a bank and then paid into a bank account.

c) Bills of exchange are used in international trade as a means of settlement. They can put the exporter in a strong legal position and can also be used to give an importer a period of credit.

d) Where goods are being exported and settlement is to be made by a bill of exchange the exporter may ask his bank to send the bill and accompanying documents for collection. The collection order which the bank sends to the importer's bank spells out what the importer must do to get the documents.

e) Bills of exchange are not the only financial documents which can be used to arrange payment. Cheques and promissory notes are also used.

f) The commercial documents most widely used in international trade are:-
1. transport documents (for example bills of lading);
2. insurance documents (certificates or policies);
3. invoices.

g) Banks have to handle documents when dealing with documentary collections but need even more expertise to deal with documents under a documentary letter of credit. This is a payment method initiated by the importer which ensures that the exporter is paid provided the right documents are produced.

h) Payment methods range from consignment of goods with payment as sales take place (which is very risky for the exporter) through safer methods like collections and documentary credits to payment in advance (which is the safest method for the exporter but the least acceptable to the importer).

STUDENT SELF-TESTING

Self Review Questions

1. What information would you expect to find in a message used to make a payment from one country to another? (4)

2. What is the difference between a 'nostro' account and a 'vostro' account? (4,5)

3. What differences are there between mail transfers and urgent transfers? (6,7)

4. Describe the steps taken in issuing a foreign draft and arranging for it to be paid. (8)

5. What is a bill of exchange and what advantages are there for an exporter arranging to be paid by bill of exchange? (10,11)

6. What financial documents other than bills of exchange is a bank likely to collect for a customer? (14)

7. Apart from transport documents what other two types of commercial document are most commonly used in international trade? (15)

8. What distinguishes a bill of lading from other kinds of transport document? (16)

9. What differences are there between documentary collections and documentary credits? (21)

10. Which method of payment is likely to suit an exporter best? (22)

Exercises (answers begin page 341)

A1. What are the differences between drafts, mail transfers and urgent transfers?

A2. What commercial documents are used in international trade? Describe each of the main categories.

A3. What are bills of exchange and why are they used in international trade?

A4. What are the main features of a documentary letter of credit, and what documents are likely to be required under its terms?

22. Finance of International Trade

INTRODUCTION

1. The last chapter looked at the range of methods of making payments abroad through the banking system. This chapter deals with the ways in which banks provide support for importers and exporters by lending money or by other associated services. Areas covered include:-

    a) countertrade;

    b) produce advances;

    c) credit insurance;

    d) bonds and guarantees;

    e) factoring;

    f) forfaiting;

    g) advice services.

Emphasis is given to the role of the government agency, the Export Credits Guarantee Department, in assisting banks to finance United Kingdom export business.

TRADING WITHOUT BORROWING

2. Some businesses are able to carry on import or export business without needing to raise money because the owners of the business have invested enough or because the business has accumulated enough profit from previous trading.

Many other businesses finance themselves in international trade as they do in domestic trade, trade within the United Kingdom, by means of credit terms. Importers of goods may make payment perhaps thirty or sixty days after goods are bought giving them time to dispose of the goods and even collect in cash from their buyers. This is common practice between businesses within one country but less usual for international finance because of the extra risks involved (as outlined in Chapter 20). Exporters can finance themselves in the opposite way by requiring payment in advance, but this is a problem too because customers will prefer to buy from suppliers who offer credit, so sales may be lost.

Another option for avoiding the need for borrowed funds is to exchange goods, to barter, rather than to deal in cash. Again the needs of exporters and importers are rather different. An exporter needs the finance to pay for acquiring or making the goods to be sold so receiving a consignment of other foreign goods is of little help unless the goods can be turned into cash very quickly. For importers swapping goods may be more sensible because what they want are the imported goods to sell before having to pay out cash; if other goods can be sent abroad in payment instead of money the only problem is how to settle up with the manufacturer of the goods used as the payment for the imports.

COUNTERTRADE

3. The term countertrade is used to describe the wide variety of possible arrangements for making payment in international trade using goods instead of money. Countertrade transactions can be defined as sales to a particular country linked to exports from that country, one part of the transaction being described as a delivery of goods and the other part as a counterdelivery.(This definition excludes bilateral trade agreements between countries intended to fix balanced annual quotas of imports and exports.)

Main forms of countertrade are:-

    1. **Barter:** goods are exchanged, usually simultaneously under one contract, without any transfer of cash. This is fairly rare in modern international trade.

    2. **Compensation Deals:** one contract covers delivery and counterdelivery but there are payments in respect of each movement of goods, usually in one currency and often after applying set-off (which means calculating the difference between the amounts owed before making payment). Delivery and counterdelivery may not be simultaneous but counterdelivery is normally within 3 years of delivery.

    3. **Counterpurchases:** there are separate contracts and invoices for delivery and counterdelivery. Delivery and counterdelivery may not be simultaneous, but counterdelivery is usually within five years of delivery. Counterpurchase is the most common form of Countertrade.

    4. **Co-operation:** countertrade based on long term agreements involving a series of contracts, for example in project financing

where exports of capital goods to set up a factory are 'traded' for imports of items produced from the factory.

The involvement of banks in countertrade arises from their aim of providing a complete service for customers. United Kingdom importers are unlikely to become involved in countertrade but exporters may meet the problem when selling to countries which have difficulty in obtaining foreign currency to pay for their purchases. Banks have specialist departments which can advise on what terms to accept and can suggest how to dispose of counter-traded goods.

USING CONVENTIONAL FINANCING

4. If importers or exporters do need to borrow money to finance their operations the possibilities open to them include the forms of finance which banks offer to all borrowers.

Importers can take an overdraft or loan to pay for goods they are buying. When sales are made the borrowing can be repaid. The bank's decision about whether to lend or not will be based on the general lending principles described in Chapter 11. Factoring might also be available as a means of raising finance as the imported goods are sold to United Kingdom buyers. This choice of conventional forms of finance meets the needs of most importers so there are few specialist forms of finance directed specifically at importers. Perhaps the most important is the produce advance referred to in the next section of the chapter.

Exporters can borrow in the form of a conventional loan or overdraft too, and for many businesses which produce goods for both the domestic and overseas markets funds may be borrowed for the general purpose of continuing production without any specific allocation of funds to the export part of the business. However there are forms of finance specifically targetted at exporters, partly because of government support for exporting.

PRODUCE ADVANCES

5. As explained in Chapter 17 a produce advance is a form of lending based on goods as security. Because importers usually buy goods in bulk and then resell them as soon as they can, they are ideal customers for produce advances if the goods handled meet the bank's requirements of being non-perishable and easily saleable.

Importers of basic commodities which are dealt with in bulk are the most likely customers for produce advances. They may well need finance because their business often depends upon small profit margins on large deals at irregular intervals, so financing by retained profits or invested capital is not always possible. Many bank branches will never come across lending in this form because it is only need-ed by dealers who trade regularly in goods which are easy to sell while having very little cash to finance themselves.

PRODUCE ADVANCES ASSESSED

6. The following table looks at the advantages and disadvantages of lending based on goods as security. These factors are particularly relevant to importers but other traders may also use produce advances.

Advantages and disadvantages of produce advances

Advantages for the Bank

1. The lending is safer than an unsecured loan or overdraft.

2. The purpose of the borrowing can be clearly identified.

3. Some control over the money and the security is possible.

Advantages for the Customer

1. Interest may be slightly less than for unsecured borrowing.

2. Borrowing might be possible where the bank would not lend unsecured.

Disadvantages for the Bank

1. There may be problems with the security, for example if the original suppliers of the goods have written a retention clause into the contract preventing the importer from owning the goods until they have been paid for.

2. If the customer is untrustworthy there may be opportunities for the goods to be sold without the bank getting its money back.

Disadvantages for the Customer

1. The extra paperwork needed to give the bank control over the goods is time-consuming.

2. Bank delays could get in the way of a sale.

EXPORTERS AND CREDIT INSURANCE

7.   All countries are keen to export their products, so in general United Kingdom importers are able to get fairly good credit terms and do not have a great need for specialist financing. For United Kingdom exporters the problem is how to win customers in competitive markets. Offering credit is often essential even though getting paid in advance would be preferable. This means that exporters generally have to face a credit risk, a risk that goods sent to a customer will not be paid for.

One likely reason for non-payment is that the buyer has become insolvent. This is a risk taken by traders selling on credit in the domestic market, but in general it is less difficult to find out about the financial problems of other United Kingdom firms than it is about foreign businesses (even though status enquiries can be carried out through banks in the same way as for local businesses). In addition to credit risk associated with insolvency there are a number of other reasons for non-payment which arise only in international trade. These include:-

a)   political decisions to prevent payments from leaving the country (referred to as a moratorium on debt);

b)   legal decisions in foreign courts (which may be very difficult and expensive to challenge);

c)   the outbreak of war;

d)   the refusal of an export licence for the goods to be sold.

Exporters who want to reduce the risk of loss can take out credit insurance. This means paying a premium to an insurer who will then pay out if loss occurs. Commercial insurance companies do provide credit insurance to cover the risk of a buyer's insolvency. More complete insurance cover for all of the risks referred to above is offered by a government agency, the Export Credits Guarantee Department.

E.C.G.D.

8.   The Export Credits Guarantee Department was set up in 1919 to help exporters by providing them with credit insurance. The department aims to charge commercial premiums so that all claims are paid out of income though since 1970 some losses have been made reducing the surplus funds built up by the department.

At its peak during the 1970s ECGD insured over a third of all United Kingdom exports. During the 1980s that proportion has fallen to about a quarter of exports (though the total value is higher than in the 1970s).

The main role of the Export Credits Guarantee Department is to provide credit insurance for businesses selling goods and services abroad, but in addition it provides:-

a)   insurance for United Kingdom businesses setting up operations overseas;

b)   insurance for lines of credit offered to foreign buyers to enable them to purchase from different United Kingdom suppliers;

c)   guarantees to banks to support loans to exporters;

d)   guarantees to banks to support the issue of bonds on behalf of exporters.

With all the forms of insurance which ECGD provides the total sum insured is less than the invoice value of the goods or services covered. The level of cover is usually 80 to 90% depending on the risks insured. This limitation on cover is intended to ensure that exporters do have an interest in pressing their customers to pay rather than just relying on the insurance policy.

E.C.G.D. SUPPORT FOR LOANS

9.   A bank which is considering lending to an exporter and wants to have security may take security in a conventional form like a mortgage of the business premises. If the exporter is using ECGD insurance to cover exported goods there are two additional kinds of security available to the lender:-

a)   an assignment of the insurance policy *or*

b)   a guarantee to the bank from ECGD.

1.   **ECGD policies as security**
ECGD credit insurance policies can be assigned as security just as life policies can. Although they have no surrender value the lender obtains the right to be paid if a claim is made on the policy. This gives the bank some protection against loss but if the exporter has not complied with ECGD requirements so that the policy is invalid the bank will not get its money back.

Note that ECGD policies are rather confusingly referred to as guarantees. For example an ECGD Specific Guarantee is an insurance policy covering a single major project.

2. **ECGD bank guarantees as security**

If an insured exporter wants to borrow and the bank wants a rather stronger form of security than an assignment of the ECGD policy an ECGD bank guarantee may be used. The exporter will be required to pay the extra cost of obtaining the guarantee. Like any other guarantee the ECGD bank guarantee is a promise to pay if the borrower fails to repay. This will normally cover the full amount lent to the customer, usually against bills of exchange or promissory notes.

If payment is made to the bank any part of the sum not covered by the credit insurance (usually 10 or 20% but the whole amount if the exporter was at fault) can be claimed back from the exporter by ECGD.

Note that the guarantees which ECGD issues to banks are known as Bank Guarantees to distinguish them from the insurance policies, so an ECGD Specific Bank Guarantee is the guarantee relating to a transaction insured under a Specific Guarantee.

The Export Credits Guarantee Department also supports lending by banks by enabling them to charge special interest rates (agreed by international convention) on deals with credit terms of two to ten years, provided the exports are not to members of the European Economic Community. ECGD pays the lending bank any extra interest which would normally have been charged on the loan above the internationally agreed rate (which depends on the particular category of lending) so the bank makes its usual profit while the customer borrows cheaply. For loans to finance trade within the EEC normal commercial rates apply, and no ECGD subsidy is available.

E.C.G.D. AND BONDS

10. For major contracts such as civil engineering projects for foreign governments or government agencies exporters often have to provide a series of bonds intended to protect the buyer government from any problems caused by the exporter's inability to complete the work. This could be costly both because of the time and effort needed to find another contractor to take over the partly finished job and because of damage to the economy through failure to complete the project on time. Bonds are promises from reliable financial institutions, such as internationally known banks, to the government or other buyer, guaranteeing specific amounts of financial compensation if problems or losses occur at different stages of the process.

Example

For a major project lasting two years there may be different bonds covering a number of different stages in the process. The following diagram illustrates possible requirements imposed by a buyer on the contractor.

Contract Bonds and Guarantees

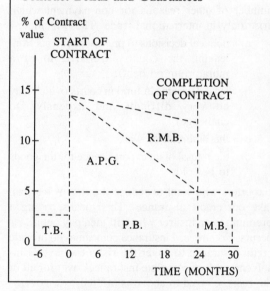

The illustration shows on the vertical axis possible amounts of cover as a percentage of the total contract value, so for a $100 million contract the first of the bonds shown would be for $2.5 million. The horizontal axis shows the time scale so this bond might last for the six months until the start of the work for the contract.

The items shown in the diagram are explained below.

1. T.B. = Tender Bond (or Bid Bond)

This is a promise to pay if the exporter's

tender for the contract is accepted but the exporter then withdraws before beginning work.

2. A.P.G = Advance Payment Guarantee
This is issued when a contract has been awarded and the exporter receives a payment of some of the money in advance. The guarantee is a promise to repay this money if it is not used properly, so as the money is used to pay for work on the contract the amount of the guarantee liability reduces.

3. P.B. = Performance Bond
This is a promise to repay if the contract is undertaken but not completed properly.

4. R.M.B. = Retention Money Bond
In some contracts part of the money payable at each stage of work is kept back by the buyer in case of problems. In order to get this retention money rather than having it kept back the contractor can arrange a retention money bond which promises to repay the money that would otherwise have been kept.

5. M.B. = Maintenance Bond
A maintenance bond is a kind of continuation of a performance bond after completion of the contract. If the finished construction is faulty the buyer will be able to claim under the maintenance bond.

The role of ECGD in dealing with bonds and guarantees for contractors is not in providing the bonds but in giving protection to the banks who provide them. With most bonds banks undertake to pay on demand without having to enquire into the validity of the claim. If the exporter has arranged ECGD cover for the bond the bank will obtain immediate repayment from ECGD. The Export Credits Guarantee Department will then be entitled to reclaim the money from the exporter but will not do so unless the exporter has been at fault.

SHORT-TERM EXPORT FINANCE

11. Export Credits Guarantee Department insurance is available for short-term business, selling consumer goods, as well as for major projects, but the supporting ECGD bank guarantees for goods and services sold on less than two years' credit have now been phased out. This has led banks to introduce special short-term export schemes to assist exporters

who might otherwise have used the ECGD bank guarantee to help them to borrow.

Some of the bank schemes introduced since the phasing out of ECGD short-term bank guarantees:-

a) allow the exporter to sell on credit terms with ECGD credit insurance to cover losses from bad debts *and*

b) offer the advantage of providing finance without recourse (which means that if the debtors do not pay it is not the exporter who has to stand the loss).

The bank can deal with the administration of the ECGD policy to save work for the exporter. In effect the exporter may be as well protected as exporters with ECGD bank guarantees, but less money is paid to ECGD and more to the customer's own bank.

For small exporters it is possible to obtain cover for debts under a general ECGD credit insurance policy in the name of the bank and this can give 100% cover rather than just the 80 or 90% which ECGD usually provides.

EXPORT FACTORING

12. Just as businesses can sell their debts to a factoring company if they trade in this country so exporters selling on credit terms can sell their debts. The same kind of conditions apply as for domestic factoring (described in Chapter 14) though smaller factoring companies may not have the international experience to assess the quality of debts they are offered by exporters.

FORFAITING

13. For businesses which deal with much larger export deals with credit spread over a number of years an idea similar to factoring is to sell a series of bills of exchange or promissory notes covering the credit period. This is known as forfaiting.

Forfaiting is finance provided by buying bills of exchange or other financial documents *without recourse* to the seller. Note that this is in contrast to discounting bills of exchange where the bank offering a discounting service does have recourse to the seller if the drawer of the bill fails to pay.

The characteristics of forfaiting
1. Interest is at a fixed rate determined at the time the bills are bought.

2. Transactions appropriate for forfaiting are normally for capital goods. (Bills must relate to trade, and cannot be merely a means of raising finance.)

3. The normal period covered by forfaiting arrangements is from three to five years, sometimes as long as eight.

4. The bills or promissory notes are usually in a series with maturity dates at regular intervals, for example every six months.

5. The costs to the customer are:-
   a) a commitment fee;
   b) interest linked to rates in the Euro-currency markets;
   c) a premium related to risk, e.g. higher for unstable countries.

6. The financial documents used are 'guaranteed', either because they are promissory notes of a reputable financial institution or, if bills of exchange, because they are 'avalised', signed by a bank undertaking primary responsibility for payment.

FACTORING AND FORFAITING COMPARED

14. This table looks at the differences between the two services.

Forfaiting	Factoring
1. For capital goods.	1. For consumer goods.
2. Bills or promissory used.	2. Invoices, not financial documents used.
3. No administrative service.	3. Sales ledger accounting provided.
4. Medium term credit.	4. Open account, short term credit.
5. By definition a non-recourse facility.	5. Non-recourse an available option.

Both forfaiting and factoring involve the purchase of debts, but they are suited to different kinds of export business.

ADVICE SERVICES

15. Apart from providing ordinary forms of business finance and a range of specialist forms of finance banks are able to help importers and exporters by offering advice on many aspects of

foreign trade. The following list looks at some of the most important of these.

1. **Foreign Exchange**
   Banks can give advice to their customers about such issues as the advantages and disadvantages of invoicing in foreign currency, the problems of exchange risk and solutions to these problems. (See also Chapter 20.)

2. **Documentation and methods of payment**
   Advice here covers areas such as the kind of documents to call for under a documentary credit and the choice to be made between different payment methods. (See also Chapter 21.)

3. **Forms of Finance**
   Banks need to be able to make recommendations to their customers about which forms of finance best suit their needs.

4. **Exchange Control**
   In 1979 the numerous regulations restricting the making of payments from the United Kingdom were suspended, so exchange control is now rarely a problem for importers paying for goods. For exporters exchange control regulations imposed by other countries can still be a problem and banks can obtain up-to-date information about any restrictions.

5. **Contacts**
   Banks pass on information about customers looking for trading partners abroad to help to make new business possible. Status enquiries (see Chapter 7) can also be taken on businesses abroad to give customers guidance about whether to enter a contract or offer credit.

6. **Other sources of help**
   Banks can also advise their customers about other forms of assistance like the British Overseas Trade Board, and they can encourage exporters to use the services of the Export Credits Guarantee Department.

COMPETITORS OF THE BANKS

16. For the major United Kingdom banks the main competition in the provision of finance for international trade comes from other banks, in particular the foreign banks operating in London. Some

merchant banks also have particular expertise in some forms of financing for international trade.

Apart from banks competition comes from export houses. These are specialist businesses which can help other companies to export successfully by taking over a number of the tasks which need to be done. In comparison to banks they are much more likely to become involved in the administrative aspects of exporting, as well as providing financial assistance.

The following list describes briefly the main kinds of export house.

1. Export Finance Houses which deal mainly with financing export deals and arranging credit terms.

2. Confirming Houses which act on behalf of foreign buyers and arrange to ship goods which they have bought.

3. Export Managers which can take over all the functions of an export department including marketing and assessing the credit risk of potential customers.

4. Export Merchants which act on their own behalf as principals in buying goods and then selling them so that for the United Kingdom manufacturer any deal is just like other domestic business.

SUMMARY

17. a) Exporters need finance to pay for acquiring or making goods for export. Importers need finance to pay for goods before they are sold. For some businesses this finance is available from internal sources.

b) Where international trade takes place by means of exchange of goods rather than by changing goods for money this is known as countertrade. It takes a variety of forms from simple barter to more complex arrangements.

c) One of the specialist forms of finance available to importers, in addition to the forms of finance all businesses can use, is a produce advance. This uses imported goods as security for borrowing.

d) Traders face greater risk in selling on credit to overseas buyers than to domestic buyers and therefore may choose to take out credit insurance.

e) ECGD, the Export Credits Guarantee Department is a government department which is the major provider of credit insurance in the United Kingdom.

f) Export Credits Guarantee Department helps banks to provide finance for exports:-
1. through the use of credit insurance policies as security;
2. by providing guarantees to banks to make sure their lending is repaid;
3. by making up the interest when banks lend at the internationally agreed concessionary rates for exports on extended credit.

g) Export Credits Guarantee Department also helps exporters involved in major projects by giving guarantees to banks to enable them to issue bonds, such as performance bonds, on behalf of their customers.

h) The Export Credits Guarantee Department has reduced its role in supporting lending for exports on short credit terms but the banks have introduced schemes of their own to help their customers.

i) Export factoring can help customers selling consumer goods abroad by enabling them to raise cash against their invoices.

j) Forfaiting is a method of financing longer term projects by selling bills of exchange or promissory notes.

k) Banks also help their importer and exporter customers by giving advice on a variety of aspects of international trade including exchange control regulations and contacts with overseas businesses.

l) Apart from other banks export houses are leading competitors in providing export advice and financial assistance.

STUDENT SELF-TESTING

Self Review Questions

1. What is countertrade? (3)

2. What are the main advantages for banks of lending in the form of a produce advance? (5)

3. What is credit risk? (7)

4. What do the letters E.C.G.D. stand for? (7)

5.   State two of the risks apart from insolvency of the buyer which are covered by ECGD credit insurance. (7)

6.   In what two ways can ECGD act as a form of security for bank lending? (9)

7.   How else does ECGD help to finance exports? (9)

8.   What is the difference between a tender bond and a performance bond? (10)

9.   What are the main differences between factoring and forfaiting? (14)

10.   What are export houses? (16)

Exercises (answers begin page 342)

A1.   A friend of yours works for a business importing grain in bulk and selling it to mills for processing. It seems that the business is sometimes held back by lack of funds to invest in stocks when prices are low. Your friend asks whether there are any special schemes available to help importers in this position. Explain how a bank might be able to help in these circumstances, and describe what conditions the customer would need to meet.

A2.   What different kinds of bonds and guarantees are likely to be issued in connection with a major construction project abroad? Who issues them and why are they needed?

A3.   Sellwright Ltd is a business which deals in British-made video equipment. A large part of the company's turnover comes from exports to wholesalers in Western European countries. The directors are looking for a form of financing related to their export business which can improve their cash flow without adding to the level of their borrowing from the bank. They usually sell on credit terms of less than one year. What form of export finance would be most appropriate and why?

A4.   What are export houses and to what extent do they compete with banks?

23. International Finance

INTRODUCTION

1. The purpose of this chapter is to explain briefly some of the terminology of international finance and to describe the role of banks in providing specialist services for major customers operating internationally. The chapter covers the currencies used in international finance, the kinds of investments which can be made and the risks for businesses operating internationally. Methods of dealing with risk are also considered.

This is the last of the chapters which deals specifically with the syllabus for Banking Operations 1.

INTERNATIONAL CUSTOMERS

2. Banking on an international scale involves enormous sums of money so the kind of customers which banks deal with are customers investing or spending very large sums measured in millions of pounds or millions of dollars. Some of the investors may be exceptionally wealthy individuals but most will be companies. The international users of funds are nearly all companies, many of them multinationals with operations in several countries. Governments and government agencies also make use of the international markets to raise money for their spending programmes.

The international markets are designed to enable investors to place funds for periods which suit their needs. As with any investors obtaining a good rate of return is a priority and the large sums mean that rates are good. For the users it is also important that the costs of arranging finance are not too high.

Customers in the international markets do not necessarily use banks as conventional financial intermediaries, taking deposits and providing loans. More commonly the banks are investment banks rather than commercial banks, helping the users of funds to find investors to place money directly into securities issued by the users. The banks' income comes from fees rather than interest and banks negotiate their terms with the corporate treasurers or finance directors of the large companies.

CURRENCIES IN INTERNATIONAL FINANCE

3. Because financial services are international, money markets do not just trade in their own local currency. The most widely traded international currencies, bought and sold in all the leading money markets in the world, are:-

a) the United States dollar (because the United States is the largest economy in the world and because dollars have a long-established role as an international currency);

b) the Japanese yen (because the Japanese economy is exceptionally strong and Japanese investment abroad is greater than that of any other country);

c) the pound sterling (because London has become a major financial centre and because the pound has a very long tradition of being an international currency).

Other leading currencies include the Deutsche mark and the Swiss franc because both countries have strong economies. Because all of these currencies are important internationally they have come to be traded outside their own country. For example a very large volume of loans and deposits in dollars are made through banks in London. Currencies traded in this way are known as Eurocurrencies (as described later in the chapter).

There are also a number of artificial currencies known as composite currencies, which are used to some extent in international finance.

COMPOSITE CURRENCIES

4. Composite currencies are not used by any one country but are used as an accounting device for agreeing payments between countries. They are called composite currencies because they are based on the idea of a 'basket of currencies' and they have a value related to the values of the component currencies which are included in the 'basket'. A major fluctuation in value of one of the currencies will only have a minor effect on the value of the composite currency, so the main function of such currencies is to reduce the risk of sudden variations in value.

The most important composite currencies are:-

a) European currency units *and*

b) special drawing rights.

1. **European Currency Units** (ECUs)
    The European Currency Unit is based on the currencies of the European Community. At the end of 1985, for example, an ECU consisted of:-

0.0878	Pounds sterling
0.719	Deutsche marks
1.31	French francs
3.71	Belgian francs
0.14	Luxembourg francs
140	Italian lira
0.256	Dutch guilder
0.219	Danish kroner
0.00871	Irish punts
1.15	Greek drachma

    This gave an overall value of an ECU as about 59 pence in sterling.
    The ECU is used in some of the financial transactions of the European Economic Community and is used by some major businesses, particularly in Italy which has suffered from a weak currency. Travel cheques are also available in ECUs.

2. **Special Drawing Rights** (SDRs)
    Special Drawing Rights are an artificial currency created by the International Monetary Fund in 1970 and based on the currencies of the major trading nations of the world. Originally there were 16 currencies used to calculate the value of the SDR but in 1981 this was simplified to include only:-

    > United States dollars;
    > Deutsche marks;
    > Pounds sterling;
    > French francs;
    > Japanese yen.

One of the drawbacks of any composite currency is that it must ultimately be converted back into a national currency in order to pay wages or pay for goods and services.

EUROCURRENCIES

5.   A Eurocurrency, unlike the composite currencies just described, is not an artificial currency. Eurocurrency is defined as currency outside the control of the authorities of the country of which it is the currency.

Usually, as explained in Chapter 21, payments abroad are based on messages which transfer the ownership of currency without actually moving the currency from one country to another. If the owner of a currency in one country is a bank in another country that bank can control the currency deposit, lending it to other people if it chooses to do so.

> **Example**
>
> Commercial Bank in London receives a payment in dollars from the United Bank of Denver for a customer who wants to place the dollars on deposit rather than using them to buy pounds. Commercial Bank now has a claim on United Bank of Denver and can make a loan of those dollars. The Eurocurrency has been created.
>
> Commercial Bank offers interest on the deposit and charges interest on the loan without being affected by any restriction imposed by the United States government. The dollars are therefore outside the control of the authorities who would normally deal with the dollar.

The idea of Eurocurrency began originally when United States restrictions limiting the interest paid on deposits made it impossible for holders of dollars to get a good rate of return by depositing dollars directly with banks in the United States. Foreign depositors therefore placed deposits with banks which were free from restriction, particularly banks in London. Eastern European countries also preferred to place deposits with banks outside the United States because of political tension between the United States and the U.S.S.R. during the 1950s and 1960s.

Eurodollars were therefore the first major Eurocurrency and the prefix 'Euro' indicated that the currency was placed with European banks rather than United States banks. Now the term 'Euro' is much wider and has lost its original sense; for example Japanese yen placed with banks in Australia are Euroyen even though neither country is part of Europe.

All of the leading currencies of the world are traded as Eurocurrencies and London is the main trading centre for most of them. The important exception is Eurosterling, which must by definition be traded outside the United Kingdom; Paris is the main centre.

TRADING IN EUROCURRENCIES

6.   Central banks like to control their own currency and influence its exchange rate and the interest rates paid on it. When a currency is traded in the Eurocurrency market some of this control disappears. When a United States manufacturer exports goods payment may be made in foreign currency used to buy dollars or it may be made in Eurodollars which become ordinary domestic dollars once they are owned by the U.S. company. Rates paid on Eurocurrency loans and deposits are usually very close to rates paid on the same currency domestically. There is no separate foreign exchange market because the question of whether a deposit is a Eurocurrency or not is merely a question of ownership. Eurocurrency deposits can change hands several times as they are lent or used to make payment. Similarly new Eurocurrency deposits can be created at any time as funds pass into the control of a foreign bank.

Much of the trading in Eurocurrencies is like trading in domestic money markets. Lending is on a large scale and very often for quite short periods of time, overnight or a few days. The borderline between domestic trading and Eurocurrency trading is of significance to the monetary authorities trying to control their own currency but makes little difference to the customer such as the treasurer of a major business unless regulations are unusually restrictive as they were in the United States when the Eurodollar market began.

SHORT-TERM OPERATIONS

7.   When corporate treasurers have surplus funds to invest short term they will usually be well aware of the range of possibilities. Even for private investors banks are not likely to be active advisers since short-term investment on a large scale is generally the preserve of professionals. Any private investor with as much as £500,000 or £1 million to invest for a few days or weeks would be expected to deposit the money at money market rates through a bank, probably in local currency though possibly as a Eurocurrency deposit.

Banks do have a more prominent role in the short-term international markets in helping corporate treasurers who want to raise large quantities of money. For amounts in sterling of up to about £100 million banks can provide:-

a)   overdrafts;

b)   money market loans;

c)   acceptance credits (see Chapter 14);

d)   issues of commercial paper (which are securities issued by a company to investors, usually in denominations of £500,000 or £1 million for periods of one week to one year).

Similar facilities can also be offered in other leading currencies, and banks advise their customers on the advantages and disadvantages of taking currency borrowing. Where finance is provided in the form of securities, as with sterling or dollar commercial paper, the bank deals with selling the paper to investors, including corporate treasurers looking for a good investment for their own surplus short-term funds. In addition the bank may underwrite the issue, guaranteeing that the customer will get the funds required even if there are not enough buyers.

LONG-TERM OPERATIONS

8.   Long-term investors, placing large sums of money for a year or more, may choose to invest in securities quoted on a stock market because such securities can be sold easily if the money is needed more quickly than expected. This gives a reasonable degree of safety except for the one important disadvantage that prices can fluctuate so losses may occur if a sale becomes necessary when prices are low.

In spite of the marketability of quoted stocks and shares some long-term investors prefer to look for alternative investments in order to escape from one or more of the other drawbacks of quoted securities explained below.

1.   The investor's name becomes known because it appears on the register of shareholders (unless the holding is made through a nominee company).

2.   Tax is usually deducted from dividends at source so it is difficult to avoid paying; claiming any refunds may be a slow process.

3.   Returns depend upon the profitability of the company in which funds are invested, except for investments in the now relatively unusual quoted loan stocks and debentures (where a set rate of interest is paid).

Some of these drawbacks can be avoided by investing funds in other ways, for example in Eurobonds. Eurobonds take their name from the fact that they are sold in countries which use a different currency from the currency being borrowed (similar to the idea of Eurocurrency described earlier in the chapter). British companies can therefore use Eurobonds to raise sterling from investors outside the United Kingdom.

Domestic bonds, issued by a company to attract funds from local investors in domestic currency, can be used as a way of raising money but are less popular than Eurobonds because:-

a) one of the main purposes of using bonds is to allow foreign investors to receive an income free from United Kingdom tax;

b) companies large enough to issue bonds can usually raise money from local investors through the domestic stock market;

c) bond issues are usually aimed at markets with very little regulation.

See also Chapter 2 on securities for major companies and Chapter 3 on bonds and interest rates.

EUROBONDS

9.   A Eurobond is a form of security issued in the currency of one country to sell to investors in other countries (unlike shares which are usually sold mainly to domestic investors through a stock market).

Eurobonds are issued partly to cut out financial intermediaries which might charge more for raising the same amount of money and partly so that the borrower has a more diversified range of sources of funding. Choosing to issue Eurobonds may be also a matter of speed because some other forms of security take much longer to arrange; a Eurobond issue may take as little as a month from start to finish and there is little formal documentation.

A company wanting to issue a Eurobond will usually approach a number of banks to see which will offer the best deal. The final choice will depend on:-

a)   the interest rate to be charged;

b)   other costs such as arrangement fees;

c)   the customer's relationship with the bank;

d)   the reputation of the bank in the Eurobond market.

The businesses which can issue Eurobonds are mostly well-known names considered to be very good credit risks. Amounts raised in this way are usually between £20 million and £500 million but larger amounts are possible. Often the borrowing is for seven years or more and interest, normally at a fixed rate, is paid to the investors at regular intervals, sometimes every six months but more commonly once a year.

The most widely used currency for Eurobond issues is the dollar, normally accounting for over half the money raised in the Eurobond market. Other popular currencies are the Deutsche mark and the pound sterling, but the Japanese yen has also become extremely important. In 1986 for the first time a greater value of funds was raised in yen than in any other currency apart from the dollar, equivalent to about $18 billion out of a total market of around $170 billion.

An investor in a Eurobond is issued with a certificate in the same way that a shareholder in a company receives a certificate, but the money is only lent and does not form part of the borrowing company's permanent capital. Eurobond certificates are normally bearer securities which means that the holder has the right to the interest and ultimate repayment of the debt. Because of this the certificates are usually held in a central clearing house rather than personally looked after by the investor. Interest payments, usually free of all taxes, are dealt with by the clearing house.

EUROBONDS AND LOANS

10.   Before the development of the Eurobond market borrowers on the international markets had relied on banks for their funds. The move towards securitisation has reduced the role of banks as lenders but has enabled them to increase their business as arrangers of Eurobond issues (a business which has become so competitive that it is not always very profitable).

However Eurobonds have not completely replaced loans as a form of international funding. Some situations remain where bank loans are more suitable than issues of securities. This list looks at some of these key areas.

1. **Syndicated loans for
   large-scale borrowing**
   Because Eurobond issues have to be sold
   to large numbers of separate investors it is
   difficult for the market to cope with enormous sums of money. Banks can deal with
   very large sums, too large for any one bank
   to handle, by forming syndicates, groups
   of banks which each agree to contribute a
   proportion of the total sum the borrower
   needs. One bank or a small group of banks
   takes a leading role as organiser of the loan
   and other banks are invited to participate.
   The circle can be widened enough to meet
   the needs of any borrower. All participants
   take a share in the interest paid on the loan
   and share the risk of any bad debts. The lead
   bank obtains extra income for its work in
   arranging the loan.

2. **Project finance for special situations**
   Banks also have a part to play in providing
   finance for the more risky projects which
   would not appeal to direct investors like the
   buyers of Eurobonds. Where an organisation has a particular project or plan which
   will generate income if it is successful bank
   credit analysts have the skill and experience
   to assess the risk of the project in a way
   which an outside investor would not be able
   to do. Many banks have developed particular expertise in some industries, for
   example in judging the viability of new oil
   pipelines or chemical processing plants.

3. **Underwriting securities**
   Even if a company wants to raise funds by
   selling bonds, accepted bills of exchange or
   commercial paper a bank may end up as the
   lender because the paper does not sell. The
   market for securities fluctuates and there are
   times when only the most highly regarded
   companies in the world can find willing investors. When a lesser known multinational
   or a company with only a national reputation arranges an issue of securities of any
   kind it can avoid the risk of not getting the
   money it needs by paying a bank, usually
   the bank arranging the issue, a fee to act
   as underwriter. This means that the bank
   takes on a commitment to provide the funds
   if the securities are not bought by other
   investors.

DEALING WITH RISK

11.   As businesses grow large they face an increasing level of risk, but also access to a wider range
of techniques which can be applied to reduce risk.
A small exporter will usually have to convert export
earnings into sterling as soon as possible, regardless
of exchange rate movements, because the cash is
needed to pay the workforce; for a United Kingdom
based multinational foreign earnings might be:-

   a) held on deposit abroad until rates are
      favourable;

   b) used to set up a new factory abroad nearer
      to the markets;

   c) lent to a foreign company which has spare
      cash from its exports to the United Kingdom
      in exchange for a loan in sterling from that
      company.

Large companies can also make use of techniques
provided by banks and financial markets to help them
to deal with risk, and banks have an important role
as advisers to companies. Some of the services which
banks provide to reduce risk are cheap enough to
benefit any business but more sophisticated services
are only suitable for the largest companies. For
example forward exchange contracts (described in
Chapter 20) are available to most creditworthy
importers and exporters, but more specialised
contracts offered through the London International
Financial Futures Exchange are only bought and sold
in large denominations and therefore are only
suitable as a protection against risk for major
companies.

The main risks of concern to businesses operating
internationally are exchange risk and interest-rate
risk, and these are dealt with in the sections which
follow the description of the London International
Financial Futures Exchange.

LONDON INTERNATIONAL
FINANCIAL FUTURES EXCHANGE

12.   The London International Financial Futures
Exchange was set up in 1982 as a centre for trading
in financial contracts. One of the purposes of such
trading is to give businesses protection against
exchange risk.

Businesses using LIFFE options for this purpose pay
a premium for the right to buy or sell a specified
security or currency in the future. For a buyer, if

the market price is lower than the contracted price when the security or currency is required the contract can be cancelled, but if the price is higher the option to buy can be exercised at the agreed price, avoiding paying more. The option, the contract to be able to buy, can itself be sold to another investor.

Many of the traders on LIFFE are speculators judging which way interest rates or exchange rates are going to move. Because there are speculators willing to deal there is a ready market for traders using the exchange to buy protection from their business risks, exchange risk or interest-rate risk.

The main contracts dealt with on the London International Financial Futures Exchange are:-

a)   long-term interest rate contracts, e.g. based on the interest rate for British government stock;

b)   short-term interest rate contracts, e.g. based on the interest rate for 3 month Eurodollars;

c)   currency options, e.g. based on the exchange rate for the pound against the dollar;

d)   a futures contract based on the movement of share prices on the stock exchange.

As the London International Financial Futures Exchange continues to develop it has added to the range of contracts which can be traded and has set up links with other financial futures exchanges in other parts of the world.

EXCHANGE RISK

13.   Exchange risk (defined in Chapter 20) is a concept which covers three separate ideas:-

a)   economic exposure;

b)   transaction exposure;

c)   translation exposure.

1.   **Economic exposure**
This means the risk that changes in the relative strengths of different economies will affect the value of foreign earnings. For example from the point of view of a major United Kingdom exporter like Jaguar cars if the United States economy becomes very weak the dollars the company earns will be less valuable. Banks cannot help very much with this kind of risk because only the exporter can decide on an appropriate policy. Setting up a factory in the United

States might be a solution because the dollar earnings would then be used to pay for wages and other expenses in dollars.

2.   **Transaction exposure**
This is the exchange risk for a particular deal or transaction. If a consignment of cars is sold when the rate for the dollar is 1.40 to the pound and the rate changes to 1.60 to the pound before the dollars are received, a deal which was expected to be profitable may make a loss. Here banks can be of direct help by offering:-

a)   forward contracts;

b)   currency options.

The company itself may take steps to avoid the problem by invoicing in sterling or by using the dollars to buy raw materials. The company may also protect its own position by entering into a contract on the London International Financial Futures Exchange or one of the similar financial futures exchanges abroad.

3.   **Translation Exposure**
For companies operating in more than one country one problem is that annual accounts have to be produced in the home country showing all assets valued in one currency. The major banks themselves, with subsidiaries in many different countries, face the same problem. Assets priced in yen or in francs need to be shown valued at their equivalent in sterling in the annual accounts, and even if the assets are unchanged the sterling equivalent may fluctuate violently from one year to the next. Some steps can be taken to reduce the effects of rate changes on the balance sheet by acquiring liabilities to correspond to the assets, but the cost of doing this may be high and many businesses feel that such 'paper' risks can be safely ignored.

INTEREST-RATE RISK

14.   Businesses which are financed partly by borrowing face a risk, considered in Chapter 6, that interest rates may change leaving the form of borrowing originally entered into as an expensive way of obtaining funds in comparison to other kinds of borrowing.

If borrowing is taken at a fixed rate of 9% per annum when general interest rates are at 10 or 11% the risk is that if general rates fall to 7% the borrowing is more expensive than it needed to be. To complicate matters different currencies attract different interest rates, mainly because of different expectations about inflation. In addition companies are able to borrow more cheaply through some markets than others, for example because of a local reputation.

Risk from changes in interest rates can be reduced by borrowing short-term and switching from one form of borrowing to another as rates change, but this is no protection against the possibility that long-term fixed interest borrowing might have been the cheapest. In addition it has the drawback that the borrower may find difficulty in raising money as each loan comes to an end.

HEDGING INTEREST-RATE RISK

15. The most widely used method of hedging (or taking protection) against the risk of interest-rate changes is to ensure that a range of different kinds of loan are taken out so that no interest-rate movement can have a disastrously bad effect. By having a variety of fixed and variable rate loans and some variety of different currencies the corporate borrower can feel fairly safe.

More specific forms of protection are also available. The following list describes some of the most important possibilities.

1. **Roll-over loans**
   A roll-over loan is a loan which is long-term but based on interest rates for short-term borrowing. The sum required is lent short-term, for example over 6 months with the interest rate linked to 6-month LIBOR, but at the end of the 6 months the borrowing is renewed automatically (or rolled-over) for a further 6 months based on the new LIBOR rate. Over the whole period of the loan the borrower avoids paying interest much above the market rate (though there is equally no opportunity for getting very cheap funds, which can happen where borrowing is at a fixed interest rate).

2. **Forward rate agreements**
   If a borrower has a view that interest rates are going to rise in the future it may be possible to enter into a forward rate agreement (or FRA) with the bank to set a rate for future borrowing. If rates do rise the customer will gain by having locked into a lower rate before taking the loan. The bank charges the customer for the forward rate agreement but the saving on interest will be more than enough to compensate for this charge if the borrower's prediction of the interest rate change is correct.

3. **Swaps**
   If a company can get a very good deal borrowing at a fixed rate but really requires variable rate borrowing the risk of being tied to an unacceptable fixed rate can be avoided by arranging a swap with another business in the reverse position. Banks act as brokers matching up partners in such swap transactions, and the customer does not need to worry about the partner failing to pay any cash which is due because of the difference in rates; the bank will make sure payments are made.
   The effect of an interest rate swap of this type is that a customer borrowing variable rate funds can arrange to pay a fixed rate of interest just as though a fixed rate loan had been arranged (and vice versa for the other party involved). The advantage is that each party to the swap can get the borrowing required at a slightly lower cost than by borrowing directly, because each is using the comparative advantage the other has in a particular kind of borrowing.

More complicated hedging methods can also be arranged, for example swaps with borrowers taking loans in different currencies as well as with different kinds of interest rate. These can provide a hedge against exchange risk as well as interest-rate risk. Some of the contracts which can be bought through LIFFE and other futures exchanges can also be used as hedges against changes in interest rates.

SUMMARY

16. a) The main customers for international financial services are major companies, often multinationals. Banks deal with the corporate treasurers or finance directors of such companies.

b) Leading currencies in world money markets are the United States dollar, the Japanese yen and the pound sterling.

c) Artificial composite currencies are used to reduce exchange rate fluctuations. These currencies include the ECU and the SDR. One weakness of such composite currencies is that they cannot be used to pay for goods and services except on a large scale.

d) A eurocurrency is a currency which is outside the control of the authorities of the country of which it is the currency, for example dollars deposited with a bank in the United Kingdom.

e) Short-term investors in the international financial markets are usually professionals, but banks regularly provide advice for businesses seeking funds.

f) Long-term investors may choose to use international markets because they are less regulated than domestic stock markets.

g) Eurobonds are mostly issued in the range £20 million to £500 million and for periods of five years or more, in some cases up to thirty years.

h) In spite of the trend towards securitisation bank lending on an international scale remains important for:-
   1. large syndicated loans;
   2. project finance;
   3. underwriting securities issues.

i) Major risks for international businesses include exchange risk and interest-rate risk. Large companies can hedge these risks in a number of ways including:-
   1. forward contracts;
   2. currency options;
   3. LIFFE contracts;
   4. forward rate agreements;
   5. swaps.

STUDENT SELF-TESTING

Self Review Questions

1. What are the three leading international currencies? (3)

2. What is an ECU? (4)

3. What is a eurocurrency? (5)

4. If a bank underwrites a security issue what does it do? (7)

5. State two of the disadvantages of investing in quoted securities. (8)

6. What is a Eurobond? (9)

7. What are syndicated loans? (10)

8. What is LIFFE? (12)

9. What is the difference between transaction exposure and translation exposure? (13)

10. What is an interest-rate swap? (15)

Exercises (answers begin page 343)

A1. Mr Kennedy, the Treasurer of Maglite plc, a major customer of your branch, has written the following letter to your manager.

Dear John,

We are currently having some problems with our sales to France because of competition on prices from local suppliers. As this seems to be a short-term phenomenon associated with the strength of the pound there seems to be no serious economic exposure which would justify changing our plans for expansion in the French market.

Essentially the problem is partly one of translation exposure since our premises in Paris now need to be shown in our accounts at a different value (which does not worry us unduly) but more importantly a matter of transaction exposure on individual deals.

In effect we sell to our subsidiary sales organisation in France and give them a good period of credit, so we want to hedge the exchange rate risk while prospects for the franc look so poor. Can you let me have some information on the currency options you are now offering so that I can see how these will compare with the forward contracts we are used to.

Yours sincerely,

Answer the following questions.

1. What is economic exposure?

2. Why do businesses often consider translation exposure to be of fairly limited significance?

3. What is 'hedging'?

4. What other ways are there of hedging exchange-rate risk apart from forward contracts and options?

A2. What are the most important currencies in the world? What factors make a currency important in world terms?

A3. 'Bank lending will not disappear just because there is a trend towards greater securitisation'. To what extent is this view confirmed by the continuing need for certain types of international lending?

A4. What are composite currencies? Explain your answer with reference to one of the main examples.

24. General Banking Services

INTRODUCTION

1. This chapter is the first of a series dealing with the services which banks offer to their customers. This material forms part of the syllabus of the Banking Operations 2 examination. Since banking services are changing all the time to meet the changing needs of customers it is important for students to keep up-to-date by reading about new services as they are introduced.

The services covered in this chapter are those which banks provide for all customers rather than those specifically intended for personal customers (which are covered in the next chapter) or those for business users (described in Chapter 26).

The main services covered are:-

a) those associated with operating bank accounts;

b) looking after valuables;

c) dealing in shares;

d) operating unit trusts;

e) trustee and executor work.

OPERATING A BANK ACCOUNT

2. As explained in Chapter 7 it is normally by opening an account that someone becomes a customer of a bank. This applies equally to businesses and to individuals.

At its simplest the service a bank provides is to take in the customer's money and give it back when the customer asks for it. In practice matters are far more complicated as a number of the previous chapters have indicated. Even for a very simple deposit account there will be the additional feature that interest is paid on the account and there may be a number of associated services such as:-

a) regular statements;

b) credit open arrangements;

c) a cash dispenser card;

d) automated payments.

For current accounts the range of associated services is even wider because in addition to any of the services available to deposit account holders current account customers expect to have a cheque book and may also have:-

a) a cheque guarantee card;

b) eurocheques.

Each of these services is explained in more detail in the sections which follow.

STATEMENTS

3. A statement of account is simply a document showing the transactions which the bank has recorded on the customer's account. Statements were originally handwritten documents checked against the bank's own hand-written records, but now they are produced by computer, usually overnight (while the computer system is not handling the large volume of account enquiries which are dealt with during normal business hours) ready to send out to customers the next day. From the customer's point of view they are not necessarily completely up-to-date because they cannot show cheques which have been written out but not yet paid.

Many Automated Teller Machines (see Chapter 25) are also able to produce mini-statements which give a listing of recent transactions but with less detail than a full statement. This may enable banks to provide full statements less often, saving on stationery and postage costs. More advanced technology also enables banks to provide customers with access to information about their accounts through other means; see the section on home banking in Chapter 25.

Note that in the United Kingdom unlike some other countries there is no legal requirement for customers to check their statements or to bring any errors to the bank's attention.

CREDIT OPEN ARRANGEMENTS

4. A customer at one branch who wants to draw out money at another branch can make an arrangement to do so known as a credit open. The account-holding branch will notify the other branch of the amount which can be withdrawn, for example £100 a week, and will provide a specimen signature.

This service has declined in importance because so many customers now have cheque guarantee cards or cash dispenser cards (both of which are described later in the chapter) enabling them to obtain cash from machines or other banks. A customer approaching the bank for advice about how to arrange to draw out cash elsewhere is more likely to be offered the appropriate card rather than offered a credit open arrangement, but the system is suitable for companies wanting to draw out wages in cash regularly from branches other than their own.

Credit open arrangements can also be made with branches of banks abroad (as explained in Chapter 19) though this too has become fairly unusual.

CASH DISPENSER CARDS

5.   A cash dispenser or Automated Teller Machine is a machine from which a customer can draw out cash, usually located on the outside wall of a bank branch though some are inside branches or in shops or factories. Other services are also available, and are detailed in Chapter 25 since they are mainly designed for personal customers.

The cards used for Automated Teller Machines are plastic cards with a magnetic strip which carries identification data. When a customer inserts the card into a machine and keys in the correct Personal Identification Number (PIN) the machine is activated and enables the customer to choose from the services available.

Because the cards can be used to obtain cash (and are sometimes also designed to act as cheque guarantee cards or credit cards) there is a danger that they may be fraudulently used if they get into the wrong hands. To reduce the risk banks make use of the latest technology to make the cards as safe as possible. Apart from the protection provided by the fact that customers are requested to memorise their personal identification numbers the cards are made with special features which are difficult to forge such as magnetic codes 'watermarked' into the plastic or the familiar holograms.

More sophisticated cards known as 'smart cards' have also been developed. These incorporate a microchip and can therefore store very large amounts of information. Banks in some countries already use them as Automated Teller Machine cards.

AUTOMATED PAYMENTS

6.   The term automated payments refers to any payment which does not involve the transfer of a document from one place to another. From a customer's point of view the ability to receive automated payments is a valuable service because it means, for example, that a salary can be paid directly into a bank account. In addition most accounts have the facility of making automated payments out of the account to other people so that the customer does not have to write out cheques regularly to the same payee for such items as a monthly rates bill or an annual subscription.

The most common forms of automated payment used by personal customers are regular payments by standing order or direct debit. The essential difference between these two kinds of payment is that:-

a)   a standing order is sent out by the bank on the instructions of the customer providing there are sufficient funds in the account;

b)   a direct debit is claimed from the bank by the organisation which is to receive payment, in accordance with terms agreed with the customer (which makes the system more flexible, for example coping with variable amounts, and gives the recipient of the payment far more control over income and any bad debts). A claim can be rejected if there are no funds to pay it or if the customer cancels the agreement.

The most common form of automated payment used by businesses is payment through the automated credit clearing operated by BACS, formerly Bankers Automated Clearing Services Limited. Business customers use these payments for wages to their employees as well as for payments between businesses.

SPECIALISED PAYMENT SYSTEMS

7.   In addition to the widely used automated payments there are a number of systems for special kinds of automated payments. The following list covers the most important of these.

1.   Clearing House Automated Payments System (CHAPS)
The CHAPS computer network came into operation in 1984 to enable large payments to be made from one bank to another on the same day using computer messages. This replaced a system of transfers by telephone messages. Messages keyed in at one branch of a bank (or in some cases at terminals operated by major customers of the bank) are transmitted to the bank which is to receive payment. The recipient bank sends back an acknowledgement message and the customer can be credited with the funds straightaway.

When the system was set up payments had to be for amounts between £10,000 and £100,000 but the upper limit has now been removed so that any payment over £10,000 can now be sent through CHAPS.

2. Society for Worldwide Interbank Financial Telecommunication (SWIFT)
    SWIFT was established in 1973 to carry international payment messages. (See Chapter 21 for more details.) SWIFT is also used for electronically transmitted letters of credit and settlement for securities such as Eurobonds.

3. Electronic Funds Transfer at Point Of Sale (EFTPOS)
    EFTPOS is a general term for methods of making payment for goods or services through electronic payment terminals linked directly to bank accounts. There is not yet an agreed system operated by all banks as there is with CHAPS or SWIFT. Different banks are working on their own methods based on plastic cards and a number of pilot schemes have been set up. It is expected that a more general national scheme will eventually come into operation.

CHEQUE BOOKS

8. Apart from the services already described, perhaps the most important facility for customers with current accounts (and similar more specialised accounts like the budget accounts and revolving credit accounts described in Chapter 12) is the use of a cheque book.

Students who have taken the preliminary stage of the Banking Certificate will already be familiar with cheques and their role as payment instruments in the banking system. The following table summarises briefly the features of cheques.

Features of cheques

1. Banks issue cheques in books, usually of 25 or 30 cheques, though larger books are available for business customers.

2. Each cheque can be completed by the customer and when it is signed it is a valid bill of exchange payable at sight by the bank it is drawn on. Cheques like other bills of exchange are negotiable instruments. (See

Chapter 4 for an explanation of this concept.)

3. The main legislation covering cheques is the Cheques Act 1957, though some parts of the Bills of Exchange Act 1882 still apply.

4. One of the most important areas in which cheques are treated differently from other bills of exchange is in crossings on cheques, words written across the cheque to alter its significance in some way. Important crossings include:-
    a) parallel lines, the most simple form of crossing (normally pre-printed onto cheques), meaning that the cheque must be paid into a bank account and cannot be cashed by the payee as an open (or uncrossed) cheque can be;
    b) the words 'not negotiable' which mean that the cheque cannot be treated as a negotiable instrument, a protection for the drawer of the cheque if it gets into the wrong hands and therefore often used when cheques for large sums are sent by post.

5. Cheques can be transferred by endorsing them, which means signing them on the back. This gives the new holder all the rights possessed by the person who has endorsed the cheque. With negotiable cheques a holder may obtain a better title than the person who has transferred the cheque. In practice endorsement is not often needed because most cheques are paid into bank accounts directly by the payee. Where a payee does not have a bank account the cheque can be endorsed so that it can be paid into someone else's account.

CHEQUE GUARANTEE CARDS

9. Shopkeepers are cautious about taking cheques from customers they do not know because the customer may take goods and then order the bank to stop payment of the cheque. This countermand of a cheque cannot relieve the customer of the debt but it does make it difficult for the shopkeeper to obtain payment; taking legal action is slow and expensive, and may be of little use against someone who has no money.

To give greater security to shopkeepers and others who take the risk of providing goods or services against cheques which have not been cleared banks issue cheque guarantee cards to customers they consider trustworthy. The bank guarantees payment of cheques up to a set limit, which for nearly all banks is £50, provided that all the terms stated on the card are complied with by the person taking the cheque. This improves the service banks offer their account-holders because it makes their cheques more acceptable, but the main weakness of the system is the £50 limit on transactions. Many customers do spend more than £50 at a time but most banks are unwilling to agree to higher limits because of the risk of increased losses from fraud, although creditworthy customers do have the alternative of using a credit card, which can have a much higher limit. Cheque cards take the same form as credit cards and the plastic cards used for cash dispensers or Automated Teller Machines, and some banks combine some or all of these functions into one card.

Eurocheque cards are a more specialised form of cheque guarantee card and are considered more fully in Chapter 19.

Until the Building Societies Act 1986 gave new powers to building societies only banks were able to issue cheque guarantee cards. Now the building societies are providing competition in this area with new forms of current account offering cheque books and cheque guarantee cards.

CASH HANDLING

10.   Banks have an important role to play in society as handlers of cash. This is a service which benefits the whole community, not just bank customers because cash can only be an effective method of payment if:-

a)   organisations like supermarkets which receive large amounts of cash can dispose of the cash quickly and safely;

b)   organisations like companies with employees paid weekly can obtain large amounts of cash from a safe source.

Banks have secure branch premises and large bullion centres where the inflows and outflows of cash at different branches can be evened out. This means that the role of banks is not just a matter of keeping cash safe for their own customers but of controlling the flow of cash in the economy. Although building societies and money shops are beginning

to compete in this field they have not had a major impact because banks are better equipped to handle cash on a very large scale.

SAFE CUSTODY

11.   In addition to looking after cash for customers banks can also look after other valuables. Customers can deposit boxes containing their treasured possessions such as precious metals and jewellery without the bank knowing what has been deposited. Some bank branches provide safe-deposit boxes or lockers and most branches can handle small boxes and sealed parcels as well as envelopes containing valuable documents like share certificates or deeds. Often documents are not sealed up because the customer may want the bank to deal with them at some time, for example sending out the deeds to a solicitor. This is particularly important with wills.

Customers are normally charged a fee each year for items kept in safe custody and may also have to pay each time they wish to withdraw or re-deposit items. The service is mainly of value to personal customers because businesses which need security for their valuables are likely to have their own safes or strong rooms.

Banks face competition in this field, particularly in major cities, from specialist safe-deposit companies which provide well protected lockers in which customers can place valuables. These companies usually charge more than banks, but the fact that large quantities of valuables are brought together in one site does make such centres a tempting target for criminals.

SHARE DEALING

12.   Banks have acted on behalf of their customers for many years in buying and selling shares. Since the Big Bang (described in Chapter 2) the service has been more actively promoted because:-

a)   many banks have taken over security dealers (formerly stockbrokers) so that they now take all the commission paid by the customer rather than sharing it with an independent dealer;

b)   some banks have also acquired share dealing subsidiaries which act not simply as agents in buying and selling but as market makers in stocks and shares, buying and selling on their own behalf;

c) the market for stocks and shares has increased as the government has sold off many businesses formerly owned by the state;

d) more people have become shareowners than ever before following the privatisations and the changes in the stock market rules (with an estimated 20% of the adult population owning some shares by the end of 1987).

From the customer's point of view the procedure for buying or selling shares is simple. The bank takes a written authority from the customer and the bank then gets the best price available in the market at the time (unless the customer chooses to set a specific price limit for the deal). The customer receives a contract note shortly after the deal has taken place showing the price agreed and the date of the transaction and in due course receives the money from the sale or the certificate for the shares purchased.

For any companies which buy and sell securities regularly it will be more usual to trade through an established security dealer rather than through the branch of a bank, but the security dealer may itself be a bank subsidiary. Few of the firms of stockbrokers which existed before the Big Bang have remained independent because most of them have felt the need for extra capital only available from a larger organisation like a bank.

UNIT TRUST DEALING

13.   Banks can also buy and sell units in unit trusts for their customers. Essentially this is a similar service to buying and selling shares, but the Financial Services Act 1986 has made matters a little more complicated because of the rules about polarisation (explained in Chapter 7). (In practice it is mainly personal customers who buy units in unit trusts, but unit trusts provide work for banks in other ways too, as managers and as trustees.)

Some financial institutions including many building societies have decided to maintain fully the role of independent advisers in the field of unit trusts (for example because they do not own companies managing unit trust funds). Of the major banks only National Westminster Bank has taken this course selling its own unit trust management subsidiary to one of the large unit trust specialists MIM Britannia. This policy means that branch staff can give advice on the buying and selling of unit trusts managed by any other organisation, and can make profit by earning commission from doing so.

In contrast many banks have opted to sell their own brand of unit trusts (which means in effect selling units in a trust managed by the bank) and are not able to give advice about competitor products. Where banks have chosen this path the role of the branch manager has changed significantly as a result. Such a policy does not mean that no independent advice can be given, but banks have to run independent subsidiary companies to give advice; branches can only pass on the advice and are not allowed to comment on it to help to persuade their customers to buy or sell.

UNIT TRUST MANAGEMENT

14.   As explained in Chapter 2 banks are among the organisations which manage unit trusts, competing with independent unit trust groups like M & G. Fund managers usually form part of the staff of a merchant banking subsidiary or a separate unit trust management subsidiary. The role of fund managers is to decide about purchases and sales of shares to make the best use of the funds invested by the unit holders. The aim is to increase the value of the funds invested so that the unit holders can get a return on their investment, as a dividend paid out regularly or as capital growth, the increase in the value of the units.

The fund management company makes its profit from the difference between the price at which unit holders buy the units, the offer price, and the price at which the fund managers buy back units, the bid price. The size of funds under management is also seen as an important measure of a fund management company's success, and if high returns are earned for unit holders new investors are more likely to put their money into the company's units.

UNIT TRUST TRUSTEESHIP

15.   Trustees of unit trust funds have a less active role than the fund managers. They are not involved in the day-to-day decision-making about which shareholdings to buy or sell.

The role of trustees in a unit trust, generally carried out by banks or insurance companies, is to monitor the work of the fund managers to make sure that the interests of the unit holders are protected.

Although banks act as both managers and trustees they cannot take on both roles for the same unit trust fund because the trustees must be completely independent of the managers.

OTHER TRUSTEE WORK

16.   Major banks have been involved in trustee work for many years, because anyone setting up a trust of any kind needs to be sure that the assets left in trust will be safely and prudently looked after. Banks are in a strong position to act as trustees because:-

a)   they are corporate bodies and therefore will not create legal problems by dying before the trust assets have been disposed of;

b)   they have staff who are experienced in handling assets held in trust;

c)   they are accessible because of their branch networks (even though the trustee specialists are not based in the branches).

Trusts may be set up by individuals, for example under the terms of a will as described in Chapter 8, or by businesses, for example in order to operate a company pension scheme for employees. Whatever the scale of the operation bank trustee experts can be employed to look after the assets in trust. These assets are often in the form of stocks and shares, and the trustees may be given discretion to manage them in the way that unit trust fund managers deal with unit trust assets.

EXECUTORSHIP

17.   Acting as an executor of a will is often linked with becoming a trustee as explained in Chapter 8 (and is included in this chapter for that reason although it is a service for personal customers). When banks are named as executors it is the trustee department staff who deal with the will and the estate of the deceased. The work involved consists of collecting together all the information about assets held by the deceased and then making the arrangements to pass on those assets or the cash obtained from realising the assets in accordance with the terms of the will.

For complicated estates involving assets in many different forms the service of professional executors can be invaluable. For smaller estates where the only major asset is a house a relative named as executor may be able to cope adequately. It is towards customers with substantial estates that banks direct the marketing of their executorship service.

The main competition for executorship business comes from solicitors, and in general the charges which banks make for the service are rather higher than solicitors' charges (to the extent that the banks have been criticised by consumer organisations like the National Consumer Council).

SUMMARY

18. a)   Customers with all types of account expect to receive regular statements detailing transactions on the account.

b)   With most types of deposit customers can also arrange:-
1.   to draw out money from another branch through a credit open arrangement;
2.   to use a plastic card to withdraw cash from Automated Teller Machines;
3.   to make automated payments, for example by standing order or direct debit.

c)   Cheque books are one of the most useful features of current accounts and similar types of account. Cheques are negotiable instruments and the main legislation covering their use is the Cheques Act 1957. Cheques are more acceptable in shops when supported by a cheque guarantee card.

d)   Banks are able to look after valuables from cash (which is handled on behalf of major traders and employers as well as personal customers) to personal valuables like jewellery and share certificates.

e)   Banks provide a service of buying and selling shares on behalf of customers. This service has become more important following the changes in Stock Exchange rules known as the Big Bang.

f)   Banks also deal with unit trusts, buying and selling them for customers, managing unit trust funds and acting as trustees for other managers' unit trusts.

g)   Executor and trustee work includes:-
1.   dealing with the estates of people who have appointed the bank as executor;
2.   operating trusts which result from wills;
3.   operating many other kinds of trust such as pension funds.

STUDENT SELF-TESTING

Self Review Questions

1.   Are customers legally required to check that their statements are correct? (3)

2.   What are the main differences between standing orders and direct debits? (6)

3.   What do the letters EFTPOS stand for? (7)

4.   Why might a customer cross a cheque 'not negotiable'? (8)

5.   What is the main drawback of most cheque guarantee cards? (9)

6.   Why are personal customers more likely to use the safe custody service than business customers? (11)

7.   Why has greater emphasis been given to the sharedealing service which banks provide since the Big Bang? (12)

8.   How have the rules on polarisation affected banks which sell unit trusts? (13)

9.   Banks can act as managers of some unit trusts and trustees of others. What is the main difference between these two roles? (14,15)

10. Who are the main competitors of banks in providing executorship services? (17)

Exercises (answers begin page 344)

A1. What was the Big Bang and what difference has it made to the services which banks offer their customers?

A2. What are unit trusts and what different roles do banks perform in connection with unit trusts?

A3. What are the main banking services normally offered to all customers whether they are businesses or private individuals?

A4. What is a trustee, and why do banks act as trustees?

25. Personal Banking Services

INTRODUCTION

1. Many of the services considered in the last chapter are used extensively by personal customers though they are widely available for business customers too. This chapter is concerned with the services used by personal customers which are rarely appropriate for business users. The borderline is not a clear one because sole traders running small businesses may have financial needs similar to those of personal customers.

The emphasis in this chapter is on specialist forms of advice and help which banks can provide for personal customers. The main areas covered are:-

   a) taxation;
   b) insurance;
   c) pensions;
   d) investment.

Personal customers also make use of the deposit and lending services considered in earlier chapters (see in particular Chapter 12) and the chapter considers developments which are of particular concern to personal customers in operating their accounts. The last part of the chapter deals with consumer protection and the role of the banking ombudsman.

ADVICE SERVICES

2. Once banks had become established as deposit-takers and lenders customers began to see bank staff as experts who could give advice on all financial matters. Often advice was provided free of charge, but today banks have become more conscious of the cost of providing advice as the need for greater expertise has led to more and more specialisation. Customers too are gradually becoming used to the idea of paying for banking expertise in the way that they might pay for the services of other professionals like solicitors or accountants.

Advice services have therefore become an important source of revenue to banks in their own right, but some forms of advice are still provided free. Free services are likely to continue in future to some extent because:-

   a) giving advice may lead to other more profitable business, for example commission from selling life insurance;

   b) customers offered advice may be valued customers who give the bank a lot of other profitable business (so that 'free' advice is subsidised by other sources of income);

   c) free services can be promoted to improve a bank's image as helpful and caring.

TAXATION ADVICE

3. For most personal customers of banks completing a tax return form is a chore but is not necessarily very complicated or difficult. For a small minority whose tax affairs are much more complicated it may be helpful to get professional advice. Banks can provide this advice and give assistance in collecting together all the information that the tax inspectors need about interest and dividends. Advice can also be provided for customers about the tax implications of going to work abroad or about the technicalities of inheritance tax and how it may affect money left in a will.

Although the bank's taxation experts do not operate at branch level but are based in regional centres, the branches have an important role in identifying potential customers. Ideally these should be people who will want to use taxation advice over a number of years because they are wealthy enough to be able to make substantial savings by getting the best advice.

The main competitors for the banks in providing taxation advice are accountants though some solicitors specialising in tax law also offer advice to wealthy personal clients.

INSURANCE ADVICE

4. The major banks all have large insurance subsidiaries which make use of the branch network as a way of contacting potential clients. Like other insurance brokers the banks can arrange all forms of insurance including insurance for business purposes rather than for personal customers. Personal customers are most likely to want advice about:-

   a) car insurance;
   b) travel insurance (considered in Chapter 19);
   c) household contents insurance;
   d) buildings insurance;
   e) life insurance.

Banks may act as independent brokers or they may sell their own insurance products, policies which they underwrite or which are underwritten by an insurance company with which the bank has an agreement to act as a distributor. Most banks have chosen, under the Financial Services Act, to use their branches as tied sales outlets rather than independent advisers, but branches can still obtain quotations for customers from an independent insurance broking subsidiary, in some cases using a direct computer line to get the best quotations instantly. Banks are most keen to sell life insurance policies because these attract high levels of commission. Other forms of insurance are available but are generally less actively promoted. In addition to obtaining quotations banks can supply copies of policy documents and answer customers' questions about the cover provided.

Competition in giving insurance advice and arranging policies comes mainly from specialist insurance brokers, but some insurance companies market their own policies directly to the public to cut out the broker. Specialist organisations also compete; for example the motoring organisations are very active in selling car insurance and building societies are strong in selling house contents and buildings insurance and endowment insurance connected with mortgages (explained in Chapter 12).

INSURANCE COVER

5.   In addition to acting as insurance brokers (selling policies underwritten by other organisations) some banks also operate subsidiaries which are insurance companies, underwriting their own policies.

Such policies are marketed mainly through the branch network (though other distribution methods are used). Where the bank is the insurer providing insurance cover itself, profit is made from the premiums charged rather than from commission. This means that the bank's income is considerably higher but there are also higher outgoings in paying out claims to policy holders.

Insurance companies owned by banks compete directly with other insurance companies offering policies covering the same kinds of risk. Competition also comes from Lloyds, the insurance market in which policies are underwritten by syndicates of wealthy individuals rather than by limited companies.

PENSIONS

6.   Pensions advice is often linked to insurance advice because customers who are entitled to set up their own pension schemes can do so through a personal pension plan which is a form of insurance contract. The insurance specialists employed by banks can give guidance about the choices available. Banks can also help businesses to set up pension schemes (part of their trustee work referred to in the previous chapter), but the market for personal pensions is likely to grow as government legislation encourages more people to make their own arrangements.

Personal pension plans can take several forms.

1.   Pensions based on an annuity can be obtained by taking out a life insurance contract to obtain a guaranteed lump sum at retirement. This sum is then used to purchase an annuity, but the amount of income, the pension, will depend on the rates available at the time of retirement.

2.   Pensions based on a managed fund are the most popular because they offer the highest potential for growth (though risks are correspondingly high). Pension contributions are used to buy units in a fund and at retirement the units are used to buy an annuity (as with an insurance contract for a guaranteed lump sum).

3.   Guaranteed pensions can also be obtained by entering into a contract to receive regular payments after retirement. Bonuses may be added to the guaranteed minimum but there is no certainty that they will keep pace with inflation.

Banks which have insurance company subsidiaries can offer these services directly, in competition with other insurance companies. Other banks act simply as advisers, like any other insurance brokers, putting a customer in touch with a suitable company in order to earn commission.

INVESTMENT ADVICE

7.   The areas outlined so far in this chapter, taxation, insurance and pensions, are all specific concerns of customers thinking about how to invest their money. At a more general level customers may need advice about the whole idea of investment.

Personal customers who have inherited or won large sums of money or customers who have built up wealth from their savings may know nothing about investment or how to approach the subject.

Banks cannot make investment decisions for their customers because any approach to investment is a matter of personal attitudes and beliefs, but branch managers and specialist advisers can make sure that customers give adequate attention to the important issues.

The process of deciding about a full range of investments is known as portfolio planning. The following list covers some of the key questions to consider in portfolio planning, and any investment adviser should make sure that clients think about these factors.

1. Is safety and security more important than a high rate of return? If so this will mean avoiding the more speculative forms of investment.

2. Is income more important than capital growth? Before 1988 there could be tax advantages in taking a return in the form of capital gain rather than income.

3. How well do existing investments (such as life insurance or pensions) fit in with current income and future needs? Appropriate arrangements for insurance may need to be considered before starting to plan more risky investments.

4. Do personal or family circumstances create particular requirements? For example the investment may be intended to provide protection for a family.

5. Are investments to be made from a lump sum or from income?

6. To what extent will tax considerations affect planning? The customer's rate of income tax and the effects of capital gains tax and inheritance tax may need to be considered.

7. What kind of time scale is appropriate? This is related to a customer's age but also depends on personal preferences, since some customers will want to keep a high proportion of assets in liquid form to allow for short-term changes in circumstances.

8. Do any ethical considerations need to be taken into account? There is a growing trend towards ethical investment and many customers prefer to avoid investing in organisations of which they do not approve, for example companies involved in arms dealing.

From a customer's point of view another crucial question is whether the adviser has a good reputation. This may be judged by a past record of giving successful advice, but it is also important to consider whether the advice is impartial or whether the adviser is selling a particular range of products.

INVESTMENT SERVICES

8. The investment advice which banks give will often lead to the use of services for which banks charge. For the kind of wealthy customers who are most likely to seek advice about investment the bank may offer a range of facilities. The following list outlines some of the most important.

1. **Money-market investment**
   As a short-term measure while other plans are being drawn up any substantial sum of money can be invested on the money markets to earn a higher rate of interest than on an ordinary bank deposit account (as described in Chapter 6).

2. **Buying National Savings investments**
   For many customers with money to invest it will make sense to put some of the funds into National Savings because the government offers favourable tax treatment to investors. Some National Savings products are completely tax free while others pay interest gross so that tax is only payable later, or for some people not at all. Banks can deal with National Savings investments for their customers giving advice on appropriate investments and handling the paperwork.

3. **Buying other investments**
   As explained in the last chapter banks can arrange to buy stocks and shares. Wealthy investors are likely to be advised to purchase a range of different investments because this spreads the risk of loss. The investments may include unit trusts, government stocks and building society accounts as well as shares in quoted companies or other more unusual forms of investment. In all cases banks can make all the arrangements on behalf of their customers.

273

4. **Personal Equity Plans (PEPs)**

    Some customers may choose to invest through personal equity plans, which can only be operated through approved plan managers. The leading banks are among the institutions which are authorised to act as plan managers. Although the rules of PEPs are complicated the basic idea is simply that regular savings can be used to invest directly in shares. There are some tax benefits in using a PEP but these are not substantial in comparison to the management fees which have to be paid.

5. **Investment Management**

    For investors operating on a large scale the bank can deal with the whole of the customer's portfolio of investments. The customer can obtain the benefit of the expertise of bank investment managers by entering into a investment management agreement, either:-

    a) on a discretionary basis where the bank's specialists are authorised to make all the decisions about buying and selling investments; *or*

    b) on a non-discretionary basis seeking the approval of the customer before making any changes in the portfolio.

Competitors in arranging investments for customers include merchant banks, particularly those that specialise in fund management, accountants and securities dealers.

INDEMNITIES FOR LOST SHARE CERTIFICATES

9. If a customer wants to sell a shareholding in a company but finds that the share certificate has disappeared or been destroyed the company will be cautious about issuing a duplicate certificate because of the risk of fraud; the shareholder might try to sell the shares twice. The company will therefore normally seek protection by requiring an *indemnity* from a bank or other financial institution confirming that the company will be reimbursed if any loss occurs.

Banks therefore provide a service to customers by issuing indemnities to companies in respect of lost share certificates. The customer is normally charged a fee for the service. Before issuing an indemnity the bank takes a *counter-indemnity* from the customer so that if any payment has to be made it will be the customer who is ultimately responsible for the money. Because the bank may have to rely on the counter-indemnity the service is only available to creditworthy customers. Once the bank has given its indemnity the company will issue a duplicate certificate enabling the customer to sell the shareholding.

Apart from banks the major providers of indemnities are insurance companies.

PERSONAL ACCOUNTS AND NEW TECHNOLOGY

10. The next few sections of this chapter look at some of the recent developments in operating accounts for personal customers which have become possible through the use of new technology. The main areas discussed are:-

    a) Automated Teller Machines;

    b) Debit cards;

    c) Home banking.

For a more general view of the deposit-taking and lending services which banks offer see Chapter 6 and the chapters on lending, in particular Chapter 12 on Personal Lending.

AUTOMATED TELLER MACHINES

11. In the 1960s United Kingdom banks began to provide customers with cash dispensers which could be used outside normal banking hours to draw out limited sums in cash. The success of these machines led banks to improve their design to give greater flexibility both in the amounts of cash available and in the range of services provided.

These more modern machines, using plastic cards with information about the customer recorded on a magnetic strip, came to be known as Automated Teller Machines or ATMs because they took on many of the roles of a teller or bank cashier. Today the range of services which they offer includes:-

    a) making cash withdrawals (usually up to a pre-set limit determined for each individual customer);

    b) ordering a statement;

    c) checking the balance of the account;

    d) ordering a new chequebook;

    e) obtaining a printout of recent entries on the account;

f) changing the personal identification number (PIN) used to operate the card;

g) depositing cheques;

h) depositing cash;

i) making payment of bills (to pre-arranged payees).

Most of the machines are situated outside bank or building society branches and offer at least the first three of the services listed. Many banks also have simpler machines situated inside branches. These are cheaper to install but are not normally available for such long hours.

One of the most important developments for customers has been the establishment of joint networks of machines so that customers of one institution can use machines of other institutions for cash withdrawals and in some cases for other services too. The main networks are:-

a) National Westminster Bank and Midland Bank (the oldest link-up, which now also includes Trustee Savings Bank);

b) Lloyds Bank and Barclays Bank;

c) The Link group (which includes National Girobank and many building societies and smaller banks);

d) The Matrix group (which consists of several larger building societies).

The merger of the Nationwide Building Society and the Anglia Building Society in 1987 means that there is now a connection between the Link and Matrix groups.

A further stage in the development of Automated Teller Machines is to use them more actively to market services. Pilot schemes have already been operated with Automated Teller Machines linked to interactive video equipment which customers can use to learn about the benefits of a particular bank service through a series of questions and answers. Machines can also help a customer to find out whether a loan application will be accepted by going through the details to work out a credit score (as explained in Chapter 12).

AUTOMATED TELLER MACHINES ASSESSED

12. Automated Teller Machines represent a significant change in the banking industry because they offer a method of delivering bank services to customers without the need for contact between customers and staff. This has important implications some of which are considered in the following summary.

Advantages and disadvantages of Automated Teller Machines

Advantages for the Bank

1. There is a saving in costs because staff are not needed for routine tasks.

2. The machines have the capacity to cope with very high volumes of work.

3. Outlets for banking services can be provided in a wide choice of locations, not restricted to branch sites.

Advantages for the Customer

1. Service is very quick.

2. Machines are available in many locations, particularly with network-sharing agreements.

3. Machines are in operation when branches are shut, some of them for twenty-four hours a day.

Disadvantages for the Bank

1. There is a loss of personal contact with customers which may make selling other services more difficult.

2. 'Brand loyalty' is more difficult to maintain as customers can use machines provided by competitors.

Disadvantages for the Customer

1. Service is impersonal.

2. There have been claims of accounts being debited when no money has been drawn out (referred to later in this chapter).

3. It may be difficult to keep track of transactions because machines do not always produce printed records of cash withdrawals.

DEBIT CARDS

13. A credit card, as described in Chapter 12, is a card which is accepted as a method of payment but can also be used to obtain credit because the monthly bill does not have to be paid in full. In contrast debit cards are charged to a bank account which means they are used to make payments from funds which the cardholder owns. Cards used in

Automated Teller Machines already act as debit cards but banks have now developed the technology to allow customers to use debit cards to pay for goods in shops. In effect they take the role of a cheque but with greater potential for reducing the volume of paper which banks have to handle because they can be adapted for use in Electronic Funds Transfer at Point Of Sale (EFTPOS) systems.

The first of these cards to be widely issued, the Barclays Connect card, had an unsuccessful launch because of problems over charges to shops handling the card. In the longer term such cards will probably be as common as credit cards and there may be little to distinguish between the two because:-

a) some credit cards can already be used to deposit funds and earn interest;

b) debit cards used in machines can already be used to create overdrafts and are therefore a way of taking credit.

The main distinction may be that credit card transactions are charged to an account used only for such payments while a debit card can be used on an account which is also used as a normal bank account.

A further development which is already technically possible, but not yet available on a wide scale in the United Kingdom, is the use of debit or credit cards to make payments electronically by linking shops to banks' computers. This is the most likely form in which EFTPOS will be introduced (see Chapter 24).

HOME BANKING

14.   Bank customers have always been able to carry out some banking operations at a distance, for example by writing to the bank to arrange for money to be transferred from one account to another or to ask for a bank statement. Home banking uses new technology to speed up this kind of distance banking.

The first bank to offer a home banking service on a national scale in the United Kingdom was the Bank of Scotland. The system which they devised required a small home computer linked to a television screen and used telephone lines to carry messages. The main facilities available were checking balances and carrying out transfers between accounts.

Further progress has now been made by the Bank of Scotland and by other major banks. Building societies are also competitors in this field and have been since the earliest days when the Bank of

Scotland ran a pilot scheme with the Nottingham Building Society. Smaller devices which link up directly with a telephone are now available and in some cases all that is needed is a telephone with pushbutton controls. This has, of course, reduced the cost to customers. The range of services has also been increased. Some home banking services now offer facilities for:-

a)   ordering statements;

b)   checking balances;

c)   carrying out transfers between accounts;

d)   paying bills (to pre-arranged payees).

CONSUMER PROTECTION

15.   Interest in consumer affairs has been growing in recent years and banks, as suppliers of services to consumers, have not escaped attention. In 1983 the National Consumer Council, (NCC), produced a major report, 'Banking Services and the Consumer', and since then the NCC and other consumer groups have continued to monitor changes in banking and their effects on personal customers. For example criticisms were made of the proposal by Midland Bank (referred to in Chapter 7) to bring in a written contract for customers, because its terms were not of benefit to consumers.

Important issues for consumers include:-

a)   the apparent lack of competition between banks in some fields such as opening hours;

b)   the way in which references or status enquiries are dealt with without a customer's knowledge;

c)   the failure of banks to inform customers in advance of charges to be deducted from their accounts;

d)   the lack of adequate legal protection for customers if errors occur on their accounts (for example showing withdrawals of cash which the customer claims did not occur);

e)   the introduction of new technology such as EFTPOS without safeguards for customers.

Bankers should be aware of these concerns felt by consumers and consumer groups.

THE BANKING OMBUDSMAN

16.   One of the recommendations of the NCC report 'Banking Services and the Consumer' was that banks in the United Kingdom should establish an

ombudsman to deal with customers' complaints. This recommendation was accepted and in 1985 the first banking ombudsman was appointed. Personal customers who do not get their complaints dealt with satisfactorily by their bank can now turn to the ombudsman.

The ombudsman is financed by the banks which have chosen to participate in the scheme (and these include the 'big four' and most other major banks) so customers do not have to pay for his services. However his recommendations are made independently of the banks although they have agreed to be bound by his decisions including any awards of compensation originally up to £50,000, increased in 1988 to £100,000. Customers are not bound to accept the ombudsman's opinion and may take legal action if they are still not satisfied that they have been fairly treated.

The ombudsman does not have power to investigate refusals by banks to lend money but he can deal with other problems about customers' accounts. In the first year following his appointment he heard about 800 complaints and the largest number of these, over 1 in 10, were disputes about withdrawals from cash dispensers.

SUMMARY

17. a)   Giving advice to customers about financial matters can help banks as well as customers because it can lead to profitable business or an improved image.

b)   Tax advice is available for customers whose tax affairs are particularly complicated.

c)   Banks are involved in insurance, not only in giving advice, but also as brokers arranging insurance policies for customers and in many cases as insurers through ownership of insurance company subsidiaries. Within the field of insurance personal pensions are an important growth area.

d)   General investment advice is available from banks. Guidance on portfolio planning depends on answers to a number of key questions about the customer's needs and financial background.

e)   Intending investors can also be assisted in putting their money into the appropriate investments, ranging from short-term money-market investment to a managed portfolio.

f)   If a customer has lost a share certificate the bank can issue an indemnity to the company to enable a duplicate to be provided.

g)   New technological advances have improved the facilities offered through Automated Teller Machines. However they do have some drawbacks including the loss of personal contact between bank and customer.

h)   Debit cards, which could take over the role of cheques as a method of payment, are now available to customers. They can be used in much the same way as credit cards but are linked to a bank account rather than an account used only for credit card payments.

i)   Home banking using telephone lines to enable a customer to operate an account from home is now offered by a number of banks and building societies.

j)   Consumer issues have become important to personal customers and banks should be aware of areas of concern. The appointment of a banking ombudsman has given customers someone to turn to if the bank does not deal with their complaints satisfactorily.

STUDENT SELF-TESTING

Self Review Questions

1.   When banks give free advice what possible benefits can they gain? (2)

2.   Who are the main competitors of banks in giving taxation advice? (3)

3.   What kind of insurance normally earns the highest commissions for brokers? (4)

4.   What is a personal pension plan based on a managed fund? (6)

5.   What is portfolio planning? (7)

6.   What is the difference between discretionary and non-discretionary investment management? (8)

7.   What are the main advantages for banks of providing Automated Teller Machines for customers? (12)

8.   What is a debit card? (13)

9.   What is home banking? (14)

10. What is the main source of complaints handled by the banking ombudsman? (16)

Exercises (answers begin page 345)

A1. Mr Prescott comes into your branch to tell you that he has just won £100,000. He asks whether it is safe for him to invest in stocks and shares. What questions should you ask him and what advice would you give him?

A2. Answer the following letter from Mrs Morecroft, a highly valued customer.

Highcroft
Valley Lane
Richmond
Surrey

Dear Sir

I was recently intending to sell my shareholding in ICI and discovered that the certificate which I kept in a cupboard at home had been eaten by mice.

Can you tell me what I should do about it?

Yours faithfully

J Morecroft (Mrs)

A3. How important a development in the provision of services to customers is the Automated Teller Machine?

A4. Why do banks offer advice to personal customers on insurance and pensions?

26. Banking Services for Business

INTRODUCTION

1. Businesses use many of the general services outlined in Chapter 24 but banks have also developed specific services for business users just as they have for personal customers. Banks have given particular attention to forms of finance suited to business needs and these are covered in the chapters on lending, particularly Chapter 14.

In providing services for personal customers banks aim to meet the needs of large numbers of people with fairly standardised products. In providing services for businesses there is much more scope for tailoring services to meet the needs of one particular customer who will, of course, be expected to pay for the special treatment received.

This chapter deals with some of the specialist services other than loans which banks provide for businesses. The areas covered are:-

a) Business Advisory Services;
b) Account-handling services;
c) Advice about finance;
d) Merchant banking services;
e) Registrar work;
f) Data processing;
g) Cash management;
h) Guarantees and bonds;
i) Insurance;
j) Credit cards.

BUSINESS ADVISORY SERVICES

2. Many banks now offer a Business Advisory Service intended mainly for fairly small businesses which do not have a large enough staff to have expertise in all aspects of business. Although different banks have different approaches to this kind of work in general any business, whether a bank customer or not, can approach the bank and ask its experts in small business management to review the operation of the business. The business advisers can then suggest ways of improving the planning, marketing, financing or administration of the business.

The service is usually subsidised by the bank rather than being a source of profit because it is considered good for the bank's image and a possible source of profitable relationships in the future. Customers can often make use of the service free of charge and may be recommended to seek help if they are borrowing money and having difficulty in making repayments.

New businesses about to begin trading may also get advice about how to approach their preliminary planning, including such areas as costing, budgeting and promotion.

The main competitors of banks in this field are accountants. Many of the larger accountancy firms have specialist management consultancy units which can tackle business problems for clients of all sizes.

ACCOUNT-HANDLING SERVICES

3. For businesses which are customers banks can provide all of the general services associated with operating a bank account. In order to meet the special needs of some business organisations banks offer various extra facilities. Two widely used options are nightsafes and special cheque-books.

1. Nightsafes
   Customers which handle very large amounts of cash such as shops and petrol stations may wish to avoid storing the cash overnight on their own premises. They can therefore arrange access to the bank's nightsafe which means that sealed containers of cash can be delivered to the bank after it has closed. The contents are then checked by bank staff the following day.

2. Special cheque-books
   Some companies choose to have specially designed chequebooks for promotional purposes. For very large companies which issue thousands of cheques a year special machine-written cheques are also available using facsimile signatures rather than original signatures for each cheque.

These are essentially variations on the normal services available to all customers, adapting a standard service to meet the needs of large-scale users.

Competition between banks in offering account-handling services is becoming fiercer as more foreign banks enter the market, but although banks compete among themselves in services offered and charges made for business accounts there is little competition outside banking. Building societies may start to attract small business customers but at present banks have a significant lead over non-bank competitors in running business accounts.

ADVICE ABOUT FINANCE

4. As emphasised in the chapters on lending, banks are not simply the providers of loans or other forms of finance which their customers ask for. One of the most important roles which bank staff undertake is to give advice about the kind of finance most suited to a business's needs. Advice is also given to personal borrowers but there is a special need for advice where business customers are concerned because of the wide range of possibilities.

For small businesses advice may be available at branch level and the range of options may not be much greater than for a personal customer who wants to borrow. For larger businesses a bank's merchant banking subsidiary may be called in and the advice may be much more wide-ranging covering such areas as:-

a) the organisation of the business (for example as a public company rather than a private company);

b) short-term finance such as overdrafts and alternatives like acceptance credits (described in Chapter 14) or commercial paper (referred to in Chapter 4);

c) medium-term and long-term loans;

d) capital structure including the question of gearing, the proportion of borrowed funds to invested funds;

e) possible sources of capital.

OTHER MERCHANT BANKING SERVICES

5. In addition to giving business customers advice about how and where to obtain loans or capital merchant banks operate in many other fields. As explained in Chapter 1 they have a tradition of dealing with acceptances of bills of exchange and of issuing securities for companies. They are now active in so many other kinds of business that no list can cover all of their work, but the main areas include:-

a) investment management work, for example as fund managers running unit trusts or pension funds;

b) business advisory services and management consultancy;

c) advice on takeovers and mergers;

d) advice on management buyouts where managers of a business raise funds to purchase the business from its previous owners;

e) advising on import and export business;

f) foreign exchange and money-market dealing;

g) dealing in bullion or basic commodities.

In some of the activities such as dealing in bullion the merchant bank may act on its own behalf to make money, but all of these services can also be provided for customers.

Foreign banks are among the major competitors in most of these areas of business, and there are also more specialised businesses competing in some fields, for example money brokers competing in the money markets or accountancy firms competing as management consultants.

REGISTRAR WORK

6. United Kingdom law requires companies to keep a register of shareholders, and this can be a huge administrative task for a company with a large number of shareholders. Businesses the size of National Westminster or Barclays have well over 100,000 shareholders and some of the leading industrial companies have far more. If the trend towards wider share ownership continues the administrative work load will become even greater.

For small companies the work will usually be done as part of the Company Secretary's job. Some large companies also carry out all their registrar work internally by setting up a registrar's department, but many large companies choose to pass on the work to a bank. Bank registrars have the staff and equipment to deal with large-scale operations and have a good reputation for protecting confidential information.

The tasks that bank registrars take on for customers include:-

a) maintaining the register of shareholders' names and addresses;

b) dealing with dividend payments to shareholders (and interest to holders of debentures or loan stocks);

Section 2 26 Banking Services for Business

c) issuing share certificates;

d) dealing with correspondence to shareholders, from copies of the annual report and accounts to notices of rights issues, bonus issues or takeover bids;

e) counting shareholders' votes, including votes at meetings and proxy votes sent in by post;

f) providing annual accounts and other information required each year by the Registrar of Companies.

The advantages to the customer of using a bank as a registrar are that:-

a) there are savings in staff;

b) the company has no problem in coping with any extra workload;

c) using a bank's technology and expertise may save money.

DATA PROCESSING

7. One of the reasons that banks are able to provide an efficient registrar service for companies, often more cheaply than the company could do the work itself, is that the banks' computer systems are able to cope with enormous amounts of data. The power of banks' computers enables them to offer data processing services to business customers who do not have direct access to the equipment needed for large scale computing.

Originally the most popular purpose for which businesses used the banks' computer services was to deal with wages and salaries. Computerised payroll calculations are much quicker and more accurate than manual calculations; pay slips and all the documentation needed for tax purposes can be produced automatically. In addition banks are able to use the data from a client's payroll to make payments to the bank accounts of the employees through BACS (referred to in Chapters 1 and 24).

Customers can also use bank computer services for any computing task which they want carried out independently or confidentially, so even customers with their own computers may choose to use the service. Apart from payroll work important uses include:-

a) sales ledger processing including sending out bills to customers;

b) bought ledger processing including making payments to suppliers;

c) stock control and planning of production or purchasing;

d) financial planning and forecasting;

e) share registration work (as described above).

There is some competition in this field from specialist computer bureaux which own data processing equipment in order to handle data for other people, but many businesses use their own internal data-processing departments and these could be considered the most effective competition keeping business away from banks.

CASH MANAGEMENT

8. The data-processing services described above are based on the fact that bank computers can handle enormous quantities of data in batches, often processed overnight. One of the other important characteristics of computer technology is speed, and it is the speed with which data can be handled that has enabled banks to offer a cash management service to major customers.

A cash management service enables the customer to obtain up-to-date balances of a number of different accounts, possibly in different currencies and in different parts of the world. This means that a corporate treasurer can make decisions about transfers between accounts or about short-term investment plans on the basis of accurate information. At one time a number of telephone calls would have been needed to put together information which can now be obtained from a computer terminal linked to the bank's computer system.

In its most sophisticated form cash management enables the corporate treasurer to use the computer terminal to make payment instructions, for example placing surplus funds on deposit in the money markets or providing details of payments to be made through BACS (which has the facility to handle direct computer input from customers or computer tapes prepared by customers as well as input from the banks which belong to the clearing system).

Some major computer manufacturers compete with the banks in providing cash management systems.

GUARANTEES AND BONDS

9. When businesses are involved in large contracts they may need to issue guarantees to the organisa-

tions or agencies for which they are working. For example a civil engineering contractor building a bridge may need to arrange for the issue of a performance bond to the local authority which is paying for the construction work; this entitles the authority to claim money if the work is faulty or is not completed. A promise from the contractor is not acceptable because failure to complete the work might well be because the business has gone into liquidation. The local authority would therefore want a guarantee from an organisation of undoubted financial strength, and this is most likely to mean a major bank. The contractor can therefore ask its bank to issue a bond on its behalf.

Banks take a risk in issuing bonds just as they do in lending money, but the liability is only a contingent liability, which means that the bank only has to pay if a claim is made because of some problem. Banks make money by charging fees for the bonds which they issue, and obtain some protection from loss by:-

a)   assessing the creditworthiness of customers before agreeing to issue bonds for them;

b)   taking a counter-indemnity from the customer for any bond or guarantee issued.

Apart from building and civil engineering projects in this country the main use for bonds is in large-scale export deals. More details of the kinds of bonds used are given in Chapter 22.

Insurance companies are the main competitors of banks in issuing bonds and guarantees.

INSURANCE

10.   As explained in Chapter 25 banks act as insurers and as insurance brokers. This enables them to sell insurance for business purposes as well as for personal customers. Particularly important areas are:-

a)   fire insurance including loss-of-profits cover so that if premises are damaged by fire the business can claim some of the money lost because trading has been prevented;

b)   'key-man' insurance covering the lives of important employees or company directors because if they die the loss of their talents could cause financial loss to the business.

Banks are keen to ensure that their business customers are well insured because when businesses

borrow money their ability to repay may suffer if problems occur for which they have not got adequate insurance cover.

Whatever the insurance needs of a business banks can arrange appropriate policies, and may underwrite the risk through a subsidiary insurance company. The competition in this field, as for insurance sold to personal customers, comes from other insurance brokers and insurance companies.

CREDIT CARDS

11.   Although credit cards may seem to be a service to personal customers rather than to businesses (and are described in Chapter 12 on Personal Lending) there are ways in which banks offer a credit card service to businesses.

1.   **Agreements to accept credit cards**
     If a business wants to arrange to accept credit card payments a representative of the credit card company will negotiate an agreement by which the business undertakes to pay commission on all credit card sales in return for permission to accept card payments. The business may gain in spite of the commission because:-
     a)   credit card vouchers paid into a bank account can be treated as cash and there is no waiting time for clearance as there is with cheques;
     b)   displaying the credit card sign may attract more customers.

2.   **Credit card systems**
     Some very large retailers like Debenhams or Marks and Spencer choose to have their own in-house credit card either in addition to accepting bank credit cards or as the only card they will take. Often it is banks which provide the service of setting up such systems including checking the creditworthiness of applicants for cards, issuing cards and carrying out all the accounting. There is competition in this field from some finance houses which specialise in running credit card systems for shops, but banks have a large share of the business.

3.   **Business expenses cards**
     Standard Access or Visa credit cards can be issued for businesses which employ staff such as sales representatives who travel

widely, and frequently spend money for business purposes. Each card is allocated to an employee and all expenditure is charged to one account in the name of the business. The business receives a detailed statement showing what each employee has spent, and the bill is then paid each month (unlike personal credit cards which do not have to be repaid in full). In effect it is more strictly a charge card scheme, like American Express or Diners Club which offer this kind of payment service for both business and personal users, rather than a credit card designed to provide short-term credit.

SUMMARY

12. a) Many banks provide a Business Advisory Service for helping small businesses with planning and organising themselves to operate profitably.

b) Banks offer some specialist services to businesses in operating accounts. These include:-
   1. nightsafes;
   2. special chequebooks.

c) Banks give advice to businesses about finance as well as providing loans or arranging issues of securities.

d) Merchant banks, including the merchant bank subsidiaries of commercial banks, offer a wide range of advice and dealing services for customers.

e) Registrar work includes keeping a register of shareholders and dealing with the correspondence that has to be sent out to them.

f) Because banks have large computer systems they are able to offer data processing facilities to customers, for example carrying out their payroll calculations.

g) Computer technology also enables banks to offer major companies a cash management service for keeping track of balances held in different places through a terminal linked to the bank's computer.

h) Banks issue guarantees and bonds on behalf of customers when they are involved in major projects like building or civil engineering work.

i) As insurance brokers, and in some cases as owners of insurance companies, banks can help businesses with all their insurance needs including:-
   1. fire insurance with loss of profits cover;
   2. 'key-man' insurance for top personnel.

j) Banks can help businesses by offering credit card facilities:-
   1. to enable them to take payments by credit card;
   2. to run complete in-house credit card systems;
   3. to use credit cards for staff paying business expenses.

STUDENT SELF-TESTING

Self Review Questions

1. Who are the main competitors of banks in providing business advisory services? (2)

2. What is a nightsafe? (3)

3. What is gearing? (4)

4. State four services commonly provided by merchant banks. (5)

5. What are the advantages of using a bank as a company registrar? (6)

6. What advantages are there for companies in using a bank's data processing service for calculating the payroll? (7)

7. What is a cash management service? (8)

8. Why might a construction company ask a bank to issue a performance bond on its behalf? (9)

9. Why do businesses take out 'key-man' insurance? (10)

10. How can businesses benefit by accepting credit card payments? (11)

Exercises (answers begin page 346)

A1. What specialist services do banks offer to business customers apart from finance and advice about borrowing or raising capital?

A2. Mr Gregory, the Company Secretary of one of your major customers, Weldwell plc, tells you that the number of shareholders on the company register has nearly doubled in the last two years and his staff are barely able to cope.

What service can your bank offer in order to overcome this problem? How would you explain the benefits to Mr Gregory?

A3.   Ms Parsons is the Sales Director of a local company which banks with you. She used to come in once a month to draw out cash for expenses for her sales team, but now that the company employs more staff and covers a wider area she has to come in more frequently. How can the bank help her to maintain control over spending by her sales representatives while reducing her need to handle cash?

A4.   What are merchant banks and what services do they offer?

27. Interviews

INTRODUCTION

1. This final chapter of the text deals with interviewing in banking. It begins by looking at the types of interview which bank staff may be involved in. Further sections of the chapter deal with:-

   a) preparing and beginning interviews;
   b) constraints on interviews;
   c) communications in interviews;
   d) resolving conflict in interviews;
   e) achieving objectives in interviews.

THE IMPORTANCE OF INTERVIEWS IN BANKING

2. Interviewing skills are needed by staff in many industries and fields of activity; in banking there are two major factors which make interviews particularly important.

   1. **Staffing levels**
      The major banks employ very large numbers of staff, as many as 80,000 in banks as large as Barclays and National Westminster. Even in smaller banks people are an essential resource, and this means that managers and supervisors need to have the skills to deal with staff. All supervisory staff have responsibility for encouraging their staff to work well to meet the goals of the organisation.

   2. **The type of work**
      For lower level staff, who do not have responsibility for the work of other people, interviewing skills may seem less important, but the growing emphasis on marketing and the increasing use of automation for routine jobs mean that junior staff are more and more likely to have to deal with customers. Such contact with customers requires a knowledge of interpersonal skills including interviewing techniques.

FORMAL AND INFORMAL INTERVIEWS

3. Any exchange of ideas and information between people is an interview, whether in the context of work or between friends, but interviews at work are rather different from social exchanges because at least one party will have specific aims in mind.

If the aims to be achieved are particularly important or strongly felt the person concerned may make arrangements to hold a formal interview. For example a customer wanting to borrow money may ask to see the bank manager and will agree on a specific time and place for the meeting. Similarly a manager who is dissatisfied with the performance of one of his or her staff might well call in the person concerned for a formal interview to discuss the problem. These kind of situations, very often involving two people in a relatively private environment, enable both sides to plan and be prepared for the interview.

When the term interview is used it is often these formal situations which come to mind, but for many junior staff such occasions are rare. This does not mean that they are not concerned with interviews. Informal interviews occur wherever a member of staff deals with a customer or a more senior colleague. It is in these informal situations that staff have most opportunity to use interviewing skills to achieve their goals and the goals of the organisation. For example when a customer comes in to a branch to ask for information the member of staff may enter into a conversation which helps to identify the customer's financial needs, an essential first step in good marketing. Obtaining this information requires interviewing skill.

The distinction between formal and informal interviews is not always clear but in general informal interviews, which take place with little specific preparation or planning, are likely to be more frequent than formal interviews.

PERSONNEL INTERVIEWS

4. Many of the kinds of interview which seem most important to staff are interviews concerned with staff matters rather than with customers. Sometimes such interviews are carried out by specialist personnel managers, trained in dealing with staff and staff problems. In other circumstances line managers, for example branch managers or assistant managers who have a direct line of command to the staff who work for them, may carry out personnel interviews as part of their general responsibility for their staff.

The following list outlines some of the most important kinds of personnel interview.

1. **Interviews for new recruits**

   Recruitment interviews are only a stage in a longer process of decision-making about the kinds of staff which the organisation needs, how to attract them and how to select the best applicants. Recruitment interviews are usually based on an application form completed in advance by the candidate for the job, and this gives both the applicant and the interviewer material on which to base the interview.

   Some employers choose to widen the scope of the recruitment interview to include more informal assessment as well as a limited time in a formal situation. Informal interviewing may take place over a meal or at a group discussion between a number of candidates.

2. **Interviews for promotion**

   In the past the United Kingdom clearers have usually appointed higher level staff by promoting from within rather than bringing in outsiders. To some extent this pattern is changing as:-

   a)   competition from other banks attracts some of the better internal candidates;

   b)   banks diversify and need staff with new kinds of expertise;

   c)   so much technical expertise is required that bankers used to working in the branch network cannot always be easily trained to the right level.

   Where jobs are suitable for internal applicants banks often use the system of 'paging' which means using a circular to managers to ask them whether they have suitable staff whom they can recommend for a particular post. Candidates put forward by their managers can then be called for interview having had a chance to consider what the new job will be like.

3. **Appraisal interviews**

   Most banks use a regular system of appraisal to:-

   a)   help managers to monitor the performance of their staff;

   b)   make sure staff know what they need to do to improve their performance.

Often managers will need to complete some kind of appraisal form describing the performance of the member of staff, and the interview is then a discussion of the opinions the manager has recorded on the form. Members of staff may then be asked to sign the form to confirm that they have discussed it, and if they feel that the comments are unfair they may have the opportunity to add their own views.

4. **Salary review interviews**

   Although some banks link appraisal interviews to decisions about staff salaries most personnel management theorists feel that this is not an advisable policy because staff under appraisal are likely to be far more defensive and hostile to the interviewer's criticisms if they feel threatened with a loss of salary. This may defeat the object of appraisal which is intended partly to encourage self-criticism as a means to improving performance. Some banks therefore have quite separate interviews for appraisal and salary reviews.

5. **Disciplinary interviews**

   When a manager feels that a member of staff has broken the rules of the organisation some action needs to be taken. A first step is likely to be an informal interview as a friendly warning. If this is ignored a more formal interview will be held. The exact procedures to be followed will depend on the bank's own rules but in general they are likely to follow the guidelines on disciplinary procedure recommended by ACAS (the Advisory Conciliation and Arbitration Service). In practice this will mean that if there is no improvement in behaviour a series of interviews will be needed before a member of staff is dismissed. Normally the member of staff will have the right to have a friend present at such interviews, a role often taken on by trade union officials on behalf of members.

6. **Grievance interviews**

   The reverse of a complaint by a manager about staff is a complaint brought by a member of staff against a manager, for example because of unfair treatment. Again banks have formally laid down procedures for dealing with such grievances, and trade union representation is often possible.

At a less formal level personnel staff may visit branches and departments from time to time simply to talk to staff to see whether there are any aspects of work about which they are unhappy. Discussions of this kind can reduce the need for formal grievance interviews.

CUSTOMER INTERVIEWS

5.   For many bank staff talking to customers takes up a high proportion of their working time, and the number of staff for whom this is true is likely to increase as banks become more marketing orientated.

The following list outlines some of the most important types of customer interview.

1. **Telephone enquiries**
   One of the most simple forms which an interview can take is a telephone enquiry from a customer. The manner in which staff deal with telephone calls can have an important role in creating an impression, good or bad, about the friendliness and efficiency of the bank.

2. **Face-to-face enquiries**
   Staff who have to deal with customers at the bank counter or at desks within the public area of a bank branch are frequently involved in interviews ranging from the most simple transactions to longer, more detailed discussions of bank services which may lead to a sale.

3. **Sales interviews**
   If a customer comes to a bank with a clear view of a specific service which he or she wants to buy a member of the bank staff will be able to provide the required service without needing to exercise any particular skill in selling. More often customers are unsure about:-
   a)   their own needs;
   b)   the services which the bank can offer to meet those needs;
   c)   how to choose the most suitable service.
   Bank staff are therefore likely to have an active role in controlling a sales interview to make sure that the customer obtains the right knowledge and understands what choices can be made. Sales staff also need to be aware of the possibility of cross-selling, selling services to meet other needs which only become apparent in discussing the customer's position.

4. **Complaints**
   One of the most difficult kinds of interview to handle is a complaint from a customer. Usually junior staff will be expected to refer complaints to higher authority, partly because this helps the complainant to feel that the complaint is being taken seriously and partly because more experienced staff are likely to have greater knowledge of possible solutions to any problem raised. Occasionally the situation is reversed with a bank having to criticise its customer, for example for persistently writing out cheques when there is no money in the account. Again senior staff will usually take on responsibility for such interviews, which may lead to the closure of a customer's account.

PREPARATION FOR INTERVIEWS

6.   One of the most important aspects of any interview is preparation. As the previous sections have shown interviews can take many forms and some are easier to prepare for than others, but even the most informal interview should not be approached without some preparation. Being prepared to deal with a telephone enquiry may require only a few simple factors, for example:-

a)   controlling breathing rather than picking up the receiver while out of breath;

b)   concentration on what the caller says rather than trying to carry on with some other piece of work;

c)   developing a broad enough knowledge of the bank and its organisation to know how to deal with calls.

This last point implies that being well prepared for general enquiries needs constant work to keep up to date, for example in having a good knowledge of bank products.

For more formal interviews preparation is likely to be much more detailed and specific. If a customer has made an appointment to discuss a loan the lending officer should prepare by:-

a) looking at the bank's records about the customer, in particular any previous correspondence, details of earlier borrowing and current information on balances;

b) studying any information already provided by the customer in connection with the proposed loan, for example the latest balance sheet of the business, in order to assess what the customer really needs;

c) preparing any information or documentation which will be needed during the interview, for example loan application forms for the customer to sign if agreement is reached, or details of bank services which may be relevant to the customer's needs;

d) making sure that the physical environment for the interview is as comfortable as possible;

e) arranging for an uninterrupted discussion, for example by telling the switchboard operator not to put through any calls.

All of these steps help to make sure that the interview is as successful as possible. This means that the interviewer is likely to achieve his or her objectives, which might include:-

a) identifying the customer's real needs;

b) giving fair consideration to the request;

c) providing appropriate advice;

d) selling suitable services.

If an interviewer does not plan properly and does not have clear objectives in mind problems may arise because:-

a) the customer may feel unfairly treated;

b) a loan may be agreed without adequate consideration of the problems;

c) the customer's real needs may not be met;

d) the customer may get the impression that the bank is inefficient and badly organised.

BEGINNING INTERVIEWS

7.   All of the preparation for an interview may be wasted, however carefully it has been done, if the interview itself starts badly.

For a fairly informal interview a good impression can be created from the outset by a welcoming smile and a friendly greeting to put the interviewee at ease. The principle of putting the other person at ease is particularly important with personnel interviews, for example in recruiting new staff. To get an applicant for a job to talk in a comfortable and relaxed way about himself or herself means getting the interview off to a good start, 'breaking the ice' perhaps by talking about the sports and hobbies which the candidate has referred to in the application form. For many jobs applicants are interviewed by a panel of people and part of the opening stage of the interview is for the leader of the panel to introduce each panel member. The expressions which they adopt can also help to determine whether the atmosphere is suitably relaxed. Some interviewers choose to begin proceedings in a deliberately aggressive manner but this is generally only suited to special circumstances.

In some cases explaining the background to the interview may also be a part of the opening stage, for example in disciplinary interviews where the member of staff may need to be put in the picture about the exact details of alleged misdemeanours and the penalties which are likely to be imposed if there is no improvement in behaviour.

CONSTRAINTS ON INTERVIEWS

8.   In whatever way an interview has begun there will be certain constraints on the conduct of the interview. In particular the parties involved will have some idea in advance of what ground the interview will cover. Such expectations should not be seen as too severe a limitation. For example in a sales interview the interviewer should be aware of the possibility of introducing new ideas when the opportunity arises (and this is the essence of good cross-selling). However to change too abruptly from matters originally put forward for discussion may make the customer feel that he or she is being side-tracked, so the participants' perceptions of the purpose of the interview do represent some kind of constraint.

Another important factor is time. Time is limited and valuable so interviewers need to be very conscious of how long it is taking to obtain information or put over ideas. Even if an interview does not have a specific deadline time needs to be used efficiently, though the emphasis on getting to the point of an interview must be balanced against the fact that in many interviews it is essential to make sure that an interviewee does not feel pressured or rushed into a decision.

The relative power of different parties to an interview may also prove a constraint on how the interview develops. A customer who is rather intimidated by dealing with a powerful institution like a bank may have difficult in putting over a good case. Similarly junior members of staff may be unwilling to express their true feelings to senior staff.

COMMUNICATIONS IN INTERVIEWS

9.   Essentially any communication is a two-way process with a message directed from one party to another in order to obtain a response. Feedback from the recipient of the message then leads to further response. Interviews are no exception to this general pattern; in comparison to many other forms of communication feedback is extremely rapid.

The following list looks at some of the range of communications skills which interviewers need.

1.   **Asking questions**
Asking questions seems such a simple idea that it is easy to overlook the skill which is needed to ask questions effectively.
In recruitment interviews the interviewer is usually in a position of power and authority and is able to direct the interview by asking questions. Often the most useful in meeting the interviewer's objectives are open-ended questions which have no short simple answer, for example questions about an applicant's beliefs or feelings. Closed questions which just require factual responses or answers of yes and no tend to discourage dialogue.
In interviews with customers asking the right questions may be even more difficult because one of the interviewer's aims is to find out what the customer's real needs are, and these may differ from the customer's own perceptions.

2.   **Giving information**
An interviewer is rarely just an interrogator seeking information by asking questions. Usually part of the role of the interviewer is to give information, for example to a job applicant about the kind of work to be done and about the organisation.

In customer interviews giving information clearly and accurately may be of special importance because to sell a service to a customer on the basis of false, incomplete or misleading information may lead to very serious problems. At the very least the customer may be dissatisfied with the bank's service and choose to buy financial services elsewhere. At worst the bank may face legal liability for the bad advice it has given.

3.   **Leading the discussion**
An important technique, particularly in sales interviews, is to lead the customer from one area of interest to another. By asking questions like 'What if ...?' or 'Have you thought about ...?' the customer can be encouraged to identify additional needs. Such questions can reinforce the bank's image as caring and concerned about its customers and can help to sell additional services.

4.   **Listening**
In all interviewing it is important to listen effectively. This means being aware of the feelings behind words that are spoken, and being able to make use of the other person's comments, for example to pick up points they have made in order to introduce new information.

5.   **Persuading**
The aim of much communication is to put over a point of view so that someone else will accept it, to persuade someone else, usually in order to achieve a change in behaviour. For example in a sales interview the interviewer tries to persuade the potential buyer that the product is suitable and worth buying so that a sale takes place. To be effective at persuading requires a belief in the message put over and a determination to get the interviewee to agree.

NON-VERBAL COMMUNICATION

10.   In addition to having the skills of verbal communication already discussed interviewers should be capable of using and assessing non-verbal communication (or body language). Just as language itself differs from person to person and from society

to society so body language has its variations which make it difficult to generalise about. However there are some features of body language which can be interpreted in Western society as having broadly similar meanings.

In 'reading' body language there are many different elements which make up the complete message. If all the features signal the same kind of feelings or attitudes the overall message may be fairly clear even if individual details are confusing.

1. **Physical appearance**

    A person's size, shape and build give some indication of what he or she may be like as a character, but more important information comes from the physical features over which people have more control, how neat, tidy and clean they are, what kind of clothes they wear and how they choose to change their appearance, for example by make-up or hairstyle. However there is a danger for interviewers that they may be prejudiced about certain kinds of appearance or style, which may mean that smart, conventionally dressed people are more likely to get bank loans than other people.

2. **Posture**

    In many formal interviews the interviewer will offer the interviewee a chair. Just how the interviewee sits during the interview may be an important indicator of attitudes. To pull the chair up close and lean forward towards the interviewer may suggest a confident and involved interest in what is going on. To sit more rigidly, turned partly away from the interviewer and with arms tightly crossed may suggest a closed, uninvolved attitude which may need to be overcome before real progress can be made in the interview.

3. **Voice**

    The way in which people use their voices can also reveal something of their feelings and views. This may give the words they use a quite different meaning. For example softness of voice may suggest uncertainty even if positive views are being put forward, or exaggerated speed in speaking may be a sign of nervousness. Body language and the spoken language need to be interpreted together.

4. **Body movements**

    Some of the automatic body movements which are basic functional mechanisms can be affected by feelings; breathing and blinking may be speeded up, for example, in moments of stress or anxiety. Many other movements are also largely involuntary indicators of emotion. Some people may tap a finger or foot when feeling impatient or frustrated; others may blush with embarrassment or laugh nervously. More conscious movements can also be indicators of feeling, like scratching one's head when puzzled or lighting up a cigarette when under stress.

Experts on body language can identify such signals quickly and get a good view of how people feel by looking at the range of their nonverbal messages. For interviewers, with rather less expertise, it is important to be aware that body language has a part to play in judging how an interview is developing. If an interviewee 'switches off' body language will make this clear even if questions are still being answered. Non-verbal communication can also give away feelings which an interviewee is trying to hide. A characteristic example is when someone looks away while telling a lie (though, of course, experienced liars may well have learnt not to do this). In personnel interviews a junior member of staff may verbally agree with the supervisor or manager out of respect or fear but may show a different opinion through body language; this can guide the supervisor to follow up the problem.

RESOLVING CONFLICT IN INTERVIEWS

11. In any interview there is a risk of conflict between the parties because of differences in objectives or in perceptions. To be successful in handling interviews it is useful to have a range of techniques to choose from in order to deal with any conflict which arises.

Where the conflict arises from a difference in perceptions conflict may be resolved by promoting a change in attitude of one party or both parties. For example at an appraisal interview a member of staff may feel that he or she is being unfairly criticised for absenteeism; conflict over this may be resolved if evidence is available of genuine illness, which may make the supervisor or manager see the member of staff in a different light. Similarly where a customer is not persuaded that a particular bank service will really meet his or her needs providing extra information or reviewing the product's benefits may change the customer's view.

Where a conflict is the result of differing objectives resolution may come in the form of a compromise. A customer who is dissatisfied about having to pay any bank charges may be placated if the bank agrees to refund some of the money charged.

An important technique for management in dealing with conflict is to impose a solution if the conflict is with someone who has less power or authority. This may mean refusing a member of staff time off or declining a customer's request for a loan. Where this method is used it may leave the manager with a sense of having achieved the objective of the interview and having come out as a 'winner', but unless good reasons for the decision are given the other party may feel a sense of injustice as the 'loser'. The advantage of compromise solutions is that both sides can feel that they have won.

In cases of serious conflict, where the interview is specifically intended to tackle a major problem like a disciplinary matter, a longer term approach to conflict may be needed. Procedures may be agreed at the interview for reducing the problem in the future and for monitoring progress.

ACHIEVING INTERVIEW OBJECTIVES

12. Measuring the success of any interview is difficult, though it can be made easier by setting clear goals to be achieved. Such objectives may help an interviewer to concentrate on what is important in the interview and may give guidance in directing the interview to a conclusion.

In selling interviews the primary goal for the interviewer is to sell a product, and specific techniques can be used to achieve this aim. The interviewer may:-

a) make sure the product does meet the customer's minimum requirements;

b) concentrate on the benefits of the product;

c) come up with convincing answers to any objections raised by the customer;

d) assess the moment when the customer is willing to say yes to the deal;

e) complete or 'close' the sale by getting the customer to sign.

SUMMARY

13. a) Interviews are important in banking because:-
     1. staff are an essential resource, often used in large numbers;
     2. much work that staff carry out consists of interviews with customers.

b) Interviews can be broadly classified as formal or informal.

c) Major types of personnel interview include:-
     1. recruitment and promotion interviews;
     2. appraisal and salary review interviews;
     3. discipline and grievance interviews.

d) Among the most important customer interviews are sales interviews.

e) Most kinds of interview require some preparation. More formal interviews often need detailed, specific preparation.

f) Often when beginning an interview a major concern of the interviewer is to put the interviewee at ease.

g) During interviews the participants' perceptions may be a constraint on how the interview develops. Time may also be a limiting factor.

h) Interviews require a wide range of communications skills, from asking questions and giving information to identifying and interpreting body language.

i) Where conflict arises in an interview it is useful to have a range of methods of resolving the conflict, of which compromise is often the most appropriate.

j) The success of interviews can often only be judged if clear objectives are set in advance.

STUDENT SELF-TESTING

Self Review Questions

1. What is the difference between a formal interview and an informal interview? (3)

2. Why is it recommended that salary review interviews should be held separately from appraisal interviews? (4)

3.   What is the difference between a disciplinary interview and a grievance interview? (4)

4.   What is cross-selling? (5)

5.   What problems may occur if a sales interview is held without adequate preparation? (6)

6.   Describe two main constraints which can affect the way an interview develops. (8)

7.   State four of the important communications skills needed by interviewers. (9)

8.   In what way is physical appearance an important part of body language? (10)

9.   State two methods of resolving conflict in interviews. (11)

10. Why should an interviewer set objectives before conducting an interview? (12)

Exercises (answers begin page 347)

A1.   What problems are likely to arise if an interview is inadequately prepared? Illustrate your answer with reference to specific kinds of interview.

A2.   'Only personnel managers need to be trained in interviewing.' To what extent do you agree with this view?

A3.   How can a knowledge of non-verbal communication help interviewers?

A4.   The manager of your branch is planning to hold a training session on interviewing skills for all staff as a way of improving branch profitability. What aspects of interviewing would you expect to be emphasised, and why?

Section 3
The Revision Section

Examination technique

Revision summaries

Sample question papers with commentary

Mock examination papers

Examination Technique

INTRODUCTION

If you get full marks in every examination you take you do not need to read this section of the text. If, on the other hand, you are human it is worth your while to think about the reasons why people do badly in examinations. You can improve your chances of success by getting all the simple things right.

BASIC PREPARATION

Well before the examination you need to put in plenty of hard work. By the time you read this section you should have studied all the material for Section 2 of the text, and you should be familiar with the syllabus. You should also have tackled a large number of questions on the material to become familiar with the technique of organising your answers in a logical manner. There should be no serious gaps in your knowledge. You should make use of this revision section as actively as possible.

DO NOT just read through what the revision summaries tell you that you should know. For example the summary for Chapter 1 tells you that you should be able to describe the role of the discount houses in the banking system. Make sure that you can do this by WRITING DOWN what you can remember about the role of the discount houses. Then check what you have written against the text, and concentrate on memorizing any points you missed out or got wrong. Do this for every area referred to in the revision summaries.

IMMEDIATELY BEFORE THE EXAMINATION

Make sure that you:-
   a) know exactly when and where the examination is to be held;
   b) can get there in good time; check your travel arrangements!
   c) have all the equipment you need;
      − your examination entry slip
      − your calculator (and spare battery)
      − your pens, pencils and ruler
      − your watch
      − anything else you feel you need like sweets or cigarettes.

IN THE EXAMINATION ROOM

Relax and take a few deep breaths. Tell yourself that you are calm and confident. You have all the equipment you need and you have done enough work to pass. Now it is a matter of getting things right on the night.

Before you start writing:-
   a) read the whole examination paper very carefully;
   b) make sure you understand the instructions;
   c) decide which questions you are going to answer;
   d) decide what order you will answer the questions in, generally starting with the easiest;
   e) decide how much time to allocate to each question based on the mark allocations, allowing at least some time for re-reading;
   f) underline key words in the questions you are going to tackle;
   g) think carefully about what the examiner had in mind in setting each question.

When tackling questions:-
   a) write a brief plan outlining the key points;
   b) make sure the points are organised in a logical sequence;
   c) be as concise as possible;
   d) concentrate on what the question wants rather than writing the answer you know to a rather different question;
   e) write legibly;
   f) while writing leave plenty of space between paragraphs so that you can add any later thoughts.

When you have finished writing:-
   a) re-read what you have written and cross out anything which does not make sense;
   b) add any other ideas you have thought of;
   c) make sure you have completed all the formalities, entering details of the examination and your name and Institute membership number where required;
   d) make sure you have attached any extra sheets you have used;
   e) use any further time for more re-reading rather than leaving early.

EXAMINERS' COMMENTS

Examiners regularly complain about the same failings in candidates. Make sure that you know what the common problems are so that you can avoid them.

Among the most frequent causes of failure are:-

a)   failure to read the question;

b)   failure to answer the question as set;

c)   poor planning of answers;

d)   poor planning of time;

e)   inclusion of irrelevant material;

f)   poor writing;

g)   guessing at topics to revise rather than studying the whole syllabus.

Avoid these problems and you should do well.

Revision Summaries

CHAPTER 1: The Banking System

ESSENTIAL KNOWLEDGE

At the end of your studies you should be able to:-
1. define what a bank is;
2. describe the 1979 and 1987 Banking Acts;
3. explain how the Bank of England categorises banks;
4. define the term Licensed Deposit Taking Institution;
5. explain the concept of deposit protection (or deposit insurance);
6. compare the functions of different kinds of banks including:-
    a) the central bank;
    b) clearing banks;
    c) foreign banks;
    d) merchant banks;
7. describe the role of discount houses in the banking system;
8. explain what fringe banks are;
9. describe the National Savings Bank;
10. explain how the banking system is changing.

CHAPTER 2: Financial Intermediaries

ESSENTIAL KNOWLEDGE

At the end of your studies you should be able to:-
1. define what a financial intermediary is;
2. compare the features of different financial intermediaries including:-
    a) credit unions;
    b) friendly societies;
    c) building societies;
    d) insurance companies;
    e) pension funds;
    f) unit trusts;
    g) investment trusts;
    h) finance houses;
3. explain the differences between traditional lending and securities;

4. describe different kinds of commonly used securities;
5. assess the importance of the securities industry to banks;
6. describe the markets in which securities are traded;
7. explain how businesses can raise money through the stock market.

CHAPTER 3: Monetary Policy; Control of the Banking System

ESSENTIAL KNOWLEDGE

At the end of your studies you should be able to:-
1. explain why government tries to control the banking system;
2. define monetary policy;
3. identify the main measures of the money supply;
4. describe the policies put forward in the 'Competition and Credit Control' document;
5. compare the purposes and effects of the major tools of monetary policy:-
    a) reserve asset ratios and cash ratios;
    b) special deposits;
    c) influence over interest rates;
    d) directives;
6. explain what eligible banks are;
7. distinguish between nominal interest rates, yields and real interest rates;
8. outline the factors influencing interest rates;
9. explain how changes in interest rates affect banks.

CHAPTER 4: The Money Markets

ESSENTIAL KNOWLEDGE

At the end of your studies you should be able to:-
1. name the main money markets in the United Kingdom;
2. define Certificates of Deposit;
3. explain the concept of negotiability;
4. define Local Authority Bills;

5.   define Bills of Exchange (or commercial bills);

6.   define Treasury Bills;

7.   compare the different forms of 'paper' used in the money markets;

8.   interpret press reports about the money markets.

CHAPTER 5: The Balance Sheet of a Bank
ESSENTIAL KNOWLEDGE

At the end of your studies you should be able to:-

1.   define what a balance sheet is;

2.   explain how and why a bank balance sheet is unusual;

3.   describe the various assets and liabilities which appear in bank balance sheets;

4.   explain why there is a conflict between liquidity and profitability;

5.   analyse bank balance sheets in terms of:-

   a)   total capital : total liabilities %;

   b)   free equity : advances %;

   c)   advances : deposits %;

6.   describe items which appear in a bank's published annual report and accounts.

CHAPTER 6: The Range of Banking Business
ESSENTIAL KNOWLEDGE

At the end of your studies you should be able to:-

1.   explain the needs of depositors;

2.   compare current accounts, deposit accounts and money market deposits;

3.   explain the needs of borrowers;

4.   compare overdrafts, structured loans and loan accounts;

5.   explain how and why deposits and lending services are changing;

6.   explain the role of branch networks in:-

   a)   taking deposits;

   b)   giving loans;

   c)   operating a payments system;

7.   assess how branch networks are changing;

8.   analyse strategies open to banks.

CHAPTER 7: Bank and Customer; The Legal Relationship
ESSENTIAL KNOWLEDGE

At the end of your studies you should be able to:-

1.   define what a contract is;

2.   describe the terms of the contract between bank and customer;

3.   quote relevant case law;

4.   explain the legal problems involved in opening and closing accounts;

5.   explain why banks need to keep customers' affairs secret;

6.   state the circumstances in which information about customers can be given to other people;

7.   describe the procedures for giving bankers' opinions (replies to status enquiries);

8.   summarise the main legal risks which banks face in their normal business;

9.   identify important legislation affecting banks;

10. assess how the banker-customer contract is changing.

CHAPTER 8: Types of Customer
ESSENTIAL KNOWLEDGE

At the end of your studies you should be able to:-

1.   explain what is meant by a personal account;

2.   describe the effects on the bank account of a customer's:-

   a)   death;

   b)   bankruptcy;

   c)   mental incapacity;

3.   explain the terms power of attorney and mandate;

4.   compare sole accounts, joint accounts and accounts for minors;

5.   compare business accounts for sole traders and partnerships;

6.   identify types of business which keep funds in trust for clients;

7.   distinguish between executors, administrators and trustees;

8.   identify types of unincorporated bodies which use bank accounts.

CHAPTER 9: Corporate Customers
ESSENTIAL KNOWLEDGE

At the end of your studies you should be able to:-
1. define what a company is;
2. identify different types of company;
3. distinguish between the Memorandum of Association and the Articles of Association;
4. describe the role of directors of companies;
5. describe procedures for opening, operating and closing company accounts;
6. distinguish between administrators, administrative receivers and liquidators.

CHAPTER 10: Marketing Financial Services
ESSENTIAL KNOWLEDGE

At the end of your studies you should be able to:-
1. define what marketing is;
2. describe the particular problems of marketing financial services;
3. explain the role of the marketing plan and its component parts;
4. distinguish between market research and marketing research;
5. explain the importance of the main elements of the marketing mix:-
    a) product;
    b) price;
    c) place;
    d) promotion;
6. assess the importance of personal selling in banking;
7. define market segmentation and identify different approaches to it;
8. explain the marketing philosophy and assess its effect on banks.

CHAPTER 11: Principles of Lending
ESSENTIAL KNOWLEDGE

At the end of your studies you should be able to:-
1. assess how important lending is to major banks;
2. describe methods used to reduce risk in lending;
3. identify different approaches to lending;

4. explain the importance of the main factors to assess in making lending decisions:-
    a) purpose;
    b) amount;
    c) period;
    d) expertise;
    e) repayments;
    f) security;
5. identify other factors influencing lending decisions;
6. appreciate the need to re-shape some lending propositions.

CHAPTER 12: Personal Lending
ESSENTIAL KNOWLEDGE

At the end of your studies you should be able to:-
1. define what credit scoring is;
2. assess the advantages and disadvantages of credit scoring in different circumstances;
3. explain the basic needs of personal borrowers;
4. describe and assess the advantages and disadvantages of:-
    a) overdrafts;
    b) personal loans;
    c) revolving credit accounts;
    d) budget accounts;
    e) credit cards;
5. distinguish between credit cards and gold cards;
6. identify different kinds of mortgage (house purchase loan) and explain their advantages and disadvantages;
7. describe the main provisions of the Consumer Credit Act 1974 and the impact of the act on banks.

CHAPTER 13: Commercial Lending
ESSENTIAL KNOWLEDGE

At the end of your studies you should be able to:-
1. explain why commercial lending decisions are often more difficult than personal lending decisions;
2. list different reasons for which businesses borrow;
3. define what working capital and trading finance are;
4. identify problems businesses are likely to face when:-
    a) financing fixed assets;
    b) taking over another business;

5.   define what goodwill is;

6.   explain why the 'ultra vires' principle can be a problem for banks;

7.   define what 'hard core' borrowing is;

8.   compare the use by businesses of overdrafts and loans.

CHAPTER 14: Forms of Finance
ESSENTIAL KNOWLEDGE

At the end of your studies you should be able to:-

1.   describe the role of branches and specialist departments in providing finance for customers;

2.   describe and assess the advantages and disadvantages of:-

a)   leasing;

b)   hire purchase;

c)   factoring;

d)   discounting bills of exchange;

e)   acceptance credits;

f)   issuing securities;

g)   venture capital;

3.   identify suitable forms of finance to meet specific customer needs.

CHAPTER 15: Balance Sheets and Company Accounts
ESSENTIAL KNOWLEDGE

At the end of your studies you should be able to:-

1.   appreciate the need to consider what a business does when judging a set of accounts;

2.   appreciate the importance of profitability, liquidity and capital in assessing businesses;

3.   use balance sheet figures to calculate:-

a)   the current ratio;

b)   the acid-test (or liquidity) ratio;

c)   the gearing ratio;

4.   assess the importance of different balance sheet items;

5.   use profit and loss account figures to calculate:-

a)   net profit/sales % (or net profit margin);

b)   gross profit/sales % (or gross profit margin);

c)   retained cash flow;

6.   use balance sheet and profit and loss account figures to calculate return on capital employed;

7.   assess the changes in a business shown in a funds flow statement;

8.   interpret a set of accounts using appropriate ratios;

9.   make lending decisions on the basis of information which includes accounting data.

CHAPTER 16: Security for Lending
ESSENTIAL KNOWLEDGE

At the end of your studies you should be able to:-

1.   assess the advantages and disadvantages of taking security when lending;

2.   state the principles of good security;

3.   distinguish between legal charges and equitable charges;

4.   distinguish between fixed charges and floating charges;

5.   distinguish between direct security and third-party security;

6.   describe and assess the advantages and disadvantages of the main types of security:-

a)   guarantees;

b)   stocks and shares;

c)   life policies;

d)   registered land;

e)   unregistered land;

f)   mortgage debentures;

7.   list other forms of security;

8.   outline the procedures for taking security, releasing security and realising security.

CHAPTER 17: Lending Situations
ESSENTIAL KNOWLEDGE

At the end of your studies you should be able to:-

1.   tackle case studies relating to lending;

2.   describe methods used for controlling lending;

3.   describe methods used for recovering lending;

4.   describe the procedures for forms of lending based on security:-

a)   produce advances;

b)   bridging loans.

CHAPTER 18: The Background to International Banking
ESSENTIAL KNOWLEDGE

At the end of your studies you should be able to:-

1.   describe the development of international banking;

2.   assess the role of London as a financial centre;

3.   appreciate the difficulty of distinguishing between foreign banking services and international banking services;

4.   describe the international debt crisis and assess its effect on United Kingdom banks;

5.   define what securitisation is and explain how it has affected international banking;

7.   assess the strength of the leading United Kingdom banks as competitors in international banking.

CHAPTER 19: Travel Facilities
ESSENTIAL KNOWLEDGE

At the end of your studies you should be able to:-

1.   describe how banks show foreign exchange rates for currency;

2.   calculate sterling equivalents of foreign currency and vice versa;

3.   describe and assess other main travel services provided by banks:-

   a)   travel cheques;
   b)   credit open arrangements;
   c)   travellers' letters of credit;
   d)   eurocheques;
   e)   credit cards;

4.   identify other travel services which banks provide.

CHAPTER 20: Foreign Exchange
ESSENTIAL KNOWLEDGE

At the end of your studies you should be able to:-

1.   list the factors which make foreign trade more risky than domestic trade;

2.   define what is meant by exchange rates;

3.   list factors which affect exchange rates;

4.   distinguish between spot rates and forward rates;

5.   distinguish between discounts and premiums;

6.   distinguish between fixed forward exchange contracts and option forward exchange contracts;

7.   explain other methods of reducing exchange risk including pure (or true) currency options;

8.   explain the relationship between forward exchange rates and interest rates;

9.   explain how and why government tries to influence exchange rates;

10.   describe the scale of foreign exchange business;

11.   interpret press reports on foreign exchange.

CHAPTER 21: Payments Abroad
ESSENTIAL KNOWLEDGE

At the end of your studies you should be able to:-

1.   explain in what sense payments abroad are messages;

2.   distinguish between sterling payment messages and currency payment messages (with reference to 'nostro' and 'vostro' accounts);

3.   explain the differences between mail transfers, urgent transfers and drafts;

4.   describe the role of SWIFT in making payments abroad;

5.   assess the advantages and disadvantages of using bills of exchange in making payments abroad;

6.   describe the banking procedure for handling collections;

7.   list the information normally found in a collection order;

8.   distinguish between clean collections and documentary collections;

9.   describe the main documents used in international trade;

10.   describe the banking procedure for handling documentary letters of credit;

11.   distinguish between documentary collections and documentary credits;

12.   list methods of settlement available to importers and exporters.

CHAPTER 22: Finance of International Trade
ESSENTIAL KNOWLEDGE

At the end of your studies you should be able to:-

1.   define what countertrade is;

2.   assess the advantages and disadvantages of produce advances;

3.   define what credit insurance is;

4.   describe the role of ECGD;

5.   identify different types of bonds and guarantees issued by banks;

6.   distinguish between export factoring and forfaiting;

7.   describe different forms of advice offered by banks to importers and exporters;

8.   identify major competitors of banks in export finance.

CHAPTER 23: International Finance
ESSENTIAL KNOWLEDGE

At the end of your studies you should be able to:-

1.   describe the kinds of customers who use international banking services;

2.   identify examples of:-

a)   major international currencies;

b)   composite currencies;

c)   eurocurrencies;

3.   distinguish between the short-term and long-term investment and borrowing facilities offered to international customers;

4.   define what eurobonds are;

5.   identify situations in which the trend towards securitisation has not removed the need for bank lending;

6.   identify different forms of exchange risk;

7.   explain the role of LIFFE;

8.   identify methods of hedging against exchange risk and interest-rate risk.

CHAPTER 24: General Banking Services
ESSENTIAL KNOWLEDGE

At the end of your studies you should be able to:-

1.   describe the services offered to all types of account-holders;

2.   distinguish between CHAPS, SWIFT and EFTPOS;

3.   describe the features of cheques;

4.   describe other bank services including:-

a)   safe custody;

b)   share dealing;

c)   unit trust dealing, management and trusteeship;

d)   trustee work;

e)   executorship.

CHAPTER 25: Personal Banking Services
ESSENTIAL KNOWLEDGE

At the end of your studies you should be able to:-

1.   describe advice services offered to personal customers including:-

a)   taxation advice;

b)   insurance advice;

c)   pensions advice;

d)   investment advice;

2.   describe the services offered to customers in connection with:-

a)   insurance and pensions;

b)   investment;

3.   explain how and why banks issue indemnities for lost share certificates;

4.   assess how personal banking services are changing because of:-

a)   Automated Teller Machines;

b)   debit cards;

c)   home banking;

5.   explain how growing interest in consumer affairs has affected banks;

6.   describe the role of the banking ombudsman.

CHAPTER 26: Banking Services for Business
ESSENTIAL KNOWLEDGE

At the end of your studies you should be able to:-

1.   describe banking services for business including:-

a)   business advisory services;

b)   account-holding services;

c)   advice about finance;

d)   registrar work;

e)   data processing services;

f)   cash management services;

g)   guarantees and bonds;

h)   insurance services;

i)   credit services;

2.   list additional services offered by merchant banks.

CHAPTER 27: Interviews
ESSENTIAL KNOWLEDGE

At the end of your studies you should be able to:-

1.   assess the importance of interviews in banking;

2.   distinguish between formal and informal interviews;

3.   list different types of personnel interview;

4.   list different types of customer interview;

5.   explain the need to prepare for interviews;

6.   identify important constraints on interviews;

7. describe the communication skills used in interviews;

8. define what is meant by non-verbal communication (body language);

9. describe methods of resolving conflict in interviews;

10. describe techniques used for achieving objectives in interviews.

Sample Examination Papers

BANKING OPERATIONS 1: Examination Paper November 1987
(reproduced by kind permission of the Chartered Institute of Bankers)

The Chartered Institute of Bankers

STAGE 1

BANKING CERTIFICATE EXAMINATION–
FINAL SECTION

BANKING OPERATIONS I–
INTERNATIONAL AND LENDING

5 November, 1987

N.B.
1. Read the instructions on the cover of the answer book.
2. **Answer FIVE questions: TWO from Section A, THREE from Section B.**
3. CANDIDATES MUST SATISFY THE EXAMINER IN BOTH SECTIONS OF THE PAPER.
4. The number in brackets after each question indicates the marks allotted. Where questions are subdivided, the figure shown after each subdivision indicates the number of marks allotted to that part of the question.
   In awarding marks the examiner will look for answers which show (*a*) an appreciation of the significance of the question and (*b*) a reasoned practical approach to the problem.
5. Tabulated answers (i.e. statements in listed note form) are acceptable.
6. Silent electronic calculators may be used in this examination. Whether or not candidates use them, it is in their interest to show the basic figures from which their calculations are made.
7. Time allowed: three hours.

8. 15 minutes' reading time is allowed at the beginning of the examination when candidates may write on this paper but NOT in the answer book.

SECTION A

Answer TWO questions only from this section; 20 marks per question

1.—Both 1(a) and 1(b) must be answered.

(a) All parts ((i) to (x)) must be attempted; Write the number of each part ((i), (ix) etc.) and ONE of A, B or C in your answerbook.

(i) One month forward, a foreign currency is at a premium over sterling. Does this mean that a UK exporter will receive:

A More sterling for his foreign currency receipts in one month's time than exchanged at the spot rate now.

B Less sterling for his foreign currency receipts in one month's time than exchanged at the spot rate now.

C The same either way?

(ii) What is a Eurocurrency:

A A deposit in a European currency held in the country of issue.

B A deposit in any major market currency held outside the country which issued the currency.

C A deposit in any major market currency held in the country which issued the currency?

(iii) At which rate does a bank usually sell to its customer a specified amount of one currency in exchange for another currency:

A Lower than that at which it will buy.

B Higher than that at which it will buy.

C Average of day's range from financial press.

(iv) In order to carry out International transactions, a bank must maintain accounts with other banks overseas. If a UK bank maintains its Spanish pesetas with banks in Spain, are they called:

A Vostro account.

B Votre account.

C Nostro account?

  (v) A forward option exchange contract must be performed:

A Between two specified dates.

B Anytime at the customer's option.

C The customer has the option not to perform the contract.

 (vi) Which of the under-mentioned risks is **not** covered by ECGD insurance?

A Blocking of payment in buyer's country.

B Damage to or destruction of goods.

C Insolvency or default of payment by buyer.

(vii) Contract guarantees may be required by overseas buyers in case of default by the exporter. Who gives the undertaking to pay on demand?

A The bank to the buyer.

B The exporter to the buyer.

C The bank to the exporter.

(viii) What do INCOTERMS define?

A International companies terms of trade.

B The duties/responsibilities of the sellers/buyers to each other and also at what stage in the movement of goods the risk of handling, transportation and insurance passes from seller to buyer.

C The regulations covering banking accounts (both lending and borrowing of international currencies) in the Eurocurrency market.

 (ix) The foreign exchange market is conducted:

A In Lombard Street.

B In the Stock Exchange.

C Over the telephone?

  (x) Negotiable instruments include:

A Bills of lading.

B Movement certificates.

C Certificates of deposit.

(10)

(*b*) Your customers, Classic Shoes Limited, have the opportunity to export for the first time. Explain to the Directors the major advantages and disadvantages of Forward Contracts. (10)

(Total marks for this question – 20)

2.—A customer of your bank, Mr Stavros Costas, runs a small business in the High Street, Dainty Linens Ltd. Mr Costas has a cousin in Cyprus who exports hand-made lace, and has offered to trade with your customer on open account. Mr Costas has never imported previously and seeks your advice.

(*a*) Name three ways in which your customer can settle with his cousin in Cyprus on open account. What are the benefits and drawbacks of each method to Mr Stavros Costas and his cousin? (15)

(*b*) Assuming that the goods are purchased FOB, what primary documents must accompany the customs entry form before your customer can take delivery? (5)

3.—You receive the following letter from your customer, Miss Imelda Dumpling:

Dear Sir,

As you may know, I am a teacher at the local girls' Secondary School. When term ends in July, I have the opportunity of spending four weeks' holiday with a former pupil and her husband in Spain.

I estimate that I shall need approximately £1,000 for living expenses and spending money.

Will you please advise me of the most economical and safe way of taking money with me for this purpose.

Yours faithfully

I. DUMPLING (Miss)

Required:

Prepare brief notes outlining the alternative services you would recommend to this customer and the benefits and drawbacks of each.

(20)

SECTION B

*Answer THREE questions only
from this section;
20 marks per question*

4.—You receive a telephone call from your customer, Paul Jones, asking whether you will advance him the 10% deposit towards the purchase of a new home costing £52,000. A mortgage of £30,000 has been arranged. On further inquiry you learn that he has received an offer for his present home of £37,500, and there is an outstanding mortgage of £11,000.

(*a*) What are the advantages and disadvantages to Mr Jones of entering into a bridging loan for the new house purchase? (5)

(*b*) How should the bank safeguard its position? (7)

(*c*) Assuming that you agree to lend to Mr Jones, what are the options concerning the amount to be advanced? (8)
(Total marks for question–20)

5.—Your Manager has asked you to review personal account unauthorised overdrafts at the branch and tell him of any adverse trends. What sort of evidence will you be looking for? If the situation appears serious on a particular account, what recommendations will you make to the Manager? (20)

6.—*You must answer 6(a), 6(b) and 6(c).*

(*a*) All parts ((i) to (v)) must be attempted. Write the number of each part ((i), (iv) etc.) and ONE of A, B or C in your answerbook.

(i) When lending for the purchase of fixed assets, a bank must ensure that:

A Sufficient profits will be made to generate the cash to repay the advance within the life of the asset purchased.

B All taxes have been paid on the purchase.

C The cost of purchase is shown in the balance sheet as a current asset for that year.

(ii) Your customer, Mr Winder, owns the family home which he occupies with his wife and his 17 year old student daughter.

Which one of them is presumed to have an equitable interest:

A Mr Winder.

B Mrs Winder.

C The daughter?

(iii) A finance house is likely to provide finance to individuals for:

A House purchase.

B Hire purchase of a consumer durable.

C Purchase of shares for privatised industry?

(iv) A creditor holding the following security does not have the power of sale:

A A lien.

B A pledge.

C A mortgage.

(v) What is credit scoring:

A The application of a points system to identify high credit balance customers.

B A device which measures the statistical probability that credit will be repaid.

C The calculation of average percentage borrowings on credit cards in relation to limits marked? (5)

(*b*) Roland Smith and Ron Elliott maintain separate, private accounts with your branch. Today, they have called to see you and you have agreed an unsecured loan of £17,500 in their joint names.
What are the technical considerations to protect the bank's position? (5)

(*c*) Your Manager has invited you to sit in on an interview with your customer, Joe Bloggs, who has requested a loan towards the refurbishment of his kitchen. What are the three criteria of the perfect banking advance? Describe how you would examine the loan request to ensure that it met these criteria. (10)
(Total marks for question–20)

7.(*a*)—Your customers, Fields Limited, have been experiencing trading difficulties recently. For four years, the bank has held a debenture which gives a first fixed charge on fixed assets and debtors, and a floating charge on the remainder.

Using the following figures produced by your customer, calculate what the bank would receive should a receiver be appointed.

Liabilities		Assets	
Bank	15,500	Leasehold premises	5,000
Corporation tax	1,000	Fixed machinery	1,600
Creditors	10,200	Vehicles	4,100
(Inc. £2,000 with		Fixtures and fittings	500
reservation of title)			
Directors' loans	1,800	Stock	5,000
PAYE & NI	3,100	Debtors	4,500
	31,600		20,700

NOTE: (i) Assume that the assets realise the values shown in the statement.

(ii) You are not required to apply any value judgements to the figures.

(iii) *Ignore the provisions of the Insolvency Act 1986.*

(18)

(b) What other problems can arise with Debentures? (2)

(Total marks for question—20)

BANKING OPERATIONS 2: Examination Paper November 1987
(reproduced by kind permission of the Chartered Institute of Bankers)

The Chartered Institute of Bankers

STAGE 1

BANKING CERTIFICATE EXAMINATION– FINAL SECTION

BANKING OPERATIONS II–

9 November, 1987

N.B. 1. Read the instructions on the cover of the answer book.

2. At the end of this examination, do **not** fill in column 1 on the cover of the answer book, but leave it blank.

3. This examination paper has **FOUR** Sections. Candidates should attempt all four sections.
Section A: Answer **ALL** parts of question 1 in this section (**one** mark per part)
Section B: Answer **ALL** parts of question 2 in this section (**25** marks in all)
Section C: Answer **TWO** questions only (**15** marks per question)
Section D: Answer **ONE** question only. Your answer should be in essay form. (**25** marks).

4. In **Sections A and B** a fresh page should **not** be used for the answer to each part of the question. **In Sections C and D** you should begin each answer on a fresh page.

5. In Sections B and C, tabulated answers (i.e. statements in listed note form) are acceptable, unless the question specifies a different format.

6. Time allowed: three hours.

7. 15 minutes' reading time is allowed at the beginning of the examination when candidates may write on this paper but NOT in the answer book.

SECTION A

Answer ALL parts of this question. Write the number of each part ((i), (ix) etc.) and ONE of A, B, C or D in your answerbook. Do not use a fresh page for each part of the question.

1. *(i)* The Deposit Rate of interest offered by clearing banks is usually:

A The same as Base Rate.

B The same as LIBOR.

C About two per cent above Base Rate.

D About two per cent below Base Rate.

(ii) In connection with life assurance policies, the principal advantage of an endowment policy over a whole life policy is:

A The premiums are lower.

B Tax relief is available on premiums.

C The assured does not have to die before benefit is paid.

D Benefits are payable to a third party.

(iii) The term 'special deposits' in a bank's balance sheet refers to:

A Deposits from important customers.

B Money which the Bank of England has required to be placed with itself.

C Deposits for which the bank issues a certificate.

D Deposits which the bank has made with other banks.

(iv) The main source from which a discount house borrows is:

A Private individuals.

B Other commercial banks.

C The Bank of England.

D The Government.

(v) Investors in Industry Group Plc is owned by:

A Merchant banks.

B Clearing banks and the Bank of England.

307

C A consortium of industrial companies.

D The Stock Exchange.

(vi) If goods have been purchased by means of a credit card and prove faulty, a customer can claim reimbursement from the credit card company:

A In no circumstances.

B When the cash price would have been more than £100 and less than £30,000.

C When the retailer refuses compensation.

D When the cash price would have been less than £10,000.

(vii) A husband and wife operate a joint current account with a mandate for either to sign. If the wife advises the bank of a marital dispute, who may withdraw money from the account?

A The wife only.

B The husband only.

C Both husband and wife signing jointly.

D Neither party until the dispute is resolved?

(viii) When using a Eurocheque card and cheque to obtain cash in a bank the cheque should be made out in:

A Sterling.

B The currency of the country where it is being cashed.

C The currency of the country where the bank account is maintained.

D U.S. Dollars.

(ix) The expression 'return on equity' for a clearing bank refers to:

A A measure of the level of dividends paid.

B The profits of the bank's equity investment subsidiary.

C The profits of the bank as a percentage of its capital base.

D The level of interest charged to customers.

(x) Following the Bank of England paper 'Monetary Control–Provisions' in 1981, the clearing banks had to hold a certain percentage of their eligible liabilities in interest-free non-operational accounts at the Bank of England. Was this percentage between 1981 and 1987:

A ½%.

B 1½%.

C 2½%.

D 3%?

(xi) Bankers' Automated Clearing Services Ltd. is principally concerned with:

A Clearing cheques under agency arrangements.

B Processing giro credits and direct debits.

C Special presentations.

D The settlement of the town clearing.

(xii) The Clearing House Automated Payments System is limited to payments of a certain value. Are these:

A of £10,000 and over.

B of £100,000 and over.

C of less than £1,000,000.

D of over £1,000,000?

(xiii) For which of the following reasons may a cheque for £50 in conjunction with a cheque card be returned unpaid:

A It is post-dated.

B Is is not signed by the customer.

C There are insufficient funds on the account.

D Payment has been countermanded by the customer.

(xiv) The term 'eligible bank' means:

A The bank is eligible to take deposits from the public.

B The bank's acceptance on a bill of exchange makes it suitable security for borrowing from the Bank of England.

C The bank is eligible to deal on the inter-bank market.

D The bank is eligible to lend to sovereign states.

(xv) The Banking Ombudsman is empowered to make awards to aggrieved customers of the banks:

A With no upper limit.

B Up to £5,000.

C Up to £50,000.

D Up to £100,000.

(xvi) Which of the following would probably form the largest asset in a clearing bank's balance sheet:

A Cash and short-term funds.

B Advances to customers.

C Current, deposit and other accounts.

D Premises and equipment?

(xvii) A quoted company may make a 'rights issue' in order to:

A Avoid paying a dividend.

B Raise additional capital.

C Give shareholders a higher dividend.

D Increase the price of its shares on the Stock Market.

(xviii) The maximum monthly payment to a Save As You Earn scheme is:

A £10.

B £20.

C £50.

D £100.

(xix) The minimum capital required for public limited company status is:

A £2.

B £10,000.

C £50,000.

D £100,000.

(xx) Which of the following is to be found in the Memorandum of Association of a limited company:

A The objects of the company.

B The duties of the directors.

C The borrowing powers of the directors.

D Details of the issue of shares?

(Total marks for this question – 20)

SECTION B

2.—*Read the following extract from the Financial Times and answer all the parts of the question at the end of the passage.*

BANKS COUNT THE COST OF CAPITAL

The fallacy that equity capital is a cheap form of funding has long since been exploded. The calculation of the true cost of equity is an exercise perhaps best left to mathematicians, who can squabble over their methods. And to many companies it does not much matter what the exact figure might be. But to the banks the question is crucial because their balance sheets, and hence a large part of their businesses, are skyscrapers of loans constructed on the foundation of equity.

There has been a growing recognition by the clearers, prompted by the Bank of England's increasing emphasis on primary capital in the measurement of banks' strength, that the return on equity capital is a key ratio. All four made clear with their preliminary results that a prime objective was to sustain or improve that return. Gone, apparently, are the days when merely building up the balance sheet was every banker's aim. And no wonder that "other operating income" has become a more important line in the revenue account.

Lloyds Bank has led the way by publishing an estimate that its cost of equity capital is 17 per cent. This figure, supplied to Lloyds by the London Business School, is based on the yield required by the market for a notionally risk-free investment, gilt-edged stock, plus a risk premium calculated by reference to market and share price volatility. This might not be a fashionable method during a raging bull market, when reminders of the risks inherent in investment are unwelcome, and it happens to produce a figure conveniently below Lloyds' after tax return on equity of 18.5 per cent. Nor does it bear much relation to the immediate payout on the shares. But in the sense that it represents the return demanded by investors before they will put their capital in Lloyds' rather than anyone else's hands, it provides Lloyds' management with a valuable financial discipline.

Earning a return greater than that cost of equity could prove tougher as the banks increase their capital bases while the new capital adequacy rules are phased in. New capital cannot in practice be put to full use straight away. National Westminster's rights issue last spring

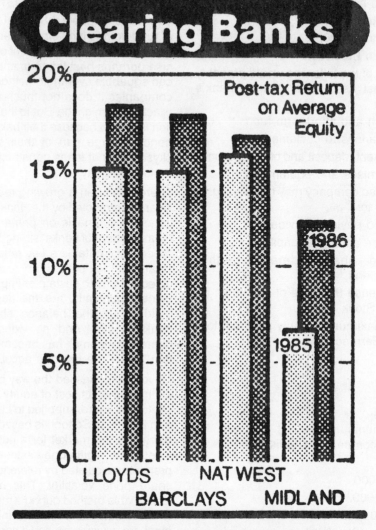

Clearing Banks

Post-tax Return
on Average
Equity

1986

1985

LLOYDS   NAT WEST
BARCLAYS   MIDLAND

(from the Lex Column, *Financial Times*, 9 March 1987)

surely restrained the rise in its after-tax return and Midland must be acutely conscious of the effect.

It is thus particularly annoying for the banks that the perpetual floating rate note market has chosen this period to perish. It became even more clear as prices of these instruments tumbled, that they had provided an exceptionally cheap form of primary capital. Indeed, in so far as perpetuals could only be counted as primary capital because they were akin to equity, even though they masqueraded as debt, their yields were so far below Lloyds' theoretical 17 per cent

that the investors who bought them cannot be as sophisticated as supposed. It may be that some new instrument can be devised to take their place in the primary capital hierarchy, but whatever it is will be more apparently equity and therefore more expensive.

At the same time the uncertainty created by Brazil's decision to stop paying interest to banks on all but short term loans poses a threat to banks' capital bases. With Brazil's debt quoted at 68 per cent of face value and Mexico's at 58 per cent in the secondary market, the banks are arguably underprovisioned on their loans to rescheduling countries. In the very unlikely event that the worst comes to the worst, the banks' primary capital would start to be chipped away. And if the foundations shrink, the upper storeys have to reduce at up to 20 times the rate.

(i) Why should there be 'no wonder' that 'other operating income' has become more important to the clearing banks? (5)

(ii) Why is gilt-edged stock regarded as a notionally risk-free investment? (5)

(iii) Why might 'share price volatility' not be particularly relevant to the calculation of a 'risk premium' in a 'raging bull market'? (5)

(iv) Why does return on equity measurement of performance provide Lloyds' management with a valuable financial discipline? (5)

(v) Why is earning a return greater than the cost of equity tougher as banks increase their capital base? (5)

(Total marks for question – 25)

SECTION C

Answer TWO questions only from this section

3.—Your manager tells you that a personal customer is calling to query the amount of his bank charges. In a paragraph, outline the items of information which you think your manager would need to know to help him in his preparation for this interview. (15)

4.—Your branch has decided to use the granting of house mortgages as the prime target for increasing the cross-selling of bank products and services. Prepare brief notes for a meeting, identifying a maximum of five products/services which could be promoted and your reasons for linking each with house purchase. (15)

5.—A Mr Smith has written to the branch asking advice on the investment of an unspecified amount of money. His account has only been open a short while and, whilst satisfactory, gives no clue as to his needs. Draft a brief letter to Mr Smith, offering to meet him, in which you outline the basic information you will need to consider in order to assess his needs (15)

SECTION D

Answer ONE question only from this section.

Your answer should be in essay form.

6.—Outline the principal characteristics of the various methods which a business may use to pay wages direct to its employees' bank accounts. Indicate the factors which would determine which method would be most suitable, giving examples. (25)

7.—There comes a time during a sales presentation or contract negotiation meeting when sufficient information is available for a decision to be made.

Describe the principle 'closes' which are available to a sales representative or a negotiator in that position. Discuss the acceptability of these techniques in banker/customer negotiations. (25)

8.—For many years, banks have taken references on individuals opening accounts. Discuss the reasons for this practice; explain why some banks have discontinued it; and describe the systems they have introduced to replace it. (25)

Commentary on Sample Papers

BANKING OPERATIONS 1:
Commentary on November 1987 paper

This paper, like the sample Banking Operations 1 paper in Section 1 of the text, is divided into two sections, international banking and lending, with greater weight given to lending because candidates have to tackle two (out of three) questions on international banking and three (out of four) on lending.

Q1. Multiple choice and forward contracts

The emphasis on multiple choice questions is lower than in the May 1987 paper because the ten multiple choice questions are only allocated one mark each. Most students should earn high marks here if they have studied thoroughly, though as with most multiple choice questions some of the wrong answers may seem quite plausible. Part b) of the question asks about the advantages and disadvantages of forward contracts, and requires a straightforward answer, ideally a list of numbered points.

Q2. Part a) of this question deals with the three basic methods of settlement, urgent transfer, mail transfer and draft, which should be familiar to every student. For each method a full answer would cover advantages and disadvantages for both importer and exporter.

Part b) asks about the documents used, and assumes a knowledge of the exact meaning of Free on Board.

Q3. This question is a straightforward assessment of the travel facilities suitable for a holiday in Spain, and a full response should cover the advantages and disadvantages of cash, travel cheques and Eurocheques. For twenty marks there seems rather less to say here than to earn fifteen marks for the first part of the previous question.

Q4. This is quite a complicated question on bridging finance for a customer who is moving house, but the question is helpfully divided up into three parts to guide the candidate through the material to be covered. In this question a calculator might prove useful though the figures are not complicated. The customer's present mortgage of £11,000 could be paid off in full to enable the new mortgage to be taken out, or the bank could lend £5,200 now and a further £46,800 to make up the full purchase price with repayment coming from the £30,000 mortgage

and the net sale proceeds of £26,500 (leaving £4,500 for all the associated expenses).

Q5. This is a much more difficult question for most students because it is open-ended. The key concept here is control, but to earn the twenty marks available by discussing different aspects of control over personal overdrafts requires a high level of knowledge.

Q6. Like question 1 this question includes an element of multiple choice but only for five marks. Part b) of the question asks about a loan in joint names. As in the May 1987 paper the examiner has used the term 'technical considerations' here. Comment is therefore needed on the concept of joint and several liability, perhaps with reference to the Civil Liability (Contribution) Act and certainly with reference to the wording of bank mandates and loan application forms. It might also be appropriate to point out that in view of the amount the borrowing is not a regulated agreement under the Consumer Credit Act. No consideration should be given to security because this is specifically excluded by the wording of the question.

Q7. This question deals with the technicalities of realising debenture security, and includes such issues as reservation of title and preferential claims which seem to require a higher level of knowledge than any of the other questions in the paper.

Part b) of the question asks about other problems, implying that the figures show the bank to be undersecured (£14,600 of assets to cover £15,500 owed) but the points to make about this second part of the question also seem to require a very high level of knowledge, for example about the rules on a 'hardening period'. The examiner may, however, have been prepared to award marks for more mundane points like the need for registration and the possible concern about bad publicity.

BANKING OPERATIONS 2:
Commentary on November 1987 paper

This paper is very close in format to the Banking Operations 2 paper in Section 1 of the text. It is divided into four sections, Section A carrying 20 marks, Section B 25 marks, Section C 30 marks and Section D 25 marks.

Section A. Multiple choice

This section consists of twenty multiple choice questions covering a wide range of areas of the syllabus, many of them fairly specifically factual rather than testing basic concepts.

Section B. Comprehension

This section is based on a passage from the Financial Times, but answers do need to show background knowledge about the banking environment and the stock market as well as understanding of the text. The five parts to Question 2 are compulsory so gaps in candidates' knowledge are likely to be exposed.

Section C. Short case studies

In this section there is a choice of two questions out of three.

Q3. This question deals with bank charges and the information a manager would need to deal with a customer querying charges. A good answer to the question might make reference to the importance of preparing for interviews and the techniques for dealing with complaints as well as outlining the methods banks use for calculating charges for personal customers.

Q4. This question looks at the cross-selling of services related to house mortgages. Candidates are asked to suggest five services which would be appropriate, which means that 3 marks are allocated to each so the amount of detail required is not very great. To earn good marks candidates would need to explain why each service is connected with buying a house.

Q5. This is a fairly straightforward question about information needed from a customer before beginning to give any investment advice.

Section D. Essay

This section gives candidates a choice of one essay out of three, each of which is for 25 marks, a quarter of the paper.

Q6. This is quite a tough question about different approaches to paying wages direct to employees' bank accounts. The question asks for examples, which implies that a good answer would discuss different kinds of business, or perhaps more appropriately different sizes of business, to explain why their needs would be different, and to identify different ways in which banks can be of help.

Q7. This question deals with a fairly specialised aspect of interviewing, the 'close' of a sales interview. There is some scope for introducing material about the marketing of financial services and the concept of the trust which customers put in banks as experts in financial matters, but essentially the focus of the essay is fairly narrow.

Q8. This is the most straightforward of the three essays because it can be broken down easily into a structure, dealing first with the legal background to taking references and the protection of the Cheques Act, then with the disadvantages of this procedure, particularly the cost, and finally with current practice.

Mock Examination Papers

You should attempt these papers under simulated examination conditions, working without books and notes and keeping strictly to the time limit. Mark your answers by referring *afterwards* to the suggested answers. Do not mislead youself by marking too generously. ONLY GIVE MARKS IF YOU HAVE EARNED THEM.

Answers are provided in Section 4.

MOCK EXAMINATION: BANKING OPERATIONS 1

ATTEMPT BOTH SECTIONS OF THE PAPER

Time Allowed: 3 hours

15 minutes reading time is allowed.

Section A

Answer TWO questions from this section.

1. Write down the question number and the option (a,b,c or d) that you think is correct.

i. A payment in French francs from the United Kingdom to France can be made by arranging for a French bank to:-
a) debit the nostro account of a United Kingdom bank;
b) credit the nostro account of a United Kingdom bank;
c) debit the nostro account and credit the vostro account of a United Kingdom bank;
d) credit the nostro account and debit the vostro account of a United Kingdom bank.

ii. Which of these is not a guarantee?
a) a bid bond;
b) a performance bond;
c) an advance payments guarantee;
d) an ECGD guarantee.

iii. Countertrade means paying for:-
a) exports by a counterdelivery of goods;
b) exports through the over-the-counter market;
c) imports by borrowing from a countertrade bank;
d) imports through the over-the-counter market.

iv. A documentary letter of credit provides a payment guaranteed by:-
a) the advising bank;
b) ECGD;
c) the issuing bank;
d) the correspondent bank.

v. One of the factors making London a leading financial centre is that it has the world's largest:-
a) turnover in stocks and shares;
b) number of Japanese banks in one city;
c) deposits of Eurosterling;
d) market in foreign exchange.

vi. In the United Kingdom financial futures can be traded through:-
a) LME;
b) LIFFE;
c) LMFFE;
d) LFFME.

vii. The safest way of taking money abroad is:-
a) a traveller's letter of credit;
b) traveller's cheques;
c) eurocheques;
d) cash.

viii.The principal in a documentary collection:-
a) receives the documents from the advising bank;
b) has to pay the accepted bill of exchange;
c) gives his bank instructions about the collection order;
d) is usually an importer.

ix. Which of the following statements is true?
a) Forfaiting is an alternative name for export factoring;
b) Forfaiting is appropriate for longer-term deals than factoring;
c) Forfaiting is appropriate for shorter-term deals than factoring;
d) Forfaiting is appropriate for smaller-value transactions than factoring.

x. ECGD stands for:-
a) Exchange Credit Guarantee Department;
b) Exchange Credits and Guarantees Division;
c) Export Credits and Guarantees Department;
d) Export Credits Guarantee Department.

(20)

2. a. Define the following terms:-
i) Premium;
ii) Discount;
iii) Bid Bond;

314

iv) Performance Bond;
v) Retention Monies Bond.

(10)

b. What are the main advantages and disadvantages of taking Eurocheques rather than travel cheques when going on holiday abroad?

(10)

3. Your good customer, Propelrite Ltd, has entered into a contract to buy supplies from abroad for the first time. The German exporter has asked for payment to be by documentary letter of credit using a bill of exchange at thirty days sight.

Write brief notes on the explanation you would give to your customer about:-

a. the nature of a documentary credit;

(12)

b. the purpose of using a bill of exchange at thirty days sight.

(8)

Section B

Answer THREE questions from this section.

4. a. Your manager, Mrs Whitwell, has been asked by Barfield Toys Ltd to provide a loan of £30,000 towards the purchase of a grocery shop in the town centre. Mrs Whitwell comments to you that she is concerned that the borrowing may be 'ultra vires'. What does this mean and how can you find out if Mrs Whitwell is right?

(6)

b. Your customers, Brown & Co, a firm of accountants, offer you a choice of security for a loan of £8,000 which your manager has authorised. They have put forward three proposals:-

i) a charge over a portfolio of shares owned by the firm in six major quoted companies (value £10,000);

ii) a charge over a life policy taken out by Mr Brown, the senior partner, on his own life (surrender value £7,000);

iii) a guarantee to be given by Mr Brown to cover all the debts of the partnership.

Which of these options would you prefer, and why?

(14)

5. a. What are the advantages and disadvantages for customers of revolving credit accounts?

(5)

b. What is a regulated agreement under the Consumer Credit Act?

(5)

c. What are the main differences between repayment mortgages and endowment mortgages?

(5)

d. What is goodwill and what does the term mean when you see it as an item in the balance sheet of a business?

(5)

6. Your customer, Speedwell Ltd, has produced the balance sheet and profit and loss account figures, (see overleaf), and now requests a loan of £3,000 for new machinery, to be repaid over three years.

From your branch records you are aware that similar profit figures were recorded last year and the business has grown steadily.

Assuming that you are satisfied about the purpose of the loan what can you learn:-

a. from the balance sheet to help you to decide whether to lend?

(15)

b. from the profit and loss account to help you to judge whether the business can afford to repay.

(5)

7. Write down the question number and the option (a,b,c or d) that you think is correct.

i. Which would you expect to have the lowest interest rate?

a) bank base rate;
b) bank deposit rate;
c) LIBOR;
d) mortgage rate.

ii. In a balance sheet of a manufacturing company a stock of finished goods appears as:-

a) a fixed asset;
b) a current asset;
c) working capital;
d) work-in-progress.

iii. Land is a good form of security because it is:-

a) easy and cheap to charge;
b) quick and easy to realise;
c) divided into two categories, registered and unregistered;
d) likely to maintain or increase its value.

iv. An acceptance credit is:-

a) a form of lending based on bills of exchange;
b) a kind of insurance policy issued by ECGD;
c) a method of making payments abroad;
d) a form of factoring suited to large companies.

Balance Sheet of Speedwell Ltd as at the end of last month

Fixed Assets	At Cost	Depreciation to date	Net
	£	£	£
Freehold Property	30000	0	30000
Machinery	4500	1500	3000
Fixtures and Fittings	4000	600	3400
	38500	2100	36400

Current Assets			
Stock/Work in Progress	1220		
Finished Goods	2315	3535	
Debtors		4110	
Bank		2000	
Cash		1025	10670
			47070

financed by:-

Capital		
Ordinary Shares	25000	
Reserves	8000	
Retained Profits	345	33345

Long-term liabilities		
Mortgage		4500

Current liabilities		
Creditors	4325	
Divident due	2500	
Tax due	1485	
Accruals	915	9225
		47070

Figures from the Profit and loss account for the past year

Sales	37850
Gross Profit	9665
Net Profit	4876
after charging depreciation	750

v.   Overtrading means:-
a)   selling goods which the vendor does not own;
b)   turning over stock faster than other comparable businesses;
c)   borrowing too much for the amount of security provided;
d)   increasing turnover beyond the level the business can finance.

vi. Venture capital is a form of finance provided:-
a) to businesses wanting to explore new markets;
b)   as loans to small businesses by investment trusts;
c)   in the form of share capital instead of a loan;
d)   through the Bank of England in order to obtain tax relief.

vii. Which of the following is normally at a fixed rate of interest?

a) an overdraft;

b) a revolving credit account;

c) a personal loan;

d) a house purchase loan.

viii. The gearing of a company is:-

a) the relationship between loan capital and shareholders' funds;

b) the relationship between current assets and fixed assets;

c) the level of investment in plant, machinery and other equipment;

d) the level of investment in other companies through shareholdings.

ix. A bridging loan is a form of finance which is:-

a) provided for the construction industry;

b) intended to provide long-term finance;

c) expected to be self-liquidating;

d) covered by the issue of a bank guarantee.

x. The basic difference between a guarantee and an indemnity is that:-

a) a guarantee covers debts by minors;

b) an indemnity covers debts which are not legally enforceable;

c) an indemnity must be in writing and signed;

d) companies are not legally permitted to give indemnities.

MOCK EXAMINATION: BANKING OPERATIONS 2

ATTEMPT ALL SECTIONS OF THE PAPER

Time Allowed: 3 hours

15 minutes reading time is allowed.

Section A

Answer ALL questions. Each question carries ONE mark. Write down the question number and the option (a,b,c or d) that you think is correct.

1.   The articles of association lay down:-

a.   what a company can do;

b.   how the company raises finance;

c.   what the directors can do;

d.   how the directors operate the bank account.

2.   The ACORN approach to market segmentation is based on:-

a.   the age range a customer comes into;

b.   the kind of lifestyle of the customer;

c.   the type of housing the customer lives in;

d.   the financial services a customer uses.

3.   Qualitative directives were used by the Bank of England to:-

a.   take money out of the banking system;

b.   increase interest rates;

c.   encourage banks to hold more cash;

d.   promote lending to particular sectors of the economy.

4.   A cheque drawn on the Birmingham branch of Lloyds Bank and paid in at the Chester branch of Barclays Bank passes through:-

a.   the clearing department of Lloyds Bank;

b.   the clearing department of the Bank of England;

c.   the Clearing House Automated Payments System;

d.   the Bankers' Automated Clearing.

5.   A produce advance is a type of loan intended to help:-

a.   exporters to sell their produce abroad;

b.   exporters to exchange their goods for foreign produce;

c.   importers to buy produce in bulk;

d.   importers to buy securities.

6.   A bid bond is issued by a bank when a customer:-

a.   has lost a share certificate;

b.   is tendering for a major contract;

c.   is trying to get advance payment on a major contract;

d.   has had a car impounded by a foreign court.

7.   Items deposited with banks for safe custody are:-

a.   uninsured unless the customer takes out insurance;

b.   insured by the bank taking the item;

c.   covered by the deposit protection scheme;

d.   covered by the Bank of England's insurance.

8.   Which one of the following could count as a regulated agreement under the Consumer Credit Act 1974?

a.   lending an amount over £15,000;

b. lending by way of overdraft;

c. lending for export finance;

d. lending to a limited company.

9. When using leasing as a form of finance for new equipment, customers:-

a. become owners of the equipment as soon as all the payments are made;

b. have to pay a deposit, usually of about 25% of the cost;

c. claim back V.A.T. as soon as the equipment is delivered;

d. have the option to continue payments at a lower level after a primary period.

10. The rules which prevent banks from selling their own products while also acting as independent financial advisers are based on:-

a. the Data Protection Act;

b. the Companies Act;

c. the Consumer Credit Act;

d. the Financial Services Act.

11. In a bank's consolidated balance sheet the largest asset will normally be:-

a. advances;

b. deposits;

c. investments;

d. premises and equipment.

12. A discount house is a kind of bank which:-

a. offers loans at a discount to other banks;

b. competes in the house-purchase loan market;

c. deals in bills of exchange and Treasury bills;

d. acts as lender of last resort.

13. Which of these items is *not* a form of 'paper' traded in the money markets?

a. certificate of deposit;

b. commercial bill;

c. treasury bill;

d. treasury stock.

14. Which of the following should be treated as a trust account?

a. solicitor's office account;

b. insurance broker's broking account;

c. accountant's partnership account;

d. doctor's private account.

15. A unit trust is a form of investment for which:-

a. fund managers sell units to investors;

b. unit prices are quoted on the stock exchange;

c. the value of units is linked to inflation;

d. unit holders are exempt from all tax.

16. A bank is required to provide statements of account to every party to a joint acount unless they agree to share one statement. This is a requirement of:-

a. the Bills of Exchange Act;

b. the Cheques Act;

c. the Consumer Credit Act;

d. the Financial Services Act.

17. Banks and other financial institutions have had to make a decision about whether to act as independent financial advisers or be tied to selling one brand of financial services. This principle is known as:-

a. diversification;

b. a niche strategy;

c. centralisation;

d. polarisation.

18. A bill of exchange is:-

a. an unconditional order in writing signed by the person to whom it is addressed;

b. an unconditional order in writing signed by the person giving it;

c. a conditional order in writing signed by the person giving it;

d. a conditional order in writing signed by the person to whom it is addressed.

19. The case of Tournier v. National Provincial and Union Bank of England dealt with:-

a. stopped cheques;

b. conversion;

c. disclaimer clauses;

d. secrecy.

20. The 1987 Banking Act changed the status of of licensed deposit-takers by:-

a. barring them from taking deposits;

b. treating them like other banks;

c. requiring them to apply for new licences;

d. excluding them from the Deposit Protection Scheme.

Section B

Answer ALL questions. Each question carries FIVE marks.

Read the following passage and answer all the questions which relate to it.

Almost exactly a year after Big Bang came the great stock market crash of 1987, when prices fell on stock markets all round the world and many small investors hastily sold their shareholdings and put their cash into banks and building societies which they felt were safer. Ultimately only measures by the United States government were able to reassure investors worldwide that imbalances in international trade were going to be corrected, and even the formal announcement of appropriate measures left many investors unconvinced. Following the crash the United Kingdom money markets were in turmoil with interest rates being cut by government to restore confidence that industry would not be too badly affected by falling share prices. Once the Bank of England had cut its rates the major clearing banks followed and building societies too reduced the cost of mortgages.

Building societies found that they had plenty of funds flowing in from investors, perhaps because small investors were scared away from putting their money into equities. Because of this the cuts in interest rates did not lead to concern among the building societies about a fall in income. Expected outflows of cash for the proposed sell-off of BP shares did not materialise.

21. What was Big Bang?

22. Why would a cut in interest rates be seen as restoring confidence?

23. Why do banks and building societies follow the lead of the Bank of England in cutting interest rates?

24. What effect would a cut in building society rates normally have on building society income, and why?

25. Why is a reduction in building society income a problem for building societies?

Section C

Answer TWO questions only. Each question carries FIFTEEN marks.

26. A customer asks you about the different kinds of mortgage which are available. Write brief notes outlining what you would tell him.

27. The manager is due to see a customer who has recently won a large sum of money. What questions would you expect him/her to ask the customer before giving any advice about how to deal with the money?

28. Write a reply to the following letter received by your manager, Mrs Jacobs.

Dear Mrs Jacobs

As you know the shop I bought two years ago is now trading quite successfully, but I feel that I could increase my turnover if I could take payments from credit card holders. Would there be any risk to me in doing this, and how can I find out more?

Yours faithfully

Mr P Evans

Section D

Answer ONE question only, in essay form. Each question carries TWENTY-FIVE marks.

29. To what extent has securitisation affected banks?

30. How have banks been changed by adopting a marketing philosophy?

31. Why are interviewing skills important to bank staff?

Section 4

Solutions to end-of-chapter exercises

Chapter 1

Solutions to end-of-chapter exercises

A1. 1. The fringe banking crisis was the crisis in the United Kingdom banking system in 1973-74 when a number of institutions which were not full banks got into difficulties, mainly as a result of lending money to companies involved in property speculation. The leading banks, the big clearing banks, helped to finance a rescue operation organised by the Bank of England.

2. Prudential supervision is the supervision of the banking system carried out by the central bank in order to make sure that banks are operating sensibly (or prudently). This reduces the risk of banks going into liquidation. Methods used include capital adequacy ratios and regular reporting to the central bank.

3. The two categories of deposit-takers under the 1979 Banking Act were:

a) banks (or recognised banks) *and*

b) licensed deposit-taking institutions.

4. It can be helpful for the banking system as a whole if the Bank of England can influence who owns banks because this makes the system more stable. The Bank of England can make sure that banks are not owned by companies inexperienced in financial services which might introduce unsafe competitive practices. The Bank of England is also concerned about the risk of banks being controlled by owners who might act against the best interests of the country.

5. It is a matter of opinion which are the most important changes. The removal of the two-tier system of categorising banks might be seen as a major change because it gives scope for freer competition between different institutions, but other changes could be mentioned here too.

A2. Introduction

A definition of the phrase 'central bank'.

Main sections of the answer cover basic functions including:-

a) banker to other banks;

b) banker to the government;

c) adviser to the government;

d) representative of the country in international financial affairs;

e) influence on the money supply (implementing government monetary policy);

f) lender of the last resort.

Other roles to be mentioned include:-

a) note issuing;

b) banker to some private institutions and individuals;

c) supervisor of other financial institutions.

Conclusion

The Bank of England carries out all of the functions which any central bank performs, plus a range of other roles shared by only some other central banks.

A3. Introduction

A definition of a British overseas bank.

Main sections of the answer cover:-

a) the changing pattern of international banking (see also Chapter 18);

b) the former overseas banks merged into United Kingdom banks (with examples);

c) the former overseas banks which are now foreign-owned (with examples);

Conclusion

The concept of British Overseas Bank is no longer of great importance in United Kingdom banking, though Standard Chartered does remain as one example.

A4. Introduction

A definition of a clearing bank.

Main sections of the answer cover:-

a) an explanation of the concept of a clearing house (with reference to APACS);

b) explanation of the increase in the number of institutions wanting to participate in the clearing system;

c) summary of the reasons for change including:

1. new technology;

2. competition;

3. deregulation, e.g. of building societies.

Conclusion

Since clearing banks are defined as banks participating directly in a payment clearing system the status of banks as clearing banks must change as payment systems change.

Chapter 2

Solutions to end-of-chapter exercises

A1. Introduction

An explanation of the idea of managed funds into which investors can put money. Main sections of the answer cover:-

a) legal status (company compared to trust);

b) nature of the investment (marketable shares compared to units);

c) valuation (supply and demand compared to pricing related to underlying securities; n.b. possibility of discounts);

d) method of selling (through market or to unit managers);

e) dealing costs;

f) promotion;

g) minor differences like availability of savings plans.

Section on the importance of these differences covering:-

a) investor perceptions;

b) size of total funds invested;

c) range of specialist funds.

Conclusion

The similarities between the two kinds of financial intermediary are probably as important as the differences.

A2. Introduction

A definition of a credit union.

Main sections of the answer cover:-

a) features of credit unions:-
1. size;
2. limits on amounts lent and invested;
3. other limitations.

b) competition between all financial intermediaries;

c) representation of banks and credit unions at local level;

d) competition in small-scale lending.

Conclusion

The differences are so important that competition is not severe. Credit unions may complement banks by offering financial services where banks would not want to lend.

A3. Introduction

A definition of a financial intermediary.

Main sections of the answer cover:-

a) the role of the stock market as:-
1. a market place (though no longer a trading floor);
2. a self-regulating organisation of dealers.

b) the absence of basic financial intermediation since:-
1. deposits are not taken from the public;
2. users of funds do not borrow from the stock market.

c) the way in which the stock market does match up the needs of investors and users of funds.

Conclusion

The stock market has a role as a financial intermediary only in a very limited sense, and might be better considered as an alternative to using a financial intermediary.

A4. Introduction

An explanation of the idea of using securities, certificates which can usually be traded.

Main sections of the answer cover:-

a) advantages for issuers:
1. flexibility in choice between interest or dividend;
2. opportunity to obtain permanent share capital;
3. cheapness through cutting out middleman.

b) advantages for investor:-
1. flexibility in waiting for repayment or selling;
2. possible capital growth;
3. high returns because middleman is cut out.

c) disadvantages for the issuer:-

1. investors may not want to buy;

2. relationship with usual lenders may be affected.

d) disadvantages for the investor:-

1. getting money back may be more uncertain;

2. capital losses may occur.

Conclusion

Where major companies issue securities there may be significant advantages for both issuer and investor.

Chapter 3

Solutions to end-of-chapter exercises

A1. 1. The phrase 'new monetary sector' refers to all banks and other deposit takers included in a new definition brought in by the Bank of England following the 1979 Banking Act. This definition was intended to ensure fair treatment of similar institutions, and was important, too, for statistics kept by the Bank of England about bank lending.

2. Eligible liabilities are basically the deposits placed with banks by their customers, defined to exclude deposits made between banks in order to avoid double-counting.

3. When the Bank of England buys bills from the discount houses the price it pays is not the face value of the bills but a lower amount to allow for the interest payable over the period from the sale until the maturity date of the bill. Lower prices therefore represent higher interest rates. The Bank of England is able to influence interest rates by deciding what prices it is willing to pay for bills. The discount houses themselves buy bills from other banks at prices which will enable them to make a profit so they determine the interest banks can obtain on their liquid assets.

4. MLR stands for Minimum Lending Rate, which was the rate at which the Bank of England would lend to discount houses as lender of last resort. The rate used to be published regularly so that all lenders could estimate the rates they ought to charge. By announcing any change in the rate the Bank of England could signal to all financial institutions that it wanted to see a general change in interest rates in the economy.

5. The purpose of the Special Deposits scheme was to restrict bank lending from time to time by taking away liquid assets from all banks so that they could not safely lend more money.

A2. Introduction

Banks formally announce interest rates of a number of kinds including base rates and deposit rates.

Main sections of the answer cover:-

a) external influences on interest rates:

1. expectations about inflation;

2. economic growth;

3. exchange rates.

b) government decisions about interest rate policy through the Bank of England;

c) decisions of individual banks designed to attract deposits or encourage borrowers;

d) effects of competition between banks and with other financial institutions.

Conclusion

Interest rates are essentially the price of money and are determined by supply and demand. Banks do have decisions to make but these are within limits set by the external forces of the market.

A3. Introduction

When interest rates are high banks do charge more for their loans and income per pound lent is higher.

Main sections of the answer cover the disadvantages to banks of high rates:-

a) less customers will want to borrow;

b) more borrowing will be repaid early;

c) cost of obtaining funds to lend will be higher;

d) instability may mean customers are less able to plan expansion of their businesses.

Conclusion

Bank do not necessarily want interest rates to be high even though they can earn more with less lending.

A4. Introduction

Liquid assets are a base from which lending can take place in the knowledge that depositors will be able to get their money when they want it.

Main sections of the answer cover the way in which special deposits and ratios reduce liquidity:-

a) the steps in reducing liquidity by taking special deposits;

b) the steps in reducing liquidity by imposing a liquid asset ratio scheme;

c) the use of a cash ratio scheme.

Alternatives to describe briefly include:-

a) directives;

b) influence on interest rates;

c) penalty schemes like the Supplementary Special Deposits scheme.

Conclusion

Not all methods of monetary control work in the same way and not all are used at the same time.

Chapter 4

Solutions to end-of-chapter exercises

A1. Introduction

A definition of a money market, and brief comparison with other financial markets.

Main sections of the answer cover the different money markets:-

a) certificate of deposit market;

b) local authority bill market;

c) commercial bill market;

d) treasury bill market;

e) interbank market;

f) commercial paper market;

g) discount house market.

Conclusion

The changing patern of money markets depends on financial intermediaries and financial instruments.

A2. Introduction

A definition of a certificate of deposit.

Main sections of the answer cover features of CDs including:-

a) negotiability and marketability;

b) liquidity;

c) flexibility in choice of currency and maturity;

d) interest rates and tax position.

Conclusion

Certificates of deposit are only one of the important forms of 'paper' used in the money markets.

A3. Introduction

An explanation of the concept of 'paper' and its use in the money markets.

Main sections of the answer cover areas of difference including:-

a) issuers;

b) maturities;

c) amounts;

d) currencies.

Conclusion

Similarities between the different forms of paper are also important.

A4. Introduction

A definition of Treasury bills.

Main sections of the answer cover:-

a) the volume of bills issued;

b) the role of government and the 'official' discount house market;

c) the tradition of using Treasury bills;

d) the significance of Treasury bill rate for other rates.

Conclusion

Treasury bills are only one of the forms of 'paper' used in the money markets but **may** have a special role because they are issued by government.

Chapter 5

Solutions to end-of-chapter exercises

A1. 1. Liquid assets (including investments and cheques in course of collection) 3710
Total assets 7700
Liquid assets: Total assets = 48%
(If investments are excluded the figure is 44%).

2. Advances 3090
Deposits 5500
Advances: Deposits = 56%

3. Free equity:-
Capital and reserves − Premises and equipment
600 − 500 = £100 million

4. Omega Bank is clearly diferent from commercial banks like the big clearers because liquidity is much higher and the advances to deposits ratio is much lower. Another difference is simply that the figures are smaller than for the big United Kingdom clearing banks.

5. The figures suggest a merchant bank dealing in short-term assets and making much of its profit from activities other than lending.

A2. Introduction

The basic feature of banks is that they act as financial intermediaries taking deposits and providing loans, so these are major items in their balance sheets.

Main sections of the answer cover special features of bank balance sheets:-

a) the level of cash and liquid assets;

b) level of debtors/borrowers;

c) low level of stock;

d) level of creditors/depositors;

e) level of capital in relation to size.

Conclusion

Most trading and manufacturing businesses are likely to have balance sheets very different from bank balance sheets.

A3. Introduction

Banks are trying to meet the needs of depositors and the needs of shareholders (among other groups).

Main sections of the answer cover:-

a) aims of shareholders (mainly concerned with profitability):-
  1. high return on investment;
  2. safe and continuing return.

b) aims of depositors (more concerned with liquidity):-
  1. safety of deposits;
  2. ability to get money when required;
  3. interest on funds deposited.

c) the fact that conflict can arise because interests are not the same.

Conclusion

Conflict can be resolved fairly effectively because only if a bank is safe will it continue to attract deposits and therefore make profit from loans.

A4. Introduction

An explanation of the concept of capital.

Main sections of the answer cover:-

a) the banks' need for capital;

b) the difficulty of measuring capital;

c) methods of assessing capital adequacy:-
  1. the amount of capital;
  2. the ratio of capital to other liabilities;
  3. the amount of free equity;
  4. allowing for loan capital;
  5. allowing for risks which capital may need to cover.

Conclusion

Bank supervisors like the Bank of England have a serious problem in deciding how much capital is adequate.

Chapter 6

Solutions to end-of-chapter exercises

A1. Introduction

Deposit-taking originally meant looking after depositors money safely, but other features are now important to depositors.

Main sections of the answer cover:-

a) features which depositors look for, including:-
  1. safety;

2. speed of accessibility;

3. choice of methods of obtaining access;

4. interest.

b) changes taking place in:-

1. improved speed of accessibility (because of technology);

2. wider choice of methods (because of technology);

3. higher interest (because of competition);

4. more kinds of account (through competition and technology).

Conclusion

Changes in the whole of the financial services industry have created pressure for change in specific areas like deposit-taking.

A2. Introduction

A brief summary of the purposes for which money is borrowed.

Main sections of the answer cover factors affecting choice:-

a) flexibility to repay when it is convenient;

b) simplicity of knowing how much to repay each month (conflict with point a)?);

c) availability of funds;

d) low interest (though this can be overlooked by customers);

e) flexibility to change from one kind of loan to another.

Conclusion

The main factors are flexibility and simplicity, but these may pull in opposite directions.

A3. Introduction

A brief comment on the characteristics of the branch network.

Main sections of the answer cover:-

a) advantages of a large network:-

1. access to customers;

2. outlets for selling services;

3. adaptability to local needs.

b) disadvantages of a large network:-

1. resources tied up;

2. cost of staff;

3. difficulty of maintaining standards and good communications.

Conclusion

A view should be expressed about the balance between advantages and disadvantages.

A4. Introduction

A definition of diversification.

Main sections of the answer cover the forms of diversification being adopted by clearing banks:-

a) a continuation of basic banking services;

b) development of insurance services;

c) unit trust business;

d) involvement in the securities industry;

e) travel agency;

f) estate agency;

g) overseas markets.

Conclusion

Diversification is a suitable strategy for the clearing banks because of their branch networks and current range of services.

Chapter 7

Solutions to end-of-chapter exercises

A1. 1. Replying to status enquiries is not a breach of the bank's contractual duty of confidentiality because the bank's right to give replies is an implied term of the banker-customer contract.

2. The disclaimer clause is the phrase 'for your private use and without responsibility on the part of the bank or its officials'.

3. The Unfair Contract Terms Act 1977 may make disclaimer clauses unenforceable which could leave the bank liable for damages to the enquirer, or possibly the customer, if the information given is inaccurate or misleading. There has not yet been a case to decide the present legal position.

4. No. A customer of Lloyds Bank has probably asked the bank to make the enquiry. It is the customer which is considering offering credit and the information in the reply will be passed on by Lloyds Bank.

5. The reply is not very favourable and suggests that the amount is far too high and would present serious difficulties for BP & Co Ltd.

A2. Introduction

A brief summary of the requirements for forming a contract.

Main sections of the answer cover:-

a) the basic relationship of debtor and creditor;

b) the duties of the bank including:-

1. repayment of money directly or on the basis of instructions to pay third parties;

2. maintaining secrecy;

3. giving reasonable notice to close an account;

4. giving notice before changing bank procedures.

c) the duties of the customer including:-

1. applying to the bank to get money back;

2. exercising care in giving instructions.

Conclusion

There is now a move towards the use of written contracts and where these are used the terms are clear express terms rather than the implied terms referred to here.

A3. Introduction

Explanation of the idea of legal risk as the risk that a bank may be taken to court and may lose a case and incur some penalty like payment of damages.

Main sections of the answer cover:-

a) risks on opening accounts including:-

1. claims for conversion if bank is negligent (quote leading cases);

2. claims from a trustee in bankruptcy if a customer is an undischarged bankrupt (see Chapter 8);

3. liability to third parties if the account is for a company which has not completed all the right formalities.

b) risks on closing accounts including:-

1. claims for breach of contract if inadequate notice is given;

2. claims for libel if cheques are returned marked 'No account'.

Conclusion

The legal relationship between bank and customer is complicated, and there are special difficulties at the point at which the contract begins or ends.

A4. Introduction

The general rule of secrecy was established by the Tournier case.

Main sections of the answer cover:-

a) the major exceptions to the rule of secrecy:-

1. compulsion of law;

2. public duty;

3. the interest of the bank;

4. with the customer's consent.

b) how status enquiries fit into the category of customer's consent:-

1. what a status enquiry is;

2. the tradition of providing replies.

Conclusion

There has been criticism of the system of status enquiries because customers do not know about them, but it is still considered that banks are not at risk of any claim for breach of contract if they disclose information to other banks in reply to formal enquiries.

Chapter 8

Solutions to end-of-chapter exercises

A1. Introduction

A definition of a mandate as an instruction to a bank about how to operate an account.

Main sections of the answer cover:-

a) the types of mandates;

b) the need for mandates (where there is more than one account-holder or signatory);

c) the basic information contained in mandates:-

1. signing instructions;

2. liabilities of the parties (e.g. joint and several liability for debts, liability for guarantees etc.).

Conclusion

Although some of the information in mandates does not add to a bank's legal rights it is useful to clarify the legal relationships where the bank has more than one customer to deal with.

A2. Introduction

Personal representatives are people who deal with the assets and liabilities of someone who has died.

Main sections of the answer cover:-

a) types of personal representative:-

1. executors;

2. administrators.

b) effects on banks:-

1. assets 'frozen' until court appoints personal representatives;

2. personal representatives have power to dispose of the deceased's assets, including bank balances and items held in safe custody;

3. personal representatives will be asked to repay money owed by the deceased.

c) banks need to check that personal representatives have been validly appointed.

Conclusion

The powers of personal representatives are given to them on appointment by a court. A bank is therefore protected in its dealings with personal representatives only if they are validly appointed.

A3. Introduction

Trust accounts are accounts in which funds are controlled by one person or group of people (the trustee or trustees) for the benefit of others (the beneficiaries of the trust).

Main sections of the answer cover:-

a) implications including:-

1. money cannot be used by trustees for their own debts;

2. banks have to take care that trust funds are not misused;

3. beneficiaries may have a claim on the funds if anything happens to the trustees.

b) examples with suitable explanations of each:- (any three from these)

1. charitable trusts;

2. club accounts held in the name of the treasurer;

3. solicitors' clients accounts;

4. insurance brokers' broking accounts;

5. estate agents' clients accounts;

6. securities dealers' or investment advisers' clients accounts.

Conclusion

Special care needs to be taken over trust accounts because of the possibility of the bank incurring a liability to the beneficiaries of the trust.

A4. Introduction

The basic problem for a bank is that if a customer is mentally incapacitated this terminates the bank's mandate, which implies that the bank can no longer operate the account.

Main sections of the answer cover:-

a) difficulty in deciding whether mental illness amounts to incapacity;

b) problems which may arise if the bank is wrong in its judgement:-

1. breach of contract and/or libel if cheques are returned without reason.

2. possible breach of contract and liability to refund money if cheques are paid which should have been returned.

Conclusion

The best solution is to get a medical certificate as evidence of mental incapacity and arrange for a receiver to be appointed to look after the customer's affairs.

Chapter 9

Solutions to end-of-chapter exercises

A1. 1. Three of the areas covered by a partnership mandate are:-

a) who the partners are;

b)   who can sign on the account;

c)   the liability of all partners for debts which any of them incur.

2. The main legislation covering companies is the Companies Act 1985.

3. The Memorandum of Association states the external rules of the company and the Articles deal with the internal rules.

4. 'Ultra vires' means beyond the powers of (the company).

5. Section 9 of the European Communities Act means that if anyone dealing with a company does not know what its objects clause covers they should not suffer as a result of actions which are 'ultra vires' the company. Banks may be unable to benefit from this protection because they do see the Memorandum of Association for any company customer.

b)   advantages for members:-

1. possible benefits with limited risk of loss;

2. opportunity to decide on the level of risk which is acceptable.

c)   advantages for companies:-

1. possibility of attracting a wide range of shareholders;

2. total investment available is higher because shareholders can invest without great risk;

3. clear distinction between owners and managers is possible.

Conclusion

The advantages are so great that limited companies have become the dominant form of business organisation in Western society.

A2.   Introduction

Both Administrators and Administrative Receivers need to be qualified insolvency practitioners under the Insolvency Act 1986.

Main sections of the answer cover:-

a)   the differences:-

1. purpose of appointment (to get business out of difficulty or to realise assets);

2. source of request for appointment;

3. powers.

b)   the circumstances for appointing an Administrator.

c)   the circumstances for appointing an Administrative Receiver.

Conclusion

If an Administrator is appointed this prevents the appointment of an Administrative Receiver.

A3.   Introduction

Most companies are incorporated with limited liability, usually limited by issuing shares.

Main sections of the answer cover:-

a)   explanation of the concept of limited liability;

A4.   Introduction

The essential difference between partnerships and companies is that companies have a legal existence in their own right.

Main sections of the answer cover:-

a)   banking considerations on the death of a company director, for example:-

1. the company can continue to trade;

2. no action is needed unless rules require a new director;

3. cheques signed by the deceased director are valid.

b)   banking considerations on the death of a partner, for example:-

1. the mandate is terminated;

2. a new mandate will be needed;

3. continuing partners should confirm cheques signed by the deceased.

c)   account opening procedures (e.g. evidence of a company's existence);

d)   account operating procedures (e.g. changes in signatories to account routine for companies, but usually requiring a new mandate for partners).

Conclusion

Companies can carry on in spite of the death of directors because they are separate legal entities. Partnerships are not separate from the partners so when a partner dies new relationships need to be created.

Chapter 10
Solutions to end-of-chapter exercises

A1. Introduction

A brief explanation that the marketing mix covers the four areas of product, price, promotion and place.

Main sections of the answer cover important marketing considerations for banks, giving some indication of their importance:-

a) product;

b) price;

c) promotion;

d) place;

e) other possible concerns:-

    1. public relations;

    2. personnel;

Conclusion

The traditional factors certainly are important in marketing banking services but they should not be seen as the only areas of concern.

A2. Introduction

A brief definition of a situation analysis.

Main sections of the answer cover:-

a) the situation analysis as a starting point in a marketing plan;

b) the relevance of the situation analysis to decisions on:-

    1. marketing objectives;

    2. product;

    3. price;

    4. promotion;

    5. place or distribution;

    6. resource allocation.

Conclusion

Because the situation analysis is a basic starting point it has implications for all aspects of the marketing plan.

A3. Introduction

A definition of market segmentation.

Main sections of the answer cover a selection of different approaches to segmentation (with reasons why each can be considered appropriate):-

a) personal versus business customers;

b) socio-economic groupings for personal customers;

c) ACORN classification for personal customers;

d) life-style/age-group segmentation for personal customers.

Conclusion

Different forms of segmentation meet different needs.

A4. Introduction

A definition of market research.

Main sections of the answer cover:-

a) use of market research in banking:-

    1. to look at demand among specific groups or market segments;

    2. to question customers about services provided;

    3. to pilot new services;

b) differences between market research and marketing research, for example:-

    1. the assessment of all markets;

    2. the attention paid to broader marketing objectives;

    3. the implications for the whole of the marketing mix.

Conclusion

Banks are making increasing use of market research and developing more sophisticated marketing research in order to meet customer needs more effectively.

Chapter 11
Solutions to end-of-chapter exercises

A1. Introduction

Banks are risk-takers because lending money involves risk.

Main sections of the answer cover methods of reducing risk, in each case commenting on effects on profit:-

a) insurance, where cost may reduce profit or be passed on to customer;

b) training, where cost usually reduces profit;

c) setting limits and monitoring lending, usually affecting profit;

d) spreading risk, with some possible effect on profit;

e) using local knowledge, which may be costly in staff time.

Conclusion

It is always difficult to balance risk against profit, because spending too much money to reduce risk will make profit lower than suffering some loss from bad debts.

A2. Introduction

The period of borrowing is one of the crucial factors to look at in assessing lending. Longer periods imply higher risk because there is more time in which things can go wrong.

Main sections of the answer cover:-

a) the extent of the difference in time, including:-

1. small difference between 2 months and 6 months;

2. risk not proportionately greater (i.e. not 3 times as risky);

3. little effect where such a small sum is involved.

b) the need to compensate for extra risk, including:-

1. possibility of different interest rate;

2. possibility of a different arrangement fee;

3. likelihood of charging more per month to short-term borrower.

Conclusion

Banks tend to charge more for higher risk lending but where differences are very small as in the example in the question it may well be the short-term borrower who has more expensive borrowing because of the principle of charging an arrangement fee.

A3. Introduction

This question assumes that there may be someone who can be seen as an ideal borrower. In practice aiming for a spread of risk means that different kinds of borrowers are needed. However certain personality factors may be judged as desirable.

Main sections of the answer cover valued characteristics such as:-

a) honesty and integrity;

b) carefulness about money;

c) good organisation and planning about money;

d) hard-work and commitment to do well;

e) determination to overcome problems;

f) ability in business or at work.

Conclusion

From a lender's point of view character is only one of many factors to consider. Even in looking at the individual borrower such matters as family connection or appearance may have a bearing, and usually lenders take a much wider view of the situation.

A4. *Comment*

The statement to be assessed here is difficult to justify because it is either obvious or wrong. Examples will be needed to support any argument.

Introduction

The period of borrowing is one of the key factors to be considered in any lending situation.

Main sections of the answer cover the links between the period of borrowing and other considerations:-

a) purpose:-

1. example, e.g. business obtaining stock for Christmas;

2. example, e.g. period of borrowing needed to buy a house.

b) source of repayments:-

1. example, e.g. business borrowing to buy new machinery which will generate new income;

2. example, e.g. one month overdraft for customer to repay from salary.

Conclusion

The principle put forward, that there is a link between period and both purpose of borrowing and source of repayment, is clearly valid if the information is available. For more open-ended borrowing like credit card advances the purpose of borrowing may be irrelevant.

Chapter 12

Solutions to end-of-chapter exercises

A1. Introduction

All three forms of borrowing are used for personal spending over short periods of time.

Main sections of the answer cover:-

a) advantages of overdrafts;

b) advantages of revolving credit accounts;

c) advantages of budget accounts;

d) disadvantages of overdrafts;

e) disadvantages of revolving credit accounts;

f) disadvantages of budget accounts.

Conclusion

Different forms of borrowing will suit different people according to their personal circumstances.

A2. Introduction

A brief definition of credit scoring.

Main sections of the answer cover:-

a) the concept of setting a score which determines whether a loan is agreed or not;

b) moving the score to alter levels of lending and bad debts;

c) determining a balance between gaining profitable business and suffering losses;

d) explanation of why the lowest level of debt is not the best:-

  1. over-cautious approach;

  2. loss of business to competitors;

  3. possible desire for market share.

Conclusion

There is some justification for the statement made, though some people see credit-scoring as a way of saving staff time on easy lending decisions rather than as a way of determining the level of bad debts.

A3. Introduction

Customers have differing needs so to offer only one form of finance would not meet the requirements of all customers.

Main sections of the answer cover:-

a) circumstances in which overdrafts are appropriate:-

  1. very short term finance;

  2. where the borrower needs flexibility;

  3. where borrowing may not be taken up at all;

  4. where the customer already pays bank charges.

b) circumstances in which personal loans are appropriate:-

  1. longer borrowing over a few years;

  2. where knowing the repayments is important;

  3. where the customer expects interest rates to rise.

Conclusion

Apart from the factors which may influence a customer to ask for a personal loan or an overdraft the bank itself may wish to consider the form of lending it prefers. Personal loans give more control over lending because the regular repayments can be monitored.

A4. Introduction

The Consumer Credit Act 1974 was brought in to protect consumers from unscrupulous lenders. The effects on banks have been wide-ranging.

Main sections of the answer cover:-

a) features which make a loan a regulated agreement, including:-

  1. the borrower not a company;

  2. the amount below £15,000;

3. loan not used for international finance;

4. loan not a mortgage from a specialist lender.

b) reasons why it matters that an agreement is regulated, including:-

1. need for standard documentation (though overdrafts are excluded);

2. protections for the customer;

3. extra requirements on banks (e.g. default notices).

Conclusion

Although customers are given extra legal protections under the Consumer Credit Act, in practice people who deal with reputable banks have not benefitted significantly from the legislation. More paperwork is needed so service may be slower and more complicated than before.

Chapter 13

Solutions to end-of-chapter exercises

A1. Introduction

A definition of working capital as the capital available to finance the day-to-day running of a business.

Main sections of the answer cover:-

a) the calculation of working capital as current assets minus current liabilities;

b) the relationship between working capital and total capital (i.e. allowing for financing of fixed assets);

c) main components of working capital, stock, debtors, cash, creditors;

d) the need for an increase in these items when turnover increases (with example in figures);

e) the need for extra working capital because of changes in the component parts.

Conclusion

Only in the exceptional case of a business with creditors exceeding debtors and stock will a rise in turnover mean a reduced need for working capital.

A2. 1. *Balance Sheet of Growers Ltd with loan account*

	£
Fixed Assets	25000
Current Assets	8000
Current Liabilities	(7000)
	26000
Capital	
Shares	10000
Reserves	8000
Long-term Liabilities	8000
	26000

2. *Comparison of loan and overdraft*

	£ (loan)	£ (overdraft)
Fixed Assets	25000	25000
Current Assets	8000	8000
Current Liabilities	(7000)	(12000)
	26000	21000
Capital		
Shares	10000	10000
Reserves	8000	8000
Long-term Liabilities	8000	3000
	26000	21000

3. Current ratio with a loan, $8000:7000 = 1.14:1$

Current ratio with an overdraft, $8000:12000 = 0.67:1$

4. The difference in current ratios suggests that the use of a loan would leave the liquidity of the business little changed, but if an overdraft is taken the business will find that the current liabilities outweigh current assets and may make it difficult for the business to meet its debts.

A3. Introduction

One of the basic considerations when looking at any lending situation is whether the amount is right.

Main sections of the answer cover:-

a) why the manager might believe the amount is too low, for example:-

1. other costs may need to be added on;

2. there is no margin for error if prices rise;

3. new machinery will lead to an increase in turnover so more working capital may be needed.

b) the ways of checking on the amount, including:-

1. obtaining a breakdown of all expected costs;

2. specifically asking about increased turnover;

3. carrying out calculations based on increased sales.

Conclusion

One of the main reasons for businesses asking for too little money is that they do not allow sufficiently for the extra working capital needed if turnover increases. Calculation of extra working capital can be based on expected increases in debtors, stock and creditors.

A4. Introduction

A definition of 'ultra vires' as beyond the powers of (the company).

Main sections of the answer cover:-

a) the role of the objects clause in the memorandum of association;

b) the principle that activity not included in the objects clause is not permitted and therefore not valid;

c) the unenforceability of debts for 'ultra vires' purposes;

d) the circumstances in which banks face a problem, for example where:-

1. they have seen the memorandum (which is usual);

2. they cannot obtain protection from the rule in Turquand's case;

3. the company decides not to repay;

4. personal claims on the directors are unlikely to be enforceable.

Conclusion

A change in the 'ultra vires' law is expected in the next few years, but until it comes in banks need to be conscious of the potential problems.

Chapter 14

Solutions to end-of-chapter exercises

A1. Introduction

Leasing and hire purchase are both forms of finance for fixed assets which banks offer to customers, usually through subsidiary companies.

Main sections of the answer cover:-

a) similarities between the two forms of finance, for example both are:-

1. alternatives to a loan;

2. paid in instalments;

3. often offered through a finance house.

b) differences between the two, including:-

1. who owns the asset financed;

2. the tax position in each case;

3. the need for a deposit;

4. the position at the end of the basic period of the finance.

Conclusion

These are two similar services which will suit different customers according to their own tax position and other requirements.

A2. Introduction

A brief definition of factoring.

Main sections of the answer cover:-

a) main features of factoring including its different forms:-

1. sales ledger service;

2. credit control;

3. loans against invoices;

4. non-recourse factoring.

b) circumstances in which factoring is suitable, for example where:-

1. debtors are a major asset;

2. sales take place regularly in large amounts (£500 plus);

3. sales are to a limited number of known clients;

4. total turnover is £1 million or more;

5. the business is short-staffed in sales ledger administration.

Conclusion

Factoring is a valuable service to many businesses but is not widely accepted because of its unfavourable image.

A3.   Introduction

The options considered here are only available to major companies because small businesses would not be dealing in large enough amounts.

Main sections of the answer cover:-

a)   advantages of acceptance credits;

b)   advantages of issuing securities;

c)   disadvantages of acceptance credits;

d)   disadvantages of issuing securities.

Conclusion

Acceptance credits are often seen as an alternative to large-scale borrowing on overdraft. Issuing securities is usually only appropriate for longer-term finance instead of a loan.

A4.   Introduction

A brief definition of venture capital as finance by acquiring shares.

Main sections of the answer cover:-

a)   main features of venture capital:-

1. offered mainly to new or expanding businesses;

2. often considered most suitable for high technology businesses;

3. appropriate for companies which are likely to become public companies in time;

4. often combined with finance in the form of a loan.

b)   how banks get their money back:-

1. by receiving dividends once profits are made;

2. by selling all or part of the shareholding when the company is 'floated'.

Conclusion

Venture capital is a fairly small part of bank financing but an important facility for many businesses which are not able to take on the burden of extra debt interest.

Chapter 15

Solutions to end-of-chapter exercises

A1.   Introduction

Different approaches to lending are possible. In general banks are interested in the whole situation including purpose, amount, period, experience, repayments and security.

Main sections of the answer cover:-

a)   the most valuable information obtained from balance sheets, including details of:-

1. liquidity;

2. profitability;

3. capital strength.

b)   other information including:-

1. past management performance;

2. assets available as security.

c)   the main omissions, notably:-

1. personal qualities of the managers;

2. outside influences such as competition or changing technology.

Conclusion

Balance sheets are a valuable source of information in assessing lending propositions but the final decision about whether to lend should take into account other factors.

A2.   Introduction

An explanation of the concept of profitability.

Main sections of the answer describe and assess the suitability of key ratios:-

a)   net profit/sales;

b)   gross profit/sales;

c)   return on capital employed.

Conclusion

No single profit ratio can give a detailed picture of how a business is operating, but by looking at several different calculations a clearer view may emerge.

A3.   1. Company A appears to be the manufacturer and Company B the finance company.

2. The evidence on which this conclusion is based comes from:-

1. fixed assets (more needed for a manufacturer);
2. stock (not normally held by a finance company);
3. debtors (the main asset of a finance company);
4. capital (probably needed more by a manufacturer);
5. long-term liabilities (more likely as funding for a finance company);
6. current liabilities (since the finance company would take deposits).

A4. Introduction

A definition of liquidity.

Main sections of the answer cover:-

a) strengths of the current ratio (covering all current assets);
b) strengths of the acid-test ratio (adjusted for illiquid assets);
c) weaknesses of current ratio (assuming stock is saleable);
d) weaknesses of acid-test ratio (possibly undervaluing stock).

Conclusion

Like all ratios the current ratio and acid-test ratio need to be treated with caution; they have value in making comparisons between businesses or in looking at trends rather than as figures in their own right.

Chapter 16
Solutions to end-of-chapter exercises

A1. Introduction

Security in this context means assets or claims on assets which a lender can take to make sure it gets its money back if the loan is not repaid.

Main sections of the answer cover basic qualities of good security:-

a) easy to value (life policy, quoted shares);
b) valuable, with rising value (life policy, land);
c) easy to charge (guarantee, life policy);
d) realisable (quoted shares, life policy).

Conclusion

Most security does not meet all the criteria of good security.

A2. Introduction

All of the terms in the question refer to forms of security.

Main sections of the answer cover:-

a) a charge, the general term for a lender's claim over an asset;
b) a legal mortgage, the most effective form of charge, as applied to:-
   1. stocks and shares;
   2. land.
c) an equitable mortgage:-
   1. less complicated to take;
   2. giving less powerful control to the lender.

Conclusion

Charges can be categorised in various ways. The distinction between a full legal mortgage and a less effective equitable mortgage is particularly important.

A3. Introduction

The term stocks and shares covers a wide variety of different financial claims with differing characteristics.

Main sections of the answer cover features of good security:-

a) easy to value (unless unquoted);
b) unstable in value though may rise (if the company grows);
c) fairly easy to take a charge (particularly an equitable charge);
d) easy to realise (if a legal charge has been taken).

Conclusion

Stocks and shares can be good security but they do pose some problems. Part-paid shares in an unquoted company may be quite unsatisfactory, but a selection of shareholdings in different quoted companies could be very suitable.

A4. Introduction

Many life policies are not suitable as security because they have no surrender value or because beneficiaries of the policy are unable or unwilling to sign away their rights.

Main sections of the answer cover features of policies which can be charged:-

a) a surrender value is payable so valuation is easy;

b) the value shold rise as premiums are paid;

c) policies are easy to charge (by completing a charge form and sending it to the company);

d) policies are easy to realise (by submitting an encashment form and the policy to the company).

Conclusion

If a policy can be charged it is probably a very good form of security.

Chapter 17

Solutions to end-of-chapter exercises

A1. *Comment*

All of these case study questions are open-ended and examiners will usually give credit for good ideas even if these are not specifically what was expected in an answer. Do try to make sure that where a question is structured (divided into separate parts) you answer each part separately.

1. The bank would require further information about any aspects of the proposal which seem uncertain or problematical, for example:-

a) the terms of the contract;

b) the timings (e.g. when material will be bought);

c) any other costs to be incurred;

d) the amount of other business the firm is doing;

e) how profitable the deal will be;

f) what security the firm can offer, if any.

2. Possible problems include:-

a) delays, perhaps because of other contractors;

b) rising material costs;

c) increases in other costs;

d) the council claiming that the work is below standard;

e) a change in plans on the part of the council;

f) financial problems for the council.

A2. 1. Important questions for the manager to ask include:-

a) what exactly does the purchase price cover?

b) what is the shop like? (condition, location, potential etc.);

c) why is the shop being sold?

d) can the Blackstocks cope with two shops? how?

e) will they take on more staff?

f) how much do they want to borrow?

g) what costs have they included? (any cash flow forecast?);

h) have they allowed for extra working capital?

i) how long do they think they will need to borrow for?

j) are repayments to come from profit from the new shop or from both shops?

k) will the premises be offered to the bank as security?

If the manager feels that the proposal seems promising information will also be needed about the solicitors acting on behalf of the Blackstocks and the vendors, and exact details of the address.

2. Other important factors are:-

a) the manager's assessment of the character, capability and commitment of the customers;

b) the local economic environment;

c) the accounts of the shop to be bought;

d) the accounts of the Blackstocks' present shop.

A3. *Comment*

Detailed research into the customer's background would not be usual in circumstances like these because the amount is small and the matter is urgent.

1. The manager (or a clerk acting on the manager's behalf) would check that:-

a) there had been no previous problems with the account;

b) the account records show that Gareth is a student;

c) Gareth's parents are still considered valued customers;

d) Gareth is over 18 (likely if he is at university).

2. Factors which support a decision to lend include:-

a) the valuable family connection;

b) the expected source of repayment (a student grant);

c) Gareth's future earnings potential.

A4. Introduction

In one sense lending is easy because it requires no more than the decision to say yes to a customer's request.

Main sections of the answer cover:-

a) factors which make the lending decision difficult including:-

1. the need to assess the overall situation;

2. the need to make sure that the bank's regulations are complied with;

3. the desire to avoid losing the bank's money.

b) factors which make control difficult including:-

1. lack of contact with customers (except when regular payments are coming in);

2. difficulty of setting up control procedures.

c) factors which make recovery difficult including:-

1. the borrower's lack of money to repay;

2. disappearance of bad debtors;

3. problems in realising any security.

Conclusion

Control and recovery of lending are certainly difficult. Lending can be treated as an easy matter but the more care that is taken in lending the less problems there will be with control and recovery.

Chapter 18

Solutions to end-of-chapter exercises

A1. Introduction

London has a long tradition as an international financial and trading centre.

Main sections of the answer cover changes since the Second World War:-

a) the increase in foreign exchange business;

b) the increased presence of foreign banks;

c) the high level of international lending;

d) changes in the United Kingdom securities market;

e) the development of the city as the third centre between the time zones of New York and Tokyo;

f) the expansion of major British banks into international markets;

g) the growth of the Eurocurrency markets (see Chapter 23).

Conclusion

Although much of the importance of London as a financial centre is based on traditional factors like the shipping and insurance markets new developments have taken place and the environment is constantly changing.

A2. Introduction

A brief explanation of the phrase 'international debt crisis'.

Main sections of the answer cover:-

a) the protection banks obtain from a strong domestic branch network:-

1. good reputation;

2. continuing source of deposits;

3. high proportion of lending to customers who will repay.

b) the effects of the debt crisis on United Kingdom banks including:-

1. the likelihood that some debts will never be repaid;

2. the reduction in profit from writing off debts;

3. the possibility of actual trading losses, reducing capital.

Conclusion

United Kingdom banks have so far shown that they have the strength to cope with bad debts associated with lending to poor countries, but it is not true that they have been unaffected.

A3. *Comment*

This question is a problem because the distinction between foreign services and international services is an arbitrary one.

Introduction

The purpose of distinguishing between foreign services and international services could be to consider how to organise or market the different kinds of service.

Main sections of the answer cover:-

a) a possible definition of foreign services:-

   1. provided through a branch network (with specialist departments);

   2. provided for businesses of any size and individual customers;

   3. might include e.g. travel services, payments abroad.

b) a possible definition of international services:-

   1. provided through head office;

   2. provided for very large businesses, often multinationals;

   3. might include Eurobond issues, swaps etc. (see Chapter 23).

Conclusion

However the two areas of business are defined there is overlap between them as many services provided through head offices are also offered to some customers through branches.

A4. Introduction

Clearly not all United Kingdom banks can claim to be international and the question therefore relates specifically to those which are large enough to operate worldwide.

Main sections of the answer cover the ways of assessing whether a bank is international (with reference to how well United Kingdom banks match up):-

a) strong home base (which most international banks need);

b) operations in many countries (true of major United Kingdom banks);

c) presence in major international financial centres;

d) wide range of loans internationally;

e) overall size (the area in which United Kingdom banks are weakest in comparison to their rivals).

Conclusion

In all respects except absolute size the biggest United Kingdom banks are very definitely international banks.

Chapter 19

Solutions to end-of-chapter exercises

A1. 1. A foreign clerk needs to check that:-

a) the notes seem genuine;

b) the bank can accept the denominations offered;

c) there is no limit on the amount of currency the bank will change.

Calculations:-

$400 \div 10.49 = 38.13$	37.13
$600 \div 3.24 = 185.19$	184.19

Total amount received
in sterling is   £221.32

The price of a Maltese pound is higher than the price of a pound sterling according to the rate table.

Calculations:-

Buy $1000 \div 0.54 = 1851.85$	1851.85
Sell $1000 \div 0.52 = 1923.08$	1923.08

Profit from buying then selling is   £71.23

A2. 1. Calculations:-

Buy $30 \div 2.84 = 10.56$
Buy $90 \div 9.33 = 9.65$

The bank pays out most sterling for the 30 Deutsche marks;

2. Calculations:-

Sell $500 \div 9.30 = 53.76$	54.76
Sell $800 \div 10.78 = 74.21$	75.21

Total bill for the
two currencies is   £129.97

A3. Introduction

If a customer is travelling in the United States the Eurocheque scheme will not apply and a credit-open facility at one bank will be inappropriate. Cash will be needed but other less risky methods of taking money are required.

Main sections of the answer cover the two most suitable methods:-

a) U.S. dollar travel cheques because:-

    1. money can be refunded if they are lost;

    2. they can be used for hotel bills and some purchases;

    3. they can be cashed at many banks.

b) a credit card because:-

    1. major credit cards are widely accepted in the United States;

    2. money does not have to be paid out in advance;

    3. cash may be obtained if necessary.

Conclusion

The main aims of the customer are convenience and safety. Using travel cheques and a credit card should meet these requirements well.

A4. Introduction

A customer travelling round Belgium, Holland and France needs to be able to draw out cash in different currencies and from different places.

Main sections of the answer cover:-

a) problems of credit open facility:-

    1. limited to a named place;

    2. complicated to arrange.

b) problems of a traveller's letter of credit:-

    1. so unusual that it may not be accepted;

    2. complicated to arrange;

    3. complicated to use.

c) preferable alternatives include:-

    1. some foreign cash;

    2. sterling travel cheques;

    3. eurocheques and eurocheque card.

Conclusion

The customer is concerned with flexibility and acceptability when arranging to draw cash while abroad. The old-fashioned methods are less appropriate because they are now not widely accepted.

Chapter 20

Solutions to end-of-chapter exercises

A1. 1. A change in French economic policy may alter the views of potential buyers and sellers of francs and this alters the exchange rate of the franc.

2. The exchange rate of the franc is simply the price of the franc in terms of another currency. If the price of the franc rises in relation to the pound this is the same as saying that the price of the pound falls in relation to the franc.

3. Pressure on the dollar means that dollars were being sold in greater quantities than they were being bought, which leads to a fall in the price of the dollar.

4. Early selling refers to sales of pounds for other currencies.

A2. Introduction

Exchange risk is the risk of loss caused by changes in exchange rates.

Main sections of the answer cover:-

a) the importance of exchange risk:-

    1. because it can turn profit into loss;

    2. because it can make import and export business unacceptably risky;

b) methods of reducing exchange risk:-

    1. forward foreign exchange contracts;

    2. currency options;

    3. operating a currency account.

c) methods of avoiding exchange risk:-

    1. sterling invoicing;

    2. avoiding deals with countries which do not trade in sterling.

Conclusion

Banks can play a major part in helping businesses to reduce exchange risk.

A3. Introduction

An exchange rate is the price of one currency in terms of another.

Main sections of the answer cover important influences on rates:-

a) relative strength of economies (only partly controlled by each government);

b) speculative demand for either currency (affected to only a limited extent by government buying or selling its own currency);

c) relative interest rates (only partly controlled by each government);

d) business expectations about inflation (affected but not controlled by government policy).

Conclusion

In the short-term a government can affect exchange rates by buying or selling currency but in the longer term the influences are largely outside government control.

A4. Introduction

The forward exchange market is the market in which currencies are bought and sold for delivery at a later date, usually 1, 3 or 6 months ahead.

Main sections of the answer cover:-

a) what a premium is (higher price, lower rate);

b) the difference in interest rates (lower in Japan to give a premium);

c) the larger the difference in rates the higher the premium (which can be calculated as the equivalent of an interest rate).

Conclusion

The relationship between premiums (or discounts) and interest rates is a fairly precise mathematical relationship. If any difference occurs between the premium and what it ought to be (based on the difference in interest rates) speculators would soon buy whichever currency was seen as a bargain, so adjusting the price.

Chapter 21

Solutions to end-of-chapter exercises

A1. Introduction

Drafts, mail transfers and urgent transfers are the three basic methods of settlement used to make payments abroad.

Main sections of the answer cover:-

a) features of drafts including:-

1. a payment message authorising payment of the draft;

2. the draft document issued to a customer to send;

3. the matching up of the draft and the authorisation message.

b) features of mail transfers including:-

1. payment consisting only of the message;

2. the message sent by airmail or non-urgent SWIFT.

c) features of urgent transfers including:-

1. payment consisting only of the message;

2. the message sent by telex or urgent SWIFT.

Conclusion

The three methods give a choice to customers in speed and cost; each will be the most appropriate in some circumstances.

A2. Introduction

Commercial documents are documents used by businesses in international trade. They can be distinguished from financial documents used to obtain payment.

Main categories (to be described as fully as possible):-

a) insurance documents:-

1. certificates;

2. policies.

b) invoices;

c) transport documents:-

1. bills of lading (documents of title);

2. way bills etc. (not documents of title).

d) other documents *(though it is not clear whether the question requires this further information)*, e.g.;

1. certificates of origin;

2. inspection certificates.

Conclusion

There are three main categories of commercial document used in international trade, though many other documents are also used.

A3. Introduction

A bill of exchange is a financial document used to obtain payment.

Main sections of the answer cover:-

a) features of bills of exchange, e.g. that they are:-

1. written by the person who is to receive the money;

2. negotiable;

3. often payable at a future date.

b) reasons for using bills of exchange including;

1. possibility of using term bills to give an importer credit;

2. stronger legal protection for an exporter if an importer accepts a bill;

3. protection because default on a bill is seen as very serious;

4. opportunity to use an accepted bill to raise money.

Conclusion

Although using sight bills of exchange may have few advantages term bills can give benefits to both importer and exporter.

A4. Introduction

A documentary credit is intended as a compromise agreement on payment between an importer and an exporter in order to meet the needs of both parties.

Main sections of the answer cover:-

a) main features including:-

1. the importer requests the bank to issue a letter of credit;

2. the importer specifies the documents required;

3. the exporter is guaranteed payment if the right documents are produced;

4. the importer is committed to paying if the documents are right.

b) usual documents including:-

1. insurance documents;

2. invoices;

3. transport documents;

4. financial documents.

Conclusion

By specifying the documents to be used the importer has some control over the goods. For example documents may be required which show that independent checks have been made on the quality of the goods before despatch.

Chapter 22

Solutions to end-of-chapter exercises

A1. The bank may be able to help in the circumstances described here by offering a produce loan.

This helps by providing finance secured by the imported goods.

Conditions the customer would need to meet include:-

a) agreeing to give the bank a charge over the goods;

b) being assessed as credit-worthy;

c) insuring the goods adequately;

d) showing evidence that no-one else has a claim to the goods;

e) completing a letter of pledge in favour of the bank;

f) finding a buyer for the goods.

A2. Introduction

Bonds or guarantees are promises of payment if certain conditions are met or certain circumstances arise.

The main categories of bonds and guarantees used in connection with construction projects abroad are:-

a) tender bonds;

b) advance payment guarantees;

c) performance bonds;

d) retention money bonds;

e) maintenance bonds.

The answer should also cover:-

a) banks as issuers (with reasons);

b) why they are needed (the buyer's point of view).

Conclusion

Issuing bonds and guarantees is an important bank service to major customers.

A3. The situation described here seems suitable for export factoring. This is appropriate because:-

a) the goods traded are consumer goods;

b) bank borrrowing will not be increased;

c) the credit terms are short, less than one year;

d) the business may want:-

1. non-recourse financing;

2. help with sales ledger administration.

(See also Chapter 14 on general aspects of factoring).

A4. Introduction

A definition of an export house.

Main sections of the answer cover ways in which export houses compete with banks:-

a) giving advice (on documentation, methods of payment etc.);

b) providing finance;

c) assessing credit-worthiness of trading partners.

Other areas to refer to are fields in which export houses provide non-banking services:-

a) marketing;

b) handling goods;

c) dealing with shipping companies etc.

Conclusion

Export houses are far more specialised than banks and in their areas of specialisation they provide a wider range of services than banks.

Chapter 23

Solutions to end-of-chapter exercises

A1. 1. Economic exposure is the risk of loss because of a change in exchange rates affecting the general pattern of trade of a business.

2. Translation exposure is often seen as being of little significance because balance sheets at one point in time give an arbitrary view of business performance.

3. 'Hedging' is action taken to counter a risk of loss, for example from exchange rate movements, by entering into an agreement or transaction which will fix the profit the business will make.

4. Alternative forms of hedging exchange rate risk are:-

a) to operate a currency account, paying bills from foreign currency earnings;

b) to enter into financial futures contracts.

A2. Introduction

In general it is accepted that the most important currencies in the world are the United States dollar, the Japanese yen and the pound sterling.

Main sections of the answer cover factors which make currencies important:-

a) size of domestic market;

b) size of stock market and its openness to foreign investors;

c) use of the currency by multinational companies;

d) use of the currency in international lending;

e) importance of financial centres using the currency;

f) use of the currency in international trade.

Conclusion

Some of the reasons for the importance of currencies come from a tradition of economic strength, but established currencies often continue in importance even if economic strength declines.

A3. Introduction

A definition of securitisation.

Main sections of the answer cover:-

a) the need for lending rather than securities in some circumstances;

b) lending to underwrite securities;

c) lending for specific projects;

d) large syndicated loans.

Conclusion

The trend towards securitisation will not remove entirely the need for international lending.

A4. Introduction

A brief definition of a composite currency.

Main sections of the answer cover:-

a) features of composite currencies including:-

1. the idea of a 'basket of currencies';

2. valuation according to the values of component currencies.

b) advantages of using composite currencies including:-

1. reduction of fluctuations in exchange rates;

2. acceptability in many different countries.

c) the relationship between the above factors and a specific example of a composite currency, for example the ECU.

Conclusion

Composite currencies have certain advantages but are not widely used because they cannot replace ordinary currencies for everyday purposes like paying wages or buying services.

Chapter 24

Solutions to end-of-chapter exercises

A1. Introduction

The Big Bang is the term used to describe the introduction of a number of major changes in the rules governing the Stock Exchange.

Main sections of the answer cover:-

a) the changes made in Stock Exchange rules (see Chapter 2);

b) the effects on banks as organisations (in particular their acquisition of securities dealing firms);

c) the effects on the service banks offer:-

1. increased activity because of wider share ownership;

2. increased promotion of share dealing services;

3. banks subsidiaries acting as market makers, trading in shares they own.

Conclusion

The Big Bang has made the stock market in the United Kingdom more open and has enabled banks to become more active participants.

A2. Introduction

A definition of a unit trust.

Main sections of the answer cover:-

a) banks as fund managers;

b) banks as dealers selling unit trust products (referring to the issue of polarisation);

c) banks as trustees.

Conclusion

Although banks are not able to act as trustees and managers of the same funds they do take on the role of trustees for funds managed by others. Their role in selling unit trusts depends on the status of their branches as independent advisers or tied agents.

A3. *Comment*

This question is difficult because it is so open-ended that it is unclear what information would be needed to give a complete answer.

Introduction

The basic banking services are taking deposits, offering loans and providing a payments service.

Main sections of the answer cover:-

a) taking deposits, in particular operating accounts for customers;

b) offering loans (though the kinds of loan offered are not necessarily the same for personal and business customers);

c) providing a payments system;

d) other services including:-

1. looking after valuables;

2. buying and selling investments.

Conclusion

The range of banking services is enormous and though many are offered to all customers most take varying forms according to the market segment at which they are aimed.

A4. Introduction

A trustee is someone who has control over assets which are held for the benefit of someone else, the beneficiary of the trust.

Main sections of the answer cover:-

a) circumstances in which trusts are needed;

b) why banks act as trustees (to make profit);

c) why banks are considered suitable as trustees, for example because:-

1. they do not die;

2. they are considered honest and reliable;

3. they are experienced in the work.

Conclusion

Bank trustee departments have the experience and skills to be effective as trustees for all types of trust, and are often appointed in preference to individual trustees.

Chapter 25
Solutions to end-of-chapter exercises

A1. Introduction

The implication of the question is that you are dealing with a customer who is not used to handling such large sums as £100,000.

Basic questions to ask about are:-

a) the customer's preference for safety rather than high returns;

b) the choice between income and capital growth;

c) what investments, if any, the customer owns;

d) family circumstances;

e) an appropriate time scale;

f) any ethical considerations.

The kind of advice to give is:-

a) to think carefully about the questions raised;

b) to keep at least some money available for emergencies;

c) to aim for a good spread of risk (if he decides to make his own investments);

d) to consider getting the bank to deal with the investment decisions by means of an investment management agreement.

Conclusion

The bank has a good opportunity here to meet its customer's needs in a variety of ways, not just in giving advice but also in selling profitable services.

A2. The letter to Mrs. Morecroft should cover:-

a) the possibility of issuing an indemnity;

b) the need for her to contact the company to request a new certificate;

c) the need for her to sign a counter-indemnity to the bank when the bank completes the company's indemnity;

d) the suggestion that she should keep her certificates at the bank in future.

A3. Introduction

An Automated Teller Machine is a machine through which a customer can obtain cash and use a variety of other bank services by means of a plastic card which activates the machine.

Main sections of the answer cover factors which make the ATM important:-

a) legal considerations (use of a Personal Identification Number rather than a signature to give the bank payment instructions);

b) improved access to cash (longer hours and, with networks, more locations);

c) improved access to other services, and more and more of them;

d) reduction in bank costs through:-

1. reduced staffing;

2. more automation of transactions to cope with higher volumes of work.

Conclusion

The ATM has been an important development in providing services because it has created new services as well as changing the way existing services are supplied.

A4. Introduction

Insurance and pensions are only two of many areas in which banks provide advice to their customers.

Main sections of the answer cover key reasons for giving advice:-

a) to help meet customers' needs, building up a client relationship;

b) to improve the bank's image:-

1. as helpful and friendly;

2. as expert in the field of insurance and pensions;

c) to achieve sales in these profitable areas of business.

Conclusion

Whichever path banks choose under the polarisation rules of the Financial Services Act they will continue to act as advisers to customers, either through branch staff or through separate subsidiary companies.

Chapter 26

Solutions to end-of-chapter exercises

A1. Introduction

Business customers are very important users of bank services, particularly finance services.

Main sections of the answer cover specific business services:-
a) advice services;
b) account-handling services;
c) foreign and international services;
d) registrar work;
e) data processing;
f) cash management;
g) guarantees and bonds;
h) insurance services;
i) credit cards.

Conclusion

The business services used by any individual business will depend on its own special needs and requirements.

A2. The service which would clearly be of benefit to Mr. Gregory is the bank's registrar service. This service should be described briefly.

The main benefits for Mr. Gregory are:-
a) saving in time;
b) accuracy in recordkeeping;
c) capacity to cope with high volumes of work (mergers, takeovers etc.);
d) saving in staff;
e) possible cost saving.

A3. The service which would be of most use to Ms. Parsons in the circumstances described is a company credit card. The way in which this works is that:-
a) cards are issued to individual sales representatives;
b) all spending is charged to one account in the name of the company;
c) the company can identify who has spent what from a monthly statement;
d) the company settles the bill when its statement is received.

The major benefits to the company are that:-
a) there is no need to draw out cash for expenses;
b) all items of expenditure are identified clearly;
c) payment is only made after expenses have been incurred.

A4. Introduction

Defining merchant banks is difficult because each has its own range of services.

Main sections of the answer cover services which merchant banks commonly offer:-
a) advice about forms of finance;
b) arranging methods of raising finance:-
1. loans (often as leader of a syndicate of lenders);
2. acceptance credits (see Chapter 14);
3. securities issues.
c) investment management;
d) management consultancy and business advice;
e) advice on takeovers, mergers and buy-outs;
f) advice on import and export business;
g) dealing on the foreign exchange market and money markets;
h) dealing in bullion and basic commodities.

Conclusion

A merchant bank is a bank which carries out a number of the activities outlined, though many of them specialise in only a few fields. The major clearing banks own merchant banking subsidiaries to act as their specialists in some areas, particularly corporate finance.

Chapter 27
Solutions to end-of-chapter exercises

A1. Introduction

Interviews can take many forms ranging from informal conversations to formal discussion, and in general the more formal the interview the more complicated the preparation that is needed.

Main sections of the answer cover:-

a) the interviewer failing to understand the interviewee, for example:-
   1. misjudging a job applicant;
   2. misunderstanding a customer's needs.

b) the interviewer looking badly organised, for example:-
   1. being interrupted frequently;
   2. not having the right information to give the interviewee.

c) the objectives of the interview not being met, for example:-
   1. failing to explain a product's benefits adequately;
   2. failing to tell an applicant what a job entails.

d) the outcome of the interview being a mistake, for example:-
   1. lending money in inappropriate circumstances;
   2. appointing the wrong person for a job.

Conclusion

Because interviews can go wrong in so many ways it is important to reduce the risk of problems by adequate planning and preparation.

A2. Introduction

Personnel managers are specialist managers who deal with staff and their problems. Their interviewing skills need to be well developed.

Main sections of the answer cover:-

a) personnel work carried out by non-specialists, including:-
   1. managers interviewing their own staff;
   2. lower level supervisors dealing with staff;
   3. ordinary members of staff dealing with their colleagues.

b) interviews with customers, including:-
   1. customer enquiries;
   2. sales interviews.

Conclusion

Although personnel managers need a particularly high level of skill in interviewing, bank staff at all levels are likely to find interviewing skills useful.

A3. Introduction

Interviewers, who may be bank staff at all levels of the organisation, are trying to communicate effectively, both in putting across their ideas and in understanding the thoughts and ideas of the people they interview.

Main sections of the answer cover ways in which non-verbal communication can help:-

a) explanation of the concept of body language;

b) body language supporting what an interviewee says;

c) body language conflicting with what an interviewee says;

d) body language used directly by the interviewer.

Conclusion

Most interviewers can make use of body language as a way of judging whether what an interviewee says reflects how he or she feels. More expert interviewers may also use their own body language to put over their ideas more effectively.

A4. Introduction

The interviewing skills to be emphasised in a branch training session will be those of most direct relevance to improving branch profits, and will therefore tend to exclude staff interviews.

Main sections of the answer cover:-

a) asking questions and listening intelligently in order to identify customer needs;

b) leading the discussion towards specific bank products;

c) explaining product benefits clearly;

d) closing a sale.

Conclusion

The interview skills which will help to improve branch profits are those which lead to successful sales of bank products. Interview training should concentrate on these areas but needs to be backed up by good training in product knowledge.

MOCK EXAMINATION:
Banking Operations 1
Solutions

Q1. i:a ii:d iii:a iv:c v:d
vi:b vii:c viii:c ix:b x:d

Q2.

a) i. A premium is the difference between the spot rate for a currency and the forward rate for the currency. If a premium is payable it is deducted from the spot rate to calculate the forward rate (because a premium means a higher price which is the same as a lower rate). From a United Kingdom point of view a premium occurs when the interest rate for the foreign currency is lower than for sterling, i.e. where the foreign currency is stronger than sterling.

ii. A discount is the difference between the spot rate and the forward rate, but is added to the spot rate to calculate a forward rate because a discount, or lower price, means a higher exchange rate. From a United Kingdom point of view a discount occurs when the interest rate for the foreign currency is higher than for sterling, because the foreign currency is weaker than sterling.

iii. A bid bond is a form of guarantee issued by a bank (or other financial institution such as an insurance company) when a customer is bidding or tendering for a major contract. The buyer, the person or organisation intending to pay for the work to be done, will want a guarantee to make sure that no money is lost if a bid is accepted but then withdrawn (which could mean that the process of inviting tenders has to be repeated). The guarantee needs to be from a reputable institution and is paid for and arranged by the bidder. A bid bond may also be known as a tender bond.

iv. A performance bond is a form of guarantee, again usually issued by a bank in connection with a major contract. The contractor, the bank's customer, is often required to obtain a guarantee from the bank so that the buyer can claim money if the work is unfinished (for example because the contractor goes into liquidation) or unsatisfactory. The guarantee is arranged and paid for by the contractor.

v. A retention monies bond is also a form of guarantee issued by a bank. In some contracts the buyer will be entitled to keep back some of the money payable to the contractor until a certain amount of work has been done. If the contractor wants to obtain the money earlier, for example to pay for materials used in the contract, the money which would have been retained (the retention monies) can be released in exchange for a guarantee from a bank. This promises to repay the buyer if the money is not used to carry out the work on the contract. The contractor arranges and pays for the bond.

b) Eurocheques and travel cheques

Advantages of Eurocheques for the customer:-

i. There is no need to decide in advance how much money to take because Eurocheques are drawn on the balance of the customer's current account (but with travel cheques a decision has to be made about how much to take).

ii. No payment needs to be made in advance except for a small fee to obtain a booklet of Eurocheques and the cheque guarantee card (but with travel cheques payment in full plus commission is made beforehand).

iii. Commission is only paid on Eurocheques when they are used.

iv. The customer's account is not debited until well after a payment has been made because of the long clearance time.

v. Eurocheques are often more acceptable in shops than travel cheques.

vi. Exchange commission will only need to be paid once, but with travel cheques in foreign currency the customer may have to pay two lots of exchange commission on any unused cheques.

Disadvantages of Eurocheques for the customer:-

i. If the Eurocheques are lost or stolen a refund is not available as it is with travel cheques.

ii. Eurocheques can only be cashed in limited amounts each day.

iii. Eurocheques are not accepted in as many countries as travel cheques.

iv. The exchange rate for a Eurocheque cannot be fixed in advance as it can with a travel cheque in foreign currency.

From a bank's point of view there may be additional drawbacks to Eurocheques, for example the risk of fraud.

Q3.

a) A documentary letter of credit is:-

i.   a letter drawn up by a bank known as the issuing bank;

ii.   based on instructions from a customer, usually an importer, known as the applicant;

iii.   guaranteeing that payment will be made to the beneficiary usually an exporter;

iv.   provided that the beneficiary complies with the conditions laid down in the letter of credit;

v.   which require the beneficiary to produce specified documents (determined by the applicant when entering into the original underlying contract with the beneficiary);

vi.   by a particular date.

This means that the exporter has protection against non-payment if the correct documents are produced (irrespective of the condition of the goods).

The importer, in this case Propelrite Ltd, will be responsible for all the bank's charges for issuing the letter of credit and handling the documents.

The procedures for dealing with the documentary credit are laid down in the International Chamber of Commerce 'Uniform Customs and Practice' regulations accepted by banks of all major trading countries.

b) A bill of exchange at thirty days sight is a document drawn up by the exporter, the person who is to receive payment.

The bill will be paid thirty days after it has been seen and accepted by the importer, which means that Propelrite have a period of thirty days credit instead of having to pay straightaway.

From the exporter's point of view it is better than a straightforward credit agreement because an accepted bill of exchange is a firm commitment to pay. In this case it may be our bank which accepts the bill under the terms of the letter of credit, but Propelrite will have a commitment to us which they cannot escape from.

The exporter may want to use a bill of exchange simply because of the extra legal rights obtained from the bill.

If the amount of the bill is large enough the exporter may want to obtain cash without having to wait thirty days, by selling the bill at a discount to his own bank.

Q4.

a) i.   'Ultra vires' means beyond the powers of, and refers here to borrowing which is beyond the powers of the company.

ii.   Some actions are permissible for a company but are beyond the powers of the directors, though here it seems to be the company's powers which are in question.

iii.   The company's powers are detailed in the objects clause of the Memorandum of Association.

iv.   The objects clause lists all the things which the company can do. For a toy company selling toys and quite possibly making them will be included, but selling groceries may not be.

v.   Any activity not specifically covered by the objects clause is 'ultra vires' the company and the company is not allowed to do it unless the objects clause is changed.

vi.   This is important to banks because if money is lent for a purpose which is 'ultra vires' the company, the borrowing does not have to be repaid.

vii.   To make sure that this does not happen the bank should check what is written in the Memorandum of Association, consulting a legal expert if necessary. (A copy of the Memorandum and Articles of Association should be held in the branch records from the time the account was opened but the bank should check that this is up-to-date.)

b) The choice between the three proposals for security depends on the advantages and disadvantages of each.

i.   The portfolio of shares is easy to value by looking up the prices in the press. The security may well rise in value as the companies grow, but a major drawback is that the prices could also fall sharply, even though the shares are not all in the same company.

Taking a charge over the shares would be fairly quick and easy to do, particularly if a memorandum of deposit is used to give an equitable charge. Taking a full legal charge would be more expensive and complicated, involving transferring the shares into the name of a bank nominee company. Realising the shares would be reasonably straightforward even with an equitable charge because the stock market ensures that there are always buyers available.

ii.   The life policy would also be easy to value because the surrender value can be obtained by contacting the insurance company, and unlike stocks and shares life policies can be expected to rise steadily in value as further premiums are paid. The bank can make sure that this happens by dealing with the premium payments by standing order. Taking a charge over the policy should be easy if there are no specific restrictions, and a full legal assignment is not complicated to arrange. Realising the policy would then be quite simple, requiring the bank to send the policy, charge form and an encashment form to the company.

The present value of the life policy is below the amount of borrowing but as time goes by the surrender value will increase and the amount owed will probably fall. There is no serious problem of lack of security unless default on the borrowing occurs very quickly.

iii.   A guarantee is easy to value and easy to take as security, but in this situation has no real value at all because Mr Brown, as a partner, is already fully liable for the debts of the partnership. A guarantee from someone who is not a partner could be of value, though it might be difficult to realise; a guarantee from any partner gives no additional security.

The choice between the three options can therefore be narrowed down to a choice between two. The life policy seems preferable because it is easier to obtain a full legal charge and because it is more certain to provide assets of a high enough value if it ever becomes necessary to realise the security.

Q5.

a)   A revolving credit account is an account into which the account holder pays a regular sum of money, usually each month, and is given a credit limit, an amount by which the account can be overdrawn. As repayments are made of any borrowing the right to borrow is renewed.

Advantages for the Customer

i.   Most services provided with a current account are available.

ii.   Borrowing is very flexible.

iii.   Interest is paid on credit balances.

Disadvantages for the Customer

i.   Borrowing may be quite expensive.

ii.   If the credit limit is fully used repayment may take a very long time.

b)   An agreement to provide credit counts as a regulated agreement under the Consumer Credit Act 1974 if:-

i.   the borrower is an individual or group of individuals (i.e. not a company);

ii.   the amount is below £15,000;

iii.   the loan is not used to finance international trade;

iv.   the lending is not mortgage lending by a specialist lender.

This means that most bank loans and overdrafts are regulated agreements, but overdrafts are a special case because they are exempt from the rule that other regulated agreements such as loans have to take the form of a standard signed document.

c)   Main differences between repayment mortgages and endowment mortgages.

i.   Regular payments under repayment mortgages include repayment of capital borrowed, as well as the interest. With endowment mortgages regular instalments are only interest on the loan.

ii.   The capital sum with an endowment mortgage is repaid at the end of the period of the mortgage from an endowment assurance policy.

iii.   The sum paid to the house owner when an endowment assurance policy matures is likely to be more than the amount owed on the loan so an extra lump sum is obtained.

iv.   With a repayment mortgage the amount of interest reduces (and the amount of capital

351

paid back usually increases) so that tax relief is less later on than when the loan is first taken out, but with an endowment mortgage the tax relief is only affected by changes in interest rates and tax rates.

v.   Sometimes lenders charge different rates for repayment mortgages and endowment mortgages, though since 1986 it has become normal practice to charge the same rate of interest for both kinds of mortgage.

d)   Goodwill is the extra value a business has over and above the value of the net assets which it owns, because it is an established going concern and has customers who are willing to come back to it.

The more a trader depends on repeat business the more valuable goodwill is likely to be. When goodwill appears in a balance sheet this means that money has been paid for the goodwill. This shows that the business must have changed hands at some time, with a buyer agreeing to pay more for the business than the agreed value of the physical assets.

Usually goodwill in a balance sheet is 'written down' by deducting the amount from profits until it no longer appears, so the presence of a figure for goodwill in a set of accounts will usually show either that the business has changed hands recently or that the business has not been very profitable since it changed hands.

Q6.

a)   i.   The business owns freehold property and this may now be worth more than the £30,000 paid for it.

ii.   Other fixed assets have been depreciated and the figure for machinery, now valued at £3,000 suggests that the new machinery may be an upgrading of the machinery previously used.

iii.   The total of fixed assets is financed partly by a mortgage of £4,500 but mainly by the share capital and reserves.

iv.   The balance sheet does not give much useful information about the stock and debtors but these figures related to the turnover could be used to calculate that stock is turned over roughly every 30 days and debtors take about 40 days to pay.

Stock turnover =
    stock ÷ cost of goods sold × 365
    = 2315 ÷ (37850 — 9665) × 365
    = 29.97 days
Credit period allowed to debtors =
    debtors ÷ sales × 365
    = 4110 ÷ 37850 × 365
    = 39.63 days

n.b. such calculations do not give much meaningful information on their own; changes in stock turnover or credit allowed can be significant but can only be calculated from a series of sets of accounts.

v.   The figure for bank and cash amounts to over £3,000 so it seems likely that the business is intending to contribute some money towards the purchase of the new machinery. The bank needs to know what the total cost will be.

vi.   The capital section of the balance sheet confirms that profits have been made in the past. Apart from the figure of £345 for retained profits the reserves of £8,000 may well be from profit.

vii.   The amount owed on the mortgage is far less than the value of the property owned so the company has an 'equity' in the property of at least £25,500.

viii.   The surplus value of the property means that if required the bank could take a second mortgage as security.

ix.   The creditors figure is of no special significance; if the figure for purchases had been included it would have been possible to calculate the period of credit taken, but this too would have meant little without comparative figures.

x.   The dividend is 10% of the share capital.

xi.   Current assets cover current liabilities, giving a current ratio of 10670:9225 = 1.16:1.

xii.   Liquid assets do not quite cover current liabilities, giving an acid-test ratio of 7135:9225 = 0.78:1.

xiii.   Overall the liquidity of the business is not very strong but there does not seem to be any serious problem as long as the company can continue to sell its stock.

xiv.   Overall profitability, as evidenced by the reserves and the dividend in the balance sheet, seems quite satisfactory.

xv. Overall the capital position of the business seems very strong with a very small proportion of the funding of the company coming from borrowing, £4,500 out of a total capital employed of £37,845, less than 12%.

b) i. The profit and loss account shows that the gross profit is 25.5% of sales turnover, a figure which would be of more value if the comparable figures for previous years were available.

ii. The net profit is 12.9% of turnover, so the difference, 12.6% of turnover, is used up in expenses.

iii. The retained cash flow is £(4876 + 750) = £5,626, which suggests that the business could easily cope with a £3,000 loan even if the period of borrowing were only a year.

iv. Overall the business is making adequate profit to repay the proposed borrowing.

v. What the figures cannot show is whether future profits will be as good.

Q7. i:b ii:b iii:d iv:a v:d
vi:c vii:c viii:a ix:c x:b

MOCK EXAMINATION:
Banking Operations 2

Solutions

Q1. c

Q2. c

Q3. d

Q4. a

Q5. c

Q6. b

Q7. a

Q8. b

Q9. d

Q10. d

Q11. a

Q12. c

Q13. d

Q14. b

Q15. a

Q16. c

Q17. d

Q18. b

Q19. d

Q20. b

Q21. Big Bang was the name given to the changes made in the rules of the Stock Exchange in October 1986. The main changes were:-

a) to allow outside organisations to own members of the Stock Exchange (which meant that many banks took over firms of securities dealers);

b) to end the distinction between brokers and jobbers so that all Stock Exchange members could choose whether to carry on in one role or to act as both agents for their clients and as market-makers buying and selling securities in their own right;

c) to end the system of fixed commissions.

Q22. A cut in interest rates would be seen as restoring confidence because:-

a) lower interest rates make costs lower for industry as a whole (since industry relies on borrowed funds);

b) lower interest rates make returns on shares relatively attractive which should encourage more people to buy shares, slowing down the fall in share prices;

c) lower interest rates are generally a sign of a strong economy (which does not need to offer high interest rates in order to attract funds from abroad).

Q23. Banks and building societies follow the lead of the Bank of England because:-

a) if a bank fails to cut interest rates this would mean that competitors could undercut by offering cheaper loans, and profitable business could be lost;

b) any bank or building society with unusually high rates will attract deposits but find difficulty in lending the money to anyone;

c) the Bank of England's decisions on rates are accepted by the markets as an influential guideline.

Q24. A cut in building society rates would normally reduce income because:-

a)   investors would look for better returns on their investment elsewhere, for example from banks or National Savings;

b)   income from interest would also fall because of the lower rates charged to borrowers.

Q25. A reduction in income for building societies is a problem because:-

a)   the less money that comes in the less lending can be done, and it is lending which enables building societies to create 'profit';

b)   the less money that is received from depositors the more that will need to be raised through the money markets (and building societies have limits imposed on them to prevent them from relying heavily on the money markets).

Q26.

a)   A mortgage is a popular name for a house-purchase loan secured by a mortgage over the house.

b)   Mortgage borrowing is usually over a long period of time, twenty or twenty-five years, though repayment is often made earlier because house-owners move, repaying one loan before starting another.

c)   The two main types of mortgage are repayment mortgages and endowment mortgages.

d)   A mortgage is:-
i.   a loan over an agreed period of time;
ii.   with interest charged at a variable interest rate;
iii.   with the borrower making regular payments to the lender, usually once a month;
iv.   tax relief is available on the interest on borrowing for such house-purchase loans provided certain conditions are met.

e)   A repayment mortgage is a mortgage for which:-
i.   the regular payments consist partly of capital and partly of interest (with the proportion of interest reducing over the period of the borrowing;
ii.   tax relief is greatest in the early stages when most interest is paid;
iii.   at the end of the period the regular instalments will have paid off the whole debt;

iv.   the lender normally requires the borrower to take out life insurance to make sure that repayment will be made even if the borrower dies (and this is normally in the form of a 'mortgage protection policy', a term life policy covering an amount which reduces as the amount owed on the mortgage is reduced).

f)   An endowment mortgage is a kind of mortgage for which:-
i.   the regular payments consist entirely of interest;
ii.   tax relief is roughly equal through the period of the borrowing, affected only by changes in interest rates and/or changes in tax rates;
iii.   repayment of the capital is made at the end of the period from the proceeds of an endowment insurance policy;
iv.   an endowment insurance policy (rather more expensive than a 'mortgage protection policy') has to be taken out and assigned to the lender as part of the mortgage agreement, with the amount of the insurance covering the amount of the borrowing;
v.   when the endowment policy matures the cash received should pay off the capital owed on the mortgage and give the borrower an extra lump sum.

g)   An alternative to repayment mortgages and endowment mortgages is a pension mortgage. This is similar to an endowment mortgage, but is based on a personal pension insurance policy which gives additional tax benefits for people who are entitled to take out such policies.

Q27. If a customer has a large sum of money and needs investment advice it is important to begin by assessing the customer's priorities. The following key questions can help to judge what investments might be suitable.

a)   Is safety and security more important than a high rate of return? If so this will mean avoiding the more speculative forms of investment.

b)   Is income more important than capital growth?

c)   How well do existing investments (such as life insurance or pensions) fit in with current income and future needs? Appropriate arrangements for insurance may need to be considered before starting to plan more risky investments.

d) Do personal or family circumstances create particular requirements? For example the investment may be intended to provide protection for a family.

e) Are investments to be made from a lump sum or from income? Here the former seems more likely.

f) To what extent will tax considerations affect planning? The customer's rate of income tax and the effects of capital gains tax and inheritance tax may need to be considered.

g) What kind of time scale is appropriate? This is related to a customer's age but also depends on personal preferences, since some customers will want to keep a high proportion of assets in liquid form to allow for short-term changes in circumstances.

h) Do any ethical considerations need to be taken into account? There is a growing trend towards ethical investment and many customers prefer to avoid investing in organisations of which they do not approve, for example companies involved in arms dealing.

Q28. Dear Mr Evans

Thank you for your recent letter. I agree that you could benefit from an increase in turnover if you accepted credit card payments from your customers. You might also find that you reduce risk because when you take credit card payments you can be sure of getting the money provided that you follow the credit card company's instructions; this makes the system safer for you than taking cheques where amounts can only be guaranteed if they are within the limit covered by a cheque guarantee card. For unusually large amounts paid by credit card you can get a quick telephone approval.

I will arrange for the representative of our credit card company to call and see you to discuss the terms and conditions and answer any questions you may have. You may also wish to contact other credit card companies to arrange to accept their cards.

Yours sincerely

pp Mrs Jacobs

Q29. An introduction to this answer should cover the meaning of the term 'securitisation'.

Further sections should deal with:-

a) changes in bank deposit-taking (tending to reduce because of the desire by investors to get better returns by placing money directly with users of funds);

b) factors helping to encourage depositors to keep funds with banks (such as the fluctuations in the stock market);

c) changes in bank lending (tending to reduce because users of funds prefer to go direct to investors to reduce cost);

d) factors helping to maintain bank lending (such as the requirement for very large sums which investors cannot meet at short notice);

e) changes in bank income (tending to move from interest to fees);

f) the continuing importance of interest income.

The conclusion should summarise and weigh up these factors, possibly emphasising that change is continuing steadily.

Q30. An introduction to this answer should describe briefly the meaning of the phrase 'marketing philosophy'.

Further sections should deal with:-

a) marketing planning and its links with strategic goals;

b) the need for a situation analysis to determine where the marketing effort starts from;

c) the marketing view of the product range as being determined by customer needs rather than what banks choose to provide;

d) the marketing view of pricing as influenced by customer perceptions;

e) the new emphasis on the need for adequate and suitable promotion;

f) the new emphasis on appropriate distribution methods;

g) the development of marketing information systems rather than just smaller-scale market research projects;

h) the increase in staff training about marketing including selling skills.

The conclusion should emphasise that marketing affects all aspects of the organisation, not just the staff who deal with customers.

Q31. An introduction to this answer should comment on the range of situations in which bank staff use interviewing skills.

Further sections should deal with:-

a) the skills used in getting to know customers and understand their needs for financial services;

b) the techniques of persuading customers to buy the bank's products;

c) the skills needed for dealing with customer complaints;

d) the need for interviewing skills in dealing with other staff.

The conclusion should emphasise that in banking personal and social skills are particularly important because customers see bank staff as experts rather than just as sales staff.

Section 5

Exercises and Questions without answers

Note: A lecturers' guide giving answers to all exercises and questions from this section is available free to lecturers adopting this manual as a course text.

CHAPTER 1: THE BANKING SYSTEM

B1. What is deposit protection insurance? What provisions are there for protecting deposits with banks in the United Kingdom?

B2. What is merchant banking and how does it differ from commercial banking?

B3. Discount houses are different from other banks. What are the differences and why are they important?

CHAPTER 2: FINANCIAL INTERMEDIARIES

B1. Read this passage and answer the questions which follow.

The major investors in Investment Trusts are the financial institutions, but ordinary members of the investing public could consider them a good investment too.

Unit trusts are far better known to the general public, but management charges may be lower with investment trusts and there is the possible advantage of obtaining the underlying securities at a discount. If you ask at your high street bank they are likely to point you in the direction of their own range of unit trusts. Ask them about investment trusts and see how they react.

Investment trusts have many of the advantages of unit trusts and, although you may not be able to buy them in monthly instalments, if you have a lump sum to invest you should not rule out investment trusts as part of your portfolio.

    1. State what you understand by the phrase 'financial institutions'.

    2. Why are unit trusts better known to the general public?

    3. What does the phrase 'at a discount' mean in this context?

    4. Why do banks often have a range of unit trusts rather than just one?

    5. List three of the benefits to investors shared by investment trusts and unit trusts.

B2. Is the development of the Unlisted Securities Market and the third market an indication that the stock market and financial institutions were failing to meet the needs of smaller businesses?

B3. Why are insurance companies and pension funds considered as financial intermediaries when members of the public cannot open accounts with them as they can with banks or building societies?

CHAPTER 3: CONTROL OF THE BANKING SYSTEM: MONETARY POLICY

B1. When the Bank of England issues directives what kind of instructions can it give and how effective are these instructions?

B2. What makes an 'eligible bank' different from any other bank? What special role do eligible banks have in the United Kingdom banking system?

B3. To what extent is the length of time for which money is lent or invested a determinant of interest rates, given that base rates for different kinds of lending do not always change at the same time?

CHAPTER 4: THE MONEY MARKETS

B1. Read this passage and answer the questions which follow.

The money markets had a troubled day yesterday as news came in of the latest increase in the U.S. deficit, which brought about pressure for higher interest rates.

During the morning prices fell most sharply in long-dated Commercial Bills as the Bank of England showed no sign of intervening. Trading in C.D.s was thin.

In late trading prices became firmer as buyers came in to take advantage of the day's falls.

1. What connection is there between higher interest rates and lower prices of commercial bills?

2. How does the Bank of England 'intervene' in the money markets?

3. What are C.D.s?

4. Why should there be more buyers if prices have been falling?

5. Explain why news about the U.S. deficit might have a bearing on the money markets in the U.K.

B2.   How do Bank of England policies affect the prices of C.D.s and commercial bills?

B3.   Are the money markets a tool of the government's economic policy or an independent determinant of the conditions in which government operates?

CHAPTER 5: THE BALANCE SHEET OF A BANK

B1.   If a bank wants to make more profit by lending more what other effects does this have on the bank's balance sheet?

B2.   What is capital adequacy and how can ratios be used to judge a bank's capital strength in comparison to its competitors?

B3.   What would you expect to find in the full set of published accounts of a banking group apart from the balance sheet representing the assets and liabilities of the bank itself?

CHAPTER 6: THE RANGE OF BANKING BUSINESS

B1.   Read this passage and answer the questions which follow.

The easiest strategy to see and understand is a 'niche' strategy. For very large banks like the 'big

four' this is not really a possibility because they are so heavily committed in so many fields from investment banking to credit cards and cash dispensers. They are stuck with large branch networks whether they like it or not, and they therefore need to develop a strategy which uses the branches as effectively as possible. That means selling successfully.

Branches are already becoming more like financial supermarkets, some of them having in-branch share-shops, some of them offering instant insurance quotations. Diversification is hitting the branches hard; staff need to acquire new skills and knowledge very rapidly as the range of services becomes wider than ever before.

1. What is a 'niche' stategy?

2. What is investment banking?

3. What disadvantages are there in having a large branch network?

4. What do you understand by the term 'financial supermarket'?

5. What new skills do you think staff need as a result of diversification?

B2.   What factors are leading to changes in the basic deposit-taking and lending services which banks provide?

B3.   How can a strategy of diversification help the major clearing banks to make the best use of their branch networks?

CHAPTER 7: BANK AND CUSTOMER: THE LEGAL RELATIONSHIP

B1.   Why does it matter whether the relationship of bank and customer is one of debtor and creditor?

B2.   What are the advantages and disadvantages to banks of relying on a contract with implied terms rather than having a formal written contract?

B3.   What is negligence and why is it an important concept for bankers? Illustrate your answer with reference to situations in which banks may face claims for negligence?

CHAPTER 8: TYPES OF CUSTOMER

B1.   Read this passage and answer the questions which follow.

Estate Agents now have to keep their clients money in trust in a separate account from their own money. The Estate Agents Act 1979 also made it a statutory requirement that customers of estate agents should receive interest on their deposits (except for very small deposits or interest amounting to less than £10).

The idea that clients money should be kept separate makes it easier for agents to ensure that clients get the interest to which they are entitled, but it also has the added advantage of offering some protection if the estate agent becomes insolvent. A Trustee in Bankruptcy or Liquidator cannot take the money from a Clients Account to pay off creditors of the business.

1. What does the phrase 'in trust' mean?

2. Why has legislation been passed to make estate agents keep their clients' money in separate accounts?

3. State two other kinds of business which have to keep clients' money separately.

4. How do clients have protection if an estate agency becomes insolvent?

5. What is the difference between a Trustee in Bankruptcy and a Liquidator?

B2. What do you understand by the phrase 'termination of mandate', and in what circumstances does it occur?

B3. How are partnerships formed and dissolved? What factors do banks need to consider when opening or closing accounts for partnerships?

CHAPTER 9: CORPORATE CUSTOMERS

B1. Companies limited by shares are more common than any other type of company. What advantages are there for businesses in choosing this kind of structure?

B2. Why do banks require different information from companies when opening bank accounts than they do from partnerships?

B3. Insolvency practitioners can take on a number of roles when a company becomes insolvent. Define and explain what these roles are.

CHAPTER 10: MARKETING FINANCIAL SERVICES

B1. Read this passage and answer the questions which follow.

One of the weaknesses of the traditional approach to market segmentation is that it is not sufficiently refined. Customers of socio-economic group A are not all the same. More subtle forms of segmentation have been developed but the more complex they are the more expensive they are to research.

The psychographics approach based on life style preferences offers a wider variety of segments, but perhaps more suitable for banks in the United Kingdom is the ACORN analysis (A Classification Of Residential Neighbourhoods). This identifies different groups of people according to where they live. The assumption underlying the use of this classification to segment the market for financial services is that people in similar types of housing have similar financial needs. In practice a customer's age and family commitments may be just as good a guide. The 'nest-builder' is likely to have different needs from the student or the 'empty-nesters', couples whose children have left home. In any case whatever divisions are considered appropriate it may well be more important to adapt the marketing mix to the target market than to have a clear label to apply to it.

1. Define market segmentation.

2. What does the phrase 'socio-economic group A' mean?

3. What does the term 'nest-builder' mean in this context?

4. In what ways do the financial needs of a student differ from those of an 'empty-nester'?

5. What is the marketing mix?

B2. Do you consider personal selling to be part of the promotional activity of a bank or part of the distribution system? Why?

B3. If a bank adopts a marketing philosophy what does this mean and what effect would you expect it to have?

CHAPTER 11: PRINCIPLES OF LENDING

B1. 'Banks take an unnecessary risk in lending money when they can make profit by providing services.' Discuss.

B2. Mr. Peters has an income of £1,100 a month and regular outgoings of £850. He wants to take a loan over one year to buy a new car, replacing his old one. You calculate that the repayments for the sum he wants to borrow will come to £250 a month.

How would you react to his proposal and what options would you suggest to him?

B3.   List the kinds of situation in which a bank should refuse to lend money. Give examples to illustrate each category which you identify.

CHAPTER 12: PERSONAL LENDING

B1.   How important has the Consumer Credit Act been in protecting the interests of personal customers borrowing from major banks?

B2.   The values which underlie credit scoring systems have been criticised as highly conservative and potentially discriminatory. Should banks be concerned about this, and what can they do to minimise the problems?

B3.   Over the last few months Mr. Jenkins has drawn out money from his account before his monthly salary has been received. He is paid direct to the account and receives £700 net a month. He has arranged to come in to see your manager about an overdraft, and you have checked the bank's records about him. You have established that:-

   a)   3 months ago he made a large purchase of travellers cheques and currency, apparently for a holiday in Spain;

   b)   2 months ago you had an enquiry from a finance house about his suitability to undertake repayment of £220 a month to purchase a car, and it seems that he has gone ahead with this deal;

   c)   his standing orders include payments to a television rental company of £40 a month and two high street shops of £50 and £32 a month, all of which have been started in the last three months.

You carried out a credit-scoring check on Mr. Jenkins when he opened the account two years ago and his rating then was high enough for you to be willing to lend. What aspects of the information given above might make you less keen to lend, and why?

CHAPTER 13: COMMERCIAL LENDING

B1.   You manager receives the following letter from a customer and asks for your reactions.

Dear Sir,

As you know I am looking for a small shop to purchase now that I have taken early retirement, and I think I've found just the one.

I've looked at the accounts for the past 3 years but there's hardly been any change each year. The vendor, Mr. R. Gray, tells me that he paid £80,000 for the goodwill two years ago, and it must be worth more than that by now so he's asking £85,000 on top of the value of the stock and premises.

Profits aren't very good but with the accomodation included Mr. Gray reckons he lives comfortably by taking out £5,000 a year in drawings.

Can we talk it over when I'm next in the branch?

Yours faithfully

Comment on your customer's ideas, particularly about the concept of goodwill.

B2.   Any lending decision is difficult, even for loans to personal customers. What extra factors make it even harder to judge whether a loan to a business should be agreed?

B3.   What costs need to be taken into account if a bank lends money to a company in order to pay for new vehicles?

CHAPTER 14: FORMS OF BANK FINANCE

B1.   How does 'buying' bills of exchange differ from 'buying' the general debts of a company?

B2.   Why might a business choose to acquire assets through leasing or hire purchase rather than by taking a loan?

B3.   What alternatives are there to loans for businesses needing extra cash?

CHAPTER 15: BALANCE SHEETS AND COMPANY ACCOUNTS

B1.   'Capital strength is the most important feature of a business which wants to borrow' To what extent do you agree with this view?

B2.   What can a balance sheet tell a lender about a business?

B3.   What is Return on Capital Employed? Why is it so important and why is it so difficult to calculate?

CHAPTER 16: SECURITY FOR LENDING

B1.   What are the special features of land as security?

B2. Compare and contrast life policies and stocks and shares as forms of security.

B3. What factors make guarantees different from most other common forms of security?

CHAPTER 17: LENDING SITUATIONS

B1. Mr. P. Reynolds is a customer of your branch He is 29 years old and has had an account with you for 11 years. He lives at 166 Wellesley Road, Colchester, a house which he purchased 6 years ago with the help of a building society mortgage of £15,000. He is now being moved by his employers to Norwich, and he has found a house there which he wants to buy for £48,000. He expects to get £35,000 for his present house and the Halifax Buliding Society has agreed a mortgage on the new property of £30,000, the maximum on which he can get tax relief.

What questions would you want to ask Mr. Reynolds before agreeing to his request for a bridging loan?

B2. 'Essentially all businesses have the same borrowing needs.' Discuss.

B3. Study the following cash forecast and answer the questions which follow.

Amounts in £ thousands

MONTHS	1	2	3	4	5	6
Opening Cash	100	20	(35)	(92)	(103)	(90)
+ Receipts	—	30	30	70	100	140
Sub-total	100	50	(5)	(22)	(3)	50
− Payments	80	85	87	81	87	90
Closing Cash	20	(35)	(92)	(103)	(90)	(40)

1. What evidence is there that this is a new business?

2. If the forecasts are accurate at what stage will the business need to borrow most from the bank?

3. How quickly would you expect the business to be operating in credit, and why?

4. How can this information help a banker to decide whether to lend or not when it is only a forecast?

CHAPTER 18: THE BACKGROUND TO INTERNATIONAL LENDING

B1. 'The Trustee Savings Bank is stronger than the big four because it does not have the same exposure to international debt problems.' Discuss.

B2. What effect if any do the international debt problems have on domestic banking within the United Kingdom?

B3. Is the securitisation of debt ultimately harmful or beneficial to banks?

CHAPTER 19: TRAVEL FACILITIES

B1. Why do banks provide such a wide range of services and why is travel insurance included in their range?

B2. How good a range of financial services do banks provide for travellers abroad? What one major proposal would you make to offer an improved service?

B3. A customer complains that the spread on exchange rates which your branch is offering for changing French francs is too wide, and that you expect commission too. How would you deal with this complaint?

CHAPTER 20: FOREIGN EXCHANGE

B1. Why are foreign currencies bought and sold?

B2. What special risks are there for businesses involved in foreign trade?

B3. What are the advantages and disadvantages of the different methods by which businesses can avoid exchange risk?

CHAPTER 21: PAYMENTS ABROAD

B1. In what sense are all payments abroad messages?

B2. How is a customer affected if he requests that a payment abroad should be made in currency rather than in sterling?

B3. Why would an exporter prefer to arrange for payment by means of a documentary credit rather than a documentary collection?

CHAPTER 22: FINANCE OF INTERNATIONAL TRADE

B1. What is countertrade and how might it affect a customer of yours exporting to all parts of the world?

B2. Why does ECGD matter to banks and their exporter customers?

B3. In what circumstances is forfaiting a more appropriate service than factoring?

CHAPTER 23: INTERNATIONAL FINANCE

B1. Read the following passage and answer the questions which follow.

A currency option is an agreement by which the purchaser (the bank's customer) pays a premium to acquire the right to buy from or sell to the writer of the option (the bank) a specified amount of one currency against another currency at an agreed price (rate of exchange) on or before an agreed date. These true (or pure) currency options are a more recently introduced alternative to traditional option forward contracts.

Options have a number of important advantages over the forms of hedging which were available before. There is no obligation to buy or sell currency. This means that the right to buy or sell can be exercised when conditions require it. One of the main disadvantages is that the cost is higher than for forward contracts.

Apart from the options which banks sell to their customers it is possible for businesses to use traded options – 'written' by traders in round amounts (e.g. £25 000) and bought and sold on recognised exchanges like LIFFE.

　1.　Why do businesses hedge against exchange rate risk?

　2.　What are the main differences between forward contracts and currency options?

　3.　Why do you think some businesses choose not to hedge when forward contracts or options are available to them?

　4.　What is LIFFE?

B2. What are eurocurrencies and why do they matter?

B3. What are the advantages and disadvantages to investors of using the Eurobond market?

CHAPTER 24: GENERAL BANKING SERVICES

B1. In what ways do banks discourage payments by cheque?

B2. To what extent is protecting customers' valuables a basic banking service?

B3. Describe the methods available to customers who want to draw out cash from branches other than their own.

CHAPTER 25: PERSONAL BANKING SERVICES

B1. To what extent do banks offer personal financial advice?

B2. Mr. Youlgreave, a customer who regularly uses the bank's sharedealing service, calls at the branch and says that he would like to know more about PEPs. What can you tell him?

B3. The consumer movement has had a significant impact on banking. What do you see as the three main issues of concern to consumers in their relationship with banks? How successful have banks been in tackling these issues?

CHAPTER 26: BANKING SERVICES FOR BUSINESS

B1. Mr. Lucas, who has been running his own business for just over a year, has complained that some of his most recent deals have not been as profitable as he had expected and he does not know why. He is thinking of getting a firm of accountants to come and look over his business to give him some advice. What would you say to him?

B2. Credit cards seem to be a service intended for personal customers. In what ways can banks provide a service to businesses through the use of credit cards?

B3. What use can banks make of their computer systems to offer specialist services to major customers?

CHAPTER 27: INTERVIEWS

B1. Why do bank staff need interviewing skills?

B2. What factors determine whether a selling interview is successful?

B3. 'Preparing for an interview is as important as the interview itself.' Discuss this view with reference to specific types of interview.

Index *(By reference to chapter and paragraph)*